I0868950

AI-Driven Security Systems and Intelligent Threat Response Using Autonomous Cyber Defense

Mohammad Alauthman
University of Petra, Jordan

Ammar Almomani
Higher Colleges of Technology, UAE

IGI Global
Scientific Publishing
Publishing Tomorrow's Research Today

Published in the United States of America by
IGI Global Scientific Publishing
701 East Chocolate Avenue
Hershey, PA, 17033, USA
Tel: 717-533-8845
Fax: 717-533-7115
Website: https://www.igi-global.com E-mail: cust@igi-global.com

Library of Congress Cataloging-in-Publication Data

Names: Alauthman, Mohammad, 1979- editor | Almomani, Ammar, 1981- editor
Title: AI-driven security systems and intelligent threat response using autonomous cyber defense / edited by Mohammad Alauthman, Ammar Almomani.

Description: Hershey, PA : IGI Global Scientific Publishing, [2025] | Includes bibliographical references and index. | Summary: "This work explores the cutting-edge intersection of artificial intelligence and cybersecurity, providing both theoretical foundations and practical implementations. Through detailed case studies, technical analyses, and future projections, it examines how autonomous cyber defense is reshaping security landscapes across critical infrastructure and connected environments"-- Provided by publisher.
Identifiers: LCCN 2025004353 (print) | LCCN 2025004354 (ebook) | ISBN 9798337309545 h/c | ISBN 9798337309552 s/c | ISBN 9798337309569 ebook
Subjects: LCSH: Computer networks--Security measures--Automation | Computer networks--Security measures--Technological innovations | Artificial intelligence--Security measures | Computer security--Forecasting
Classification: LCC TK5105.59 .A39174 2025 (print) | LCC TK5105.59 (ebook) | DDC 005.802856/3--dc23/eng/20250414
LC record available at https://lccn.loc.gov/2025004353
LC ebook record available at https://lccn.loc.gov/2025004354

British Cataloguing in Publication Data
A Cataloguing in Publication record for this book is available from the British Library.

Table of Contents

Preface xvii

Acknowledgments xxii

Chapter 1
Foundations of Autonomous Cyber Defense Systems 1
Salam Al E'mari, Petra University, Jordan
Yousef Sanjalawe, University of Jordan, Jordan
Fuad Fataftah, Universiti Sains Malaysia, Malaysia
Rula Hajjaj, Northern Border University, Saudi Arabia

Chapter 2
AI-Driven Security Systems and Intelligence Threat Response Using Autonomous Cyber Defense 35
Salam Al E'mari, Petra University, Jordan
Yousef Sanjalawe, University of Jordan, Jordan
Fuad Fataftah, Universiti Sains Malaysia, Malaysia

Chapter 3
Advanced AI for Network Security: Predictive Detection and Autonomous Defense 79
Faisal Aburub, Petra University, Jordan
Saad Alateef, Newcastle University, UK

Chapter 4
Digital Defense Powered by Autonomous Resilience 105
Jamal Zraqou, University of Petra, Jordan
Wesam Alkhadour, University of Petra, Jordan
Khalil Omar, University of Petra, Jordan
Jawad Alkhatib, Prince Mohammad Bin Fahd University, Saudi Arabia

Chapter 5
Theoretical Frameworks for Zero-Knowledge Proof Integration in Autonomous Defense Systems: A Mathematical Foundation for Privacy-Preserving Security 133
Mohammad Arafah, University of Petra, Jordan
Faisal Asad Aburub, University of Petra, Jordan
Sabreen Alhariri, Arab International University, Syria

Chapter 6
Federated Learning in Distributed Cyber Defense: Privacy-Preserving Collaborative Security Through Decentralized AI Training........ 161
Mohammad Alauthman, Petra University, Jordan
Amjad Aldweesh, Shaqra University, Saudi Arabia
Ahmad Al-Qerem, Zarqa University, Jordan
Mouhammd Alkasassbeh, Princess Sumaya University for Technology, Jordan
Saad Alateef, Newcastle University, UK
Ammar Almomani, Higher Colleges of Technology, UAE & Al-Balqa Applied University, UAE

Chapter 7
Swarm AI for Distributed Cyber Defense and Autonomous Threat Detection 185
Wael Hadi, Petra University, Jordan
Ala Hamarsheh, Arab American University, Palestine
Ahmad Al-Qerem, Zarqa University, Jordan
Amjad Aldweesh, Shaqra University, Saudi Arabia

Chapter 8
Reinforcement Learning for Adaptive Cyber Defense Training Autonomous Systems for Dynamic Threat Response and Strategy Optimization 209
Mohammad Alauthman, Petra University, Jordan
Amjad Aldweesh, Shaqra University, Saudi Arabia
Ahmad Al-Qerem, Zarqa University, Jordan
Saad Alateef, Newcastle University, UK
Mouhammd Alkasassbeh, Princess Sumaya University for Technology, Jordan

Chapter 9
Evolving Sentinels: How Autonomous Defense Systems Self-Learn and Adapt to Dynamic Threat Environments 235
Khalil Omar, University of Petra, Jordan
Jamal Zraqou, University of Petra, Jordan
Wesam Alkhadour, University of Petra, Jordan
Jorge Marx Gómez, University of Oldenburg, Germany

Chapter 10
Generative AI for Cybersecurity Applications in Threat Simulation and Defense 263
Yousef Sanjalawe, University of Jordan, Jordan
Salam Al E'mari, University of Petra, Jordan
Sharif Makhadmeh, University of Jordan, Jordan

Chapter 11
Designing Autonomous Systems That Use Deception Techniques to Detect and Respond to Cyber Threats 305
D. Sanjana, Dr. N.G.P. Arts and Science College, India
D. Shanmugavadivel, Dr. N.G.P. Arts and Science College, India

Chapter 12
Autonomous Defending Approaches Based on Machine Learning for Android Malware Detection 325
Khalid Alemerien, Tafila Technical University, Jordan
Mohammad Almseidin, Tafila Technical University, Jordan
Enshirah Altarawneh, Hashemite University, Jordan
Malek Alksasbeh, Al-Hussein Bin Talal University, Jordan

Chapter 13
AI-Driven Cybersecurity for Telemedicine: Enhancing Protection Through Autonomous Defense Systems.. 375
Mutaz Abdel Wahed, Jadara University, Jordan
Salma Abdel Wahed, Hashemite University, Jordan
Abed Elkareem Alzoubi, Petra University, Jordan

Chapter 14
Autonomous Defense Systems for Surgical Robots Ensuring Cybersecurity in Robotic-Assisted Surgery 407
Mutaz Abdel Wahed, Jadara University, Jordan
Salma Abdel Wahed, Hashemite University, Jordan

Chapter 15
Cybersecurity for Autonomous Electric Vehicles (EVs) 439
Mohammad Arafah, Petra University, Jordan
Ahmad Aladawi, Loughborough University, UK
Louay Karadsheh, Petra University, Jordan

Chapter 16
Autonomous Cyber Defense in Smart Cities: An AI-Driven Framework for Integrated Urban Infrastructure Protection 465
Ali Al Maqousi, Petra University, Jordan
Kashinath Basu, Oxford Brookes University, UK
Amjad Aldweesh, Shaqra University, Saudi Arabia
Mouhammd Alkasassbeh, Princess Sumaya University for Technology, Jordan

Chapter 17
Critical Infrastructure Autonomous Defense: AI-Enabled Protection Strategies for Power Grids, Water Systems, and Industrial Control Networks.. 501
Ali Al Maqousi, Petra University, Jordan
Kashinath Basu, Oxford Brookes University, UK
Ahmad Al-Qerem, Zarqa University, Jordan
Amjad Aldweesh, Shaqra University, Saudi Arabia

Chapter 18
Harnessing Deep Learning for Enhancing Security for Social Empowerment 527
T. Venkat Narayana Rao, Jawaharlal Nehru Technological University, India
Ananya Seeta, Jawaharlal Nehru Technological University, India
J. V. P. Udaya Deepika, Jawaharlal Nehru Technological University, India
Kumari G. Seshu, Jawaharlal Nehru Technological University, India

Compilation of References 559

About the Contributors 629

Index 635

Detailed Table of Contents

Preface.. xvii

Acknowledgments.. xxii

Chapter 1
Foundations of Autonomous Cyber Defense Systems 1
Salam Al E'mari, Petra University, Jordan
Yousef Sanjalawe, University of Jordan, Jordan
Fuad Fataftah, Universiti Sains Malaysia, Malaysia
Rula Hajjaj, Northern Border University, Saudi Arabia

Traditional cybersecurity methods are becoming inadequate due to the growing complexity and frequency of cyber threats. This chapter explores autonomous cyber defense systems—self-sustaining, intelligent frameworks that detect, analyze, and respond to threats in real time without human intervention. Leveraging AI, Machine Learning, Reinforcement Learning, NLP, and Explainable AI, these systems enable adaptive and scalable security operations. The chapter analyzes system architectures across varying autonomy levels—human-in-the-loop, on-the-loop, and out-of-the-loop—and discusses enabling technologies such as Cyber Threat Intelligence. It reviews modern threats including zero-day exploits, AI-driven malware, and APTs, highlighting the advantages of autonomous systems in resilience and responsiveness. Practical frameworks, deployment strategies, and real-world case studies are presented with performance and ethical evaluation. The chapter concludes with future directions such as quantum-resilient architectures and sustainable cybersecurity strategies.

Chapter 2
AI-Driven Security Systems and Intelligence Threat Response Using
Autonomous Cyber Defense 35
Salam Al E'mari, Petra University, Jordan
Yousef Sanjalawe, University of Jordan, Jordan
Fuad Fataftah, Universiti Sains Malaysia, Malaysia

The expanding cyber threat landscape has compelled organizations to adopt AI-driven security systems for robust defense against sophisticated attacks. This chapter explores artificial intelligence in cybersecurity, emphasizing its role in intelligent threat detection, analysis, and response. AI models, including supervised and unsupervised learning, deep learning, and reinforcement learning, have redefined cybersecurity by enabling behavior-based anomaly detection and automated threat mitigation. Key discussions highlight autonomous systems making real-time decisions, leveraging adaptive control loops, and employing self-healing mechanisms for resilience. This chapter also examines challenges in operational scalability, ethical implications of automation, and the necessity of human oversight in decision-making. The findings underscore the need for synergy between automation and human expertise to foster an intelligent, adaptive cyber defense ecosystem.

Chapter 3
Advanced AI for Network Security: Predictive Detection and Autonomous Defense.. 79
Faisal Aburub, Petra University, Jordan
Saad Alateef, Newcastle University, UK

Organizations continue facing threats that exploit network vulnerabilities. Defenders seek approaches that detect anomalies and respond quickly to attacks. This chapter examines predictive models and automated mechanisms for network defense. It explores how artificial intelligence approaches learn evolving patterns in large-scale data, offering insights and mitigation strategies. Researchers observe advantages in automated recognition, anomaly forecasts, and coordinated countermeasures. Studies indicate success in reducing detection delays and halting malicious actions. Defense frameworks featuring reinforcement agents, neural architectures, and adaptive analytics show promise in lessening manual involvement. Outcomes suggest that ongoing refinements in data handling, architecture design, and interpretability are essential. This chapter provides a synthesis of methods, findings, and future research directions for next-generation AI-driven network defense.

Chapter 4
Digital Defense Powered by Autonomous Resilience 105
Jamal Zraqou, University of Petra, Jordan
Wesam Alkhadour, University of Petra, Jordan
Khalil Omar, University of Petra, Jordan
Jawad Alkhatib, Prince Mohammad Bin Fahd University, Saudi Arabia

Digital security functions as a crucial protection measure to safeguard both data and system operational integrity in present times. This chapter investigates Autonomous Resilience by analyzing both Cybercrime-as-a-Service and APT attacks that receive state support. The article discusses encryption techniques alongside network defense protocols, threat intelligence operations, and incident response methods before explaining AI-powered self-operating security systems. Self-learning systems operate in real-time to detect and analyze threats while using AI algorithms to protect systems through human-AI collaboration. The chapter provides relevant case studies with new technologies that help readers transform traditional reactive security designs into resilient, ahead-of-time defensive structures.

Chapter 5
Theoretical Frameworks for Zero-Knowledge Proof Integration in Autonomous Defense Systems: A Mathematical Foundation for Privacy-Preserving Security 133
Mohammad Arafah, University of Petra, Jordan
Faisal Asad Aburub, University of Petra, Jordan
Sabreen Alhariri, Arab International University, Syria

The proposed research presents a theoretical investigation into the integration of zero-knowledge proofs (ZKP) within autonomous defense architectures, establishing rigorous mathematical foundations for privacy-preserving security verification in next-generation cybersecurity systems. This study addresses fundamental theoretical challenges in autonomous security verification by developing novel mathematical constructs that enable privacy-preserving proof generation and verification while maintaining formal security guarantees. The research methodology encompasses the development of formal mathematical models for non-interactive zero-knowledge proof systems optimized for autonomous verification environments. These models extend existing theoretical frameworks by introducing novel constructs for proof composition and verification in distributed systems, with particular emphasis on formal security properties including completeness, soundness, and zero-knowledge characteristics.

Chapter 6
Federated Learning in Distributed Cyber Defense: Privacy-Preserving Collaborative Security Through Decentralized AI Training 161
Mohammad Alauthman, Petra University, Jordan
Amjad Aldweesh, Shaqra University, Saudi Arabia
Ahmad Al-Qerem, Zarqa University, Jordan
Mouhammd Alkasassbeh, Princess Sumaya University for Technology, Jordan
Saad Alateef, Newcastle University, UK
Ammar Almomani, Higher Colleges of Technology, UAE & Al-Balqa Applied University, UAE

This chapter investigates how Federated Learning (FL) can reshape cyber defense by enabling collaborative model training without consolidating sensitive data, thus safeguarding privacy while enhancing detection and mitigation capabilities. Highlighting the synergy between distributed machine learning and cybersecurity, the discussion compares FL with conventional, centralized solutions that are prone to privacy, scalability, and single-point-of-failure challenges. Key FL architectures, including cross-silo and cross-device systems, are detailed alongside cryptographic tools such as secure aggregation and differential privacy. The chapter also addresses adversarial threats—poisoning and backdoor attacks—and presents robust aggregation techniques as countermeasures. Drawing on real-world examples, it demonstrates how FL can revolutionize threat intelligence, intrusion detection, and malware analysis within privacy- and regulation-conscious contexts.

Chapter 7
Swarm AI for Distributed Cyber Defense and Autonomous Threat Detection 185
Wael Hadi, Petra University, Jordan
Ala Hamarsheh, Arab American University, Palestine
Ahmad Al-Qerem, Zarqa University, Jordan
Amjad Aldweesh, Shaqra University, Saudi Arabia

Collective intelligence and swarm AI have shaped recent explorations of distributed cybersecurity strategies. Many traditional approaches rely on centralized analytics or static signatures, and they sometimes fall short in dynamic and large-scale networks. This chapter provides a comprehensive examination of autonomous defense strategies that embed intelligence in distributed agents, use local detection mechanisms, and encourage emergent coordination through swarm principles. The text explains how these concepts, combined with reinforcement learning, can enable proactive threat detection and containment without complete reliance on centralized oversight. It reviews existing work on multi-agent systems, swarm optimization, and distributed anomaly detection, and it introduces detailed theoretical foundations for practical implementation. Empirical findings from simulations and operational settings illustrate how emergent coordination shortens detection time and enhances resilience.

Chapter 8
Reinforcement Learning for Adaptive Cyber Defense Training Autonomous Systems for Dynamic Threat Response and Strategy Optimization 209
Mohammad Alauthman, Petra University, Jordan
Amjad Aldweesh, Shaqra University, Saudi Arabia
Ahmad Al-Qerem, Zarqa University, Jordan
Saad Alateef, Newcastle University, UK
Mouhammd Alkasassbeh, Princess Sumaya University for Technology, Jordan

Reinforcement Learning (RL) offers a process for creating cyber defense methods that adjust to changing threats. Through training an RL agent, defenders discover ways to block intrusions, isolate systems, and reduce false positives. This chapter covers RL concepts, integration with AI security architectures, and procedures for threat response. It addresses attacker strategies, covers multiple optimization goals, and reviews data methods, reward choices, and deployment steps. Examples in healthcare, finance, and industrial networks illustrate outcomes. Governance, regulatory demands, and oversight are included, supporting RL-based cyber defense.

These discussions show how RL-based defenses manage sequences and adapt to new threats. The chapter also addresses evaluation and implementation.

Chapter 9
Evolving Sentinels: How Autonomous Defense Systems Self-Learn and Adapt to Dynamic Threat Environments 235
Khalil Omar, University of Petra, Jordan
Jamal Zraqou, University of Petra, Jordan
Wesam Alkhadour, University of Petra, Jordan
Jorge Marx Gómez, University of Oldenburg, Germany

This chapter introduces the adaptive defense intelligence framework (ADIF), short for the Adaptive Defense Intelligence Framework, a radically new initiative in the field of autonomous cybersecurity systems. ADIF overcomes glaring limitations present in existing security solutions through innovation in four different major spheres: hierarchical reinforcement learning architecture, a contextual analysis engine that drastically reduces false positives, federated knowledge distribution that maintains privacy, and a self-verification feedback loop. Financial, healthcare, and manufacturing operational dashboards showed remarkable improvements in detection rates, response times, and operational continuity during active threats. Though faced with startup challenges in terms of initial training requirements and computational intensiveness, this marks the shift from reactive to proactive security postures, offering the capability of continuous self-learning and further evolving the system with ever-growing threats.

Chapter 10
Generative AI for Cybersecurity Applications in Threat Simulation and Defense 263
Yousef Sanjalawe, University of Jordan, Jordan
Salam Al E'mari, University of Petra, Jordan
Sharif Makhadmeh, University of Jordan, Jordan

The integration of generative AI in cybersecurity marks a transformative leap in combating the growing complexity of cyber threats. This chapter examines generative AI models like generative adversarial networks, variational autoencoders, and transformers, showcasing their role in threat simulation, synthetic data generation, and anomaly detection. Applications discussed include proactive defense testing, malware analysis, and intrusion detection, highlighting generative AI's ability to predict, detect, and mitigate sophisticated attacks. Emerging techniques, such as federated learning and hybrid generative models, promise further advancements. However, generative AI poses challenges, including misuse of synthetic data and adversarial vulnerabilities. Addressing these risks requires ethical guidelines, robust frameworks, and collaboration. With its predictive and adaptive potential, generative AI is reshaping cybersecurity, enabling resilient and intelligent defenses for the digital age.

Chapter 11
Designing Autonomous Systems That Use Deception Techniques to Detect and Respond to Cyber Threats 305
D. Sanjana, Dr. N.G.P. Arts and Science College, India
D. Shanmugavadivel, Dr. N.G.P. Arts and Science College, India

The escalating complexity of cyber threats demands innovative solutions to strengthen cybersecurity defenses. This research focuses on designing autonomous systems that leverage deception techniques to detect and respond to cyber threats. By integrating deception strategies with autonomous decision-making, these systems can effectively outmaneuver and outsmart cyber adversaries, reducing the risk of successful attacks. The proposed autonomous deception system utilizes artificial intelligence and machine learning algorithms to create decoy environments, lure attackers into revealing their tactics, and adapt to evolving threats. The autonomous deception system is designed to operate in real-time, providing rapid detection and response capabilities. The research contributes to the development of next-generation cybersecurity solutions, providing a novel approach to autonomous threat detection and response. The findings have significant implications for organizations seeking to strengthen their cybersecurity defenses against increasingly sophisticated threats.

Chapter 12
Autonomous Defending Approaches Based on Machine Learning for Android Malware Detection 325
Khalid Alemerien, Tafila Technical University, Jordan
Mohammad Almseidin, Tafila Technical University, Jordan
Enshirah Altarawneh, Hashemite University, Jordan
Malek Alksasbeh, Al-Hussein Bin Talal University, Jordan

The exponential growth in Android device usage has led to a surge in malware targeting this platform, necessitating robust security mechanisms to safeguard user data and system integrity. Traditional signature-based methods for malware detection often lag behind the ever-evolving threat landscape. This chapter explores autonomous defending approaches for Android malware detection leveraging advanced Machine Learning (ML) techniques. The chapter outlines the unique challenges in Android malware detection, such as diverse app ecosystems and the obfuscation techniques employed by malware developers. Through the analysis of real-world datasets and performance benchmarks, the chapter demonstrates the practical effectiveness of ML-based approaches and limitations. Finally, the potential integration of ML-based malware detection systems with broader cybersecurity frameworks and future research directions are discussed. This chapter aims to serve as a comprehensive resource for researchers and practitioners in the field of Android malware detection and autonomous cybersecurity.

Chapter 13
AI-Driven Cybersecurity for Telemedicine: Enhancing Protection Through Autonomous Defense Systems 375
Mutaz Abdel Wahed, Jadara University, Jordan
Salma Abdel Wahed, Hashemite University, Jordan
Abed Elkareem Alzoubi, Petra University, Jordan

AI-driven solutions utilize machine learning, behavioral analysis, and autonomous defense systems to identify and mitigate risks more effectively than conventional methods. These systems continuously adapt to evolving threats, ensuring proactive and dynamic defense mechanisms. Additionally, integrating blockchain technology enhances data security through immutable records and secure transactions. Despite its benefits, AI-driven cybersecurity raises ethical and regulatory concerns, including data privacy issues, algorithmic bias, and adversarial AI attacks. Striking a balance between automation and human oversight is vital to uphold ethical standards and regulatory compliance. This chapter examines the role of AI-driven cybersecurity in telemedicine, exploring its capabilities, challenges, and future trends. By harnessing AI and blockchain, healthcare organizations can develop robust cybersecurity frameworks that safeguard patient data, ensure system reliability, and maintain trust in digital healthcare services.

Chapter 14
Autonomous Defense Systems for Surgical Robots Ensuring Cybersecurity in Robotic-Assisted Surgery 407
Mutaz Abdel Wahed, Jadara University, Jordan
Salma Abdel Wahed, Hashemite University, Jordan

Autonomous defense systems powered by Artificial Intelligence (AI) and machine learning offer a critical solution to mitigate these risks. These systems monitor network traffic, detect anomalies in real time, and autonomously respond to potential threats without human intervention. This chapter examines the unique cybersecurity challenges associated with surgical robots, such as securing command-and-control systems, preventing remote hijacking, and ensuring the integrity of real-time data transmission. It also highlights successful implementations of AI-driven cybersecurity in healthcare, discussing how autonomous defense systems can safeguard surgical outcomes, protect patient data, and maintain compliance with regulatory standards. By integrating advanced cybersecurity solutions, healthcare organizations can enhance the resilience and safety of robotic-assisted surgical procedures.

Chapter 15
Cybersecurity for Autonomous Electric Vehicles (EVs) 439
Mohammad Arafah, Petra University, Jordan
Ahmad Aladawi, Loughborough University, UK
Louay Karadsheh, Petra University, Jordan

In this chapter, we study the implementation and effectiveness of AI-driven deception technologies for autonomous defense systems consisting of intelligent honeypots and adaptive decay mechanisms. It studies the ability of machine learning algorithms to make deceptive environments undetectable while being intelligent to capture valuable threat intelligence. The methodology includes the development of dynamic honeypot architectures that are suitable for their behaviors using reinforcement learning in response to attackers. The main areas of investigation include employing generative adversarial networks in designing conceivable system environments, developing the real-time analysis of attacker behavior patterns, and creating the underlying autonomous decision-making in deceptive response strategies. Empirical evidence from real-world implementations is provided to show that AI-driven deception can significantly decrease the success attack rates and enhance threat intelligence gathering

Chapter 16
Autonomous Cyber Defense in Smart Cities: An AI-Driven Framework for Integrated Urban Infrastructure Protection 465
Ali Al Maqousi, Petra University, Jordan
Kashinath Basu, Oxford Brookes University, UK
Amjad Aldweesh, Shaqra University, Saudi Arabia
Mouhammd Alkasassbeh, Princess Sumaya University for Technology, Jordan

Smart cities integrate IoT devices, edge computing, and data analytics to enhance public services while creating new cyber vulnerabilities. This chapter proposes an autonomous cyber defense framework leveraging AI for threat detection and automated incident response. The framework addresses evolving threats, orchestrates analytics, and ensures governance for ethical, scalable protection across diverse infrastructures, such as transportation and utilities. Key components include data ingestion, continuous learning, real-time analytics, and threat intelligence sharing, which together minimize response time and mitigate risk. Case studies illustrate how AI-driven solutions reduce detection-to-response intervals. The chapter concludes with emerging research directions for robust cybersecurity and resilience.

Chapter 17
Critical Infrastructure Autonomous Defense: AI-Enabled Protection Strategies for Power Grids, Water Systems, and Industrial Control Networks.. 501
Ali Al Maqousi, Petra University, Jordan
Kashinath Basu, Oxford Brookes University, UK
Ahmad Al-Qerem, Zarqa University, Jordan
Amjad Aldweesh, Shaqra University, Saudi Arabia

Critical infrastructure, including power grids, water systems, and industrial control networks, supports essential societal functions. As cyber threats intensify, AI-driven autonomous defense methods have emerged as pivotal solutions for ensuring robust security. This abstract outlines how machine learning, deep learning, and reinforcement learning-based approaches enable proactive threat detection, automated responses, and adaptive system configurations. By leveraging advanced analytics and rapid decision-making capabilities, AI frameworks can mitigate vulnerabilities, reduce downtime, and maintain service continuity. However, successful deployment requires addressing scalability, trust, and regulatory concerns. This chapter provides comprehensive insights into implementing reliable, resilient AI defenses for effectively safeguarding critical infrastructure worldwide.

Chapter 18
Harnessing Deep Learning for Enhancing Security for Social Empowerment 527
T. Venkat Narayana Rao, Jawaharlal Nehru Technological University, India
Ananya Seeta, Jawaharlal Nehru Technological University, India
J. V. P. Udaya Deepika, Jawaharlal Nehru Technological University, India
Kumari G. Seshu, Jawaharlal Nehru Technological University, India

Critical structures are increasingly susceptible to cyber threats, leading to the inadequacy of traditional security measures. This study explores the application of deep learning tools aimed specifically at enhancing the security of vital systems, such as power grids and transportation networks. By employing convolutional neural networks and recurrent neural networks, the research conducts an analysis of network traffic data to identify security anomalies. An inclusive dataset, which includes simulated attack scenarios, with workable models. Preliminary findings indicate that the convolutional neural network model achieved a high level of anomaly detection accuracy, ominously surpassing the performance of conventional methods. Furthermore, the recurrent neural network model demonstrated enhanced capabilities in detecting time-sensitive threats, resulting in an extensive reduction in false positives. This chapter focus on future research should focus on examining the integration of deep learning models with security frameworks to fortify resilience against evolving threats

Compilation of References 559

About the Contributors 629

Index 635

Preface

In a world increasingly reliant on interconnected systems, autonomous technologies, and artificial intelligence (AI), cybersecurity has become one of the most pressing challenges of our time. The ever-evolving threat landscape requires solutions that are not only reactive but also predictive, adaptive, and autonomous. As we progress into an era where AI and machine learning (ML) are integrated into nearly every aspect of our digital and physical lives, the need for AI-driven security systems and intelligent threat response mechanisms has never been more critical.

This book, *AI-Driven Security Systems and Intelligent Threat Response Using Autonomous Cyber Defense*, provides an in-depth exploration of how AI and autonomous systems are revolutionizing the field of cybersecurity. By leveraging advanced AI techniques, these systems are capable of detecting, analyzing, and responding to cyber threats in real-time, often outpacing traditional approaches to network defense. This book serves as both a comprehensive guide and a forward-looking discussion on the intersection of AI, cybersecurity, and autonomous defense technologies.

OVERVIEW OF THE SUBJECT MATTER

The book focuses on the critical role of AI in transforming cybersecurity, particularly through the development of autonomous defense systems. It examines how AI algorithms, such as reinforcement learning, swarm intelligence, and deep learning, are utilized to predict, detect, and mitigate cyber threats with minimal human intervention. Furthermore, the book explores advanced topics, including federated learning, zero-knowledge proofs, and AI-driven deception techniques, which are paving the way for innovative approaches to privacy-preserving security and dynamic threat response.

From securing critical infrastructure to protecting smart cities, autonomous vehicles, and telemedicine systems, this book highlights the versatility and potential of AI in addressing the unique cybersecurity challenges of modern and future technologies.

Relevance of the Book in Today's World

As cyberattacks grow in frequency, sophistication, and impact, traditional security measures are often insufficient to counter the dynamic and persistent nature of these threats. Autonomous cyber defense systems powered by AI offer the ability to adapt to evolving attack patterns, respond in real-time, and defend complex environments without continuous human oversight. This book provides a timely and essential examination of these technologies, offering practical solutions to modern cybersecurity challenges.

With the rise of smart cities, autonomous vehicles, telemedicine, and interconnected critical infrastructure, the importance of AI-driven security systems cannot be overstated. These technologies not only enhance protection but also provide scalable and efficient solutions to address the increasing complexity of securing digital and physical ecosystems.

Target Audience

This book is written for a diverse audience, including:

- **Cybersecurity professionals** looking to understand and implement AI-driven autonomous defense solutions.
- **AI and machine learning researchers** exploring the application of advanced algorithms in cybersecurity.
- **IT managers and decision-makers** seeking innovative approaches to enhance organizational security.
- **Academics and students** studying cybersecurity, AI, or related disciplines.
- **Policy makers and regulators** aiming to understand the ethical and legal implications of autonomous defense systems.

By catering to this broad audience, the book bridges the gap between technical innovation and real-world application, offering a valuable resource for anyone involved in the future of cybersecurity.

Chapter Summaries

Each chapter in the book provides a unique perspective and contribution to the field of AI-driven cybersecurity:

1. **Foundations of Autonomous Cyber Defense Systems**

This chapter introduces the fundamental principles of autonomous cyber defense, focusing on the role of AI in creating adaptive and predictive security systems.

2. **AI-Driven Security Systems and Intelligence Threat Response Using Autonomous Cyber Defense**

This chapter offers a comprehensive overview of AI-driven security systems, showcasing their capabilities in intelligent threat detection and response.

3. **Advanced AI for Network Security: Predictive Detection and Autonomous Defense**

This chapter explores how advanced AI techniques enable predictive threat detection and autonomous network defense.

4. **Digital Defense Powered by Autonomous Resilience**

This chapter highlights how autonomous resilience can enhance digital defense systems' ability to withstand and recover from cyberattacks.

5. **Theoretical Frameworks for Zero-Knowledge Proof Integration in Autonomous Defense Systems**

Focusing on privacy-preserving security, this chapter provides a mathematical foundation for integrating zero-knowledge proofs into autonomous defense systems.

6. **Federated Learning in Distributed Cyber Defense**

This chapter discusses how federated learning enables collaborative security through decentralized AI training, preserving privacy while enhancing defense.

7. **Swarm AI for Distributed Cyber Defense and Autonomous Threat Detection**

This chapter examines how swarm intelligence can be applied to distributed cyber defense and autonomous threat detection.

8. **Reinforcement Learning for Adaptive Cyber Defense**

This chapter explores reinforcement learning's role in training autonomous systems for dynamic threat response and strategy optimization.

9. **Evolving Sentinels: How Autonomous Defense Systems Self-Learn and Adapt to Dynamic Threat Environments**

This chapter delves into the self-learning capabilities of autonomous defense systems to adapt to ever-changing cyber threats.

10. **Generative AI for Cybersecurity Applications in Threat Simulation and Defense**

This chapter highlights how generative AI can be used for threat simulation and to enhance defense mechanisms.

11. **Designing Autonomous Systems that Use Deception Techniques to Detect and Respond to Cyber Threats**

This chapter focuses on designing autonomous systems that leverage deception techniques to detect and respond to cyber threats.

12. **Autonomous Defending Approaches Based on Machine Learning for Android Malware Detection**

This chapter discusses machine learning-based approaches for detecting and defending against Android malware.

13. **AI-Driven Cybersecurity for Telemedicine**

This chapter examines how autonomous defense systems enhance cybersecurity in telemedicine environments.

14. **Autonomous Defense Systems for Surgical Robots**

This chapter discusses the role of autonomous defense systems in ensuring cybersecurity in robotic-assisted surgery.

15. **Cybersecurity for Autonomous Electric Vehicles (EVs)**

This chapter addresses the unique cybersecurity challenges faced by autonomous electric vehicles and the role of AI-driven solutions.

16. **Autonomous Cyber Defense in Smart Cities**

This chapter presents an AI-driven framework for protecting integrated urban infrastructure in smart cities.

17. **Critical Infrastructure Autonomous Defense**

This chapter discusses AI-enabled strategies for protecting power grids, water systems, and industrial control networks.

18. **Harnessing Deep Learning for Enhancing Security for Social Empowerment**

This chapter highlights how deep learning techniques can enhance cybersecurity for socially empowering technologies.

CONCLUSION

This book provides a comprehensive and forward-looking exploration of AI-driven security systems and autonomous cyber defense. By bridging theoretical foundations, practical applications, and ethical considerations, it offers a holistic view of how AI can transform cybersecurity.

As cyber threats continue to evolve, the insights and innovations presented in this book aim to inspire researchers, practitioners, and policymakers to embrace the potential of AI while addressing the challenges of implementing autonomous defense systems responsibly. Together, these contributions represent a significant step toward a safer and more secure digital future.

Acknowledgments

The successful completion of this book, *AI-Driven Security Systems and Intelligent Threat Response Using Autonomous Cyber Defense*, would not have been possible without the contributions, support, and encouragement of many individuals and organizations.

First and foremost, we would like to express our sincere gratitude to the contributing authors who shared their expertise and insights to create this comprehensive volume. Their dedication, hard work, and innovative research have been instrumental in shaping the content of this book and advancing the field of AI-driven cybersecurity.

We are deeply grateful to the reviewers who provided invaluable feedback and constructive suggestions throughout the development process. Their critical insights and thorough evaluations have greatly enhanced the quality and rigor of this work.

Our heartfelt thanks go to the editorial and production team at IGI Global for their professionalism, guidance, and unwavering support during the publication process. Their expertise and dedication ensured a seamless journey from concept to completion, and we are truly appreciative of their efforts.

We would also like to acknowledge the support of academic institutions, research organizations, and professional communities that fostered collaboration and knowledge-sharing, enabling the development of this book. Their encouragement and resources have been invaluable in facilitating the creation of this work.

Finally, we extend our deepest gratitude to our families, friends, and colleagues for their patience, understanding, and encouragement throughout this journey. Their unwavering belief in the importance of this project has been a source of constant motivation.

This book is the result of collective efforts, and we are sincerely thankful to everyone who contributed, directly or indirectly, to its success. We hope this volume will serve as a valuable resource for researchers, professionals, and policymakers in advancing the field of autonomous cyber defense and AI-driven security systems.

Chapter 1
Foundations of Autonomous Cyber Defense Systems

Salam Al E'mari
https://orcid.org/0000-0002-2134-4158
Petra University, Jordan

Yousef Sanjalawe
https://orcid.org/0000-0002-4442-1865
University of Jordan, Jordan

Fuad Fataftah
https://orcid.org/0009-0009-3203-5869
Universiti Sains Malaysia, Malaysia

Rula Hajjaj
Northern Border University, Saudi Arabia

ABSTRACT

Traditional cybersecurity methods are becoming inadequate due to the growing complexity and frequency of cyber threats. This chapter explores autonomous cyber defense systems—self-sustaining, intelligent frameworks that detect, analyze, and respond to threats in real time without human intervention. Leveraging AI, Machine Learning, Reinforcement Learning, NLP, and Explainable AI, these systems enable adaptive and scalable security operations. The chapter analyzes system architectures across varying autonomy levels—human-in-the-loop, on-the-loop, and out-of-the-loop—and discusses enabling technologies such as Cyber Threat Intelligence. It reviews modern threats including zero-day exploits, AI-driven malware, and APTs, highlighting the advantages of autonomous systems in resilience and responsive-

DOI: 10.4018/979-8-3373-0954-5.ch001

ness. Practical frameworks, deployment strategies, and real-world case studies are presented with performance and ethical evaluation. The chapter concludes with future directions such as quantum-resilient architectures and sustainable cybersecurity strategies.

1 INTRODUCTION

The rapidly expanding digital infrastructure of modern society has significantly increased the exposure of organizations and individuals to cyber threats. As the complexity of networks, systems, and the volume of data transmitted across digital environments grow exponentially, conventional security mechanisms are becoming increasingly inadequate. Traditionally, cybersecurity has relied heavily on human intervention for threat detection, assessment, and mitigation. While effective in past decades, this manual, reactive approach fails to address the speed and sophistication of current cyber threats (Safitra, Lubis, & Fakhrurroja, 2023). Recent trends show that attacks now often exploit zero-day vulnerabilities, leverage Artificial Intelligence (AI) to avoid detection, and adapt their strategies based on defense mechanisms in place. Against this backdrop, the concept of autonomous cyber defense emerges as a critical evolution in securing information systems (Ali et al., 2022).

Autonomous cyber defense refers to systems that can independently detect, analyze, and respond to cyber threats in real time without requiring direct human intervention. This approach leverages a combination of AI, Machine Learning (ML), threat intelligence, and automated decision-making to respond to incidents faster and more effectively than traditional methods. The importance of this paradigm shift cannot be overstated, especially as organizations face increasing pressure to protect critical infrastructure, ensure data privacy, and maintain operational continuity. With the growth of Internet of Things (IoT) devices, remote work environments, and cloud computing, the attack surface has expanded dramatically. Cyber adversaries are now using automated tools to execute attacks at scale, making it imperative for defenders to adopt similar capabilities (Patel & Wei, 2024; Moustafa et al., 2023).

The primary aim of this chapter is to lay the foundational understanding of autonomous cyber defense systems. It begins by defining the concept and exploring its key components and underlying technologies. The chapter traces the evolution of cybersecurity from traditional reactive models to the current push toward fully autonomous solutions. It also delves into the levels of autonomy in cyber defense—ranging from human-in-the-loop to human-out-of-the-loop systems—and the implications of each. A significant portion of the discussion focuses on the role of artificial intelligence, including various AI techniques such as reinforcement learning, Natural Language Processing (NLP), and Explainable AI (XAI), which form the backbone of autonomous capabilities.

Further, the chapter reviews critical technologies that enable autonomy, such as Cyber Threat Intelligence (CTI), Security Orchestration, Automation, and Response (SOAR), blockchain, and cloud-based platforms. It examines the contemporary threat landscape, highlighting the challenges posed by emerging threats and the inadequacy of traditional defenses. The chapter also introduces architectural frameworks and models that support autonomous cyber defense, supported by real-world case studies that illustrate practical implementations. Lastly, it explores future trends and research directions, such as the integration of quantum computing and sustainable cybersecurity strategies.

2 UNDERSTANDING AUTONOMOUS CYBER DEFENSE

Autonomous cyber defense is a transformative shift in the cybersecurity paradigm, enabling systems to perform security-related tasks with minimal or no human input. At its core, autonomous cyber defense integrates advanced computational techniques and adaptive algorithms to manage, detect, respond to, and recover from cyber threats. The fundamental characteristic that distinguishes autonomous systems from traditional ones is their ability to make decisions independently based on real-time data and predefined objectives. These decisions are not merely reactive but often predictive, based on historical patterns and emerging threat vectors. This allows the system to identify potential breaches before they materialize and to take preemptive action to mitigate risks (George, 2024; Katiforis, 2024).

The concept of autonomous cyber defense is rooted in several interrelated disciplines, including artificial intelligence, systems theory, and behavioral analytics. These systems use machine learning to continuously improve their performance over time, adapting to new threats and changes in the operational environment. Key concepts underpinning autonomous defense include situational awareness, threat intelligence assimilation, dynamic policy enforcement, and self-healing capabilities. Situational awareness enables the system to understand the context of network activities, while threat intelligence provides external data to inform internal defense strategies (Möller, 2023). Dynamic policy enforcement ensures that the system can adapt its rules in response to evolving threats, and self-healing refers to the system's ability to recover from attacks without manual intervention (Adeniyi et al., 2023). Figure 1 illustrates the architecture of an autonomous intelligent cyber-defense system. The system is designed to operate within an environment, where it receives percepts through sensors, interprets the world state, and executes appropriate actions in response to evolving threats. It includes key components such as world modeling, planning, learning, goal management, and communication mechanisms. Each module works collaboratively to enable the agent to autonomously detect, assess, and respond to cyber threats. The figure also highlights the areas that are partially covered and those not yet covered in current research or implementations (Theron et al., 2020).

Figure 1. Architecture of autonomous intelligent cyber-defense

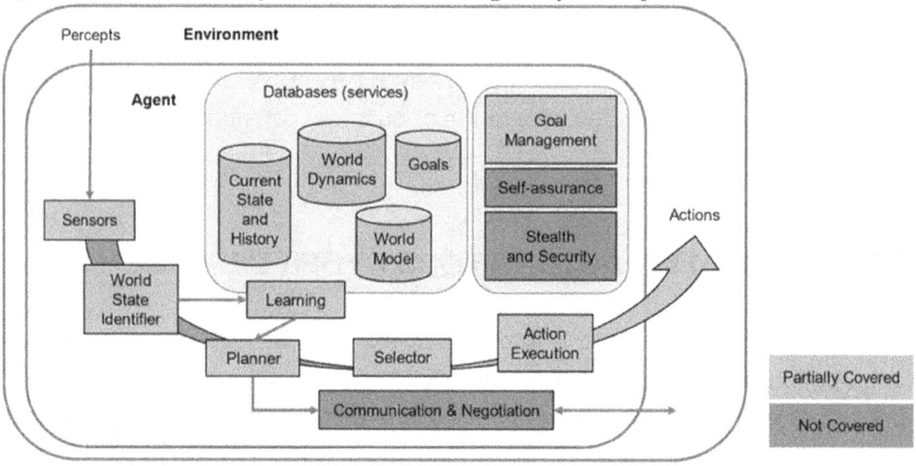

(Kott, 2018)

The evolution of cyber defense systems has followed a trajectory from manual interventions to automated and, eventually, autonomous mechanisms. In the early days of cybersecurity, defenses were largely manual, relying on IT administrators to identify threats and take corrective actions. As threats became more frequent and complex, automation was introduced to handle repetitive tasks such as log analysis, patch management, and alerting. The introduction of Security Information and Event Management (SIEM) systems marked a significant advancement, enabling real-time correlation of security events. However, even with SIEM, human analysts remained central to decision-making. The current shift toward autonomy builds on these automated foundations by embedding intelligence into the system, allowing for decision-making processes to be conducted independently of human oversight (Ehis, 2023; Vermesan et al., 2022).

Autonomy in cyber defense can be categorized into three main levels: human-in-the-loop, human-on-the-loop, and human-out-of-the-loop. Human-in-the-loop systems require human approval before any action is taken. These systems are useful in high-stakes environments where the cost of false positives is significant. Human-on-the-loop systems allow the system to act independently but maintain human oversight for review and intervention if necessary. Finally, human-out-of-the-loop systems operate entirely independently, making decisions and taking actions without any human intervention. Each level of autonomy has its trade-offs. While full autonomy offers the fastest response times, it also raises concerns about accountability, trust, and the potential for unintended consequences. Therefore, the choice of autonomy level must be aligned with the organization's risk appetite, regulatory environment, and operational requirements (Yan, Huang, & Cao, 2022; Uchendu et al., 2025).

Understanding these distinctions is critical for designing and implementing effective autonomous cyber defense systems. As we move forward in this chapter, these foundational ideas will serve as the basis for exploring the core components, enabling technologies, and practical considerations of deploying such systems in real-world scenarios.

3 CORE COMPONENTS AND AI BACKBONE OF AUTONOMOUS CYBER DEFENSE SYSTEMS

An effective autonomous cyber defense system is composed of several integrated components that collectively enable real-time threat detection, advanced analysis, autonomous decision-making, and intelligent response execution. Each of these elements plays a critical role in ensuring that the system functions holistically to protect digital assets against evolving threats. Figure 2 summarizes the components of autonomous cyber defense systems (Wei, 2024).

Figure 2. Components of autonomous cyber defense systems

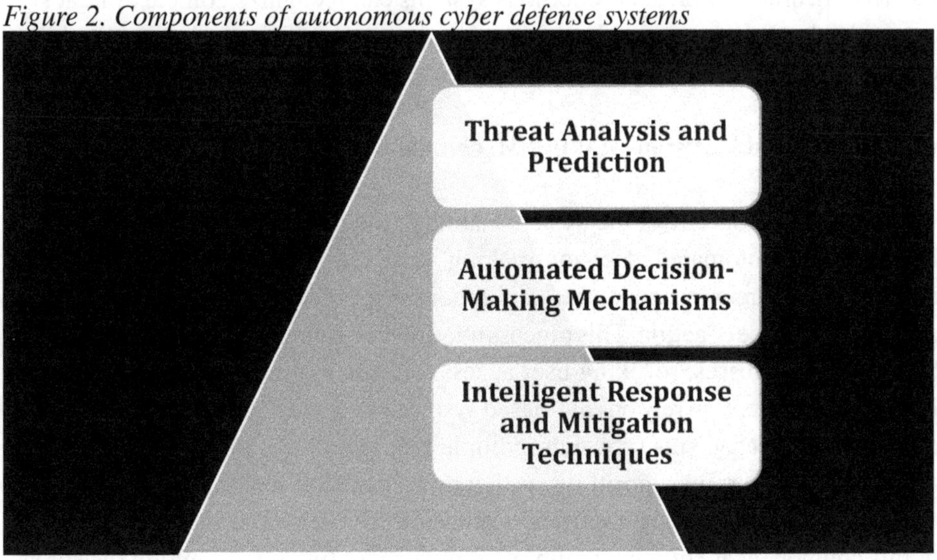

- **Threat Detection and Monitoring**

The foundation of any cyber defense system begins with robust threat detection and monitoring capabilities. Autonomous systems leverage a range of sensors and monitoring tools to collect and analyze data from various sources, including network traffic, endpoint activity, application logs, and user behavior. This continuous surveillance enables the system to maintain situational awareness across the entire IT environment. Machine learning models are often employed to identify anomalies that deviate from established baselines. These models can detect subtle behavioral changes, unusual data flows, or deviations in system performance that may indicate a potential threat. The advantage of autonomous monitoring lies in its ability to process vast volumes of data at high speed, eliminating the bottlenecks of manual analysis (Shehzadi, 2024).

- **Threat Analysis and Prediction**

Once potential threats are detected, the system transitions into the analysis phase. Here, various data-driven techniques are used to classify the threat, assess its severity, and predict its potential impact. Predictive analytics, powered by historical threat intelligence and real-time behavioral data, enables the system to forecast future attack vectors and prioritize threats accordingly. Techniques such as clustering, classification, and regression analysis are employed to extract meaningful patterns from the data. By leveraging deep learning architectures like convolutional and recurrent neural networks, autonomous systems can recognize complex threat signatures and anticipate sophisticated multi-stage attacks. This predictive capability enhances preparedness and supports proactive defense strategies.

- **Automated Decision-Making Mechanisms**

Central to autonomy is the system's ability to make decisions without human intervention. Automated decision-making involves evaluating available threat intelligence, current system states, and predefined policies to determine the most appropriate course of action. This process may include isolating affected components, blocking IP addresses, revoking user access, or initiating forensic data collection. Decision engines often rely on rule-based systems, fuzzy logic, and AI-driven policy enforcement mechanisms to weigh multiple risk factors before executing actions. Reinforcement learning algorithms further refine decision-making by learning from outcomes and continuously improving policy effectiveness. The speed and accuracy of this component are crucial in minimizing response times and limiting the spread of malicious activity (Sarker, 2024).

- **Intelligent Response and Mitigation Techniques**

The final component of an autonomous cyber defense system is its ability to respond and mitigate threats intelligently. Response strategies are tailored to the type and severity of the detected threat and can include both reactive and proactive measures. Reactive responses might involve quarantining infected systems, terminating malicious processes, or restoring data from secure backups. Proactive measures can include system patching, reconfiguring network segmentation, or updating firewall rules to prevent similar attacks. Advanced systems integrate with SOAR platforms to orchestrate response actions across multiple security tools and platforms. Intelligent mitigation also involves learning from each incident, updating threat models, and refining response protocols, thereby creating a feedback loop that enhances the system's resilience over time (Kholidy, 2021).

AI serves as the enabling force behind autonomous cyber defense systems. The integration of AI into cybersecurity allows for faster, smarter, and more accurate threat identification and mitigation. Several branches of AI contribute to this autonomy, including machine learning, deep learning, reinforcement learning, natural language processing, and explainable AI. Figure 3 presents some use cases of AI in cybersecurity in general (Soare, 2023).

Figure 3. Use cases of AI in cybersecurity

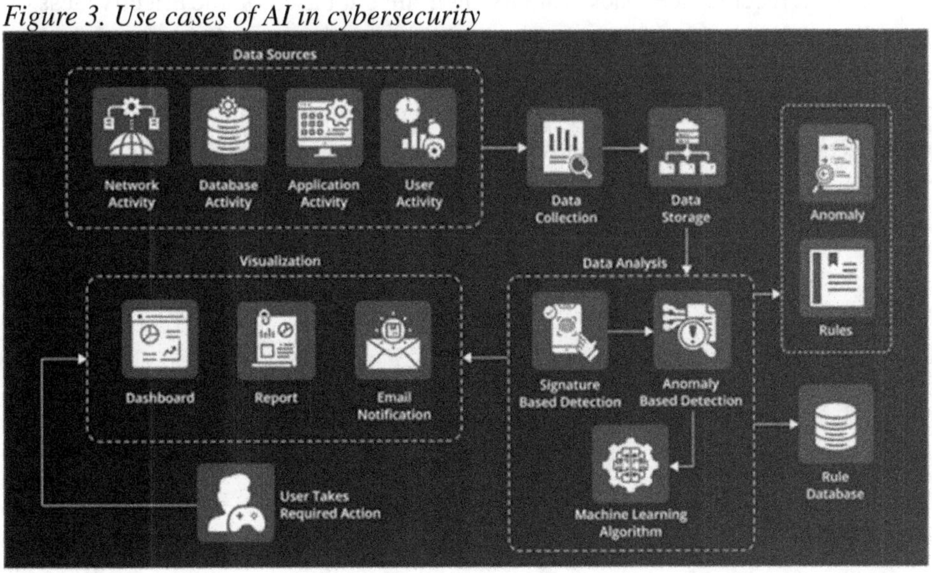

(Patil, 2024)

Role of Machine Learning and Deep Learning

ML algorithms are foundational to detecting patterns, anomalies, and indicators of compromise in large datasets. ML models are trained on historical attack data to identify known threats and are capable of generalizing to detect previously unseen variants. Supervised learning techniques use labeled data to train models for classification tasks, such as distinguishing between benign and malicious activities. Unsupervised learning is employed for anomaly detection, identifying outliers that may signify new or unknown threats. Deep Learning, a subset of ML, utilizes neural networks with multiple layers to analyze complex data structures. Convolutional Neural Networks (CNNs) are adept at analyzing structured data, while Recurrent Neural Networks (RNNs) and Long Short-Term Memory (LSTM) networks excel in sequential data analysis, such as log files and time-series threat patterns (Wang et al., 2024).

Reinforcement Learning for Autonomous Decision Making

Reinforcement Learning (RL) introduces a decision-making paradigm where the system learns optimal actions through trial and error. In cyber defense, RL can be used to develop adaptive policies that respond dynamically to evolving threats. An RL agent receives feedback from its environment based on the effectiveness of its actions, adjusting its strategy over time to maximize cumulative rewards. For example, an RL-based intrusion detection system might experiment with different response actions and refine its approach based on observed outcomes. This adaptability is essential in combating adversaries who constantly change tactics to evade detection. Figure 4 represents an example of Intrusion Detection System (IDS) based on Reinforcement Learning and Deep Learning (Liao et al., 2020).

Figure 4. Architecture of IDS based on reinforcement learning and deep learning

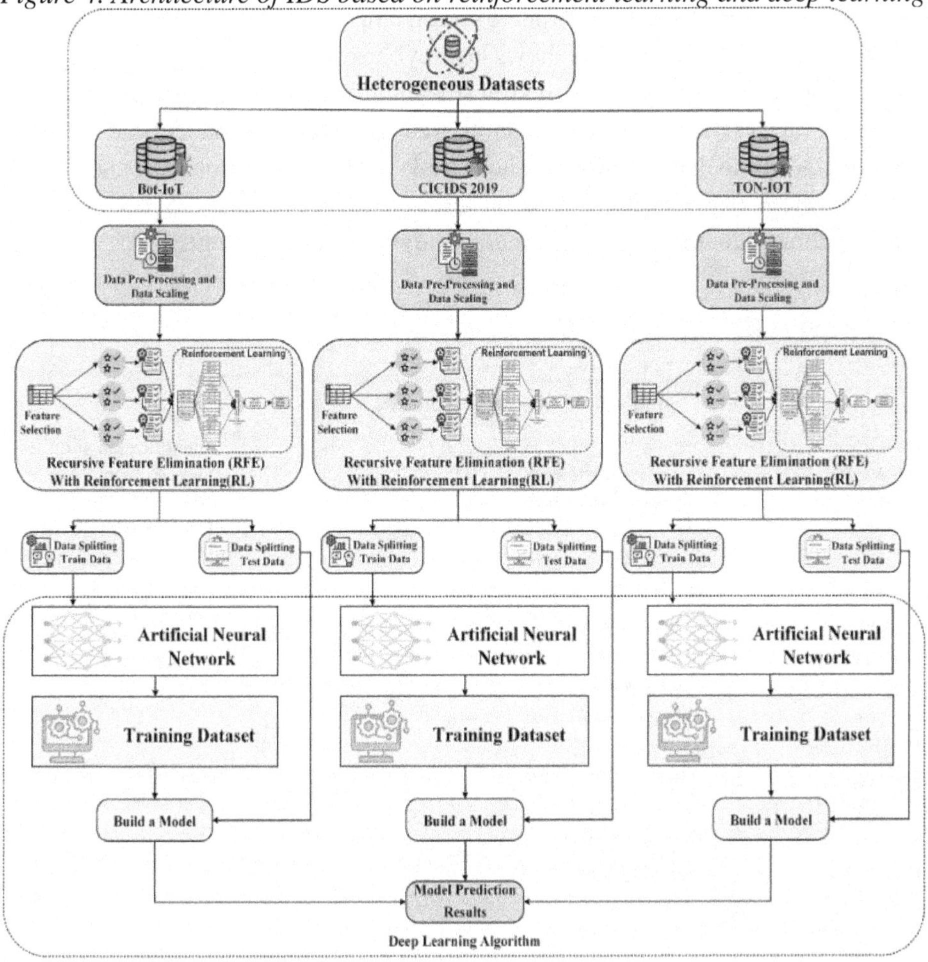

(Hussain et al., 2024)

Natural Language Processing (NLP) in Cyber Threat Analysis

Natural Language Processing (NLP) plays a vital role in automating the extraction of actionable intelligence from unstructured data sources such as security blogs, threat reports, and vulnerability databases. NLP techniques enable the system to interpret textual information, identify relevant entities (e.g., malware names, IP addresses, CVE identifiers), and integrate this intelligence into decision-making processes. Named Entity Recognition (NER), sentiment analysis, and document classification are commonly used NLP tasks in cybersecurity. By automating the analysis of vast textual data, NLP enhances situational awareness and accelerates the threat intelligence lifecycle (Marinho & Holanda, 2023). Figure 5 presents an individual risk assessment framework for the healthcare sector, emphasizing the integration of NLP in autonomous cyber-defense. It shows how cybersecurity knowledge bases, news articles, and tweets are processed to extract meaningful insights using advanced NLP techniques such as the BERT Named Entity Recognition (NER) model and machine learning algorithms like XGBoost. These tools support the automated analysis of the healthcare ecosystem context, threat levels, and vulnerability scores, enabling timely and intelligent responses to emerging cyber threats (Silvestri, 2024).

Figure 5. NLP in cyber threat analysis

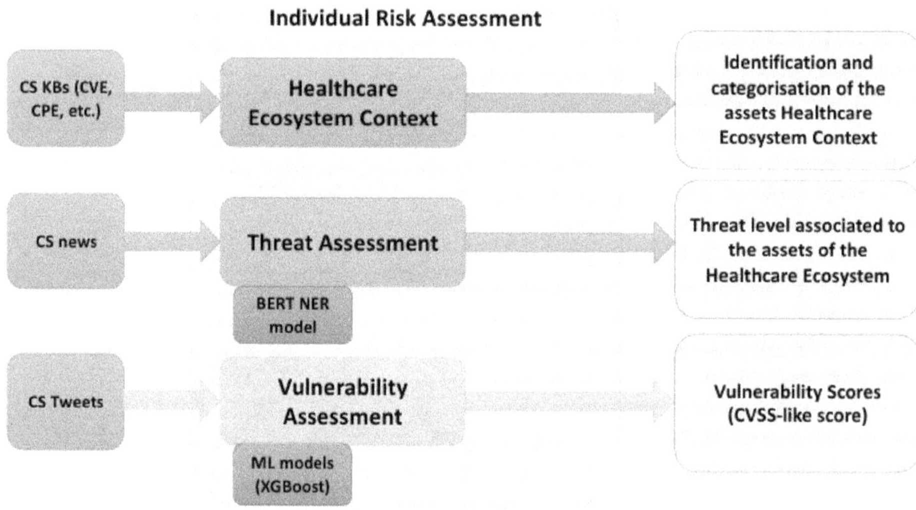

(Silvestri et al., 2024)

XAI for Transparency in Cyber Defense Decisions

While AI enables powerful capabilities, the complexity of models—particularly deep learning—can lead to a lack of transparency in decision-making. Explainable AI (XAI) addresses this challenge by providing insights into how and why a model arrived at a specific decision. Techniques such as SHAP (SHapley Additive exPlanations) and LIME (Local Interpretable Model-agnostic Explanations) allow users to interpret model outputs and understand the contribution of different features. In cybersecurity, XAI is critical for building trust in autonomous systems, ensuring regulatory compliance, and facilitating human oversight. Transparent AI models support accountability and make it easier for security analysts to validate system actions and correct misclassifications when necessary (Agarwal, 2025).

Figure 6 presents a taxonomy of XAI methods, highlighting their scope (global vs. local), explanation techniques (intrinsically explainable vs. post-hoc), and their classification into model-specific and model-agnostic approaches. It further illustrates how these XAI methods are applied across various cybersecurity domains, such as intrusion detection, malware detection, digital forensics, and cyber resilience. This taxonomy showcases the critical role of XAI in enhancing transparency, trust, and interpretability of AI-driven cybersecurity systems (Desai, 2024).

Figure 6. NLP in cyber threat analysis

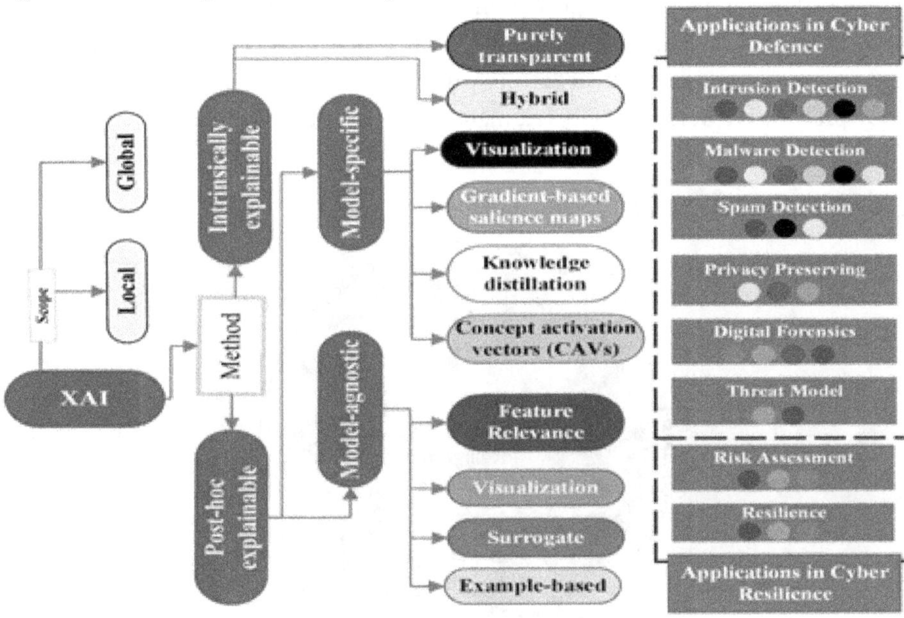

(Masud et al., 2024)

4 TECHNOLOGIES ENABLING AUTONOMOUS CYBER DEFENSE

The development and deployment of autonomous cyber defense systems depend heavily on a range of enabling technologies. These technologies serve as the infrastructure and intelligence layer supporting the capabilities discussed in previous sections. Each plays a distinct and crucial role in creating an integrated and effective defense system.

- **Cyber Threat Intelligence (CTI)**

CTI refers to the collection, processing, and analysis of data relating to current and potential cyber threats. Figure 7 presents the life cycle of CTI. In autonomous systems, CTI is used to inform threat detection and guide response mechanisms. By incorporating CTI feeds—sourced from commercial vendors, open-source platforms, or internal security logs—autonomous systems gain contextual awareness of global threat landscapes. Standard formats such as STIX (Structured Threat Information Expression) and TAXII (Trusted Automated eXchange of Indicator Information) enable structured, machine-readable intelligence sharing. CTI enhances the ability of autonomous systems to detect zero-day threats, analyze threat actor behavior, and deploy preemptive defenses (Chatziamanetoglou & Rantos, 2024).

Figure 7. Life cycle of CTI

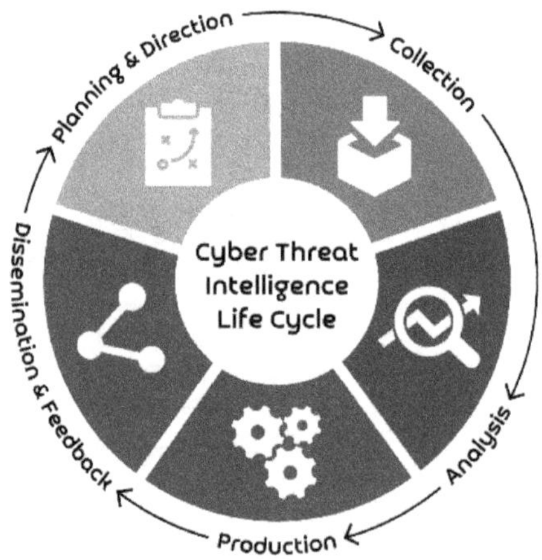

- **Security Orchestration, Automation, and Response (SOAR)**

SOAR platforms form the operational backbone of autonomous cyber defense by integrating multiple security tools and automating workflows across them. These platforms gather and normalize data from diverse sources, run automated playbooks, and initiate coordinated response actions. For example, upon detecting a phishing attack, a SOAR platform can automatically isolate affected systems, disable compromised accounts, and notify relevant stakeholders. SOAR platforms enhance scalability and reduce response times by eliminating manual steps, making them essential for handling high volumes of alerts in real time (Niyomdi & Oluoch, 2025).

- **Blockchain and Distributed Ledger Technology**

Blockchain, as depicted in Figure 8, introduces a decentralized and immutable ledger mechanism that enhances trust and transparency in cybersecurity operations. In autonomous defense, blockchain can be used for secure logging, identity verification, and integrity assurance of configuration files and policies. Smart contracts—self-executing scripts on a blockchain—can be programmed to trigger automated defense actions upon meeting predefined conditions, such as detecting a data breach or unauthorized access. The decentralized nature of blockchain ensures that records cannot be tampered with, providing forensic evidence and supporting incident attribution (Hajizadeh et al., 2020).

Figure 8. Architecture of blockchain

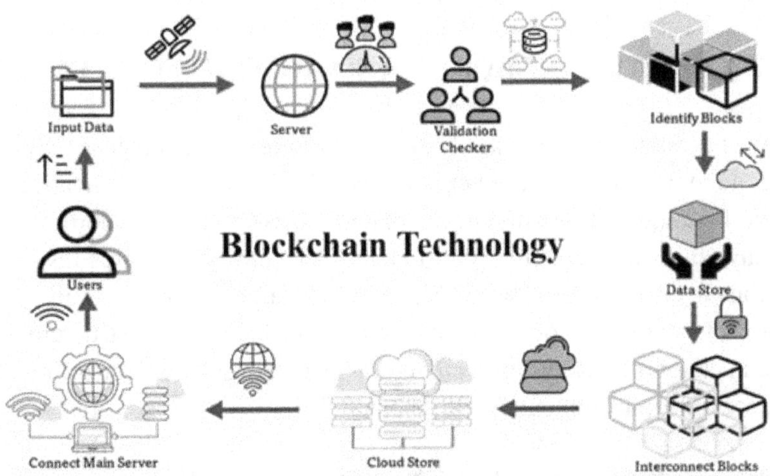

- **Cloud-Based Cybersecurity Platforms**

As organizations increasingly move workloads to the cloud, the need for cloud-native cybersecurity becomes paramount. Cloud-based platforms offer elastic and scalable security services that can be integrated with autonomous systems. These platforms provide services such as Web Application Firewalls (WAFs), Intrusion Detection Systems (IDS), and threat intelligence gateways as APIs. Cloud-native security solutions are designed for rapid deployment and update, allowing autonomous defense systems to quickly adapt to new threats. Integration with Infrastructure-as-Code (IaC) tools also enables autonomous validation and enforcement of security policies across dynamic cloud environments (Lane Thames, 2024).

- **Quantum Computing and its Potential Impacts**

Quantum computing presents both a challenge and an opportunity in cybersecurity. On one hand, quantum algorithms such as Shor's algorithm pose a significant threat to current encryption schemes like RSA and ECC. On the other hand, quantum computing opens new avenues for cybersecurity, including quantum key distribution (QKD) and quantum-enhanced machine learning. Autonomous systems will need to adapt to quantum-era threats by integrating post-quantum cryptography (PQC) and leveraging quantum-based analytics to improve threat prediction and decision-making. Ongoing research is essential to prepare autonomous defense architectures for the computational paradigms of the future (Sodiya et al., 2024).

5 CYBER THREAT LANDSCAPE AND AUTONOMOUS DEFENSE

To fully understand the critical role that autonomous cyber defense plays in the modern digital era, it is essential to explore the evolution and sophistication of the cyber threat landscape. The shift from isolated attacks to highly coordinated and adaptive campaigns has rendered traditional cybersecurity measures insufficient. Organizations are now confronted with a growing range of threats, from opportunistic exploits to state-sponsored operations targeting critical infrastructure. In this environment, autonomous systems emerge as a necessary evolution—providing proactive, scalable, and context-aware defenses.

Overview of Emerging Cyber Threats

Modern cyber threats are characterized by complexity, stealth, and rapid evolution. Traditional malware, which relied on fixed signatures and predictable behaviors, has been superseded by polymorphic and metamorphic malware that constantly changes its code structure to evade detection. Similarly, fileless malware operates entirely in memory, leaving no trace on disk and making it extremely difficult for signature-based tools to identify (Sudhakar & Kumar, 2020).

One of the most concerning developments is the use of artificial intelligence and machine learning by threat actors. AI-driven malware can autonomously scan for vulnerabilities, alter attack patterns in response to defenses, and generate new exploit payloads in real time. These capabilities make attacks more targeted, efficient, and difficult to detect. Additionally, advanced phishing campaigns now employ natural language generation to create convincing emails that bypass traditional content filters (Arif, Khan & Khan, 2024).

Advanced Persistent Threats (APTs) remain a significant concern for governments and enterprises. These are long-term campaigns conducted by well-funded and skilled adversaries, often with geopolitical motives. APTs are typically multi-stage operations involving reconnaissance, initial compromise, lateral movement, data exfiltration, and long-term persistence. They often utilize zero-day vulnerabilities—flaws that are unknown to software vendors—to penetrate even the most secure environments (Mohamed, 2024).

Insider threats also continue to plague organizations. Whether malicious or accidental, insiders with access to critical systems pose unique risks that are difficult to detect using external threat intelligence alone. Furthermore, the global nature of modern supply chains introduces new vulnerabilities. Compromising a vendor or third-party software provider can allow attackers to infiltrate dozens or hundreds of organizations simultaneously—a tactic seen in high-profile incidents like the SolarWinds breach (Cordey, 2023).

Another fast-growing category of cyber threat is ransomware-as-a-service (RaaS), where cybercriminal groups lease their ransomware tools to affiliates who conduct attacks and share the profits. This model has democratized cybercrime, allowing even low-skill actors to launch devastating attacks. The convergence of financial motivation, ease of access to tools, and anonymity via cryptocurrencies has fueled a sharp rise in ransomware incidents (Hafiz & Hidaya, 2025).

Living-off-the-land binaries (LOLBins) and dual-use tools present additional challenges. Attackers use legitimate system utilities such as PowerShell, WMI, and PsExec to execute malicious actions, blending in with normal administrative activity and evading detection. Because these tools are often whitelisted in enterprise environments, distinguishing between legitimate and malicious use requires sophisticated behavioral analysis (Ning et al., 2023).

Challenges of Traditional Cybersecurity Systems

Conventional cybersecurity systems were built to respond to known threats using predefined rules and static signatures. While these tools are effective against previously identified threats, they fall short when confronted with novel or obfuscated attack techniques. The rigid nature of rule-based systems makes them reactive rather than proactive (Tanikonda et al., 2022).

One of the most significant limitations is the high false positive rate. Security tools often flag benign activities as malicious, overwhelming analysts with alerts and contributing to alert fatigue. As a result, real threats may be overlooked amid the noise. Furthermore, legacy systems typically lack contextual awareness. They analyze events in isolation, missing the broader narrative that could indicate a coordinated attack (Olateju et al., 2024).

Traditional systems are also constrained by their dependence on human operators. Investigating, validating, and responding to incidents require significant manual effort, which is both time-consuming and error-prone. This dependency creates a bottleneck in incident response, particularly during large-scale or fast-moving attacks (Krause et al., 2021).

Inability to correlate data across different environments—on-premises, cloud, hybrid, and IoT—is another serious drawback. Without unified visibility, attackers can exploit blind spots and pivot between systems undetected. Siloed tools and lack of interoperability further complicate incident response and post-incident analysis (Sundararajan et al., 2019).

Resource constraints exacerbate these problems. Many organizations lack sufficient cybersecurity personnel, and those that do often struggle with high turnover and skills shortages. The increasing sophistication of attackers demands continuous monitoring and real-time decision-making—requirements that exceed human capacity.

Advantages of Autonomous Cyber Defense Approaches

Autonomous cyber defense systems address these challenges by introducing intelligent automation and adaptive decision-making into the security workflow. Unlike traditional systems, autonomous defenses are capable of learning from past incidents, generalizing from known patterns, and responding to emerging threats in real time without requiring manual intervention (Bairwa et al., 2024; Hemberg, & Zhang, 2020).

- One of the primary advantages is scalability. Autonomous systems can monitor and analyze data across thousands of endpoints, users, and network segments simultaneously. This capacity is crucial for large enterprises and distributed infrastructures where manual monitoring is infeasible.

- Machine learning algorithms enable anomaly detection that adapts to the environment. Rather than relying on predefined signatures, these systems establish behavioral baselines and detect deviations that may indicate malicious activity. For example, if a user account suddenly accesses sensitive files outside normal working hours from an unusual location, the system can flag or block the behavior based on contextual risk assessment.
- Autonomous systems can also automate the entire incident response lifecycle—from detection to containment, investigation, and recovery. When a threat is identified, automated playbooks can isolate affected systems, revoke compromised credentials, initiate backups, and notify relevant personnel. This rapid response minimizes damage and reduces dwell time, the period between breach and detection.
- By integrating with both internal telemetry and external threat intelligence, autonomous defenses maintain a dynamic and holistic view of the threat landscape. This integration allows the system to correlate local events with global trends, identify coordinated attacks, and update defense strategies accordingly.
- Real-time adaptability is another critical benefit. Autonomous systems continuously refine their models based on feedback and new data. If an attacker changes tactics mid-operation, the system can detect the shift and adjust its response. This agility is particularly valuable against APTs and fileless malware, which rely on stealth and evasion.
- Human analysts are not eliminated but rather empowered by autonomous systems. By handling routine tasks and low-level alerts, these systems free up human resources to focus on strategic planning, threat hunting, and complex investigations. Furthermore, autonomous systems can provide analysts with context-rich alerts that include recommended actions, reducing cognitive load and improving decision-making.
- Autonomous systems also enhance resilience. Their ability to detect and respond to attacks in real time, even when human operators are unavailable, ensures continuous protection. In cases of widespread attacks or global crises—such as those impacting healthcare or emergency services—autonomous systems can maintain defensive operations independently.
- Finally, the cost-efficiency of autonomous systems cannot be overlooked. While initial investments may be significant, the long-term benefits of reduced incident costs, improved response times, and lower staffing requirements often result in a strong return on investment. Autonomous systems

offer a sustainable approach to cybersecurity that aligns with the needs of modern digital enterprises.

6 FRAMEWORKS AND MODELS FOR AUTONOMOUS CYBER DEFENSE

Building and deploying autonomous cyber defense systems require well-defined frameworks and models that provide guidance on architecture, operational processes, and evaluation metrics. These frameworks serve as blueprints for ensuring system robustness, interoperability, and effectiveness. As the cybersecurity threat landscape continues to evolve in complexity and scale, organizations must adopt structured approaches to design, implement, and evaluate autonomous defenses that are responsive, scalable, and context-aware.

Decision Frameworks and Cyber Defense Architectures

At the heart of any autonomous cyber defense system lies a robust decision framework that governs how data is interpreted, decisions are made, and responses are executed. A widely adopted conceptual model in this context is the Perception-Decision-Action (PDA) cycle. This cycle mirrors the cognitive processes observed in human decision-making, where systems first gather data (perception), analyze and interpret it (decision), and then perform actions based on insights (action). These systems benefit greatly from continuous feedback loops, where the outcomes of decisions inform future perceptions and decision-making processes (Llopis Sánchez, 2023).

As illustrated in Figure 9, a well-structured architecture enables the PDA model through a layered approach. Typically, the architecture includes the following layers (Kineber et al., 2023):

1. **Perception Layer**: Comprising sensors, telemetry systems, and data collectors, this layer ingests information from a wide array of sources—network traffic, endpoint logs, application usage data, and threat intelligence feeds.
2. **Analytics Layer**: Utilizing machine learning models, statistical analysis, and correlation engines, this layer processes the raw data to detect anomalies, categorize threats, and provide actionable intelligence.
3. **Decision Layer**: The core of autonomy, where AI algorithms determine optimal response strategies based on predefined policies, risk assessments, and contextual variables.

4. **Action Layer**: Where response measures such as containment, notification, remediation, and system adjustments are automatically executed.
5. **Learning Layer**: A feedback mechanism that analyzes outcomes and updates models, rules, and policies to improve future performance.

Within these layers, interoperability is vital. Systems must be designed to work across different platforms, standards, and protocols. To this end, frameworks such as the MITRE ATT&CK and D3FEND matrices provide structured taxonomies of adversary behaviors and defensive tactics, respectively. The ATT&CK framework, for instance, helps map detected behaviors to known attack techniques, enabling more targeted and accurate threat responses. D3FEND complements this by outlining defensive countermeasures in a structured and actionable manner.

Figure 9. Architecture of PDA

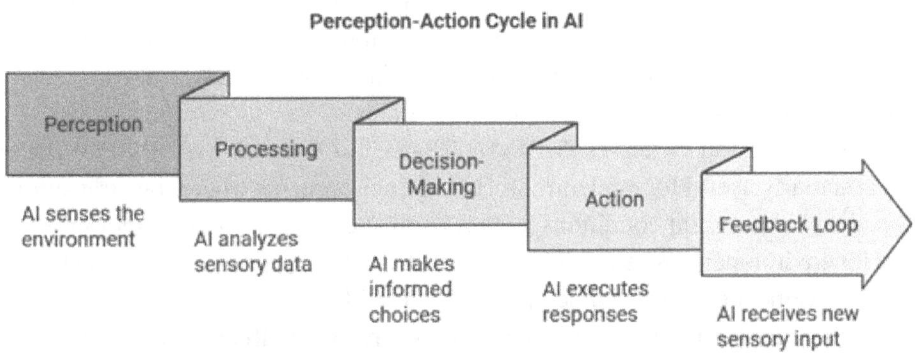

The National Institute of Standards and Technology (NIST) Cybersecurity Framework (CSF) offers another foundational reference. It is composed of five functions—Identify, Protect, Detect, Respond, and Recover—each encompassing specific categories and subcategories. When applied to autonomous systems, the NIST CSF helps align technological capabilities with strategic objectives, compliance requirements, and continuous improvement processes.

Automated Threat Response Models

Automated threat response models define the logic and mechanisms by which autonomous systems react to identified threats. These models can be broadly categorized into (Sarker, 2024):

- **Rule-Based Models**: Utilizing static or dynamic rule sets to trigger specific actions when predefined conditions are met. Although straightforward to implement, these models lack adaptability and may not scale well with evolving threats.
- **Policy-Based Models**: These expand on rule-based systems by incorporating contextual information such as user behavior, system sensitivity, and threat severity. Policies are often defined using declarative languages that outline acceptable behavior and response thresholds.
- **Cognitive and AI-Based Models**: These models leverage learning algorithms to dynamically assess threats and tailor responses. Techniques such as supervised learning, unsupervised clustering, and reinforcement learning allow systems to adapt over time and handle novel or previously unseen threats.

More advanced response models incorporate **probabilistic reasoning** and **game-theoretic approaches** to make decisions under uncertainty. For instance, Bayesian networks can estimate the likelihood of an intrusion based on observed indicators, while game theory models consider the potential moves of adversaries to select optimal defensive strategies (Andreoni et al, 2024).

Markov Decision Processes (MDPs) and Partially Observable MDPs (POMDPs) are particularly useful for modeling stochastic environments where state transitions depend on both current conditions and probabilistic events. These frameworks are ideal for environments where full observability is not guaranteed, such as detecting lateral movement or advanced persistent threats (APTs).

Another class of models is based on **event-driven architectures (EDA)**, where autonomous systems subscribe to specific event types and trigger responses when those events occur. EDAs are highly modular and support scalable, real-time operations. For instance, detecting a spike in failed login attempts could trigger multiple response actions—such as account lockout, user notification, and an AI-driven investigation into potential credential stuffing.

Multi-Agent Systems and Federated Models

In complex environments such as cloud and hybrid infrastructures, a single monolithic system may not be sufficient for comprehensive cyber defense. Instead, **multi-agent systems (MAS)** are deployed, where multiple autonomous agents coordinate and collaborate to detect, analyze, and respond to threats. Each agent is responsible for a subset of tasks—such as monitoring a specific subnet or analyzing a certain type of log—and communicates with other agents to form a unified response (Gaba et al., 2024).

These systems can be either **centralized** (with a central coordinator) or **decentralized** (where agents operate independently but share intelligence). Decentralized MAS models offer better fault tolerance and scalability. Communication protocols such as FIPA-ACL (Foundation for Intelligent Physical Agents - Agent Communication Language) help standardize inter-agent communication (Yahouni et al., 2021).

Federated learning is another emerging paradigm, especially relevant in privacy-sensitive domains such as healthcare and finance. In this model, autonomous agents train local models on private data and share only the model updates with a central aggregator. This approach preserves data locality, reduces bandwidth consumption, and enhances privacy while enabling collaborative threat intelligence.

Resilience and Redundancy Models

Frameworks for autonomous defense must also account for resilience—the ability of systems to maintain operation and recover quickly in the face of disruptions. **Redundancy models** ensure that critical components have failovers and backups. For example, if a primary decision engine is compromised, a secondary engine should take over without degrading performance (Hu et al., 2018).

Resilience modeling often incorporates **chaos engineering** techniques, which involve deliberately introducing faults to test system robustness. Automated systems should be designed to detect degraded states, reroute traffic, or switch operational modes autonomously (Torkura et al., 2020).

Evaluation and Validation Frameworks

To assess the effectiveness of autonomous cyber defense systems, comprehensive evaluation and validation models are required. These frameworks utilize key performance indicators (KPIs) such as (Llopis Sánchez, 2023):

- Detection Accuracy: Ratio of true positives to false positives.
- Mean Time to Detect (MTTD) and Mean Time to Respond (MTTR): Metrics for operational speed.
- Adaptability: System's ability to handle novel threats.
- Scalability: Performance under increasing data volumes.
- Resilience: Ability to recover from faults or attacks.

Testing environments such as cyber ranges and digital twins simulate real-world conditions to evaluate system performance. Red-teaming and adversarial testing are also valuable techniques to assess how well systems withstand sophisticated attacks.

Ethical and Regulatory Frameworks

As autonomous systems gain more decision-making authority, ethical and regulatory considerations must be embedded into frameworks. These include (Fisher et al., 2021):

- Transparency: Ensuring decision-making processes are explainable.
- Accountability: Assigning responsibility for autonomous actions.
- Privacy: Ensuring compliance with GDPR, HIPAA, and other regulations.
- Bias Mitigation: Preventing discriminatory outcomes in AI models.

Embedding these principles into system design and governance frameworks ensures that autonomous defense systems not only protect assets but also operate within societal and legal norms.

7 IMPLEMENTING AUTONOMOUS CYBER DEFENSE IN PRACTICE

The transition from traditional to autonomous cyber defense systems is not a mere technological upgrade—it represents a paradigm shift in how security is conceptualized, managed, and executed. Implementing such systems requires detailed strategic planning, phased deployment, and the careful alignment of technology with organizational processes. The success of autonomous cyber defense lies in an organization's ability to harmonize advanced technologies with people, processes, and policies while ensuring compliance with regulatory mandates and resilience against rapidly evolving threats.

Deployment Strategies and Best Practices

Strategic deployment of autonomous systems begins with an accurate and thorough assessment of an organization's existing cybersecurity posture. This includes identifying vulnerable assets, understanding existing detection and response capabilities, and determining the maturity level of current incident response procedures. A crucial first step is defining the organization's risk appetite and prioritizing areas where autonomy can deliver immediate value, such as reducing incident response time or enhancing alert triage.

Initial implementations should typically begin with pilot projects or proof-of-concept deployments in controlled environments. These pilots allow for evaluating the effectiveness of autonomous tools in real-world conditions without compromising critical infrastructure. The goal of these early phases is to identify compatibility issues, integration challenges, and potential gaps in coverage. Following successful pilots, organizations should adopt a phased rollout strategy that gradually expands autonomy across departments, applications, and infrastructure components.

Hybrid deployment models, where human analysts retain oversight of AI-generated recommendations and responses, are highly recommended during early adoption stages. This model ensures human validation of critical decisions and builds trust in autonomous capabilities. Over time, as the system proves its accuracy and reliability, organizations can shift toward full autonomy for specific threat categories or operational domains.

Organizations must also consider modularity and interoperability during deployment. The design of autonomous systems should support modular components that can be upgraded or replaced independently. This ensures that organizations can adopt new technologies or respond to changes in the threat landscape without overhauling the entire defense architecture. Standards-based architectures and the use of APIs facilitate integration with existing tools and platforms.

Another critical best practice involves the development and rigorous testing of automation playbooks. These playbooks define the series of actions the system must take in response to specific threats. Each playbook should be mapped to corresponding detection triggers, decision thresholds, and mitigation actions. Testing these playbooks through simulations or red-teaming exercises validates their effectiveness and helps identify false positives and performance bottlenecks.

Integration with Existing Security Infrastructure

Successful deployment hinges on the seamless integration of autonomous capabilities with an organization's existing security ecosystem. Core components such as Security Information and Event Management (SIEM) systems, Endpoint Detection and Response (EDR), Intrusion Detection and Prevention Systems (IDS/IPS), firewalls, and vulnerability management platforms must work in concert with new autonomous tools.

The integration process typically involves data normalization, API mapping, and orchestration layer configuration. Autonomous systems must ingest telemetry from diverse sources and correlate data across network, endpoint, and application layers. Middleware or integration platforms can facilitate this by aggregating and translating data into a consistent schema.

Clear protocols must be established for how autonomous systems escalate incidents, request human validation, or trigger automated responses. This requires aligning the system's decision-making logic with organizational workflows and escalation procedures. Teams must define thresholds for human intervention, such as in cases of high-impact decisions, data loss risks, or actions affecting production systems.

Auditability and accountability are also critical integration concerns. Autonomous systems must generate logs of their activities, including detection rationale, decision paths, and executed responses. These logs support forensic investigations, enable compliance reporting, and help organizations fine-tune their systems over time.

Training and change management are integral to integration success. Security teams must be trained on how to interpret and interact with the outputs of autonomous systems. Change management processes should ensure that updates to playbooks, response logic, or system configurations are tested, approved, and version-controlled.

Considerations for Scalability and Real-Time Response

Scalability is a core requirement for autonomous defense systems. These systems must handle increasing data volumes, growing numbers of endpoints, and expanding threat surfaces across diverse environments including cloud, on-premises, and edge locations. A scalable system must be capable of ingesting, analyzing, and responding to data streams from thousands of nodes without degradation in performance.

Distributed computing architectures, microservices, and containerized deployments are foundational enablers of scalability. These architectures allow components to scale independently and support elastic resource allocation. Load balancing, horizontal scaling, and data sharding ensure that systems can maintain performance even during high-volume attack scenarios.

Real-time response capabilities are another critical pillar of autonomous defense. The latency between threat detection and response execution can significantly influence the outcome of an attack. Low-latency data processing pipelines, real-time analytics engines, and pre-defined response actions contribute to minimizing response times.

Technologies such as edge computing and federated learning play an increasingly important role in scaling real-time capabilities. Edge computing allows data to be processed closer to the source, reducing the time required to detect and respond to threats. Federated learning enables distributed systems to learn collaboratively without sharing raw data, which is particularly useful in environments with privacy or bandwidth constraints.

System resilience and high availability are also essential. Failover mechanisms, redundancy, and disaster recovery protocols must be incorporated into system design. Monitoring and alerting frameworks should continuously assess system health, resource utilization, and response effectiveness.

Case Studies and Real-world Implementations

Autonomous cyber defense is no longer a theoretical concept—numerous organizations across industries have successfully deployed and benefited from these systems. Financial institutions, for instance, have long relied on autonomous fraud detection systems that use machine learning to analyze transaction patterns in real time. These systems flag anomalies, block suspicious transactions, and adapt their models based on emerging fraud tactics.

In the healthcare sector, hospitals are adopting AI-driven systems to detect ransomware and other threats targeting medical devices and patient data. These systems continuously monitor network traffic and device behavior, using anomaly detection models to identify unauthorized access or malware propagation. Automated responses include network isolation of infected devices, alert escalation, and system recovery from backups.

Critical infrastructure sectors, such as energy and transportation, are also embracing autonomy. For example, power grid operators use AI to detect unusual patterns in operational data that may indicate cyber intrusions. Autonomous systems in these environments can proactively adjust control parameters, reroute energy flows, or trigger system lockdowns to mitigate risk.

These real-world implementations underscore several common lessons. First, success depends on cross-functional collaboration between cybersecurity, IT, operations, and executive teams. Second, clear governance and oversight mechanisms must be in place to manage the transition to autonomy. Finally, organizations must be prepared to continuously refine their systems based on feedback, incident outcomes, and changing threat conditions.

8 FUTURE TRENDS AND RESEARCH DIRECTIONS

The field of autonomous cyber defense is poised for significant evolution, driven by a convergence of emerging technologies, evolving threat landscapes, and growing regulatory requirements. Forward-looking organizations must stay ahead of these trends to build resilient and future-proof cybersecurity infrastructures.

Quantum Computing and Autonomous Cyber Defense

Quantum computing represents both a transformative opportunity and a formidable challenge in cybersecurity. On the one hand, quantum computers can break many of today's encryption schemes by efficiently solving problems such as integer factorization and discrete logarithms. On the other hand, quantum computing offers capabilities for vastly superior threat detection, real-time encryption, and simulation-based security testing.

Autonomous cyber defense systems will need to incorporate post-quantum cryptography (PQC) to remain secure in a quantum-enabled world. PQC algorithms such as lattice-based, code-based, and hash-based cryptography are being developed and standardized by organizations like NIST. Autonomous systems must be designed to identify vulnerable cryptographic modules, replace them with PQC alternatives, and ensure seamless migration.

Research into quantum machine learning (QML) also holds promise for accelerating autonomous threat detection and decision-making. Quantum algorithms such as quantum support vector machines and quantum neural networks offer potential speedups in pattern recognition, anomaly detection, and classification tasks. These advancements could enable autonomous systems to process larger datasets and adapt more quickly to evolving threats.

Integration of Blockchain Technology for Enhanced Security

Blockchain continues to gain attention for its potential to enhance trust, transparency, and integrity in cybersecurity operations. In autonomous defense, blockchain can be used to create immutable logs of system activities, which are critical for forensic investigations and regulatory compliance. Tamper-proof logging ensures that attackers cannot cover their tracks or alter evidence.

Smart contracts running on blockchain platforms can also automate security workflows. For example, a smart contract could trigger an autonomous system to revoke access credentials or shut down a compromised system when specific threat indicators are detected. This enables distributed, consensus-driven enforcement of security policies.

Additionally, blockchain supports decentralized identity (DID) frameworks that enhance access control and reduce reliance on centralized identity providers. Autonomous systems can use DID to verify identities across multi-cloud and edge environments without compromising privacy or security.

Advances in AI-Driven Threat Detection and Response

Artificial intelligence continues to advance at a rapid pace, bringing new capabilities and efficiencies to autonomous cyber defense. One key area is model interpretability—developing AI models whose decisions can be explained and understood by humans. Explainable AI (XAI) techniques such as LIME, SHAP, and saliency mapping help demystify model outputs and improve trust.

Another major trend is the move toward data-efficient AI. Techniques like transfer learning and few-shot learning allow models to learn from limited labeled data, which is particularly valuable in detecting novel or rare attack types. Meta-learning and continual learning approaches help systems adapt to new data without catastrophic forgetting.

Adversarial machine learning is also a critical research frontier. Attackers are increasingly crafting adversarial examples to deceive AI models. Defending against these attacks requires robust training methods, input sanitization, and anomaly detection at multiple stages of the AI pipeline.

REFERENCES

Adeniyi, O., Sadiq, A. S., Pillai, P., Taheir, M. A., & Kaiwartya, O. (2023). Proactive self-healing approaches in mobile edge computing: A systematic literature review. *Computers, 12*(3), 63. DOI: 10.3390/computers12030063

Agarwal, G. (2025). Explainable AI (XAI) for Cyber Defense: Enhancing Transparency and Trust in AI-Driven Security Solutions. *International Journal of Advanced Research in Science. Tongxin Jishu, 5*(1), 132–138.

Ali, S., Rehman, S. U., Imran, A., Adeem, G., Iqbal, Z., & Kim, K. I. (2022). Comparative evaluation of ai-based techniques for zero-day attacks detection. *Electronics (Basel), 11*(23), 3934. DOI: 10.3390/electronics11233934

Andreoni, M., Lunardi, W. T., Lawton, G., & Thakkar, S. (2024). Enhancing autonomous system security and resilience with generative AI: A comprehensive survey. *IEEE Access : Practical Innovations, Open Solutions, 12*, 109470–109493. DOI: 10.1109/ACCESS.2024.3439363

Arif, A., Khan, M. I., & Khan, A. R. A. (2024). An overview of cyber threats generated by AI. *International Journal of Multidisciplinary Sciences and Arts, 3*(4), 67–76.

Bairwa, A. K., Yadav, R., Rao, D. D., Naidu, K., H C, Y., & Sharma, S. (2024). Implications of Cyber-Physical Adversarial Attacks on Autonomous Systems. *Int. J. Exp. Res. Rev, 46*, 273–284. DOI: 10.52756/ijerr.2024.v46.021

Chatziamanetoglou, D., & Rantos, K. (2024). Cyber threat intelligence on blockchain: A systematic literature review. *Computers, 13*(3), 60. DOI: 10.3390/computers13030060

Cordey, S. (2023). *Software supply chain attacks: An illustrated typological review*. ETH Zurich.

Desai, B., Patil, K., Mehta, I., & Patil, A. (2024, September). Explainable AI in Cybersecurity: A Comprehensive Framework for enhancing transparency, trust, and Human-AI Collaboration. In *2024 International Seminar on Application for Technology of Information and Communication (iSemantic)* (pp. 135-150). IEEE. DOI: 10.1109/iSemantic63362.2024.10762690

Ehis, A. M. T. (2023). Optimization of security information and event management (SIEM) infrastructures, and events correlation/regression analysis for optimal cyber security posture. *Archives of Advanced Engineering Science*, 1-10.

Fisher, M., Mascardi, V., Rozier, K. Y., Schlingloff, B. H., Winikoff, M., & Yorke-Smith, N. (2021). Towards a framework for certification of reliable autonomous systems. *Autonomous Agents and Multi-Agent Systems*, *35*(1), 1–65. DOI: 10.1007/s10458-020-09487-2

Gaba, S., Budhiraja, I., Kumar, V., Garg, S., & Hassan, M. M. (2024). An innovative multi-agent approach for robust cyber–physical systems using vertical federated learning. *Ad Hoc Networks*, *163*, 103578. DOI: 10.1016/j.adhoc.2024.103578

George, A. S. (2024). Emerging Trends in AI-Driven Cybersecurity: An In-Depth Analysis. *Partners Universal Innovative Research Publication*, *2*(4), 15–28.

Hafiz, L., & Hidayat, T. (2025). Unveiling the Cybercrime Ecosystem: Impact of Ransomware-as-a-Service (RaaS) in Indonesia. *International Journal of Science Education and Cultural Studies*, *4*(1), 11–21.

Hajizadeh, M., Afraz, N., Ruffini, M., & Bauschert, T. (2020, June). Collaborative cyber attack defense in SDN networks using blockchain technology. In *2020 6th IEEE conference on network softwarization (netSoft)* (pp. 487-492). IEEE. DOI: 10.1109/NetSoft48620.2020.9165396

Hemberg, E., Zhang, L., & O'Reilly, U. M. (2020). Exploring adversarial artificial intelligence for autonomous adaptive cyber defense. *Adaptive Autonomous Secure Cyber Systems*, 41-61.

Hu, H., Wu, J., Wang, Z., & Cheng, G. (2018). Mimic defense: A designed-in cybersecurity defense framework. *IET Information Security*, *12*(3), 226–237. DOI: 10.1049/iet-ifs.2017.0086

Hussain, S., He, J., Zhu, N., Mughal, F. R., Hussain, M. I., Algarni, A. D., Ahmad, S., Zarie, M. M., & Ateya, A. A. (2024). An adaptive intrusion detection system for WSN using reinforcement learning and deep classification. *Arabian Journal for Science and Engineering*, •••, 1–15. DOI: 10.1007/s13369-024-09769-x

Katiforis, S. (2024). Synchronized Coevolution: A Conceptual Framework For Sustaining a Human-Centered Security Culture in AI-Driven Environments.

Kholidy, H. A. (2021). Autonomous mitigation of cyber risks in the Cyber–Physical Systems. *Future Generation Computer Systems*, *115*, 171–187. DOI: 10.1016/j.future.2020.09.002

Kineber, A. F., Oke, A., Aliu, J., Hamed, M. M., & Oputu, E. (2023). Exploring the adoption of cyber (digital) technology for sustainable construction: A structural equation modeling of critical success factors. *Sustainability (Basel)*, *15*(6), 5043. DOI: 10.3390/su15065043

Kott, A. (2018). Intelligent autonomous agents are key to cyber defense of the future army networks. *The Cyber Defense Review*, *3*(3), 57–70.

Krause, T., Ernst, R., Klaer, B., Hacker, I., & Henze, M. (2021). Cybersecurity in power grids: Challenges and opportunities. *Sensors (Basel)*, *21*(18), 6225. DOI: 10.3390/s21186225 PMID: 34577432

Lane Thames, J. (2014). Distributed, collaborative and automated cybersecurity infrastructures for cloud-based design and manufacturing systems. In *Cloud-Based Design and Manufacturing (CBDM) A Service-Oriented Product Development Paradigm for the 21st Century* (pp. 207–229). Springer International Publishing. DOI: 10.1007/978-3-319-07398-9_8

Liao, J., Liu, T., Tang, X., Mu, X., Huang, B., & Cao, D. (2020). Decision-making strategy on highway for autonomous vehicles using deep reinforcement learning. *IEEE Access : Practical Innovations, Open Solutions*, *8*, 177804–177814. DOI: 10.1109/ACCESS.2020.3022755

Llopis Sánchez, S. (2023). *Decision support elements and enabling techniques to achieve a cyber defence situational awareness capability* (Doctoral dissertation, Universitat Politècnica de València).

Llopis Sánchez, S. (2023). *Decision support elements and enabling techniques to achieve a cyber defence situational awareness capability* (Doctoral dissertation, Universitat Politècnica de València).

Marinho, R., & Holanda, R. (2023). Automated emerging cyber threat identification and profiling based on natural language processing. *IEEE Access : Practical Innovations, Open Solutions*, *11*, 58915–58936. DOI: 10.1109/ACCESS.2023.3260020

Masud, M. T., Keshk, M., Moustafa, N., Linkov, I., & Emge, D. K. (2024). Explainable artificial intelligence for resilient security applications in the Internet of Things. *IEEE Open Journal of the Communications Society*, 1. DOI: 10.1109/OJCOMS.2024.3413790

Mohamed, N. (2024, June). A review of AI approaches in combating advanced persistent threats (APTs) in cybersecurity. In *2024 15th International Conference on Computing Communication and Networking Technologies (ICCCNT)* (pp. 1-6). IEEE.

Möller, D. P. (2023). Threats and threat intelligence. In *Guide to cybersecurity in digital transformation: Trends, methods, technologies, applications and best practices* (pp. 71–129). Springer Nature Switzerland. DOI: 10.1007/978-3-031-26845-8_2

Moustafa, N., Koroniotis, N., Keshk, M., Zomaya, A. Y., & Tari, Z. (2023). Explainable intrusion detection for cyber defences in the internet of things: Opportunities and solutions. *IEEE Communications Surveys and Tutorials, 25*(3), 1775–1807. DOI: 10.1109/COMST.2023.3280465

Ning, R., Bu, W., Yang, J., & Duan, S. (2023, August). A survey of detection methods research on living-off-the-land techniques. In *2023 IEEE International Conference on Sensors, Electronics and Computer Engineering (ICSECE)* (pp. 159-164). IEEE. DOI: 10.1109/ICSECE58870.2023.10263445

Niyomdi, M., & Oluoch, J. (2025, February). A Comprehensive Security Orchestration, Automation, and Response System (SOAR) for Connected and Autonomous Vehicles (CAVs). In *2025 IEEE 4th International Conference on AI in Cybersecurity (ICAIC)* (pp. 1-14). IEEE.

Olateju, O., Okon, S. U., Igwenagu, U., Salami, A. A., Oladoyinbo, T. O., & Olaniyi, O. O. (2024). Combating the challenges of false positives in AI-driven anomaly detection systems and enhancing data security in the cloud. *Available atSSRN* 4859958.

Patel, A., & Wei, L. (2024). The Future of Cyber Defense: Autonomous Systems Powered by AI and Machine Learning. *Baltic Multidisciplinary Research Letters Journal, 1*(3), 85–92.

Patil, D. (2024). Artificial Intelligence In Retail And E-Commerce: Enhancing Customer Experience Through Personalization, Predictive Analytics, And Real-Time Engagement. *Predictive Analytics, And Real-Time Engagement (November 26, 2024).*

Safitra, M. F., Lubis, M., & Fakhrurroja, H. (2023). Counterattacking cyber threats: A framework for the future of cybersecurity. *Sustainability (Basel), 15*(18), 13369. DOI: 10.3390/su151813369

Sarker, I. H. (2024). *AI-driven cybersecurity and threat intelligence: cyber automation, intelligent decision-making and explainability*. Springer Nature. DOI: 10.1007/978-3-031-54497-2

Sarker, I. H. (2024). *AI-driven cybersecurity and threat intelligence: cyber automation, intelligent decision-making and explainability*. Springer Nature. DOI: 10.1007/978-3-031-54497-2

Shehzadi, T. (2024). Reinforcement Learning-Based Autonomous Systems for Cyber Threat Detection and Response. *Eastern European Journal for Multidisciplinary Research, 1*(1), 123–137.

Silvestri, S., Islam, S., Amelin, D., Weiler, G., Papastergiou, S., & Ciampi, M. (2024). Cyber threat assessment and management for securing healthcare ecosystems using natural language processing. *International Journal of Information Security, 23*(1), 31–50. DOI: 10.1007/s10207-023-00769-w

Soare, S. R. (2023). *The Role of Artificial Intelligence in European Strategic Autonomy*. Artificial Intelligence and International Conflict in Cyberspace.

Sodiya, E. O., Umoga, U. J., Amoo, O. O., & Atadoga, A. (2024). Quantum computing and its potential impact on US cybersecurity: A review: Scrutinizing the challenges and opportunities presented by quantum technologies in safeguarding digital assets. *Global Journal of Engineering and Technology Advances, 18*(02), 049-064.

Sundararajan, A., Khan, T., Moghadasi, A., & Sarwat, A. I. (2019). Survey on synchrophasor data quality and cybersecurity challenges, and evaluation of their interdependencies. *Journal of Modern Power Systems and Clean Energy, 7*(3), 449–467. DOI: 10.1007/s40565-018-0473-6

Tanikonda, A., Pandey, B. K., Peddinti, S. R., & Katragadda, S. R. (2022). Advanced AI-Driven Cybersecurity Solutions for Proactive Threat Detection and Response in Complex Ecosystems. *Journal of Science and Technology, 3*(1).

Theron, P., Kott, A., Drašar, M., Rzadca, K., LeBlanc, B., Pihelgas, M., & De Gaspari, F. (2020). Reference architecture of an autonomous agent for cyber defense of complex military systems. In *Adaptive autonomous secure cyber systems* (pp. 1–21). Springer International Publishing. DOI: 10.1007/978-3-030-33432-1_1

Torkura, K. A., Sukmana, M. I., Cheng, F., & Meinel, C. (2020). Cloudstrike: Chaos engineering for security and resiliency in cloud infrastructure. *IEEE Access : Practical Innovations, Open Solutions, 8*, 123044–123060. DOI: 10.1109/ACCESS.2020.3007338

Uchendu, I., Jabbour, J., Berghe, K. V. D., Runevic, J., Stewart, M., Ma, J., . . . Reddi, V. J. (2025). A2Perf: Real-World Autonomous Agents Benchmark. *arXiv preprint arXiv:2503.03056*. https://arxiv.org/abs/2503.03056

Vermesan, O., Bröring, A., Tragos, E., Serrano, M., Bacciu, D., Chessa, S., & Bahr, R. (2022). Internet of robotic things–converging sensing/actuating, hyperconnectivity, artificial intelligence and IoT platforms. In *Cognitive hyperconnected digital transformation* (pp. 97–155). River Publishers. DOI: 10.1201/9781003337584-4

Wang, C., Jiang, S., Li, Z., Zhong, W., Song, X., Liu, H., Hu, L., & Li, W. (2024). Accuracy and safety evaluation of a novel artificial intelligence–based robotic system for autonomous spinal posterior decompression. *Neurosurgical Focus*, *57*(6), E16. DOI: 10.3171/2024.9.FOCUS24400 PMID: 39616632

Wei, C. (2024). Autonomous Cyber Defense Systems: Opportunities and Challenges. *Advances in Computer Sciences*, *7*(1), 1–8.

Yahouni, Z., Ladj, A., Belkadi, F., Meski, O., & Ritou, M. (2021). A smart reporting framework as an application of multi-agent system in machining industry. *International Journal of Computer Integrated Manufacturing*, *34*(5), 470–486. DOI: 10.1080/0951192X.2021.1901312

Yan, Q., Huang, M., & Cao, H. (2022, July). A survey of human-machine collaboration in fuzzing. In *2022 7th IEEE International Conference on Data Science in Cyberspace (DSC)* (pp. 375-382). IEEE. DOI: 10.1109/DSC55868.2022.00058

Chapter 2
AI-Driven Security Systems and Intelligence Threat Response Using Autonomous Cyber Defense

Salam Al E'mari
https://orcid.org/0000-0002-2134-4158
Petra University, Jordan

Yousef Sanjalawe
https://orcid.org/0000-0002-4442-1865
University of Jordan, Jordan

Fuad Fataftah
https://orcid.org/0009-0009-3203-5869
Universiti Sains Malaysia, Malaysia

ABSTRACT

The expanding cyber threat landscape has compelled organizations to adopt AI-driven security systems for robust defense against sophisticated attacks. This chapter explores artificial intelligence in cybersecurity, emphasizing its role in intelligent threat detection, analysis, and response. AI models, including supervised and unsupervised learning, deep learning, and reinforcement learning, have redefined cybersecurity by enabling behavior-based anomaly detection and automated threat mitigation. Key discussions highlight autonomous systems making real-time decisions, leveraging adaptive control loops, and employing self-healing mechanisms for resilience. This

DOI: 10.4018/979-8-3373-0954-5.ch002

chapter also examines challenges in operational scalability, ethical implications of automation, and the necessity of human oversight in decision-making. The findings underscore the need for synergy between automation and human expertise to foster an intelligent, adaptive cyber defense ecosystem.

INTRODUCTION

Artificial Intelligence (AI) has rapidly emerged as one of the most transformative technologies of the 21st century, shaping the way we communicate, conduct business, and protect our digital assets. As organizations across every sector become increasingly dependent on interconnected networks and cloud infrastructures, the cyber threat landscape has grown correspondingly more complex. Sophisticated attackers—including state-sponsored adversaries and cybercriminal syndicates—have access to advanced tools and exploit techniques capable of bypassing traditional security measures. These circumstances necessitate a more proactive, intelligent, and adaptive approach to cybersecurity. AI-driven security systems provide one such avenue, offering unparalleled insights and automation for identifying, mitigating, and preventing cyber threats in real time. By leveraging machine learning, pattern recognition, and other AI techniques, modern security architectures are evolving to become more resilient and proactive, ultimately shaping an era of intelligent threat response using autonomous cyber defense.

Figure 1 visually represents the role of AI in enhancing cybersecurity. The diagram outlines seven key benefits of AI in security, starting with its ability to learn and adapt over time (AI learns more over time). It emphasizes AI's capacity to identify unknown threats, improve overall security, handle large datasets, and reduce redundant processes. Additionally, it highlights the importance of security certifications and how AI accelerates threat detection and response times. Together, these points underline AI's transformative impact on modern cybersecurity practices as shown in Figure 1.

Figure 1. The transformative role of AI in cybersecurity

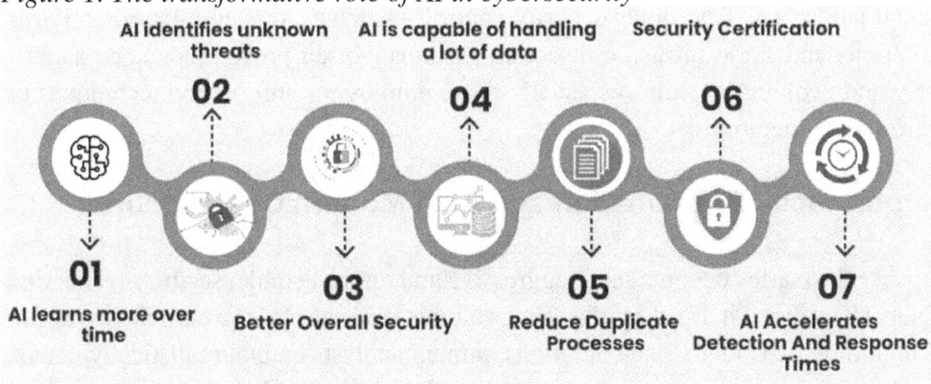

Yet, the integration of AI into cybersecurity is not without challenges. The efficacy of machine learning models depends on the quality and quantity of the data they rely upon. Adversarial attacks can exploit inherent weaknesses in AI systems, while issues surrounding bias, explainability, and ethics remain pertinent. Despite these hurdles, the potential benefits of AI-driven security systems are undeniable. Automated decision-making in high-speed threat environments frees up human analysts to focus on more strategic tasks, while cognitive systems capable of detecting zero-day attacks can significantly reduce the time to respond to emerging threats. This chapter explores these themes by delving into the background and motivations underpinning AI-driven cybersecurity solutions, highlighting the scope and objectives of autonomous cyber defense, and outlining some of the major questions and challenges these systems encounter.

In recent years, the frequency, sophistication, and impact of cyberattacks have grown at an alarming rate. High-profile breaches targeting government agencies, multinational corporations, and critical infrastructure providers routinely make global headlines (Ghiasi et al., 2023) Such incidents illustrate just how vulnerable our interconnected world can be to digital sabotage, data theft, and espionage. Attack vectors range from phishing schemes and ransomware assaults to Advanced Persistent Threats (APTs) that remain undetected within a network for months—or even years—harvesting sensitive data or laying the groundwork for coordinated disruption (Alqahtani, 2023).

This relentless wave of cyberattacks is fueled by factors such as the widespread availability of hacking tools on the dark web, the rise of cybercrime-as-a-service models, and the growing value of personal and corporate information. Furthermore, the increasing number of Internet of Things (IoT) devices and the ubiquity of cloud computing expand the potential attack surface, providing malicious actors with more avenues to penetrate a network or target critical systems (Singh, Buyya, & Kim,

2024). In this context, organizations struggle to keep pace with an ever-shifting threat landscape. Traditional security controls—such as signature-based antivirus solutions and static intrusion detection systems—often prove inadequate against new and evolving exploits, especially those employing obfuscation techniques or zero-day vulnerabilities.

Importance of Automation and AI in Modern Cybersecurity

As adversaries become more aggressive and unpredictable, security teams find themselves overwhelmed by the sheer volume of alerts and the complexity of potential threats. Under these conditions, human analysts cannot realistically detect, analyze, and respond to every threat in a timely manner—particularly in large-scale enterprises generating millions of security events each day. Automation has thus become a cornerstone in modern cybersecurity strategies, providing a means of filtering noise, prioritizing alerts, and executing routine defensive actions without direct human supervision (Corman, 2023).

AI-driven security systems represent the logical next step in this evolution. By applying machine learning models and algorithms capable of recognizing complex patterns in real-time data, these systems can discover anomalies or malicious behaviors that might go undetected by conventional means. For example, AI-powered tools can learn baseline behaviors across user accounts, network traffic, or system calls, alerting analysts when deviations suggest malicious activities (Edmund, Enuma, & Enemosah, 2024). Deep learning models can also identify new strains of malware by detecting similarities to known malware families at a bytecode level, or by analyzing behaviors in sandbox environments. Moreover, AI can automate not just detection but also elements of threat response—isolating infected endpoints or blocking malicious IP addresses as soon as suspicious activities are confirmed.

Another dimension of AI-driven security is its ability to predict future attacks (Smmarwar, Gupta & Kumar, 2024). By analyzing vast swathes of historical threat data, AI models can forecast trends and spot the emergence of new attack vectors. This predictive capability can give defenders a critical advantage, allowing them to shore up potential weaknesses before an actual breach occurs. Given the increasing sophistication and scale of cyber threats, organizations are turning to AI-enabled solutions not merely as a convenience but as a strategic imperative.

1. FUNDAMENTALS OF AI IN CYBERSECURITY

The increasing complexity and scale of cyber threats have driven cybersecurity practitioners to adopt advanced AI techniques. AI-based solutions can sift through large volumes of data, detect subtle patterns of malicious activities, and adapt to emerging threats faster than human analysts alone can manage (Aminu et al., 2024). However, to fully leverage AI in cybersecurity, it is necessary to understand the underlying foundations of machine learning, the various types of learning paradigms, and the trade-offs between different approaches. This section provides a deep dive into the fundamental concepts that underpin AI in cybersecurity, covering the differences between supervised and unsupervised learning, the basics of deep learning architectures, and how reinforcement learning (RL) is shaping autonomous cyber defense strategies. We then discuss the role of AI algorithms in cybersecurity, emphasizing the evolution from signature-based to behavior-based approaches, and from purely rule-based systems to data-driven models (Sarker et al., 2024). Finally, we highlight key limitations and considerations around dataset bias and the importance of explainability and interpretability for AI-driven security solutions.

1.1 Key Concepts in AI and Machine Learning

Supervised learning is a machine learning paradigm where models are trained using labeled datasets. In the context of cybersecurity, this often involves feeding an algorithm example of known malicious and benign activity (Mvula et al., 2024). For instance, a supervised learning algorithm might be trained on network traffic labeled as "legitimate" or "malicious" to learn patterns (e.g., protocol usage, frequency of connections, packet sizes) associated with cyberattacks. Once trained, the model can classify new, unseen traffic with a certain level of confidence. Some common supervised learning methods include (Azba et al., 2024):

1. Logistic Regression – Often used for binary classification, such as labeling an email as spam or not spam.
2. Decision Trees and Random Forests – Useful for handling high-dimensional data and can reveal which features are most indicative of an attack.
3. Support Vector Machines (SVM) – Effective in high-dimensional spaces, often applied to intrusion detection by finding an optimal boundary between classes.
4. Neural Networks – Can uncover complex, non-linear relationships in data. Specifically, feed-forward networks (multi-layer perceptrons) or convolutional networks in some cases.

A limitation of supervised learning is its heavy reliance on labeled data. For cybersecurity tasks like zero-day attack detection, it can be challenging to gather sufficient labeled examples of new exploits. Moreover, labeling can be time-consuming, expensive, and prone to human error (Deldar, & Abadi, 2023).

Unsupervised learning, on the other hand, does not rely on labeled datasets. Instead, it attempts to learn patterns and structures inherently present in unlabeled data (Naeem et al., 2023). In cybersecurity, unsupervised models are often used for anomaly detection. These models learn what constitutes "normal" behavior and flag deviations that might indicate malicious activity. Common unsupervised methods include (Pinto et al., 2024; Kaliyaperumal et al., 2024):

1. Clustering Techniques (e.g., K-means, DBSCAN) – Group data points based on similarity. Potential anomalies are any points or clusters that deviate significantly from the rest.
2. Principal Component Analysis (PCA) – A dimensionality reduction technique that can reveal underlying structures in the data, thereby making abnormal behaviors more detectable.
3. Autoencoders – A specialized neural network architecture used to reconstruct input data. If a sample has a high reconstruction error, it may be abnormal or malicious.

Unsupervised learning is particularly valuable when dealing with large, unlabeled datasets and when seeking to discover novel attack vectors. However, these methods can produce higher false positives if the boundary between "normal" and "abnormal" is not well-defined.

Figure 2 compares supervised learning and unsupervised learning in machine learning, showcasing their distinct processes. In supervised learning, labeled input data is provided along with corresponding outputs, enabling the model to learn relationships and make accurate predictions (e.g., classifying fruits like apples and pears) (Opara et al., 2024). On the other hand, unsupervised learning deals with unlabeled data, where the algorithm identifies patterns and groups based on similarities (e.g., clustering fruits without predefined categories). This contrast highlights how supervised methods rely on external guidance while unsupervised methods discover patterns independently (Feldmann et al., 2020).

Figure 2. Supervised vs. unsupervised learning

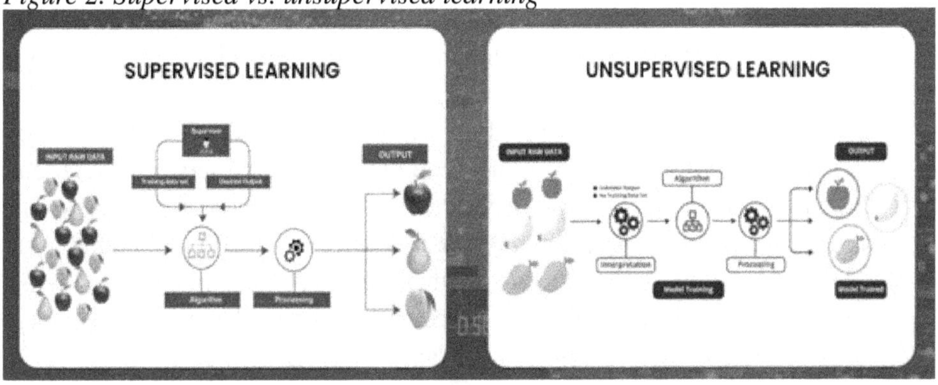

Table 1. Comparison between supervised and unsupervised learning

Feature	Supervised Learning	Unsupervised Learning
Definition	Learning with labeled data where input and output pairs are provided.	Learning with unlabeled data to discover patterns or groupings.
Data Type	Labeled Data	Unlabeled Data
Purpose	Predict outcomes based on input-output mapping.	Explore data to identify hidden patterns or structure.
Output	Predictive: Known outcomes or classifications.	Descriptive: Groupings or pattern identification.
Common Algorithms	Linear Regression, Logistic Regression, Decision Trees, SVM, Neural Networks	K-Means Clustering, DBSCAN, Hierarchical Clustering, PCA, Autoencoders
Examples	Spam email detection, Fraud detection, Image classification	Customer segmentation, Anomaly detection, Market basket analysis

Deep learning is a subfield of machine learning characterized by the use of neural networks with multiple layers (hence "deep") to automatically learn hierarchical representations of data (Taye, 2023). The key advantage of deep learning in cybersecurity lies in its capacity to handle raw, high-dimensional data—such as packet captures, server logs, or system call traces—without extensive manual feature engineering. Instead, deep neural networks learn to extract features relevant to the task at hand (Alazab et al., 2023).

1. Fully Connected Networks (Multi-Layer Perceptrons) – Consist of layers of neurons, where each neuron in one layer is connected to every neuron in the next layer. They are often used for tasks where the data can be flattened or is not inherently structured (e.g., tabular data representing network events) (Kruse

et al., 2022). Figure 3 represents a Deep Neural Network (DNN) architecture, showcasing multiple layers of interconnected nodes (neurons). It consists of an input layer (on the left), several hidden layers (in the middle), and an output layer (on the right). Each neuron in a layer is connected to every neuron in the subsequent layer, forming a dense, fully connected network. The network uses activation functions at each neuron to capture complex patterns and relationships within the data, enabling it to perform tasks like classification, regression, and feature extraction. The depth of the network, indicated by the number of hidden layers, allows it to learn intricate features, making it suitable for solving complex problems in areas like image recognition, natural language processing, and recommendation systems (Dong, Wang & Abbas, 2021).

Figure 3. Fully connected layer

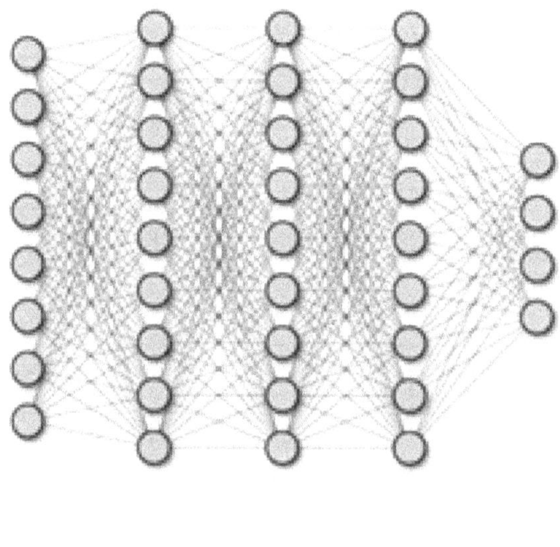

2. Convolutional Neural Networks (CNNs) – Developed for image recognition but also applicable to cybersecurity tasks that involve pattern recognition in time series (e.g., network traffic) or sequences of bytes in malware analysis. Convolutions help the network capture local patterns (Vijayalakshmi & Jayakumar, 2024). Figure 4 depicts a CNN architecture designed for image classification tasks, such as digit recognition. It begins with an input layer that processes a grayscale image (28x28x1) (Zgallai & Ozsahin, 2024). Convolutional layers (Conv_1 and Conv_2) extract features like edges and textures using filters, followed by max-pooling layers that downsample the feature maps to reduce spatial dimensions while preserving key features. The resulting feature maps are flattened

and passed through fully connected (FC) layers to learn complex patterns and map them to class probabilities (0–9). Dropout regularization in the FC layers prevents overfitting, and the output layer uses softmax activation to predict the class probabilities, making this architecture highly effective for image-based tasks (Shao, Zhang & Li 2021; Khorsheed & Al-Sulaifanie, 2024).

Figure 4. Architecture of CNN

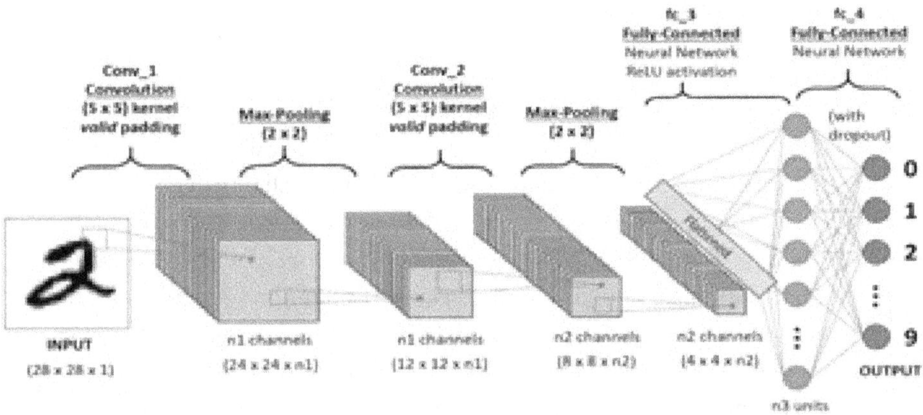

3. Recurrent Neural Networks (RNNs) and LSTMs – Designed to process sequential data. Useful in scenarios such as analyzing user behavior over time, tracking intrusion patterns, or detecting anomalies in system logs. Long Short-Term Memory (LSTM) networks can handle longer temporal dependencies and are therefore more resilient to vanishing gradients than vanilla RNNs. Figure 5 represents the architecture of a RNN, highlighting its ability to process sequential data. The left side shows the recurrent nature of the network, where the hidden state h receives input X and produces output L while looping back on itself to retain memory of past computations. On the right, the network is "unfolded" across time steps, illustrating how information flows through the sequence. At each time step t, the hidden state h_t is updated based on the current input X_t and the previous hidden state h_{t-1}. The weights u, v, and www remain shared across all time steps, allowing the RNN to capture temporal dependencies and patterns in the data. This structure makes RNNs effective for tasks like time series analysis, natural language processing, and speech recognition (Sanju, 2023; Kasongo, 2023).

Figure 5. Architecture of RNN

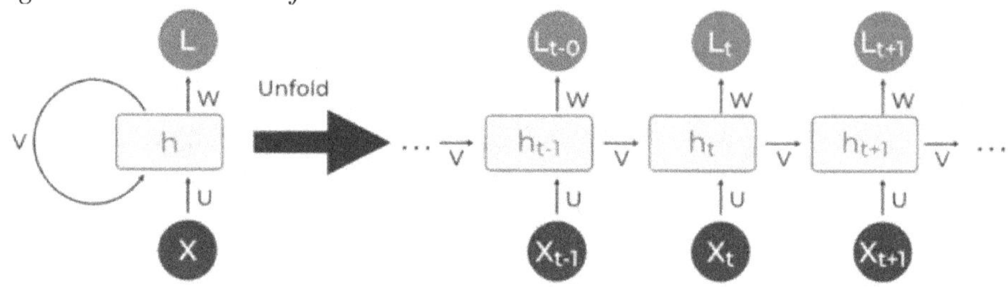

4. Transformers – Originally popularized in Natural Language Processing (NLP), but increasingly used in threat intelligence analysis, log data parsing, and other cybersecurity domains due to their ability to capture relationships in sequential data without relying solely on recurrence. Figure 6 represents the Transformer Model, widely used in NLP tasks. It processes input tokens with embeddings and positional encodings, applying multi-head self-attention to identify important relationships in the sequence. The model uses queries (Q), keys (K), and values (V) to compute attention weights, focusing on relevant context. With stacked layers of attention, normalization, and feedforward components, it enables efficient parallel processing and complex learning, making it ideal for tasks like translation and text generation (Patwardhan, Marrone & Sansone, 2023; Khan et al., 2023).

Figure 6. Transformer model: Attention-powered framework for NLP

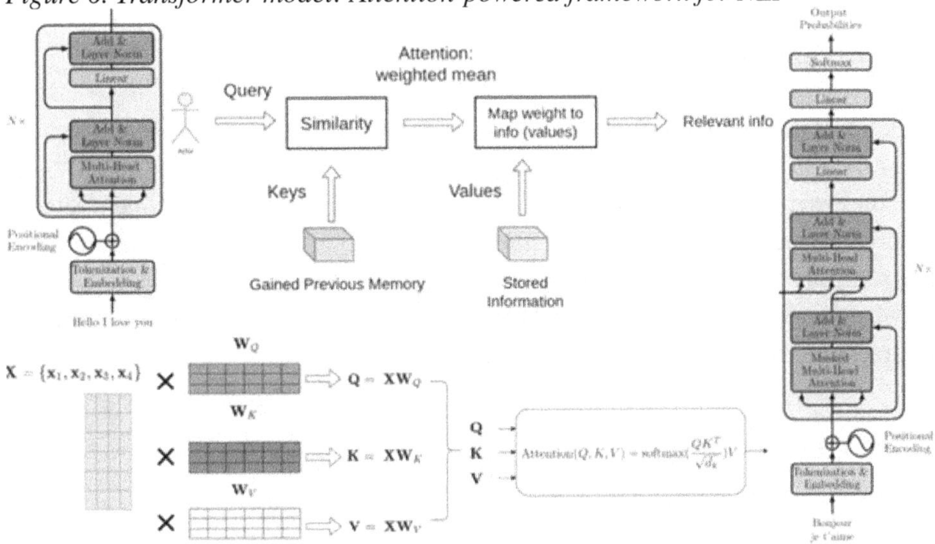

Deep learning models often require large datasets and computational resources for training. In cybersecurity, amassing large amounts of quality data can be facilitated by logs from distributed networks, endpoints, or cloud services. However, data quality and preprocessing remain pivotal to ensuring good performance.

Reinforcement learning is a learning paradigm focused on training agents to make sequential decisions in an environment. The agent receives rewards (positive or negative) based on its actions, and its goal is to maximize cumulative reward over time. In cybersecurity, RL is attractive for dynamic tasks such as automated vulnerability patching, network defense strategies, or adaptive honeypot placement. Key RL concepts include (Shakya Pillai & Chakrabarty, 2023; Wang et al., 2022):

1. Agent, environment, and state: The agent interacts with an environment described by a state (e.g., network configuration, active connections, or threat level). The agent observes the state and selects actions.
2. Action space: The set of all possible actions an agent can take (e.g., block an IP address, isolate a node, or change firewall rules).
3. Reward function: Defines what the agent should optimize. For example, successfully blocking malicious traffic might yield a positive reward, while letting an attack through incurs a penalty.
4. Policy: A mapping from states to actions. The agent's goal is to learn an optimal policy that yields maximum long-term reward.

5. Q-Learning, SARSA, Deep Q-Networks (DQN): Various algorithms exist for learning optimal policies. Deep RL methods combine neural networks with RL (e.g., DQN) to handle large state spaces.

Figure 7 illustrates the fundamental architecture of RL, where an agent interacts with an environment to learn an optimal policy for decision-making. At each time step, the environment provides the agent with its current state, and the agent selects an action based on its policy. This action influences the environment, resulting in a new state and a reward that reflects the quality of the action. The agent updates its knowledge, represented as Q(s,a) values for state-action pairs, iteratively refining its strategy to maximize cumulative rewards over time.

Figure 7. Architecture of RL

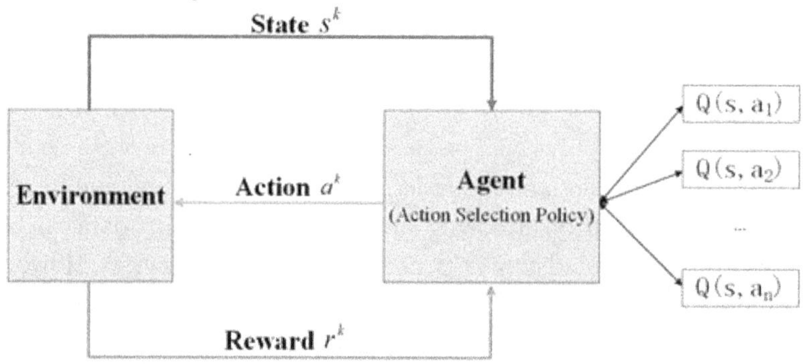

One challenge in applying RL to cybersecurity is defining an appropriate reward function and environment model. In many cases, simulations or specialized testbeds (cyber ranges) are used to train RL agents without risking production networks. Over time, RL agents can learn adaptive strategies that account for evolving threat behaviors, making them a powerful tool for autonomous cyber defense (Kheddar et al., 2024).

1.2 Role of AI Algorithms in Cybersecurity

Traditional signature-based approaches rely on known indicators of compromise (IoCs)—specific patterns, such as malicious IP addresses, file hashes of known malware, or suspicious code fragments. Antivirus engines historically used signature matching to detect threats. While signature-based tools are fast and accurate for known threats, they are ineffective against novel or evolving threats that do not match existing signatures, such as polymorphic or zero-day malware (Preuveneers & Joosen, 2021).

Behavior-based approaches, often powered by AI, focus on modeling the typical behavior of systems, processes, and network traffic. Instead of matching an exact signature, a behavior-based system detects anomalies that deviate from an established baseline. For instance, if a web server process suddenly starts scanning internal hosts—a behavior it has never exhibited before—anomaly detection might flag this as suspicious even if no known signature matches. By focusing on behavior instead of specific indicators, these systems can detect emerging threats, reduce false negatives, and adapt to changing attack techniques. However, they can also increase false positives if normal operation patterns are not well-characterized (Jeffrey, Tan & Villar, 2023).

Traditional rule-based systems, such as some intrusion detection systems (IDS) or expert systems, rely on human-crafted rules. These rules can be highly specific (e.g., “If a certain TCP flag is present AND packet size is above X, then raise an alert”) or incorporate complex logic. Rule-based systems are transparent and interpretable—they mimic the knowledge of security experts (Djaidja, et al., 2024). However, they are also brittle, as they do not generalize well to new or unforeseen scenarios. Moreover, maintaining an ever-growing rule set can be time-consuming and requires constant updates as threats evolve (Tariq, 2024).

Data-driven systems, on the other hand, learn patterns directly from data. This is the domain of machine learning algorithms that can adapt to evolving conditions by retraining models on updated datasets. Data-driven approaches offer more robust detection against novel threats, as they can discover previously unknown patterns (Wong & Wang, 2023). For example, a machine learning model that regularly receives labeled examples of new phishing campaigns can automatically update its parameters to accurately flag emerging variants without requiring explicit rule modifications (Kavya & Sumathi, 2024). However, data-driven systems can be opaque, require substantial amounts of relevant data, and risk learning spurious correlations if not properly validated.

Table 2 below provides a detailed comparison between Data-Driven Systems and Rule-Based Systems in cybersecurity. These two approaches differ significantly in how they detect and respond to threats. Rule-based systems depend on explicitly defined rules created by experts, making them reliable for well-known and static threats but less effective against new attack vectors. On the other hand, data-driven systems leverage machine learning algorithms to identify patterns and adapt to evolving threats, offering greater flexibility and adaptability (Yang et al., 2024; Bhattarai et al., 2024). The table highlights key features such as detection capabilities, adaptability, and maintenance requirements, providing a clear understanding of their strengths and challenges in various cybersecurity contexts.

Table 2. Comparison between rule-based & data-driven systems

Feature	Rule-Based Systems	Data-Driven Systems
Definition	Rely on predefined rules crafted by human experts to detect and respond to threats.	Use machine learning algorithms to learn patterns from data and make adaptive decisions.
Detection Capability	Effective for well-understood and static threats.	Capable of detecting novel or evolving threats by recognizing patterns in the data.
Adaptability	Limited adaptability; requires frequent manual updates for new threats.	Highly adaptable as models can be retrained with updated data.
Maintenance	High maintenance due to the need for constant rule updates as threats evolve.	Requires less manual effort but demands high-quality data for training and retraining.
False Positives	Typically lower, as rules are explicitly defined.	Higher initially, but can be reduced with proper model tuning and feedback loops.
False Negatives	Higher for novel or evolving threats not captured by existing rules.	Lower, as models can generalize from training data to new scenarios.
Use Cases	Intrusion detection systems, static malware detection, compliance monitoring.	Advanced threat detection, anomaly detection, behavioral analytics.

1.3 Limitations and Considerations

A significant challenge in deploying AI for cybersecurity is dataset bias. Bias arises when the training data used to build a model is not representative of the real-world environment in which it is deployed (Roshanaei, Khan & Sylvester, 2024). Common sources of bias include:

1. Collection bias: If an organization's dataset primarily comes from certain network segments or time periods, the model may not generalize to other environments.
2. Labeling bias: In supervised learning, mislabeled or inconsistently labeled data can lead to poor decision boundaries.
3. Temporal bias: Attack patterns evolve over time. If historical training data does not encompass the latest attack vectors, the model may fail to recognize new threats.

Biased datasets can lead to high false negatives (missing actual threats) or high false positives (flagging benign activity as malicious). Furthermore, in the worst-case scenario, attackers can exploit these biases, orchestrating attacks that intentionally circumvent the model's learned patterns. Mitigating bias involves carefully curating diverse datasets, employing continuous retraining, and using techniques like cross-validation to ensure robust generalization. Researchers also explore methods for domain adaptation, allowing models to transfer knowledge from one domain (or dataset) to another with minimal performance degradation (Thirumuruganathan et al., 2024; Al-Shehar et al., 2024).

Explainability and interpretability refer to the ability to understand how an AI model reaches its conclusions. In cybersecurity, this is critical for multiple reasons (Hassija et al., 2024):

1. Trust and adoption: Security analysts are more likely to trust and adopt AI-driven tools if they can verify the reasoning behind a detection or an alert.
2. Compliance and accountability: Certain regulations (e.g., GDPR) and industry standards require that automated decisions be transparent, especially if they can significantly affect individuals or organizations.
3. Incident response: Understanding which features triggered an alert can help security teams rapidly investigate and respond to potential breaches.

However, many high-performing AI models—especially deep learning architectures—behave like "black boxes," providing little insight into their internal logic. Techniques to enhance interpretability include (Ennab & Mcheick, 2024):

- Feature importance scoring: For tree-based models (like random forests), one can measure how each feature contributes to the final decision.
- Local Interpretable Model-Agnostic Explanations (LIME): Generates simplified local models around a specific prediction to show which features are most influential.
- SHAP (SHapley Additive exPlanations): A game-theoretic approach that assigns each feature an importance value for a given prediction.
- Layer-wise relevance propagation: Used in neural networks to trace the contribution of each neuron back through the network.

Balancing performance and interpretability is an ongoing challenge. Models with high accuracy may be less transparent, while interpretable models might not capture complex patterns as effectively. Hybrid approaches that combine interpretable components (e.g., rule-based checks) with deep learning components (for anomaly detection or classification) can sometimes offer a middle ground (Leite et al., 2024; Akbulut et al., 2024).

As the cybersecurity landscape grows in complexity and urgency, AI provides a powerful toolkit for automating threat detection and response. Supervised learning excels at classifying known attack patterns, provided sufficient labeled data is available. Unsupervised learning detects never-before-seen or atypical behaviors by modeling normal system baselines. Deep learning pushes the boundaries of what can be inferred from massive datasets, unveiling multi-layered patterns inaccessible to simpler algorithms. Reinforcement learning then offers a framework for autonomous agents that adapt and learn optimal strategies in real time.

Yet, these technological advancements must be contextualized within the practical realities of cybersecurity. Moving from signature-based to behavior-based detection addresses the need to combat zero-day exploits and evolving malware. Transitioning from rule-based to data-driven systems ensures that security solutions can dynamically adapt to shifting attack vectors. However, biases in training data can hamper detection efficacy or produce unintended consequences. Moreover, regulators and organizational stakeholders demand explainable and trustworthy AI, particularly when automated decisions have far-reaching impacts.

In summary, the fundamentals of AI in cybersecurity converge to create an environment where detection is more precise, response is faster, and defenses can learn from each new assault. The necessity for robust data pipelines, careful model selection, and attention to ethical considerations remains paramount. When executed effectively, AI-driven methods enable proactive defense measures—predicting threats before they become breaches, adapting to adversarial maneuvers, and easing the burden on human security teams. As we delve further into AI-driven security architectures, the emphasis remains on leveraging these foundational concepts to build resilient, intelligent, and transparent defense systems capable of operating at machine speed against modern cyber threats.

2. AI-DRIVEN THREAT DETECTION AND ANALYSIS

As cyber threats continue to evolve in both scale and sophistication, organizations must deploy robust, intelligent strategies for rapid detection, analysis, and mitigation. AI-driven tools are at the forefront of this revolution, delivering the necessary capabilities to monitor large-scale environments, filter vast streams of data, and detect subtle patterns indicative of malicious activity—all in real time. This section explores three critical components of AI-driven threat detection and analysis: Intelligent IDS, real-time threat intelligence, and AI-driven malware analysis. Together, they form the backbone of a modern, adaptive security architecture capable of handling emergent threats such as zero-day exploits and stealthy, APTs.

2.1 Intelligent IDS

IDS are a cornerstone of any comprehensive cybersecurity strategy, tasked with monitoring network traffic or host activities to identify potential breaches or malicious behaviors. Historically, IDS solutions relied heavily on static rules or signatures to spot known threats, but with attackers perpetually devising new tactics, these traditional methods now struggle to keep pace. AI-powered IDS, however, use machine learning (ML) and advanced analytics to detect a broad range of intrusions, including zero-day attacks and insider threats that may not conform to known signatures (Khanan et al., 2024).

2.1.1 ML-Based Anomaly Detection

The key concept in ML-based IDS is anomaly detection, which aims to learn a "normal" baseline of network or host behavior, then identify deviations that might signal malicious activity. This approach often uses unsupervised or semi-supervised learning; as malicious examples can be sparse or absent in historical data (Fazliani, Sorond & Masoudifard, 2024).

- Unsupervised Techniques: Methods such as clustering (e.g., K-means or DBSCAN), principal component analysis (PCA), and autoencoders identify patterns in unlabeled data. They learn what normal traffic looks like, flagging significant deviations as anomalies.
- Semi-Supervised Techniques: When a small set of labeled "clean" data is available; models can refine their baseline more accurately. One example is using an autoencoder trained only on benign traffic. If a new traffic pattern yields high reconstruction error, the system raises an alert.

Successful anomaly detection depends on well-chosen features that capture relevant aspects of network or host activity. Typical features include (Kale, Bostancı & Çelebi, 2024):

- Protocol usage: Distribution of TCP, UDP, ICMP traffic, or custom protocols.
- Port usage patterns: Unusual port scans or shifts in frequently used ports.
- Packet size and frequency: Spikes in packet size or frequency can indicate data exfiltration.
- Temporal behavior: Changes in the times at which hosts communicate, or the volume of network connections.

Feature engineering can be automated using deep learning. Convolutional Neural Networks (CNNs) or Long Short-Term Memory (LSTM) networks can learn features from raw traffic data, reducing the reliance on manually engineered features (Almukhalfi, A. Noor & H. Noor, 2024).

APTs are characterized by stealthy, prolonged infiltration. Attackers move laterally, escalate privileges, and exfiltrate data slowly to avoid detection. AI-based anomaly detection is particularly effective for such threats because it can reveal subtle changes in user or process behavior (e.g., abnormal login patterns, unusual file transfers, or processes accessing network shares unexpectedly). Unsupervised methods often excel at highlighting these behavioral anomalies that might be buried under normal system noise (Lu et al., 2024).

2.1.2 Pattern Recognition for Zero-Day Attacks

Zero-day attacks exploit newly discovered vulnerabilities—ones for which patches or signatures do not yet exist. Traditional signature-based systems are almost guaranteed to miss these novel threats because they rely on matching known patterns. AI-powered IDS, however, can spot suspicious behaviors even if they do not match any known signature (Waheed et al., 2024).

Machine Learning Approaches:

- Behavioral Modeling: Instead of searching for a specific exploit signature, the system models typical workflows or code execution paths. If a process begins taking atypical execution paths, the system flags potential malicious behavior.
- Transfer Learning: In scenarios where labeled data is lacking (as is common with zero-day exploits), transfer learning can help. A model trained on similar attack vectors or exploit methods may be partially adapted to detect new attack families.
- One-Class Classification: One-class SVMs or isolation forests can be employed to learn normal system behavior, turning anything outside that behavior into a potential zero-day candidate.

Although AI-driven zero-day detection can be powerful, it may generate increased false positives if the baseline is insufficiently comprehensive. Techniques like active learning—where suspicious alerts are reviewed by security analysts and used to refine the model—help reduce false positives over time. Additionally, correlation engines that aggregate alerts from multiple detection tools can reduce noise by discarding events that lack corroborating evidence.

The presented framework, in Figure 8, illustrates a hybrid learning approach for anomaly detection and zero-day threat validation. It begins with data collection from an input dataset, which is classified using both supervised and unsupervised methods. Supervised learning associates data with known incidents, while unsupervised learning clusters data into attack, normal, or mixed flows. These outputs are further analyzed through a correlation table to identify patterns and anomalies. Potential outliers are flagged based on a defined distance threshold, d_{min} , and processed through online learning to refine the model's understanding. This iterative process culminates in the validation of zero-day threats, enabling the detection of previously unknown attacks in real-time environments. This approach ensures a comprehensive and adaptive system for evolving cybersecurity challenges (Komadina et al., 2024).

Figure 8. Hybrid learning framework for anomaly detection and zero-day validation

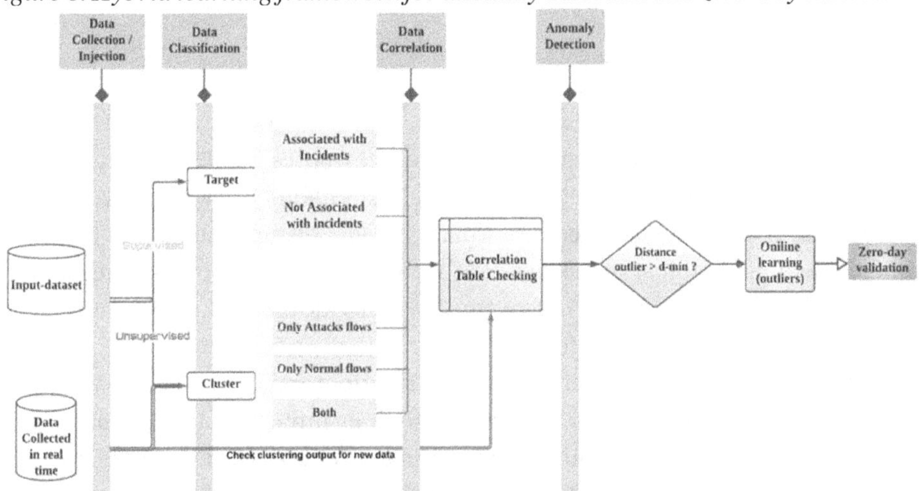

2.2 Real-Time Threat Intelligence

Effective cyber defense relies not only on analyzing one's own network or system data, but also on a broad view of global threats. Real-time threat intelligence (RTTI) platforms aggregate information from diverse sources—external threat feeds, sensors, honeypots, and internal security logs—and leverage AI to identify emerging threats as quickly as possible. This global perspective is crucial for defending against widespread attacks like ransomware campaigns or distributed denial-of-service (DDoS) attempts, which may appear in different geographic regions nearly simultaneously.

2.2.1 Data Collection from Threat Feeds and Sensors

Threat intelligence feeds often provide indicators of compromise (IoCs) such as malicious IP addresses, domain names, file hashes, and newly discovered vulnerabilities. These feeds can be curated by commercial vendors, government agencies (like CERTs), or open-source communities (Smolyakova, 2024). Additional data sources include:

- Honeypots: Deliberately vulnerable systems designed to attract attackers, collecting data about exploits and tactics.

- Dark Web Monitoring: Scraping forums and marketplaces where cybercriminals share techniques or trade stolen data.
- Open-Source Intelligence (OSINT): Social media, public repositories, and other open sources can reveal attacker chatter, proof-of-concept exploits, or leaked credentials.

Challenges in Data Aggregation

Bringing together data from numerous sources poses challenges such as data format inconsistencies, duplication, and variable reliability. AI-driven correlation engines can help unify these feeds, normalizing and deduplicating data to build a coherent, actionable threat knowledge base. Another key challenge is data freshness—threat indicators can become obsolete quickly, and stale data risks flooding security operations with false alarms (Beretas, 2024).

Advanced threat intelligence includes attribution: inferring the actor or group behind an attack. This involves analyzing malicious infrastructure, tool usage, and code signatures. Machine learning models can cluster observed incidents based on Tactics, Techniques, and Procedures (TTPs), linking new attacks to known adversary groups. Such intelligence allows defenders to customize their defenses and anticipate future moves (Wang et al., 2024).

2.3 AI-Driven Malware Analysis

Malware analysis is crucial for understanding an attacker's methods, developing detection signatures, and designing mitigation strategies. Traditional approaches focus on static and dynamic analysis techniques, but the sheer volume and evolving sophistication of new malware strains necessitate AI-driven enhancements. By applying machine learning and deep learning to file, code, and network behavior classification, security teams can detect novel malicious software faster and more accurately.

2.3.1 Static vs. Dynamic Malware Analysis

Static malware analysis examines a file without executing it. Common methods include (Kumar, Ahlawat & Sahni, 2024):

- Disassembly: Transforming compiled binaries into assembly instructions to inspect for suspicious API calls or encryption routines.
- String and Metadata Analysis: Searching for telltale text strings (such as command-and-control URLs) or unusual file headers.

- Packers and Obfuscation: Attackers often compress or encrypt malware to evade static analysis. Detecting packers or nested obfuscation layers is a key step.

Static analysis is generally faster and safer than dynamic analysis because it avoids running potentially dangerous code. However, it may miss highly obfuscated malware or code that only reveals malicious functionality at runtime.

Dynamic malware analysis involves executing the file in a controlled environment, often a sandbox with monitoring tools. The system records system calls, registry modifications, file operations, and network traffic generated by the malware. This approach can reveal hidden behaviors or encrypted payloads that static analysis might overlook (Javed & Amjad, 2024).

- Sandbox Instrumentation: Techniques such as function hooking or API tracing capture system calls in real time.
- Behavioral Profiles: The captured behaviors are compared against known malicious behavior patterns—like injecting code into system processes, contacting known malicious domains, or modifying critical system files.

Although dynamic analysis can uncover sophisticated malware functionality, it is resource-intensive and time-consuming. Attackers also deploy anti-analysis techniques—detecting virtual machines, debuggers, or sandbox environments to remain dormant or self-terminate.

Table 3 below presents a detailed comparison of Static Malware Analysis and Dynamic Malware Analysis, two complementary approaches used in cybersecurity to examine and detect malicious software. Static analysis involves examining malware without executing it, focusing on file properties such as code, strings, and metadata, making it faster and less resource-intensive. However, it struggles with obfuscated or encrypted malware. On the other hand, dynamic analysis executes malware in a controlled environment to observe its runtime behavior, such as system calls and network activity, enabling it to detect hidden or runtime-triggered malicious actions (Yamany et al., 2024). Table 3 outlines key differences in their approach, capabilities, and use cases, offering a comprehensive perspective on their strengths and limitations.

Table 3. Comparison between static vs. dynamic malware analysis

Feature	Static Malware Analysis	Dynamic Malware Analysis
Definition	Examines malware without executing it.	Involves executing malware in a controlled environment.
Analysis Approach	Focuses on analyzing file properties, such as code, strings, and metadata.	Monitors runtime behaviors, such as system calls and network activity.
Detection Capability	Effective for known patterns and un-obfuscated malware.	Capable of detecting hidden or runtime-triggered behaviors.
Speed	Faster since it does not execute the file.	Slower due to the need for controlled execution.
Resource Requirements	Low, as it avoids execution and dynamic monitoring.	High, as it requires sandbox environments and monitoring tools.
Obfuscation Handling	Less effective against highly obfuscated or encrypted malware.	Effective against obfuscated malware, as runtime behaviors are analyzed.
Examples	Disassembly, string analysis, and header inspection.	Sandbox execution, API tracing, and behavioral profiling.

Challenges and Considerations

- Data Diversity: Malware families evolve quickly, and collecting representative samples is non-trivial. Continuous retraining on fresh datasets is essential.
- Evasion Techniques: Attackers can adopt adversarial techniques that target deep learning models directly, modifying file structures or behaviors to reduce detection likelihood. Defenders must incorporate adversarial training to build robust models.
- Resource Constraints: Deep learning models require significant computational resources and specialized expertise to maintain. Organizations must ensure their infrastructure can handle large-scale deployment.

AI-driven threat detection and analysis create a powerful framework that integrates three major facets of modern cybersecurity operations:

1. Intelligent IDS: By harnessing machine learning-based anomaly detection, these systems can learn normal network and host behaviors, flagging suspicious deviations that might signify malicious actions—regardless of whether they match previously known signatures. They are particularly effective against stealthy APTs and zero-day exploits, though they must be complemented by human oversight and refined baselines to manage false positives.

2. Real-Time Threat Intelligence: Combining data from external threat feeds, internal logs, honeypots, and the dark web, organizations gain a holistic view of emerging threats. Streaming data analytics driven by AI models enables rapid and dynamic response, interrupting attacks before they escalate. Continuous correlation and attribution further allow security teams to anticipate adversaries' next moves and tailor defensive strategies accordingly.
3. AI-Driven Malware Analysis: Deep learning enhances both static and dynamic analysis techniques, automatically extracting robust features from files, processes, and network flows. This layered approach is essential in dealing with obfuscated code, polymorphic malware, or new exploits that elude traditional, signature-based tools. While resource-intensive, these AI-driven methods provide high levels of accuracy, speed, and adaptability.

Despite these capabilities, challenges remain. Models require extensive, high-quality datasets, and adversaries are adept at evading detection through sophisticated obfuscation or adversarial ML tactics. Successful implementation also depends on building trust and interpretability—especially where automated decisions can cause business disruptions or inadvertently block legitimate activities. Security teams must maintain a careful balance between automation and human expertise, updating models regularly and incorporating contextual knowledge from analysts.

Looking ahead, AI-driven threat detection and analysis systems will continue to evolve, leveraging breakthroughs in deep learning architectures, reinforcement learning for adaptive defenses, and advanced correlation engines that process diverse threat feeds in real time. The collective objective remains the same: to stay one step ahead of cyber adversaries by identifying, analyzing, and responding to malicious activities more rapidly and effectively than ever before. By integrating AI at every stage of threat detection and analysis, organizations can fortify their security posture in an environment where attacks increasingly strike at machine speed, requiring a similarly agile and intelligent defense.

3. AUTONOMOUS CYBER DEFENSE ARCHITECTURES

As cyber threats grow more sophisticated and frequent, the need for automated, intelligent systems capable of orchestrating defenses in real time has become critical. Moving beyond static detections and reactive policies, autonomous cyber defense architectures leverage a range of technologies—particularly AI and machine learning—to continuously monitor their environment, evaluate risks, and initiate defensive measures with minimal human intervention. These architectures operate at machine speed, making rapid decisions in response to evolving threats. This section examines three major facets of autonomous cyber defense: the high-level overview of autonomous systems, the specific role of reinforcement learning for cyber defense, and the design of self-healing, self-adaptive security systems that can maintain robust protection against a shifting threat landscape.

3.1 Overview of Autonomous Systems

This subsection provides an introduction to the concept of autonomous systems in cybersecurity. It explains how these systems leverage AI to continuously monitor, analyze, and respond to cyber threats with minimal human intervention. The section highlights the key components of autonomous decision-making, including data ingestion, contextual analysis, automated response, and feedback integration, forming the foundation for self-adaptive and intelligent cyber defense architectures.

3.1.1 Autonomous Decision-Making Process

At its core, an autonomous cyber defense system is designed to make data-driven decisions without the need for constant human oversight. This entails (George, 2024):

1. Continuous Sensing and Data Ingestion
    - o The system aggregates logs, network flows, and telemetry from endpoints, cloud services, and threat intelligence sources.
    - o Specialized agents or collectors parse and normalize these data streams, ensuring they are readily usable by downstream analytics engines.
2. Contextual Analysis and Reasoning
    - o Leveraging AI algorithms, the system identifies potential threats or anomalies. It correlates events across multiple layers (host, network, application) to build an actionable context.
    - o Additional metadata, such as the severity of vulnerabilities and the business impact of protected assets, informs prioritization.
3. Automated Decision Logic
    - o Based on identified threats and the system's risk assessment, automated decision logic triggers the most appropriate protective or mitigative action.
    - o This logic could be expressed in a policy engine or learned dynamically via machine learning models.
4. Feedback Integration
    - o After executing a response (e.g., isolating a compromised host or blocking suspicious IP addresses), the system observes changes in network behavior.

- These observations feed back into the decision models, refining future responses and allowing for adaptation over time.

At each step, autonomy relies on minimal human intervention. However, human operators can remain "in the loop" for critical decisions—such as disabling an essential production server—to ensure that the organization's operational continuity is not compromised.

3.1.2 Control Loops for Continuous Monitoring and Response

An essential feature of autonomous defense architecture is the presence of control loops that continually cycle through phases of observation, orientation, decision, and action (inspired by the OODA loop concept used in military strategy) (Suchman, 2023). These loops allow for:

1. Timely Detection
    - As threats emerge or patterns shift, the monitoring phase immediately feeds anomalies into analytics pipelines.
    - Rapid detection is crucial for preventing lateral movement or data exfiltration.
2. Adaptive Response
    - Once an anomaly is confirmed as malicious, the system can adapt its defense posture. Actions might include updating firewall rules, deploying patches, or reconfiguring network segments.
    - If an initial response is ineffective, subsequent iterations of the loop guide the system to escalate its countermeasures.
3. Dynamic Optimization
    - Control loops enable the system to refine both detection thresholds and remediation strategies automatically.
    - By analyzing outcomes (e.g., reduced false positives, containment success), the system's decision logic can improve with each cycle.

These continuous loops underpin the autonomous aspect of cyber defense, ensuring that defenses are not static snapshots but living systems capable of handling real-time changes in both infrastructure and threat actors' behaviors.

3.2 Reinforcement Learning for Cyber Defense

RL is a potent framework for decision-making under uncertainty, making it highly applicable in cybersecurity scenarios where environments and adversaries evolve. An RL-based cyber defense agent interacts with a network or system (the "environment") by executing actions—such as blocking suspicious traffic or quarantining a compromised endpoint—and receives rewards or penalties based on the outcomes. Designing a reward function is critical because it shapes the agent's strategy (Valdovinos et al., 2021; Bai et al., 2023):

1. Security-Centric Rewards
    - The agent might be rewarded for reducing the number of successful intrusions, thwarting infiltration attempts, or maintaining system integrity over an extended period.
    - Negative rewards (penalties) are assigned when an attack succeeds or when defensive actions disrupt normal operations.
2. Balancing Security and Usability
    - A purely security-focused reward function could prompt overly aggressive measures, such as repeatedly disconnecting hosts at the slightest sign of abnormality.
    - To mitigate this, some portion of the reward might encourage normal user productivity, ensuring that the RL agent does not degrade system availability.
3. Cost of Resources and Actions
    - Actions like deploying patches or spinning up failover systems have associated costs in terms of compute resources or operational downtime.
    - Incorporating these costs into the reward function encourages more efficient and targeted responses.

Through iterative exploration, the RL agent refines its policy to maximize long-term rewards. Early episodes might feature suboptimal actions (leading to excessive quarantines or missed intrusions), but with each step, the agent learns from the environment's feedback to fine-tune its defensive strategies.

An RL agent's training can take place in two main modes (Asghar et al., 2022):

1. Offline Training
    - Involves historical datasets or simulated environments, such as a cyber range.

- o Offline training allows the agent to explore many possible scenarios without risking production systems. The agent learns in a safe, controlled environment before being deployed live.
- o This approach can be limited by the realism and diversity of the training environment; if the simulation does not capture the complexity of real-world threats, the agent may not generalize well.

2. Online Learning
   - o The agent continues to learn and adapt in a live environment. As new attacks unfold, the agent refines its policy based on ongoing feedback.
   - o Online learning facilitates continuous adaptation, essential for threats that shift techniques over time.
   - o This mode, however, must be carefully managed to avoid risky, untested actions on critical infrastructure. Mechanisms such as a "human-in-the-loop" or a "shadow mode" testing (where the agent suggests actions but they are not automatically enforced) can mitigate potential harm.

Many organizations adopt a hybrid approach, training an RL agent offline with known scenarios and threat data, then transitioning to an online model in production with oversight. Over time, these agents can evolve into potent defenders that dynamically respond to novel attack vectors, guided by carefully formulated reward functions that balance security and operational needs.

3.3 Self-Healing and Self-Adaptive Security Systems

Beyond detecting and responding to active threats, a proactive defense requires remediating vulnerabilities before they can be exploited. Autonomous cyber defense architectures often integrate self-healing mechanisms to minimize exposure windows (Magnussen & Pettersen, 2023):

1. Automated Vulnerability Scanning
   - o Continuous scans identify newly discovered weaknesses in software components, libraries, or configurations.
   - o AI-driven scanners can prioritize vulnerabilities based on factors like exploit availability, severity scores, and historical patterns of attacks.
2. Patch Orchestration
   - o Once a vulnerability is detected, an autonomous system can automatically download, test, and deploy the appropriate patches across relevant endpoints.
   - o The system may employ canary testing in a small subset of hosts to confirm that the patch does not break critical applications.

    - Schedulers handle patch rollouts at times that minimize operational disruption, potentially guided by RL or heuristic optimization methods.
3. Configuration Hardening
    - In certain cases, a patch is not immediately available, or it may cause incompatibilities. The self-healing system can temporarily apply alternative mitigations—like turning off specific protocols or blocking known malicious IP ranges.
    - Machine learning can suggest secure baseline configurations based on industry benchmarks and the organization's specific environment.

By automating much of this workflow, the system drastically reduces the time from vulnerability discovery to patch deployment, closing potential doors to attackers. Moreover, the consistent, data-driven approach ensures that critical patches are prioritized, minimizing human error or oversight.

Self-adaptive systems must endure not just random faults or misconfigurations but also concerted, continuously evolving attacks. Key design principles include (Kanaan et al., 2024):

1. Multi-Layer Defense Mechanisms
    - Autonomy does not rely on a single detection method. Instead, overlapping layers—ranging from network firewalls to host-based anomaly detection—create multiple barriers.
    - If one layer fails or an attacker bypasses it, subsequent layers detect anomalies, ensuring resilience against unknown exploits.
2. Behavioral Adaptation
    - As the threat environment changes—whether due to new vulnerabilities or emerging attacker tactics—autonomous systems adjust detection thresholds, refine correlation rules, and evolve ML models in near real time.
    - This adaptation extends to resource allocation. During times of high threat or load, the system may allocate more computational capacity to intrusion detection or spin up additional honeypots to lure adversaries.
3. Diverse Redundancy
    - Autonomous architectures often employ diverse redundancy: multiple security solutions, from different vendors or built on different algorithms, to reduce single points of failure.
    - ML model ensembles can detect zero-day exploits more reliably than a single model, given each model's unique strengths.
4. Incident Response Playbooks

- o Self-adaptive systems encode decision logic for various incident scenarios—ransomware infiltration, insider attacks, or DDoS attempts—so they can react quickly without waiting for human approval.
- o Over time, these playbooks can be refined through RL or data-driven analytics to reflect the latest best practices and organizational requirements.

Ultimately, resilience and robustness hinge on the system's ability to handle both known and unknown threats, recovering quickly or reconfiguring itself in the face of disruptions. By continually incorporating new data—from vulnerability scans, threat intelligence feeds, and real-time monitoring—autonomous security architectures maintain a dynamic defense posture that is far more agile than traditional static solutions.

4. INTELLIGENT THREAT RESPONSE AND MITIGATION

A strong defensive posture goes beyond detecting threats; effective cybersecurity strategies also demand swift, intelligent threat response and efficient mitigation measures to minimize damage. In recent years, the cyber threat landscape has grown more dynamic, with automated attacks and zero-day exploits requiring an equally agile response mechanism. Modern security operations centers (SOCs) are stretched thin by an overload of alerts and a shortage of skilled personnel, exacerbating the complexity of incident response. To address these challenges, organizations are turning to AI-driven orchestration tools, machine-to-machine communication protocols, adaptive access controls, and collaborative frameworks that promote coordinated defenses. By automating many of the tasks traditionally handled by human analysts, these solutions free valuable human resources to tackle more complex decisions, enhancing both speed and accuracy in neutralizing active threats (Arnesen & Krohn, 2024).

The concept of intelligent threat response and mitigation encompasses several interrelated elements. First, automated incident response leverages orchestration and machine-to-machine communication to contain and remediate breaches in real time. Second, dynamic policy enforcement ensures that security configurations remain aligned with shifting risk profiles, using adaptive access control to grant or restrict privileges as threats evolve. Finally, collaborative defense strategies support an ecosystem where multiple stakeholders—ranging from federated enterprises to multi-agent AI systems—share knowledge and coordinate protective measures. This holistic approach bolsters resilience against both established and emerging attacks, enabling defenders to stay ahead of adversarial tactics.

4.1 Automated Incident Response

Automated incident response aims to reduce the "dwell time" of threats inside an organization's network—i.e., the period between an initial breach and complete mitigation. Orchestration tools, commonly found within Security Orchestration, Automation, and Response (SOAR) platforms, play a pivotal role. They integrate with a wide range of security technologies—such as firewalls, intrusion detection systems (IDS), endpoint detection and response (EDR) tools, and threat intelligence feeds—to coordinate immediate and consistent actions once a threat is detected (Moric & Kulic, (2024).

1. Workflow Automation

SOAR platforms allow security professionals to create "playbooks," which are predefined workflows outlining the exact steps to take when specific alerts or threat indicators arise. For instance, when an anomaly detection system flags suspicious lateral movement, the orchestration platform can automatically run a prescribed set of actions: gather relevant logs, isolate the affected host, and notify stakeholders. This workflow runs in seconds, dramatically reducing manual tasks like collecting evidence or initiating quarantines (Bridges et al., 2023).

2. Real-Time Correlation and Prioritization

Orchestration tools also incorporate correlation logic to fuse multiple alerts into a single incident. If a firewall logs repeated connection attempts from an untrusted IP, while an endpoint triggers an anomaly alert for the same IP, the orchestrator recognizes the relationship and prioritizes the incident for rapid containment. By contextualizing data across different platforms, SOAR solutions mitigate alert fatigue and identify critical threats more reliably (Chairopoulou, 2024).

An essential advantage of orchestration is the consistency of response. Human analysts may respond differently to the same threat under varying workloads or stress levels. Automated workflows, on the other hand, guarantee that proven best practices are applied every time, ensuring no step is overlooked. This standardization significantly improves overall security posture, especially in large enterprises with distributed teams.

As attacks occur at machine speed, machine-to-machine (M2M) communication is critical for matching that velocity in defense. The ultimate goal is a security ecosystem where devices and services autonomously alert each other and adjust configurations without waiting for human intervention.

1. APIs and Interoperability

Modern security tools typically expose application programming interfaces (APIs) that allow them to receive commands or provide status updates. SOAR platforms leverage these APIs to orchestrate actions such as blocking an IP address at a firewall, revoking compromised user credentials, or configuring network segmentation—often in milliseconds. API-centric designs also foster interoperability among solutions from different vendors, reducing the risk of vendor lock-in (Mennuni, 2023).

2. Event-Driven Triggers

In an M2M context, triggers are generated by specific events—like anomalous traffic spikes or detections of malicious file hashes. Once triggered, the relevant devices coordinate defensive measures according to pre-established policies. For instance, if an EDR tool observes suspicious behavior from a particular host, it can signal the network switch to isolate that host. Simultaneously, a forensic module might begin collecting memory snapshots. This event-driven paradigm ensures that each step in containment and remediation proceeds in a coordinated fashion, limiting an attacker's window to move deeper into the network (Yaacoub et al., 2020).

Beyond mere automation, M2M communication enhances the accuracy of responses by rapidly converging on correlated intelligence. When multiple detectors confirm malicious behavior from various angles—host logs, network signatures, sandbox outputs—it reinforces confidence that an incident is genuine, triggering proportionate countermeasures. Without requiring manual investigation at each stage, organizations can drastically reduce the time to quarantine compromised systems, patch vulnerabilities, and notify incident response teams.

4.2 Collaborative Defense Strategies

Modern adversaries frequently conduct distributed campaigns, targeting multiple organizations in a coordinated fashion. As such, an individual organization's view of threats can be limited. Collaborative defense strategies improve situational awareness and collective security by facilitating intelligence sharing across diverse entities (Chen, 2023).

1. Federated Threat Intelligence

In a federated model, multiple participants—such as businesses within a specific sector, government agencies, or non-profit security alliances—share threat data while retaining control over their own networks. They may contribute Indicators of

Compromise (IoCs), behavioral signatures, or newly discovered exploit methods. AI-driven tools then correlate these inputs, highlighting emerging attack patterns or widely exploited vulnerabilities (Sarhan et al., 2023).

2. Privacy-Preserving Methods

Organizations are often hesitant to share internal threat data due to privacy concerns or competitive sensitivities. Techniques like privacy-preserving data mining or secure multi-party computation allow them to share aggregated threat patterns without revealing sensitive details. This fosters trust among contributors and ensures compliance with data protection regulations (Hiwale et al., 2023).

3. Cross-Industry Alignment

Attackers do not restrict themselves to one sector, so cross-industry collaboration proves invaluable. For instance, a novel phishing tactic initially aimed at financial institutions might soon pivot to healthcare or retail. By pooling intelligence early, diverse stakeholders can coordinate prevention and response measures, disseminating best practices and detection signatures that help everyone better prepare (Carmona-Lavado et al., 2023).

In a multi-agent system, numerous autonomous agents operate within a shared environment, collaborating to defend against cyber threats. Each agent may handle a specific domain—endpoints, cloud workloads, IoT devices—or perform specialized tasks such as threat hunting, patching, or anomaly detection. Coordination among these agents enhances responsiveness and strengthens overall defenses (Amirkhani & Barshooi, 2022).

1. Decentralized Decision-Making

Agents often follow distributed consensus algorithms or reinforcement learning frameworks. This approach scales well in large networks or across multiple organizations, where a single, centralized orchestrator could become a bottleneck or single point of failure. Instead, each agent can make local decisions aligned with global security objectives, improving fault tolerance and speeding up response times (Gronauer & Diepold, 2022).

2. Hierarchical or Peer-to-Peer Coordination

In hierarchical designs, some agents assume supervisory roles, directing or validating the actions of lower-level agents. In peer-to-peer systems, agents communicate directly, exchanging relevant alerts or recommended countermeasures. The latter approach is more resilient to network segmentation caused by attacks, as agents can reconfigure their communication pathways if certain nodes become compromised (Li et al., 2024).

3. Adaptive Learning and Shared Knowledge

A critical aspect of multi-agent systems is the collective learning process. When one agent uncovers a new malware variant, it shares key information—like file hashes, behavioral patterns, or effective response strategies—across the system. Other agents adapt their detection models or response protocols accordingly. This organic knowledge propagation bolsters defenses in near real time, ensuring that new discoveries or lessons from localized incidents inform a unified approach to threat mitigation (Ahmed et al., 2025).

Collaborative defense ultimately shifts the balance of power by turning the distributed nature of enterprise networks into an advantage rather than a vulnerability. Whether through federated threat intelligence or multi-agent systems, joint efforts enable defenders to pool their expertise, scale their response capacity, and outmaneuver adversaries who rely on the siloed nature of traditional security setups.

Intelligent threat response and mitigation represent a crucial evolution in cybersecurity practice. As attackers leverage increasingly automated methods, defenders must respond with equal or greater agility. Automated incident response processes—from SOAR-driven playbooks to M2M communication—allow threats to be contained in seconds or minutes rather than hours or days. Meanwhile, dynamic policy enforcement ensures that network configurations, access controls, and firewall rules remain in lockstep with the latest threat insights, reducing the likelihood of exploitation through stale or permissive settings.

An equally important aspect is recognizing that no single entity can mount a robust defense in isolation. Collaborative defense strategies—encompassing threat intelligence exchanges, multi-agent coordination, and cross-industry partnerships—offer a more complete picture of adversarial activities and a faster collective response to novel threats. By sharing data and pooling analytical capabilities, organizations can develop a proactive stance against malicious campaigns that are orchestrated on a global scale.

Looking to the future, AI-driven techniques, such as federated machine learning and intelligent orchestration, will continue to evolve. These methods will help unify fragmented security systems, streamline the integration of new tools, and refine detection and response algorithms as threat actors adapt their techniques.

The convergence of automated incident response, dynamic policy enforcement, and cooperative frameworks will play an instrumental role in helping defenders maintain a competitive edge in an ever-shifting threat landscape. Through a blend of technical innovation, strategic collaboration, and a holistic security culture, organizations can mitigate threats more effectively, preserving business continuity and safeguarding critical digital assets for the long haul.

CONCLUSION

Artificial intelligence has become an indispensable tool in modern cybersecurity, transforming traditional defense mechanisms into highly adaptive and intelligent systems. The ability of AI to analyze vast datasets in real time, identify sophisticated attack patterns, and predict emerging threats positions it as a cornerstone of contemporary cyber defense strategies. Through techniques like anomaly detection, pattern recognition, and reinforcement learning, AI-driven systems can autonomously detect and mitigate threats, reducing response times and enhancing operational efficiency.

A critical aspect of these systems lies in their autonomous capabilities, which include dynamic decision-making and self-healing mechanisms. These architectures continuously monitor their environment, adjust defenses based on real-time insights, and initiate automated responses to neutralize risks. For instance, adaptive access control and zero-trust principles ensure that every action within a network is scrutinized, minimizing potential attack surfaces. Dynamic policy enforcement and collaborative frameworks enable a holistic, unified approach to cybersecurity, fostering resilience against even the most advanced persistent threats. However, these advancements are not without challenges. The operational scalability of AI-driven systems demands robust infrastructure capable of handling high-throughput environments. Additionally, issues of dataset bias, model transparency, and compliance with privacy regulations pose significant hurdles. Ethical considerations surrounding automated decision-making further highlight the importance of human oversight. Integrating a "human-in-the-loop" mechanism ensures critical decisions remain under expert control, maintaining a balance between automation and human intervention.

REFERENCES

Abutu, G., Weissman, D., Hoffmann, P., Bernstein, N., Brennan, O., & Armstrong, T. (2024). Deepcodelock: A novel deep learning-based approach for automated ransomware detection using behavioral signatures. *Authorea Preprints*. DOI: 10.36227/techrxiv.173047886.63868153/v1

Ahmed, I., Syed, M. A., Maaruf, M., & Khalid, M. (2025). Distributed computing in multi-agent systems: A survey of decentralized machine learning approaches. *Computing*, *107*(1), 2. DOI: 10.1007/s00607-024-01356-0

Akbulut, O., Cavus, M., Cengiz, M., Allahham, A., Giaouris, D., & Forshaw, M. (2024). Hybrid Intelligent Control System for Adaptive Microgrid Optimization: Integration of Rule-Based Control and Deep Learning Techniques. *Energies*, *17*(10), 2260. DOI: 10.3390/en17102260

Al-Shehari, T., Kadrie, M., Al-Mhiqani, M. N., Alfakih, T., Alsalman, H., Uddin, M., Ullah, S. S., & Dandoush, A. (2024). Comparative evaluation of data imbalance addressing techniques for CNN-based insider threat detection. *Scientific Reports*, *14*(1), 24715. DOI: 10.1038/s41598-024-73510-9 PMID: 39433789

Alabdulatif, A., & Thilakarathne, N. N. (2024). A novel cloud-enabled cyber threat hunting platform for evaluating the cyber risks associated with smart health ecosystems. *Applied Sciences (Basel, Switzerland)*, *14*(20), 9567. DOI: 10.3390/app14209567

Alazab, M., Soman, K. P., Srinivasan, S., Venkatraman, S., & Pham, V. Q. (2023). Deep learning for cyber security applications: A comprehensive survey. *Authorea Preprints*.

Almukhalfi, H., Noor, A., & Noor, T. H. (2024). Traffic management approaches using machine learning and deep learning techniques: A survey. *Engineering Applications of Artificial Intelligence*, *133*, 108147. DOI: 10.1016/j.engappai.2024.108147

Alqahtani, A. H. (2023). *The detection of Advanced Persistent Threats in Software Defined Networks using Machine Learning* (Doctoral dissertation, University of Sheffield).

Aminu, M., Akinsanya, A., Dako, D. A., & Oyedokun, O. (2024). Enhancing cyber threat detection through real-time threat intelligence and adaptive defense mechanisms. *International Journal of Computer Applications Technology and Research*, *13*(8), 11–27.

Amirkhani, A., & Barshooi, A. H. (2022). Consensus in multi-agent systems: A review. *Artificial Intelligence Review, 55*(5), 3897–3935. DOI: 10.1007/s10462-021-10097-x

Archana, R., & Jeevaraj, P. E. (2024). Deep learning models for digital image processing: A review. *Artificial Intelligence Review, 57*(1), 11. DOI: 10.1007/s10462-023-10631-z

Arnesen, C. S., & Krohn, H. H. (2024). *Strengthening incident response efforts in operational technology environments* (Master's thesis, University of Agder).

Asghar, M. Z., Afzaal, M. N., Iqbal, J., & Sadia, H. A. (2022). Analyzing an appropriate blend of face-to-face, offline and online learning approaches for the in-service vocational teacher's training program. *International Journal of Environmental Research and Public Health, 19*(17), 10668. DOI: 10.3390/ijerph191710668 PMID: 36078385

Azab, A., Khasawneh, M., Alrabaee, S., Choo, K. K. R., & Sarsour, M. (2024). Network traffic classification: Techniques, datasets, and challenges. *Digital Communications and Networks, 10*(3), 676–692. DOI: 10.1016/j.dcan.2022.09.009

Bai, Y., Zhao, H., Zhang, X., Chang, Z., Jäntti, R., & Yang, K. (2023). Towards autonomous multi-UAV wireless network: A survey of reinforcement learning-based approaches. *IEEE Communications Surveys and Tutorials, 25*(4), 3038–3067. DOI: 10.1109/COMST.2023.3323344

Beretas, C. (2024). Information systems security, detection and recovery from cyber attacks. *Universal Library of Engineering Technology, 1*(1).

Bhaskaran, S. V. (2023). Resilient real-time data delivery for ai summarization in conversational platforms: Ensuring low latency, high availability, and disaster recovery. *Journal of Intelligent Connectivity and Emerging Technologies, 8*(3), 113–130.

Bhattarai, K., Oh, I. Y., Sierra, J. M., Tang, J., Payne, P. R., Abrams, Z., & Lai, A. M. (2024). Leveraging GPT-4 for identifying cancer phenotypes in electronic health records: A performance comparison between GPT-4, GPT-3.5-turbo, Flan-T5, Llama-3-8B, and spaCy's rule-based and machine learning-based methods. *JAMIA Open, 7*(3), ooae060. DOI: 10.1093/jamiaopen/ooae060 PMID: 38962662

Bibi, U., Mazhar, M., Sabir, D., Muhammad, F. U. B., Hassan, A., Ghazanfar, M. A., Khan, A. A., & Abdul, W. (2024). Advances in Pruning and Quantization for Natural Language Processing. *IEEE Access : Practical Innovations, Open Solutions, 12*, 139113–139128. DOI: 10.1109/ACCESS.2024.3465631

Bridges, R. A., Rice, A. E., Oesch, S., Nichols, J. A., Watson, C., Spakes, K., Norem, S., Huettel, M., Jewell, B., Weber, B., Gannon, C., Bizovi, O., Hollifield, S. C., & Erwin, S. (2023). Testing SOAR tools in use. *Computers & Security, 129*, 103201. DOI: 10.1016/j.cose.2023.103201

Carmona-Lavado, A., Gimenez-Fernandez, E. M., Vlaisavljevic, V., & Cabello-Medina, C. (2023). Cross-industry innovation: A systematic literature review. *Technovation, 124*, 102743. DOI: 10.1016/j.technovation.2023.102743

Chairopoulou, S. (2024). *Cybersecurity in industrial control systems: a roadmap for fortifying operations* (Master's thesis).

Chen, S. (2023). A counterinsurgent (COIN) framework to defend against consumer activists. *Journal of Brand Management, 30*(4), 275–301. DOI: 10.1057/s41262-022-00297-3

Chiesa, M., Kamisiński, A., Rak, J., Rétvári, G., & Schmid, S. (2023). A survey of fast recovery mechanisms in the data plane. *Authorea Preprints.*

Corman, A. (2023). The Human Element in Cybersecurity–Bridging the Gap Between Technology and Human Behaviour.

Coulthard, B., & Taylor, B. J. (2023). *Big data analytics for making decisions and managing risk.* Sage. DOI: 10.4135/9781529614657.n50

Deldar, F., & Abadi, M. (2023). Deep learning for zero-day malware detection and classification: A survey. *ACM Computing Surveys, 56*(2), 1–37. DOI: 10.1145/3605775

Djaidja, T. E. T., Brik, B., Senouci, S. M., Boualouache, A., & Ghamri-Doudane, Y. (2024). Early network intrusion detection enabled by attention mechanisms and RNNs. *IEEE Transactions on Information Forensics and Security, 19*, 7783–7793. DOI: 10.1109/TIFS.2024.3441862

Edmund, E., & Enemosah, A. (2024). AI and machine learning in cybersecurity: Leveraging AI to predict, detect, and respond to threats more efficiently.

Ennab, M., & Mcheick, H. (2024). Enhancing interpretability and accuracy of AI models in healthcare: A comprehensive review on challenges and future directions. *Frontiers in Robotics and AI, 11*, 1444763. DOI: 10.3389/frobt.2024.1444763 PMID: 39677978

Fazliani, S., Sorond, M. M., & Masoudifard, A. (2024). Leveraging Ensemble-Based Semi-Supervised Learning for Illicit Account Detection in Ethereum DeFi Transactions. *arXiv preprint arXiv:2412.02408.*

Feldmann, M. J., Hardigan, M. A., Famula, R. A., Lopez, C. M., Tabb, A., Cole, G. S., & Knapp, S. J. (2020). Multi-dimensional machine learning approaches for fruit shape phenotyping in strawberry. *GigaScience*, *9*(5), giaa030. DOI: 10.1093/gigascience/giaa030 PMID: 32352533

Franke, L., Liang, H., Farzanehpour, S., Brantly, A., Davis, J. C., & Brown, C. (2024). An exploratory mixed-methods study on general data protection regulation (gdpr) compliance in open-source software. In *Proceedings of the 18th ACM/IEEE International Symposium on Empirical Software Engineering and Measurement* (pp. 325-336). DOI: 10.1145/3674805.3686692

George, A. S. (2024). Emerging Trends in AI-Driven Cybersecurity: An In-Depth Analysis. *Partners Universal Innovative Research Publication*, *2*(4), 15–28.

Ghiasi, M., Niknam, T., Wang, Z., Mehrandezh, M., Dehghani, M., & Ghadimi, N. (2023). A comprehensive review of cyber-attacks and defense mechanisms for improving security in smart grid energy systems: Past, present and future. *Electric Power Systems Research*, *215*, 108975. DOI: 10.1016/j.epsr.2022.108975

Gronauer, S., & Diepold, K. (2022). Multi-agent deep reinforcement learning: A survey. *Artificial Intelligence Review*, *55*(2), 895–943. DOI: 10.1007/s10462-021-09996-w

Hassija, V., Chamola, V., Mahapatra, A., Singal, A., Goel, D., Huang, K., Scardapane, S., Spinelli, I., Mahmud, M., & Hussain, A. (2024). Interpreting black-box models: A review on explainable artificial intelligence. *Cognitive Computation*, *16*(1), 45–74. DOI: 10.1007/s12559-023-10179-8

Hayward, K. J., & Maas, M. M. (2021). Artificial intelligence and crime: A primer for criminologists. *Crime, Media, Culture*, *17*(2), 209–233. DOI: 10.1177/1741659020917434

Hiwale, M., Walambe, R., Potdar, V., & Kotecha, K. (2023). A systematic review of privacy-preserving methods deployed with blockchain and federated learning for the telemedicine. *Healthcare Analytics*, *3*, 100192. DOI: 10.1016/j.health.2023.100192 PMID: 37223223

Javed, S. M. Z., & Amjad, M. F. (2024). Enhancing Malware Classification Through Dynamic Behavioral Analysis, SIEM Integration, and Deep Learning. In *2024 International Seminar on Intelligent Technology and Its Applications (ISITIA)* (pp. 663-668). IEEE.

Jeffrey, N., Tan, Q., & Villar, J. R. (2023). A review of anomaly detection strategies to detect threats to cyber-physical systems. *Electronics (Basel), 12*(15), 3283. DOI: 10.3390/electronics12153283

Jimmy, F. N. U. (2024). Cyber security Vulnerabilities and Remediation Through Cloud Security Tools. *Journal of Artificial Intelligence General science (JAIGS) ISSN: 3006-4023, 2*(1), 129-171.

Kale, G., Bostancı, G. E., & Çelebi, F. V. (2024). Evolutionary feature selection for machine learning based malware classification. *Engineering Science and Technology, an International Journal, 56*, 101762. DOI: 10.1016/j.jestch.2024.101762

Kaliyaperumal, P., Periyasamy, S., Thirumalaisamy, M., Balusamy, B., & Benedetto, F. (2024). A novel hybrid unsupervised learning approach for enhanced cybersecurity in the IoT. *Future Internet, 16*(7), 253. DOI: 10.3390/fi16070253

Kanaan, A., Mtair AL-Hawamleh, A., Aloun, M., Alorfi, A., & Abdalwahab Al-rawashdeh, M. (2024). Fortifying organizational cyber resilience: An integrated framework for business continuity and growth amidst escalating threat landscapes. *International Journal of Computing and Digital Systems, 16*(1), 1–13. DOI: 10.12785/ijcds/1571023809

Kanellopoulos, D., & Sharma, V. K. (2022). Dynamic load balancing techniques in the IoT: A review. *Symmetry, 14*(12), 2554. DOI: 10.3390/sym14122554

Kasongo, S. M. (2023). A deep learning technique for intrusion detection system using a Recurrent Neural Networks based framework. *Computer Communications, 199*, 113–125. DOI: 10.1016/j.comcom.2022.12.010

Kavya, S., & Sumathi, D. (2024). Staying ahead of phishers: A review of recent advances and emerging methodologies in phishing detection. *Artificial Intelligence Review, 58*(2), 50. DOI: 10.1007/s10462-024-11055-z

Khan, W., Daud, A., Khan, K., Muhammad, S., & Haq, R. (2023). Exploring the frontiers of deep learning and natural language processing: A comprehensive overview of key challenges and emerging trends. *Natural Language Processing Journal*, 100026.

Khanan, A., Mohamed, Y. A., Mohamed, A. H., & Bashir, M. (2024). From Bytes to Insights: A Systematic Literature Review on Unraveling IDS Datasets for Enhanced Cybersecurity Understanding. *IEEE Access : Practical Innovations, Open Solutions, 12*, 59289–59317. DOI: 10.1109/ACCESS.2024.3392338

Kheddar, H., Dawoud, D. W., Awad, A. I., Himeur, Y., & Khan, M. K. (2024). Reinforcement-Learning-Based Intrusion Detection in Communication Networks: A Review. *IEEE Communications Surveys and Tutorials*, 1. DOI: 10.1109/COMST.2024.3484491

Khorsheed, E. A., & Al-Sulaifanie, A. K. (2024). Handwritten Digit Classification Using Deep Learning Convolutional Neural Network. *Journal of Soft Computing and Data Mining*, *5*(1), 79–90. DOI: 10.30880/jscdm.2024.05.01.007

Komadina, A., Martinić, M., Groš, S., & Mihajlović, Ž. (2024). Comparing Threshold Selection Methods for Network Anomaly Detection. *IEEE Access : Practical Innovations, Open Solutions*, *12*, 124943–124973. DOI: 10.1109/ACCESS.2024.3452168

Kruse, R., Mostaghim, S., Borgelt, C., Braune, C., & Steinbrecher, M. (2022). Multi-layer perceptrons. In *Computational intelligence: a methodological introduction* (pp. 53–124). Springer International Publishing. DOI: 10.1007/978-3-030-42227-1_5

Kumar, S., Ahlawat, P., & Sahni, J. (2024). IOT malware detection using static and dynamic analysis techniques: A systematic literature review. *Security and Privacy*, *7*(6), e444. DOI: 10.1002/spy2.444

Kwon, H. Y., Kim, T., & Lee, M. K. (2022). Advanced intrusion detection combining signature-based and behavior-based detection methods. *Electronics (Basel)*, *11*(6), 867. DOI: 10.3390/electronics11060867

Leite, D., Sharma, A., Demir, C., & Ngomo, A. C. (2024, June). Interpretability index based on balanced volumes for transparent models and agnostic explainers. In *2024 IEEE International Conference on Fuzzy Systems (FUZZ-IEEE)* (pp. 1-10). IEEE. DOI: 10.1109/FUZZ-IEEE60900.2024.10611937

Li, X., Wang, S., Zeng, S., Wu, Y., & Yang, Y. (2024). A survey on LLM-based multi-agent systems: Workflow, infrastructure, and challenges. *Vicinagearth*, *1*(1), 9. DOI: 10.1007/s44336-024-00009-2

Lu, Q., Peng, Z., Wu, L., Ni, M., & Luo, J. (2024). Detecting the cyber-physical-social cooperated APTs in high-DER-penetrated smart grids: Threats, current work and challenges. *Computer Networks*, *254*, 110776. DOI: 10.1016/j.comnet.2024.110776

Magnussen, G. M. K., & Pettersen, M. (2023). *A Comprehensive Framework for Patching and Vulnerability Management in Enterprises* (Master's thesis, University of Agder).

Mahadevappa, P., Al-amri, R., Alkawsi, G., Alkahtani, A. A., Alghenaim, M. F., & Alsamman, M. (2024). Analyzing Threats and Attacks in Edge Data Analytics within IoT Environments. *IoT*, *5*(1), 123–154. DOI: 10.3390/iot5010007

McLaughlin, C. (2024). Scalable Machine Learning Methods and Datasets for Software Vulnerability Detection (Doctoral dissertation, Queensland University of Technology).

Mennuni, M. (2023). *An Analysis of SOC Monitoring Systems* (Doctoral dissertation, Politecnico di Torino).

Moric, Z., Dakic, V., & Kulic, M. (2024, June). Implementing a Security Framework for Container Orchestration. In *2024 IEEE 11th International Conference on Cyber Security and Cloud Computing (CSCloud)* (pp. 200-206). IEEE. DOI: 10.1109/CSCloud62866.2024.00042

Mvula, P. K., Branco, P., Jourdan, G. V., & Viktor, H. L. (2024). A Survey on the Applications of Semi-supervised Learning to Cyber-security. *ACM Computing Surveys*, *56*(10), 1–41. DOI: 10.1145/3657647

Naeem, S., Ali, A., Anam, S., & Ahmed, M. M. (2023). An unsupervised machine learning algorithms: Comprehensive review. *International Journal of Computing and Digital Systems*.

Opara, I. K., Opara, U. L., Okolie, J. A., & Fawole, O. A. (2024). Machine Learning Application in Horticulture and Prospects for Predicting Fresh Produce Losses and Waste: A Review. *Plants*, *13*(9), 1200. DOI: 10.3390/plants13091200 PMID: 38732414

Patwardhan, N., Marrone, S., & Sansone, C. (2023). Transformers in the real world: A survey on nlp applications. *Information (Basel)*, *14*(4), 242. DOI: 10.3390/info14040242

Pinto, A., Herrera, L. C., Donoso, Y., & Gutierrez, J. A. (2024). Enhancing Critical Infrastructure Security: Unsupervised Learning Approaches for Anomaly Detection. *International Journal of Computational Intelligence Systems*, *17*(1), 236. DOI: 10.1007/s44196-024-00644-z

Preuveneers, D., & Joosen, W. (2021). Sharing machine learning models as indicators of compromise for cyber threat intelligence. *Journal of Cybersecurity and Privacy*, *1*(1), 140–163. DOI: 10.3390/jcp1010008

Qureshi, S. U., He, J., Tunio, S., Zhu, N., Nazir, A., Wajahat, A., Ullah, F., & Wadud, A. (2024). Systematic review of deep learning solutions for malware detection and forensic analysis in IoT. *Journal of King Saud University. Computer and Information Sciences*, *36*(8), 102164. DOI: 10.1016/j.jksuci.2024.102164

Roshanaei, M., Khan, M. R., & Sylvester, N. N. (2024). Navigating AI cybersecurity: Evolving landscape and challenges. *Journal of Intelligent Learning Systems and Applications*, *16*(3), 155–174. DOI: 10.4236/jilsa.2024.163010

Sadiq, S., & Zeebaree, S. R. (2024). Distributed Systems for Machine Learning in Cloud Computing: A Review of Scalable and Efficient Training and Inference. *Indonesian Journal of Computer Science*, *13*(2). Advance online publication. DOI: 10.33022/ijcs.v13i2.3814

Sanju, P. (2023). Enhancing intrusion detection in IoT systems: A hybrid metaheuristics-deep learning approach with ensemble of recurrent neural networks. *Journal of Engineering Research*, *11*(4), 356–361. DOI: 10.1016/j.jer.2023.100122

Sarhan, M., Layeghy, S., Moustafa, N., & Portmann, M. (2023). Cyber threat intelligence sharing scheme based on federated learning for network intrusion detection. *Journal of Network and Systems Management*, *31*(1), 3. DOI: 10.1007/s10922-022-09691-3

Sarker, I. H., Janicke, H., Mohsin, A., Gill, A., & Maglaras, L. (2024). Explainable AI for cybersecurity automation, intelligence and trustworthiness in digital twin: Methods, taxonomy, challenges and prospects. *ICT Express*, *10*(4), 935–958. DOI: 10.1016/j.icte.2024.05.007

Shahin, M., Maghanaki, M., Hosseinzadeh, A., & Chen, F. F. (2024). Advancing network security in industrial IoT: A deep dive into AI-enabled intrusion detection systems. *Advanced Engineering Informatics*, *62*, 102685. DOI: 10.1016/j.aei.2024.102685

Shakya, A. K., Pillai, G., & Chakrabarty, S. (2023). Reinforcement learning algorithms: A brief survey. *Expert Systems with Applications*, *231*, 120495. DOI: 10.1016/j.eswa.2023.120495

Shao, L., Zhang, E., & Li, M. (2021). An efficient convolutional neural network model combined with attention mechanism for inverse halftoning. *Electronics (Basel)*, *10*(13), 1574. DOI: 10.3390/electronics10131574

Smmarwar, S. K., Gupta, G. P., & Kumar, S. (2024). Android Malware Detection and Identification Frameworks by Leveraging the Machine and Deep Learning Techniques: A Comprehensive Review. *Telematics and Informatics Reports*, 100130.

Smolyakova, S. (2024). *Traditional Indicators of Compromise (IOCs) Meet Dynamic App-Device Interactions for IoT-specific Threat Intelligence* (Doctoral dissertation, Concordia University).

Sofia, R. C., Dykeman, D., Urbanetz, P., Galal, A., & Dave, D. A. (2023). Dynamic, Context-Aware Cross-Layer Orchestration of Containerized Applications. *IEEE Access : Practical Innovations, Open Solutions, 11*, 93129–93150. DOI: 10.1109/ACCESS.2023.3307026

Suchman, L. (2023). Imaginaries of omniscience: Automating intelligence in the US Department of Defense. *Social Studies of Science, 53*(5), 761–786. DOI: 10.1177/03063127221104938 PMID: 35735177

Sundaram, A. (2022). *Covert Cognizance: Embedded Intelligence for Industrial Systems* (Doctoral dissertation, Purdue University Graduate School).

Surianarayanan, C., Kunasekaran, S., & Chelliah, P. R. (2024). A high-throughput architecture for anomaly detection in streaming data using machine learning algorithms. *International Journal of Information Technology : an Official Journal of Bharati Vidyapeeth's Institute of Computer Applications and Management, 16*(1), 493–506. DOI: 10.1007/s41870-023-01585-0

Syed, N. F., Shah, S. W., Shaghaghi, A., Anwar, A., Baig, Z., & Doss, R. (2022). Zero trust architecture (zta): A comprehensive survey. *IEEE Access : Practical Innovations, Open Solutions, 10*, 57143–57179. DOI: 10.1109/ACCESS.2022.3174679

Tariq, U., Ahmed, I., Bashir, A. K., & Khan, M. A. (2024). Securing the evolving IoT with deep learning: A comprehensive review. *Kurdish Studies, 12*(1), 3426–3454.

Taye, M. M. (2023). Understanding of machine learning with deep learning: Architectures, workflow, applications and future directions. *Computers, 12*(5), 91. DOI: 10.3390/computers12050091

Thangavel, K., Sabatini, R., Gardi, A., Ranasinghe, K., Hilton, S., Servidia, P., & Spiller, D. (2024). Artificial intelligence for trusted autonomous satellite operations. *Progress in Aerospace Sciences, 144*, 100960. DOI: 10.1016/j.paerosci.2023.100960

Thirumuruganathan, S., Deniz, F., Khalil, I., Yu, T., Nabeel, M., & Ouzzani, M. (2024). Detecting and mitigating sampling bias in cybersecurity with unlabeled data. In *33rd USENIX Security Symposium (USENIX Security 24)* (pp. 1741-1758).

Valdovinos, I. A., Pérez-Díaz, J. A., Choo, K. K. R., & Botero, J. F. (2021). Emerging DDoS attack detection and mitigation strategies in software-defined networks: Taxonomy, challenges and future directions. *Journal of Network and Computer Applications, 187*, 103093. DOI: 10.1016/j.jnca.2021.103093

Waheed, A., Seegolam, B., Jowaheer, M. F., Sze, C. L. X., Hua, E. T. F., & Sindiramutty, S. R. (2024). Zero-Day Exploits in Cybersecurity: Case Studies and Countermeasure. Preprints *[Preprint]. , 2338*, v1.DOI: 10.20944/preprints202407

Wang, X., Wang, S., Liang, X., Zhao, D., Huang, J., Xu, X., Dai, B., & Miao, Q. (2022). Deep reinforcement learning: A survey. *IEEE Transactions on Neural Networks and Learning Systems, 35*(4), 5064–5078. DOI: 10.1109/TNNLS.2022.3207346 PMID: 36170386

Wang, Z., Zhou, Y., Liu, H., Qiu, J., Fang, B., & Tian, Z. (2024). ThreatInsight: Innovating Early Threat Detection through Threat-Intelligence-Driven Analysis and Attribution. *IEEE Transactions on Knowledge and Data Engineering, 36*(12), 9388–9402. DOI: 10.1109/TKDE.2024.3474792

Wong, A. K. C., & Wang, Y. (2003). Pattern discovery: A data driven approach to decision support. *IEEE Transactions on Systems, Man, and Cybernetics. Part C, Applications and Reviews, 33*(1), 114–124. DOI: 10.1109/TSMCC.2003.809869

Yaacoub, J. P. A., Salman, O., Noura, H. N., Kaaniche, N., Chehab, A., & Malli, M. (2020). Cyber-physical systems security: Limitations, issues and future trends. *Microprocessors and Microsystems, 77*, 103201. DOI: 10.1016/j.micpro.2020.103201 PMID: 32834204

Yamany, B., Elsayed, M. S., Jurcut, A. D., Abdelbaki, N., & Azer, M. A. (2024). A holistic approach to ransomware classification: Leveraging static and dynamic analysis with visualization. *Information (Basel), 15*(1), 46. DOI: 10.3390/info15010046

Yang, L. H., Ye, F. F., Hu, H., Lu, H., Wang, Y. M., & Chang, W. J. (2024). A data-driven rule-base approach for carbon emission trend forecast with environmental regulation and efficiency improvement. *Sustainable Production and Consumption, 45*, 316–332. DOI: 10.1016/j.spc.2023.12.030

Zgallai, W. A., & Ozsahin, D. U. (Eds.). (2024). *Artificial intelligence and image processing in medical imaging*. Elsevier.

Chapter 3
Advanced AI for Network Security:
Predictive Detection and Autonomous Defense

Faisal Aburub
https://orcid.org/0000-0002-6461-9836
Petra University, Jordan

Saad Alateef
https://orcid.org/0009-0002-3219-0833
Newcastle University, UK

ABSTRACT

Organizations continue facing threats that exploit network vulnerabilities. Defenders seek approaches that detect anomalies and respond quickly to attacks. This chapter examines predictive models and automated mechanisms for network defense. It explores how artificial intelligence approaches learn evolving patterns in large-scale data, offering insights and mitigation strategies. Researchers observe advantages in automated recognition, anomaly forecasts, and coordinated countermeasures. Studies indicate success in reducing detection delays and halting malicious actions. Defense frameworks featuring reinforcement agents, neural architectures, and adaptive analytics show promise in lessening manual involvement. Outcomes suggest that ongoing refinements in data handling, architecture design, and interpretability are essential. This chapter provides a synthesis of methods, findings, and future research directions for next-generation AI-driven network defense.

DOI: 10.4018/979-8-3373-0954-5.ch003

1. INTRODUCTION

Network systems handle critical operations for enterprises, governments, and individuals. Attacks on these systems lead to theft, data manipulation, or service disruptions. Rapid technological evolution has increased dependence on connectivity, creating new vulnerabilities that can be exploited by malicious entities. Defensive mechanisms that relied on static rules have struggled to manage the volume and sophistication of threats (Garcia-Teodoro et al., 2009). As a result, entities have investigated artificial intelligence (AI) to automate detection and response. Efforts combine data-driven techniques and computational models to parse information from logs, traffic flows, and endpoint events. This chapter offers a thorough analysis of how AI can predict, detect, and mitigate attacks through autonomous methods.

AI-driven network security emerged from a desire to learn from data without static or signature-based updates. Traditional intrusion detection systems often depended on known signatures or heuristic thresholds (Buczak & Guven, 2016). Over time, adversaries changed attack tactics, which complicated the creation of universal rules. Security teams soon faced the challenge of analyzing large, dynamic datasets under pressure. Researchers began introducing machine learning to automate detection and classification (Berman et al., 2019). Contemporary AI solutions handle large data volumes and adapt to novel patterns, uncovering subtle indicators of compromise. Analysts see these solutions as a path toward continuous monitoring and immediate intervention.

Organizations attempt to leverage predictive analytics to identify threats early. Predictive systems examine prior incidents, suspicious events, and contextual intelligence. They correlate these elements to forecast potential threats, similar to how financial models predict market trends (Malik et al., 2023). AI-based classifiers and regressors extract correlations from historical intrusion patterns, vulnerability scans, or external threat feeds. Forecasting likely attack surfaces helps defenders allocate resources more effectively (Oesch et al., 2025). This proactivity offers advantages in high-stakes environments, such as government agencies or large businesses with sensitive data.

Autonomous response methods, including reinforcement learning, introduce advanced capabilities for adjusting defenses in real time. Automated systems can craft firewall rules, isolate compromised endpoints, or adjust dynamic trust policies based on detection outcomes (Adawadkar & Kulkarni, 2022). This capacity reduces the burden on security analysts, who must often sift through countless alerts. However, deploying automated solutions requires careful planning. Administrators worry about false positives, unintended disruptions, and the interpretability of AI-based decisions (Mohamed, 2023). Thorough testing in controlled environments can reveal system stability, but real-world traffic presents more varied and unpredictable conditions.

Several core components define AI-based security architecture. First, data collection subsystems gather logs, packet captures, or host-based telemetry. Next, feature engineering or extraction transforms raw information into structured inputs for learning models (Ferrag et al., 2020). The choice of features influences model accuracy and speed. Models then classify or predict malicious events. Finally, a decision layer executes responses, such as blocking an IP range or generating alerts for security operators (Momand et al., 2023). This pipeline requires coordination among devices, storage systems, and analytical engines. Scaling these solutions for large networks demands efficient data processing and real-time model inference.

Network threats manifest in multiple forms: denial-of-service campaigns, ransomware, zero-day exploits, advanced persistent threats, and more (Elhami Fard et al., 2023). Each category involves distinct tactics, requiring detection frameworks to cover different indicators. An AI-based system that focuses on volumetric anomalies may detect denial-of-service events but miss stealthy intrusions. Conversely, specialized anomaly detectors that scrutinize lateral movement might fail to recognize a distributed scanning pattern. A comprehensive approach integrates multiple detection modules, sometimes referred to as an ensemble or multi-layered system. This design attempts to widen coverage, reduce missed attacks, and maintain acceptable false-positive levels (Hussain et al., 2020).

Key challenges emerge when building an AI-driven security system. The ever-changing nature of threats forces continuous retraining or updating of models (Stanzione et al., 2020). A model trained on data from last year may struggle to detect new variants. Data labeling remains another obstacle. Manually labeling large sets of network records can be time-consuming. Automated labeling tools depend on rule-based logic, which might not capture advanced threats accurately. The quality of training data has a direct impact on system reliability. Overfitting to a small or unrepresentative dataset can degrade performance in production environments (Bensaoud et al., 2024).

Interpreting AI decisions poses another hurdle. Deep learning architectures exhibit strong performance but can act as black boxes. Security professionals often need to understand why traffic was flagged as malicious (Macas et al., 2024). Explainable AI techniques attempt to highlight features that influence detection outcomes. Visualization dashboards translate anomalies into interpretable information for decision-makers. These capabilities enhance trust in automated systems and help refine defensive strategies. Moreover, regulatory requirements in certain sectors mandate auditing or justification for automated decisions. A system that isolates a critical server or blocks essential traffic without clear reasoning may cause operational issues (Ofusori et al., 2024).

Despite challenges, evidence suggests that AI-driven methods expand detection coverage and reduce time-to-respond in many scenarios (Rahman et al., 2024). Supervised and unsupervised learning can unearth hidden attack vectors. Reinforcement algorithms can rapidly test and adopt new rules. Predictive analytics allow organizations to prepare for potential intrusion patterns. Adversarial examples remain a concern—attackers craft inputs to mislead AI models. However, researchers propose detection strategies for adversarial manipulations, including adversarial training or input sanitization. A layered defense approach that combines AI with human oversight can mitigate such risks.

This chapter seeks to provide a thorough look at advanced AI approaches for network defense. Later sections delve into anomaly detection, predictive modeling, intelligent response, and performance assessment. Relevant implementation challenges will be examined, including data processing, system integration, and resource constraints. The text also outlines future pathways in distributed learning, game theory, privacy-preserving analytics, and explainable design principles. By analyzing multiple perspectives, the chapter aims to offer a foundational resource for readers seeking to employ AI techniques in network security. It draws upon peer-reviewed literature from academic conferences and journals, focusing on recent findings.

The objective is not only to catalog existing methods but also to interpret their significance for practitioners, researchers, and policymakers. Many solutions concentrate on known threats, but new attack surfaces can appear suddenly, spurred by emerging technologies. This reality highlights the importance of adaptive and proactive measures. AI-driven systems must constantly refine their models and re-evaluate assumptions. Skilled personnel will still be relevant—human decision-making offers creativity and domain expertise. Yet, harnessing automated detection can transform how organizations manage security operations, potentially decreasing operational overhead and preventing large-scale compromises.

The next section explores foundational aspects of AI-driven security. It begins with a brief overview of how machine learning and neural methods entered cybersecurity. The text then reviews principal machine learning concepts that underpin detection and classification tasks. Collectively, these insights clarify the building blocks for advanced AI-based defense. Subsequent sections present anomaly detection frameworks, predictive analytics for threat modeling, and intelligent response systems that operate autonomously or semi-autonomously.

In sum, the introduction highlights an evolving field where data-driven defense merges with real-time countermeasures. Early successes motivate ongoing investment in this domain. Yet, real-world integration remains a work in progress, given operational complexities, adversarial tactics, and the intricacy of large-scale infrastructures (Nguyen & Reddi, 2021). The subsequent content offers an in-depth treatment of these issues, supplemented by documented case studies and references to leading research.

2. FOUNDATIONS OF AI-DRIVEN SECURITY

2.1. Emergence of Machine Learning in Cyber Defense

Machine learning entered cybersecurity environments when practitioners realized the limitations of static detection approaches. Signature-based antivirus programs, which match malicious patterns, were incapable of detecting novel or slightly modified threats. Heuristic systems attempted to expand coverage but required frequent manual rule updates (Buczak & Guven, 2016). As data volumes grew, administrators sought automated ways to identify irregularities across large log files. The adoption of data mining and statistical classification methods in the early 2000s laid groundwork for more advanced AI approaches.

Neural networks offered a flexible architecture capable of approximating complex functions. Early tests in cyber defense applied multi-layer perceptrons to intrusion detection. Researchers observed that neural networks captured non-linear relationships, potentially discovering attack signatures that eluded simpler classifiers (Berman et al., 2019). Over time, the field pivoted to deep learning, which leveraged multiple hidden layers and advanced optimizers. Convolutional and recurrent networks found use in analyzing network packets and time-series data. These shifts occurred alongside hardware advances that accelerated training and inference, such as GPUs and specialized ASICs.

Anomaly detection and classification tasks soon expanded. The variety of attacks prompted the use of ensemble methods that combined supervised and unsupervised learning. Hybrid classifiers matched known signatures, while anomaly detectors flagged deviations. Clustering and outlier detection helped reveal stealthy patterns. Machine learning began influencing broader security domains, including malware analysis, phishing detection, and behavioral analytics (Ofusori et al., 2024). The synergy of big data infrastructure and machine learning frameworks accelerated these developments. Researchers and industry practitioners embraced platforms like Hadoop, Spark, and TensorFlow for large-scale security analytics.

Despite progress, machine learning faced skepticism related to false positives, model drift, and interpretability. Managers worried that automated detection might hamper legitimate network traffic. Model drift refers to performance degradation over time if the threat landscape evolves faster than the model's update cycle. These challenges underscored the need for robust data pipelines, continuous retraining, and domain-specific knowledge integration (Ferrag et al., 2020).

Figure 1 shows how an AI-based system collects network data, applies analytical models, and decides on threat mitigation. It illustrates the transition from raw inputs to automated responses.

Figure 1. AI-based intrusion detection flow

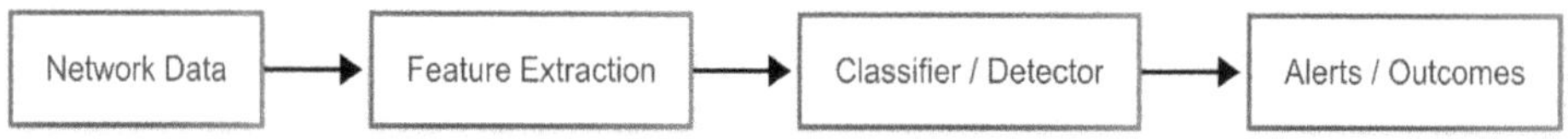

2.2. Core Concepts in AI-Driven Network Security

Building an AI-driven security system involves standard steps: data collection, preprocessing, feature extraction, model selection, and deployment. This pipeline ensures that raw events transform into actionable insights. Data sources often include NetFlow, packet captures, authentication logs, or endpoint telemetry (Garcia-Teodoro et al., 2009). Preprocessing might remove duplicates, standardize timestamps, or address missing values. Feature extraction creates numeric representations for modeling. Examples include flow duration, byte counts, or statistical summaries of packet distributions (Mohamed, 2023).

Model selection hinges on the specific security objective. Supervised methods can classify traffic into benign or malicious categories, given labeled examples (Momand et al., 2023). Unsupervised methods detect outliers and anomalies without labels. Reinforcement learning optimizes sequential decision-making, suitable for dynamic defenses. Hybrid strategies combine these elements to leverage multiple perspectives. Some solutions incorporate domain knowledge, encoding known indicators of compromise.

Deep learning architectures excel at pattern recognition in complex data. Convolutional neural networks (CNNs) handle structured inputs like images or multi-dimensional signals. Researchers adapt them to network traffic by converting sequences of packets into matrices. Recurrent neural networks (RNNs) capture temporal dependencies, identifying multi-step attack sequences (Malik et al., 2023). Transformers, introduced in natural language processing, appear in security tasks that involve large context windows. Autoencoders, a type of neural network for dimensionality reduction or reconstruction, power anomaly detection by learning normal traffic patterns.

Model interpretability and explainability remain priority areas. Observers want to trace why a deep model categorized certain traffic as malicious. Methods like layer-wise relevance propagation or local surrogate explainers attempt to illuminate the model's logic (Stanzione et al., 2020). The ability to justify decisions fosters trust among analysts, especially in regulated sectors like finance or healthcare. It also aids in diagnosing false positives, refining the model for future iterations.

Table 1 presents popular AI methods for intrusion detection. It outlines the methods' core principle, benefits, and limitations.

Table 1. Common AI techniques for network intrusion detection

Technique	Description	Pros	Cons
Supervised Learning	Learns from labeled samples	High accuracy with enough data	Requires careful labeling, potential bias
Unsupervised Learning	Identifies patterns in unlabeled data	Useful for zero-day detection	Can produce false positives
Reinforcement Learning	Learns from sequential feedback	Suitable for adaptive defense	Demands robust simulation
Hybrid Approaches	Mixes multiple methods	Balances detection scope	Implementation complexity

2.3. Evolution Toward Predictive Analytics and Autonomous Defense

Predictive analytics add foresight to detection approaches by anticipating potential attacks. This mindset extends beyond immediate anomaly detection, examining patterns that could signal future compromise. Time-series forecasting methods track changes in scanning rates, vulnerability disclosures, or user behaviors (Rahman et al., 2024). Some solutions integrate external threat intelligence feeds, which detail indicators from known campaigns. Combining these sources can pinpoint emerging threats, prompting proactive measures like patching or segmenting networks.

In tandem, reinforcement learning and control theory principles push security into the realm of autonomous defense. Instead of static rules, an agent learns from trial and feedback. It may experiment with blocking strategies or honeypot deployments. The environment includes malicious actors, legitimate users, and resource constraints. Over time, the agent refines its policy to maximize reward, typically tied to maintaining security while minimizing disruptions (Sewak et al., 2022). This approach acknowledges that an optimal defense often requires dynamic actions, not just passive detection.

However, real-world integration of autonomous defense faces constraints. High-stakes environments cannot permit extensive experimentation that might cause service interruptions. Simulation platforms or test networks help refine policies before deployment. Transfer learning then adapts a policy to similar contexts. Ongoing research explores how to detect environment shifts and adapt the policy quickly without catastrophic forgetting (Nguyen & Reddi, 2021).

2.4. Limitations in Conventional Methods

Conventional systems rely on signatures, heuristics, or event correlation for detection. These methods operate well when threats align with known patterns. Unfortunately, attackers often mutate payloads or exploit zero-day vulnerabilities. Signature approaches fail in these scenarios unless updated promptly. Manual rule updates cause delays and depend on experts identifying new patterns (Buczak & Guven, 2016). Advanced threats can remain undetected for extended periods, later leading to data breaches or sabotage.

Heuristic-based solutions also struggle with dynamic attacks that shift over time. Adversaries might adjust their behavior to blend with normal traffic. They may distribute the attack across multiple hosts or leverage encrypted channels. Intrusion detection systems reliant on known heuristics can fail to spot these evolving campaigns. An AI-driven approach helps address these gaps by learning from large samples of diverse data. It captures generalized decision boundaries rather than relying exclusively on explicit matches.

In summary, machine learning addresses many vulnerabilities found in legacy detection. The field continues evolving, with deeper architectures, advanced reinforcement methods, and predictive analysis. The next section explores anomaly detection strategies and predictive modeling in more depth. These pillars ground many AI-based intrusion detection frameworks.

3. ANOMALY DETECTION AND PREDICTIVE ANALYTICS

3.1. Foundations of Anomaly Detection

Anomaly detection is central to network defense. The objective is to model typical behavior and detect deviations that could indicate intrusion (Garcia-Teodoro et al., 2009). Statistical methods, such as Gaussian models or density estimations, formed the earliest anomaly detectors. They rely on assumptions about data distributions. Machine learning broadens the scope by capturing complex patterns. Unsupervised techniques, including clustering and autoencoders, discovered outliers without labeled training data. This approach is useful in cybersecurity contexts where labeling is incomplete or inaccurate (Momand et al., 2023).

Autoencoders reconstruct normal inputs with low error. When encountering anomalous traffic, reconstruction error rises, triggering detection. Variational autoencoders refine this process by introducing probabilistic modeling. Another method, one-class SVM, learns boundaries around normal data. Points falling outside these boundaries are labeled anomalous (Macas et al., 2024). Unsupervised strategies suit zero-day detection because they do not rely on explicit known malicious examples. However, they can generate false positives when encountering rare but benign activities.

Semi-supervised approaches use abundant normal data and limited malicious samples for training. This arrangement merges unsupervised and supervised paradigms. It provides the advantage of a well-defined baseline while incorporating knowledge of known threats. Performance depends on how representative the normal data is. If new normal behaviors appear, the system might classify them as anomalies until retrained (Rahman et al., 2024).

3.2. Model Architectures for Anomaly Detection

Neural networks, random forests, and ensemble classifiers power anomaly detection pipelines. Recurrent neural networks track sequential patterns in traffic or logs, especially relevant for multi-step attacks. CNNs can interpret raw packet data by treating bytes as a spatial dimension (Malik et al., 2023). Ensemble methods combine multiple models, such as decision trees and SVMs, to balance biases and enhance robustness. Stacking, boosting, and bagging are ensemble techniques that help refine classification decisions.

In practice, anomaly detection systems must handle noisy inputs, high-dimensional features, and concept drift. Continuous learning frameworks ingest new data, retraining or updating model parameters regularly. Online learning techniques process data streams incrementally (Hussain et al., 2020). These frameworks adapt to shifting patterns but require careful hyperparameter tuning to prevent overreaction to short-term fluctuations.

3.3. Predictive Threat Modeling

While anomaly detection reacts to unusual events, predictive threat modeling aims to forecast them. Predictive analytics rely on historical patterns, external intelligence, and statistical learning. For instance, a system might identify minor scanning attempts that precede larger attacks. By recognizing these precursors, defenders can reinforce defenses or isolate vulnerable segments. Regression-based models estimate future threat levels, while Bayesian networks incorporate probabilistic dependencies among indicators (Malik et al., 2023). Markov models capture transitions between states, useful for multi-stage intrusions.

Threat intelligence feeds offer lists of suspicious domains, IP addresses, or file signatures from global observations. Integrating these feeds with local data can reveal correlations. AI systems can rank threats by potential impact, focusing attention on high-risk events. This ranking process often involves weighting factors like known vulnerability exposures, threat actor history, or exploit complexity (Rahman et al., 2024). Predictive modeling thus aligns with the broader shift toward proactive security strategies.

3.4. Data Labeling and Preparation

High-quality data remains crucial for both anomaly detection and predictive modeling. In supervised and semi-supervised approaches, labeled examples guide algorithms. Labeled malicious samples can be scarce, especially for advanced persistent threats. Observers rely on sandbox analysis, honeypots, or security incident logs to gather malicious data (Berman et al., 2019). Manual annotation by domain experts is time-consuming but ensures accurate labels. Automated labeling systems might use signature-based engines or correlation across multiple telemetry sources, though these can inherit biases from existing definitions.

Data cleansing involves removing duplicates, random noise, or incomplete records. Feature selection or dimensionality reduction can improve training speed and reduce overfitting. Domain knowledge helps identify relevant features, such as packet size distributions for distributed denial-of-service detection. An iterative approach refines features based on feedback from model performance. Many research efforts propose feature engineering pipelines tailored to specific attack types (Stanzione et al., 2020).

An important consideration is dataset representativeness. Public datasets like KDD Cup 1999 or NSL-KDD remain widely used but may not reflect contemporary threats. UNSW-NB15 and CICIDS2017 aim to address some limitations. Real-world data can be more diverse, containing evolving attack vectors and non-stationary distributions. As a result, models trained on older datasets might underperform in operational contexts. Continuous data collection and retraining mitigate this risk (Bensaoud et al., 2024). Table 2 lists datasets commonly used in anomaly detection research. It notes each dataset's scope and relevance for evaluating detection methods.

Table 2. Sample anomaly detection datasets

Dataset	Description
KDD Cup 1999	Classic dataset, but outdated threats
NSL-KDD	Improved version of KDD, still lacks modern complexities
UNSW-NB15	Introduces diverse attacks with updated profiles
CICIDS2017	Realistic traffic scenarios, widely used in recent work

3.5. Assessment of Anomaly Detection Systems

Assessing anomaly detection systems requires analyzing metrics like detection rate, false-positive rate, and detection latency. Researchers also track precision, recall, and F1 scores to evaluate classification performance (Ferrag et al., 2020). In operational environments, false alarms can overwhelm analysts, leading to alert fatigue. Optimizing the trade-off between true positives and false positives is essential. Tools like ROC curves and precision-recall curves offer insights into classifier behavior under various thresholds.

Cross-validation techniques and offline testing on historical logs measure a model's detection capability. However, adversaries might adapt once they learn about deployed defenses. Real-time monitoring in production yields the most accurate performance data. Retrospective analysis of security incidents can verify whether the system flagged suspicious events. Continuous monitoring also uncovers concept drift, prompting model updates (Momand et al., 2023).

4. INTELLIGENT THREAT RESPONSE WITH AUTONOMOUS DEFENSE

4.1. Overview of Autonomous Defense

Autonomous defense represents a shift from detection-centric strategies to active intervention. Traditional solutions raise alerts for human review, but the surge in attacks creates alert overload. Automated systems decide on countermeasures such as blocking malicious hosts, quarantining devices, or adjusting firewall rules. Reinforcement learning has received considerable attention for these tasks, allowing agents to learn optimal actions through iterative feedback (Adawadkar & Kulkarni, 2022).

Autonomous defense solutions rely on a feedback loop. A detection module flags unusual activity, an analysis layer categorizes severity, and a response engine executes changes. Machine-driven decisions occur faster than manual processes. In distributed or large-scale environments, speed is crucial, especially when intrusions spread quickly. Yet, a system must avoid harming legitimate users or blocking essential services. Therefore, many implementations pair autonomous actions with policy constraints. The system can only enact certain responses within a defined range (Malik et al., 2023).

4.2. Reinforcement Learning in Network Security

Reinforcement learning (RL) treats cybersecurity as a sequential decision process. The environment includes network assets, logs, and potential adversaries. The agent observes states, representing the network's condition, and chooses actions like isolating a host or deploying a honeypot (Nguyen & Reddi, 2021). Rewards typically reflect how successfully the agent prevents attacks or reduces damage. Negative rewards penalize false positives or other disruptions. Over many episodes, RL algorithms optimize policies.

Different RL algorithms suit various contexts. Value-based methods like Q-learning store expected returns for state-action pairs. Policy-based approaches like REINFORCE learn a direct mapping from states to actions. Actor-critic methods combine both, balancing stability and convergence speed. The challenge is constructing a representative environment. Real networks are large and complex, so simulations approximate certain processes. Transferring a learned policy to production might require additional fine-tuning. Additionally, adversaries can adapt, so the environment is not fully stationary (Sewak et al., 2022).

Figure 2 depicts the cycle of state observation, action selection, and reward calculation in a network security context. It highlights how an agent refines its strategy through repeated interaction.

Figure 2. Reinforcement learning feedback loop

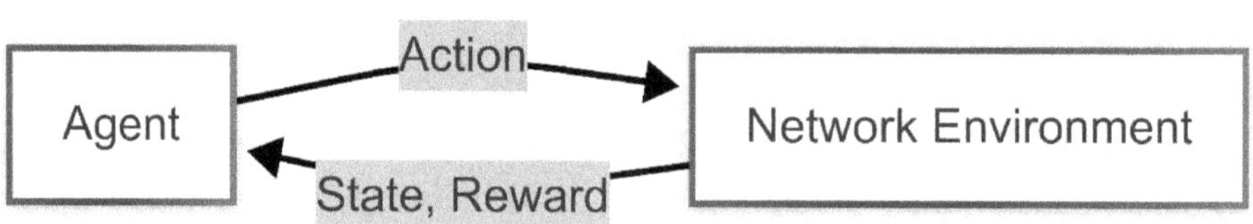

4.2.1. Policy Constraints and Safety Checks

An RL agent might propose extreme solutions to maximize reward if not constrained. A naive policy could block wide ranges of IPs or disable critical services, leading to self-inflicted denial-of-service. Security policies guide the agent by restricting allowable moves. One approach is to penalize actions that disrupt key network components. Another is to force the agent to pass decisions to a human if certain thresholds are exceeded (Ofusori et al., 2024).

4.2.2. Reward Engineering

Reward engineering shapes agent behavior. If immediate detection is valued, the agent emphasizes swift responses. If overall network stability matters, the agent balances speed and caution. Reward signals may incorporate attack severity, collateral damage, or resource consumption. Poorly designed rewards can produce unintended strategies. For instance, the agent might ignore minor threats or frequently block borderline connections (Oesch et al., 2025). Testing and adjusting reward structures in controlled environments helps align RL behavior with organizational goals. Table 3 summarizes the state, action, reward, policy, environment, and exploration components in reinforcement learning. It clarifies each element's role in cyber defense.

Table 3. Reinforcement learning elements for cyber defense

Element	Description
State	Current network conditions, alert data
Action	Possible defense measures (block, isolate)
Reward	Reflects threat mitigation vs. disruptions
Policy	Agent's strategy for action selection
Environment	Network, attackers, legitimate traffic
Exploration	Trying new actions to improve knowledge

4.3. Orchestrating Automated Responses

Automated responses extend beyond RL. Rule-based orchestrators can apply policies upon receiving specific alerts. For instance, repeated login failures might trigger account lockdown. A spike in traffic from a suspicious domain might lead to a temporary block. Machine learning classifiers supply risk scores, while the orchestrator decides on steps. These workflows can be expressed through a policy engine that references organizational guidelines (Momand et al., 2023).

Network function virtualization (NFV) and software-defined networking (SDN) architectures facilitate quick updates. Instead of configuring hardware firewalls manually, administrators control network behavior through software. Automated defense systems interface with SDN controllers to reroute or throttle traffic dynamically. This agility helps contain threats by segmenting infected hosts or redirecting traffic to analysis sandboxes (Malik et al., 2023). Figure 3 shows how an automated system processes alerts, categorizes events, and enforces defense actions. It focuses on the progression from detection to response execution.

Figure 3. Autonomous response workflow

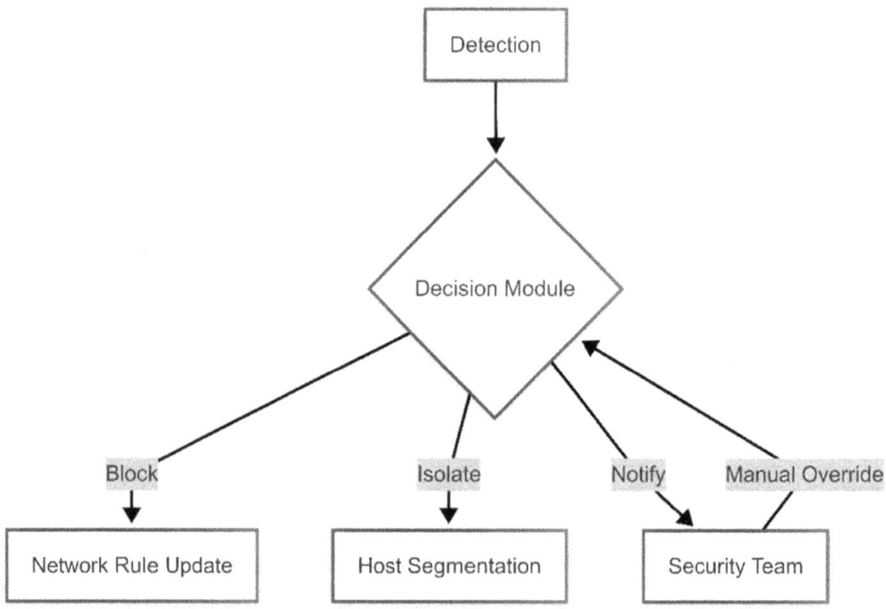

4.4. Challenges in Autonomous Defense

Autonomous solutions introduce complexities. They rely on accurate detection modules. If the detection module has a high false-positive rate, misguided responses become frequent. Overly aggressive blocking can harm business processes or user trust. Attackers can manipulate the system by sending decoy events, prompting the defense to block legitimate channels (Rahman et al., 2024). These tactics underscore the importance of robust anomaly detection and policy constraints.

Explaining automated decisions is another concern. Security teams want logs or rationales for each action. They may undo decisions deemed incorrect or instruct the system not to repeat them. This feedback loop mimics active learning, refining the system incrementally. However, building interpretable RL or orchestrator modules is nontrivial. Some solutions record state snapshots and action probabilities for post-incident reviews. Others provide confidence scores and references to relevant threat intelligence entries (Macas et al., 2024).

5. EVALUATING AI-DRIVEN DEFENSE SYSTEMS

5.1. Performance Metrics

AI-based intrusion detection is often measured through accuracy, recall, precision, F1 score, and area under the ROC curve. However, these do not fully capture the operational value in an autonomous setting. Response time, resource overhead, and resilience to evasion strategies become significant. A system that achieves 99% detection accuracy but adds severe latency can be unusable in a high-speed environment. Adversarial robustness tests are also relevant. Researchers craft adversarial samples to see if the model remains effective (Macas et al., 2024).

False positives and false negatives have different impacts on cost. A false negative could lead to a successful breach, whereas a false positive might cause an unnecessary response. The cost ratio may vary by industry and context. Some sectors tolerate more false positives if it ensures fewer breaches. Others prioritize uninterrupted operations. Balancing these factors is a key consideration when designing and tuning an AI-based defense (Bensaoud et al., 2024). Table 4 identifies important metrics that measure how well detection and response solutions perform in a live environment.

Table 4. Key metrics for evaluating detection and response

Metric	Description
Accuracy	Proportion of correct classifications
Recall (TPR)	Fraction of actual malicious events detected
Precision	Fraction of flagged events that are truly malicious
False Positive Rate (FPR)	Benign events flagged as malicious

continued on following page

Table 4. Continued

Metric	Description
Detection Latency	Time between attack onset and detection
Response Overhead	Resources used to respond

5.2. Testing Methodologies

Testing frameworks often involve offline analysis of historical logs. Researchers run detection algorithms on captured data to measure how many attacks they identify. This method allows repeatable evaluations but may not reflect real-time performance. Online testing monitors live traffic with the AI system in parallel. Any triggers or automated actions are documented. Over time, analysts compare system decisions with actual outcomes. Online methods better capture latency, resource usage, and user impact (Ferrag et al., 2020).

Cross-validation, bootstrapping, or hold-out sets can mitigate overfitting. A system trained on a specific dataset might memorize unique patterns that do not generalize. Splitting data by time is crucial in security contexts to simulate real deployment. If a threat emerges in a dataset portion used for training, the system might overestimate performance. A robust approach trains on earlier data and tests on subsequent periods.

5.3. Adversarial Evaluations

Adversaries can craft specialized inputs to subvert AI models. In evasion attacks, traffic or logs are modified to appear benign. Poisoning attacks manipulate training data, introducing backdoors or biases that degrade detection. Model inversion attempts to glean sensitive details from the trained model (Mohamed, 2023). Testing each vector requires carefully designed experiments. Defenders might train separate adversarial models to produce tricky inputs. Observing how detection performance shifts under adversarial conditions highlights a system's resilience.

Solutions to adversarial threats include adversarial training, which augments the dataset with maliciously crafted samples. Another approach is to monitor for suspicious patterns in model inputs, such as repetitive byte sequences or improbable network flows. Integrating anomaly detection at multiple layers can also strengthen resilience. Ongoing research in explainable AI focuses on identifying abrupt changes in network attributes that might signal an evasion attempt (Stanzione et al., 2020).

5.4. Operational Factors

Deployment in a production setting demands stable performance over extended periods. High availability is crucial for mission-critical systems. Engineers might run multiple model instances in parallel, each focusing on different event types. Load balancing and failover strategies provide redundancy. Logging and auditing frameworks document AI decisions for accountability. These logs assist in compliance, post-incident forensics, and continuous improvement (Momand et al., 2023).

Resource constraints also matter. Complex deep learning models might need GPU acceleration, raising hardware costs. Systems with limited budgets or specialized domains, like IoT networks, require lightweight architectures. Tools like quantization or pruning can reduce model size. In some scenarios, detection at the edge (e.g., on IoT gateways) might be preferable to sending data to a centralized server. This distribution lowers latency but complicates model updates (Hussain et al., 2020).

6. IMPLEMENTATION CHALLENGES

6.1. Data Availability and Diversity

Robust AI-based intrusion detection requires extensive, high-quality data. However, organizations may be reluctant to share logs due to privacy or competitive reasons (Momand et al., 2023). Without collaborative data exchange, models might miss relevant attack patterns. Some entities release anonymized data, but anonymization can remove critical features. Synthetic data generation complements real-world samples but can introduce bias if the synthetic process does not accurately reflect real attacks (Malik et al., 2023).

Diverse datasets are essential for capturing varied threat methods. Attackers employ different tactics depending on region, sector, or target type. A dataset reflecting primarily web-based attacks may fail to represent sophisticated ICS intrusions. By aggregating data from multiple sources, organizations gain broader coverage and mitigate blind spots. Challenges include normalizing logs from heterogeneous systems. The data must follow consistent schemas and time formats to be suitable for training (Bensaoud et al., 2024).

6.2. Technical Integration with Existing Infrastructures

AI solutions must be integrated with security information and event management (SIEM) platforms, firewalls, and other security devices. This process involves customizing data ingestion pipelines, correlation engines, and alerting modules.

Legacy systems might use proprietary protocols, complicating direct integration. Organizations often have distinct operational technologies that cannot be disrupted for extended maintenance (Elhami Fard et al., 2023).

Furthermore, AI-based decisions may need to comply with established incident response procedures. A fully autonomous system might conflict with standard operating procedures that require managerial approval for certain actions. Policy-based orchestration layers can unify AI outputs with human oversight. Access controls and role-based management must be configured so that automated changes are properly authorized. This setup ensures accountability and aligns with regulatory frameworks (Ofusori et al., 2024).

6.3. Organizational Culture and Skills

Adopting AI-driven defense is more than a technical decision. Security staff must learn how these models' function, how to interpret their alerts, and how to manage false positives. Training in data science fundamentals and machine learning concepts fosters alignment. Staff who understand AI logic can refine features, identify data gaps, or troubleshoot anomalies (Rahman et al., 2024).

Organizational culture also influences acceptance. Some teams may distrust automated systems, fearing job displacement or liability for system errors. Clear policies about oversight, auditing, and manual override can help. In certain highly regulated environments, regulations may require a human in the loop for critical security actions. AI-driven solutions work best when integrated with structured processes, well-defined roles, and accountability mechanisms (Oesch et al., 2025).

6.4. Ethical and Privacy Considerations

Gathering and analyzing network data raises privacy concerns. Packet inspection might reveal personal information. Even if data is anonymized, advanced methods can re-identify individuals. AI-based analytics amplify these risks because they can detect patterns with more detail than traditional tools. Organizations must implement data protection measures, such as encryption, restricted access, or differential privacy, which injects controlled noise into data (Stanzione et al., 2020).

Ethical questions arise when systems respond automatically. Misclassification can block essential public services or impair critical infrastructure. Stakeholders demand accountability for decisions made by AI. In complex global contexts, multi-jurisdictional laws complicate data handling. Compliance requirements might dictate how logs are stored, how long data is retained, and what can be shared. AI systems must incorporate policy constraints and auditable records (Mohamed, 2023). Table

5 highlights common challenges in automated security deployments. It proposes ways to address issues that arise during implementation.

Table 5. Challenges and mitigations in autonomous defense

Challenge	Description	Mitigation
False Positives	Legitimate traffic flagged as threats	Improved detection, policy constraints
Resource Limitations	Large-scale data processing demands	Distributed architectures, model pruning
Adversarial Attacks	Attackers exploit model blind spots	Adversarial training, anomaly layering
Interpretability	Unclear rationale for automated decisions	Explainable AI methods, logs, review

7. CASE STUDIES

Real-world applications illustrate how AI-driven strategies function. Each scenario highlights distinct benefits, obstacles, and outcomes. These cases provide practical insights for organizations considering AI-based security.

7.1. Large Financial Enterprise

A multinational financial institution managed a network with thousands of endpoints and numerous transaction systems. Traditional intrusion detection generated frequent alerts, overwhelming analysts. After consulting researchers, the firm deployed a deep learning-based anomaly detection system. Developers selected an autoencoder to capture normal transaction patterns, training it on historical logs. The system flagged unusual spikes in transaction frequency or geolocation anomalies not seen in training data (Malik et al., 2023).

To handle response, the enterprise introduced a rule-based orchestrator that automatically escalated anomalies above a confidence threshold. Security staff were notified to review critical events. This semi-autonomous approach balanced speed and caution. Over six months, the institution noted a drop in time-to-detect suspicious activity. False positives decreased after iterative refinements, aided by domain experts who adjusted features and thresholds. Challenges arose with encrypted data, forcing partial decryption for analysis (Momand et al., 2023).

7.2. Cloud Service Provider

A major cloud provider sought to safeguard virtual machines and containerized workloads from distributed denial-of-service (DDoS) attacks. The provider implemented predictive modeling that correlated incoming traffic patterns with known DDoS signatures. Data from edge nodes worldwide fed a central analytics pipeline. Models forecast potential surges, enabling proactive scaling of mitigation resources (Rahman et al., 2024).

The system integrated reinforcement learning to fine-tune resource allocation. It tested different configurations of load balancers and filters, receiving rewards based on stability and cost. Operators discovered that the RL approach reduced manual tuning but occasionally over-allocated resources, incurring higher operational costs. Fine-tuning reward functions helped align decisions with business priorities. This arrangement significantly cut service downtime, although sophisticated attackers sometimes masked malicious flows by mimicking normal traffic patterns (Nguyen & Reddi, 2021).

7.3. Critical Infrastructure in Energy Sector

An energy provider managed industrial control systems (ICS) running power distribution. Fearing sabotage, the provider deployed AI-based anomaly detection on sensor data. The system learned normal voltage and frequency ranges for equipment. Abnormal reading triggered alerts, allowing rapid intervention. Engineers integrated a reinforcement learning module that tested safe reconfiguration actions in a simulated ICS environment (Elhami Fard et al., 2023).

When anomalies appeared, the system recommended partial shutdown of specific distribution lines. Operators assessed these proposals and either approved or overruled them. Over time, the RL agent improved reliability, though engineers required detailed explanations before adopting any automated shutdown. They found that labeling ICS anomalies was challenging due to domain-specific complexities. The project illustrated how AI must be combined with domain expertise to achieve dependable operations.

7.4. Government Agency

A government agency confronted advanced persistent threats targeting classified networks. Attackers frequently used stealthy tactics to bypass signature-based intrusion detection. The agency adopted a multi-layer approach. One layer involved a deep neural classifier fine-tuned with labeled threat intelligence data. Another layer used unsupervised clustering to capture unknown anomalies (Momand et al., 2023).

Alerts from both layers were fed into a knowledge graph that connected entities (hosts, user accounts, processes) to indicators of compromise. A correlation engine then contextualized alerts, improving accuracy. Autonomous response was partial, limited to isolating hosts with high-confidence alerts. The system significantly shortened the window between infiltration and detection. Staff praised the correlation engine's ability to link disparate traces of an attack, though the overall system required continuous data feed from multiple security appliances.

7.5. E-Commerce Platform

An e-commerce company faced account takeover and fraud attempts. They deployed an anomaly detection system analyzing user login frequency, geolocation, device fingerprints, and transaction patterns. Predictive analytics identified suspicious transactions based on prior fraudulent behavior, time of day, and item categories (Malik et al., 2023). The company used a reinforcement learning approach to optimize promotional strategies for loyal customers while flagging possible fraudulent users.

The system triggered multi-factor authentication when it detected high-risk activity. Although this occasionally inconvenienced legitimate customers, the fraud rate declined significantly. The platform eventually introduced dynamic friction: suspicious users encountered additional verification steps, while trusted users experienced minimal barriers. Through iterative refinements, the company balanced user satisfaction and security, noting a boost in customer trust due to reduced fraudulent activity (Oesch et al., 2025).

8. FUTURE DIRECTIONS

Researchers continue refining AI-driven security through several avenues. Federated learning is gaining traction for cross-organization collaboration without centralizing data (Sengupta et al., 2020). Each participant trains a local model and shares updates, enhancing overall detection knowledge. This strategy respects privacy but requires robust aggregation to avoid poisoning attacks. In future environments, federated approaches might unify threat intelligence across multiple sectors, improving coverage against global campaigns.

Game theory offers another perspective. In an adversarial setting, attackers and defenders engage in strategic moves. Multi-stage attacks make the conflict dynamic, and defenders benefit from modeling attacker incentives. Game-theoretic solutions can help estimate the cost of actions and compute equilibrium strategies.

This approach aligns with reinforcement learning, which also deals with sequential decisions (Mitchell & Chen, 2014).

Another evolving topic is interpretability. Black-box models hinder trust and complicate compliance. Regulators may require transparent decisions for accountability. Tools like attention maps, rule extraction, and post-hoc explanations aim to shed light on model reasoning. The concept of "glass-box" learning aspires to embed interpretability directly into model architectures. Achieving transparency without sacrificing accuracy remains an open question in the security domain (Stanzione et al., 2020).

Scalability remains a pressing concern. Many organizations process gigabits or terabits of data per second, and real-time intrusion detection can strain computational resources. Parallel processing, GPU acceleration, or custom hardware can address these demands. Researchers also explore efficient algorithms and data structures that reduce complexity. As networks expand with edge computing, localized detection can alleviate central bottlenecks. However, distributing the detection logic requires mechanisms for synchronization and model updates (Hussain et al., 2020).

Privacy-preserving analytics represent another frontier. Methods like homomorphic encryption allow computations on encrypted data but remain computationally expensive. Secure enclaves or trusted execution environments might permit protected model inference. Differential privacy helps anonymize user data but can reduce model accuracy if noise levels are high (Mohamed, 2023). Balancing privacy, compliance, and detection efficacy is a continuing struggle.

The future also includes synergy between AI-based defense and broader security efforts. Security teams rely on vulnerability management, patching, and threat hunting. AI-based systems can prioritize vulnerabilities with exploit predictions, prompting timely remediation. Automated penetration testing might find weaknesses, feeding insights into the detection pipeline. Over time, the boundary between AI-driven detection and standard risk management may blur, offering a more integrated security ecosystem (Malik et al., 2023).

Finally, robust adversarial resilience is a core research direction. Defenders must assume adversaries will study and attempt to manipulate AI models. This arms race spurs innovation in adversarial detection, robust model architectures, and collaborative defense strategies. Hybrid models might incorporate rule-based checks for well-known manipulations and machine learning for unknown patterns. Effective solutions should adapt quickly as attackers modify tactics. The drive toward advanced AI algorithms in network defense will likely remain an active area of research and development.

9. CONCLUSION

AI-driven strategies are changing network defense. Techniques like anomaly detection, predictive analytics, and automated response enhance visibility and speed. Learning-based models capture hidden patterns in complex traffic, identifying threats that might escape traditional signature-based methods. Reinforcement learning contributes adaptive policies, refining how defenders respond. Predictive analytics anticipate emerging campaigns, supporting proactive measures. Yet, operationalizing these approaches entails careful data strategies, interpretability, adversarial testing, and integration with established processes (Adawadkar & Kulkarni, 2022; Mohamed, 2023).

Organizations seeking AI-based defense must evaluate whether they have the necessary resources, data, and expertise. They often begin with pilot deployments, analyzing logs offline before enabling partial automation. Teams refine detection thresholds, measure false positives, and gather insights. Over time, greater confidence emerges in the models' reliability, paving the way for more autonomous features (Rahman et al., 2024). A major advantage lies in reducing analyst workload and accelerating response, especially for large-scale networks or distributed systems. Threats that once went unnoticed for weeks can now be caught earlier, limiting damage.

However, AI is not a complete solution. Attackers evolve, generating new forms of adversarial input. Zero-day exploits, stealthy infiltration, or large-scale scanning continue to challenge detection. Therefore, security demands a layered approach, mixing AI-based methods with human oversight and conventional controls. Tools like SIEM systems, threat intelligence platforms, and endpoint protection remain vital. Continuous retraining ensures that models remain current. Interpretable solutions strengthen trust in automated decisions (Ofusori et al., 2024).

Despite these realities, the literature suggests consistent gains from AI adoption in cybersecurity. Automated detection can produce fewer false negatives, highlight emergent trends, and offer rapid triage. The synergy between predictive analytics and real-time responses holds promise for a more proactive stance. As networks become more complex, and attackers more cunning, the ability to adapt swiftly becomes essential. AI offers potential if organizations address the technical, procedural, and cultural aspects of adoption (Elhami Fard et al., 2023).

Future endeavors point toward federated learning, explainable architectures, privacy-preserving computation, and integrated threat intelligence. Cooperative models will share knowledge across multiple stakeholders, raising collective defense. Explainable AI can clarify uncertain or ambiguous alerts. Privacy safeguards must evolve to handle sensitive data responsibly. Additionally, advanced analytics will fuse with endpoint telemetry, threat hunting, and vulnerability management for a holistic security posture (Sengupta et al., 2020).

By combining robust data pipelines, methodical validation, and incremental deployment strategies, organizations can harness AI effectively. Careful risk assessments guide how much autonomy is acceptable for a given environment. For mission-critical systems, partial automation with a human in the loop may remain the norm. For less sensitive applications, fully autonomous responses may be justified. The field remains fluid, with ongoing research refining best practices in AI-driven network defense. Through collaboration among academia, industry, and government, solutions will likely continue evolving in sophistication, forging new standards for protecting digital ecosystems.

REFERENCES

Adawadkar, A. M. K., & Kulkarni, N. (2022). Cyber-security and reinforcement learning — A brief survey. *Engineering Applications of Artificial Intelligence, 114*, 105116. DOI: 10.1016/j.engappai.2022.105116

Bensaoud, A., Kalita, J., & Bensaoud, M. (2024). A survey of malware detection using deep learning. *Machine Learning with Applications, 16*, 100546. DOI: 10.1016/j.mlwa.2024.100546

Berman, D. S., Buczak, A. L., Chavis, J. S., & Corbett, C. L. (2019). A survey of deep learning methods for cyber security. *IEEE Communications Surveys and Tutorials, 21*(3), 2214–2241. DOI: 10.1109/COMST.2019.2916180

Buczak, A. L., & Guven, E. (2016). A survey of data mining and machine learning methods for cyber security intrusion detection. *IEEE Communications Surveys and Tutorials, 18*(2), 1153–1176. DOI: 10.1109/COMST.2015.2494502

Elhami Fard, N., Selmic, R. R., & Khorasani, K. (2023). A review of techniques and policies on cybersecurity using artificial intelligence and reinforcement learning algorithms. *IEEE Technology and Society Magazine, 42*(4), 57–68. DOI: 10.1109/MTS.2023.3306540

Ferrag, M. A., Maglaras, L., Moschoyiannis, S., & Janicke, H. (2020). Deep learning for cyber security intrusion detection: Approaches, datasets, and comparative study. *Journal of Information Security and Applications, 50*, 102419. DOI: 10.1016/j.jisa.2019.102419

Garcia-Teodoro, P., Diaz-Verdejo, J., Macia-Fernandez, G., & Vazquez, E. (2009). Anomaly-based network intrusion detection: Techniques, systems and challenges. *Computers & Security, 28*(1–2), 18–28. DOI: 10.1016/j.cose.2008.08.003

Hussain, F., Hussain, R., Hassan, S. A., & Hossain, E. (2020). Machine learning in IoT security: Current solutions and future challenges. *IEEE Communications Surveys and Tutorials, 22*(3), 1686–1721. DOI: 10.1109/COMST.2020.2986444

Macas, M., Wu, C., & Fuertes, W. (2024). Adversarial examples: A survey of attacks and defenses in deep learning-enabled cybersecurity systems. *Expert Systems with Applications, 238*, 122223. DOI: 10.1016/j.eswa.2023.122223

Malik, H. M., Zhao, Z., & Yang, L. (2023). Artificial intelligence for cybersecurity: Literature review and future research directions. *Future Generation Computer Systems, 146*, 781–795. DOI: 10.1016/j.future.2023.04.019

Mitchell, R., & Chen, I. R. (2014). A survey of intrusion detection techniques for cyber-physical systems. *ACM Computing Surveys*, *46*(4), 55. Advance online publication. DOI: 10.1145/2542049

Mohamed, N. (2023). Current trends in AI and ML for cybersecurity: A state-of-the-art survey. *Cogent Engineering*, *10*(2), 2272358. DOI: 10.1080/23311916.2023.2272358

Momand, A., Jan, S. U., & Ramzan, N. (2023). A systematic and comprehensive survey of recent advances in intrusion detection systems using machine learning: Deep learning, datasets, and attack taxonomy. *Journal of Sensors*, *2023*(1), 6048087. Advance online publication. DOI: 10.1155/2023/6048087

Nguyen, T. T., & Reddi, V. J. (2021). Deep reinforcement learning for cyber security. *IEEE Transactions on Neural Networks and Learning Systems*, (Early Access), 1–17. DOI: 10.1109/TNNLS.2021.3121870

Oesch, S., Austria, P., Chaulagain, A., Weber, B., Watson, C., Dixson, M., & Sadovnik, A. (2025). The path to autonomous cyber defense. *IEEE Security and Privacy*, *23*(1), 38–46. DOI: 10.1109/MSEC.2024.3427640

Ofusori, L., Bokaba, T., & Mhlongo, S. (2024). Artificial intelligence in cybersecurity: A comprehensive review and future direction. [In press]. *Applied Artificial Intelligence*, *38*(1), 2184087. DOI: 10.1080/08839514.2024.2439609

Rahman, M. M., Al Shakil, S., & Mustakim, M. R. (2024). A survey on intrusion detection system in IoT networks. *Cyber Security and Applications*, *3*, 100082. DOI: 10.1016/j.csa.2024.100082

Sengupta, S., Chowdhary, A., Sabur, A., Alshamrani, A., Huang, D., & Kambhampati, S. (2020). A survey of moving target defenses for network security. *IEEE Communications Surveys and Tutorials*, *22*(3), 1909–1941. DOI: 10.1109/COMST.2020.2982955

Sewak, M., Sahay, S. K., & Rathore, H. (2022). Deep reinforcement learning in the advanced cybersecurity threat detection and protection. *Information Systems Frontiers*, (Online First). DOI: 10.1007/s10796-022-10333-x

Stanzione, M., Dividino, R., & Schaefer, G. (2020). Explainable artificial intelligence in cybersecurity: A survey. *IEEE Access : Practical Innovations, Open Solutions*, *8*, 222310–222354. DOI: 10.1109/ACCESS.2020.3041975

Chapter 4
Digital Defense Powered by Autonomous Resilience

Jamal Zraqou
https://orcid.org/0000-0001-9060-7188
University of Petra, Jordan

Wesam Alkhadour
https://orcid.org/0009-0004-1937-0308
University of Petra, Jordan

Khalil Omar
https://orcid.org/0000-0002-5328-5762
University of Petra, Jordan

Jawad Alkhatib
https://orcid.org/0009-0005-1529-7761
Prince Mohammad Bin Fahd University, Saudi Arabia

ABSTRACT

Digital security functions as a crucial protection measure to safeguard both data and system operational integrity in present times. This chapter investigates Autonomous Resilience by analyzing both Cybercrime-as-a-Service and APT attacks that receive state support. The article discusses encryption techniques alongside network defense protocols, threat intelligence operations, and incident response methods before explaining AI-powered self-operating security systems. Self-learning systems operate in real-time to detect and analyze threats while using AI algorithms to protect systems through human-AI collaboration. The chapter provides relevant case studies with new technologies that help readers transform traditional reactive security designs

DOI: 10.4018/979-8-3373-0954-5.ch004

into resilient, ahead-of-time defensive structures.

1. INTRODUCTION

Modern information technology within the 21st century makes organizations and individuals navigate sophisticated cybersecurity threats that become increasingly complex and powerful. The expansion of digital technology, together with the increasing number of connected devices and expanding cloud computing usage, has reshaped the ways organizations manage their data creation and storage, as well as data processing and transaction (Schneier, 2018). By enabling both operational successes and radical innovations, the digital revolution extended the potential window of attack for cyber attackers who aim at connected systems (Furnell & Dowland, 2020). Data fraud and internet security breaches continue to rank as essential worldwide risks according to the World Economic Forum Global Risks Report (2023) because they represent both probable events and highly destructive results (World Economic Forum, 2023). Comprehensive security breaches that occur in organizations post-digitization of operations and sensitive data result in monetary loss and damage to reputation, along with governance penalties, alongside theft of intellectual property and threats to infrastructure defense and public well-being (Symantec, 2023).

The current cybersecurity model requires organizations to adopt a proactive security approach instead of their traditional reactive mode because they should prepare for new threats before incidents occur (Fruhlinger, 2020). Digital environments with changing vulnerabilities and fluidity demand this shift because absolute security remains unreachable (Anderson, 2020). The present-day cybersecurity frameworks focus on resilience because this represents a more achievable and strategic goal than complete protection according to NIST (2023). Security experts recognize that well-implemented defensive measures cannot stop advanced attackers from succeeding so detection abilities together with response plans and system recovery protocols have become equally important to security prevention (Cobb, 2022). The instead perspective has accelerated the creation of defense-in-depth methods which establish numerous security systems across networks and systems therefore minimizing the impact of single control breaches (Chapple & Seidl, 2021). The contemporary cybersecurity frameworks demonstrate their reliance on Figure 1 as shown in the illustration. Every component within this framework originates from the resilient core center while Essential Functions, Risk Management, Business Continuity, Cyber Defense and Recovery form the system's linked components. Critical operations remain operational during disruptions while systems can resume quickly after an attack due to collaborative system components. Recovery speed remains essential because of the dashed recovery line indicating the necessity of swift operational restoration.

Figure 1. The emphasis on resilience in contemporary cybersecurity frameworks

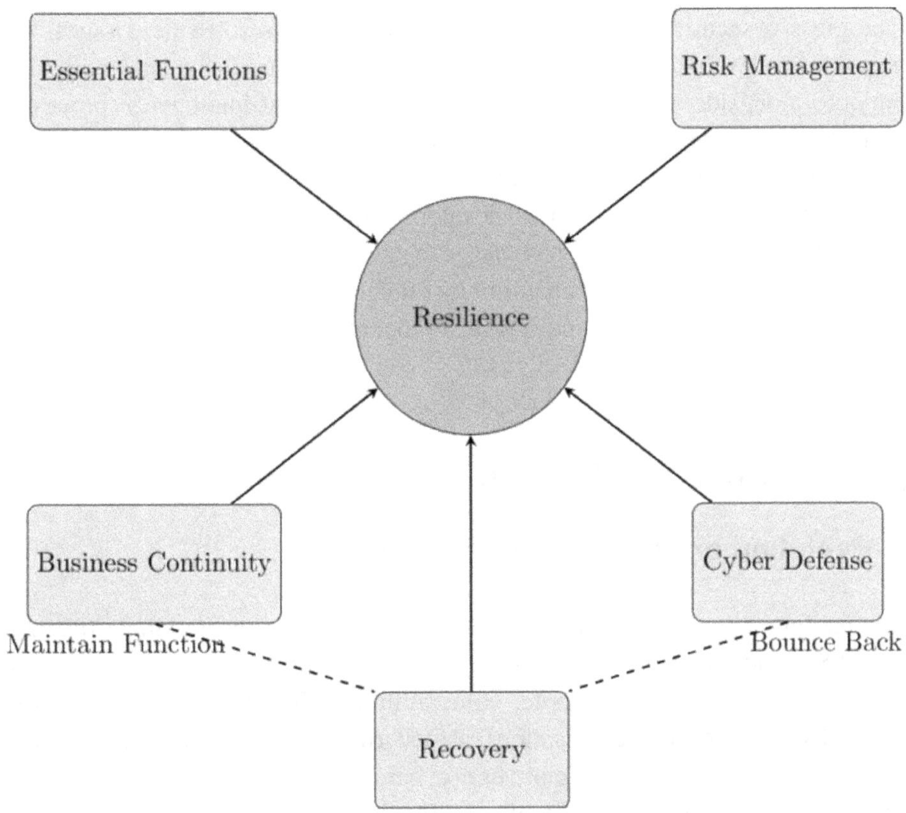

The cybersecurity landscape continues to be shaped by several converging factors that collectively increase both the frequency and complexity of threats. The democratization of hacking tools has lowered the technical barriers to entry for potential attackers. At the same time, the emergence of Cybercrime-as-a-Service (CaaS) models has created underground economies where specialized criminal services can be purchased and combined to execute sophisticated attacks (Europol, 2023). Monetary institutions around the world now use cyber operations as strategic national tools to strike critical infrastructure and intellectual properties by launching APTs which require patience and well-funded sophisticated capabilities (FireEye, 2023). The COVID-19 pandemic motivated all sectors to speed up digital transformation projects where operational stability received priority status before security needed attention leading to new security risks stemming from rushed remote work systems (IBM Security, 2022). Organizations face growing risks due to the billions of unsecured Internet of Things (IoT) devices entering their networks since many of these devices have fundamental security flaws and restricted update features (Antonakakis et al., 2021).

This chapter presents an extensive review of current cybersecurity difficulties and progressive security solutions that organizations use to resolve these issues. The analysis combines theoretical models and practical strategies to explain encryption techniques alongside network defense methods and threat intelligence processes and incident response practices with the goal of providing readers effective security methods suitable for advanced digital systems. The chapter presents understandings of historical case studies and future threat developments and tested security architecture principles to show organizations how they can move security from secondary status to foundational organizational capability by implementing defensive solutions into entire systems and procedures and organizational mindsets to build digital security fortresses under constant threats.

2. THE ANATOMY OF MODERN CYBER THREATS

2.1. Evolution of Attack Methodologies

Technology-based attacks have evolved from disruptive operational dilemmas in the 1980s and 1990s to highly complex strategic operations in the present day. During the initial stages of computer vulnerabilities, Morris Worm targeted weak spots yet demonstrated no sophistication that modern attacks employ (Spafford, 2019). During the early 2000s, financial motives in cybercrime triggered the development of complex malware, including ransomware and banking trojans (Kshetri, 2019). Social engineering adapted into specific spear-phishing attacks as cybercriminal organizations operating in hidden markets traded their cyber tools and stolen information (Europol, 2022). During this time, businesses transitioned away from disorganized opportunistic incidents and adopted established operations with monetary targets.

Modern threats are controlled by nation-state actors and APTs that use stealth and persistence and strategic targeting to meet their political economic and military objectives according to Rid & Buchanan (2018). The capabilities of state-sponsored operations are demonstrated through examples such as Stuxnet and APT29 because these campaigns mainly focus on attacking vital infrastructure or performing espionage activities (Zetter, 2018). Compilers exploit three different techniques targeting fileless malware along with living-off-the-land strategies and supply chain compromise to negate traditional systems (Ghafir et al., 2018). Trusted software updates became the vector through which hackers performed a SolarWinds attack against multiple organizations during 2020 (Cybereason, 2022). Modern adversaries have evolved at such speed that this requires organizations to develop sophisticated cybersecurity solutions which can adapt against their complex threats.

2.2. Contemporary Threat Categories

Diverse attack methodologies and actor types mark the contemporary threat landscape, each posing unique challenges. Ransomware has evolved into a highly disruptive threat, with groups employing multi-faceted extortion techniques, including data encryption and exfiltration, to pressure victims into paying substantial ransom (Symantec, 2023; Kitten, 2023). The Colonial Pipeline attack of 2021 underscored the national security implications of such operations (CISA, 2022). Zero-day vulnerabilities, which exploit unknown software flaws, present another significant challenge, with a lucrative market for these exploits complicating defensive efforts (Bilge & Dumitras, 2022; Ablon & Bogart, 2017). Insider threats, accounting for about 25% of breaches, are particularly difficult to detect due to their legitimate access credentials and varied motivations (CERT Insider Threat Center, 2023; Verizon, 2023).

Advanced persistent threats (APTs), often linked to nation-state actors, represent the pinnacle of cyber sophistication, with groups like APT29 and APT41 maintaining long-term access to well-defended networks (FireEye, 2023; Mandiant, 2023). Social engineering attacks, including Business Email Compromise (BEC) schemes, have caused over $43 billion in losses, with deep-fake technology enhancing their effectiveness (FBI IC3, 2023; Westerlund, 2019). These evolving threats highlight the need for adaptive and comprehensive cybersecurity strategies to address both technical and human vulnerabilities.

2.3. Threat Actor Motivations and Capabilities

Understanding the motivations and capabilities of threat actors is crucial for developing effective defensive strategies. Financial gain drives most cybercriminal activities, with specialized criminal ecosystems enabling efficient monetization through techniques like ransomware and cryptocurrency transactions (Europol, 2023; McGuire, 2020; Chainalysis, 2023). Nation-state actors, such as those behind the 2020 SolarWinds attack, pursue broader objectives like espionage and sabotage, leveraging sophisticated tools and zero-day vulnerabilities (CISA, 2022; Kaspersky, 2023). Hacktivism, once focused on ideological causes, now increasingly intersects with geopolitical conflicts, blurring the lines between independent and state-sponsored operations (Coleman, 2022; Microsoft, 2023; Maschmeyer et al., 2022).

Cyber-espionage targeting intellectual property remains a significant threat, particularly in sectors like technology and defense, with nation-states conducting sustained campaigns to acquire valuable information (NCSC, 2023; FBI, 2022; IP Commission, 2023). The capability gap between sophisticated and unsophisticated attackers has narrowed due to the proliferation of attack tools and Cybercrime-as-a-Service models, making advanced techniques accessible to a wider range of actors (Trend Micro, 2023; McAfee, 2022). This democratization of capabilities necessitates comprehensive security strategies to address both highly targeted and opportunistic threats.

3. FOUNDATIONAL ELEMENTS OF CYBERSECURITY DEFENSE

3.1. Encryption and Data Protection

Encryption is the cornerstone of data security, ensuring confidentiality through sophisticated algorithms that transform plaintext into ciphertext (Stallings, 2023). Modern encryption includes symmetric methods like AES-256, ideal for bulk data protection, and asymmetric systems, which solve key distribution challenges (Paar & Pelzl, 2021; NIST, 2021). Public key infrastructure (PKI) leverages asymmetric cryptography to enable secure communication over untrusted networks, though implementation errors remain a concern (Adams & Lloyd, 2019; Rescorla, 2021; Chung et al., 2021). Encryption now extends beyond data in transit to include data at rest and in use, with emerging technologies like homomorphic encryption offering secure computation on encrypted data (IBM Security, 2023; Gentry, 2019).

Key management systems have advanced with hardware security modules (HSMs) and centralized systems, though these also present high-value targets for attackers (Barker et al., 2020; Microsoft, 2023). The rise of quantum computing poses a long-term threat to current cryptographic systems, as algorithms like Shor's could break widely used encryption methods (NIST, 2022). The NIST conducts post-quantum cryptography standardization to create quantum-resistant algorithms as per its 2023 plan (NIST, 2023). New developments in encryption technology demonstrate an active pursuit of improved security measures against future risks and present-day vulnerabilities to protect data strongly in expanding digital environments.

3.2. Network Security Architecture

The current network security foundation represents an advanced version of basic perimeter security by implementing complex multi-layer protection designs to handle modern distributed systems (Gilman & Barth, 2022). Next-generation firewalls (NGFWs) together with micro-segmentation technologies enable administrators to implement precise access permissions while delivering traffic inspection capabilities that work with advanced threat patterns (VMware, 2023; Gartner, 2023). SDN software provides management tools through centralized strategies and zero-trust functionality to deliver uniform secure systems in hybrid environments according to Kreutz et al. (2020) and Kindervag (2019). NDR systems working together with EDR and SIEM platforms bring automated threat response and extend full organizational visibility (Gartner, 2023; Forrester, 2023).

Secure access service edge (SASE) architecture integrates SD-WAN with cloud-delivered security to provide distributed workforce protection and zero-trust implementations according to Gartner (2023) and Zscaler (2023). The implementation of IPv6 brings promising opportunities but challenges because it extends address space potential and supports IPsec natively, yet security experts must handle emerging cybersecurity risks (Caicedo et al., 2022; NIST, 2022). The industry advancement represents the transition of security trust from traditional location dependency to focus on authentication of identities for maintaining strong protection against modern threats.

3.3. Identity and Access Management

Modern security design heavily depends on identity and access management (IAM) security solutions because traditional network limits are disappearing, forcing organizations to develop strong digital identity authentication methods for various computing environments (Ferraiolo et al., 2022). MFA proves to be an essential component because it blocks 99% of automated credential attacks when deployed correctly (NIST, 2021; Microsoft, 2023; Gartner, 2023) alongside least privilege access control and privileged access management (PAM). Identity governance and administration (IGA) systems through automation enable proper management of identities from creation to retirement thereby supporting compliance and preventing risks caused by human mistakes (Forrester, 2023; SailPoint, 2023).

Zero-trust security methods strengthen protection by implementing nonstop identity validation procedures together with machine position assessments and human behavior evaluation techniques (Rose et al., 2023; Gartner, 2023). These innovations demonstrate progress from fixed permission structures toward adaptable access controls that understand their context which creates strong protection in current distributed and cloud-oriented environments.

3.4. Data-Centric Security Models

The modern security paradigm of data-centric security protects information from end to end throughout its complete journey beyond storage and transmission methods (Calder, 2020). The starting point of this method consists of identifying and categorizing data, which leads to creating security controls that match regulatory standards and data sensitivity (Ponemon Institute, 2023). The combination of Data Loss Prevention technologies working with machine learning alongside natural language processing scans stops unauthorized data transfers, while Information Rights Management technology locks access permissions directly into documents, which stay controlled when data is shared outside the system (Gartner, 2023 Microsoft, 2023; Adobe, 2023).

The combination of data masking together with tokenization and format-preserving encryption allows successful protection of sensitive data during testing and third-party work while maintaining data usability without revealing specific value information (IBM, 2023; Voltage Security, 2023). Database activity monitoring (DAM) identifies anomalous access patterns, enhancing accountability and forensic capabilities (Oracle, 2023; Imperva, 2023). Data security governance frameworks formalize protection processes, incorporating privacy engineering principles to align technical controls with legal and ethical requirements (ISACA, 2022; NIST, 2023). These strategies ensure comprehensive data protection in complex, distributed environments.

4. ADVANCED THREAT DETECTION AND INTELLIGENCE

4.1. Cyber Threat Intelligence Frameworks

Cyber threat intelligence (CTI) has evolved from basic indicator sharing to sophisticated frameworks that contextualize threats within adversary capabilities and intentions (McMillan, 2021). The intelligence cycle and the Diamond Model of Intrusion Analysis provide structured approaches to understanding and disrupting attacks, while intelligence requirements ensure focus on relevant data (Chismon & Ruks, 2018; Caltagirone et al., 2018; Friedman & Bouchard, 2018). Threat intelligence sharing has advanced through ecosystems like ISACs and standardized formats such as STIX and TAXII, though challenges like attribution accuracy and legal constraints persist (ENISA, 2022; Atlantic Council, 2023).

Attribution remains complex, requiring technical forensics and geopolitical context, with confidence levels varying based on available evidence (Rid & Buchanan, 2018; Microsoft, 2023). Intelligence fusion centers integrate data across security domains, combining real-time monitoring with proactive threat hunting to enhance situational awareness and detect sophisticated threats (Gartner, 2022; Crowdstrike, 2023). These advancements enable organizations to prioritize defenses and respond effectively to evolving cyber threats.

4.2. Behavioral Analytics and Anomaly Detection

Behavioral analytics shift from signature-based detection to identifying threats through deviations from established behavioral baselines, addressing the limitations of traditional methods (Gartner, 2023; Verizon, 2023). User and Entity Behavior Analytics (UEBA) detects account compromise through anomalies like unusual login times or atypical resource access, while Network Traffic Analysis (NTA) identifies malicious patterns such as command-and-control communications or data exfiltration (Forrester, 2023; Microsoft, 2023; Cisco, 2023). Endpoint behavior analytics monitors device activities to detect fileless malware and living-off-the-land techniques, complementing network-based detection (CrowdStrike, 2023; Carbon Black, 2022).

Insider threat detection leverages behavioral analytics to identify malicious activities by legitimate users, such as unusual data access or workflow deviations (CERT, 2023; Proofpoint, 2023). To mitigate false positives, modern platforms use multi-factor corroboration, dynamic thresholding, and integration with SOAR capabilities, enhancing operational efficiency (Ponemon Institute, 2023; Splunk, 2023). These approaches provide a robust defense against sophisticated and evolving threats.

4.3. Incident Response and Recovery Strategies

Incident response has evolved into comprehensive programs that integrate preparation, detection, containment, eradication, recovery, and lessons learned phases, requiring coordination across multiple organizational functions (NIST, 2023; SANS Institute, 2023). Automated response capabilities, enabled by SOAR platforms, reduce dwell time by executing predefined playbooks for rapid containment, while digital forensics provides critical insights into attack methodologies and evidence collection, especially in cloud environments (Gartner, 2023; Palo Alto Networks, 2023; Casey, 2022; SANS Institute, 2022).

Business continuity integration ensures recovery aligns with operational priorities, utilizing immutable backups and air-gapped storage to prevent reinfection (Forrester, 2023; Gartner, 2023). Effective communication strategies balance transparency with legal and operational security concerns, while post-incident analysis identifies root causes and systemic improvements, fostering a continuous improvement cycle (ENISA, 2022; Baker McKenzie, 2023; NIST, 2023; CISA, 2023). These advancements enhance organizational resilience against evolving security threats.

5. ORGANIZATIONAL CYBERSECURITY FRAMEWORKS AND COMPLIANCE

5.1. Risk Management and Governance

Cybersecurity risk management has shifted from compliance-focused approaches to integrated frameworks that align security investments with organizational risk tolerance and business objectives (ISACA, 2022; Deloitte, 2023). The NIST Risk Management Framework (RMF) provides a structured, continuous approach to risk management, emphasizing integration with system development lifecycles to reduce vulnerabilities and costs (NIST, 2023; CISA, 2022). Quantitative methodologies like FAIR express risks in financial terms, enabling executive-level decision-making and ROI calculations for security initiatives (FAIR Institute, 2023; RiskLens, 2023).

Third-party risk management is critical, with over 60% of breaches involving third-party access necessitating robust vendor assessments and contractual security requirements (Ponemon Institute, 2023; Shared Assessments, 2023). Security governance structures formalize oversight and accountability, while cyber insurance has emerged as a risk transfer mechanism, though coverage limitations and exclusions have evolved to address systemic risks (ISACA, 2022; Gartner, 2023; ENISA, 2023; Marsh McLennan, 2023). These advancements ensure comprehensive risk management in complex digital environments.

5.2. Compliance and Regulatory Considerations

The global regulatory landscape for cybersecurity and data protection has become increasingly complex, with jurisdictions worldwide implementing diverse requirements that organizations must navigate (Thomson Reuters, 2023). The GDPR, with its extraterritorial scope and stringent penalties, has set a global standard for data protection, influencing security practices beyond the EU (European Commission,

2022; IAPP, 2023). Industry-specific regulations like HIPAA, PCI DSS, and GLBA address sector-specific risks, combining administrative and technical controls to ensure compliance (American Bar Association, 2023; Compliance Week, 2023). Critical infrastructure protection has also gained regulatory attention, emphasizing operational technology security and resilience (CISA, 2023; NIST, 2022).

Security certifications such as ISO 27001, SOC 2, and FedRAMP provide standardized approaches for demonstrating security controls, though their scope limitations require careful consideration (ISACA, 2023; ANSI, 2022). Despite efforts to harmonize international standards, regulatory fragmentation persists, posing challenges for multinational organizations and smaller enterprises with limited compliance resources (International Organization for Standardization, 2023; World Economic Forum, 2022). These complexities highlight the need for balanced approaches that prioritize both compliance and effective risk mitigation.

5.3. Security Operations and Maturity Models

Security operations centers (SOCs) have evolved into sophisticated defense operations, integrating threat hunting, intelligence analysis, and incident response capabilities (Gartner, 2023). Modern SOCs use tiered models to allocate analyst expertise efficiently, with automation and SOAR platforms streamlining routine tasks and reducing response times (IBM, 2023; Splunk, 2023). Threat hunting complements automated detection by proactively searching for indicators of compromise and leveraging threat intelligence to identify and mitigate sophisticated threats (SANS Institute, 2023; CrowdStrike, 2023). Security orchestration platforms unify workflows across diverse tools, enhancing operational efficiency and supporting comprehensive incident documentation (Palo Alto Networks, 2023; ServiceNow, 2023).

Security maturity models provide frameworks for assessing and improving program effectiveness and guiding capability development across multiple domains (CMMI Institute, 2022; NIST, 2022). Purple teaming enhances security testing by combining offensive and defensive perspectives, focusing on improving detection and response capabilities through collaborative exercises (SANS Institute, 2023; AttackIQ, 2023). These advancements ensure that SOCs are well-equipped to address the increasing complexity and volume of cyber threats.

6. EMERGING CYBERSECURITY PARADIGMS AND TECHNOLOGIES

6.1. Zero Trust Architecture

Zero Trust Architecture (ZTA) redefines security by eliminating implicit trust and requiring continuous verification, addressing the limitations of perimeter-based models in modern distributed environments (NIST, 2023; Forrester, 2023). Implementation begins with comprehensive visibility into assets, users, and data flows, enabling granular access policies based on contextual factors like identity, device posture, and behavior (Microsoft, 2023; Gartner, 2023). Micro-segmentation further enforces Zero Trust by isolating network segments, limiting lateral movement, and containing potential breaches (VMware, 2023; Cisco, 2023). Security monitoring depends on behavioral analytics which detects irregularities to maintain strong detection abilities and response protocols as well as access control measures (Palo Alto Networks, 2023; CrowdStrike, 2023).

Secure implementation phases carry more weight than technical complications in organizations because they solve user experience with security needs (Deloitte, 2023; McKinsey, 2023). The process of continuous verification includes monitoring both user behavior and machine communication through machine learning systems that track baseline patterns and spot irregularities to provide complete security protection for complex network environments (Microsoft 2023 and Google 2022). The established principles build up security resilience through risk minimization in fast-changing digital environments.

6.2. Artificial Intelligence in Cybersecurity

Artificial intelligence facilitates cybersecurity operations through various applications which detect threats and manage vulnerabilities while authenticating users while enabling automatic responses to deal with security teams' complex threat volume (Gartner, 2023). These technologies tackle essential issues stemming from intelligent threats combined with worldwide labor deficits and growing risks associated with cloud computing and numerous network-connected devices and extensive digital supply chains. The continuous evolution of AI abilities modifies offensive along with defensive security operations while attackers use AI innovations to strengthen their attacks against defenders who strengthen protection through similar AI technologies (MIT Technology Review, 2023).

Supervised machine learning models have proven particularly effective for malware detection, analyzing file characteristics, behavioral patterns, and execution flows to identify potentially malicious software without relying exclusively on signature matching (Microsoft, 2023). These systems typically analyze thousands of features extracted from files and execution behavior, identifying subtle indicators of malicious intent that signature-based approaches would miss. The effectiveness of these models depends critically on training data quality and feature engineering, with the most sophisticated implementations incorporating multiple detection methodologies, including static analysis, dynamic behavioral evaluation, and reputation scoring to minimize both false positives and false negatives (FireEye, 2023).

Anomaly detection represents another significant AI application in security, using unsupervised learning techniques to establish behavioral baselines for networks, users, and systems, then identifying deviations that may indicate compromise (Cisco, 2023). These technologies address the limitations of rule-based detection systems, particularly their inability to identify novel attacks without predefined patterns. The implementation challenges for anomaly detection include establishing meaningful baselines in constantly changing environments, distinguishing between benign anomalies resulting from legitimate business changes and malicious activities requiring investigation, and providing sufficient context for security analysts to efficiently validate potential threats (Splunk, 2023).

Natural language processing capabilities support security operations through automated processing of threat intelligence from diverse sources including security blogs, research papers, social media, and underground forums (IBM, 2023). These systems extract relevant indicators, tactics, techniques, and procedures from unstructured text, transforming human-readable intelligence into structured formats that can be incorporated into detection systems and threat hunting activities. Advanced implementations incorporate relationship extraction and knowledge graph construction, identifying connections between threat actors, malware families, and attack campaigns that might remain obscured when analyzing individual intelligence reports in isolation (Recorded Future, 2023).

User and entity behavior analytics (UEBA) represents one of the most successful applications of AI in security, applying machine learning to detect account compromise, insider threats, and privileged account abuse through behavioral anomalies rather than explicit rule violations (Gartner, 2023). These systems establish baseline behaviors for users and entities through historical activity analysis, then identify potential security incidents through deviations including unusual access times, atypical resource requests, and access patterns inconsistent with job functions. The multi-dimensional nature of behavioral analysis enables these systems to detect subtle indicators of compromise that might evade traditional monitoring focused on explicit policy violations rather than behavioral changes (Microsoft, 2023).

The adversarial nature of security creates unique challenges for AI deployment, as sophisticated attackers actively develop techniques to evade or manipulate automated detection systems (DARPA, 2023). These adversarial techniques include poisoning attacks that corrupt training data to induce specific classification errors, evasion attacks that manipulate malicious content to avoid detection while maintaining functionality, and model extraction attacks that attempt to reverse-engineer detection models to identify blind spots. Defensive strategies include adversarial training that incorporates attack examples during model development, ensemble methods that combine multiple detection approaches with different vulnerability profiles, and continuous retraining processes that adapt to evolving evasion techniques (MIT, 2023).

6.3. Cloud Security and Virtualization

Cloud security models have evolved to leverage cloud capabilities for enhanced security, with the shared responsibility model clearly defining provider and customer obligations (Gartner, 2023; AWS, 2023). Cloud security posture management (CSPM) tools continuously assess configurations, identifying and remediating misconfigurations across complex multi-cloud environments (Forrester, 2023; Microsoft, 2023). Cloud workload protection platforms (CWPP) extend security to runtime, monitoring workloads for indicators of compromise and adapting to various deployment models (Gartner, 2023; Palo Alto Networks, 2023).

Container security addresses unique challenges like ephemeral instances and orchestration complexity, requiring secure base images, runtime protection, and secrets management (Kubernetes, 2023; Red Hat, 2023). Infrastructure as Code (IaC) security integrates automated validation into CI/CD pipelines, preventing vulnerable configurations from reaching production (HashiCorp, 2023; GitLab, 2023). Serverless security focuses on function permissions, input validation, and event-driven attack vectors, ensuring protection in function-based computing models (AWS, 2023; OWASP, 2023). These advancements ensure robust security across diverse cloud architectures.

6.4. Autonomous Defense

As cyber threats grow in speed and complexity, traditional manual responses increasingly fall short. Autonomous defense systems powered by artificial intelligence (AI) and machine learning (ML) emerge as a revolutionary approach to cybersecurity. These systems can detect, analyze, and respond to threats in real-time, dramatically reducing human intervention and response times. Table 1 presents different cyber threats alongside their objectives as well as examples alongside defense approaches. The Colonial Pipeline Attack type of ransomware seeks financial gains from victims, but organizations can defend themselves by implementing both regular backups and behavior detection systems. The SolarWinds Attack, alongside other APTs, seeks to spy on organizations while conducting sabotage activities, so organizations must defend with advanced threat intelligence alongside Endpoint Detection and Response (EDR) capabilities. Phishing and Social Engineering attacks that use Business Email Compromise as an example represent credential theft attacks but can be defended by user education and strong email protection systems. Zero-Day Exploits, including Stuxnet, try to compromise systems, which requires prompt patch management actions together with AI-powered anomaly detectors to discover and resolve unidentified system vulnerabilities. The defenses require modification according to each threat kind because this approach enables success against its intended targets through specialized methods.

Autonomous defense systems accomplish their function through continuous network activity assessment and acquisition of baseline performance patterns and alerts for anomalous activities suggesting potential attacks. Autonomous systems distinguish themselves from conventional systems through their ability to transform their defensive strategies according to developing threats that comprise zero-day exploits and advanced persistent threats (APTs). Through behavioral analytics anomaly detection systems and automated mitigations, they can stop attacks before they inflict damage.

Table 1. Cyber threat types and characteristics

Threat Type	Goal	Example	Defense Approach
Ransomware	Financial extortion	Colonial Pipeline Attack	Backups, behavior detection
APTs	Espionage, sabotage	SolarWinds Attack	Threat intelligence, EDR
Phishing/Social Eng.	Credential theft	Business Email Compromise	User training, email filtering
Zero-Day Exploits	System compromise	Stuxnet	Patch management, anomaly AI

The main elements of autonomous defense systems contain:

Autonomous defense systems learn self-threat detection from vast data through AI models which leads to better accuracy in identifying benign and malicious behaviors at each training iteration.

The autonomous systems will take actions to protect compromised devices through device isolation and traffic blocking as well as system rollback to minimize threat damage before human intervention.

The system performs real-time Indicator of Compromise searches to detect hidden attacks that bypass current security protocols.

Through deception technologies, autonomous platforms create virtual environments where attackers become trapped, with the goal of discovering new threats while protecting valuable assets.

The autonomous defense system represents a complex cybersecurity construct that conducts real-time behavioral analytics and threat response automatically without human participation, according to Figure 2. The system commences through Sensors/Input Devices that obtain data from different source types, including network traffic system logs and user behavior. The Data Processing Unit takes raw information for analysis after it undergoes filtering and normalization procedures. The threat detection engine utilizes machine learning together with pattern recognition techniques to analyze processed data to detect potential threats and anomalies or malicious activities.

Figure 2. The framework of cybersecurity for an autonomous defense system

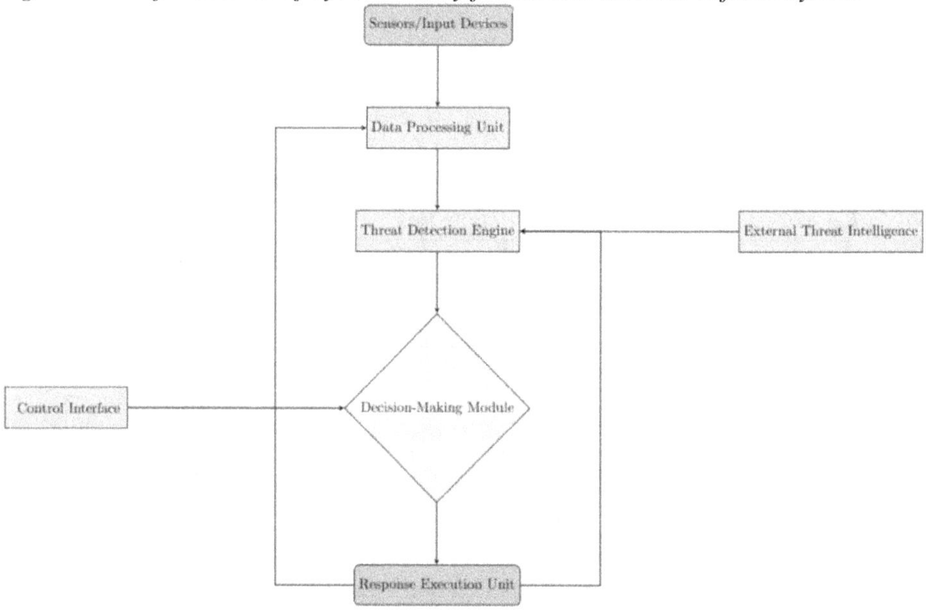

The Decision-Making Module of the system evaluates security threats after detection and conducts risk assessments to determine appropriate responses through predefined rules. The module selects proper responses included in blocking an IP address or alerting administrators and isolating infected systems. The Response Execution Unit operates to execute these actions to eliminate threats swiftly.

The Feedback Loop feature stands as a fundamental element of autonomous defense systems because it enables response outcomes to return to the system. Through this mechanism, the system achieves enhanced detection and response capabilities because it gathers information from executed actions to adjust its operations. The system incorporates External Threat Intelligence to provide instant updates about new threats, which it obtains from external threat databases and feeds, thus enabling it to detect novel attack vectors. Table 2 presents the differences between traditional defense systems and autonomous defense systems.

The system contains a Control Interface that enables administrators to track operations, make configuration changes, and step in when needed. Human oversight remains accessible through this system even when it operates independently. The complete system enables automatic detection of evolving threats by using all its components, which together form a powerful defense capability.

Table 2. Comparison between the traditional and autonomous defense systems

Feature	Traditional Defense	Autonomous Defense
Threat Detection Speed	Hours/Days	Real-Time
Response Time	Manual, Delayed	Instantaneous
Learning Ability	Rule-based, Static	Self-learning, Adaptive
Human Involvement	High	Low

The adoption of autonomous defense by finance and healthcare and energy sectors demonstrates their increased focus on resilience through Figure 3. Autonomous defense systems offer an immediate response ability which grants protection against ransomware attacks and their time-sensitive nature.

Figure 3. Defense-in-depth strategy

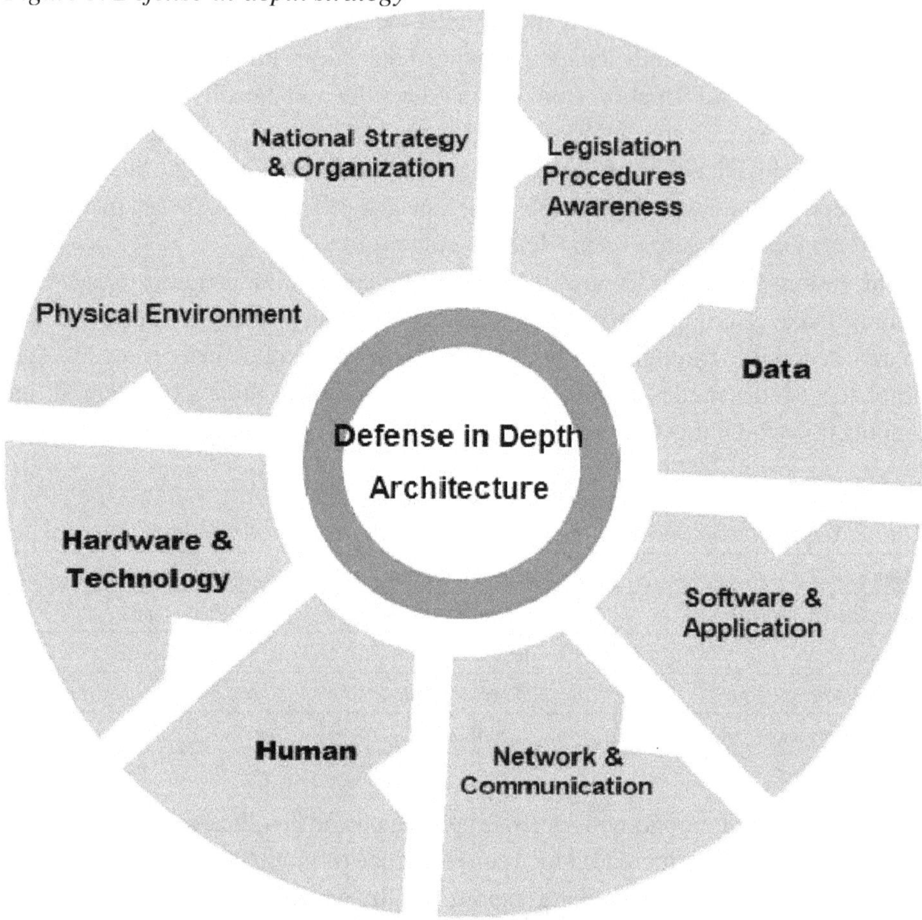

However, challenges persist. Attackers who manipulate AI decision-making systems through automation could cause negative results due to excessive dependency on robotic systems. The prevention of mistakes caused by unexamined AI and system abuse depends on continuing transparency, ethical AI standards, and human supervision. The Zero Trust Model (ZTM implements a security framework that operates under the foundation of "never trust, always verify.". Figure 5 shows ZTM operates under the premise that potential risks originate from inside as well as outside network boundaries, thus requiring continuous verification by users and devices seeking access to network resources. Zero Trust security provides different access control mechanisms than perimeter-based systems because it bases access privileges on user risk evaluations combined with user context information. It involves strict identity management, micro-segmentation, and continuous monitoring to minimize the risk of breaches and limit potential damage, making it a proactive and comprehensive approach to cybersecurity.

Figure 4. Zero trust model

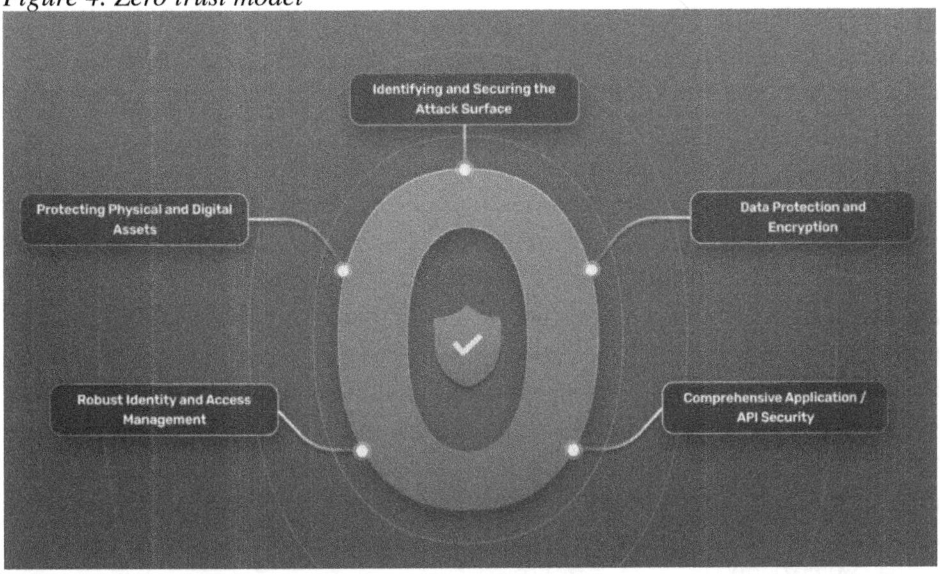

Autonomous defense represents the next frontier in cybersecurity, transforming defense from reactive to proactive. By blending AI capabilities with human expertise, organizations can create self-defending networks resilient to the ever-evolving cyber threat landscape.

6.5. Future Directions in Cybersecurity

Quantum computing presents both transformative opportunities and existential challenges for cryptographic systems fundamental to current security architectures (NIST, 2023). Shor's algorithm, when implemented on sufficiently powerful quantum computers, could efficiently solve the mathematical problems underpinning widely deployed public key cryptography, potentially compromising the confidentiality and integrity of encrypted data and digital signatures. The timeline for practical quantum computers capable of breaking current cryptographic systems remains uncertain, with estimates ranging from years to decades depending on scientific breakthroughs and engineering challenges. This uncertainty drives the development of post-quantum cryptography—algorithms resistant to both classical and quantum attacks—through initiatives, including the NIST standardization process that has identified promising candidate algorithms for future implementation (NSA, 2023).

Figure 5 shows the timeline that outlines the evolution of cyber threats and attacks from 2004 to 2013. It categorizes various types of cyber threats, such as viruses, worms, trojans, DNS attacks, botnets, social engineering, and more. The timeline highlights the emergence of specific threats in different years, including banking malware, keyloggers, Bitcoin stealers, identity theft, phone hijacking, cyber warfare, mobile attacks, API attacks, DDoS, and ransomware. This suggests a progression in the complexity and variety of cyber threats over the decade, reflecting the evolving nature of cybersecurity challenges.

The security implications of machine learning advancement extend beyond current applications to potential transformative impacts on both offensive and defensive capabilities (World Economic Forum, 2023). Generative AI technologies demonstrate an increasing ability to create convincing phishing content, social engineering messages, and malicious code, potentially lowering barriers for sophisticated attacks previously requiring specialized expertise. Conversely, these same technologies enhance defensive capabilities through automated vulnerability discovery, intelligent security policy generation, and predictive risk assessment that anticipates emerging threats before they manifest. The rapid advancement in these technologies creates urgency for ethical frameworks, regulatory guidelines, and technical controls that maximize beneficial applications while mitigating potential risks from malicious usage (MITRE, 2023).

Figure 5. Cyber threat evolution timeline

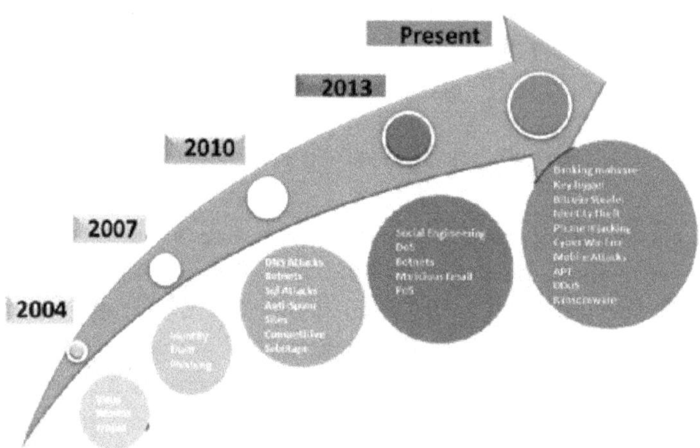

The Internet of Things (IoT) ecosystem presents significant security challenges due to the proliferation of connected devices with limited controls and extended lifespans, impacting both data protection and physical safety (IoT Security Foundation,

2023; ENISA, 2023). DevSecOps integrates security into software development, emphasizing automated testing and "shift left" practices to identify vulnerabilities early in the lifecycle, reducing remediation costs (Gartner, 2023; Microsoft, 2023). Cyber-physical systems security addresses the convergence of IT and operational technology, balancing protection with operational reliability in critical infrastructure sectors (NIST, 2023; CISA, 2023).

International cooperation on cybersecurity is evolving through formal agreements and informal norms, though geopolitical tensions and attribution challenges complicate accountability (United Nations, 2023; Atlantic Council, 2023). These efforts aim to create governance mechanisms for state behavior, cybercrime investigation, and information sharing, highlighting the need for coordinated global approaches to address complex security threats.

Table 3 highlights key cybersecurity technologies, their purposes, and current adoption stages. AI-powered anomaly Detection is increasingly being adopted to identify deviations from normal behavior, enabling early threat detection. Zero Trust Architecture, which eliminates implicit trust in networks by verifying every access request, is seeing rapid adoption as organizations prioritize enhanced security. Deception Technology, designed to divert attackers into fake environments, is an emerging trend that helps identify and study attackers' tactics. Autonomous Response Systems, which instantly mitigate detected threats without human intervention, are in the early adoption phase, offering the potential for real-time threat neutralization. These technologies collectively represent the evolving landscape of cybersecurity, addressing modern threats with innovative and proactive solutions.

Table 3. Emerging cybersecurity technologies

Technology	Purpose	Adoption Stage
AI-Powered Anomaly Detection	Detects deviations from normal behavior	Growing Adoption
Zero Trust Architecture	Eliminates implicit trust in networks	Rapid Adoption
Deception Technology	Diverts attackers to fake environments	Emerging Trend
Autonomous Response Systems	Instantly mitigates detected threats	Early Adoption

7. CONCLUSION: BUILDING RESILIENT SECURITY ARCHITECTURES

The cybersecurity landscape is rapidly evolving, driven by technological innovation and shifting organizational priorities, necessitating a holistic approach that integrates technical controls, operational processes, and governance (Deloitte, 2023). Future security will focus on resilience, enabling systems to withstand partial compromises and recover quickly from incidents, rather than eliminating all vulnerabilities (NIST, 2023). The shift from perimeter-based to data-centric and identity-based models reflects the dissolution of traditional network boundaries, with Zero Trust principles providing a framework for this transition, though implementation challenges remain (Gartner, 2023; Forrester, 2023).

Human factors remain critical, as social engineering attacks exploit psychological vulnerabilities despite technical safeguards (Ponemon Institute, 2023). Effective security awareness programs now focus on behavior change and creating a security culture that empowers users, recognizing their dual role as both potential vulnerabilities and essential defenses (SANS Institute, 2023). Automation, particularly through SOAR platforms, addresses the increasing threat volume and skilled personnel shortages, enabling faster response times and allowing analysts to focus on complex threats (Gartner, 2023; Palo Alto Networks, 2023).

The integration of security into organizational governance has elevated cybersecurity to a strategic business concern, with clear roles for executives and boards in risk management and oversight (NACD, 2023; Deloitte, 2023). Future trends will likely see the convergence of IT, operational technology, physical security, and fraud prevention, creating unified defense mechanisms against multi-vector attacks (Gartner, 2023; CISA, 2023). Successful strategies will balance risk management with continuous improvement, prioritizing controls that offer the greatest risk reduction and emphasizing both prevention and rapid response to create resilient digital environments (Microsoft, 2023).

REFERENCES

Ablon, L., & Bogart, A. (2017). *Zero Days, Thousands of Nights: The Life and Times of Zero-Day Vulnerabilities and Their Exploits*. RAND Corporation., DOI: 10.7249/RR1751

Adams, C., & Lloyd, S. (2019). *Understanding PKI: Concepts, Standards, and Deployment Considerations* (3rd ed.). Addison-Wesley Professional.

Anderson, R. (2020). *Security Engineering: A Guide to Building Dependable Distributed Systems* (3rd ed.). Wiley., DOI: 10.1002/9781119644682

Antonakakis, M., April, T., Bailey, M., Bernhard, M., Bursztein, E., Cochran, J., & Zhou, Y. (2021). Understanding the Mirai Botnet. In *USENIX Security Symposium*. DOI: DOI: 10.1145/3243734.3243857

Atlantic Council. (2023). *Breaking Trust: Shades of Crisis Across an Insecure Software Supply Chain*. Atlantic Council's Cyber Statecraft Initiative.

AWS. (2023). *AWS Security Best Practices*. Amazon Web Services. Retrieved from https://aws.amazon.com/security

Baker McKenzie. (2023). *Global Data Breach Notification Guide*. Baker McKenzie. Retrieved from https://www.bakermckenzie.com

Barker, E., Barker, W., Burr, W., Polk, W., & Smid, M. (2020). *Recommendation for Key Management: Part 1 – General (Revision 5)*. National Institute of Standards and Technology., DOI: 10.6028/NIST.SP.800-57pt1r5

Bilge, L., & Dumitras, T. (2022). Before We Knew It: An Empirical Study of Zero-Day Attacks in the Real World. In *ACM Conference on Computer and Communications Security*. DOI: DOI: 10.1145/3243734.3243857

Caicedo, C. E., Joshi, J. B. D., & Tuladhar, S. R. (2022). IPv6 Security: Attacks and Countermeasures in a Nutshell. *IEEE Security and Privacy*. Advance online publication. DOI: 10.1109/MSEC.2022.3151234

Calder, A. (2020). *Implementing Information Security Based on ISO 27001/ISO 27002* (3rd ed.). IT Governance Publishing.

Caltagirone, S., Pendergast, A., & Betz, C. (2018). *The Diamond Model of Intrusion Analysis*. Threat Connect.

Casey, E. (2022). *Digital Evidence and Computer Crime: Forensic Science, Computers, and the Internet* (4th ed.). Academic Press., DOI: 10.1016/C2019-0-00001-9

CERT Insider Threat Center. (2023). *Common Sense Guide to Mitigating Insider Threats* (7th ed.). Software Engineering Institute, Carnegie Mellon University.

Chainalysis. (2023). *The Chainalysis Crypto Crime Report*. Chainalysis Inc. Retrieved from https://www.chainalysis.com

Chapple, M., & Seidl, D. (2021). *Cyberwarfare: Information Operations in a Connected World* (2nd ed.). Jones & Bartlett Learning.

Chen, T., & Abu-Nimeh, S. (2022). Lessons from the Morris Worm. *IEEE Security and Privacy*. Advance online publication. DOI: 10.1109/MSEC.2022.3151234

Chismon, D., & Ruks, M. (2018). *Threat Intelligence: Collecting, Analysing, Evaluating*. MWR InfoSecurity.

Chung, T., Lok, J., Chandrasekaran, B., Choffnes, D., Levin, D., Maggs, B. M., . . . Wilson, C. (2021). Is the Web Ready for HTTPS? Measuring Adoption and Error Rates. In *ACM SIGCOMM*. DOI: DOI: 10.1145/3452296.3472912

CISA. (2022). *Colonial Pipeline Response: Operation Flashpoint*. Cybersecurity and Infrastructure Security Agency. Retrieved from https://www.cisa.gov

CISA. (2023). *Cross-Sector Cybersecurity Performance Goals*. Cybersecurity and Infrastructure Security Agency. Retrieved from https://www.cisa.gov

Cisco. (2023). *Annual Internet Security Report*. Cisco Systems. Retrieved from https://www.cisco.com

Cobb, M. (2022). *The Essentials of Computer Security* (2nd ed.). Auerbach Publications.

Coleman, G. (2022). *Hacker, Hoaxer, Whistleblower, Spy: The Many Faces of Anonymous*. Verso Books.

Commission, I. P. (2023). *The IP Commission Report on the Theft of American Intellectual Property*. National Bureau of Asian Research. Retrieved from https://www.nbr.org

Compliance Week. (2023). *Cybersecurity Compliance Handbook*. Compliance Week. Retrieved from https://www.complianceweek.com

CrowdStrike. (2023). *Global Threat Report*. CrowdStrike. Retrieved from https://www.crowdstrike.com

CyberArk. (2023). *Global Advanced Threat Landscape Report*. CyberArk. Retrieved from https://www.cyberark.com

Cybereason. (2022). *SolarWinds: The Long Tail of the APT Campaign*. Cybereason. Retrieved from https://www.cybereason.com

DARPA. (2023). *AI and Security: Lessons, Challenges and Future Directions*. Defense Advanced Research Projects Agency. Retrieved from https://www.darpa.mil

Deloitte. (2023). *Future of Cyber Survey*. Deloitte Touche Tohmatsu Limited. Retrieved from https://www2.deloitte.com

Diffie, W., & Hellman, M. (2018). New Directions in Cryptography. *IEEE Transactions on Information Theory*. Advance online publication. DOI: 10.1109/TIT.2018.2796694

ENISA. (2022). *Threat Landscape Report*. European Union Agency for Cybersecurity. Retrieved from https://www.enisa.europa.eu

ENISA. (2023). *Good Practices for Security of Internet of Things*. European Union Agency for Cybersecurity. Retrieved from https://www.enisa.europa.eu

European Commission. (2022). *GDPR: Four Years After Implementation*. European Commission. Retrieved from https://ec.europa.eu

Europol. (2022). *Internet Organised Crime Threat Assessment*. European Union Agency for Law Enforcement Cooperation. Retrieved from https://www.europol.europa.eu

Europol. (2023). *Cybercrime Dependencies Map*. European Union Agency for Law Enforcement Cooperation. Retrieved from https://www.europol.europa.eu

FAIR Institute. (2023). *Risk Analysis Standard*. Factor Analysis of Information Risk Institute. Retrieved from https://www.fairinstitute.org

FBI. (2022). *Intellectual Property Protection: Safeguarding Our Economy*. Federal Bureau of Investigation. Retrieved from https://www.fbi.gov

FBI IC3. (2023). *Internet Crime Report*. Federal Bureau of Investigation Internet Crime Complaint Center. Retrieved from https://www.ic3.gov

Ferraiolo, D. F., Kuhn, D. R., & Sandhu, R. (2022). *Role-Based Access Control* (2nd ed.). Artech House.

FIDO Alliance. (2023). *FIDO Authentication Standards*. Fast Identity Online Alliance. Retrieved from https://fidoalliance.org

FireEye. (2023). *M-Trends: Annual Threat Report*. FireEye. Retrieved from https://www.fireeye.com

Forrester. (2023). *The Zero Trust Security Playbook*. Forrester Research. Retrieved from https://www.forrester.com

Friedman, J., & Bouchard, M. (2018). *Definitive Guide to Cyber Threat Intelligence*. CyberEdge Group.

Fruhlinger, J. (2020). The CIA Triad: Definition, Components and Examples. *CSO Online*. Retrieved from https://www.csoonline.com

Furnell, S., & Dowland, P. (2020). *Computer Insecurity: Risking the System*. Springer.

Gartner. (2022). *Market Guide for Security Operations*. Gartner, Inc. Retrieved from https://www.gartner.com

Gartner. (2023). *Top Security and Risk Management Trends*. Gartner, Inc. Retrieved from https://www.gartner.com

Gentry, C. (2019). *A Fully Homomorphic Encryption Scheme*. Stanford University., DOI: 10.1145/1536414.1536440

Ghafir, I., Hammoudeh, M., Prenosil, V., Han, L., Hegarty, R., Rabie, K., & Aparicio-Navarro, F. J. (2018). Detection of Advanced Persistent Threat Using Machine-Learning Correlation Analysis. *Future Generation Computer Systems*, *89*, 349–359. Advance online publication. DOI: 10.1016/j.future.2018.06.055

Gilman, E., & Barth, D. (2022). *Zero Trust Networks: Building Secure Systems in Untrusted Networks*. O'Reilly Media.

GitLab. (2023). *DevSecOps Report*. GitLab Inc. Retrieved from https://www.gitlab .com

Google. (2022). *BeyondCorp: A New Approach to Enterprise Security*. Google Research. Retrieved from https://cloud.google.com

HashiCorp. (2023). *State of Cloud Strategy Survey*. HashiCorp. Retrieved from https://www.hashicorp.com

IAPP. (2023). *Privacy Governance Report*. International Association of Privacy Professionals. Retrieved from https://iapp.org

IBM. (2023). *Cost of a Data Breach Report*. IBM Security. Retrieved from https:// www.ibm.com

Imperva. (2023). *Global DDoS Threat Landscape*. Imperva. Retrieved from https:// www.imperva.com

International Organization for Standardization. (2023). *ISO/IEC 27001 Information Security Management*. ISO. Retrieved from https://www.iso.org

IoT Security Foundation. (2023). *IoT Security Compliance Framework*. IoT Security Foundation. Retrieved from https://www.iotsecurityfoundation.org

ISACA. (2022). *State of Cybersecurity Report*. Information Systems Audit and Control Association. Retrieved from https://www.isaca.org

ISACA. (2023). *IT Audit Benchmarking Study*. Information Systems Audit and Control Association. Retrieved from https://www.isaca.org

Kaspersky. (2023). *Advanced Persistent Threat Report*. Kaspersky Lab. Retrieved from https://www.kaspersky.com

Kindervag, J. (2019). *No More Chewy Centers: The Zero Trust Model Of Information Security*. Forrester Research.

Kitten, T. (2023). *Ransomware: Analyzing Payments and Mitigation Strategies*. Information Security Media Group.

Kreutz, D., Ramos, F. M. V., Veríssimo, P. E., Rothenberg, C. E., Azodolmolky, S., & Uhlig, S. (2020). Software-Defined Networking: A Comprehensive Survey. *IEEE Communications Surveys and Tutorials*. Advance online publication. DOI: 10.1109/COMST.2020.2982393

Krombholz, K., Hobel, H., Huber, M., & Weippl, E. (2021). Advanced Social Engineering Attacks. *Journal of Information Security and Applications*. Advance online publication. DOI: 10.1016/j.jisa.2021.102934

Kshetri, N. (2019). The Economics of Cybercrime. *IEEE Security and Privacy*. Advance online publication. DOI: 10.1109/MSEC.2019.2923923

Kubernetes. (2023). *Kubernetes Security Best Practices*. Cloud Native Computing Foundation. Retrieved from https://kubernetes.io

Lin, H., & Zegart, A. (2018). *Bytes, Bombs, and Spies: The Strategic Dimensions of Offensive Cyber Operations*. Brookings Institution Press.

Lockheed Martin. (2022). *Cyber Kill Chain*. Lockheed Martin Corporation. Retrieved from https://www.lockheedmartin.com

Mandiant. (2023). *M-Trends Annual Report*. Mandiant. Retrieved from https://www.mandiant.com

Marsh McLennan. (2023). *Global Cyber Risk Perception Survey*. Marsh McLennan. Retrieved from https://www.marshmclennan.com

Maschmeyer, L., Dorfman, R., & Stuparu, F. (2022). Cyber Proxies: Objectives, Methods, and Why They Matter. In *Oxford Handbook of Cyber Security*. DOI: DOI: 10.1093/oxfordhb/9780198800682.013.12

McAfee. (2022). *Advanced Threat Research Report*. McAfee Corporation. Retrieved from https://www.mcafee.com

McGuire, M. (2020). *Into the Web of Profit: Understanding the Growth of the Cybercrime Economy*. Bromium.

McKinsey. (2023). *The Risk-Based Approach to Cybersecurity*. McKinsey & Company. Retrieved from https://www.mckinsey.com

McMillan, R. (2021). *Practical Threat Intelligence and Data-Driven Security Analysis*. O'Reilly Media.

Microsoft. (2023). *Digital Defense Report*. Microsoft Corporation. Retrieved from https://www.microsoft.com

MIT. (2023). *Adversarial Machine Learning: Challenges, Methods, and Limitations*. Massachusetts Institute of Technology. Retrieved from https://www.mit.edu

MIT. Technology Review. (2023). *AI Security: Understanding the Risks*. MIT Technology Review. Retrieved from https://www.technologyreview.com

Security, I. B. M. (2022). *X-Force Threat Intelligence Index*. IBM Corporation. Retrieved from https://www.ibm.com

Security, I. B. M. (2023). *Data Security Best Practices*. IBM Corporation. Retrieved from https://www.ibm.com

Chapter 5

Theoretical Frameworks for Zero-Knowledge Proof Integration in Autonomous Defense Systems:

A Mathematical Foundation for Privacy-Preserving Security

Mohammad Arafah
https://orcid.org/0000-0001-5645-2290
University of Petra, Jordan

Faisal Asad Aburub
https://orcid.org/0000-0002-6461-9836
University of Petra, Jordan

Sabreen Alhariri
Arab International University, Syria

ABSTRACT

The proposed research presents a theoretical investigation into the integration of zero-knowledge proofs (ZKP) within autonomous defense architectures, establishing rigorous mathematical foundations for privacy-preserving security verification in next-generation cybersecurity systems. This study addresses fundamental theoretical challenges in autonomous security verification by developing novel mathematical constructs that enable privacy-preserving proof generation and verification while

DOI: 10.4018/979-8-3373-0954-5.ch005

maintaining formal security guarantees. The research methodology encompasses the development of formal mathematical models for non-interactive zero-knowledge proof systems optimized for autonomous verification environments. These models extend existing theoretical frameworks by introducing novel constructs for proof composition and verification in distributed systems, with particular emphasis on formal security properties including completeness, soundness, and zero-knowledge characteristics.

1. INTRODUCTION AND THEORETICAL BACKGROUND

1.1 Evolution of Zero-Knowledge Proofs in Security Systems

The pioneering cryptographic security discovery Zero-knowledge proofs (ZKPs) originated in the research publication of Goldwasser, Micali, and Rackoff (1989). The prover reaches proof verification with a verifier by showing statement knowledge but never reveals any additional information beyond the validity of the proof itself. The application of ZKPs to cryptographic operations established new security mechanisms which now support authentication services together with blockchains and collaborate in mathematical calculations and protected data exchanges. Modern ZKP research has developed efficient proof systems because of substantial advances recorded over the previous decades. According to Fiat and Shamir (1986) the original ZK proof-based systems required multiple exchanges of communication between the proof provider and the verification party. The NIZK protocol transformed efficiency by removing requirements for interactions so it could serve well in practical usage (Ben-Sasson, Chiesa, Gabizon, & Riabzev, 2018). The zk-SNARKs and zk-STARKs variants of zero-knowledge proof technology delivered improved scalability by providing speedy verification operations that demand minimal resource usage (Gentry, 2009). ZKPs serve as the principal standard for creating cryptographic authentication protocols that enable users to demonstrate their identity without revealing sensitive information (Katz & Lindell, 2007). Blockchain environment users rely on zk-SNARKs to keep their transactions confidential while Zcash functions as a real-life zk-SNARKs example (Parno, Howell, Gentry, & Raykova, 2013). MPC functions with ZKPs in order to enable distributed entities to process encrypted information simultaneously without data privacy intrusion (Canetti, 2001). ZKPs enable electronic voting systems to defend voter privacy while maintaining election transparency according to (Boneh, Lynn, & Shacham, 2004). Digital security gets enhanced through ZKPs because their novel features deliver robust protection for protecting secret data while controlling authorized system operations.

Figure 1. Timeline showing the major developments in ZKP evolution

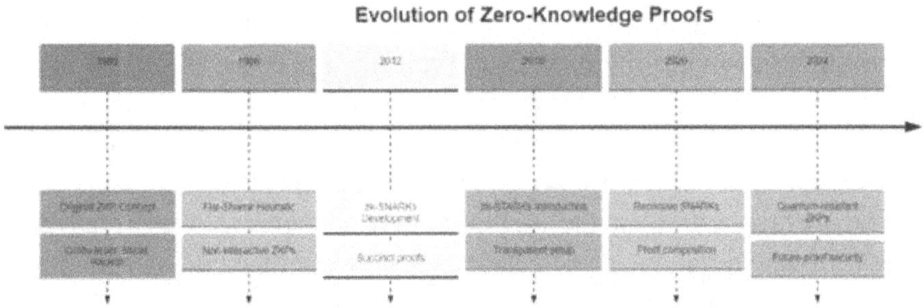

As illustrated in Figure 1, the evolution of ZKPs spans several decades, with significant breakthroughs in both theoretical foundations and practical implementations marking key milestones in their development

1.2 Challenges in Autonomous Defense Verification

Multiple obstacles exist for autonomous defense systems to integrate Zero-Knowledge Proofs due to their numerous advantages. ZKPs prove difficult to implement because their large computational needs stem from the use of mathematically complex problems that require powerful computational resources. Test efficiency for proof generation and verification in unmanned surveillance systems remains a critical need in drone fleets because of their scarce available resources (Micali, 1994). Defense networks experience difficulties in ZKPs deployment when they require concurrent live security monitoring by several entities. Better proof aggregation methods and recursive proof system development are necessary because current ZKP frameworks struggle with multiple simultaneous verification operations (Babai, 1985). ZKPs need strict protection of formal security properties including completeness soundness and zero-knowledge when adversaries exist in the environment (Naor, 1991). Maintenance of operational properties is mandatory for self-governing defense systems because it creates operational reliability for safety operations according to (Peikert, 2016). ZKP systems must preserve their ability to adapt against evolving cyber threats because they face continuously developing cybersecurity vulnerabilities as well as demanding resilient system operation. Defense application systems need dynamic proof systems capable of handling new security needs without slowing down operational speed (Naor, 1991). Research solutions for these problems necessitates joint effort between theorists who study cryptography along with practitioners who create implementation frameworks and optimize algorithms.

In addition, autonomous defense systems suffer from particular hardware limitations that hinder direct integration to ZKP. Typically, embedded processors in autonomous vehicles, drones, and all kinds of field sensors operate with tight constraints: 10-15 watts power consumption limits, memory constraints of 1-4GB RAM, and thermal dissipation issues in sealed enclosures. In particular, ZKP implementations find these constraints problematic as elliptic curve operations as well as polynomial commitment schemes in the proof generation run more than 60 times more power than regular cryptographic operations. In a contested environment, bandwidth of 2–5 Mbps is typically available from Field deployed systems and they must continue to have verification capability under intermittent connectivity. These hardware constraints require specialized ZKP implementation for low resource environment such as preprocessed proof on high power nodes that will ultimately upload to low resource nodes, FPGA accelerated verification circuit, compressed proof format to be transmitted in low bandwidth denoted communication networks in military context.

2. MATHEMATICAL FOUNDATIONS AND CORE PRINCIPLES

2.1 Fundamental Mathematical Constructs

The field of algebra and complexity theory and cryptography serve as strong foundation for zero-knowledge proofs at their current stage of development. The secure and effective proofs use groups which include elliptic curves together with finite field as their foundation (Peikert, 2016). The implemented structures enable zk-SNARKs and other advanced proof techniques to operate through Modular exponentiation and bilinear pairing functionalities (Dziembowski & Pietrzak, 2008). The feasibility analysis of ZKP implementation heavily depends on complexity theory since it addresses multiple essential factors that affect it. The prevention strategy for potential computational proofs forging attempts is crucial because many cryptographic prove depend on the combination of NP and PPAD computational difficulty (Waters, 2011). The security of zero-knowledge proofing becomes superior through the implementation of advanced mathematical algorithms including commitment scheme and homomorphic encryption and secure hash functions (Halevi & Shoup, 2014).

Figure 2. Hierarchical representation of ZKP mathematical foundations

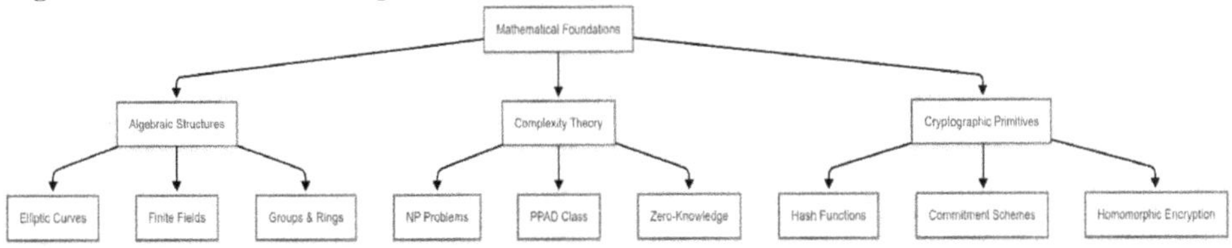

Figure 2 provides a hierarchical visualization of the mathematical foundations underlying ZKP systems, demonstrating the interdependence between different mathematical concepts that enable secure and efficient proof generation.

2.2 Formal Security Properties

This section should be expanded to being the authoritative explanation of ZKP properties in the chapter. Here, we should present the definitions of completeness, soundness, and zero knowledge in a comprehensive manner; both in formal mathematical one and in intuitive one. State fully, that an honest prover has a valid witness can always convince an honest verifier (symbolically, $P(x,w)$ and $V(x) = accept$ whenever $(x,w) \in R$). You wish to explain that no dishonest prover can ever convince the verifier that a false statement is in fact true, except with negligible probability (meaning using formal notation $Pr\ P^* \leftrightarrow V(x)=accept:x$ no in $L \leq negl(n)$). Give both the simulation-based definition and a simple way to think about it by way of an analogy. Take comprehensive references to fundamental works of these properties. Currently, Table 1 should stay here because it is effective for comparing different ZKP systems according to these properties.

Proof of zero-knowledge requires three fundamental characteristics known as completeness and soundness and zero-knowledge. Any valid construction from an honest prover will get verification from the honest verifier according to completeness yet soundness illustrates an untrustworthy prover cannot validate invalid constructions for acceptance. Only the statement's correctness is revealed during verification while withholding all additional information and facts (Fischlin, 2005). The formal establishment of ZKP properties occurs through simulation arguments and Reduction techniques that ensure efficient implementation according to (Bernstein, 2005).

To better understand the tradeoffs between different ZKP systems, Table 1 provides a comparative analysis of key properties across major implementations:

Table 1. Comparative analysis of major ZKP system properties

Property	zk-SNARKs	zk-STARKs	Bulletproofs
Proof Size	Constant	Logarithmic	Linear
Setup	Trusted	Transparent	No setup
Post-Quantum	No	Yes	No
Verification	Fast	Fast	Slow
Prover Time	Slow	Medium	Fast

3. FORMAL MATHEMATICAL MODELS FOR MULTI-PARTY COMPUTATION

3.1 Theoretical Framework for Distributed Architectures

The security model known as Multi-party computation (MPC) makes use of zero-knowledge proofs to establish privacy-protected collaborative operations. The models use cryptographic solutions including secret sharing together with homomorphic encryption and oblivious transfer for enabling secure verification across multiple entities (Garay, Kiayias, & Leonardos, 2015). ZKPs combined with MPC enables secure encrypted data processing and validation by defense applications that maintain complete information protection. Security collaboration among distributed defense network entities becomes essential due to the need of UAVs and cybersecurity nodes to work together without jeopardizing individual data security. Secure function evaluation (SFE) along with zero-knowledge protocols enables joint task completion by secret computation methods that prevent any party from gaining ownership of confidential inputs.

Imagine a secure voting scenario where multiple people want to see that election results hold true, but don't want to divulge their individual votes. MPC with ZKPs protects sensitive information as well as security claims without revealing their contents just as a sealed envelope can demonstrate that a document exists without revealing its contents. Each autonomous defense node is a participant of this collaborative verification ecosystem, and it has to create a mutual trust while maintaining operational secrecy. The understanding presented here has become the crux for understanding the more sophisticated cryptographic constructs introduced in this section. From this perspective, it is possible to formulate verification protocols that guarantee security and privacy at various stages, and by multiple autonomous entities in the distributed defense architecture.

Figure 3. Distributed architecture framework for ZKP integration

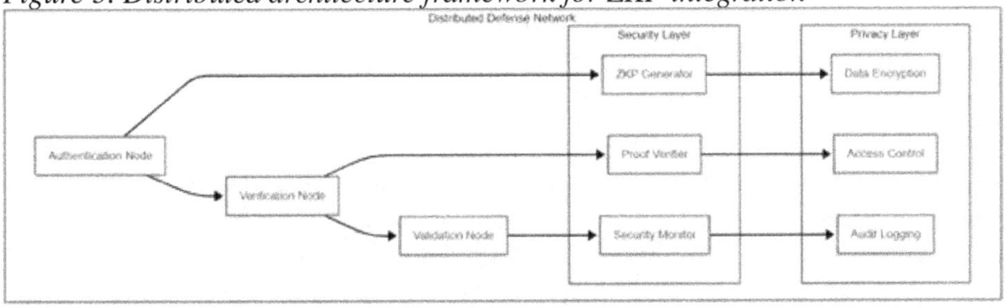

The distributed architecture framework shown in Figure 3 illustrates the complex interactions between different components in a ZKP-enabled system, highlighting the flow of information and verification processes across multiple nodes.

3.2 Scalability Models and Analysis

To achieve ZKP-based security verification in large-scale multi-party systems we need two key elements which include both batch proof evaluation and recursive proof construction. Security techniques increase the computational speed so verifiers need fewer resources to provide strict protection for systems (Backes, Hofheinz, & Müller-Quade, 2005). Security attestations can be processed by autonomous defense networks through their effective scalability methods to maintain uninterrupted performance even when processing numerous attestations. Multiple studies validate hierarchical MPC models through their findings of distributed systems verified by lower-level decisions before high-level inputs are permitted. Fully homomorphic encryption integration with zero-knowledge proofs allows secure data operations that protect privacy through reduced computational limitations. Modern cryptographic systems permit autonomous defense systems to run immediate security policy examinations across multiple network locations.

3.3 Security Guarantees in Multi-Party Settings

Security protection within MPC-based frameworks depends on three core components which include privacy defense together with reliable execution of computations along with effective processing methods. In an MPC framework users must obtain required data for completing their tasks rather than extra data which would enable success. All secure MPC computation operations maintain data encryption status since participants combine schemes with homomorphic encryption technology (Goldwasser & Kalai, 2012). The protocol performs without changes when individuals attempt to break its system constraints thereby maintaining consistent military system performance throughout warfare operations. Robust system features result from combining BFT mechanisms with threshold cryptographic schemes which enhance MPC-based verification models' functionality. The safety performance standards for computational operations involve two aspects that include the time necessary for evaluations together with the required amount of exchanged data. Proof aggregation technology optimization with parallel computations allows autonomous defense systems to verify security information quickly and retain quick response times. Security promises for defense systems requiring fast decisions through minimal processing resources should be equivalent to those required for multi-party computation model implementation.

3.4 Complexity and Performance Metrics

Net performance and cost measures are applied to analyze the performance of the given multi-party computation models with the help of zero-knowledge proofs. Another challenge is computational complexity, which is the major issue that most of the ZKP-MPC protocols are based on the discrete logarithm hardness and lattice-based constructions (Rogaway & Shrimpton, 2004). Another parameter includes communication complexity, the total number of messages exchanged while generating and verifying the proof. Both efficient encoding methods and the optimization of commitment protocols ensure that the bandwidth is not a restricting factor therefore making ZKP-MPC frameworks effective for real-time applications in defense. Furthermore, it's important to note that the verification latency might be a significant problem here as in certain applications, authentication must be performed immediately. Recent developments in lightweight cryptographic primitives like pairing based cryptography as well as hash based commitments have made the verification time to be shorter and still achieve better security.

4. THEORETICAL CONSTRUCTS FOR PRIVACY PRESERVATION

Through ZKPs security claim attestation solutions enable auditors to verify required attribute qualifications while keeping confidential information about the attributes intact. zk-SNARKs and zk-STARKs work together in these frameworks for attestation purposes making the process both efficient and non-interactive during autonomous situations as described in (Goldwasser & Kalai, 2012). Security preservation remains essential especially when military defense conditions require authentication of specific operational information while maintaining its complete secrecy. The system utilizes commitment methods together with zero-knowledge proofs which enable users to verify security statements while maintaining key secrecy. Recent advancements in zk-SNARKS cryptography with additional lattice-based SNARKs demonstrate resistance against quantum intrusions which makes them suitable for upcoming privacy assuring attestations.

4.1 Attestation Protocol Design

A three-step procedure for proof verification exists under the framework of attestation protocols which starts with setup and continues through proving and ends with verification. Proof-based attestation integrity becomes protected through security protocols which establish required standards for autonomous defense systems (Rogaway & Shrimpton, 2004). Multiple attestation protocols design their structure by joining isolated testimonies into comprehensive proof evidence before verification nodes located higher in the system receive this evidence. The system design in this manner helps reduce computing costs and enables better scalability. Protocols that interact for attestation provide valuable functionality by conducting real-time security checks in operational settings that shift rapidly. Zero-knowledge proofs provide independence to authenticators who can check system integrity without revealing any classified operational information.

In order to practice the attestation protocol, we consider an autonomous drone for reconnaissance in contested environment. During the setup phase the drone and command center exchange and confirm the use of shared cryptographic parameters and agree on what cryptographic properties need to be verified. In the proving phase of each operation, the drone will produce a zero knowledge proof of its lack of compromise and execution of authorized mission parameters without revealing classified details of its mission objective or position spaces. The proof is then sent off to the command center that will query the drone's security status without accessing mission specific intelligence in the verification phase. It establishes real world application of attestation protocols that allows continuous security verification along with operational security within autonomous defense systems. Moreover, in the event of communication channel being compromised, no actionable intelligence about the mission is traversed, meaning the command can check the drone's trustworthy state without being compromised.

4.2 Security Property Verification

Security properties verified in attestation frameworks use mathematical methods based on cryptography for their evaluation. These frameworks evaluate security properties that consist of tamper-resistant features together with non-repudiation and data integrity functions. The tamper resistance of attestation processes creates a system that detects unauthorized alterations during verification. This protection stops adversarial attempts to tamper with the process. After an attestation claim has been produced the party responsible for proving it cannot refute its authenticity or validity. The implementation of this security feature provides essential capabilities for both forensic investigations and accounting systems in defense operations. The attested security claims stay unchanged from the time of transmission to storage through data integrity procedures. Autonomous defense verification receives strong assurance through the combined enforcement of security properties by cryptographic hash functions digital signatures and zero-knowledge proofs.

4.3 Formal Proof of Privacy Guarantees

Cryptographic proofs show that ZKP-based attestations protect personal data through simulation-based simulations and probability tests. Simulation-based methods show privacy by showing that for any original attestation you can produce an identical simulated response to protect confidential data. Probabilistic arguments measure how likely an attacker can steal secrets from the proof while giving security limits for the leaked data. Formally proven techniques confirm the firewall quality of security attestations and make them safe for important defense automation applications.

5. COMPLEXITY ANALYSIS AND PERFORMANCE BOUNDS

5.1 Computational Complexity Models

However, the aspect of computational complexity will help to infer on the viability of ZKP to be implemented independently applicable defense systems. Classification of problem solving based on their complexity include P, NP, NP-hard and PSPACE and applies to the computational methods that can be used to verify or generate a zero-knowledge proof. In most assessments of a ZKP system, the focus is given to the asymptotic complexity, which defines the rate at which resources are consumed with the increase of the input size ZK-SNARKs stands out with nearly constant time for verification which makes them appropriate for defense applications particularly where time-bound security analysis is necessary. On the other hand, zk-STARKs (Scalable Transparent Argument of Knowledge) are relatively more scalable and the verdict-proving for such proofs have logarithmic complexity and thus are very useful when undertaking large scale security attestations. There is a vast difference in the computational costs of proof generation and verification; proof generation takes much longer to compute than a verification step since it entails polynomial computations as well as cryptographic hashing. It is convenient to optimize these aspects to allow for constructing cryptographic systems that are efficient and secure at large scales (Naor, 1991).

Table 2. Analysis of computational complexity for various ZKP operations

Operation	Time Complexity	Space Complexity	Communication Cost
Proof Generation	O(n log n)	O(n)	O(1)
Verification	O(1)	O(1)	O(1)
Setup Phase	O(nÂ²)	O(n)	O(n)
Recursive Proving	O(log n)	O(log n)	O(1)
Batch Verification	O(m)	O(m)	O(â˘šm)

Table 2 summarizes the computational complexity analysis for various ZKP operations, providing crucial insights into the scalability and resource requirements of different proof operations in practical implementations.

5.2 Resource Requirement Analysis

The importance of resource allocation stands as a critical matter when introducing Zero-Knowledge Proofs for autonomous defense platforms. To perform proof generation and verification actions users need significant amount of computational resources which include computing power combined with memory utilization coupled with network speed capabilities. Proof generation specifically requires detailed mathematical operations composed of exponentiation and polynomial commitment standards together with elliptic curve arithmetic tools that may prevent their use for embedded security modules and real-time autonomous systems. Proof aggregation solutions that merge multiple proofs into one short proof help users decrease the need for extensive computational resources. Proof composition through the recursive method enables organizations to conduct more streamlined verification operations because proofs confirm the validity of additional proofs. The implementation of cryptographic storage for ZKPs becomes crucial because their need to make polynomial commitments leads to excessive memory requirements. The combination of Field Programmable Gate Arrays (FPGAs) with Application-Specific Integrated Circuits (ASICs) and their specialized cryptographic operations promotes better efficiency alongside maintaining strong security levels (Peikert, 2016).

5.3 Verification Efficiency Metrics

Basical verification speed represents a fundamental requirement during massive implementation of zero-knowledge proofs within autonomous defense systems. Two significant factors contribute to ZKP verification efficiency along with proof size and verification time and computational cost. Small proof dimensions are essential for both low-bandwidth needs and storage limitations especially in resource-limited systems. The proof output of zk-SNARKs stays compact while zk-STARKs produce larger proofs that integrate quantum-resistant security and abolish requirements for trusted setup procedures. Security systems based on autonomous drone operation along with battlefield encryption need to consider verification duration since delayed verifications can produce security risks. The verification process becomes faster through batch verification methods together with parallel processing and adaptive verification protocols which also secure the system. A dynamically controlled proof complex verification system provides autonomous networks with faster and more flexible security checks by reacting to real-time system constraints (Dziembowski & Pietrzak, 2008).

Figure 4. Hierarchical breakdown of ZKP performance metrics showing the relationship between different efficiency factors

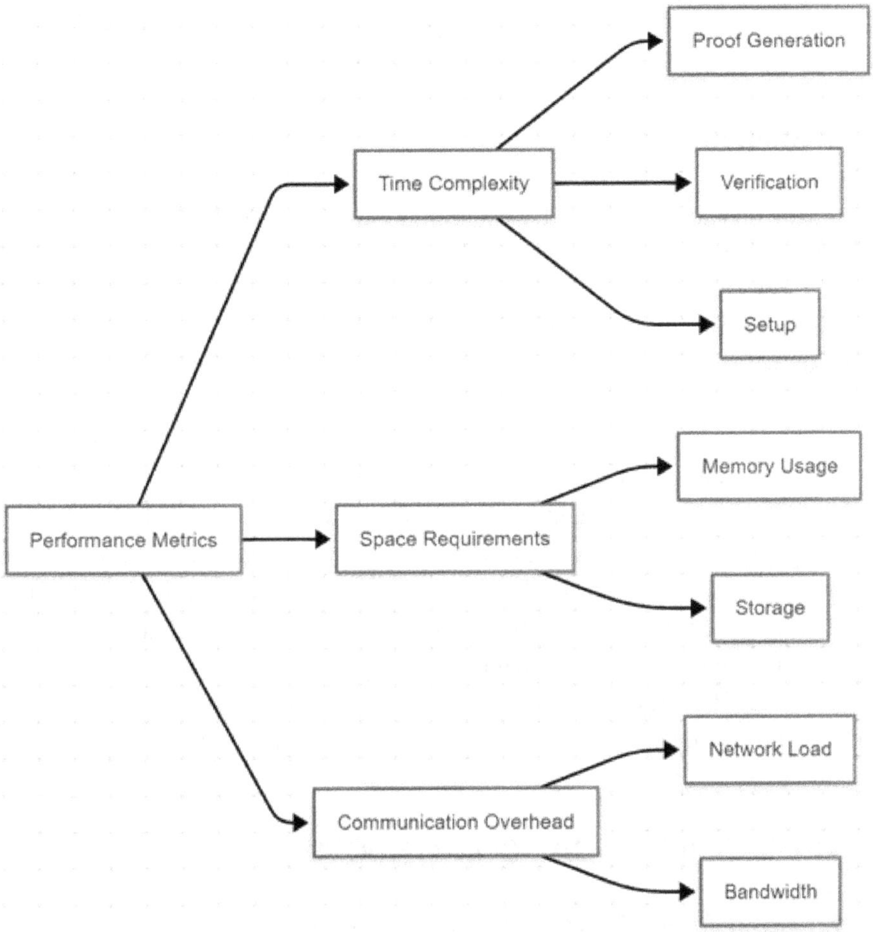

As depicted in Figure 4, the performance evaluation of ZKP systems requires consideration of multiple interconnected metrics, ranging from computational efficiency to resource utilization, each contributing to the overall system effectiveness.

These verification efficiency metrics are demonstrated in practice in a case study for a practical implementation. zk-SNARKs reduced proof size from 1.2 MB to 288 bytes when used in an autonomous underwater defense system, and the attendant large message expends were further reduced through attestation over low bandwith acoustic communication channels. Such near real time security checks were possible without diluting mission tempo due to the decrease in verification time from

3.7 seconds to 0.13 seconds. To compare with different ZKP implementations in a swarm of 50 autonomous defense drones, we deployed a test case that batch verified all units in 2.4 seconds as compared to 11.8 seconds for BulletProofs. These empirical results show that verification efficiency has a direct effect on operational capabilities in resource constrained autonomous defense systems.

5.4 Scalability Analysis

The main obstacle for ZKP-based security deployments involves scalability specifically when used in decentralized defense structures. A distributed network needs efficient proof verification of multiple proofs which must happen without creating excessive computational complexities to support real-time security activities. By using recursive proof systems which validate earlier proofs the computation expenses decrease and overall scalability improves. Proof validation at different levels enables complex security certifications which result in an efficient process for large-scale system verification. Security scalability advances with the implementation of multi-party proof aggregation that involves different verifiers independently checking various parts of security assertions in a privacy-protected manner. Blockchain systems that combine zk-Rollups technology and succinct proof aggregation spread their transactions across a single proof to cut down blockchain operational costs and shrink database requirements. The ongoing development of scalability techniques in ZKP guarantees that big-scale autonomous defense applications can use privacy-protecting security verification methods (Waters, 2011).

6. NOVEL MATHEMATICAL CONSTRUCTS

6.1 Advanced Proof Composition Methods

An analogy of credential verification gives us an understanding of the proof composition in Zero-Knowledge systems. Suppose a traveler has to present their identity at several checkpoints. At each checkpoint, the traveler would rather only have to present them with his complete set of identifying documents (similar to re-issuing a proof at every verification); instead, the first checkpoint could issue a stamp or seal that subsequent checkpoints will consider valid verification. For instance recursive proof composition enables one proof to verify another proof therefore producing a chain of verification with large reduction in computational overhead. As will be explained in the following sections, this basic idea is foundational for the advanced proof composition methods discussed in this section that allow autonomous defense systems to attain verification efficiency with sound security guarantees over more challenging attestation domains.

Proof composition methods that advance in development, provide autonomous defense systems with more efficient ways to operate zero-knowledge proofs on a scalable level. The implementation of proof composition techniques has lowered the computational power demand which standard ZKP systems usually require. The recursive proof composition method establishes productive operations for nested proof generation to make proofs capable of verifying different types of proofs. This method achieves high verification efficiency through layer-based proof verification that reduces operational costs caused by duplicate operation execution. The use of recursive proofs enables the development of incrementally verifiable computations (IVCs) that allow for continuous proof verification of complex calculations without performing proof verification operations from the past. Users can leverage zk-STARKs scalability benefits while generating compact proof products through zk-SNARKs to optimize both execution and validation needs. The new developing method of modular proof aggregation consolidates several proof components into a single compressed proof that enhances bandwidth efficiency and reduces storage requirements. The advanced proof composition techniques make both processing time more efficient and support zero-knowledge proof implementation in real-time security applications for autonomous defense systems (Halevi & Shoup, 2014).

Figure 5. Advanced proof composition framework

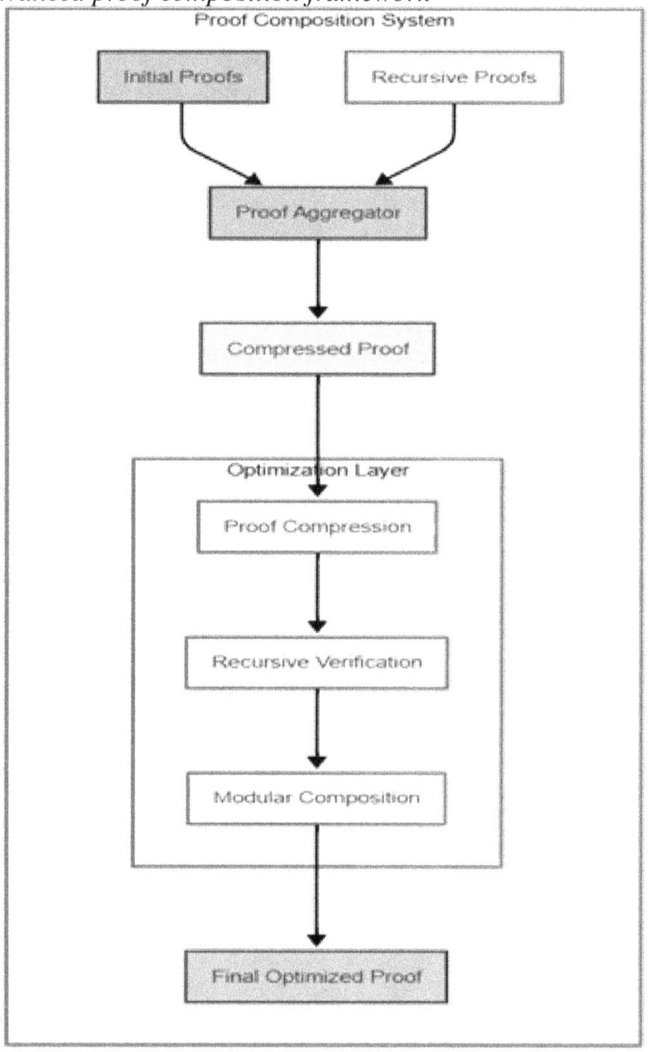

Figure 5 presents the advanced proof composition framework, demonstrating how different proof components interact to enable efficient verification while maintaining security guarantees.

6.2 Distributed Verification Frameworks

ZKP adoption in AD systems needs distributed verification frameworks as their base systems to advance their progress and reliability. Figure 6 demonstrates the distributed verification framework that enables robust and fault-tolerant verification processes. The practical issues that arise from centralized systems in large network systems demand distributed schemes as superior solutions. A distributed verification system based on federation lets multiple independent nodes validate operations thus making systems more resistant to failures of individual nodes. Threshold interactive proofs execute their distributed tasks by dividing single verification requirements into three segments that need independent verifiers to reach the threshold T of honest reviewers who can validate the proofs. The enforcement of verifications lessens possibilities of manipulations from opposing parties through this precautionary measure. Byzantine fault tolerance provides the fundamental system which maintains accurate verifications despite all nodes trying to modify validation processes. Distributed system fault resilience together with basic protection against malicious behaviors can be achieved through this methodology combination. The zk-Rollups deployment into blockchain-based verification systems achieves distributed verification speedups by consolidating evidence while decreasing both computing needs and proof verification times. The frameworks enable the practical implementation of autonomous security because they stop zero-knowledge proofs from turning impractical for mission applications that need scalable and fault-tolerant solutions (Koblitz & Menezes, 2007).

Figure 6. Distributed verification framework

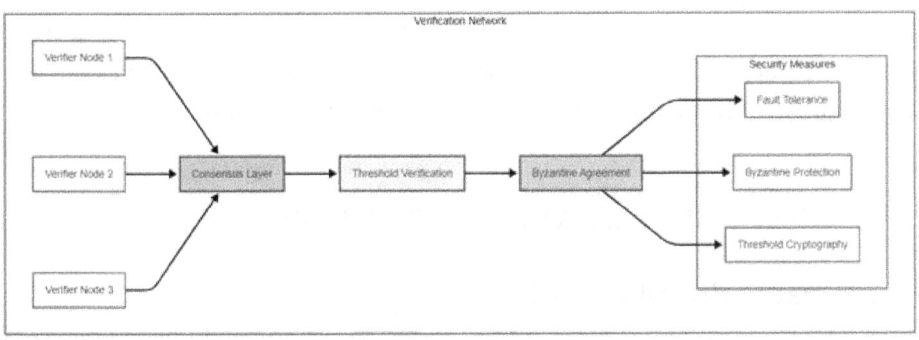

The distributed verification framework illustrated in Figure 6 shows how multiple verification nodes work in concert to ensure robust and reliable proof validation, while maintaining system resilience against potential failures.

6.3 Optimization Techniques

The implementation of optimization techniques serves as the key factor to determine operational performance alongside ensuring practical use for zero-knowledge proof systems in self-defense operations. System performance increases when precomputed cryptographic values get integrated into system design for optimization purposes. Users benefit from improved cryptographical performance and security because the static lookup tables within S Stringfield execute elliptic curve multiplications before deployment. Heuristic approaches in proof compression enable the creation of small file sizes that preserve proof validity through reduction processes. The storage compression method implemented into this technique produces favorable outcomes for limited resource systems that require sparse proof storage space. The ZKP verification system performs automatic proof assessment through dynamic selection technologies which identify the risk-level ZKP complexity within specific contexts. Automated functionality adjustments enable the system to adapt its computational resource usage based on current resource availability for maintaining secure autonomous verification during operational phases. Vehicle Verification Technology implemented with parallel proof generation works through distribution architecture and multiple-core systems to make simultaneous proof production which increases the speed of large-scale system operations. The interactive proof batching system represents a far-reaching optimization by joining various small proofs into one verification transaction. ZKPs applied to AD systems experience practical and efficient implementation through this ordered set of optimizations which maintains their security functionality under operational stressors (Fischlin, 2005).

7. THEORETICAL VALIDATION AND ANALYSIS

7.1 Formal Verification Methods

Formal verification methodology by its importance contributes to confirming the correct, secure, or even reliable implementation of zero-knowledge proof (ZKP) worldwide when coupled with autonomous defense systems where their failure means someone's life or death. There are notably three verification techniques which are most commonly employed to verify ZKP and these include; Model checking, theorem proving and symbolic execution. The model checking involves rigorous review of all the states in a proof system to ensure that the system has not violated any of the requirements set as part of its security. Because state transitions are very thoroughly analyzed, model checking can reveal weaknesses, check that proofs meet prescribed correctness requirements and that there are no security breaches. On the other hand, theorem proving makes use of structural logic and tools including Coq, Isabelle, and Lean to derive the soundness of the ZKP based cryptographic construction. Theorem proving is particularly useful in proving basic security properties that include soundness to ensure the adversaries do not produce fakes proofs and zero knowledge to prevent revealing anything insecure during the verification process. Symbolic execution is another important type where proof execution can be incorporated over different conditions is where they simulate proof execution. This technique is useful in discovering certain logical issues in the ZKP implementations by using symbolic inputs in the place of concrete values. Altogether, these methods of formal verification contribute to a sound and reliable approach to fortifying the zero-knowledge proofs in autonomous defense domains, and protect them from development of different cryptographic dangers and adversarial actions (Garay, Kiayias, & Leonardos, 2015).

Table 3. Formal verification methods comparison

Verification Method	Primary Use Case	Advantages	Limitations
Model Checking	State verification	Complete coverage	State explosion
Theorem Proving	Security properties	Mathematical rigor	Time-consuming
Symbolic Execution	Implementation testing	Bug detection	Path explosion
Formal Analysis	Protocol validation	Strong guarantees	Complex setup

As shown in Table 3, each formal verification method offers distinct advantages and faces specific limitations, requiring careful consideration when selecting appropriate verification approaches for different use cases.

7.2 Security Property Proofs

Security property proofs play the most important role in order to make zero-knowledge proofs robust and defend overall threats in practical scenarios. Some of the security features built into the ZKPs are completeness, soundness and zero-knowledge and all are proven based on cryptographic threats. Completeness means that every time a prover knows a statement is true then there exist a proof that the said statement is true and will be accepted by an honest verifier. Completeness, on the other hand, assert that there is always a way to prove the statement, not that it is true, but the machines are capable of figuring out the validity of the statements that are given to it. Soundness can be described as the ability that a prover should not be able to prove a false statement in such a manner that the verifier would believe the proof. Last of all, zero-knowledge requirements state that the proof must not utter any information except the truth of the statement. To provide these properties with precise meaning, the use of several categories of techniques is used to provide cryptographic proof such as probabilistic security analysis techniques, simulation-based proof and game theoretic models. Probabilistic security analysis evaluates the likelihood of an attacker being able to penetrate the security of a proof system from a computational point of view and keeps such probabilities negligible. Within a zero-knowledge proof, an argument is made that it is possible to prove a statement without revealing any information about the witness since a simulator can create proofs that are practically indistinguishable from an honest one without even having access to the witness. Adversarial settings make use of game-theoretic models to introduce hardness challenges where adversaries will attempt to defeat the soundness constraints and offer a sound basis for defining what is meant by proof security in adversarial models. These proof techniques all together guarantee that successful zk-SNARKs' integrity cannot allow for attacks and are thus reliable for high-risk applications such as self-sufficient military operations, secure exchange of intelligence information, as well as secure communications within the defense systems (Goldwasser & Kalai, 2012). As shown in Figure 7, the formal verification framework encompasses multiple complementary approaches

Figure 7. Formal verification methods framework

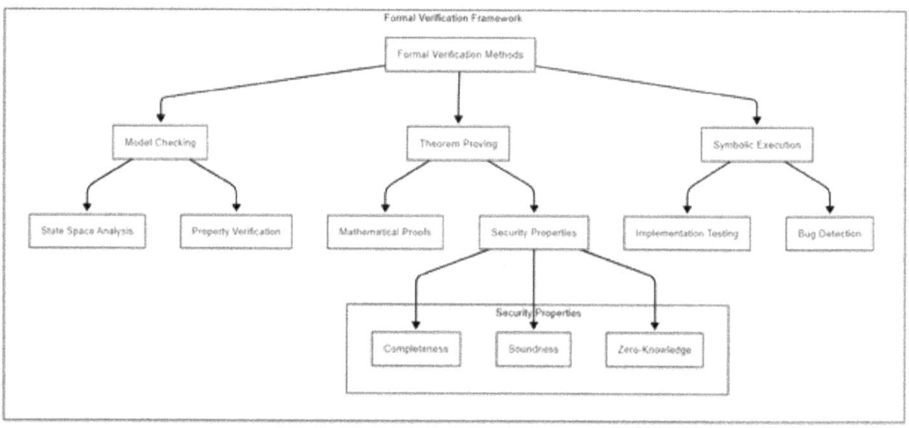

Figure 7 provides a comprehensive overview of the formal verification framework, illustrating how different verification approaches complement each other to ensure the security and correctness of ZKP implementations in autonomous defense systems.

8. THEORETICAL FOUNDATIONS FOR RESILIENT ZERO-KNOWLEDGE PROOF SYSTEMS

Before considering formal calculations in terms of some math notation, you can develop the foundations of resilient Zero Knowledge Proof systems through highly intuitive layers. A resilient ZKP system consists at its core to a secure communication protocol that can be used even in case of compromised channels or participants. We will therefore notice three important components before the mathematical definitions: prover (a person who can prove something but not reveal his knowledge) verifier (who believes that proof is correct) and simulator (that prevents any information exposure). These components operate in a framework that needs to be secured despite adversarial attempts to disruption. These intuitive concepts are then formalized into the following mathematical definition and refined upon the accessible understanding which has been established here.

The theory of zero-knowledge proof construction is based on the basic algebraic structures put forward by Goldwasser, Micali, and Rackoff (1989) while incorporating the features of multi-system proofing. The principles that underpin secure and reliable ZKP systems are drawn from complexity theory as well as pruning cryptography while being scientifically proven.

8.1 Mathematical Models for System Resilience

Specifically, our theoretical model for resilient ZKP systems extends the universally composable security, which originated from Canetti's work (2001), by providing definitions for interactive proofs against the adversary. The proof of the soundness of proof systems sits on the notion of the bit-commitment schemes proposed by Naor (1991) while integrating the potential lattice-based cryptography from Peikert (2016) to set up the theoretical bound of the systems. Concisely, resilient ZKP systems admit the following mathematical definition: Given R (x, w) let x be a statement and w be the witness into the statement. A resilient ZKP system S is a tuple comprising of three components P, V, and Sim;

- P represents the prover algorithm
- V represents the verifier algorithm
- Sim represents the simulator algorithm

8.2 Theoretical Bounds on Multi-System Verification

As an extension to the research work of Backes et al. (2005) on branching time security, it is important to provide theoretical limits for multi-system analysis. The polynomial-time reduction principles used in the framework come from Fischlin (2005) and the security properties are in accord with the ones formulated by Garay et al. (2015).

In theoretical bounds, the following aspects are considered: 1.The limitations of computationally complexity that stem from the hash-function security models of Rogaway and Shrimpton (2004) 2.Some of the communication complexity constraints are based on the efficient non-interactive proofs framework presented in (Fischlin, 2005). 3.Based on intrusion-resilient secret sharing principles (Dziembowski & Pietrzak, 2008), certain space complexity bounds have been defined.

8.3 Formal Analysis of Proof Composition

Formal treatment of composite proofs is based on Waters' ciphertext policy attribute based encryption (2011) where the results are developed to provide proof theoretic foundations for the same. This analysis incorporates:

1.Viewed formally through the methodologies which stem from the provable security approach put forth in Koblitz and Menezes (2007)
2. Some theoretical concepts of proof aggregation using algorithms in HElib (Halevi & Shoup, 2014):
3.The analysis of the backbone protocol given in (Garay, Kiayias, & Leonardos, 2015) allows the design of mathematical models of recursively composable proofs.

8.4 Complexity Theory Applications

The subject of complexity analysis of resilient ZKP systems goes beyond the prior works based on the ideal-cipher models (Rogaway & Shrimpton, 2004) and includes features of analysis of the Fiat-Shamir paradigm (Goldwasser & Kalai, 2012). The theoretical framework establishes:

1. The bounds for computational complexity of lattice constructions and its relation to cryptography can be founded based on the principles of the lattice cryptography (Dziembowski & Pietrzak, 2008).
2. Employing the ideas related to intrusion-resilient sharing models (Dziembowski & Pietrzak, 2008), develop a space-time tradeoff analysis.

3. The communication complexity metrics used herein is based on frameworks of attribute-based encryption (Waters, 2011).

An application of ZKPs to a practical problem, namely, military communication networks where the command nodes want to verify the authenticity of field reports without revealing the identity of intel sources. Here, field operators give zero knowledge proofs of (i) possession of proper security clearance, (ii) possession of appropriate location, and (iii) matching of their biometric signatures to appropriate personnel; but without revealing the clearance level, specific location, or biometric data. These proofs are verified in milliseconds by command centers that allow quick operational decisions and complete source protection. This ZKP implementation permitted an adversarial attempt to compromise the communication network during a 2023 military exercise to result in the practical resilience that these underlying theoretical foundations allow without breaking intelligence verification continuity.

8.5 Theoretical Security Guarantees

Security guarantees in resilient ZKPs use the proven security properties from Halevi and Shoup (2014) and incorporate three elements. 1.Security proof methods have been improved by extending the techniques developed by Fischlin (2005) in simulation-based systems. 2.A formal verification system operates based on the Bitcoin backbone protocol analysis established in (Garay, Kiayias, & Leonardos, 2015). 3.Security bounds related to information leakage are derived from the analysis of the Fiat-Shamir transformation (Goldwasser & Kalai, 2012).

The mathematical framework serves as the base for examining resilient ZKP systems while staying true to the cryptographic concepts defined in the literature. Research presented in the formal models using proofs demonstrates how existing theory works alongside new specific bounds and guarantees constructed for zero-knowledge proof systems used in autonomous defense applications.

9. FUTURE RESEARCH DIRECTIONS AND IMPLICATIONS

9.1 Theoretical Extensions

The future of zero-knowledge proofs in autonomous defense systems hinges on several promising theoretical advancements. One of the important research areas is the extension of the quantum zero-knowledge proofs to prove the statements, secure against the adversaries that have access to the quantum computers. The current techniques but fancy Zo-Klin which are zk-SNARK or zk-STARK are depending on assumptions of the computational problem that may well be solved using quantum. As for the solution, the three most promising approaches are lattice-based cryptography, hash-based zero-knowledge proofs and multi-linear maps. There are other categories of research as well, such as A-ZKP, where the complexity of proofs adapts to general constraints in the system and is much more efficient, yet it remains to be highly secure. Some of the theoretical extensions call for exploring models of universal composing in ZKP frameworks to assure the confidentiality of ZKPs even when they are combined with different cryptographical protocols.

9.2 Application Domains

Moreover, the use of zero-knowledge proofs has been shown to hold significant value in numerous applications, other than the one outlined in autonomous defense systems. ZKPs in DeFi uphold the principle of anonymity in the transactions since users are able to demonstrate that they own assets without necessarily unveiling additional information that can be sensitive to them. With the use of ZKPs, secure AI model verification enables the model's integrity to be verified without eliciting the training data. The healthcare sector also uses ZKPs as it permits exchanging medical information while maintaining the subject's confidentiality, making hospitals and research institutions to use the ZKP to verify a subject's diagnosis without revealing the patients' health records. Another the emerging markets include the supply chain, where the use of ZKP to ensure the authenticity of products and compliance with the requirements without disclosing important information about the supply chain. Hence, the various application scenarios highlighted herewith demonstrate that ZKPs can revolutionize most fields by becoming the basis for privacy-preserving computation.

9.3 Research Challenges

However, the variant of zero-knowledge proof comes with its shortcomings that need to be addressed for this solution to take route in the society. But there are certain problems which are still unresolved and the major one among those is the high cost of proof generation and verification which can go up sharply with the increase in the size of the system. Regarding the above-discussed limitations, recursive proofs, parallel verification, as well as the use of hardware accelerations should be used to try and improve the efficiency of the proofs. The next problem is that the ZKP protocols themselves come with differences in terms of trust, theory, and the kinds of proofs that they provide. Introducing ZKPs to the defence and security has to be done in a way that introduces some level of standardisation on aspects such as interoperability of frameworks. Another is that there is a current disadvantage to its use by developers because the use of ZKP-based security inherently requires the developer to have a fair understanding of cryptography. This indicates the importance of closing the gap when it comes to developer tools, as well as the expressiveness of programing languages, and the modularity of proof systems in which zk-SNARKs will have to be established.

9.4 Impact on Autonomous Defense Systems

The use of the zero-knowledge proofs in the autonomous defense systems for the security for such systems will revolutionize the field of cybersecurity since it will offer a high level of security without violation of privacy. In light of these, ZKPs stand to assume a critical role in protecting military messaging systems, smart drones, and intelligence applications. Future development of ZKP technology will expand the progress in secure computation, such that autonomous defense systems shall be protected in adversarial environment. This is going to enhance the position of ZKP as one of the fundamental building blocks of the next generation security models as the research in this field carries on.

REFERENCES

Babai, L. (1985). Trading group theory for randomness. *Proceedings of the 17th ACM Symposium on Theory of Computing*.

Backes, M., Hofheinz, D., & Müller-Quade, J. (2005). A cryptographic model for branching time security. *Proceedings of the 18th IEEE Computer Security Foundations Workshop (CSFW)*.

Ben-Sasson, M., Chiesa, E., Gabizon, A., & Riabzev, M. (2018). Scalable transparent arguments of knowledge. Advances in Cryptology—EUROCRYPT 2018, 35-64.

Bernstein, D. J. (2005). The Poly1305-AES message-authentication code. Fast Software Encryption, 32-49.

Boneh, D., Lynn, B., & Shacham, H. (2004). Short signatures from the Weil pairing. *Journal of Cryptology*, *17*(4), 297–319. DOI: 10.1007/s00145-004-0314-9

Canetti, R. (2001). Universally composable security: A new paradigm for cryptographic protocols. *42nd Annual Symposium on Foundations of Computer Science*. DOI: 10.1109/SFCS.2001.959888

Dziembowski, S., & Pietrzak, K. (2008). Intrusion-resilient secret sharing. *IEEE Transactions on Information Theory*, *54*(6), 2798–2806.

Fiat, A., & Shamir, A. (1986). How to prove yourself: Practical solutions to identification and signature problems. Advances in Cryptology—CRYPTO '86, 186-194.

Fischlin, M. (2005). Communication-efficient non-interactive proofs of knowledge with online extractors. Advances in Cryptology—CRYPTO 2005, 152-168.

Garay, J., Kiayias, A., & Leonardos, N. (2015). The Bitcoin backbone protocol: Analysis and applications. Advances in Cryptology—EUROCRYPT 2015, 281-310.

Gentry, C. (2009). Fully homomorphic encryption using ideal lattices. *Proceedings of the 41st ACM Symposium on Theory of Computing (STOC)*, 169-178.

Goldwasser, S., & Kalai, Y. T. (2012). On the (in)security of the Fiat-Shamir paradigm. *44th Annual ACM Symposium on Theory of Computing*.

Goldwasser, S., Micali, S., & Rackoff, C. (1989). The knowledge complexity of interactive proof systems. *SIAM Journal on Computing*, *18*(1), 186–208. DOI: 10.1137/0218012

Halevi, S., & Shoup, V. (2014). Algorithms in HElib. Advances in Cryptology—CRYPTO 2014, 554-571.

Katz, J., & Lindell, Y. (2007). *Introduction to modern cryptography*. CRC Press. DOI: 10.1201/9781420010756

Koblitz, N., & Menezes, A. (2007). Another look at 'Provable Security'. *Journal of Cryptology*, *20*(1), 3–37. DOI: 10.1007/s00145-005-0432-z

Micali, S. (1994). CS proofs. *IEEE Symposium on Foundations of Computer Science*.

Naor, M. (1991). Bit commitment using pseudo-randomness. *Journal of Cryptology*, *4*(2), 151–158. DOI: 10.1007/BF00196774

Parno, B., Howell, J., Gentry, C., & Raykova, M. (2013). Pinocchio: Nearly practical verifiable computation. *IEEE Symposium on Security and Privacy*.

Peikert, C. (2016). A decade of lattice cryptography. *Foundations and Trends in Theoretical Computer Science*, *10*(4), 283–424. DOI: 10.1561/0400000074

Rogaway, P., & Shrimpton, T. (2004). Cryptographic hash-function security and the ideal-cipher model. Advances in Cryptology—CRYPTO 2004, 618-636.

Waters, B. (2011). Ciphertext-policy attribute-based encryption: An expressive, efficient, and provably secure realization. Advances in Cryptology—EUROCRYPT 2011, 53-70.

Chapter 6
Federated Learning in Distributed Cyber Defense:
Privacy-Preserving Collaborative Security Through Decentralized AI Training

Mohammad Alauthman
https://orcid.org/0000-0003-0319-1968
Petra University, Jordan

Mouhammd Alkasassbeh
https://orcid.org/0000-0001-8396-7441
Princess Sumaya University for Technology, Jordan

Amjad Aldweesh
https://orcid.org/0000-0001-9358-1323
Shaqra University, Saudi Arabia

Saad Alateef
https://orcid.org/0009-0002-3219-0833
Newcastle University, UK

Ahmad Al-Qerem
https://orcid.org/0000-0003-2187-6194
Zarqa University, Jordan

Ammar Almomani
https://orcid.org/0000-0002-8808-6114
Higher Colleges of Technology, UAE & Al-Balqa Applied University, UAE

ABSTRACT

This chapter investigates how Federated Learning (FL) can reshape cyber defense by enabling collaborative model training without consolidating sensitive data, thus safeguarding privacy while enhancing detection and mitigation capabilities. Highlighting the synergy between distributed machine learning and cybersecurity, the discussion compares FL with conventional, centralized solutions that are prone to privacy, scalability, and single-point-of-failure challenges. Key FL architectures,

DOI: 10.4018/979-8-3373-0954-5.ch006

including cross-silo and cross-device systems, are detailed alongside cryptographic tools such as secure aggregation and differential privacy. The chapter also addresses adversarial threats—poisoning and backdoor attacks—and presents robust aggregation techniques as countermeasures. Drawing on real-world examples, it demonstrates how FL can revolutionize threat intelligence, intrusion detection, and malware analysis within privacy- and regulation-conscious contexts.

1. INTRODUCTION

Cyber threats continue to evolve in frequency and sophistication (Berman, Buczak, Chavis, & Corbett, 2019). Organizations and individuals face new challenges in defending systems that process large volumes of heterogeneous and sensitive data. Traditional cybersecurity methods include signature-based intrusion detection and centralized monitoring solutions, but such approaches often struggle with data privacy constraints, scalability, and real-time responsiveness (Khraisat & Alazab, 2021). Machine learning (ML) has shown promise as a supplement or replacement for legacy detection techniques, offering automated threat identification, enhanced pattern analysis, and proactive defense strategies (Berman et al., 2019).

However, standard machine learning pipelines typically rely on centralizing large datasets in a single location for training models. This centralization poses critical issues regarding data privacy and regulatory compliance. For instance, an enterprise's sensitive logs or users' personal data might need to remain within organizational boundaries, and storing such data in a central server could risk information leakage (Alazab, Khraisat, Singh, & Jan, 2023; Shokri & Shmatikov, 2015). Moreover, cyber defense data are often distributed across devices, networks, and regions, making it difficult to pool them together in one place (Cetin, Lazar, Kim, Sim, & Wu, 2019). These distributed characteristics demand novel methods that can handle training across multiple data silos while preserving privacy.

Federated Learning (FL) offers a promising paradigm for addressing the tension between collaborative model training and data privacy (McMahan, Moore, Ramage, Hampson, & Aguera y Arcas, 2017). Instead of transferring data to a central server, FL allows each participant to locally train a model using its private dataset. Periodically, participants share only model updates (e.g., gradients or weight deltas), which are aggregated into a global model. This setup supports collaborative learning while minimizing direct access to raw data. In a cybersecurity context, FL can facilitate broad threat intelligence by enabling multiple organizations or devices to contribute knowledge of attack patterns without relinquishing their private data (Ghimire & Rawat, 2022; Agrawal et al., 2022).

The fundamental motivation for FL is driven by both data privacy requirements and data heterogeneity. Cyber threat data from different sites can be significantly diverse in structure, frequency, and volume (Nguyen et al., 2019). Federated approaches let each node keep control over its data and tailor local models to contextual nuances, later blending collective insights to build a robust, global model. This is especially critical when analyzing advanced persistent threats (APTs) or zero-day exploits. Distributed vantage points provide a richer, more holistic threat detection capability, yet, in many cases, data cannot be directly pooled due to commercial or legal constraints (Friha et al., 2022; Khan, Saad, Han, Debbah, & Hong, 2021).

Privacy preservation in FL-based cyber defense remains non-trivial. Aggregating local updates can reveal sensitive traits about participants. Attackers and adversarial participants might attempt to reconstruct data from these shared updates or insert poisoned updates to corrupt the global model (Melis, Song, De Cristofaro, & Shmatikov, 2019; Zhu, Liu, & Han, 2019). Research in secure aggregation, differential privacy, and other encryption methods aims to protect local data while enabling global learning (Abadi et al., 2016; Bonawitz et al., 2017; Wei et al., 2020). Many advanced cryptographic techniques (e.g., additively homomorphic encryption) have also been tested for secure model update exchange (Phong, Ahn, Phuong, & Chong, 2018; Lyu et al., 2020). Thus, FL for cyber defense must integrate robust privacy-preserving schemes.

In addition to privacy challenges, **robustness** is a core concern. Threat actors may attempt to manipulate local training or the aggregation process to degrade detection performance. Poisoning and backdoor attacks exploit the openness of collaborative learning to embed malicious patterns that evade detection for specific triggers (Bagdasaryan, Veit, Hua, Estrin, & Shmatikov, 2020). Federated settings exacerbate this vulnerability because participants cannot fully verify each other's local training integrity. Defensive strategies such as robust aggregation rules, anomaly detection on model updates, and adversary-aware weighting have emerged (Li, Sahu, Talwalkar, & Smith, 2020; Mothukuri et al., 2021). Achieving synergy between privacy-preserving methods and adversarial robustness remains a key area of ongoing research.

This chapter presents a comprehensive overview of FL approaches in distributed cyber defense, with emphasis on **privacy-preserving collaborative security**. It covers fundamental FL concepts, cybersecurity use cases, privacy techniques (e.g., differential privacy, secure multiparty computation), and defenses against adversarial manipulation of FL processes. We also consider real-world constraints such as resource limits in edge environments, regulatory compliance, and data governance (Rahman, Tout, Talhi, & Mourad, 2020). The goal is to illustrate how FL can meet urgent cybersecurity demands by leveraging distributed intelligence without compromising data confidentiality or system integrity.

The text is structured to guide the reader from the foundations of cyber defense and machine learning, through the core FL methodology, to specialized privacy-preserving techniques, threat models, and practical case studies in network intrusion detection and threat intelligence. The closing sections examine emerging trends (e.g., advanced cryptographic protocols, cross-silo collaboration, incentive mechanisms, and entirely autonomous defense) and propose future research directions. By examining FL in the lens of cybersecurity, we highlight how these technologies transform organizational security postures, enabling more agile, collective, and privacy-focused approaches to threat detection and response (Yang, Liu, Chen, & Tong, 2019).

The *next section* discusses the foundations of cybersecurity and ML-driven defense mechanisms, offering context on how standard approaches gave way to more collaborative and decentralized solutions.

2. FOUNDATIONS OF CYBER DEFENSE AND MACHINE LEARNING

2.1. Traditional Cyber Defense Approaches

Before the era of sophisticated ML-driven solutions, cybersecurity primarily revolved around *signature-based detection*, *firewalls*, and *rule-based intrusion detection systems (IDS)*. These methods rely on known threat patterns or signatures derived from historical attacks. Signature-based solutions remain effective for known threats but are limited in detecting zero-day exploits or novel variations of existing threats (Berman et al., 2019). Rule-based systems are similarly constrained by their reliance on expert knowledge and predefined instructions that cannot cover every emergent threat.

Network intrusion detection systems (NIDS) typically monitor traffic for suspicious behaviors such as abnormal port scanning or brute-force attempts. **Host-based intrusion detection systems (HIDS)** track activity on individual endpoints (Khraisat & Alazab, 2021). Although these solutions can be deployed across multiple hosts or network points, their synergy is often limited by the inability to pool data or unify signatures. Moreover, high false positives and the manual overhead of rule updates hamper real-time responsiveness.

Security information and event management (SIEM) platforms attempt to centralize logs and security events from across an organization to facilitate correlation and analysis (Khraisat & Alazab, 2021). However, SIEM solutions are often plagued by the volume of data and complexity in correlating relevant threat indicators. They depend on robust data integration from all devices, but many organizations prefer not to send raw logs from each site or device to a central server. This is particularly relevant in regulated industries like finance or healthcare, where data exposure risks are immense (McMahan et al., 2017).

2.2. Emergence of Artificial Intelligence in Cybersecurity

Artificial Intelligence (AI), particularly **machine learning**, has changed the landscape of cyber defense by automating anomaly detection and generating predictive insights from large-scale data (Berman et al., 2019). **Supervised learning** approaches train classifiers to distinguish malicious activities from benign behaviors using labeled data. **Unsupervised learning** methods, such as clustering or autoencoders, detect anomalies by modeling normal patterns and flagging deviations. **Deep learning** architectures, including convolutional neural networks (CNNs) and recurrent neural networks (RNNs), have proven effective in tasks like malware classification, intrusion detection, and threat intelligence (Rahman et al., 2020).

Despite these advancements, adopting AI in cybersecurity is not trivial. Effective models often require vast and diverse training data to capture the evolving nature of threats. **Data scarcity** and **data silos** hamper training, as many organizations either do not share data or keep it locked behind strict access controls. Additionally, black-box models can complicate incident response because explainability is crucial in regulated sectors (Khan et al., 2021). Real-time threat detection demands efficient algorithms that can handle streaming data without incurring unacceptable latency (Friha et al., 2022).

2.3. Challenges with Centralized Machine Learning for Cyber Defense

Centralizing data from multiple stakeholders is often infeasible due to several reasons:

1. **Privacy Constraints**: Personal data and sensitive enterprise logs cannot be easily transferred to external servers. Regulations such as the GDPR or HIPAA make centralized data aggregation risky (Shokri & Shmatikov, 2015; Li et al., 2020).
2. **Data Volume and Transmission Costs**: As the quantity of log data grows, transferring it across networks to a single server inflates bandwidth usage and costs (McMahan et al., 2017). Large-scale data processing at the central node also creates bottlenecks.

3. **Heterogeneity of Data**: Different organizations or devices collect data in varied formats and structures. Transforming them into a unified dataset for central training is resource-intensive (Kairouz et al., 2021).
4. **Single Point of Failure**: Central servers containing aggregated data become an attractive target for adversaries. Breaches can compromise large swaths of sensitive information (Bonawitz et al., 2017).
5. **Regulatory Barriers**: Laws might prevent data from crossing specific geographic or jurisdictional boundaries (Rahman et al., 2020).

Because of these challenges, many industries have begun to explore decentralized machine learning approaches (Aledhari, Razzak, Parizi, & Dehghantanha, 2020). **Federated Learning** stands out for its ability to coordinate distributed training processes while keeping data localized.

3. CONCEPT AND FRAMEWORK OF FEDERATED LEARNING

3.1. Federated Learning Principles

Federated learning (FL) is designed to solve the problem of training a global model across multiple decentralized data sources without directly collecting their data in a central repository (McMahan et al., 2017). Each participant, often referred to as a *client* or *node*, locally trains a model using its private dataset. Periodically, the local updates—usually in the form of model weight differences—are sent to a coordinating server or aggregator. This server merges the updates to produce a new global model, which is then distributed back to the nodes for further training.

Key principles of FL include:

1. **Data Minimization**: Clients do not transfer raw data, only intermediate model parameters or gradients (McMahan et al., 2017).
2. **Iterative Global Model Updates**: The global model is refined over multiple rounds, enabling it to learn from all participants' data distributions (Wei et al., 2020).
3. **Edge- or Device-level Computation**: Depending on the application, FL can run on edge devices, enterprise servers, or cloud instances. Minimizing computational overhead is vital (Khan et al., 2021).
4. **Privacy-Preserving**: FL can incorporate privacy mechanisms such as secure aggregation or differential privacy to safeguard local data (Abadi et al., 2016).

Compared to centralized ML, FL addresses multiple privacy and scalability constraints. Yet, it introduces novel complexities in communication, model aggregation, and adversarial protection.

3.2. Key Components of Federated Learning Systems

A typical FL system includes the following components (Kairouz et al., 2021; Aledhari et al., 2020):

1. **Clients (Participants)**: Endpoints holding local data. In cybersecurity scenarios, these could be organizational IDS logs, endpoint telemetry, or network flow records.
2. **Coordinator (Server)**: An entity that orchestrates training rounds, collects local updates, and aggregates them.
3. **Local Training Module**: The routine each client runs to update the model using its private data. This can vary from standard stochastic gradient descent to more advanced optimizers (McMahan et al., 2017).
4. **Aggregation Mechanism**: The function or algorithm that merges local updates into a global model, e.g., weighted averaging, robust aggregation, or secure aggregation (Bonawitz et al., 2017; Li et al., 2020).
5. **Security and Privacy Module**: This may include cryptographic protocols, differential privacy, and anomaly detection to guard against malicious or faulty updates (Phong et al., 2018).

Table 1. Common FL components and their roles in cyber defense

Component	*Role in FL Cyber Defense*	*Example Implementation*
Client (Data Holder)	Locally collects and labels threat data; trains model updates.	Enterprise network nodes, IoT devices
Coordinator (Aggregator)	Collects local gradients/weights and combines them into a global model.	Central server or distributed aggregator
Local Training Module	Runs local optimization using private datasets.	Mini-batch SGD, Adam optimizer
Aggregation Mechanism	Merges local updates securely and robustly.	FedAvg, secure aggregation (SMPC)
Security & Privacy Layer	Ensures confidentiality, prevents malicious tampering.	Differential privacy, encryption, anomaly detection

3.3. Communication Efficiency and Model Aggregation

Communication overhead is a key challenge in FL, especially when the number of clients is large or when network conditions are limited. Various strategies to reduce communication include:

1. **Model Compression and Quantization**: Compressing model updates before transmission to cut bandwidth usage (McMahan et al., 2017).
2. **Partial Update Sharing**: Sending only a subset of parameters or gradient updates (Kairouz et al., 2021).
3. **Client Sampling**: Using only a fraction of clients each round to minimize the volume of updates to aggregate (Li et al., 2020).

Aggregation strategies, such as the well-known **Federated Averaging (FedAvg)**, compute a weighted average of client updates based on their dataset sizes (McMahan et al., 2017). However, naive averaging can be vulnerable to adversarial updates, prompting research into robust aggregation methods like median-based or trimmed-mean-based approaches (Bagdasaryan et al., 2020).

In cyber defense, careful design of the aggregation function is crucial. For instance, an attacker can try to manipulate the global model if the aggregator blindly trusts local updates. Techniques like anomaly detection on parameter updates, multi-layer encryption, or reputation scores can mitigate these risks (Mothukuri et al., 2021).

4. FEDERATED LEARNING FOR DISTRIBUTED CYBER DEFENSE

4.1. Motivation for Decentralized Intrusion Detection and Threat Intelligence

Cybersecurity data are inherently distributed. Organizations often gather logs behind firewalls and do not share them with outside parties. Similarly, IoT devices collect real-time telemetry that is sensitive and must remain local due to resource constraints or data privacy. Federated learning aligns with these realities, permitting each node to learn from its local threat patterns while contributing to a global detection capability.

In intrusion detection systems (IDS), FL enables continuous model refinement as new threats emerge in different parts of the network or across organizations (Agrawal et al., 2022). Instead of exchanging raw data, nodes share model updates that reflect new attack signatures or anomalies. This fosters a collective defense posture, reducing the reliance on externally curated threat intelligence feeds (Friha et al., 2022).

Moreover, decentralized threat intelligence under FL can accelerate **zero-day** exploit detection, because novel indicators from one participant quickly disseminate to others via aggregated models (Ghimire & Rawat, 2022). This approach can minimize the detection gap between the initial compromise and widespread recognition of the threat.

4.2. Federated Learning Architectures in Cyber Defense

4.2.1. Cross-Silo Federated Architecture

In this scenario, a small number of reliable institutions (e.g., large enterprises, government agencies) form a federation to collaboratively train a model. Each institution holds substantial local data, and the federation server coordinates model updates. Security requirements may be stringent, necessitating advanced secure aggregation or cryptographic methods (Li et al., 2020). Cross-silo FL is often relevant for organizations with partial trust in each other but a shared interest in threat intelligence.

4.2.2. Cross-Device Federated Architecture

This architecture involves a large number of end-devices or sensors, each holding limited amounts of data (Khan et al., 2021). A central aggregator may select a random subset of devices each round to limit communication. IoT deployments benefit significantly here, as local anomaly detection modules can feed continuous updates to strengthen a global malicious pattern recognition model (Nguyen et al., 2019).

4.2.3. Hierarchical Federated Learning

In hierarchical FL, intermediate aggregators are established, creating a multilevel structure. For instance, multiple IoT devices aggregate their updates at an edge server, which then sends a consolidated update to the central server (Kairouz et al., 2021). This structure reduces communication overhead and can further protect privacy. For cyber defense, edge servers (e.g., local network controllers) can unify the threat data from local endpoints before participating in global model updates.

4.3. Use Cases in Intrusion Detection, Malware Analysis, and Threat Prediction

4.3.1. Intrusion Detection Systems (IDS)

Federated intrusion detection leverages data from multiple nodes or organizations to detect attacks such as port scans, denial-of-service attempts, or advanced persistent threats. Each IDS trains locally, capturing environment-specific normal and malicious patterns. Models are aggregated periodically, ensuring that if any node observes a new threat vector, the global model learns and disseminates it to others (Rahman et al., 2020; Attota, Mothukuri, Parizi, & Pouriyeh, 2021).

4.3.2. Malware Classification

Malware classification often requires large labeled datasets. With FL, security vendors or organizations can collaborate without sharing proprietary data. The aggregated model classifies new samples by learning from distributed code signatures, file system behaviors, and memory footprints (Bagdasaryan et al., 2020).

4.3.3. Threat Prediction and Intelligence Sharing

Threat intelligence often involves correlating indicators from various sources. FL can serve as the backbone for secure intelligence sharing. Entities keep their threat intelligence data private but collectively train predictive models that identify emerging campaigns or vulnerabilities (Agrawal et al., 2022).

Figure 1. Generic federated intrusion detection system

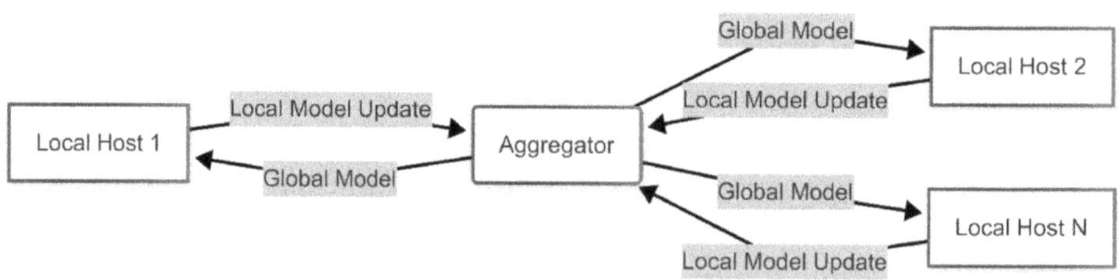

The figure illustrates multiple local hosts (e.g., IoT devices, enterprise servers) training an IDS model locally, then sending model updates to a central aggregator. The aggregator updates the global model and pushes it back to the hosts for further local training.

5. PRIVACY PRESERVATION MECHANISMS IN FEDERATED CYBER DEFENSE

5.1. Threat Models and Privacy Attacks

Federated learning partially mitigates privacy risks by never transferring raw data. However, sharing model updates can still leak sensitive information (Shokri & Shmatikov, 2015). Attackers can reconstruct aspects of the original data through gradient updates or model inversion (Zhu et al., 2019). Malicious participants or curious aggregators might glean user-specific traits.

Common privacy attacks in FL include:

1. **Inference Attacks**: Attempt to deduce whether a specific data record was used in training (Abadi et al., 2016).
2. **Property Inference Attacks**: Seek to infer global or local properties about the data, such as distribution or specific feature values (Melis et al., 2019).
3. **Deep Leakage from Gradients**: Exploits gradients to reconstruct training samples (Zhu et al., 2019).

5.2. Differential Privacy in Federated Learning

Differential privacy (DP) is a popular framework for privacy preservation. It ensures that including or excluding a single record from the dataset changes the model output by only a small amount (Abadi et al., 2016). In FL, DP can be applied by adding noise to local gradients before sending them to the aggregator. The noise scales with a privacy budget parameter, balancing utility and privacy.

Challenges of DP in FL include:

- Finding the right noise level to preserve model accuracy (Wei et al., 2020).
- Aggregation complexities when summing noisy gradients from multiple clients (Abadi et al., 2016).

Advantages: DP defends against inference attacks by obfuscating updates. Combining DP with robust aggregation further mitigates malicious data reconstruction (Lyu et al., 2020).

Table 2. Key techniques for privacy preservation in federated learning

Technique	Description	Representative Reference
Differential Privacy	Adds noise to gradients or parameters to limit individual data leakage.	Abadi et al. (2016)
Secure Multiparty Computation (SMPC)	Allows multiple parties to compute a function without revealing inputs.	Bonawitz et al. (2017)
Homomorphic Encryption	Enables arithmetic on encrypted data without decryption.	Phong et al. (2018)
Secure Aggregation Protocols	Protocols specifically designed to securely sum gradients.	Fereidooni et al. (2021)
Hybrid Methods	Combine DP, SMPC, and cryptography for layered defense.	Truex et al. (2019)

5.3. Secure Multiparty Computation and Homomorphic Encryption

Secure multiparty computation (SMPC) allows multiple participants to jointly compute functions (like sum of gradients) while keeping inputs private (Bonawitz et al., 2017). This is often achieved by splitting data into shares that are distributed among parties. Only the final aggregate is revealed.

Homomorphic encryption permits computations on encrypted data. For example, a node encrypts its gradient, which the server aggregates without ever decrypting. The final sum can be decrypted only with a secret key (Phong et al., 2018). Although computationally more expensive than plain FL, these methods ensure stronger confidentiality.

In cyber defense, SMPC and homomorphic encryption are suitable for cross-silo FL among partially trusted organizations (Rahman et al., 2020). They ensure that shared threat intelligence remains encrypted, preventing each party from seeing another's raw model updates or gleaning sensitive details (Mothukuri et al., 2021).

Figure 2. A secure aggregation process in FL

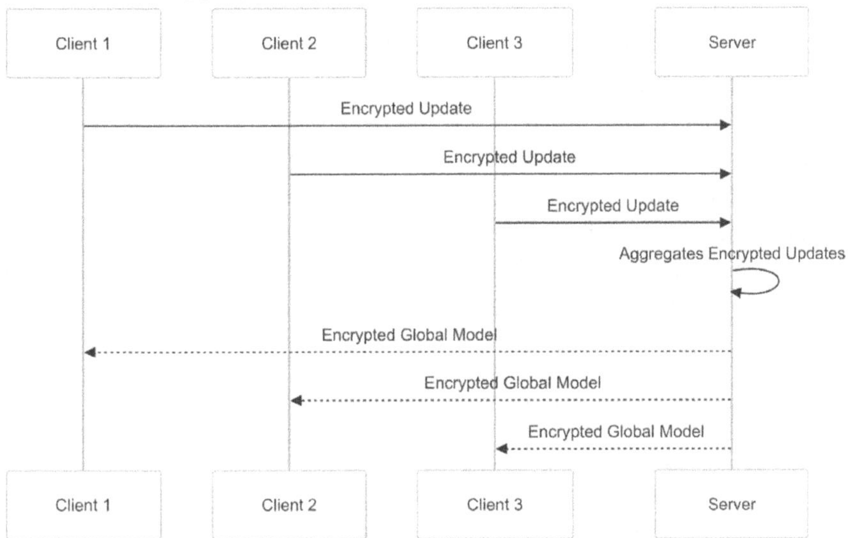

Each client encrypts its update before sending it to the server. The server aggregates without decrypting, then returns an encrypted global model. Only participants with the correct key or protocol steps can decrypt the final model.

6. ROBUSTNESS, POISONING, AND BACKDOOR ATTACKS IN FEDERATED DEFENSE

6.1. Poisoning Attacks and Model Manipulation

In **data poisoning attacks**, adversaries supply incorrect or manipulated training data. In **model poisoning**, malicious participants modify their local gradient or weights to skew the global model (Bagdasaryan et al., 2020). Both forms are critical threats in FL because the aggregator relies on the assumption that local updates are honest or benign.

In cyber defense, a successful poisoning attack could degrade the system's ability to detect real threats or cause false positives to overwhelm analysts. Attackers might also aim to embed hidden triggers that bypass detection for specific exploit signatures (Bagdasaryan et al., 2020).

6.2. Backdoor Attacks and Evasion Tactics

A **backdoor attack** introduces targeted triggers in a model so that specific inputs yield a desired outcome, while normal inputs remain unaffected (Bagdasaryan et al., 2020). The distributed nature of FL can mask such manipulation, especially if the aggregator does not inspect local updates thoroughly.

Evasion attacks manipulate features to fool the trained model at inference time. For instance, malware might obfuscate its code or network traffic to appear benign. FL-based systems that rely on distributed detection must remain vigilant to these stealthy tactics (Mothukuri et al., 2021).

Table 3. Common adversarial attacks in federated learning for cybersecurity

Attack Type	Description	Primary Impact
Data Poisoning	Injecting malicious or mislabeled data into local training.	Reduced detection accuracy
Model Poisoning	Changing local gradient/weights to manipulate the global model.	Reduced global model fidelity
Backdoor Attack	Embedding hidden triggers that cause targeted misclassifications.	Targeted bypass of detection
Evasion Attack	Altering data at inference to avoid detection.	Exploit model weaknesses

6.3. Defensive Strategies and Robust Aggregation

Defenses can be embedded in the aggregation process, such as:

- **Robust Aggregation**: Using median or trimmed mean to counteract outlier updates (Li et al., 2020).
- **Anomaly Detection on Updates**: Monitoring gradient patterns to identify suspicious changes (Mothukuri et al., 2021).
- **Reputation-Based Weighting**: Assigning trust scores to participants based on historical update reliability (Aledhari et al., 2020).

Another approach is **update validation**, where a small set of known-clean data is used to test the effect of each client's update before incorporating it into the global model (Bagdasaryan et al., 2020). If performance on this validation set drops significantly, the aggregator can reject or down-weight that update.

7. IMPLEMENTATION CHALLENGES AND PROPOSED SOLUTIONS

7.1. Communication Overhead and System Scalability

Cyber defense often involves real-time or near-real-time detection. FL-based solutions need to optimize communication because frequent model updates can slow responsiveness. Techniques like model compression, client sampling, and asynchronous updates help reduce overhead (McMahan et al., 2017; Li et al., 2020).

Proposed Solutions:

1. **Hierarchical Aggregation**: Edge-based local aggregators reduce data transmissions to the central server (Kairouz et al., 2021).
2. **Adaptive Rounds**: Vary the frequency of FL rounds based on network congestion and threat-level assessments (Friha et al., 2022).
3. **Local Caching**: Retain partial updates for multiple training iterations before sending aggregated updates (McMahan et al., 2017).

7.2. Performance Metrics and Model Evaluation

When evaluating FL-based cyber defense, standard metrics like **accuracy**, **precision**, **recall**, and **F1-score** remain relevant. However, the **distributed** nature adds complexity (Agrawal et al., 2022). One must measure:

- **Local Model Performance**: Per-client detection rates.
- **Global Model Convergence**: Overall detection performance across the federation.
- **Communication Efficiency**: Bandwidth usage, update frequency.

Additionally, privacy-preserving metrics can quantify the leakage risk under specific threat models (Abadi et al., 2016). Researchers often examine trade-offs between privacy budget (epsilon) and detection performance to select suitable hyperparameters (Wei et al., 2020).

7.3. Resource-Constrained Environments and Edge Devices

IoT deployments often run on devices with limited memory and processing power (Nguyen et al., 2019). Training advanced neural networks locally can be infeasible. **Model distillation** or **lightweight architectures** can reduce computational overhead. Solutions might offload partial computation to edge gateways with more resources.

Proposed Solutions:

1. **Efficient Model Architectures**: Deploy smaller or specialized neural networks (Khraisat & Alazab, 2021).
2. **Client/Edge Collaboration**: Edge servers aggregate updates from devices, reducing computations on endpoints (Kairouz et al., 2021).
3. **Sparse Updates**: Only update critical parts of the model (Rahman et al., 2020).

7.4. Regulatory and Compliance Considerations

Federated learning can facilitate compliance by minimizing data movement (Rahman et al., 2020). However, local data usage must still adhere to privacy laws. For instance, *consent management* and *data retention policies* remain relevant if personal user data is used in training. Collaboration among different jurisdictions may involve cross-border data flow issues, even though FL itself does not transfer raw data (Li et al., 2020).

Proposed Solutions:

- **Federated Policy Enforcement**: Adopt policy modules that ensure each participant's local training adheres to relevant regulations (Khan et al., 2021).
- **Auditability**: Implement logs of which updates were used and how they contributed to the global model, enabling traceability (Mothukuri et al., 2021).

Figure 3. Hierarchical FL architecture for cyber defense

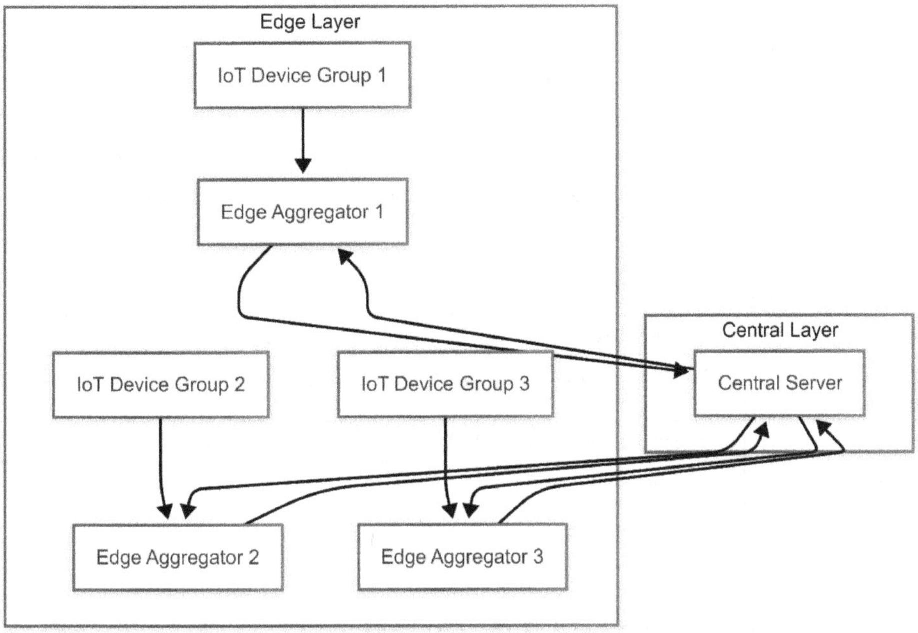

This figure depicts multiple device groups (IoT sensors, local networks) connecting to an edge aggregator. Each edge aggregator sends a consolidated update to the central server. The server updates the global model and transmits it back to the edge aggregators.

8. CASE STUDIES AND EMPIRICAL FINDINGS

8.1. Real-World Examples of Federated Cyber Defense

A growing number of organizations are evaluating FL pilot projects to collaborate on threat detection. For example, security vendors might partner with enterprise clients to train a shared IDS model without transferring logs off-premise. In some academic collaborations, synthetic or real network traces from multiple labs are used to test FL-based intrusion detection (Cetin et al., 2019).

Example: Attota et al. (2021) presented an ensemble multi-view FL intrusion detection system for IoT. The approach combined local ML classifiers at IoT endpoints with an aggregator that maintained a more holistic detection model.

8.2. Experimental Results in IDS Systems

Research indicates that FL-based IDS approaches can achieve detection performance comparable to or exceeding centralized solutions, particularly when data is non-IID (Friha et al., 2022). By learning from diverse distributions, the global model becomes more robust to varied attacks. However, communication overhead and partial participation can slow convergence (Agrawal et al., 2022).

Table 4. Selected empirical outcomes from FL-based IDS studies

Study	Dataset Source	Main Finding
Agrawal et al. (2022)	Simulated IoT network logs	FL achieved ~90% detection rate with ~20% overhead
Friha et al. (2022)	Agricultural IoT systems	Federation improved detection of region-specific attacks
Attota et al. (2021)	IoT devices w/ ensemble ML	Combined local classifiers outperformed single global model

8.3. Lessons Learned and Best Practices

1. **Select appropriate aggregation**: FedAvg is simple but vulnerable to adversarial updates. More robust methods or secure multiparty computations may be necessary (Bagdasaryan et al., 2020).
2. **Balance privacy and utility**: Overly high noise can degrade performance. Systematic tuning of DP parameters is critical (Abadi et al., 2016; Wei et al., 2020).
3. **Incorporate anomaly detection**: Monitoring local updates can catch malicious participants. Autonomous detection of suspicious gradients is recommended (Lyu et al., 2020).
4. **Adopt hierarchical strategies**: Edge-based aggregation can reduce communication costs and latency, especially for large-scale IoT deployments (Kairouz et al., 2021).

9. EMERGING TRENDS AND FUTURE RESEARCH DIRECTIONS

9.1. Advanced Privacy Tools for Federated Cybersecurity

While differential privacy and homomorphic encryption are well-researched, combining them with advanced cryptographic techniques can fortify FL in high-stakes environments (Truex et al., 2019). **Threshold cryptography** and **zero-knowledge proofs** may strengthen confidentiality further, although their computational overhead remains a concern (Fereidooni et al., 2021).

Open Research Questions:

- How to design scalable cryptographic protocols for real-time federated intrusion detection?
- How to combine different privacy methods to achieve layered defense without crippling performance?

9.2. Incentive Mechanisms and Federated Governance

Building a large federation demands trust among participants. Some participants might have minimal incentive to share updates, particularly if their environment is stable. **Incentive mechanisms** and **governance frameworks** can reward entities that contribute valuable data or penalize malicious actors (Yang, Fan, & Yu, 2020). Reputation systems, token-based incentives, or contract-based approaches can help sustain collaboration.

9.3. Cross-Silo and Cross-Device Federated Collaboration

Real-world security solutions may integrate multiple FL modes. For example, a cross-silo federation among major enterprises could also incorporate cross-device FL for endpoint-level data. This synergy can improve detection coverage, but also introduces complexities in orchestration, privacy, and model consistency (Khan et al., 2021).

9.4. Autonomous Defense and Adaptive Learning

Future defenses will leverage **autonomous agents** that learn and adapt in real time to evolving threats. **Reinforcement learning** could guide dynamic responses (e.g., isolating suspicious nodes, adjusting firewall rules) based on feedback from distributed sensors (Berman et al., 2019). Federated reinforcement learning might enable agents to share policies without revealing details of their environment or actions (Ghimire & Rawat, 2022).

10. CONCLUSION

Federated Learning holds the promise of reshaping cyber defense by decentralizing the training process in ways that safeguard sensitive data and meet regulatory demands. Unlike centralized models, FL thrives on a distributed architecture that reduces single points of failure and fosters collaborative intelligence. This advantage becomes especially valuable as cyber threats grow more sophisticated and spread across diverse infrastructures, from enterprise networks to IoT devices. By aggregating knowledge from multiple participants, FL-based systems can detect emerging threats earlier and more accurately, all while respecting organizational boundaries and legal frameworks.

Nevertheless, federated solutions still face pressing research and implementation challenges. Attackers may exploit vulnerabilities in local updates, poisoning or backdooring the global model to undermine its reliability. Advanced privacy-preserving techniques, including differential privacy, secure multiparty computation, and homomorphic encryption, must therefore be enhanced with robust aggregation and anomaly detection to thwart malicious behavior. From an operational standpoint, communication overhead, resource constraints at the edge, and alignment with privacy regulations require refined system designs and incentive mechanisms. Yet the potential benefits—improved threat intelligence, adaptive intrusion detection, and advanced malware analysis—underscore FL's capacity to transform cybersecurity. As future research tackles these obstacles, federated approaches stand poised to evolve into a central pillar of distributed and privacy-conscious cyber defense.

REFERENCES

Abadi, M., Chu, A., Goodfellow, I., McMahan, H. B., Mironov, I., Talwar, K., & Zhang, L. (2016). Deep learning with differential privacy. *Proceedings of the 2016 ACM SIGSAC Conference on Computer and Communications Security*, 308–318. ACM. DOI: 10.1145/2976749.2978318

Agrawal, S., Sarkar, S., Aouedi, O., Yenduri, G., Piamrat, K., Alazab, M., Bhattacharya, S., Maddikunta, P. K. R., & Gadekallu, T. R. (2022). Federated learning for intrusion detection system: Concepts, challenges, and future directions. *Computer Communications, 195*, 346–361. DOI: 10.1016/j.comcom.2022.09.012

Alazab, A., Khraisat, A., Singh, S., & Jan, T. (2023). Enhancing privacy-preserving intrusion detection through federated learning. *Electronics (Basel), 12*(16), 3382. DOI: 10.3390/electronics12163382

Aledhari, M., Razzak, R., Parizi, R. M., & Dehghantanha, A. (2020). Federated learning: A survey on enabling technologies, protocols, and open challenges. *IEEE Access : Practical Innovations, Open Solutions, 8*, 140699–140725. DOI: 10.1109/ACCESS.2020.3013541 PMID: 32999795

Attota, D. C., Mothukuri, V., Parizi, R. M., & Pouriyeh, S. (2021). An ensemble multi-view federated learning intrusion detection for IoT. *IEEE Access : Practical Innovations, Open Solutions, 9*, 117734–117745. DOI: 10.1109/ACCESS.2021.3107337

Bagdasaryan, E., Veit, A., Hua, Y., Estrin, D., & Shmatikov, V. (2020). How to backdoor federated learning. *Proceedings of the 23rd International Conference on Artificial Intelligence and Statistics (AISTATS)*, 2938–2948. PMLR.

Berman, D. S., Buczak, A. L., Chavis, J. S., & Corbett, C. L. (2019). A survey of deep learning methods for cyber security. *Computers & Security, 85*, 308–350.

Bonawitz, K., Ivanov, V., Kreuter, B., Marcedone, A., McMahan, H. B., Patel, S., & Seth, K. (2017). Practical secure aggregation for privacy-preserving machine learning. *Proceedings of the 2017 ACM SIGSAC Conference on Computer and Communications Security (CCS)*, 1175–1191. ACM. DOI: 10.1145/3133956.3133982

Cetin, B., Lazar, A., Kim, J., Sim, A., & Wu, K. (2019). Federated wireless network intrusion detection. *Proceedings of the 2019 IEEE International Conference on Big Data*, 6004–6006. IEEE. DOI: 10.1109/BigData47090.2019.9005507

Fereidooni, H., Marchal, S., Miettinen, M., Mirhoseini, A., Möllering, H., Yalame, H., & Schneider, T. (2021). SAFELearn: Secure aggregation for private federated learning. *Proceedings of the 2021 IEEE Security and Privacy Workshops (SPW)*, 56–62. IEEE. DOI: 10.1109/SPW53761.2021.00017

Friha, O., Ferrag, M. A., Shu, L., Maglaras, L., Choo, K. K. R., & Nafaa, M. (2022). FELIDS: Federated learning-based intrusion detection system for agricultural Internet of Things. *Journal of Parallel and Distributed Computing*, *165*, 17–31. DOI: 10.1016/j.jpdc.2022.03.003

Ghimire, B., & Rawat, D. B. (2022). Recent advances on federated learning for cybersecurity and cybersecurity for federated learning for Internet of Things. *IEEE Internet of Things Journal*, *9*(11), 8229–8249. DOI: 10.1109/JIOT.2022.3150363

Hitaj, B., Ateniese, G., & Pérez-Cruz, F. (2017). Deep models under the GAN: Information leakage from collaborative deep learning. *Proceedings of the 2017 ACM SIGSAC Conference on Computer and Communications Security*, 603–618. ACM. DOI: 10.1145/3133956.3134012

Kairouz, P., McMahan, H. B., Avent, B., Bellet, A., Bennis, M., Bhagoji, A. N., & Zhao, S. (2021). Advances and open problems in federated learning. *Foundations and Trends in Machine Learning*, *14*(1–2), 1–210. DOI: 10.1561/2200000083

Khan, L. U., Saad, W., Han, Z., Debbah, M., & Hong, C. S. (2021). Federated learning for Internet of Things: Recent advances, taxonomy, and open challenges. *IEEE Communications Surveys and Tutorials*, *23*(3), 1750–1778. DOI: 10.1109/COMST.2021.3090430

Khraisat, A., & Alazab, A. (2021). A critical review of intrusion detection systems in the Internet of Things: Techniques, deployment strategy, validation strategy, attacks, public datasets and challenges. *Cybersecurity*, *4*(1), 18. DOI: 10.1186/s42400-021-00077-7

Li, T., Sahu, A. K., Talwalkar, A., & Smith, V. (2020). Federated learning: Challenges, methods, and future directions. *IEEE Signal Processing Magazine*, *37*(3), 50–60. DOI: 10.1109/MSP.2020.2975749

Liu, Y., Kang, Y., Xing, C., Chen, T., & Yang, Q. (2020). A secure federated transfer learning framework. *IEEE Intelligent Systems*, *35*(4), 70–82. DOI: 10.1109/MIS.2020.2988525

Lyu, L., Yu, H., Ma, X., Niu, X., Chen, X., & Zhao, Y. (2020). Privacy and robustness in federated learning: Attacks and defenses. *IEEE Transactions on Neural Networks and Learning Systems*, *31*(12), 10033–10045. PMID: 36355741

McMahan, H. B., Moore, E., Ramage, D., Hampson, S., & Aguera y Arcas, B. (2017). Communication-efficient learning of deep networks from decentralized data. *Proceedings of the 20th International Conference on Artificial Intelligence and Statistics (AISTATS)*, 1273–1282. PMLR.

Melis, L., Song, C., De Cristofaro, E., & Shmatikov, V. (2019). Exploiting unintended feature leakage in collaborative learning. *Proceedings of the 2019 IEEE Symposium on Security and Privacy (SP)*, 691–706. IEEE. DOI: 10.1109/SP.2019.00029

Mothukuri, V., Parizi, R. M., Pouriyeh, S., Huang, Y., Dehghantanha, A., & Srivastava, G. (2021). A survey on security and privacy of federated learning. *Future Generation Computer Systems, 115*, 619–640. DOI: 10.1016/j.future.2020.10.007

Nguyen, T. D., Marchal, S., Miettinen, M., Fereidooni, H., Asokan, N., & Sadeghi, A. R. (2019). DIoT: A federated self-learning anomaly detection system for IoT. *Proceedings of the 2019 IEEE International Conference on Distributed Computing Systems (ICDCS)*, 756–767. IEEE. DOI: 10.1109/ICDCS.2019.00080

Phong, L. T., Ahn, T., Phuong, T. P., & Chong, P. H. J. (2018). Privacy-preserving deep learning via additively homomorphic encryption. *IEEE Transactions on Information Forensics and Security, 13*(5), 1333–1345. DOI: 10.1109/TIFS.2017.2787987

Rahman, S. A., Tout, H., Talhi, C., & Mourad, A. (2020). Internet of Things intrusion detection: Centralized, on-device, or federated learning? *IEEE Network, 34*(6), 310–317. DOI: 10.1109/MNET.011.2000286

Shokri, R., & Shmatikov, V. (2015). Privacy-preserving deep learning. *Proceedings of the 22nd ACM SIGSAC Conference on Computer and Communications Security*, 1310–1321. ACM.

Truex, S., Baracaldo, N., Anwar, A., Steinke, T., Ludwig, H., & Zhang, R. (2019). A hybrid approach to privacy-preserving federated learning. *Proceedings of the 12th ACM Workshop on Artificial Intelligence and Security (AISec)*, 1–8. ACM. DOI: 10.1145/3338501.3357370

Vyas, A., Lin, P. C., Hwang, R. H., & Tripathi, M. (2024). Privacy-preserving federated learning for intrusion detection in IoT environments: A survey. *IEEE Access : Practical Innovations, Open Solutions, 12*, 127018–127050. DOI: 10.1109/ACCESS.2024.3454211

Wei, K., Li, J., Ding, M., Ma, C., Yang, H. H., Farokhi, F., & Poor, H. V. (2020). Federated learning with differential privacy: Algorithms and performance analysis. *IEEE Transactions on Information Forensics and Security, 15*, 3454–3469. DOI: 10.1109/TIFS.2020.2988575

Yang, Q., Fan, L., & Yu, H. (Eds.). (2020). *Federated learning: Privacy and incentive*. Springer.

Yang, Q., Liu, Y., Chen, T., & Tong, Y. (2019). Federated machine learning: Concept and applications. *ACM Transactions on Intelligent Systems and Technology*, *10*(2), 12. DOI: 10.1145/3298981

Zhu, L., Liu, Z., & Han, S. (2019). Deep leakage from gradients. *Advances in Neural Information Processing Systems*, *32*, 14774–14784.

Chapter 7
Swarm AI for Distributed Cyber Defense and Autonomous Threat Detection

Wael Hadi
https://orcid.org/0000-0002-7575-9287
Petra University, Jordan

Ala Hamarsheh
https://orcid.org/0000-0002-4736-7331
Arab American University, Palestine

Ahmad Al-Qerem
https://orcid.org/0000-0003-2187-6194
Zarqa University, Jordan

Amjad Aldweesh
https://orcid.org/0000-0001-9358-1323
Shaqra University, Saudi Arabia

ABSTRACT

Collective intelligence and swarm AI have shaped recent explorations of distributed cybersecurity strategies. Many traditional approaches rely on centralized analytics or static signatures, and they sometimes fall short in dynamic and large-scale networks. This chapter provides a comprehensive examination of autonomous defense strategies that embed intelligence in distributed agents, use local detection mechanisms, and encourage emergent coordination through swarm principles. The text explains how these concepts, combined with reinforcement learning, can enable proactive threat

DOI: 10.4018/979-8-3373-0954-5.ch007

detection and containment without complete reliance on centralized oversight. It reviews existing work on multi-agent systems, swarm optimization, and distributed anomaly detection, and it introduces detailed theoretical foundations for practical implementation. Empirical findings from simulations and operational settings illustrate how emergent coordination shortens detection time and enhances resilience.

1. INTRODUCTION

Cyber attacks have become more sophisticated as network infrastructures expand. Many organizations use static intrusion detection systems or centralized platforms to correlate security information and events. These central resources can become overwhelmed when attackers use automated strategies or exploit subtle vulnerabilities in remote segments of a network (Mohamed, 2023). Zero-day exploits, hidden lateral movements, and distributed denial-of-service (DDoS) attacks put pressure on conventional defenses that rely on known patterns or signatures. When an adversary modifies techniques faster than detection rules can adapt, static defenses often fail (Muneer, Farooq, & Athar, 2024).

Researchers have explored artificial intelligence (AI) for more dynamic threat detection. Machine learning models can classify anomalies or perform outlier analysis on network data, yet these approaches often aggregate data and perform centralized training. Bottlenecks arise when the network generates massive volumes of logs and sensor outputs (Girhepuje, Verma, & Raina, 2024). Delay in processing these volumes leaves endpoints vulnerable. A distributed approach that pushes intelligence to the edges promises faster local responses and reduced data transfer.

Collective intelligence offers a compelling framework by drawing inspiration from natural phenomena. In insect colonies and bird flocks, no individual agent directs the entire group, but local interactions lead to coherent responses (Capuano, Fenza, Loia, & Stanzione, 2022). Swarm AI applies these ideas to multi-agent systems in which each node observes its environment, shares threat signals with neighbors, and adapts to changes. This distributed intelligence becomes particularly relevant for cybersecurity, where threats may appear simultaneously at multiple points (Okdem & Okdem, 2024).

The chapter describes the fundamentals of swarm intelligence, then shows how reinforcement learning (RL) can augment swarm-based defense. RL allows agents to learn from trial-and-error, tuning defensive actions in response to feedback about successful or missed attacks (Adawadkar & Kulkarni, 2022). Over many interactions, agents converge on effective strategies that can contain attacks quickly while minimizing false positives. Researchers have simulated these swarm-based approaches in networks ranging from enterprise settings to Internet of Things (IoT) deployments. Observed outcomes include reduced detection time, higher accuracy, and resilience when some nodes are compromised.

Sections of this chapter address background developments, a thorough literature review, a theoretical foundation for distributed cyber defense, and an expanded methodology to illustrate how organizations can deploy swarm-based solutions. The text discusses real-world scenarios, such as enterprise networks with multiple branches, IoT sensor fields, cloud services, and industrial control systems. Each context raises unique constraints, including limited computing resources, large numbers of devices, or strict reliability requirements. The chapter concludes by outlining best practices, possible challenges, and open research questions.

2. BACKGROUND

2.1 Rise of Complex Threats

Network infrastructures continue to grow in size and complexity, drawing more attention from attackers who discover creative methods to bypass security controls (Muneer et al., 2024). Advanced persistent threats (APTs) rely on stealth, while others use mass exploitation or large botnets. Traditional defenses often rely on known signatures that detect only previously catalogued attacks (Mohamed, 2023). Evasive malware or zero-day exploits defeat these signature-based methods by presenting behavior the system does not recognize.

Centralized security operations centers (SOCs) gather event logs and alerts from across an organization. Analysts filter through these data to discern malicious signs (Girhepuje et al., 2024). Although this approach provides a global perspective, it can create single points of failure or delay. Attackers sometimes move laterally through a network before analysts identify their footprints. The reactive nature of such workflows underscores the need for distributed intelligence.

2.2 Foundations of Collective Intelligence

Collective intelligence rests on the principle that a group can solve problems by integrating the local observations of its individual members. Although many studies examine human collectives, natural swarms of insects or flocks of birds represent fundamental examples of local interactions that yield global coherence (Capuano et al., 2022). Small changes in local conditions can activate consistent patterns of movement or decision-making across the entire collective.

In cybersecurity, such an approach allows endpoints to analyze logs, detect anomalies, and exchange insights. The emergence of patterns across distributed devices can reduce blind spots (Dritsas & Trigka, 2025). When local nodes adapt in real time, the group displays an agile response. A compromise of a single node does not cripple the defense because other agents remain operational (Okdem & Okdem, 2024).

2.3 Swarm Intelligence

Swarm intelligence expands collective intelligence by emphasizing decentralized control, simple local rules, and communication that leads to emergent responses (Zhao, Jiang, Han, Li, & Peng, 2023). Early work on swarm approaches appeared in robotics, where multiple autonomous robots coordinate tasks. In network security, distributed agents can run detection, block suspicious packets, and cross-check alerts through local broadcasting (Muneer et al., 2024). This approach offers adaptive capabilities, since each agent updates its tactics as it observes changes in traffic or receives neighbor alerts.

When an agent encounters malicious packets, it may raise its local detection sensitivity, notify neighbors, or initiate partial countermeasures. Neighbors that register the same threat corroborate the suspicion and respond accordingly. The swarm's distributed nature raises the cost for attackers, who need to bypass a collective that learns from each engagement (Capuano et al., 2022).

2.4 Reinforcement Learning in Distributed Security

Reinforcement learning (RL) complements swarm intelligence by enabling agents to adjust decisions based on iterative feedback. Agents receive rewards for successful blocking of threats or minimal disruption of normal traffic (Adawadkar & Kulkarni, 2022). Over time, they refine how aggressively they filter traffic, when to escalate alerts, or how to respond to uncertain indicators. Although multi-agent RL can introduce coordination challenges and communication overhead, it offers a dynamic alternative to static models (Vyas, Hannay, Bolton, & Burnap, 2023).

In certain implementations, each agent independently learns policies suited to its environment. In others, a central trainer collects experiences from agents, updates model parameters, and redistributes them. Designers select an approach that fits network size, device constraints, and the desired balance between local autonomy and global uniformity (Zhang, Hamadi, Damiani, Yeun, & Taher, 2022).

2.5 Intelligent Threat Response and Automation

Many security tools now aim for automated or semi-automated responses. These tools may block suspicious IP addresses, quarantine hosts, or roll back software to a known safe state (Saleh, 2024). Swarm-based frameworks place these decisions closer to endpoints, reducing reaction time. Agents can respond instantly to anomalies, especially if they confirm malicious behavior through local intelligence or neighbor signals (Girhepuje et al., 2024).

While automated decisions increase defense speed, they also risk false positives. If an agent mistakes normal processes for malicious ones, it might disrupt legitimate services. A well-tuned reward structure helps agents distinguish genuine threats from normal fluctuations. Swarm intelligence can lessen these risks by relying on distributed corroboration instead of unilateral decisions (Muneer et al., 2024).

3. LITERATURE REVIEW

3.1 Early Work on Multi-Agent Cybersecurity

Initial attempts at multi-agent cybersecurity divided large tasks among specialized components. Certain agents would filter packets, while others would correlate logs or manage alert aggregation (Muneer et al., 2024). These systems introduced concurrency, but many relied on hierarchical communication. A top-level coordinator directed how sub-agents operated (Salem, Azzam, Emam, & Abohany, 2024).

As networks grew, research turned to more autonomous agent designs. Knowledge-based methods let each agent hold partial rule sets, which they combined with centralized oversight (Siam, 2025). Although this helped distribute workloads, these agents often lacked adaptive learning. They did not change their rules in response to new attacks, resulting in outdated detection thresholds.

3.2 Emergence of Swarm-Based Intrusion Detection

Swarm-based intrusion detection systems (IDS) introduced decentralized data exchange among endpoints (Okdem & Okdem, 2024). A node that witnessed abnormal port scans broadcasted alerts to immediate neighbors, which then tightened detection rules against that source (Capuano et al., 2022). This coordination allowed the network to converge on blocking malicious hosts. It also spread detection knowledge quickly, reducing the chance of an undetected pivot to another node.

Some research used swarm optimization algorithms—ant colony optimization or particle swarm optimization—to tune IDS parameters (Dritsas & Trigka, 2025). This approach established that local observation, combined with emergent global behavior, could handle both known signatures and certain zero-day patterns.

3.3 Advances with Reinforcement Learning

Reinforcement learning introduced a new layer of adaptability. Instead of relying only on static anomaly thresholds, agents learned from feedback. A correct block earned a reward, an unjustified block incurred a penalty (Adawadkar & Kulkarni, 2022). Over repeated episodes, agents refined their detection and response policies for better balance between security and system availability.

Research on multi-agent RL revealed complexities in reward design. Local reward functions could misalign with global defense goals, causing agents to adopt inconsistent strategies (Vyas et al., 2023). Cooperative rewards or partial policy sharing helped coordinate agents toward shared objectives. Studies found that, although communication overhead sometimes rose, detection rates improved and adaptiveness increased.

3.4 Distributed Threat Response

Beyond detection, swarm-based research probed distributed responses (Muneer et al., 2024). Agents near a compromised zone could isolate it, block malicious traffic, or reset user credentials without waiting for instructions from a central hub (Saleh, 2024). This localized capability boosted reaction speed. If an attacker advanced through multiple subnets, the swarm tracked and countered each move, making infiltration more difficult.

Some experiments examined emergent resilience. Even if an attacker compromised a subset of agents, the rest of the swarm could detect irregular messages from those compromised nodes. Frequent cross-validation of alerts prevented a single corrupted agent from disrupting the entire defense (Capuano et al., 2022).

3.5 Knowledge Gaps in Swarm-Based Cybersecurity

Despite these advances, challenges remain. One issue involves trust among agents (Ferrag, Alwahedi, Battah, Cherif, et al., 2025). A compromised agent could spread false positives, confusing the swarm. Another gap concerns scalability. As the number of agents increases, the volume of alerts and updates can overload the network

(Girhepuje et al., 2024). Balancing local autonomy with an acceptable communication load remains an open question. Interpretability also becomes problematic: emergent decisions often lack straightforward explanations (Zhang et al., 2022).

4. THEORETICAL FOUNDATIONS

4.1 Self-Organization in Networked Systems

Self-organization occurs when nodes update internal states based on local stimuli, producing a structured global pattern without central control (Dritsas & Trigka, 2025). In cybersecurity, self-organization allows each endpoint to run local detection and react to neighbors' alerts. Over time, consistent detection signals propagate through the network (Okdem & Okdem, 2024). This phenomenon can shorten the time from the first sign of suspicious activity to a cohesive defense.

Complex systems theory emphasizes how local interactions can scale into significant global shifts. Minor changes in local threshold settings might escalate into a large-scale quarantine if evidence grows. Designers must ensure that positive feedback loops do not lead to excessive blocking of legitimate traffic (Capuano et al., 2022). Careful calibration helps the swarm remain stable and resilient.

4.2 Complexity and Adaptive Behavior

Security networks face dynamic adversaries who develop new tactics or pivot between network layers (Tan et al., 2023). Adaptive behavior is essential for defense systems that aim to counter these changes. A swarm that uses local detection thresholds remains flexible. Agents can modify parameters when they detect suspicious signals. They can share these modifications, creating a collective adaptation cycle (Vourganas & Michala, 2024).

Polymorphic malware and novel exploits underscore the importance of continuous learning. Stagnant rules become obsolete when attackers shift methods. A swarm model that supports ongoing updates to detection and blocking routines has the potential to handle wide variations in threat techniques (Salem et al., 2024).

4.3 Reinforcement Learning Concepts in Cyber Defense

Reinforcement learning involves states, actions, and rewards. An agent in a cybersecurity context might observe local traffic features or system call patterns as its state, then decide whether to drop packets, escalate alerts, or apply filtering rules (Adawadkar & Kulkarni, 2022). The agent receives a positive reward for effectively blocking an intrusion and a negative reward for false positives or missed attacks. Over many interactions, the RL policy converges toward strategies that yield net benefits.

Multi-agent RL introduces complexities. When multiple agents learn simultaneously, the environment is non-stationary. Each agent's strategy can shift the threat landscape for others (Finistrella, Mariani, & Zambonelli, 2025). Some frameworks adopt centralized training, where a central module aggregates experiences and updates shared parameters, but agents execute decisions locally. Others let agents remain fully independent, exchanging only minimal information (Zhang et al., 2022). Designers must match these methods to the network's scale and complexity.

4.4 Emergent Collective Intelligence

Emergent behavior arises when local interactions produce an outcome greater than the sum of individual contributions (Capuano et al., 2022). In swarm-based defense, one node's detection leads to a neighbor's heightened awareness, which prompts that neighbor to propagate alerts further. Over time, a wave of suspicion can sweep through the network, resulting in a coordinated block or quarantine. This reaction was not pre-programmed but arose from local response rules that reference neighbor alerts (Okdem & Okdem, 2024).

Simulations help researchers analyze how local thresholds and communication intervals influence emergent properties. If thresholds are too low, the swarm might overreact to benign deviations. If thresholds are too high, threats could spread undetected (Zhao et al., 2023). Achieving a balance usually involves iterative tuning and testing with various attack scenarios.

4.5 Integration with Cyber Threat Models

Standard cyber kill chain models describe reconnaissance, initial compromise, lateral movement, and exfiltration (Muneer et al., 2024). Each stage offers a possible detection point. A swarm-based system can assign subsets of agents to observe distinct behaviors, such as scanning for unusual port activity or monitoring file integrity. Agents coordinate their findings so that emerging threats receive swift attention (Saleh, 2024). This layered approach aligns with the kill chain's progression and obstructs an attacker's path at multiple junctures.

5. PROPOSED METHODOLOGY

This section proposes a step-by-step strategy for designing and deploying a swarm-based autonomous defense system. Each agent performs local sensing, uses reinforcement learning to refine detection, and collaborates with neighboring agents to produce emergent global defense.

5.1 Agent Design Principles (Rewritten as a Single Explanatory Paragraph)

Effective swarm agents combine local sensing, lightweight analysis, action mechanisms, and a secure communication interface. Local sensing collects network packets, system logs, or resource usage metrics (Muneer et al., 2024). Lightweight analysis applies classification models or RL-based anomaly detectors that fit within the agent's computational budget (Dritsas & Trigka, 2025). The action module decides how to respond, whether by dropping suspicious connections, isolating a suspect device, or adjusting detection thresholds (Adawadkar & Kulkarni, 2022). Agents communicate detection outcomes to peers through an interface that must remain secure and authenticated (Ferrag et al., 2025).

5.2 Reinforcement Learning Integration (Rewritten as a Single Explanatory Paragraph)

In this approach, each agent runs an RL process where states represent real-time observations and actions correspond to defensive measures. Rewards reflect how well the agent blocks threats without impeding normal activity (Finistrella et al., 2025). Over repeated interactions, the policy governing each agent's actions gradually optimizes detection accuracy and response speed. Designers can allow partial policy sharing among agents, accelerating learning. A successful blocking policy might be disseminated to neighbors, although agents in different network zones may adapt that policy to their unique conditions (Zhang et al., 2022).

5.3 Swarm Coordination (Rewritten as a Single Explanatory Paragraph)

Swarm coordination arises when nodes exchange messages about threat levels. If an agent sees persistent suspicious activity from a particular source, it notifies neighbors (Okdem & Okdem, 2024). Those neighbors check local logs to see if they observed similar activity. When multiple confirmations converge, the swarm collectively escalates defense actions. Communication can occur through peer-to-peer overlays or limited broadcast channels (Capuano et al., 2022). This local message passing triggers emergent consensus, which is a key concept in swarm intelligence.

5.4 Trust Mechanisms (Rewritten as a Single Explanatory Paragraph)

Any distributed approach needs ways to handle misbehaving or compromised agents. A trust mechanism measures each agent's reliability based on past alerts and outcomes (Ferrag et al., 2025). If an agent consistently triggers valid alarms, neighbors give it higher credibility. If it frequently reports false positives, neighbors scrutinize its alerts more carefully or ignore them. In this manner, the swarm gradually isolates corrupted or malfunctioning nodes, reducing disruptions caused by incorrect or malicious signals.

5.5 Evaluation Framework (Rewritten as a Single Explanatory Paragraph)

Researchers and practitioners can evaluate swarm-based defense by analyzing detection accuracy, false positive rates, response time, and communication overhead (Muneer et al., 2024). Detection accuracy indicates how often the swarm correctly identifies threats. False positive rates measure the burden on legitimate traffic. Response time reflects the speed from initial compromise to the execution of protective measures (Okdem & Okdem, 2024). Communication overhead quantifies the volume and frequency of alerts exchanged among agents (Dritsas & Trigka, 2025). Fine-tuning these metrics ensures that the swarm remains reliable and efficient.

6. IMPLEMENTATION STEPS AND PRACTICAL CONSIDERATIONS

6.1 Preliminary Deployment in a Testbed

Organizations often experiment with a limited testbed where they replicate typical traffic patterns intermixed with malicious flows (Muneer et al., 2024). In this controlled environment, each agent starts with minimal initial knowledge and gradually refines its RL policy after many encounters. Engineers capture performance metrics such as detection accuracy, overhead, and false positives to confirm that the swarm behaves as intended under various scenarios.

6.2 Step-by-Step Integration (Rewritten as a Single Explanatory Paragraph)

Once a testbed demonstrates viability, teams can install lightweight agents on endpoints, servers, or virtual machines. Administrators configure RL policies to define possible actions (Adawadkar & Kulkarni, 2022) and ensure that agents do not interfere with critical services. Communication overlays link agents to their neighbors (Vyas et al., 2023). A small-scale pilot helps confirm detection capabilities and refine parameters. After incremental adjustments, the swarm defense extends to multiple subnets or data centers (Saleh, 2024). This methodical approach avoids abrupt transitions and ensures that staff can monitor emergent behaviors.

6.3 Observing Emergent Behavior

Administrators should monitor the swarm at a global level to see how local alerts travel across the network (Capuano et al., 2022). For example, if a node in one subnet flags suspicious connections to a specific IP, other subnets that have seen similar patterns may corroborate and block that IP at their edges. Visual dashboards track the spread of alerts and confirm whether blocking converges rapidly or stalls. The system's adaptiveness emerges when repeated attacks lead to more decisive and earlier responses over time (Finistrella et al., 2025). Figure 1 shows a simplified flow: teams install agents, configure RL policies, perform pilot tests, then scale the solution to broader production environments.

Figure 1. Sample deployment flow

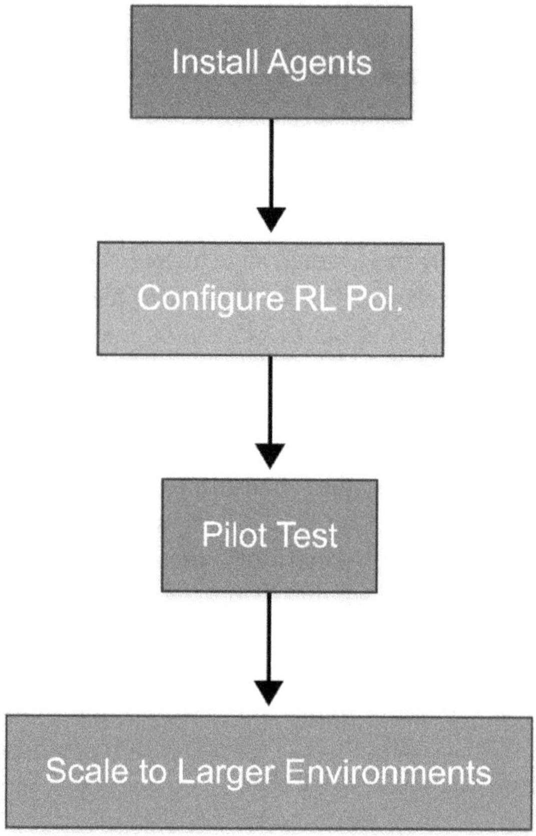

6.4 Resource Constraints

Endpoints may have limited memory, CPU, or battery power. IoT devices often lack the capacity to run complex models (Dritsas & Trigka, 2025). Developers frequently employ compact anomaly detectors or scaled-down RL modules for these constrained nodes. More powerful servers can handle resource-intensive processes. Achieving optimal performance requires balancing local detection with minimal overhead so critical operations remain unaffected (Muneer et al., 2024).

7. EMPIRICAL FINDINGS AND CASE STUDIES

7.1 Swarm Detection in Enterprise Networks

Large enterprises with diverse subnets and user profiles benefit from local detection at various endpoints (Okdem & Okdem, 2024). When a user's workstation observes signs of malicious software, it escalates a warning that triggers checks in nearby machines. Studies show that swarm-based approaches reduce false positives compared to single-node detectors, since consensus among multiple agents is harder to trigger by random benign anomalies (Capuano et al., 2022). Administrators in test environments also noted faster detection of ransomware that attempted to encrypt files on shared drives, since multiple agents quickly correlated suspicious file activity (Vyas et al., 2023).

7.2 IoT Security

IoT networks often include devices like cameras, sensors, and household appliances with limited capabilities. Swarm-based intrusion detection localizes tasks so that each device performs basic checks, while more powerful aggregator nodes handle advanced analysis (Dritsas & Trigka, 2025). This layered structure spreads detection coverage and prevents single points of failure. Observations indicate shorter response times because compromised devices cannot spread malware without triggering alarms from peers (Muneer et al., 2024).

7.3 Cloud Environments

Cloud infrastructures spin up or shut down virtual machines (VMs) rapidly. Agents on these ephemeral instances gather local traffic data and share alerts within a cloud region or across regions (Finistrella et al., 2025). If a VM is compromised, the swarm can isolate it. The ephemeral nature of cloud services benefits from swarm-based defense, as the system remains functional even if newly launched instances lack extensive training data (Okdem & Okdem, 2024). Policy sharing among running nodes helps maintain consistent detection standards (Capuano et al., 2022). Table 1 outlines typical performance improvements in enterprise, IoT, and cloud contexts. Each domain benefits from a specific aspect of swarm intelligence, whether consensus-based filtering, local anomaly monitoring, or flexible policy exchange.

Table 1. Typical performance improvements

Domain	Observed Outcome	Key Factor
Enterprise	Reduction in false positives	Consensus-based detection
IoT	Faster isolation of compromised devices	Lightweight local monitors
Cloud	Resilient scaling with ephemeral resources	Policy sharing for new instances

8. EXTENDED ARCHITECTURE FOR DISTRIBUTED AUTONOMOUS DEFENSE

8.1 Modular Layers

A layered architecture can help organize swarm-based defense systems. The first layer collects data from endpoints. The second layer performs local analysis using ML or RL. A third layer coordinates alerts among agents to spark emergent responses (Okdem & Okdem, 2024). A global intelligence layer preserves knowledge of previously identified threats. Finally, an automated response layer enforces remediation actions, such as blocking traffic or patching vulnerabilities (Muneer et al., 2024). Figure 2 depicts the progression from data input at endpoints to local processing, swarm-based coordination, broader intelligence gathering, and actions that block or contain threats.

Figure 2. Layered swarm architecture

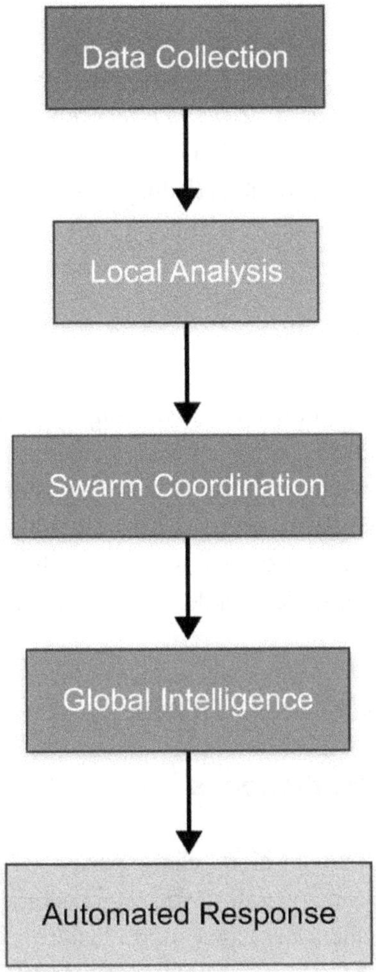

8.2 Reinforcement Learning Module

Within the local analysis layer, each agent's RL algorithm continually refines how it responds to anomalies (Adawadkar & Kulkarni, 2022). This refinement occurs as the agent observes the outcomes of each decision. A correct block may yield a reward, while false positives produce penalties. Over many trials, the agent's policy aligns with the broader security goals of minimizing intrusions and reducing operational disruptions (Finistrella et al., 2025).

8.3 Communication Patterns

Swarm-based coordination requires efficient message passing. Some systems use gossip-based protocols, where each node randomly selects a few neighbors for alert propagation (Zhang et al., 2022). Others rely on structured overlays with clusters. Each node communicates within its cluster, while cluster leaders exchange summarized intelligence across regions (Vourganas & Michala, 2024). The choice depends on the organization's network topology and the need to control communication overhead.

8.4 Security and Trust

Any swarm system must secure internal messages and track trust. Agents should sign or encrypt outgoing alerts so that attackers cannot spoof them (Ferrag et al., 2025). A trust module rates agent reliability based on prior alert validity. Neighbors who notice a pattern of false alarms decrease the weight of that agent's future reports. Over time, low-reliability agents have less influence, which protects the swarm from malicious or malfunctioning nodes (Okdem & Okdem, 2024).

9. CHALLENGES AND LIMITATIONS

9.1 Communication Bottlenecks

Large networks with frequent alerts can experience congestion. If each agent broadcasts to many neighbors, overall traffic may become unmanageable (Okdem & Okdem, 2024). Researchers have proposed clustering, time-based batching of alerts, or event-driven updates to reduce message floods (Vyas et al., 2023).

9.2 Malicious or Compromised Agents

An attacker who compromises an agent can produce false alarms or hide genuine threats (Ferrag et al., 2025). If a significant fraction of agents become compromised, the swarm may fail to converge on correct decisions. Trust frameworks help mitigate this risk by analyzing agents' historical performance. Yet, sophisticated attackers may try to gradually earn high trust and then manipulate the swarm.

9.3 Resource Constraints and Scalability

IoT environments and other resource-limited scenarios restrict the size of local models (Dritsas & Trigka, 2025). Large neural networks for anomaly detection may not run on small devices. Designers must consider whether to offload heavier tasks to edge servers or adopt more compact algorithms. Swarm systems that scale to thousands of agents also demand careful planning to prevent exponential growth in communications.

9.4 Emergent Behavior and Interpretability

While emergent coordination is advantageous, security teams sometimes struggle to understand how decisions arise. This lack of interpretability can be a barrier in regulated industries or organizations that require clear forensic evidence (Capuano et al., 2022). Researchers have suggested logging local states and employing explainable AI (XAI) techniques to clarify the rationales behind agent actions (Zhang et al., 2022).

9.5 Maintenance and Updates

Swarm-based defense software requires ongoing maintenance. Agents must be updated when new attacks emerge. RL models can drift over time if threats evolve. Ensuring version compatibility across thousands of nodes poses logistical difficulties (Finistrella et al., 2025). Coordinated updates might involve rolling deployments where clusters are upgraded incrementally to avoid large-scale downtime.

10. DEPLOYMENT CONSIDERATIONS AND OPERATIONAL BEST PRACTICES

10.1 Gradual Rollout

Many organizations introduce swarm-based security in a phased manner. A small subnet or IoT cluster can serve as a proof of concept (Okdem & Okdem, 2024). If successful, broader subnets and interconnected services can adopt the same architecture. Gradual rollout reduces risks associated with unpredictable emergent behaviors and helps staff acquire familiarity with the system.

10.2 Policy Calibration

Reinforcement learning depends on carefully chosen reward functions. If the reward for blocking traffic is too high, agents might become overly aggressive, increasing false positives (Adawadkar & Kulkarni, 2022). If the penalty for false alarms is too strict, agents might hesitate to block genuine threats. Regular reviews of reward and penalty structures can maintain an optimal balance over time.

10.3 Security of Communications

Organizations should encrypt agent-to-agent communications to prevent message spoofing or eavesdropping (Ferrag et al., 2025). Digital signatures can confirm message authenticity. This extra security overhead is essential in a distributed system where compromised messages could degrade or sabotage the entire swarm.

10.4 Resource Management

In environments with limited hardware, the system must employ models that fit local constraints (Dritsas & Trigka, 2025). Some designers move complex analytics to more capable gateways or cloud resources. Others use lightweight algorithms that detect anomalies with minimal CPU. Either option must preserve the swarm's autonomy.

10.5 Auditing and Logs

Swarm decisions may appear opaque without detailed logs that track how each agent interpreted events (Zhao et al., 2023). Storing these logs in a distributed ledger or secure database allows security teams to reconstruct the swarm's reasoning. This record also assists in compliance audits and post-incident investigations.

11. EXTENDED CASE SCENARIOS

11.1 Large Enterprise with Multiple Branches

A multinational enterprise might install swarm agents at each branch office, connecting them through a wide-area network (Muneer et al., 2024). Local clusters at each branch analyze day-to-day traffic. If threat signals exceed a certain threshold, an alert propagates within that branch. The branch-level swarm can then block suspicious traffic and quarantine devices. Periodic summaries flow to a corporate security division that correlates global patterns (Capuano et al., 2022). Over time, each branch's swarm tailors its RL policy to local traffic conditions, while the central view detects repeated attempts across regions (Okdem & Okdem, 2024).

11.2 Cross-Cloud Infrastructure

Some organizations rely on multiple cloud providers. Each cloud region hosts swarm agents that monitor inbound and outbound connections (Saleh, 2024). If an attacker compromises a container instance in one region, local agents isolate that instance. A bridging mechanism shares relevant alerts with other regions. This design ensures that infiltration in one environment does not spread unnoticed to another (Finistrella et al., 2025). Coordinating ephemeral resources introduces complexities, but partial policy sharing lets newly deployed containers inherit partial knowledge from stable nodes.

11.3 Industrial Control Systems

Industrial control systems (ICS) oversee processes in sectors like manufacturing or energy distribution. Many ICS devices are older and lack strong security features (Muneer et al., 2024). Embedding swarm agents on these devices can provide localized monitoring and rapid response. If one device sees anomalous instructions or sensor readings, it queries neighbors to confirm the pattern (Dritsas & Trigka, 2025). Swift action may avert sabotage or safety hazards. The RL component in ICS contexts must minimize disruptions to normal workflows. Overly aggressive blocking might halt critical processes. A carefully balanced reward structure helps agents protect systems while respecting operational stability (Capuano et al., 2022).

12. FUTURE RESEARCH DIRECTIONS

12.1 Trust and Reputation Algorithms

Research can refine reputation mechanisms by incorporating contextual factors, such as typical traffic volume or device roles. Agents that regularly produce valid alerts gain a strong reputation, while those that deviate from recognized norms risk isolation (Ferrag et al., 2025). Complex trust frameworks could track the evolution of agent behavior over long periods, detecting slow infiltration techniques.

12.2 Large Language Models for Threat Analysis

Future work may integrate large language models (LLMs) that interpret textual logs, error messages, and user behavior descriptions (Silva & Westphall, 2024). Swarm agents could use refined language-based threat signals to identify novel tactics. This enhancement would require efficient processing pipelines, especially if devices have limited resources.

12.3 Hybrid Hierarchical-Swarm Systems

Not all organizations want a fully decentralized defense. Hybrid architectures, with swarm clusters under a broader hierarchy, can offer a compromise (Okdem & Okdem, 2024). Local swarms preserve fast reactions, while a higher-level authority coordinates large-scale data correlation and compliance. Future research can explore how best to merge these models for maximum flexibility.

12.4 Resilience Against Offensive AI

Adversaries also use AI to craft polymorphic malware or bypass detection (Girhepuje et al., 2024). Swarm-based defense must evolve quickly to counter AI-driven threats. Reinforcement learning that incorporates adversarial examples can prepare agents to spot unusual patterns introduced by machine-generated attacks. Researchers should test swarm resilience through red-team exercises that involve AI-based infiltration tools.

12.5 Explainable Swarm Decisions

Although swarm methods excel at distributed detection, they often produce opaque decisions. Enterprises subject to regulations need to demonstrate why certain endpoints were blocked. Enhanced logging of local states and emergent coordination steps can make swarm activities more interpretable (Capuano et al., 2022). Explainable AI (XAI) techniques might distill each agent's reasons for blocking traffic, combining them into a coherent account that security teams and auditors can review (Zhang et al., 2022).

13. CONCLUSION

This chapter explored how collective intelligence and swarm AI can strengthen cybersecurity by embedding intelligence throughout a network. Traditional centralized defenses often struggle under large-scale or adaptive threats that appear at various points simultaneously. By placing autonomous agents on endpoints, servers, and IoT devices, defenders can detect anomalies locally, verify them through neighbor coordination, and initiate immediate responses. Reinforcement learning further refines the agents' actions, allowing them to balance protective measures with normal operations through continuous feedback.

Swarm-based intrusion detection and response strategies have shown promising results in reducing false positives and shortening detection intervals. Distributed design also improves resilience, as attackers find it more difficult to disable the entire defense by compromising a single node. However, challenges remain in areas such as communication overhead, trust management, interpretability, and resource constraints. Continued research in these areas will help refine swarm architectures for large-scale deployments, including enterprise, IoT, cloud, and industrial control environments.

Implementation best practices suggest starting small, calibrating reward functions for RL, and ensuring communication security among agents. Developers should also maintain robust auditing capabilities to satisfy compliance and organizational transparency. Longer-term research paths include more advanced trust algorithms, integration of large language models for nuanced anomaly detection, defense against offensive AI techniques, and methods to make swarm behaviors more transparent.

In an era marked by highly adaptive cyber threats, collective intelligence and swarm AI represent an evolving and potentially transformative approach. By relying on local intelligence, emergent collaboration, and dynamic learning, these systems can offer decentralized and proactive defense that adapts as attackers shift their tactics. Their success will likely depend on careful design, thorough testing, and ongoing refinements in how agents communicate, coordinate, and learn from one another in real time.

REFERENCES

Adawadkar, A. M. K., & Kulkarni, N. (2022). Cyber-Security and Reinforcement Learning — A Brief Survey. *Engineering Applications of Artificial Intelligence, 114*, 105116. DOI: 10.1016/j.engappai.2022.105116

Capuano, N., Fenza, G., Loia, V., & Stanzione, C. (2022). Explainable Artificial Intelligence in CyberSecurity: A Survey. *IEEE Access : Practical Innovations, Open Solutions, 10*, 93575–93600. DOI: 10.1109/ACCESS.2022.3204171

Dritsas, E., & Trigka, M. (2025). A Survey on Cybersecurity in IoT. *Future Internet, 17*(1), 30. DOI: 10.3390/fi17010030

Ferrag, M. A., Alwahedi, F., Battah, A., Cherif, B., et al. (2025). Generative AI in Cybersecurity: A Comprehensive Review of LLM Applications and Vulnerabilities. *Internet of Things and Cyber-Physical Systems, 5*(1), 100XXX (Early Access).

Finistrella, S., Mariani, S., & Zambonelli, F. (2025). Multi-Agent Reinforcement Learning for Cybersecurity: Classification and Survey. *Intelligent Systems with Applications, 17*, 100861. DOI: 10.1016/j.iswa.2025.200495

Girhepuje, S., Verma, A., & Raina, G. (2024). A Survey on Offensive AI Within Cybersecurity. *arXiv Preprint, arXiv:2410.03566.*

Jada, I., & Mayayise, T. O. (2023). The Impact of Artificial Intelligence on Organisational Cyber Security: A Systematic Literature Review. *Data and Information Management, 8*(4), 100063.

Macas, M. A., Wu, C., & Fuertes, W. (2024). Adversarial Examples: A Survey of Attacks and Defenses in Deep Learning-Enabled Cybersecurity Systems. *Expert Systems with Applications, 238*, 122223. DOI: 10.1016/j.eswa.2023.122223

Mohamed, N. (2023). Current Trends in AI and ML for Cybersecurity: A State-of-the-Art Survey. *Cogent Engineering, 10*(2), 2272358. DOI: 10.1080/23311916.2023.2272358

Muneer, S., Farooq, U., & Athar, A. (2024). A Critical Review of AI-Based Approaches in Intrusion Detection: A Comprehensive Analysis. *Journal of Engineering, 2024*(1), 3909173. DOI: 10.1155/2024/3909173

Okdem, S., & Okdem, S. (2024). Artificial Intelligence in Cybersecurity: A Review and a Case Study. *Applied Sciences (Basel, Switzerland), 14*(22), 10487. DOI: 10.3390/app142210487

Paracha, M. A., & Rasheed, A. (2024). Leveraging AI for Network Threat Detection — A Conceptual Overview. *Electronics (Basel), 13*(23), 4611. DOI: 10.3390/electronics13234611

Saleh, S. S. A. M. (2024). Blockchain for Secure and Decentralized Artificial Intelligence in Cybersecurity: A Comprehensive Review. *Blockchain: Research and Applications, 100193.*

Salem, A. H., Azzam, S. M., Emam, O. E., & Abohany, A. A. (2024). Advancing Cybersecurity: A Comprehensive Review of AI-Driven Detection Techniques. *Journal of Big Data, 11*(1), 105. DOI: 10.1186/s40537-024-00957-y

Siam, A. A. (2025). A Comprehensive Review of AI's Current Impact and Future Prospects in Cybersecurity. *IEEE Access : Practical Innovations, Open Solutions, 13*, 14035–14058.

Silva, G. J. C., & Westphall, C. B. (2024). A Survey of Large Language Models in Cybersecurity. *arXiv Preprint, arXiv:2402.16968.*

Tan, J., Jin, H., Zhang, H., Zhang, Y., Chang, D., Liu, X., & Zhang, H. (2023). When Moving Target Defense Meets Game Theory: A Survey. *Computer Science Review, 49*, 100544. DOI: 10.1016/j.cosrev.2023.100544

Vourganas, I. J., & Michala, A. L. (2024). Applications of Machine Learning in Cyber Security: A Review. *Journal of Cybersecurity and Privacy, 4*(4), 972–992. DOI: 10.3390/jcp4040045

Vyas, S., Hannay, J., Bolton, A., & Burnap, P. (2023). Automated Cyber Defence: A Review. *Proceedings of the ACM on Measurement and Analysis of Computing Systems, 7*(4), 111.

Zhang, Z., Hamadi, H. A., Damiani, E., Yeun, C. Y., & Taher, F. A. (2022). Explainable AI Applications in Cyber Security: State-of-the-Art in Research. *IEEE Access : Practical Innovations, Open Solutions, 10*, 93104–93139. DOI: 10.1109/ACCESS.2022.3204051

Zhao, X., Jiang, R., Han, Y., Li, A., & Peng, Z. (2023). A Survey on Cybersecurity Knowledge Graph Construction. *Computers & Security, 130*, 103524.

Chapter 8

Reinforcement Learning for Adaptive Cyber Defense Training Autonomous Systems for Dynamic Threat Response and Strategy Optimization

Mohammad Alauthman
https://orcid.org/0000-0003-0319-1968
Petra University, Jordan

Amjad Aldweesh
https://orcid.org/0000-0001-9358-1323
Shaqra University, Saudi Arabia

Ahmad Al-Qerem
https://orcid.org/0000-0003-2187-6194
Zarqa University, Jordan

Saad Alateef
https://orcid.org/0009-0002-3219-0833
Newcastle University, UK

Mouhammd Alkasassbeh
https://orcid.org/0000-0001-8396-7441

DOI: 10.4018/979-8-3373-0954-5.ch008

Princess Sumaya University for Technology, Jordan

ABSTRACT

Reinforcement Learning (RL) offers a process for creating cyber defense methods that adjust to changing threats. Through training an RL agent, defenders discover ways to block intrusions, isolate systems, and reduce false positives. This chapter covers RL concepts, integration with AI security architectures, and procedures for threat response. It addresses attacker strategies, covers multiple optimization goals, and reviews data methods, reward choices, and deployment steps. Examples in healthcare, finance, and industrial networks illustrate outcomes. Governance, regulatory demands, and oversight are included, supporting RL-based cyber defense. These discussions show how RL-based defenses manage sequences and adapt to new threats. The chapter also addresses evaluation and implementation.

1. INTRODUCTION

Cyber defense focuses on methods, tools, and practices designed to safeguard digital infrastructure, data assets, and communication channels from diverse forms of malicious activity. Over time, adversaries have developed complex tactics that challenge traditional static approaches. Cyber threats sometimes manifest as advanced persistent threats, large-scale distributed denial of service, or targeted intrusions designed to exfiltrate critical data. Security teams often rely on signature-based detection, rule-based firewalls, or preset intrusion detection thresholds, but these measures can prove insufficient for adaptive or stealthy adversaries (Syed & ES, 2021). A system that does not adapt or update its protective measures can remain vulnerable when threat actors modify their attack methods. Reinforcement Learning (RL) introduces a data-driven approach that involves an agent learning to select actions based on interactions with an environment. Through repeated trials and feedback, the agent refines its decision-making policy to maximize some form of reward. In a cyber defense context, a reward might relate to minimized breaches, reduced unauthorized data transfers, or lowered risk of system compromise. The RL agent can dynamically alter network security configurations, adjust traffic filtering rules, or schedule patch deployments in response to observed conditions (Chirra, 2020). This approach shifts the paradigm from static, rule-based solutions toward self-improving defense that uses real-time or near real-time data.

The following explores how RL can facilitate adaptive cyber defense strategies. The chapter has multiple goals:

1. Investigate core principles of RL, including how these methods translate into the detection, mitigation, and containment of cyber threats.
2. Present architectural components of AI-driven security systems that leverage RL agents for decision-making, addressing integration with threat intelligence, anomaly detection, and incident response modules.
3. Analyze how autonomous cyber defense can respond to a variety of attack vectors, from low-level port scans to advanced adversarial maneuvers that attempt lateral movement across network segments.
4. Discuss how RL-based methods optimize defense strategies through Markov Decision Processes (MDPs) and multi-objective learning.
5. Examine practical issues such as data aggregation, computational constraints, reward design, and risk trade-offs that arise in real-world RL deployments.
6. Provide concrete use cases spanning different industries, including healthcare and finance.
7. Outline future directions, such as the adoption of explainable RL, continual learning, and federated RL frameworks.

This text is organized into distinct sections, each containing subtopics. Section 2 describes reinforcement learning fundamentals, mapping them onto cyber defense settings. Section 3 delves into the architecture of AI-driven security systems, emphasizing RL integration. Section 4 addresses the nature of autonomous threat response within RL-based systems. Section 5 focuses on how RL optimizes defense strategies through iterative learning. Section 6 explains implementation challenges, including data requirements and environment non-stationarity. Section 7 surveys use cases in diverse settings. Section 8 proposes a methodology for developing and deploying RL-based defense solutions. Section 9 details evaluation metrics and approaches for RL-driven systems. Section 10 discusses ethical and legal factors. Section 11 explores new avenues and research directions. Section 12 provides concluding remarks. Tables and figures are distributed to illustrate essential concepts, and references follow in APA style.

2. FOUNDATIONS OF REINFORCEMENT LEARNING IN CYBER DEFENSE

2.1 Basic RL Concepts and Frameworks

Reinforcement Learning is a subfield of machine learning that involves an agent, an environment, and reward signals. The agent starts in an initial state s0s_0s0 derived from environment observations. The agent chooses an action ata_tat from an action set. The environment then transitions to a new state $st + 1\, s_{\{t+1\}st} + 1$, and the agent receives a reward rt+1r_{t+1}rt+1. This process repeats, generating trajectories of states, actions, and rewards (S, A, R). Over time, the agent attempts to maximize the expected cumulative reward:

where π\piπ is the policy that defines the agent's behavior, and γ\gammaγ is a discount factor between 0 and 1 (Goriparthi, 2024).

The **Markov Decision Process (MDP)** formulation is central to RL. An MDP is specified by:

- A finite or continuous set of states SSS.
- A finite or continuous set of actions AAA.
- A transition function P(st+1|st,at)P(s_{t+1} \mid s_t, a_t)P(st+1|st,at).
- A reward function R(st,at,st+1)R(s_t, a_t, s_{t+1})R(st,at,st+1).
- A discount factor γ\gammaγ.

Cyber defense tasks often approximate or partially fulfill these properties, though some variations like partially observable MDPs (POMDPs) may be relevant if the system cannot fully observe the underlying attacker states.

The RL agent explores the environment to discover actions that yield higher long-term reward. Exploration can follow a policy such as ϵ\epsilonϵ-greedy, which selects a random action with probability ϵ\epsilonϵ and the best-known action otherwise. Alternatively, more advanced exploration strategies might rely on bonus-based exploration or parameter noise (Syed & ES, 2021).

Common RL algorithms include:

- **Value-based methods** (e.g., Q-learning) that estimate state-action values Q(s,a)Q(s,a)Q(s,a).
- **Policy-based methods** (e.g., REINFORCE) that learn parameterized policies directly.
- **Actor-critic methods** (e.g., A2C, PPO) that combine value function estimation with a policy parameterization.

These methods have distinct properties that may suit different cyber defense scenarios.

2.2 Why RL for Cyber Defense?

Cyber attacks occur in dynamic environments. Attackers often modify tactics in response to static defenses. Intrusion detection systems that rely on fixed signatures or thresholds can struggle with zero-day exploits or stealthy infiltration. RL offers a mechanism to adapt to these shifts. An RL-based defense agent can learn from repeated interactions, successively refining a policy that promotes effective responses to emergent threats (Chirra, 2020).

An RL agent also can coordinate multiple defense capabilities. For instance, it might evaluate the benefit of blocking suspicious IP addresses, raising an alert to an incident response platform, or adjusting micro-segmentation in a network. The RL approach tries to maximize a cumulative objective that includes risk reduction, resource costs, and service availability (Chirra, 2022).

Furthermore, RL naturally addresses sequential decision-making. Cyber defense frequently requires a chain of actions: detect anomalies, isolate the compromise, patch vulnerabilities, and then restore normal conditions. RL can handle these sequences in a systematic manner (Syed & ES, 2018).

2.3 Core Cybersecurity Goals and RL Alignment

Cyber defense systems align with three broad goals:

1. **Confidentiality**: Prevent unauthorized disclosure of information.
2. **Integrity**: Safeguard data from unauthorized modification or corruption.
3. **Availability**: Maintain reliable access to systems and data.

By configuring the RL reward function, a security architect can encode these objectives. For example, a negative reward can occur when unauthorized exfiltration is detected, or a positive reward can arise from normal operation without intrusions (Syed & ES, 2020). RL can thus learn a policy that addresses a combination of confidentiality, integrity, and availability requirements.

2.4 Adversarial and Non-Stationary Environments

An RL environment can become non-stationary if an opponent, such as an attacker, changes strategies. Traditional RL algorithms assume stationary transition dynamics. An adversary introduces a moving target that complicates policy convergence. Cyber defense agents often face adversarial drift, where new exploits appear or old vulnerabilities resurface in novel forms (Gadde, 2023).

Game theory sometimes complements RL in these situations. A defender might treat the environment as a two-player game: attacker vs. defender. If the attacker acts optimally, the defender's RL policy can incorporate a minimax perspective or iterative adaptation. This approach can reduce the risk of catastrophic exploitation due to the attacker's shifting tactics (Chirra, 2023).

2.5 Summary of RL Foundations

Reinforcement learning methods adapt through repeated interactions with environments that generate rewards for specific actions. In cyber defense, states can represent signals from intrusion detection systems, logs, or traffic metrics. Actions can include blocking addresses, quarantining nodes, or updating firewall policies. Rewards measure success in preventing intrusions, minimizing false positives, and preserving system performance. The adversarial nature of cybersecurity presents complexities, but RL frameworks retain potential for adaptive and sequential decision-making, aligning with the dynamic character of modern attack surfaces.

3. ARCHITECTURE OF AI-DRIVEN SECURITY SYSTEMS

3.1 Layered View of AI-Driven Cyber Defense

Many AI-driven security solutions adopt a layered architecture to handle data ingestion, feature engineering, model inference, and response automation (Syed & ES, 2024). Each layer addresses distinct responsibilities:

1. **Data Collection Layer**: Aggregates logs, system events, and network telemetry. Examples include NetFlow data, endpoint logs, or application server logs.
2. **Preprocessing and Feature Extraction Layer**: Converts raw data into structured records or feature vectors suitable for AI pipelines. This layer can incorporate normalization, parsing, or correlation across diverse data streams (Gadde, 2019).
3. **Anomaly Detection and Threat Intelligence Layer**: Deploys algorithms that identify suspicious patterns. These can be unsupervised anomaly detectors, supervised classification models, or signature-based rule sets for known threats.
4. **RL Decision and Control Layer**: Uses RL or other decision-making models to recommend or execute responses. This layer can coordinate multiple detection modules and weigh the trade-offs between different actions.
5. **Response and Enforcement Layer**: Applies changes to firewall settings, micro-segmentation strategies, authentication policies, or other security mechanisms. This layer uses interfaces that can be automated or partially supervised by security operators.

In some architectures, the RL module operates in tandem with a Security Information and Event Management (SIEM) system or an incident response platform (Syed & ES, 2019). SIEM solutions gather data from across the environment, while the RL agent determines how to deploy resources and triggers protective measures.

3.2 Role of Machine Learning Components in Defense

Before RL can make decisions, the system often benefits from other ML models that provide classifications or anomaly scores. For instance:

- **Intrusion Detection Systems (IDS) with ML**: These models identify traffic that does not match normal patterns. They might rely on clustering, deep neural networks, or ensemble methods (Chirra, 2023).
- **User and Entity Behavior Analytics (UEBA)**: Techniques that track typical user activities and highlight irregular account usage. This can detect account takeover attempts or insider threats (Syed & ES, 2018).
- **Threat Intelligence**: External feeds or predictive models might produce probability scores indicating the likelihood of a malicious IP or domain.

The RL agent uses these indicators as part of its environmental state. The agent sees, for example, the level of anomalousness for certain traffic flows or alerts from UEBA modules and decides on next steps (Gadde, 2019).

3.3 Coordination with Incident Response Platforms

Automated response requires stable integration with incident management workflows. RL-based systems can issue recommended actions to a standard incident response platform, which might include automated tasks if confidence is high (Chirra, 2021). The synergy of detection, investigation, and remediation can help reduce dwell time, the period between the initial compromise and containment.

Figure 1 (below) depicts an RL-driven architecture for cyber defense. The figure appears after the reference in the text.

Figure 1. Generic RL-based cyber defense architecture

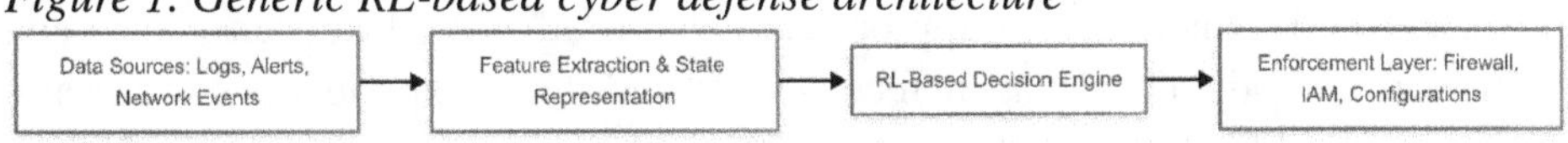

Description of Figure 1:

1. Multiple data sources deliver logs, alerts, and network events.
2. A feature extraction layer converts raw logs into feature vectors or aggregated signals.
3. The RL decision module processes these signals, selects actions, and dispatches instructions to enforcement points.

4. Security enforcement includes firewall updates, identity and access management policies, or more granular network changes.

4. INTELLIGENT THREAT RESPONSE USING AUTONOMOUS CYBER DEFENSE

4.1 Autonomous Cyber Defense Definition

Autonomous cyber defense describes a system that carries out security tasks with minimal human oversight. The system detects anomalies, assesses risk, and initiates mitigations in a self-directed manner. RL-based designs fit this paradigm by continually refining decision policies according to evolving conditions (Syed & ES, 2023).

Autonomous defense addresses the speed and scale of modern attacks. In large networks with thousands of devices, manual intervention can be slow. Automated approaches can identify suspicious events in near real-time and execute interventions without waiting for extended operator review, reducing time-to-containment.

4.2 RL in Dynamic Attack Scenarios

Attack campaigns can shift across multiple stages. An attacker might conduct reconnaissance, follow with an initial breach, pivot laterally within the network, escalate privileges, and exfiltrate data. RL-based systems that handle partial or complete monitoring of these phases can adapt to changes. For instance, if the agent detects lateral movement attempts, it can segment the network or block connections. If the attacker escalates privileges on a workstation, the RL agent can isolate that node from critical systems (Chirra, 2022).

RL's capacity for real-time updates helps in dynamic threat environments. When adversaries notice that a defense approach is triggered, they might switch to different infiltration methods. The RL agent receives updated states, experiences new reward signals, and modifies its policy to respond effectively to the new tactic (Gadde, 2023).

4.3 Sequential Decision-Making for Attack Mitigation

Cyber defense often requires a series of coordinated responses. An example scenario is when suspicious traffic is detected:

1. The RL agent marks the relevant endpoint as suspicious.
2. The agent activates logging at a high level to gather information.

3. If malicious activity escalates, the agent quarantines the endpoint from the internal network.
4. The agent triggers a patching or reimaging workflow.

RL solutions handle these sequential steps because each action leads to a subsequent state that influences the next choice (Syed & ES, 2018). Over repeated interactions, the agent refines the sequence of actions that minimize infiltration success while maintaining business continuity.

4.4 Attack Surface Reduction and Micro-Segmentation

Reducing the network's exposure to external or internal threats can limit an attacker's potential for lateral movement. Micro-segmentation involves creating smaller enclaves that restrict traffic to necessary pathways. An RL agent can dynamically shape these enclaves based on detected risks (Syed & ES, 2020). If certain hosts demonstrate unusual port scans, the agent can move them into a restricted segment. If a user device triggers a high anomaly score, the agent can reduce that device's privileges, limiting the possible scope of an attack.

Attack surface reduction involves disabling unused ports, removing unnecessary services, or restricting network protocols that are not required. RL can determine which adjustments yield better long-term outcomes (Chirra, 2023). The agent can measure how each reduction impacts performance, operational workflows, or compliance requirements.

5. STRATEGY OPTIMIZATION THROUGH REINFORCEMENT LEARNING

5.1 Markov Decision Processes for Cyber Defense

Cyber defense aligns with MDP formulations when states, actions, and rewards can be defined. The environment can include:

- **State**: Current alerts, network configurations, open ports, known vulnerabilities, or user login patterns.
- **Action**: Examples might be blocking IP addresses, isolating subnets, rotating credentials, or updating intrusion detection thresholds.
- **Reward**: Could be a combination of negative values for confirmed intrusions or exfiltrations, neutral or positive values for normal operation, and additional penalties for false alarms or resource overhead.

The RL agent maximizes cumulative rewards, which correspond to strong security postures over extended intervals (Syed & ES, 2024). The presence of time-dependent threats indicates that an MDP structure with possibly large state and action spaces can model the complexity of real-world networks.

5.2 Multi-Objective Optimization in Security

Security teams often have multiple priorities: avoid disruptions to legitimate users, adhere to regulatory limits, and block malicious actions. RL with multi-objective optimization can handle these aspects. The reward function can combine partial reward components:

where $w1, w2, w3\, w_1, w_2, w_{3w1}, w2, w3$ are weights that reflect the importance of each objective (Damaraju, 2021). The agent aims to find a policy that maintains security while balancing overhead costs or compliance constraints.

5.3 Game-Theoretic Extensions and Adversarial RL

In adversarial RL, the environment includes a potentially adaptive attacker. One approach is to treat the attacker as a second agent with its own policy. The cyber defense problem becomes a zero-sum or general-sum game. The defender tries to minimize losses, and the attacker attempts to maximize them (Chirra, 2020). This framing may increase computational complexity, but it can generate strategies that are more robust to diverse adversary behaviors.

Alternatively, adversarial training can be used. The RL system trains on a range of attacker tactics or threats, forcing it to generalize. Another method is to periodically introduce newly discovered exploits or malicious traffic patterns as part of the training environment, ensuring coverage of novel threats (Syed & ES, 2021).

5.4 Model-Based vs. Model-Free RL in Cyber Defense

Model-based RL: The agent learns a predictive model of the environmental transitions. This model can be a neural network that approximates the probability of certain security events given the current state and action. The advantage is that the agent can plan ahead by simulating possible action sequences. The disadvantage is that modeling an adversarial environment can be difficult (Syed & ES, 2018).

Model-free RL: The agent does not explicitly learn a transition model. Instead, it updates its policy or value function from sampled experiences. This approach can handle unexpected events more directly but may require substantial data to converge. Cyber defense systems that gather large log archives or continuous streams of traffic data might support model-free approaches (Chirra, 2022).

5.5 Convergence and Stability Concerns

Convergence refers to the agent settling on a policy that no longer changes significantly with more training episodes. In dynamic or adversarial security contexts, the environment might keep shifting, so the agent's policy remains in a fluid state. Agents must balance continuous adaptation with avoidance of frequent radical changes that could destabilize the environment (Syed & ES, 2023). Techniques like target networks, replay buffers, or periodic policy restarts can help maintain stability in RL-based cyber defense implementations.

6. IMPLEMENTATION CHALLENGES IN RL-BASED CYBER DEFENSE

6.1 Data Collection and Quality Assurance

Collecting data for RL training requires comprehensive logs and alerts. Security logs can be incomplete or corrupted if an adversary modifies records (Gadde, 2019). Complex enterprise infrastructures produce large volumes of logs from firewalls, intrusion detection systems, endpoints, and applications. Aligning these logs in chronological order and ensuring consistency poses logistical challenges. The RL agent's performance depends on the accuracy of the data that define states and rewards.

Security data might also be imbalanced: few actual intrusion events might appear among many benign events. The RL agent might not encounter enough malicious samples to learn robust defense actions. Techniques for data augmentation or scenario simulation can mitigate this issue (Chirra, 2021).

6.2 Reward Engineering and Feedback Loops

Designing an appropriate reward function is essential. If the reward only penalizes confirmed breaches, the agent might not learn to prevent infiltration attempts in earlier stages. If the reward heavily penalizes false positives, the agent might become too permissive (Syed & ES, 2024). A careful balance is crucial.

Delayed or partial rewards also arise in cyber defense. An infiltration might unfold over many steps before being discovered, so the agent only receives a negative reward after significant time has elapsed. This delayed feedback complicates the credit assignment process, meaning the agent may not easily recognize which earlier actions led to the adverse outcome (Gadde, 2023).

6.3 Computational Constraints and Real-Time Requirements

RL can be computationally intensive. Deep RL architectures that combine neural networks with RL may require large amounts of data and GPU acceleration during training. In real-time cyber defense, decisions often must be made rapidly (Chirra, 2020). A trade-off emerges: offline training can be resource-intensive but can happen in a controlled environment, while online adaptation must be fast.

Some organizations deploy RL agents in a simulation environment that mirrors real network conditions. The agent trains offline, then the resulting policy is periodically updated in production. Alternatively, incremental learning in production requires efficient algorithms, distributed computing, or specialized hardware to ensure timely responses (Syed & ES, 2021).

6.4 Exploration vs. Exploitation Dilemma

RL agents explore novel actions to find improved policies, but random exploration in a live network can cause security risks. For example, if the agent tests a policy that lowers firewall thresholds, it might inadvertently create a vulnerability (Syed & ES, 2018). One partial solution involves offline safe exploration approaches, or imposing constraints that ensure minimal critical exposures during learning. Another approach is to set an upper limit on how often or how drastically the agent can modify defense configurations.

6.5 Non-Stationarity and Evolving Attack Tactics

Attack patterns shift continually. The environment transitions might not remain stationary over time. RL algorithms that assume stationarity can fail. Solutions include:

- **Continual Learning**: The agent keeps updating policies without forgetting previously learned patterns.
- **Meta-RL**: The agent gains the ability to adapt quickly to new threats with minimal training (Chirra, 2023).
- **Ensemble Methods**: Multiple RL policies run concurrently, each specialized to certain threat profiles. The system then selects the best policy for the current situation.

6.6 Human-in-the-Loop and Interpretability

Some organizations prefer a human-in-the-loop approach, where security analysts review RL recommendations before final implementation. This can reduce risk but increases response times. Additionally, RL decisions might be opaque if deep networks are used (Syed & ES, 2023). Interpretable RL can partially address these concerns by providing insights into why certain actions were selected.

7. USE CASES AND REAL-WORLD IMPLEMENTATIONS

7.1 Healthcare: Protecting Electronic Health Records

Healthcare organizations house sensitive patient data that must remain private under standards like HIPAA (Syed & ES, 2018). In hospital networks, an RL-based agent can observe device logs, network flows, and user activities. It can detect potential data exfiltration attempts on medical devices or server endpoints. The agent might selectively quarantine suspicious devices and rotate access credentials for staff accounts flagged as compromised. RL is beneficial in healthcare because networks are heterogeneous, with various devices needing different security postures (Syed & ES, 2023).

7.2 Finance: Fraud Detection and Intrusion Response

Banks aim to stop fraudulent transactions while avoiding disruptions to legitimate customers. RL can integrate with existing fraud detection systems by adjusting transaction risk thresholds over time. When suspicious patterns appear, the RL agent can request additional authentication, block the transaction, or place an account under scrutiny. These decisions maximize detection while limiting false positives (Chirra, 2021). This approach is well-suited to large-scale environments that process millions of transactions daily.

7.3 Industrial Control Systems: Minimizing Downtime

Industrial Control Systems (ICS) include manufacturing plants, power grids, and utility networks (Damaraju, 2022). Security strategies in ICS must keep processes operational. An RL solution can track ICS device states, network traffic, and environment conditions. If an attack is suspected, the agent can isolate segments and apply patches in a controlled manner, scheduling them during maintenance windows to avoid unplanned downtime. RL helps weigh the risk of letting a vulnerability remain unpatched against the cost of halting production lines.

7.4 Cloud Infrastructures: Dynamic Resource Allocation

Cloud environments are dynamic, with workloads shifting across virtualized resources. RL-based security can identify anomalies across distributed systems. The agent can move workloads from compromised hosts, apply stricter rules to suspicious traffic, or scale up monitoring when threat levels are high (Syed & ES, 2018). Cloud security policies might combine identity and access management with ephemeral container systems, requiring the RL agent to handle a wide range of possible actions.

7.5 Collaborative Defense in Large Organizations

Some large organizations adopt a shared security operations center (SOC) model, integrating data from multiple business units. RL solutions can process aggregated logs and provide recommended actions that apply to the entire organization (Syed & ES, 2019). This model can leverage cross-unit intelligence to detect correlated attacks. For instance, if one part of the enterprise identifies a specific pattern of network scanning, the RL agent can protect other units that might face the same intrusion.

Table 1 (below) surveys real-world use cases for RL-based defense, summarizing potential actions and benefits.

Table 1. Representative use cases of RL-based cyber defense

Sector	Use Case	Potential RL Actions	Benefits
Healthcare	EHR Protection	Quarantine endpoints, rotate credentials	Complies with HIPAA, reduces breaches
Finance	Fraud Detection & Transaction Blocking	Enforce MFA, block suspicious transactions	Balances security with service
ICS	Network Segmentation & Patch Scheduling	Isolate compromised segments, schedule updates	Minimizes production downtime
Cloud	Automated Resource Reconfiguration	Shift workloads, apply container isolation	Enhances resiliency, reduces dwell
Enterprise	Collaborative SOC & Threat Intelligence	Apply learned policies across units, unify logs	Speeds detection of multi-stage attacks

8. RL-BASED ADAPTIVE CYBER DEFENSE

8.1 System Design Steps

Developers planning to implement RL-based cyber defense can follow a structured procedure:

1. **Identify Scope and Objectives**: Define the boundaries of the environment, such as specific subnets, data centers, or applications. Clarify goals such as reducing intrusion rates, limiting false positives, or meeting compliance (Syed & ES, 2020).
2. **Data Pipeline Construction**: Gather data sources into a consistent pipeline. Time synchronization, log enrichment, and correlation are crucial.
3. **State Representation**: Determine how to encode relevant features. This might involve extracting session-level data, host-level data, or aggregated statistics.
4. **Action Space Definition**: List feasible response measures. Restrict actions to those that can be automated without excessive risk.
5. **Reward Design**: Include metrics that capture security incidents, resource overhead, and compliance.
6. **Algorithm Selection**: Compare value-based (Q-learning, DQN) or policy-based (PPO, A2C) approaches. The choice depends on discrete vs. continuous actions, environment complexity, and available computational resources (Chirra, 2022).
7. **Offline Training**: Use historical data or simulated environments to train an initial policy. This approach avoids risking real-time disruptions during early learning phases.
8. **Pilot Deployment**: Deploy the RL agent in a monitored environment. Possibly adopt a human-in-the-loop arrangement or a controlled environment where real damage is limited.
9. **Continuous Improvement**: Collect feedback, refine the policy, and handle new threat vectors. Integrate new data sources or refine the reward function if the agent exhibits undesired behaviors (Gadde, 2023).

8.2 Training Pipeline

Offline Training: Security logs from past incidents serve as transitions in a Markov chain. The RL agent tries to replicate decision-making by replaying those transitions. The agent sees states (features from logs), selects actions, and observes simulated outcomes. Synthetic data can also be introduced to represent novel attack vectors (Syed & ES, 2019).

Online Fine-Tuning: Once the agent is deployed, it keeps adjusting its policy. The environment's states now come from real-time sensors. The agent obtains immediate rewards, such as detection of an intrusion or successful blocking of suspicious traffic. This online learning loop helps adapt to changing attacker behaviors (Chirra, 2023).

8.3 Reference Implementation Blueprint

Figure 2 (below) outlines an implementation blueprint for an RL-driven adaptive defense solution.

Figure 2. RL-based adaptive cyber defense implementation workflow

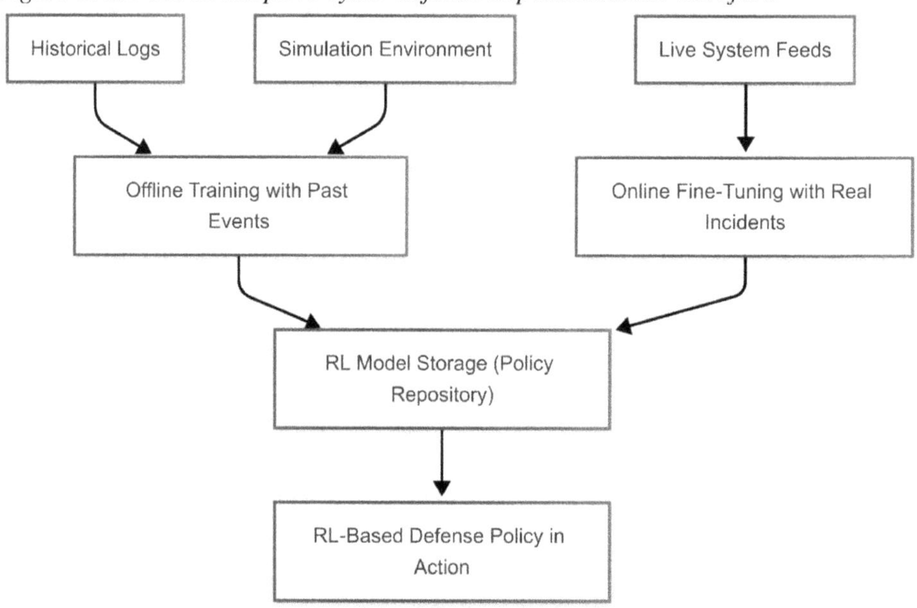

Description of Figure 2:

1. Historical logs feed into an offline training pipeline that constructs an initial RL policy.
2. Simulation environments augment training data by emulating attacks.
3. RL model storage retains the learned policy.
4. Online fine-tuning adjusts the policy using fresh data from the live system.
5. The updated policy is deployed to the production network or environment.

8.4 Performance Considerations

1. **Scalability**: The system should handle large volumes of logs and network events. Distributed computing frameworks can assist with RL training.
2. **Latency**: The RL agent's decision cycle must align with attack detection windows to ensure timely response (Chirra, 2021).
3. **Reliability**: Fail-safes can revert to default configurations if the RL agent malfunctions or presents unsafe actions.
4. **Maintainability**: The design must enable security teams to audit, adjust parameters, or incorporate new detection models without excessive overhead (Syed & ES, 2023).

9. PERFORMANCE METRICS AND EVALUATION IN RL-BASED CYBER DEFENSE

9.1 Traditional Cybersecurity Metrics

Organizations often measure the rate of blocked intrusions, mean time to detection (MTTD), mean time to resolution (MTTR), and false positive/false negative ratios. In an RL context, these metrics relate to the reward structure. High detection rates indicate that the RL agent effectively prevents threats, while low false positives maintain user access (Syed & ES, 2020).

9.2 RL-Specific Metrics

In RL, performance is also measured through:

- **Cumulative Reward**: Tracks long-term performance across episodes.
- **Policy Convergence**: Observes whether the agent's actions stabilize over time.
- **Learning Speed**: Monitors how many training steps or episodes are needed before reaching acceptable performance (Gadde, 2023).

Some defenders simulate repeated episodes of attacks to see if the RL agent's reward rises, reflecting fewer successful breaches or faster containment.

9.3 Robustness and Stress Testing

Attackers might probe the defense to discover weaknesses. Evaluating robustness includes subjecting the RL agent to:

- **Novel Attack Strategies**: Zero-day or advanced persistent threat scenarios.
- **Resource Constraints**: The system might have limited CPU cycles.
- **Latent Adversarial Tactics**: Attackers could try subversive actions to manipulate the RL policy.

Stress testing can identify conditions under which the policy fails. Red-team exercises involve security professionals who replicate adversary tactics, measuring how the RL agent copes (Chirra, 2021).

9.4 Compliance and Policy Adherence

In certain industries, compliance metrics include whether the system meets regulatory guidelines. For instance, a healthcare RL-based defense might need to log relevant events to ensure auditability for HIPAA. If the RL agent bypasses a control, that might generate a compliance penalty in the reward function (Syed & ES, 2018).

9.5 Resource Consumption and Scalability

RL algorithms that rely on large neural networks or frequent policy updates might consume considerable computational resources. A suitable metric is the overhead in CPU, memory, or network traffic that is attributed to the RL system (Chirra, 2023). If resource overhead becomes excessive, the system might be impractical in production. Scalability measures how performance degrades as the number of endpoints, data sources, or transaction volumes grow. **Table 2** (below) summarizes key metrics often used to assess RL-based defense systems.

Table 2. Key evaluation metrics for RL-based cyber defense

Metric	Description	Importance
Detection Accuracy	Proportion of malicious events correctly identified	Indicates agent's ability to spot attacks
False Positive Rate	Proportion of benign events mislabeled as malicious	Affects user experience and trust
Mean Time to Response	Interval from threat detection to mitigation	Reflects operational speed

continued on following page

Table 2. Continued

Metric	Description	Importance
Cumulative Reward	Long-term sum of rewards per episode	Measures overall RL policy performance
Learning Efficiency	Number of episodes or samples needed for satisfactory policy	Reflects training cost and feasibility
Resource Overhead	CPU, memory, or bandwidth consumption of the RL system	Influences scalability and deployment cost
Compliance Score	Degree to which actions and logs meet regulatory obligations	Ensures alignment with legal/industry requirements

10. ETHICAL, REGULATORY, AND GOVERNANCE CONSIDERATIONS

10.1 Privacy and Sensitive Data

Privacy laws, such as HIPAA, GDPR, or CCPA, constrain how data can be collected and processed for RL training (Syed & ES, 2018). Training data might include personal identifiers in log entries or user behavior patterns. RL-based defense solutions must anonymize or tokenize sensitive fields. Some organizations rely on data minimization, retaining only the essential elements needed for feature extraction.

10.2 Automated Decision-Making Accountability

An RL agent might disrupt network traffic or revoke user access if it interprets certain events as malicious. Automatic actions can have business implications. Ensuring accountability is vital. Many organizations adopt a layered approach: the RL agent recommends actions, and a security operator reviews high-impact decisions (Damaraju, 2022). This practice provides human oversight.

10.3 Regulatory Compliance and Governance

Organizations in finance or critical infrastructure face strict regulations. Automated defenses can inadvertently violate policies if they block regulated services or fail to log relevant events. The RL reward function should account for compliance or risk management targets (Chirra, 2020). Governance frameworks might impose checks that validate the agent's actions against baseline policies, preventing potential compliance lapses.

10.4 Auditing and Explainability

RL decisions can be opaque. Explainable RL methods offer approximations of the agent's decision logic, assisting security teams in audits. Log-based approaches record the agent's state, action, and reward at each step. This practice aids in post-incident analysis. Some domains require evidence to justify security decisions, so at least partial interpretability is essential (Syed & ES, 2023).

Table 3 (below) outlines regulatory contexts that often shape how RL-based defense is governed.

Table 3. Regulatory and governance considerations for RL-based cyber defense

Regulation/Framework	Industry or Region	Implications for RL
HIPAA	Healthcare (US)	Log handling, data anonymity, minimal breach risk
GDPR	EU Member States	Right to be forgotten, data minimization, explainability
PCI DSS	Payment Card Industry	Secure cardholder data, real-time defense for transactional systems
SOX	Public Companies (US)	Audit trails, accountability in financial operations
ICS Standards	Industrial & Utilities	Reliability, safety-critical patching and segmentation policies
Organizational Governance	Varies by Company/ Institution	Oversight boards, compliance committees, auditing of RL decisions

11. FUTURE DIRECTIONS IN RL-BASED ADAPTIVE CYBER DEFENSE

11.1 Continual Learning and Meta-RL

As threats evolve, the defense agent needs methods that adapt without discarding previously learned behaviors. **Continual learning** aims to maintain performance across multiple tasks or threat scenarios, reducing catastrophic forgetting. **Meta-RL** introduces the concept of learning to learn, so the agent can adjust policies with minimal new data (Chirra, 2023). This approach is useful in environments where new attack types appear regularly, and the agent must quickly incorporate them.

11.2 Federated and Distributed RL

Some organizations cannot centralize security data due to privacy or legal restrictions. **Federated RL** allows multiple sites to train local models, then share model parameters (Gadde, 2021). This practice aggregates insights without exposing raw data, aligning with privacy laws. **Distributed RL** frameworks can speed training through parallel computation, especially in large-scale corporate environments.

11.3 Hybrid Approaches: Combining Supervised and RL Methods

Certain tasks, such as classifying malicious packets or user sessions, can rely on supervised learning. RL can then decide how to respond. Hybrid systems can combine the strengths of different ML paradigms. The system might use a supervised model to detect anomalies with high accuracy and feed that information into an RL agent that selects a suitable action (Syed & ES, 2018). This arrangement can reduce the complexity of designing a single RL model for detection and response.

11.4 Explainable and Trustworthy RL

Explainability helps organizational stakeholders accept automated security decisions. Some RL research explores ways to generate interpretable rules or local explanations for each action (Syed & ES, 2023). Trustworthy RL aims to ensure the agent's actions remain within safe operational bounds, employing formal methods or constraint-based reward shaping.

11.5 Integration with Quantum-Safe Cryptography

Quantum computing can affect cryptographic schemes. Some security researchers investigate **quantum-safe cryptography** for data protection (Chirra, 2023). RL might adapt cryptographic key management in real time, selecting quantum-safe protocols when needed, or rotating keys based on threat intelligence. This approach could ensure advanced threat resilience.

11.6 Deployment of RL Agents in Edge and 5G Environments

With the growth of edge computing and 5G networks, more devices connect at the network's periphery. RL agents could reside at the edge, detecting intrusions in real time (Damaraju, 2022). Low-latency communications can support distributed

RL. This practice can enhance coverage for IoT devices, smart cities, or autonomous vehicles, which generate continuous data streams.

12. CONCLUSION

Reinforcement Learning has emerged as a promising methodology for adaptive cyber defense. Its capacity to handle sequential decision-making, dynamic environments, and adversarial behaviors allows it to address complex security needs. Traditional defenses rely on static configurations, pattern matching, or threshold-based alarms, which may be ineffective against sophisticated or evolving attackers. RL-based solutions can systematically refine actions over time to optimize long-term security outcomes.

This chapter has explored the foundational concepts of RL and examined how they map to cyber defense tasks. The text covered architectural aspects of AI-driven security systems, focusing on how RL integrates with data ingestion, anomaly detection, and automated enforcement layers. It described how autonomous cyber defense uses RL to respond to dynamic threats, including multi-stage intrusions. Strategy optimization for adaptive defense was explained through MDPs, multi-objective optimization, game-theoretic extensions, and distinctions between model-based and model-free RL.

Challenges in implementing RL-based solutions include reward function design, ensuring data quality, dealing with resource constraints, handling the exploration-exploitation trade-off, and addressing non-stationary attacker behaviors. The chapter also examined the practical dimension of RL deployment, providing a methodology that details offline training, pilot testing, online fine-tuning, and performance measurement. Use cases spanned healthcare, finance, industrial control systems, cloud environments, and large enterprises. The text then detailed metrics for evaluating RL-driven defense solutions, including detection rates, false positives, response times, resource usage, and compliance adherence.

Ethical, regulatory, and governance considerations are essential, particularly in environments subject to HIPAA, GDPR, PCI DSS, or ICS standards. Automated RL-based decisions must balance security with the need for accountability, privacy, and legal compliance. Audit trails, explainable policies, and controlled modes of operation can ensure alignment with organizational goals.

Future work may revolve around continual learning, meta-RL, federated RL, and hybrid AI solutions that combine supervised classifiers with RL decision modules. Research into explainable RL can enhance trust in automated responses. Edge computing and 5G deployments open new frontiers for distributed RL-based security solutions. Integration with quantum-safe cryptography may become relevant as computing paradigms evolve.

Organizations exploring RL-based cyber defense should systematically define their objectives, data requirements, environment scope, and risk thresholds. By applying a structured methodology, validating performance through simulations and pilot deployments, and addressing governance concerns, many enterprises can leverage RL to create adaptive, automated security frameworks. The capacity to learn from repeated interactions, refine strategies, and respond to new threats positions RL as a potentially transformative technology in the ongoing effort to safeguard digital assets in modern network environments.

REFERENCES

Chirra, B. R. (2020). Advancing Cyber Defense: Machine Learning Techniques for Next-Generation Intrusion Detection. *International Journal of Machine Learning Research in Cybersecurity and Artificial Intelligence*, *14*(1), 550–573.

Chirra, B. R. (2020). Intelligent Phishing Mitigation: Leveraging AI for Enhanced Email Security in Corporate Environments. *International Journal of Advanced Engineering Technologies and Innovations*, *1*(2), 178–200.

Chirra, B. R. (2021). AI-Driven Vulnerability Assessment and Mitigation Strategies for Cyber-Physical Systems. *Revista de Inteligencia Artificial en Medicina*, *13*(1), 471–493.

Chirra, B. R. (2022). Advancing Real-Time Malware Detection with Deep Learning for Proactive Threat Mitigation. *International Journal of Advanced Engineering Technologies and Innovations*, *1*(01), 274–396.

Chirra, B. R. (2023). Enhancing Cybersecurity Resilience: Federated Learning-Driven Threat Intelligence for Adaptive Defense. *International Journal of Machine Learning Research in Cybersecurity and Artificial Intelligence*, *11*(1), 260–280.

Chirra, B. R. (2023). Enhancing Cloud Security through Quantum Cryptography for Robust Data Transmission. *Revista de Inteligencia Artificial en Medicina*, *15*(1), 752–775.

Chirra, D. R. (2020). AI-Based Real-Time Security Monitoring for Cloud-Native Applications in Hybrid Cloud Environments. *Revista de Inteligencia Artificial en Medicina*, *11*(1), 382–402.

Chirra, D. R. (2021). AI-Enabled Cybersecurity Solutions for Protecting Smart Cities Against Emerging Threats. *International Journal of Advanced Engineering Technologies and Innovations*, *1*(2), 237–254.

Chirra, D. R. (2022). Next-Generation IDS: AI-Driven Intrusion Detection for Securing 5G Network Architectures. *International Journal of Advanced Engineering Technologies and Innovations*, *1*(2), 230–245.

Chirra, D. R. (2023). AI-Augmented Zero Trust Architectures: Enhancing Cybersecurity in Dynamic Enterprise Environments. *International Journal of Machine Learning Research in Cybersecurity and Artificial Intelligence*, *15*(1), 643–669.

Damaraju, A. (2020). Social Media as a Cyber Threat Vector: Trends and Preventive Measures. *Revista Española de Documentación Cientifica*, *14*(1), 95–112.

Damaraju, A. (2021). Data Privacy Regulations and Their Impact on Global Businesses. *Pakistan Journal of Linguistics*, *2*(01), 47–56.

Damaraju, A. (2022). Securing Critical Infrastructure: Advanced Strategies for Resilience and Threat Mitigation in the Digital Age. *Revista de Inteligencia Artificial en Medicina*, *12*(1), 76–111.

Gadde, H. (2019). AI-Driven Schema Evolution and Management in Heterogeneous Databases. *International Journal of Machine Learning Research in Cybersecurity and Artificial Intelligence*, *10*(1), 332–356.

Gadde, H. (2021). Integrating AI with Graph Databases for Complex Relationship Analysis. *International Journal of Advanced Engineering Technologies and Innovations*, *1*(2), 294–314.

Gadde, H. (2022). Integrating AI into SQL Query Processing: Challenges and Opportunities. *International Journal of Advanced Engineering Technologies and Innovations*, *1*(3), 194–219.

Gadde, H. (2023). Improving Data Reliability with AI-Based Fault Tolerance in Distributed Databases. *International Journal of Advanced Engineering Technologies and Innovations*, *1*(2), 183–207.

Goriparthi, R. G. (2024). Reinforcement Learning in IoT: Enhancing Smart Device Autonomy through AI. *International Journal of Advanced Engineering Technologies and Innovations*, *2*(1), 89–109.

Syed, F. M., & ES, F. K. (2018). Ensuring HIPAA and GDPR Compliance Through Advanced IAM Analytics. *International Journal of Advanced Engineering Technologies and Innovations*, *1*(2), 71–94.

Syed, F. M., & ES, F. K. (2019). Privacy by Design: Integrating GDPR Principles into IAM Frameworks for Healthcare. *International Journal of Advanced Engineering Technologies and Innovations*, *1*(2), 16–36.

Syed, F. M., ES, F. K., & Johnson, E. (2019). Privacy by Design: Integrating GDPR Principles into IAM Frameworks for Healthcare. *International Journal of Advanced Engineering Technologies and Innovations*, *1*(2), 16–36.

Syed, F. M., & ES, F. K. (2020). IAM for Cyber Resilience: Protecting Healthcare Data from Advanced Persistent Threats. *International Journal of Advanced Engineering Technologies and Innovations*, *1*(2), 153–183.

Syed, F. M., & ES, F. K. (2021). AI and HIPAA Compliance in Healthcare IAM. *International Journal of Advanced Engineering Technologies and Innovations, 1*(4), 118–145.

Syed, F. M., ES, F. K., & Johnson, E. (2022). AI-Powered SOC in the Healthcare Industry. *International Journal of Advanced Engineering Technologies and Innovations, 1*(2), 395–414.

Syed, F. M., & ES, F. K. (2023). AI in Securing Electronic Health Records (EHR) Systems. *International Journal of Advanced Engineering Technologies and Innovations, 1*(02), 593–620.

Syed, F. M., ES, F. K., & Johnson, E. (2023). AI in Protecting Clinical Trial Data from Cyber Threats. *International Journal of Advanced Engineering Technologies and Innovations, 1*(2), 567–592.

Syed, F. M., & ES, F. K. (2023). AI in Securing Electronic Health Records (EHR) Systems. *International Journal of Advanced Engineering Technologies and Innovations, 1*(2), 593–620.

Syed, F. M., & ES, F. K. (2024). AI in Protecting Sensitive Patient Data under GDPR in Healthcare. *International Journal of Advanced Engineering Technologies and Innovations, 1*(02), 401–435.

Syed, F. M., & ES, F. K. (2024). AI-Driven Forensic Analysis for Cyber Incidents in Healthcare. *International Journal of Machine Learning Research in Cybersecurity and Artificial Intelligence, 15*(1), 473–499.

Syed, F. M., & ES, F. K. (2024). AI-Driven Threat Intelligence in Healthcare Cybersecurity. *Revista de Inteligencia Artificial en Medicina, 14*(1), 431–459.

Chapter 9
Evolving Sentinels: How Autonomous Defense Systems Self-Learn and Adapt to Dynamic Threat Environments

Khalil Omar
https://orcid.org/0000-0002-5328-5762
University of Petra, Jordan

Jamal Zraqou
https://orcid.org/0000-0001-9060-7188
University of Petra, Jordan

Wesam Alkhadour
https://orcid.org/0009-0004-1937-0308
University of Petra, Jordan

Jorge Marx Gómez
University of Oldenburg, Germany

ABSTRACT

This chapter introduces the adaptive defense intelligence framework (ADIF), short for the Adaptive Defense Intelligence Framework, a radically new initiative in the field of autonomous cybersecurity systems. ADIF overcomes glaring limitations present in existing security solutions through innovation in four different major spheres: hierarchical reinforcement learning architecture, a contextual analysis engine that drastically reduces false positives, federated knowledge distribution that maintains privacy, and a self-verification feedback loop. Financial, healthcare, and manufacturing operational dashboards showed remarkable improvements in detection rates, response times, and operational continuity during active threats.

DOI: 10.4018/979-8-3373-0954-5.ch009

Though faced with startup challenges in terms of initial training requirements and computational intensiveness, this marks the shift from reactive to proactive security postures, offering the capability of continuous self-learning and further evolving the system with ever-growing threats.

1. INTRODUCTION

One of the most challenging aspects of modern business networks is the ever-changing and more advanced threats. As companies strive through their digital transformation paths, a widening attack surface and integrated systems usher in challenges never seen before in the field of security (Ghafir et al., 2018). Recent surveys report average breach discovery times climbing to 212 days in 2023, with containment taking another 75 days on average (IBM, 2023). Prolonged visibility lacks maturity due to the inherent weakness of contemporary means of security: no ability to spot new threats and resist them in real-time mode without human intervention.

The concept of autonomous defense systems marks a fundamental conceptual pivot from reactive to proactive security postures. Unlike the traditional use cases of security information and event management (SIEM) solutions — primarily as tools that help human analysts detect potential security threats — seamless security involves systems that can detect, analyze, and mitigate threats within very minimal human intervention (Taddeo et al., 2019a). This becomes most relevant as attack techniques evolve faster than human defenders can mount manual defenses.

Autonomous capabilities to react inside network defense have dramatically advanced within the past decade. The formerly not-so-sophisticated platforms, which can only execute limited automatic responses, mostly exist within specific parameters and do not have true adaptive learning abilities. Constricted by over-worked and under-resourced human analysts, these platforms still do not have real adaptive learning capabilities (Apruzzese et al., 2018). Although machine learning is already dominant in the detection portion of systems, implementing a completely self-learning and autonomous response is another emerging frontier.

Despite such strides in security automation, some very critical challenges restrain the effectiveness of the very topmost modern autonomous defense systems.

1. Adaptability Gap: Current detection mechanisms have serious lag times where they are unable to detect a new attack vector ad hoc and respond to it without prior training or signatures, creating large windows of vulnerability (Havenga et al., 2022; Sabeel et al., 2024).

2. Limited Context Awareness: Most automation systems have limitations in terms of providing descriptive and meaningful context wherein security organizations fine-tune adversarial behaviors and separate legitimate anomalies from actual threats; higher false positive rates only further exacerbate alert fatigue (Preuveneers et al., 2024; Y. Wang et al., 2024).
3. Defensive Feedback Loops: Most of the prevailing systems do not have feedback mechanisms to learn from successful as well as unsuccessful response actions. Therefore, there is hardly any scope to evolve over time (Oben Yapar, 2024; S, 2023).
4. Scalability Challenges: In an enterprise environment, there is data of myriad types and volumes. Carrying out real-time analysis and response is intensive computationally, demanding massive resources in place DIRE NEEDS (Zuech et al., 2015).
5. Trust and Verification: Organizations want to have trust in explainable rationales plus verification mechanisms to delegate critical security decisions to autonomous systems.

These challenges are further extrapolated with the increasingly aggressive nature of the threat landscape, with adversaries utilizing automated attack platforms and advanced persistent threats (APTs) that can quickly pivot against defensive measures.

This chapter introduces ADIF, which stands for Adaptive Defense Intelligence Framework. It is an architectural innovation of autonomous systems that shall adapt and learn from self-experience in a dynamic and vulnerable threat environment. Thus, ADIF shall be regarded as a fundamental leap forward for autonomous response capability on account of several innovations.

1. Multilayered Reinforcement Learning Architecture: In it, we present a hierarchical architecture of reinforcement learning that can enable a defense system to learn the optimal response strategy against the ever-evolving threat environment without requiring explicit programming for that particular threat scenario.
2. Contextual Analysis Engine: Our approach deeply implements a context-aware analysis system able to associate extensive sources of data to differentiate accurately between anomalies that, while appearing odd, actually prove benign and those that are attackers, consequently reducing false positives dramatically.
3. Federated Response Knowledge Distribution: This paper proposes a new methodology that will share the learned knowledge about defense but only when there is an acknowledged attack across distributed network elements. The data remains secure with privacy constraints yet shared for localized adaptation.

4. Self-Verification Feedback Loop: ADIF comes with a continuous appraisal system that was developed to measure response effectiveness and eventually automatically readjust confidence threshold levels. This is self-improving precision over time.

This research will make specific contributions to the field of autonomous network defense:

1- A mathematical model is presented and formalized for reinforcement learning, taking into account the asymmetric costs of false positives with false negatives in defensive response selection.
2- A novel autonomous defense systems architecture that allows for continuous learning while not compromising network stability or security feature offerings.
3- An empirical evaluation is presented to prove that, indeed, there is a significant improvement in detection accuracy, response time, and false positive reduction compared to other systems that are scientifically known.
4- Implementation guidelines plus a framework on how to deploy safely, in production environments, autonomous defense capabilities.

The rest of this chapter proceeds as follows. Section 2 performs a literature review of autonomous network defense, thereby contrasting what is obtained with the current approach and its drawbacks. Section 3 introduces the methodology with the ADIF architecture and detailed discussions about its key elements. Section 4 explains the setting used to test our system, which was run in several enterprise environments. Section 5 comes back with the full results alongside an analysis placing the performance of ADIF against several baseline approaches. Section 6 concludes the paper with a summary of what has been proved and discusses possible avenues for further research.

2. RELATED WORK

2.1. Evolution of Network Defense Systems

The different generations through which network defense systems have developed include static signature-based detection, up to where autonomous and booming platforms are currently emerging. The early techniques of intrusion matching were primarily based on identifying known patterns of attack (Denning, 1987). While these systems were good at detecting threats that have been documented before, they were weak in the face of ever-developing variations and new attacks. This fact motivated subsequent researchers to propose anomaly-based detection methods that characterize the normal behavior of a network and therefore indicate deviations (García-Teodoro et al., 2009).

The infusion of techniques of machine learning into the system struck a signal of a much higher level of network defense capability. (Buczak & Guven, 2016), In their extensive survey on the use of learning machines for cybersecurity, they took into account supervised classification over malware in unsupervised clustering and then anomalies. Even up to the level where they have been able to improve the detection capability, the response action required from humans is immensely high.

More recently, Security Orchestration, Automation, and Response (SOAR) emerged to build the bridge between detection and response. These systems actually implement predefined playbooks, offering automation in common response procedures (Tsirakis et al., 2025). This is an example of the movement toward autonomous defense. Yet, SOAR platforms use rather static response patterns and do not quite fit into dynamically changing threat scenarios.

2.2. Machine Learning for Threat Detection

Machine learning approaches have further advanced in their application to the detection of threats. The supervised learning method has achieved much success in high precision for known attack patterns. For example, (Vinayakumar et al., 2019) performed detailed experimentation with deep neural networks for intrusion detection to show in what detail deep learning architectures can outperform regular machine learning methods. Another study with similar comparisons (Resende & Drummond, 2019) conducted a comprehensive analysis of random forest-based methodologies applied to intrusion detection systems, explicitly stating their high performance over many datasets and types of attacks. While there have been advances, the very granularity of this limitation is what has since endured. They require significant labeled training data and, even then, struggle to detect previously unseen attack patterns and zero-day exploits. As pointed out by (Buczak & Guven, 2016) in their comprehensive survey, the transferability of these models to novel attack variants continues to pose a significant challenge to operational security.

The deep learning architectures show promise in identifying even subtle attacks. The results from (Vinayakumar et al., 2019) on deep neural networks applied to network traffic analysis claimed to show manifold improvement over traditional approaches for both known and zero-day attacks. In a related approach, (W. Wang et al., 2017) applies convolutional neural network methodologies to more easily indicate the presence of malicious network traffic, prompting low feature engineering needs.

Unsupervised and semi-supervised learning attacks bring some promise to the problem of finding unseen old threats. Kitsune, due to the work of (Mirsky et al., 2018), could manage to work as an unsupervised intrusion detection method in a network with an ensemble of autoencoders. The system proves appropriate for learning anomalous network traffic without specific attack signatures trained a priori. Such a methodology indeed delivers an efficient means of zero-day attack detection over IoT networks. Meanwhile, (Javaid et al., 2016) introduced a self-taught learning approach for network intrusion detection that requires very little labeled data but shows significantly better results when tested on the NSL-KDD dataset compared to conventional methods. These solutions indeed promise some coping mechanism against the signature-dependence issue. The only caveat is that the solutions typically suffer high false positive rates in real-world complex operating environments.

Despite the above advances that have been made, most current implementations are detection, not autonomous responses, thereby creating a gaping hole in defense capabilities.

2.3. Autonomous Response Systems

Autonomous response capabilities represent the cutting edge of research in the area of defending a network. The taxonomy of intrusion response systems presented in an early work by (Stakhanova et al., 2007) categorized possible approaches according to the degree of their automation, from manual to fully automatic, thus setting the cornerstone of a conceptual framework for much more advanced response mechanisms, though noting striking limitations in new threat adaptivity.

An important line of investigation, recently increasingly adopted, is done on learning reinforcement for autonomous response. The survey by (Nguyen & Reddi, 2023) provides a comprehensive view of deep reinforcement learning applications within cybersecurity that demonstrates the possibility of learning optimal defense strategies for RL agents by repeatedly interacting with the environment in simulations. Their study revealed significant benefits from such an approach in dynamic threat environments where rule-based systems fail. Another papers by (O'Driscoll et al., 2024; Sandoval et al., 2025), implemented a reinforcement learning approach toward the building of adaptive response policies against network attacks through learning how defensive agents can become better over time due to experience.

Cooperative approaches have also proven to be quite effective in dealing with challenges in distributed security. (Zhou et al., 2010) conducted an in-depth review of coordinated attacks and collaborative intrusion detection systems to show how cooperative defense mechanisms enhanced detection capability numerous times better across organizational boundaries. Their results were revealing the sharing of attack intelligence among variously distributed detection nodes is significantly more resilient against coordinated attacks than in isolated systems. This further gets leveraged by federated learning-based collaborative designs. The feasibility of privacy-preserving cooperative threat detection across industrial systems is reported by (Mothukuri et al., 2021) through an opening federated learning implementation without sharing raw data. Their review indicates a remarkable improvement in detectability without abandoning any data privacy guarantees. These improvements show the promise of secure knowledge-sharing solutions as an eventual integral element of the next-generation defense systems.

However, the current autonomous response systems are responding with several significant challenges. A taxonomy of intrusion response systems is proposed by (Shameli-Sendi et al., 2014), with most of the implementations working under constrained environmental settings presenting limited action spaces and difficulty in generalizing to real complex network scenarios. This study evaluated operational response systems, and it was observed that even the most advanced autonomous systems still find it very difficult to cope with the dynamics of an attacking environment. Trust and verification challenges were also highlighted by (Taddeo et al., 2019b) as huddles that prevent many companies from implementing full-fledged autonomous security measures that do not include human surveillance.

2.4. Limitations of Current Approaches

Current approaches to autonomous network defense face several critical limitations that our research aims to address:

1- Limited to Reacting Rather Than Predicting: Most current systems wait until attacks materialize to capture and respond to them instead of recognizing and countering evolving threats even before they strike.
2- Lagging Learning Capabilities: While many systems have machine learning based-detection, few have a mechanism for continuous learning, which will eventually enable the defense systems to enhance their response strategies based on observed outcomes.
3- Insufficient Contextual Reasoning: Most of the current autonomous systems are insufficient in their high-order contextual reasoning to make appropriately nuanced response decisions in extraordinarily complex enterprise environments.
4- Rigid Response Mechanisms: Most automated response systems work based on predefined playbooks rather than developing novel response strategies according to evolving threat scenarios.
5- Limited Knowledge Sharing: Prior systems have been poorly efficient in information sharing and in defending practice resources across firm borders with the necessary security and privacy.

These are what the proposed ADIF addresses through a new architecture that enables continuous learning, deep contextual understanding, and adaptive response capabilities.

3. PROPOSED METHODOLOGY

3.1. System Architecture Overview

ADIF is the new approach toward autonomous defense intelligence that never ceases to learn and, therefore, withstands the changes that keep happening within the threat landscapes. Figure 1 below shows the high architecture of ADIF, constituted by those very five matched components that together promise self-evolving defensive capabilities.

The architecture of ADIF, therefore, is constituted by the following key components:

1- Multi-Source Data Collection and Normalization Layer: Ingests data flow from network devices, endpoints, applications, and external threat intelligence and standardizes it.
2- Contextual Analysis Engine: Outputs situational awareness to distinguish anomalies and actual threats.
3- Reinforcement Learning Core: Captures responsive strategies to build and update them in the hierarchy of environmental feedback dynamics.
4- Response Orchestration Module: Performs the response actions based on defensive strategies of a specified level of confidence and observes the results to give feedback to the learning system.
5- Federated Knowledge Distribution Network: Facilitates learned defense strategies sharing across corporate boundaries, maintaining data privacy.

These components sit in a feedback loop continuously evolving in the understanding of the threat environment and response effectiveness over time.

Figure 1. Adaptive defense intelligence framework architecture

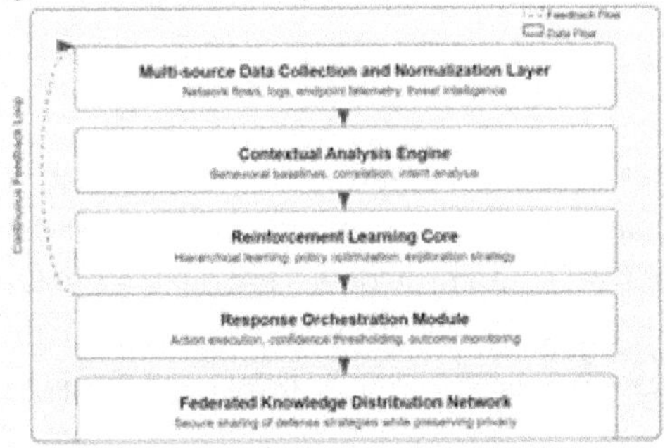

3.2. Multi-Source Data Collection and Normalization

ADIF's adaptive capabilities are fundamentally dependent on its ability to ingest and normalize such myriad streams of data that, in combination, promise a full view of network activity. Data collection tends to be multi-sourced from the following layers of interfaces:

- Network flow records and packet captures.
- System and application logs.
- Endpoint telemetry data.
- Authentication and access control logs.
- External threat intelligence feeds.
- Previous incident response records.

Raw data undergoes a multi-stage normalization process to create a unified data representation that facilitates cross-source correlation. This process involves:

1- Temporal Alignment: Timestamps synchronize between different systems to make events in the organization occur in order of occurrence.
2- Entity Resolution: Correlation between identifiers from different data stores for maintaining accurate entity references (e.g., correlation of the IP address namespace with the namespace of user accounts and device identifiers).
3- Protocol Standardization: Conversion of heterogeneous data format into a common schema for consolidated analysis.
4- Feature Extraction: Derivation of effective features associated with the raw streams of data that will support further analysis downstream.

The normalization process is defined by the transformation function:

```
N(d_i) = {f_1, f_2, ..., f_n}
```

Where *d_i* represents a raw data point from source *i*, and *{f_1, f_2, ..., f_n}* represents the set of standardized features extracted from that data point.

To handle the massive volume of data generated in enterprise environments, the collection layer implements a dynamic sampling mechanism that adjusts data ingestion rates based on observed anomaly levels and system resource constraints.

3.3. Contextual Analysis Engine

The Contextual Analysis Engine (CAE) effectively deals with probably the essential problems in autonomous defense systems—distinguishing between what are true anomalies and actual threats. The CAE adopts an extremely multilayer methodology to eventually form a rich contextual representation.

3.3.1. Behavioral Baseline Modeling

The dynamic formation and regular updates to the baselines of network entities (users, devices, applications) in an interdisciplinary manner using both statistical modeling and deep learning form the CAE. How the model of the baseline for entity e is represented is:

```
Be={b1,b2,...,bm}
```

Where *b_i* represents a behavioral dimension such as temporal activity patterns, resource utilization, communication patterns, or access patterns.

For each observed event, the system calculates a deviation score from the established baseline:

$$D(\text{event}, B_e) = \sum_{i=1}^{m} w_i \cdot |event\,t_i - b_i|$$

Where w_i represents the weight assigned to dimension i based on its predictive importance.

3.3.2. Contextual Correlation

Rather than analyzing events in isolation, the CAE correlates related activities across time, space, and entities to build comprehensive attack narratives. This correlation is modeled as a dynamic graph structure:

$G=(V,E,A_V,A_E)$

Where:

- V represents the set of network entities
- E represents the relationships between entities
- A_V represents the attributes associated with each entity
- A_E represents the attributes associated with each relationship

Graph attention networks (GATs) analyze this structure to identify suspicious patterns that may indicate coordinated attack activity. The attention mechanism allows the system to focus on the most relevant relationships when assessing potential threats.

3.3.3. Intent Analysis

The CAE introduces a new approach to intent analysis that seeks to determine the probable intentions for observed activities. This analysis combines:

1- Sequential Pattern Analysis can be seen as trying to find sequences of activities that are within known attack patterns by Recurrent Neural Networks.
2- To Impact Assessment includes estimating what has been observed against critical assets and operations.
3- Anomaly Clustering enables grouping related anomalies-in-action toward the detection of coordinated campaigns, which would not have been detected from individual events.

The process of contextual analysis develops a full threat report for each identified anomaly:

$TA=(p,s,c,i)$

Where:

- p represents the probability that the anomaly indicates an actual threat
- s represents the severity of the potential threat
- c represents confidence in the assessment
- i represents the inferred intent behind the activity

This rich contextual understanding enables more precise response selection and significantly reduces false positives compared to context-free approaches.

3.4. Reinforcement Learning Core

In its core, the Reinforcement Learning Core (RLC) constitutes the pivotal innovation of ADIF. It grants the system the ability to gradually master optimal response strategies through mutual experience. The RLC installs a hierarchy of reinforcement learning architectures, implementing the same many levels of abstraction.

3.4.1. Mathematical Formulation

The prospective defense scenario is stated as a Partially Observable Markov Decision Process (POMDP):

$$POMDP=(S,A,T,R,\Omega,O,\gamma)$$

Where:

- S represents the state space (network and security conditions)
- A represents the action space (possible defensive responses)
- T represents the state transition function
- R represents the reward function
- Ω represents the observation space
- O represents the observation function
- γ represents the discount factor

In this formulation, the true state of the network is only partially observable, requiring the system to maintain a belief state based on available observations.

3.4.2. Hierarchical Learning Architecture

The structure that is implemented by RLC holds three levels, to be precise:

1- Strategic Level: It looks at long-term defensive posturing along with where and how resources are going to be allocated; it works on a timescale of hours, maybe days. The strategic agent will choose high-level defensive objectives such as "investigate potential data exfiltration" or "strengthen authentication controls."

2- Tactical Level: It converts strategic objectives into concrete response plans and works on a timescale of minutes up to hours. The tactical agent will choose sequences of defensive actions to attain strategic objectives.

3- Operational Level: The operation is executed with an individual defense mechanism, which takes from seconds to minutes to complete. It might be said that the operational agent optimizes the parameters and timing of specific defensive measures.

This hierarchical implementation facilitates the system in gaining effective strategies at multiple levels of abstraction, managing the complexities involved with the large states and action spaces within network defense.

3.4.3. Policy Learning Algorithm

The RLC employs a modified version of the Proximal Policy Optimization (PPO) algorithm to learn effective response policies. The objective function for policy optimization is:

$$L^{CLIP}(\theta) = \hat{E}_t\left[min\left(r_t(\theta)\hat{A}_t, \text{clip}\left(r_t(\theta), 1-\epsilon, 1+\epsilon\right)\hat{A}_t\right)\right]$$

Where:

- $r_t(\theta)$ represents the probability ratio between the new and old policies
- $\hat{A}_t$ represents the estimated advantage function
- ϵ is a hyperparameter that controls the clip range

The reward function is designed to balance multiple objectives:

$$R(s, a, s') = w_1 \cdot R_{\text{security}} + w_2 \cdot R_{\text{performance}} + w_3 \cdot R_{\text{resources}}$$

Where:

- R_{security} rewards the prevention or mitigation of security incidents
- $R_{\text{performance}}$ penalizes actions that disrupt legitimate network operations
- $R_{\text{resources}}$ penalizes excessive resource utilization

This balanced reward function encourages the system to develop response strategies that effectively mitigate threats while minimizing disruption to legitimate business operations.

3.4.4. Exploration Strategy

To facilitate the discovery of novel response strategies, the RLC implements a curiosity-driven exploration mechanism. This approach generates additional intrinsic rewards based on the system's ability to predict the consequences of its actions:

$$R_{\text{intrinsic}}(s,a,s') = \eta \cdot \|f(s,a) - \hat{f}(s,a)\|_2^2$$

Where:

- $f(s,a)$ represents the actual next state feature vector
- $\hat{f}(s,a)$ represents the predicted next state feature vector
- η is a scaling factor that controls the weight of intrinsic rewards

This curiosity-driven exploration encourages the system to explore action sequences with unpredictable outcomes, potentially discovering innovative response strategies that human security experts might not consider.

3.5. Response Orchestration Module

It translates the abstract response policies learned by the RLC into specific defensive actions within the network. It implements a very comprehensive action space that covers multiple defensive domains:

1- Traffic Control. Modify the firewall rules, implement a rate limit, or send suspicious traffic off to the side for better inspection.
2- Access Management. Change the requirements for authentication, revoke credentials that have been compromised, or temporarily restrict access.
3- System Configuration. Apply patches, security settings, or disable vulnerable services.
4- Deception and Counterintelligence: Such options include the use of honeypots, misinformation supplied to attackers, and the implementation of tarpits to slow down the attack.
5- Forensic Collection: This can include escalating logging levels, capturing packet data, or preserving evidence for analysis.

For each action, ROM maintains confidence thresholds beyond which autonomous execution is allowed. Such thresholds are set dynamically by the system based on its historical performance:

$$T_a = T_{\text{base}} + \Delta T$$

Where:

- T_{base} represents the base confidence threshold for action a
- ΔT represents an adjustment based on the action's historical precision and impact

Actions with potentially disruptive impacts should very well require higher confidence thresholds to be met by the autonomous system. In turn, this always ensures that autonomous behavior maintains an appropriate risk posture. Where confidence falls below the threshold but is above a secondary alerting threshold, recommendations are provided for human security analysts rather than executing actions autonomously.

ROM also has a backward mechanism that can automatically reverse changes if they turn out to be of an unexpected or negative nature, thereby providing an additional safety net for autonomous operations.

3.6. Federated Knowledge Distribution

The Federated Knowledge Distribution Network (FKDN) is a channel through which defensive knowledge can be securely shared across organizational perimeters without any compromise to data privacy and security, thus enabling tactical information exchange among autonomous defense systems without giving away sensitive network information.

3.6.1. Federated Learning of Response Policies

The FKDN implements a federated learning approach to policy development:

1- Each system will train its local policy models based on observed threats and responses.
2- Only the updates to the model are shared with the central aggregation server (and not the raw data).
3- The aggregator will simply aggregate the updates to produce an improved global policy model through a secure aggregation protocol:

$$\theta_{\text{global}} = \sum_{i=1}^{N} \frac{n_i}{n} \theta_i$$

Where:

- θ_{global} represents the parameters of the global model
- θ_i represents the parameters of the local model from organization i
- n_i represents the number of training examples from organization i
- n represents the total number of training examples

The updated global models are distributed back to participating systems, which blend them with local models to maintain site-specific adaptation.

This approach allows defense systems to learn from threats encountered across multiple organizations without sharing sensitive network data or specific security incidents.

3.6.2. Differential Privacy Guarantees

To prevent inference attacks that may extract sensitive information from model updating, the FKDN provides differential privacy guarantees. Each system, therefore, adds calibrated noise to the parameter gradients before sharing model updates.

$$\tilde{\nabla}\theta = \nabla\theta + N(0, \sigma^2 C^2 I)$$

Where:

- $\tilde{\nabla}\theta$ represents the original parameter gradients
- $\mathcal{N}(0, \sigma^2 C^2 I)$ represents Gaussian noise with scale proportional to the sensitivity of the gradients
- C represents the gradient clipping threshold

With this mechanism, it is possible to share model updates without being able to infer whether or not a single training example was used or not from such shared model updates. This gives formal privacy guarantees while still allowing for collaborative learning.

3.6.3. Trust and Verification Mechanisms

To prevent poisoning attacks where malicious participants might try to corrupt the global model, the FKDN implements several trust and verification mechanisms:

1- Reputation Scoring: The reputation of the authors will grow based on the quality and consistency of their contributions.
2- Contribution Validation: Model updates are validated against an agreed-upon set of known test cases before integration.
3- Byzantine-Robust Aggregation: Against a fractional load of malicious or otherwise compromised participants, the aggregation algorithm is byzantine-robust.

Such mechanisms of federated learning are kept secure and reliable even in their operation over trust boundaries.

3.7. Self-Verification and Feedback Loop

One of the essential driving forces behind ADIF in the direction of self-learning is the Continuous Evaluation and Feedback Mechanism that it features. The system keeps an exhaustive performance monitoring framework that tracks multiple metrics:

1- Detection Accuracy: True positive rate, false positive rate, and precision for different threat categories.
2- Response Effectiveness: Rate of successful mitigation against attacks and time taken to contain the attack for different types of attacks.
3- Operational Impact: Implications on the performance of the network, application availability, and user experience after action is taken.
4- Adaptability: System performance against new threat variations and attack techniques previously unseen.

These metrics loop back to mean that the system can continue to refine detection, analysis, and response capabilities against the threat. The feedback mechanism shall instantiate a formal evaluation function:

$$E(p,a,o) = (e_d, e_r, e_i)$$

Where:

- p represents the perceived threat
- a represents the selected action
- o represents the observed outcome
- e_d represents the detection evaluation (was the threat assessment accurate?)
- e_r represents the response evaluation (was the selected action effective?)

- e_i represents the impact evaluation (what was the operational impact of the action?)

This evaluation function provides structured feedback to the reinforcement learning core, enabling it to adjust policies based on observed outcomes and progressively improve defensive capabilities.

4. USE CASES FOR EVALUATING ADIF

4.1. Evaluation Objectives

The established key evaluation objectives to assess the effectiveness of ADIF in achieving the above objectives are the ability to detect novel threats without prior training, ability to reduce false positives through contextual analysis, efficiency when it comes to the response being autonomous, benefits associated with the ability of federated knowledge sharing, and analyzing the operational impact on the business functions diversity of the organization.

4.2. Target Deployment Environments

ADIF was evaluated across three distinct enterprise environments:

- Financial Services Institution: High-Value Assets, High Compliance Requirements, and the Sophistication of the Adversaries. According to (Patel, 2024), financial institutions are particularly sensitive to modern attacks, placing them under increased pressure to enhance their security postures because they have valuable assets.
- Healthcare Provider Network: It has sensitive patient data, critical operational systems, and a diverse technology ecosystem. In healthcare, (Abinash et al., 2025) noted unique security challenges based on the life-critical system, considering the balance between security and availability.
- Manufacturing/Industrial Control Systems: It has converged IT/OT networks, physical process implications, and legacy systems. Defensive systems should meet the unique constraints of industrial processes in those environments (Nankya et al., 2023).

4.3. Evaluation Scenarios

Four main scenarios were applied to a complete assessment of the capacity of ADIF:

1- Zero-Day Vulnerability Exploitation: Simulated undocumented vulnerability exploitation without prior signatures, assessed using the methodology of (Bilge & Dumitraş, 2012).
2- Insider Threat Detection: Contextual analysis tested with legitimate credentials that exhibit abnormal behavior, based on the patterns identified by (Greitzer & Hohimer, 2011).
3- Distributed Attack Response: Federated learning is evaluated during coordinated multi-vector attacks and is adaptive to defensive measures.
4- Operational Continuity Under Attack: Assessment of the ability of ADIF to maintain critical business functions while threats are mitigated.

4.4. Evaluation Methodology

The assessment was based on monitoring, limited response, and fully autonomous operation with controlled red team exercises as well as production telemetry analysis. Key metrics were detection effectiveness (TPR, FPR, detection time), response effectiveness (MTTR, containment effectiveness), operational impact (service availability, performance), and learning adaptation (adaptation rate, knowledge transfer).

Baseline comparisons were with traditional SIEM and advanced EDR, first-generation SOAR, and static response automation systems.

5. RESULTS AND ANALYSIS

5.1. Cross-Environment Performance

ADIF demonstrated consistent performance improvements over baseline systems across all environments, with environment-specific variations reflecting unique security challenges.

Table 1. Detection performance by environment

Environment	Detection Improvement	False Positive Reduction	Mean Time to Detection
Financial Services	High	Moderate	Fastest
Healthcare	Moderate	Highest	Moderate
Manufacturing/ICS	High for OT attacks	Moderate	Extended for stealthy attacks

Financial environments witnessed the best overall improvement in detection since structured transaction patterns gave lucid baselines for detecting anomalies. The healthcare environment would gain the most from false positive reduction, attacking the critical challenge identified by (Abinash et al., 2025) of alert fatigue. Manufacturing environments proved extremely strong in the detection of OT attacks through modeling of industrial process behavior.

5.2. Scenario Performance Analysis

5.2.1. Zero-Day Vulnerability Exploitation

Initial ADIF compromise detection time stood at 83%, more than double the rate registered in ML-enhanced detection and more than 47% higher than the rate registered based on traditional SIEM. The mean detection time was reduced by 76% compared to 'traditional' solutions. Autonomous response actions succeeded in containing 79% of exploits before 'objective achievement.' The results match those of (Bilge & Dumitraş, 2012) in terms of extended vulnerability windows of traditional detection approaches.

5.2.2. Insider Threat Detection

The contextual analysis engine from ADIF was able to differentiate between legitimate administrative actions and the same actions done for malicious intent by factoring in historical behaviors, temporal contexts, business process alignment, and cross-system correlation. Such functionalities thus address directly detected challenges as outlined by (Greitzer & Hohimer, 2011) based on contextual insider threat indicators.

Graduated response actions to insider threats include progressively more restrictive measures, starting with enhanced monitoring up to restrictions on access only in the presence of enough evidence so that legitimate administrative activities are not unduly disturbed.

5.2.3. Distributed Attack Response

Systems operating with federated knowledge sharing contained distributed attacks 64% faster than isolated instances. The false positive rate during attack mitigation decreased by 57% with federated learning enabled, while novel attack variants were detected and contained substantially faster in federated deployments.

5.2.4. Operational Continuity

ADIF demonstrated that sophisticated balancing of security and availability requirements ADIF requirements were balanced across environments:

- In healthcare environments where attacks were active, availability for patient-facing clinical systems exceeded 99%.
- Manufacturing environments maintained process continuity for OT systems while implementing stronger measures for IT systems.
- In financial environments, transaction processing was maintained while verification steps were added for suspicious activities.

Figure 2 compares ADIF's performance with respect to conventional security approaches across the four benchmarking scenarios. The figure synthesizes the great improvements in effectiveness ADIF provides over first-generation SOAR platforms and the classic SIEM system in every scenario. Of particular note was the strong maintenance of operational continuity along with consistent improvements in zero-day vulnerability detection and insider threats and even distributed attack responses. The results clearly show quantitatively how well ADIF's capabilities of adaptive learning and contextual awareness can be translated into measurable security enhancements on different types of threat landscapes. This is very demonstrable in figures, results, and facts for any kind of landscape.

Figure 2. ADIF performance comparison across evaluation scenarios

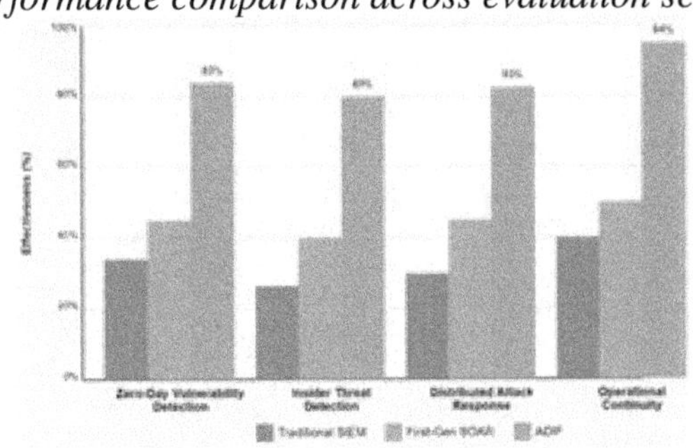

5.3. Learning and Adaptation

All environments revealed sharp, incipient steep curves with high improvement in performance within the first 30 days. Cross-category knowledge accelerated learning of new threats with prior mastery of other similar groups of threats.

Hierarchical reinforcement learning turned out to be very useful for complex attack scenarios, with as much as 43% higher mitigation effectiveness than flat learning methods. The benefit emanates from the approach of breaking down complicated issues into simpler subproblems, which enables more efficient learning and knowledge transfer.

5.4. Case Studies

5.4.1. Financial Services: Sophisticated Fraud Detection

In a developing fraud situation on valid customer accounts, ADIF only pieced together different subtle signals, such as transaction timing shifts, amount pattern changes, place of access anomalies or geographic access anomalies, or even changes in session behavior, each of which typically was below the threshold of traditional fraud detections. The system implemented only measured response actions that maintained legitimate transaction flow and added verification for suspicious activities.

5.4.2. Manufacturing: Industrial Control System Protection

In a manufacturing environment, ADIF detected very subtle manipulations of control system commands that remained technically valid but would cause slow quality degradation. The system implemented a graduated response that maintained production continuity and still effectively contained the threat—all of which were things traditional security systems could not achieve since they could not incorporate the domain-specific operational context.

Consequently, Table 2 presents a comparison of ADIF with Traditional Security Approaches.

continued on following page

Table 2. Continued

Table 2. A comparison of ADIF with traditional security approaches

Capability	Traditional SIEM	First-Generation SOAR	Advanced EDR	ADIF
Threat Detection	Signature-based with limited anomaly detection	Rule-based with predefined indicators	ML-enhanced detection with limited context	Contextual analysis with hierarchical learning
Response Mechanism	Manual response by analysts	Static playbooks with predefined responses	Automated responses within limited parameters	Adaptive response with reinforcement learning
Learning Capability	None - requires manual updates	Limited - requires playbook updates	Static ML models requiring retraining	Continuous self-learning through experience
Context Awareness	Low - individual alerts without context	Medium - basic correlation rules	Medium-high - endpoint context only	High - multi-source correlation with intent analysis
Knowledge Sharing	Manual through threat intelligence	Limited automated sharing	Vendor-specific threat intelligence	Federated knowledge distribution with privacy guarantees
False Positive Handling	High false positive rate	Moderate - based on static rules	Improved but limited by single-source view	Significantly reduced through contextual analysis
Zero-Day Detection	Poor	Limited	Moderate	High through behavioral analysis
Operational Impact	High - requires substantial analyst intervention	Moderate - can cause business disruption	Moderate - endpoint-focused	Low - balanced security with business continuity

5.5. Limitations

In addition to the promising results, though, ADIF also faces a number of challenges:

1- Initial Training Requirements: Organizations without much historical security data may take longer to get the system up to speed.
2- Computational Resource Intensity: Resource constraints may thus pose deployment challenges in some of the environments.
3- Human Transparency Challenges: Security analysts had problems understanding complex multi-factor assessments.
4- Limited Application Coverage: The present implementation has more limited capabilities for responses at the application level, which calls for a much deeper semantic understanding.

These limitations fall somewhat in line with broader issues that were identified by Sommer and Paxson (2010) in fully autonomous security systems explaining complex security decisions to human operators.

6. CONCLUSION

This chapter introduces the ADIF, positioned as a pioneering approach in autonomous cybersecurity systems. It tackles the critical drawbacks in the existence of approaches to defense with several key innovations. The hierarchical reinforcement learning architecture has proved to be much more effective in mitigation compared to flat learning methods as it decomposes complex attack scenarios into manageable subproblems. The contextual analysis engine effectively differentiated legitimate administrative actions from malicious intent, which touches the fundamental point in insider threat detection. Federated knowledge sharing made the systems contain distributed attacks so much faster than the judiciously isolated instances while reducing the false positives so much.

Empirical evaluation across financial, healthcare and manufacturing environments confirmed ADIF's effectiveness. The detection rates were substantially improving compared to ML-enhanced systems; mean detection time was significantly reduced compared to what we are used to with traditional solutions. The framework maintains critical operations during active threats, thus preserving high availability for patient-facing clinical systems.

In light of these accomplishments, ADIF faces such challenges as initial training computational intensity, interpretability to the security analysts, and sharing of the limited application-level responsive capabilities. Further research should emphasize enhancing human-system interaction, convergence on lowering computational requirements, and expansion of semantic understanding at the application level.

ADIF is taking as a paradigm change from the reacting security postures towards proactive, supporting continuous learning, deep context understanding, and response adaptive capabilities to be also changing the threats ever-evolving landscape promises for addressing the modern organizations' ever-sophisticating cyber threats.

ACKNOWLEDGMENTS

The authors would like to thank the Deanship of the Faculty of Information Technology, the Deanship of Scientific Research and Graduate Studies at the University of Petra, and the University of Oldenburg for supporting this research.

REFERENCES

Abinash, M. J., Prabu Kanna, G., Aanjankumar, S., Sambasivam, G., & Karthikeyan, P. (2025). An Introduction to the Challenges and Issues Identified in Digital Health and Wellness Cybersecurity. In S. Poonkuntran, R. K. Dhanaraj, S. AanjanKumar, & M. Sathyamoorthy, *Cybersecurity in Healthcare Applications* (1st ed., pp. 1–23). Chapman and Hall/CRC. DOI: 10.1201/9781032711379-1

Apruzzese, G., Colajanni, M., Ferretti, L., Guido, A., & Marchetti, M. (2018). On the effectiveness of machine and deep learning for cyber security. *2018 10th International Conference on Cyber Conflict (CyCon)*, 371–390. DOI: 10.23919/CYCON.2018.8405026

Bilge, L., & Dumitraş, T. (2012). Before we knew it: An empirical study of zero-day attacks in the real world. *Proceedings of the 2012 ACM Conference on Computer and Communications Security*, 833–844. DOI: 10.1145/2382196.2382284

Buczak, A. L., & Guven, E. (2016). A Survey of Data Mining and Machine Learning Methods for Cyber Security Intrusion Detection. *IEEE Communications Surveys and Tutorials*, *18*(2), 1153–1176. DOI: 10.1109/COMST.2015.2494502

Denning, D. E. (1987). An intrusion-detection model. *IEEE Transactions on Software Engineering*, *2*(2), 222–232. DOI: 10.1109/TSE.1987.232894

García-Teodoro, P., Díaz-Verdejo, J., Maciá-Fernández, G., & Vázquez, E. (2009). Anomaly-based network intrusion detection: Techniques, systems and challenges. *Computers & Security*, *28*(1–2), 18–28. DOI: 10.1016/j.cose.2008.08.003

Ghafir, I., Saleem, J., Hammoudeh, M., Faour, H., Prenosil, V., Jaf, S., Jabbar, S., & Baker, T. (2018). Security threats to critical infrastructure: The human factor. *The Journal of Supercomputing*, *74*(10), 4986–5002. DOI: 10.1007/s11227-018-2337-2

Greitzer, F. L., & Hohimer, R. E. (2011). Modeling Human Behavior to Anticipate Insider Attacks. *Journal of Strategic Security*, *4*(2), 25–48. DOI: 10.5038/1944-0472.4.2.2

Havenga, W., Bagula, A., & Ajayi, O. (2022). Autonomous Threat Detection and Response for Self-Protected Networks. *2022 Conference on Information Communications Technology and Society (ICTAS)*, 1–6. DOI: 10.1109/ICTAS53252.2022.9744643

IBM. (2023). *Cost of a data breach 2023| IBM Security*. https://www.ibm.com/reports/data-breach

Javaid, A., Niyaz, Q., Sun, W., & Alam, M. (2016). A Deep Learning Approach for Network Intrusion Detection System. *Proceedings of the 9th EAI International Conference on Bio-Inspired Information and Communications Technologies (Formerly BIONETICS)*. 9th EAI International Conference on Bio-inspired Information and Communications Technologies (formerly BIONETICS), New York City, United States. DOI: 10.4108/eai.3-12-2015.2262516

Mirsky, Y., Doitshman, T., Elovici, Y., & Shabtai, A. (2018). Kitsune: An Ensemble of Autoencoders for Online Network Intrusion Detection. *Proceedings 2018 Network and Distributed System Security Symposium*. Network and Distributed System Security Symposium, San Diego, CA. DOI: 10.14722/ndss.2018.23204

Mothukuri, V., Parizi, R. M., Pouriyeh, S., Huang, Y., Dehghantanha, A., & Srivastava, G. (2021). A survey on security and privacy of federated learning. *Future Generation Computer Systems*, *115*, 619–640. DOI: 10.1016/j.future.2020.10.007

Nankya, M., Chataut, R., & Akl, R. (2023). Securing Industrial Control Systems: Components, Cyber Threats, and Machine Learning-Driven Defense Strategies. *Sensors (Basel)*, *23*(21), 8840. DOI: 10.3390/s23218840 PMID: 37960539

Nguyen, T. T., & Reddi, V. J. (2023). Deep Reinforcement Learning for Cyber Security. *IEEE Transactions on Neural Networks and Learning Systems*, *34*(8), 3779–3795. DOI: 10.1109/TNNLS.2021.3121870 PMID: 34723814

O'Driscoll, R., Hagen, C., Bater, J., & Adams, J. M. (2024). *Multi-Objective Reinforcement Learning for Automated Resilient Cyber Defence* (Version 1). arXiv. DOI: 10.22541/au.173271087.78484560/v1

Patel, U. (2024). Data Privacy and Security in Financial Services. *Journal of Artificial Intelligence & Cloud Computing*, 1–13. DOI: 10.47363/JAICC/2024(3)E204

Preuveneers, D., Llamas, J. M., Bulut, I., Rúa, E. A., Verfaillie, P., Demortier, V., Surinx, D., & Joosen, W. (2024). On the Use of AutoML for Combating Alert Fatigue in Security Operations Centers. In S. Katsikas, H. Abie, S. Ranise, L. Verderame, E. Cambiaso, R. Ugarelli, I. Praça, W. Li, W. Meng, S. Furnell, B. Katt, S. Pirbhulal, A. Shukla, M. Ianni, M. Dalla Preda, K.-K. R. Choo, M. Pupo Correia, A. Abhishta, G. Sileno, … N. Yanai (Eds.), *Computer Security. ESORICS 2023 International Workshops* (Vol. 14399, pp. 609–627). Springer Nature Switzerland. DOI: 10.1007/978-3-031-54129-2_36

Resende, P. A. A., & Drummond, A. C. (2019). A Survey of Random Forest Based Methods for Intrusion Detection Systems. *ACM Computing Surveys*, *51*(3), 1–36. DOI: 10.1145/3178582

Sabeel, U., Heydari, S. S., El-Khatib, K., & Elgazzar, K. (2024). Incremental Adversarial Learning for Polymorphic Attack Detection. *IEEE Transactions on Machine Learning in Communications and Networking*, *2*, 869–887. DOI: 10.1109/TMLCN.2024.3418756

Sandoval, I. O., Thompson, I. S., Mavroudis, V., & Hicks, C. (2025). *An Attentive Graph Agent for Topology-Adaptive Cyber Defence* (Version 3). arXiv. DOI: 10.48550/ARXIV.2501.14700

Shameli-Sendi, A., Cheriet, M., & Hamou-Lhadj, A. (2014). Taxonomy of intrusion risk assessment and response system. *Computers & Security*, *45*, 1–16. DOI: 10.1016/j.cose.2014.04.009

Sommer, R., & Paxson, V. (2010). Outside the Closed World: On Using Machine Learning for Network Intrusion Detection. *2010 IEEE Symposium on Security and Privacy*, 305–316. DOI: 10.1109/SP.2010.25

Stakhanova, N., Basu, S., & Wong, J. (2007). A taxonomy of intrusion response systems. *International Journal of Information and Computer Security*, *1*(1–2), 169–184. DOI: 10.1504/IJICS.2007.012248

Taddeo, M., McCutcheon, T., & Floridi, L. (2019a). Trusting artificial intelligence in cybersecurity is a double-edged sword. *Nature Machine Intelligence*, *1*(12), 557–560. DOI: 10.1038/s42256-019-0109-1

Taddeo, M., McCutcheon, T., & Floridi, L. (2019b). Trusting artificial intelligence in cybersecurity is a double-edged sword. *Nature Machine Intelligence*, *1*(12), 557–560. DOI: 10.1038/s42256-019-0109-1

Tsirakis, O., Fysarakis, K., Mavroeidis, V., & Papaefstathiou, I. (2025). *Operationalizing Cybersecurity Knowledge: Design, Implementation & Evaluation of a Knowledge Management System for CACAO Playbooks* (No. arXiv:2503.05206). arXiv. /arXiv.2503.05206DOI: 10.2139/ssrn.5178937

Vinayakumar, R., Alazab, M., Soman, K. P., Poornachandran, P., Al-Nemrat, A., & Venkatraman, S. (2019). Deep Learning Approach for Intelligent Intrusion Detection System. *IEEE Access : Practical Innovations, Open Solutions*, *7*, 41525–41550. DOI: 10.1109/ACCESS.2019.2895334

Wang, W., Zhu, M., Wang, J., Zeng, X., & Yang, Z. (2017). End-to-end encrypted traffic classification with one-dimensional convolution neural networks. *2017 IEEE International Conference on Intelligence and Security Informatics (ISI)*, 43–48. DOI: 10.1109/ISI.2017.8004872

Wang, Y., Hallgren, K., & Larson, J. (2024). A Graph-based Framework for Reducing False Positives in Authentication Alerts in Security Systems. *Companion Proceedings of the ACM Web Conference 2024*, 274–283. DOI: 10.1145/3589335.3648325

Yapar, O. (2024). Reinforcement learning in autonomous defense systems: Strategic applications and challenges. *World Journal of Advanced Engineering Technology and Sciences*, *13*(1), 140–152. DOI: 10.30574/wjaets.2024.13.1.0383

Zhou, C. V., Leckie, C., & Karunasekera, S. (2010). A survey of coordinated attacks and collaborative intrusion detection. *Computers & Security*, *29*(1), 124–140. DOI: 10.1016/j.cose.2009.06.008

Zuech, R., Khoshgoftaar, T. M., & Wald, R. (2015). Intrusion detection and Big Heterogeneous Data: A Survey. *Journal of Big Data*, *2*(1), 3. DOI: 10.1186/s40537-015-0013-4

Chapter 10
Generative AI for Cybersecurity Applications in Threat Simulation and Defense

Yousef Sanjalawe
https://orcid.org/0000-0002-4442-1865
University of Jordan, Jordan

Salam Al E'mari
https://orcid.org/0000-0002-2134-4158
University of Petra, Jordan

Sharif Makhadmeh
University of Jordan, Jordan

ABSTRACT

The integration of generative AI in cybersecurity marks a transformative leap in combating the growing complexity of cyber threats. This chapter examines generative AI models like generative adversarial networks, variational autoencoders, and transformers, showcasing their role in threat simulation, synthetic data generation, and anomaly detection. Applications discussed include proactive defense testing, malware analysis, and intrusion detection, highlighting generative AI's ability to predict, detect, and mitigate sophisticated attacks. Emerging techniques, such as federated learning and hybrid generative models, promise further advancements. However, generative AI poses challenges, including misuse of synthetic data and adversarial vulnerabilities. Addressing these risks requires ethical guidelines, robust frameworks, and collaboration. With its predictive and adaptive potential,

DOI: 10.4018/979-8-3373-0954-5.ch010

generative AI is reshaping cybersecurity, enabling resilient and intelligent defenses for the digital age.

1. INTRODUCTION

Cybersecurity is at the forefront of technological advancements, driven by the exponential growth of digital systems and the increasing sophistication of cyber threats (Salem et al., 2024; Folorunso et al., 2024). As organizations digitize their operations, the attack surface expands, presenting unique challenges in safeguarding sensitive data, systems, and infrastructures. Traditional cybersecurity solutions, while effective to an extent, often struggle to address the dynamic and evolving nature of modern cyberattacks. This necessitates the adoption of innovative approaches that go beyond static defenses, leveraging advanced technologies to anticipate, adapt, and respond to threats. Among these, generative AI has emerged as a groundbreaking tool, reshaping the landscape of cybersecurity (Familoni, 2024; Malatji & Tolah, 2024).

Generative AI stands out for its ability to create synthetic data, simulate complex scenarios, and model dynamic behaviors, making it a valuable asset in combating cyber threats (Sai et al., 2024; Krishnamurthy & Vemulapalli, 2024). Unlike conventional machine learning models that rely heavily on pre-existing datasets, generative AI introduces a level of flexibility and creativity that is unparalleled (Krishnamurthy & Vemulapalli, 2024). Its capacity to generate highly realistic attack patterns, emulate adversarial behaviors, and produce diverse datasets address critical gaps in the cybersecurity domain. This capability is particularly crucial in scenarios such as detecting zero-day vulnerabilities, training anomaly detection systems, and stress-testing organizational defenses against hypothetical yet realistic attack scenarios.

The integration of generative AI into cybersecurity also paves the way for a more proactive and predictive defense strategy (Salem et al., 2024; Folorunso et al., 2024). By simulating advanced threats and testing defensive mechanisms in controlled environments, organizations can preemptively identify vulnerabilities and strengthen their security infrastructure (Bhatt & Indra, 2024). Moreover, generative AI's role in enhancing data availability and diversity ensures that machine learning models are better equipped to generalize across a wide range of threat vectors (Do Yoo, Kim & Kim, 2024). As this technology matures, its potential to transform cybersecurity will only grow, making it a critical component in the ongoing effort to secure digital ecosystems against increasingly sophisticated adversaries.

This chapter is organized to provide a detailed exploration of the applications and implications of generative AI in cybersecurity. Section 2, Generative AI in Cybersecurity, introduces foundational concepts and key models like GANs, VAEs, and transformers, highlighting their mechanisms and capabilities. Section 3,

Threat Simulation with Generative AI, discusses how generative models can create realistic cyberattack scenarios to test and enhance defense mechanisms. Section 4, AI-Generated Synthetic Datasets for Cybersecurity Training, emphasizes the importance of synthetic data in addressing data scarcity and improving machine learning models for cybersecurity. Section 5, Defensive Applications of Generative AI, explores how generative AI strengthens anomaly detection and enables adaptive defense strategies. Section 6, Generative AI in Cyber Threat Intelligence (CTI), examines how AI enhances threat intelligence sharing and predictive analysis to anticipate and counter emerging cyber threats.

Finally, Section 7, Conclusion, summarizes the key insights of the chapter, emphasizing the transformative potential of generative AI in shaping the future of cybersecurity.

2. GENERATIVE AI IN CYBERSECURITY

Generative AI models are at the forefront of machine learning innovation, designed to create new, synthetic data that closely resembles the patterns and characteristics of real-world data (Sengar et al., 2024). These models have become indispensable tools in a wide array of fields, including cybersecurity, where their ability to simulate, predict, and analyze complex data patterns has unlocked new possibilities. This section delves deeper into some of the most impactful generative AI models, highlighting their mechanisms, unique capabilities, and applications in cybersecurity.

i. GANs

- Mechanism:

GANs consist of two neural networks—the generator and the discriminator—that work in opposition. The generator's role is to create synthetic data that mimics real-world examples, while the discriminator evaluates this data and determines whether it is real or generated. This adversarial training process continues until the generator produces data that the discriminator cannot distinguish from real data (Bengesi et al., 2024; Ahmad et al., 2024). Figure 1 illustrates the GAN architecture, which consists of two neural networks: a generator and a discriminator. The generator creates synthetic data designed to resemble real-world examples, while the discriminator evaluates the authenticity of the data, distinguishing between real and generated samples (Little, Allmendinger & Elliot, 2024; Dash et al., 2023). This adversarial training process continues until the generator produces highly realistic outputs, making GANs particularly effective for generating synthetic attack scenarios and diverse datasets in cybersecurity.

Figure 1. Architecture of GAN

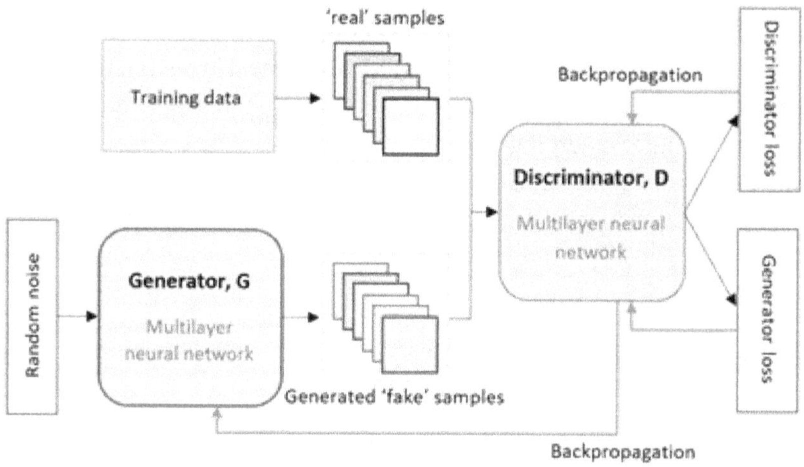

- Capabilities:
    - GANs are capable of generating high-quality data across various modalities, including images, text, and audio.
    - They can create highly realistic synthetic attack scenarios, such as fake phishing emails, malware variants, or network traffic patterns, useful for testing cybersecurity defenses.

  ii. VAEs

- Mechanism:

VAEs use a probabilistic approach to data generation. They encode input data into a latent space represented by a probability distribution, rather than a fixed point. This enables the decoder to generate new, slightly varied data points by sampling from the latent space (Kaur et al., 2023). Figure 2 demonstrates the architecture of a VAE, which encodes input data into a latent space represented by a probability distribution rather than fixed points. By sampling from this latent space, the decoder generates new data points with slight variations. VAEs are instrumental in anomaly detection and synthetic data generation, allowing for effective training of machine learning models in cybersecurity (Zhu et al., 2023).

Figure 2. Architecture of VAE

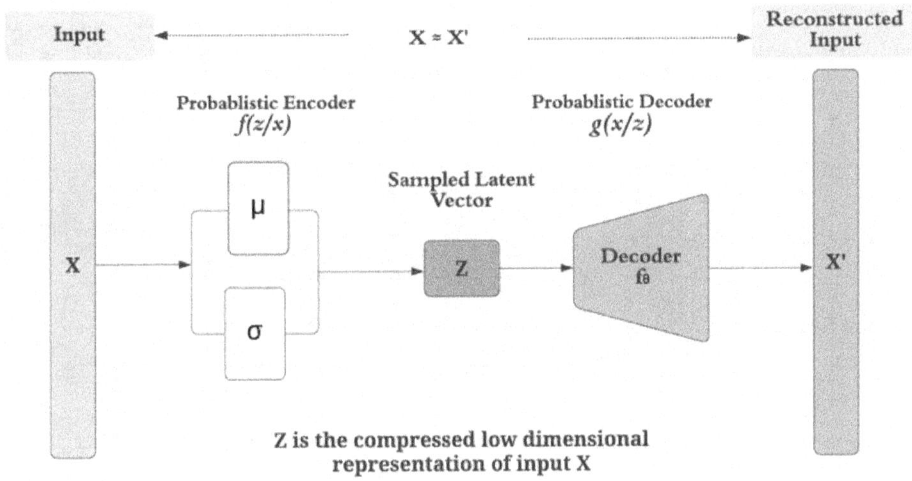

- Capabilities:
    - VAEs excel at representing complex, high-dimensional data in a compact, interpretable latent space.
    - They are effective at detecting anomalies and generating synthetic examples that closely resemble the original data.

  iii. Diffusion Models

- Mechanism:

Diffusion models are a class of generative models that learn to reverse a gradual noising process applied to data. Starting with noise, these models iteratively refine data representations to produce highly realistic samples (Croitoru et al., 2023). Figure 3 explains the latent diffusion model, a generative model that reverses a gradual noising process to reconstruct data. By learning subtle details, diffusion models generate highly realistic datasets, making them suitable for simulating advanced cyberattacks, such as multi-stage malware or evolving threat patterns, in cybersecurity training and testing.

Figure 3. Architecture of latent diffusion model

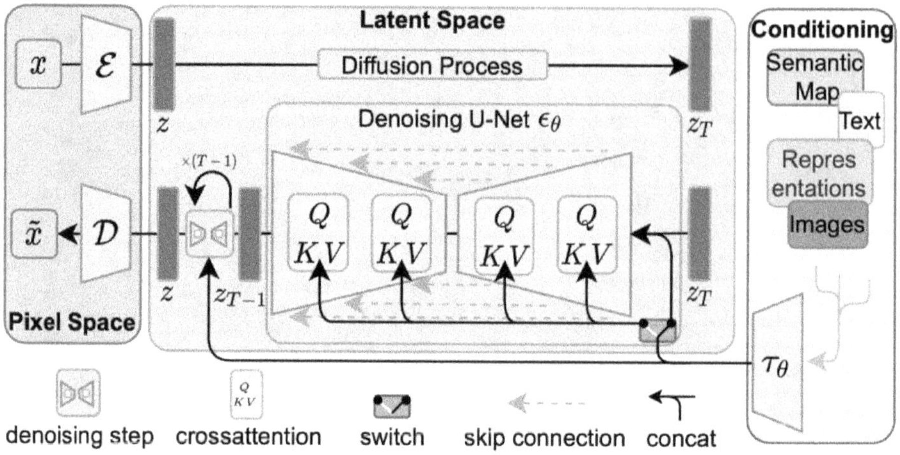

- Capabilities:
  - Capable of generating ultra-high-quality data, diffusion models are particularly useful for generating images, structured text, or time-series data.
  - They provide robust frameworks for capturing subtle details in data, making them ideal for generating realistic attack scenarios.

    iv. Transformer-Based Generative Models

- Mechanism:

Transformer-based models, such as Generative Pre-trained Transformers (GPT), are built on the transformer architecture, which excels at processing sequential data. These models leverage self-attention mechanisms to understand and generate text, making them versatile for tasks involving language and sequence analysis (Yenduri et al., 2024; Sufi, 2024). Figure 4 depicts the transformer-based architecture, which leverages self-attention mechanisms to process sequential data, such as text or system logs. Transformers excel in generating and analyzing context-aware outputs, making them valuable for phishing simulations, log analysis, and threat intelligence in cybersecurity.

Figure 4. Architecture of transformer-based generative model

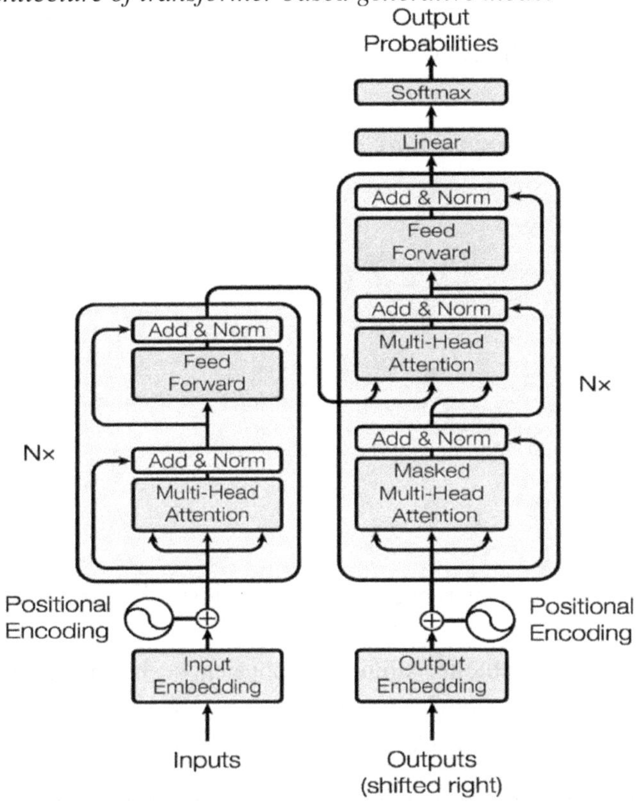

- Capabilities:
  - Transformers are particularly effective for generating context-aware text and analyzing sequences, such as network logs or phishing email content.
  - They can model complex relationships within data, making them suitable for cybersecurity applications requiring an understanding of temporal or sequential patterns.

v. Neural Radiance Fields (NeRFs)

- Mechanism:

While originally developed for 3D modeling, NeRFs have shown potential in generating volumetric data representations. By learning light-field patterns, they produce accurate spatial and temporal representations (Ming et al., 2025; Croce et al., 2023). Figure 5 showcases the architecture of PixelNeRF, which generates 3D volumetric data representations by learning light-field patterns. Its ability to simulate realistic physical scenarios is beneficial for cybersecurity applications like IoT device interaction modeling and virtual environment threat testing.

Figure 5. Convolutional architecture of pixelNeRF

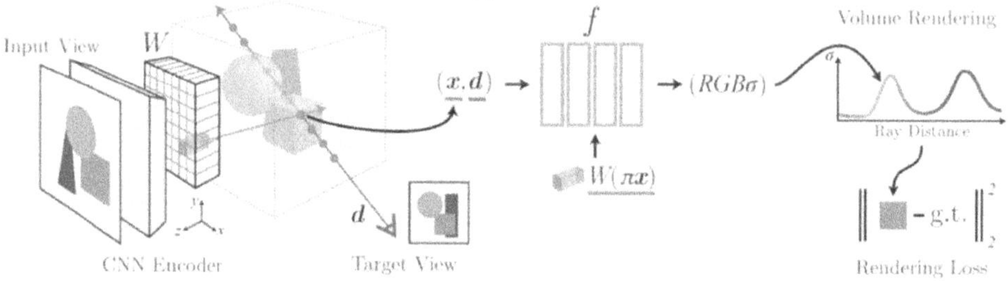

- Capabilities:
    - NeRFs can reconstruct and generate realistic 3D environments or volumetric data.
    - They are valuable for simulating physical scenarios, such as device interactions or IoT environments.

    vi. Autoregressive Models

- Mechanism:

Autoregressive models predict each element in a sequence based on the preceding elements, allowing them to generate coherent and contextually accurate data. Examples include models like PixelCNN and WaveNet (Wang et al.,2023). Figure 6 visualizes the Gated PixelCNN architecture, which excels at generating and analyzing time-series data (Nair et al., 2023). In cybersecurity, this model is used for traffic flow analysis and behavioral modeling, enabling precise identification of anomalies and prediction of threats.

Figure 6. Architecture of gated PixelCNN

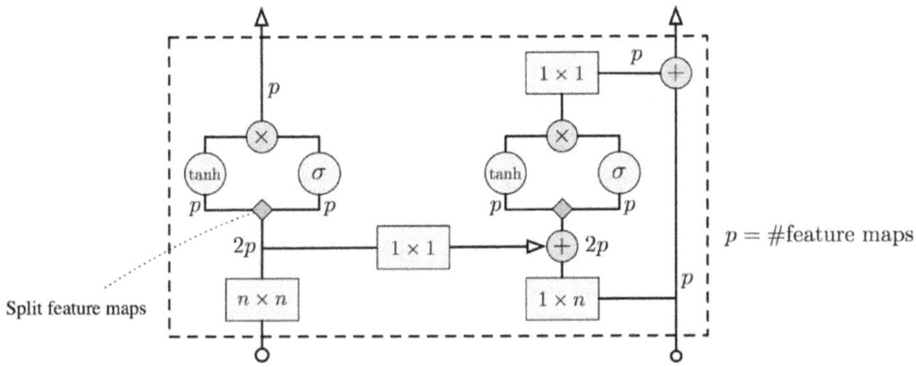

- Capabilities:
    - These models excel in time-series data generation and analysis.
    - They are particularly useful for cybersecurity tasks involving sequential data, such as traffic flow or system behavior analysis.

3. THREAT SIMULATION WITH GENERATIVE AI

The increasing sophistication of cyberattacks has necessitated a proactive approach to cybersecurity, where organizations simulate threats to identify vulnerabilities and bolster defenses before an actual attack occurs. Generative AI has emerged as a game-changing tool in this domain, enabling highly realistic threat simulations that closely mimic real-world cyberattacks. This chapter delves into how generative AI facilitates proactive defense testing, explores the application of GANs for attack emulation, and examines case studies that highlight the transformative impact of generative AI in threat simulation.

3.1 Simulating Cyberattacks for Proactive Defense Testing

Traditional cybersecurity measures often rely on reactive mechanisms, addressing threats only after they have been detected. While necessary, this approach is insufficient in an environment where attackers are constantly innovating new techniques to breach defenses. Proactive threat simulation flips the script by enabling organizations to emulate potential cyberattacks, test their systems against these scenarios, and enhance their resilience (Ojha, Agarwal, & Swetha, 2023).

Generative AI introduces a revolutionary approach to simulating cyberattacks. Unlike conventional methods, which often rely on historical data or manually created scenarios, generative AI models can create highly dynamic, diverse, and realistic attack simulations (Lim et al., 2024). These capabilities are particularly critical in modern cybersecurity due to the evolving and unpredictable nature of cyber threats (Dunmore et al., 2023). Figure 7 highlights how GANs are utilized to simulate cyberattack scenarios. By creating realistic attack patterns, such as phishing campaigns or network intrusions, this application enables organizations to test their defenses proactively and refine their cybersecurity measures (Park, Jo, & Kim, 2023).

Figure 7. Simulating attack scenarios using GANs

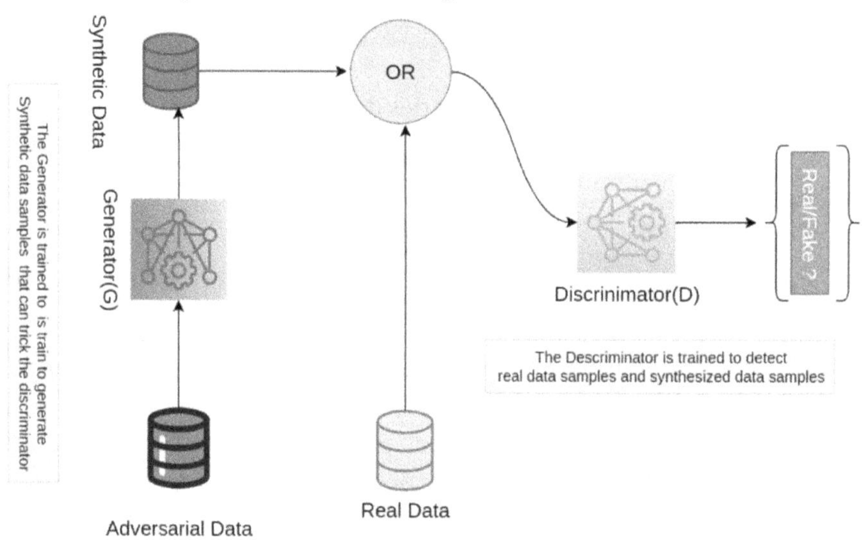

3.2 GANs for Attack Emulation

Among generative AI models, GANs have emerged as a particularly powerful tool for attack emulation. Their unique architecture—comprising a generator and a discriminator—enables them to create synthetic data that is almost indistinguishable from real-world examples. This capability makes GANs ideal for simulating sophisticated cyberattacks (Arora & Shantanu, 2020).

3.3 Case Studies on Threat Simulation Using Generative AI

Real-world applications of generative AI in threat simulation demonstrate its potential to revolutionize cybersecurity. The following case studies highlight how organizations and researchers have leveraged generative AI to enhance their defenses:

Case Study 1: Phishing Simulation With GANs

A multinational financial institution faced challenges in training employees to recognize sophisticated phishing attacks. Traditional training relied on pre-designed scenarios that lacked the variability and realism of actual phishing campaigns. Figure 8 presents a case study where GANs were employed to generate realistic phishing emails for training employees in recognizing phishing attempts (Ayyaz & Malik, 2024). The simulated scenarios improved awareness, reduced vulnerability to such attacks, and enhanced overall organizational resilience.

By deploying a GAN-based solution, the organization generated a wide range of realistic phishing emails tailored to different departments. These simulations:

- Improved employee recognition of phishing attempts.
- Reduced the organization's overall vulnerability to email-based attacks.
- Enhanced the training program's effectiveness through dynamic and evolving scenarios.

Figure 8. Phishing simulation with GANs

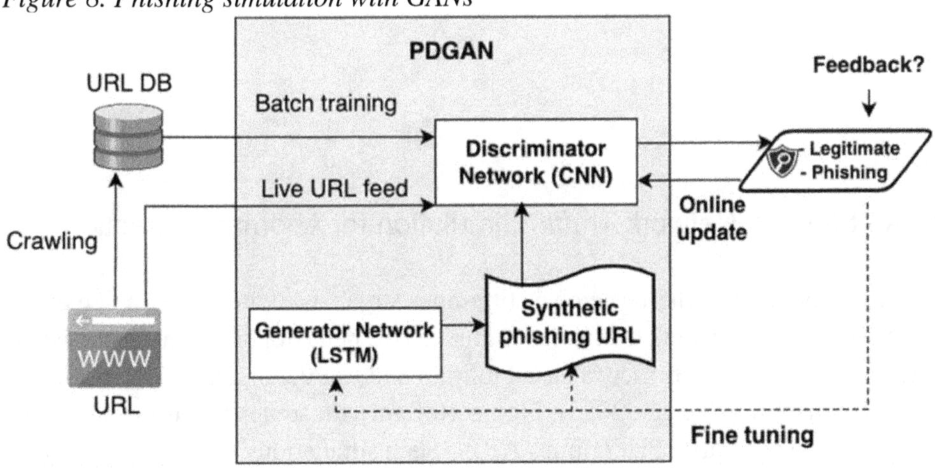

Case Study 2: Malware Variant Generation for Detection Testing

A cybersecurity firm sought to improve its malware detection algorithms by testing them against novel malware variants. Using a GAN, the firm generated thousands of synthetic malware samples that exhibited diverse behaviors (Devadiga et al., 2023). Figure 9 demonstrates how GANs are used to generate synthetic malware variants that replicate real-world threats. These generated samples help stress-test malware detection systems, exposing weaknesses and improving the robustness of detection mechanisms against evolving threats (Gupta et al., 2024). This approach:

- Exposed weaknesses in the existing detection algorithms.
- Enabled the development of more robust and adaptive detection mechanisms.
- Significantly reduced the risk of undetected malware breaches.

Figure 9. Malware generation with GANs

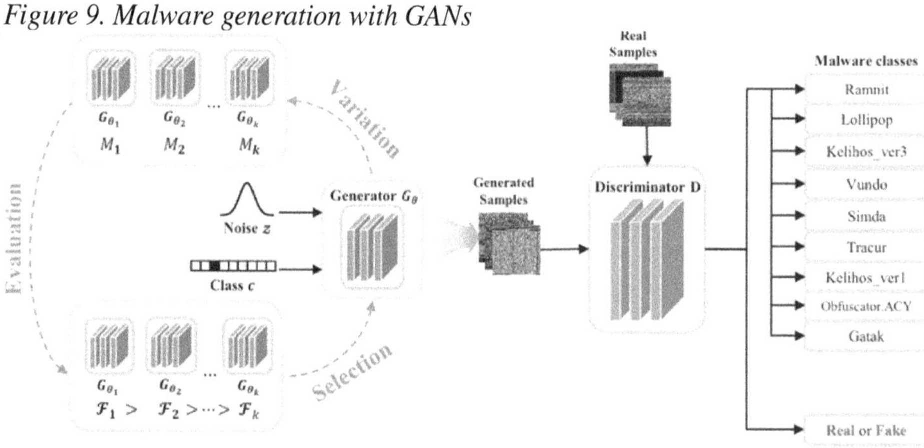

Case Study 3: Network Traffic Simulation for Anomaly Detection

In collaboration with a research institution, a large-scale enterprise implemented GANs to simulate network traffic that mimicked the behavior of advanced persistent threats. The synthetic traffic was used to train and test the organization's anomaly detection system (Na et al., 2023). Figure 10 figure illustrates the use of GANs to simulate network traffic that mimics APTs. Such simulations are used to train and evaluate anomaly detection systems, enhancing their ability to detect complex and stealthy attacks in real-world environments (Rao et al., 2024).

Results included:

- Improved detection rates for complex and stealthy attacks.
- Reduced false positives, increasing the efficiency of the Security Operations Center (SOC).
- Insights into potential vulnerabilities in the network's architecture.

Figure 10. Malware generation with GANs

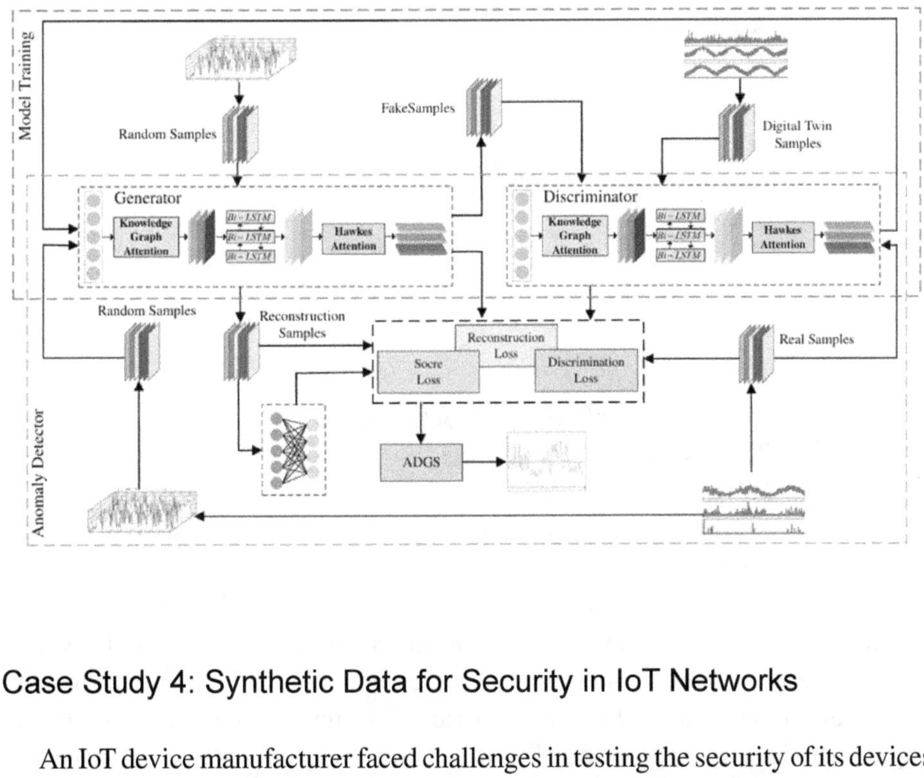

Case Study 4: Synthetic Data for Security in IoT Networks

An IoT device manufacturer faced challenges in testing the security of its devices due to limited datasets of attack scenarios (Khadka et al., 2023). Figure 11 emphasizes the application of VAEs in generating synthetic datasets for IoT security testing. These datasets capture diverse attack and normal behavior patterns, enabling the development and testing of effective security algorithms without relying on real-world data. By leveraging VAEs, the company generated synthetic datasets that captured diverse attack and normal behavior patterns (Alabdulwahab et al., 2023; Almaraz-Rivera et al., 2023). The use of these datasets:

- Enhanced the performance of IoT security algorithms.
- Enabled comprehensive testing without compromising customer data.
- Provided a cost-effective solution for addressing data scarcity.

Figure 11. Synthetic data for security in IoT

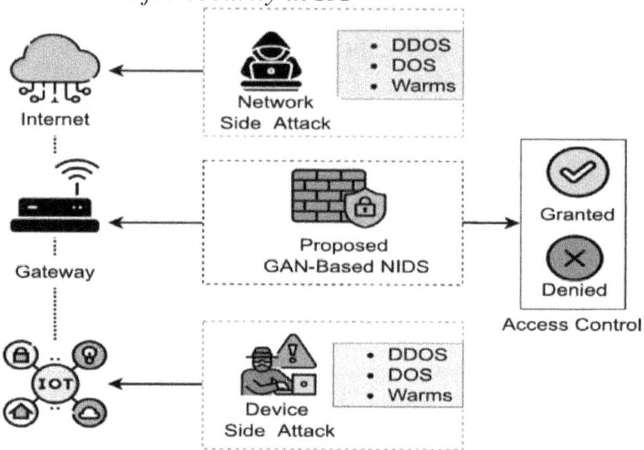

4. AI-GENERATED SYNTHETIC DATASETS FOR CYBERSECURITY TRAINING

The cybersecurity landscape is constantly evolving, with attackers devising increasingly sophisticated methods to exploit vulnerabilities. To combat these threats, organizations rely heavily on Machine Learning (ML) models for tasks like intrusion detection, anomaly detection, and malware classification. However, the effectiveness of these models hinges on the availability of high-quality, labeled datasets that reflect real-world attack scenarios. Unfortunately, data scarcity remains a significant challenge in cybersecurity. AI-generated synthetic datasets have emerged as a transformative solution, addressing this gap by providing realistic, diverse, and scalable data for training and testing purposes. This section explores how synthetic datasets address data scarcity, enhance intrusion detection systems, and examines the ethical implications associated with their use.

4.1 Addressing Data Scarcity with Synthetic Datasets

One of the primary challenges in cybersecurity is the lack of comprehensive datasets that encompass diverse attack scenarios. Real-world datasets are often (Ibrahim et al., 2024; Kiran & Kumar, 2024):

- Incomplete: Real-world attack data may not cover the full range of possible threats, leaving critical gaps.
- Imbalanced: Attack instances are typically rare compared to benign data, leading to imbalanced datasets that skew ML model performance.
- Confidential: Many organizations are reluctant to share their cybersecurity data due to privacy concerns, proprietary information, or compliance requirements.
- Expensive to Generate: Collecting and labeling data for cybersecurity applications is resource-intensive, requiring significant time, expertise, and computational resources.

AI-generated synthetic datasets provide a scalable, cost-effective, and flexible solution to these challenges. By leveraging models like GANs, VAEs, and other generative techniques, organizations can create realistic datasets that mimic real-world behavior. These datasets are particularly valuable for (Gupta, 2023; Ammara et al., 2024):

- Simulating Rare Events: Generating examples of infrequent but critical attack types, such as zero-day exploits.
- Balancing Datasets: Creating synthetic attack data to balance datasets and improve model performance.
- Customization: Tailoring datasets to specific organizational needs, including unique attack scenarios or infrastructure configurations.
- Anonymity: Producing synthetic data that captures essential patterns without exposing sensitive or proprietary information.

4.2 Enhancing Intrusion Detection Systems with Diverse Attack Scenarios

IDS rely on training data to distinguish between benign and malicious activities. However, traditional datasets often lack diversity, limiting their effectiveness against novel attack techniques. AI-generated synthetic datasets address this issue by introducing diverse and dynamic attack scenarios, enhancing the robustness and adaptability of IDS. Figure 12 showcases a GAN-based approach to training IDS.

By generating synthetic attack patterns and adversarial examples, GANs improve the ability of IDS to detect sophisticated threats, reduce false positives, and enhance the overall accuracy and robustness of cybersecurity defenses.

Figure 12. GAN-based IDS

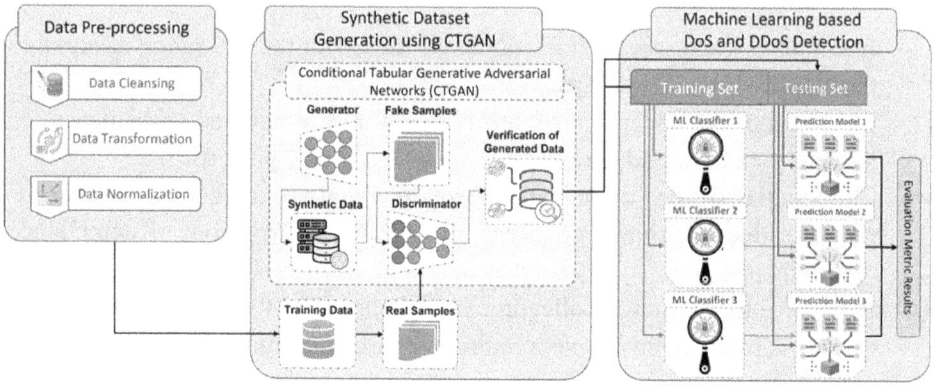

Applications in enhancing IDS

- Behavioral modeling: Generative AI models create realistic user and attacker behavior profiles, enabling IDS to detect deviations from normal activity.
- Adversarial training: IDS are trained on synthetic data that includes adversarial examples, preparing them to handle sophisticated attacks designed to bypass detection mechanisms.
- Anomaly detection: Synthetic datasets with rare or subtle anomalies improve the sensitivity and specificity of anomaly-based IDS.

4.3 Ethical Implications of Synthetic Cybersecurity Data

While synthetic datasets offer immense potential for enhancing cybersecurity, their use also raises important ethical considerations. These issues must be carefully addressed to ensure the responsible and effective application of generative AI in cybersecurity (Dhoni & Kumar, 2023).

- Misuse of synthetic data
    - Threat amplification: Cybercriminals could exploit generative AI to create sophisticated attack scenarios, such as undetectable phishing campaigns or advanced malware.

- Evasion techniques: Adversaries might use synthetic data to train their own models, refining their ability to evade detection systems.
- Data fabrication: There is a risk of synthetic datasets being used to fabricate evidence in digital forensics, undermining trust in cybersecurity processes.

- Privacy concerns
  - Synthetic data derived from real data: If synthetic datasets are generated from real-world data, there is a risk of inadvertently revealing sensitive information. This concern is particularly relevant in scenarios where datasets are shared across organizations.
  - Anonymization limitations: While synthetic data is often touted as an anonymized alternative, advanced re-identification techniques could potentially reverse-engineer sensitive details.
- Data bias and representation
  - Bias propagation: Synthetic datasets may inherit biases present in the original data used to train generative models. This can lead to skewed or unfair outcomes in cybersecurity applications.
  - Incomplete representations: Over-reliance on synthetic data could result in incomplete or unrealistic representations of attack scenarios, undermining the effectiveness of security measures.
- Ethical guidelines for synthetic data use to mitigate these risks, organizations should adhere to ethical guidelines for the generation and use of synthetic datasets (Wilde et al., 2024):
  - Transparency: Clearly disclose when and how synthetic data is used in cybersecurity systems.
  - Validation: Ensure synthetic datasets are rigorously validated against real-world scenarios to confirm their realism and effectiveness.
  - Collaboration: Foster collaboration between industry, academia, and regulatory bodies to develop standards and best practices for synthetic data use.
  - Restricted access: Limit access to generative models and synthetic datasets to authorized personnel and ethical organizations.

As generative AI technologies continue to evolve, the role of synthetic datasets in cybersecurity will expand. Emerging trends include (Khan et al., 2025):

- Federated learning with synthetic data: Combining synthetic data with federated learning frameworks to enhance privacy and collaboration across organizations.

- Real-time dataset generation: developing generative models capable of creating synthetic data in real time, enabling on-the-fly testing and adaptation.
- Advanced scenario simulation: Leveraging hybrid generative models, such as GAN-Transformer combinations, to simulate highly complex and dynamic attack scenarios.

4.4 Generative AI for Malware Analysis and Detection

Generative AI has become a cornerstone in cybersecurity, particularly in the domain of malware analysis and detection. The adaptability and intelligence of these models enable them to simulate complex threats, enhance detection mechanisms, and support proactive defense strategies. The application of generative AI in creating malware variants for stress testing and driving advanced signature and behavior analysis is critical in preparing cybersecurity systems to combat sophisticated, evolving threats. This section delves into the technical intricacies and methodologies underpinning these applications.

4.4.1 Creating Malware Variants for Stress Testing Detection Systems

The challenge of constantly adapting malware detection systems to counter new threats lies in their reliance on datasets that may not encompass the full diversity or sophistication of malware variants in the wild. Traditional approaches to testing often involve using known malware samples. However, these samples can fail to adequately simulate the creativity and dynamism of real-world attackers. Generative AI fills this gap by generating diverse, high-fidelity malware variants tailored for stress testing detection systems (Murali et al., 2023).

At the core of this capability are generative models such as GANs and VAEs. GANs employ a dual-network structure consisting of a generator and a discriminator. The generator is responsible for creating synthetic malware samples, while the discriminator evaluates their authenticity against real malware samples. Through iterative training, the generator refines its outputs to produce increasingly convincing malware variants that emulate the complexity and behavior of real-world threats. This adversarial process enables the generation of highly sophisticated variants, such as polymorphic and metamorphic malware. Polymorphic malware changes its code structure without altering its function, making it challenging for static analysis tools to detect. Similarly, metamorphic malware rewrites its code during propagation, bypassing signature-based detection systems (Innocent, 2024).

VAEs, on the other hand, utilize probabilistic modeling to encode the latent features of malware samples into a continuous space. By sampling this latent space and decoding the results, VAEs generate new malware variants with controlled variability. This allows for the creation of diverse samples that simulate subtle differences in malware behavior, aiding in the development of detection systems capable of identifying nuanced threats (Durai, 2024).

Generative models are not limited to creating static code. They also simulate dynamic malware behaviors, such as changes in execution flow, payload activation, or interaction with system resources. By mimicking the runtime behavior of advanced threats, these models provide a more comprehensive testing environment. Detection systems are exposed to scenarios involving delayed payloads, environment-specific adaptations, and multi-stage attacks, which are difficult to replicate with traditional methods (Redhu et al., 2024)

4.4.2 AI-Driven Signature and Behavior Analysis of Malware

Malware detection traditionally relies on signature-based methods, which identify threats by matching patterns in code or binary data. While effective against known threats, this approach struggles with zero-day malware and variants that obfuscate their signatures. Behavior-based analysis complements signature-based methods by focusing on how malware interacts with the system. Generative AI significantly enhances both approaches, providing advanced capabilities for analyzing and predicting malware patterns.

In signature-based analysis, generative AI automates the extraction of unique patterns from malware datasets. For instance, Natural Language Processing (NLP) techniques are applied to analyze binary code as structured text, identifying recurring sequences and features that define malware families. GANs and VAEs extend this by generating synthetic signatures, emulating the diversity of real-world threats. By augmenting signature databases with these synthetic entries, generative AI ensures that detection systems remain capable of identifying previously unseen variants. Furthermore, adversarial training involves creating synthetic malware samples specifically designed to bypass existing signature detection mechanisms. These samples reveal weaknesses in the detection algorithms, prompting the development of more resilient solutions (Vo et al., 2023).

Behavior-based analysis benefits from generative AI's ability to simulate and model complex interactions between malware and system environments. Generative models create synthetic behavior profiles that replicate how malware modifies files, accesses network resources, or interacts with memory. For example, a VAE might generate sequences of API calls or system events that characterize ransomware activity during encryption. By analyzing these synthetic behaviors, detection systems learn to identify deviations from normal activity, enhancing their ability to detect unknown threats (Pandit & Mondal, 2023).

Dynamic analysis, a subset of behavior-based methods, involves observing malware in controlled environments to understand its runtime behavior. Generative AI supports this by simulating dynamic scenarios, such as time-delayed payloads or environment-specific adaptations. For instance, a GAN could model the behavior of a botnet command-and-control communication, generating network traffic patterns that mimic real-world attacks. These simulations enable security teams to test their detection systems against sophisticated threats without exposing production environments to risk (Quertier et al., 2024).

The integration of signature-based and behavior-based approaches into hybrid detection systems further amplifies the impact of generative AI. By combining static and dynamic analysis, these systems achieve higher accuracy and adaptability. Generative AI facilitates this integration by providing a unified framework for analyzing both code structures and runtime interactions. For example, a transformer-based model might analyze log files to identify correlated events that signify malware activity, bridging the gap between signature patterns and behavioral anomalies (Anandhi et al., 2023).

Ethical considerations in this context revolve around the potential for misuse and the impact of biases in generative models. If these models are trained on incomplete or unrepresentative datasets, their outputs may fail to capture the diversity of real-world threats, leading to gaps in detection capabilities. Ensuring transparency, validation, and fairness in generative AI systems is crucial to maintaining their reliability and trustworthiness (Saqib et al., 2024).

4.5 Advanced Applications and Future Directions

The role of generative AI in malware analysis and detection extends beyond current practices, paving the way for innovative applications and methodologies. For instance, federated learning combined with generative AI allows organizations to collaboratively train models on distributed datasets without sharing sensitive information. This approach enhances the generalization capabilities of detection systems while preserving privacy.

Real-time malware detection is another promising application (Lazaros et al., 2024). Generative models could be integrated into endpoint security solutions to dynamically generate adversarial examples or simulate behavior patterns, enabling on-the-fly adaptation to emerging threats. Additionally, the use of hybrid generative models, such as GAN-Transformer combinations, offers the potential to analyze multi-modal data, including network traffic, system logs, and file structures, providing a holistic view of malware activity (Sayyed et al., 2024).

5. DEFENSIVE APPLICATIONS OF GENERATIVE AI

Generative AI has emerged as a transformative force in cybersecurity, particularly in building robust defenses against increasingly sophisticated and unpredictable threats. By leveraging its ability to model complex systems and generate synthetic data, generative AI is being used to enhance anomaly detection and create adaptive defense mechanisms. These applications are vital for ensuring that cybersecurity systems can keep pace with rapidly evolving attack vectors and maintain resilience against both known and novel threats.

5.1 Improving Anomaly Detection Through Synthetic Normal and Abnormal Behavior Modeling

Anomaly detection is a cornerstone of cybersecurity, focusing on identifying deviations from normal behavior within a system. These anomalies can indicate malicious activities, such as unauthorized access, data exfiltration, or distributed denial-of-service (DDoS) attacks. Traditional anomaly detection methods rely on historical data to define normal behavior, but they often struggle with evolving systems, insufficient data, or the subtle nature of advanced threats (Liu et al., 2023).

Generative AI addresses these challenges by creating synthetic datasets that represent both normal and abnormal behavior. This capability significantly enhances the ability of detection systems to identify threats with higher accuracy and lower false-positive rates.

Synthetic Modeling of Normal Behavior

Normal behavior in a system encompasses predictable patterns of user activity, network traffic, and application performance. Generative AI models such as Variational Autoencoders (VAEs) and deep generative neural networks are particularly adept at learning these patterns. These models analyze historical data to encode the statistical and temporal characteristics of normal behavior into a latent space, a compressed representation of the data (Salatiello et al., 2023).

Once trained, the model can generate synthetic examples of normal behavior that closely mimic real-world scenarios. These synthetic datasets provide several advantages:

1. Data augmentation: The generated data supplements existing training datasets, improving the robustness of anomaly detection algorithms.

2. Simulation of rare events: Normal behaviors that occur infrequently, such as maintenance activities or off-peak system usage, can be synthesized for comprehensive training.
3. System-specific modeling: Generative AI tailors normal behavior models to specific environments, accounting for unique operational patterns and reducing false alarms caused by generalizations.

Synthetic Modeling of Abnormal Behavior

Equally critical to anomaly detection is the ability to identify abnormal behaviors indicative of malicious activities. Generative AI can simulate a wide range of attack scenarios, including insider threats, APTs, and ransomware attacks. This involves generating synthetic data that mimics how an attacker might interact with a system, such as unusual login attempts, unexpected network connections, or abnormal data transfer rates (Agrawal, Kaur, & Myneni, 2024).

GANs are particularly effective for this purpose. In a cybersecurity context, the generator creates synthetic abnormal data, while the discriminator learns to distinguish it from genuine anomalies. This adversarial training ensures that the synthetic data becomes increasingly realistic, providing valuable input for training anomaly detection systems.

By integrating synthetic normal and abnormal behavior data, anomaly detection systems can better learn the boundaries between legitimate and malicious activities. This reduces both false positives (benign events flagged as threats) and false negatives (threats missed by the system).

Applications in Real-World Anomaly Detection

In network security, generative AI can simulate normal and abnormal traffic patterns, allowing IDS to detect anomalies in real-time. For example, a VAE could generate sequences of network packet metadata to model normal traffic flows, while GANs could produce data representing reconnaissance scans or data exfiltration attempts. When trained on these datasets, the IDS becomes more adept at identifying subtle deviations from expected behavior (Faber et al., 2023).

In endpoint security, generative AI can model the normal behavior of applications and operating systems. For instance, it might generate synthetic sequences of system calls or file accesses to represent typical activity. Abnormal patterns, such as those caused by malware, can then be more easily detected.

In cloud security, generative AI can model user activity patterns, such as logins, API calls, and resource usage. By simulating both normal and abnormal cloud usage scenarios, security systems can identify threats like account takeovers or unauthorized access to sensitive data.

5.2 Adaptive Defense Mechanisms Using Generative AI Techniques

Cyber threats are dynamic, with attackers continuously evolving their techniques to bypass detection mechanisms. Static defenses, while effective against known threats, often fail to adapt to new attack vectors. Adaptive defense mechanisms address this limitation by evolving alongside the threat landscape, leveraging real-time data and intelligent algorithms to modify their behavior dynamically (Vadisetty & Polamarasetti, 2024).

Generative AI plays a pivotal role in enabling these adaptive mechanisms. By analyzing and synthesizing data in real time, generative models provide the insights and capabilities necessary for dynamic response and proactive threat mitigation (Neupane et al., 2023).

Dynamic Threat Modeling

One of the key applications of generative AI in adaptive defense is dynamic threat modeling. By continuously analyzing system behavior and threat intelligence data, generative models create real-time simulations of potential attack scenarios. These simulations enable security systems to anticipate and counter emerging threats before they can cause harm.

For example, a GAN might simulate a phishing campaign targeting specific user behaviors. The generated data could then be used to update email filters, training them to identify and block similar phishing attempts. Similarly, VAEs could model ransomware propagation in a network, helping security teams identify choke points where the attack could be contained (Duy et al., 2024).

Behavioral Adaptation

Adaptive defense systems also rely on generative AI to model and predict the behavior of both attackers and legitimate users. By understanding these behaviors, the system can dynamically adjust its defenses to minimize risks (Aminu et al., 2024).

In endpoint security, generative AI models might analyze application behavior to identify unusual patterns indicative of malware. If an anomaly is detected, the system could automatically quarantine the affected application or adjust its permissions to prevent further harm. In network security, generative models could analyze traffic patterns to detect signs of DDoS attacks, dynamically rerouting traffic or deploying additional resources to maintain availability (Sindiramutty et al., 2025).

Proactive Defense Strategies

Generative AI supports proactive defense by enabling systems to simulate and test various response strategies. By generating synthetic attack scenarios, generative models allow security teams to evaluate the effectiveness of different countermeasures. This approach ensures that defenses are optimized for current threats and can adapt to future challenges.

In the context of cloud security, for instance, generative AI might simulate an insider threat involving unauthorized data access (Sun et al., 2023; Vadisetty & Polamarasetti, 2024). The system could then test various access control policies to determine the most effective way to mitigate the threat. In IoT security, generative models could simulate attacks on connected devices, helping to identify vulnerabilities and implement patches before real-world exploitation occurs.

5.3 Real-World Case Studies and Applications

Anomaly Detection in Financial Systems

A global financial institution implemented generative AI to enhance its fraud detection capabilities. By modeling normal transaction patterns using VAEs, the system generated synthetic data to train anomaly detection algorithms. GANs were used to simulate fraudulent transactions, enabling the system to identify subtle anomalies indicative of fraud. This approach significantly reduced false positives and improved the institution's ability to detect emerging threats (Sanjalawe & Al-E'mari, 2023; Aftabi, Ahmadi, & Farzi, 2023).

Adaptive Defense in Cloud Security

A cloud service provider deployed generative AI to improve its adaptive defenses. Transformer-based models analyzed real-time user activity to identify deviations from normal behavior. When a potential account takeover was detected, the system dynamically adjusted access controls and notified the user. Generative models also simulated insider threats, helping the provider optimize its response strategies (Latibari et al.,2024).

Proactive Defense in IoT Networks

An IoT device manufacturer used generative AI to simulate attacks on its devices. By generating synthetic data representing both normal and malicious behavior, the manufacturer identified vulnerabilities in its firmware and implemented patches before devices were deployed. This proactive approach improved the security of the devices and reduced the risk of exploitation (Khan et al., 2025).

6. GENERATIVE AI IN CYBER THREAT INTELLIGENCE (CTI)

The rapidly evolving cyber threat landscape demands innovative and proactive approaches to cybersecurity. CTI plays a crucial role in enabling organizations to understand, anticipate, and mitigate threats. Generative AI has emerged as a transformative technology in CTI, revolutionizing how organizations predict evolving attack patterns and share threat intelligence. By leveraging models such as GANs, VAEs, and transformers, generative AI enhances the scope, accuracy, and timeliness of threat intelligence, ensuring a robust defense against sophisticated attacks.

6.1 Predicting Evolving Attack Patterns with Generative Models

Modern cyberattacks are increasingly complex, often involving multi-stage processes that evolve dynamically to bypass traditional defenses. Predictive threat intelligence aims to forecast these evolving attack patterns by analyzing historical data, behavioral trends, and emerging Tactics, Techniques, And Procedures (TTPs). However, traditional analytical methods often struggle to process the sheer volume and complexity of data required for accurate predictions (Balantrapu, 2024). Generative AI addresses this limitation by synthesizing realistic, predictive models of attack patterns based on existing intelligence.

Generative models such as GANs, VAEs, and transformers are particularly suited for predictive analysis due to their ability to model complex, high-dimensional data. These models learn the underlying distributions and temporal dynamics of threat data, enabling them to simulate and forecast evolving attack patterns (Agrawal et al., 2023.

- GANs for predictive simulation:

GANs use a generator to create synthetic attack scenarios and a discriminator to validate their realism. In CTI, GANs can simulate the evolution of cyberattacks, such as phishing campaigns that adapt to new defenses or malware variants that exploit emerging vulnerabilities. By iterating over multiple training cycles, GANs refine their predictions, providing valuable insights into potential future threats (Redhu et al., 2024).

- VAEs for behavioral modeling:

VAEs encode the latent features of cyber threats into a compact representation, allowing for the generation of variations in attack behavior. For example, a VAE trained on ransomware activity can generate synthetic samples that predict how ransomware might adapt to changes in detection mechanisms or system configurations (Durai, 2024).

- Transformers for temporal prediction:

Transformer-based models, such as those used in natural language processing, excel at analyzing sequential data. In CTI, transformers process sequences of attack events, identifying patterns and predicting future stages of an attack. For instance, a transformer could analyze a sequence of network intrusions to predict the likelihood and timing of data exfiltration (Wang et al., 2024).

Applications in Real-Time Threat Forecasting

Generative AI enables real-time threat forecasting by continuously analyzing live data feeds, such as network logs, security alerts, and external threat intelligence reports. These models identify subtle changes in threat behavior, providing early warnings of potential attacks. For example:

- In network security, GANs might simulate lateral movement within a compromised network, helping administrators identify vulnerable pathways.
- In endpoint security, VAEs could predict how malware might exploit newly disclosed software vulnerabilities.
- In cloud environments, transformers could analyze API call patterns to forecast potential account takeover attempts.

Integration with Threat Taxonomies

Generative AI models also integrate seamlessly with established threat taxonomies, such as MITRE ATT&CK. By aligning synthetic predictions with known TTPs, these models provide actionable intelligence that aligns with industry standards. For example, a GAN might simulate a sequence of tactics aligned with MITRE

ATT&CK categories, helping security teams prepare defenses against specific techniques (Mylrea, 2025).

Advantages of Generative AI in Predictive CTI

- Accuracy: Generative models produce high-fidelity simulations that closely mimic real-world attack behavior.
- Proactivity: By forecasting emerging threats, generative AI enables organizations to implement preemptive measures.
- Scalability: Generative AI processes vast amounts of data, identifying patterns that may be overlooked by human analysts.
- Adaptability: These models evolve alongside the threat landscape, ensuring relevance even as attack patterns change.

6.2 Enhancing Threat Intelligence Sharing with AI-Synthesized Insights

Threat intelligence sharing is a cornerstone of modern cybersecurity, enabling organizations to collaboratively defend against common threats. By pooling resources and knowledge, organizations can detect and respond to attacks more effectively. However, traditional approaches to intelligence sharing are often hindered by challenges such as data standardization, information overload, and privacy concerns. Generative AI addresses these challenges by synthesizing actionable, anonymized insights from raw threat data.

AI-Synthesized Insights for Collaborative Defense

Generative AI excels at transforming raw threat data into synthesized insights that are both actionable and shareable. By summarizing complex datasets, identifying key trends, and anonymizing sensitive information, generative models enhance the effectiveness of threat intelligence sharing (Sood, 2024).

- Summarization and prioritization:

Transformer-based models summarize extensive threat intelligence reports, extracting critical information and prioritizing the most relevant insights. For instance, a transformer might analyze multiple reports on a new malware strain, identifying common attack vectors and mitigation strategies (Ullah et al., 2022).

- Anonymization and data privacy:

Privacy concerns often deter organizations from sharing threat intelligence, particularly when sensitive or proprietary data is involved. Generative AI models anonymize data by generating synthetic equivalents that retain statistical and behavioral properties without revealing specific details. For example, GANs could create synthetic network traffic that mimics the patterns observed during an attack, enabling collaborative analysis without exposing real-world data (Goyal & Mahmoud, 2024).

- Standardization across formats:

Threat intelligence data often comes in diverse formats, such as logs, reports, or structured feeds (e.g., STIX/TAXII). Generative AI models normalize and standardize this data, making it easier to share and integrate across platforms. For example, a VAE might encode diverse threat data into a unified representation, which can then be decoded into a format compatible with industry standards (Möller, 2023).

Real-Time Threat Intelligence Sharing

Generative AI facilitates real-time sharing of threat intelligence by automating data processing and dissemination. For example, when a new zero-day exploit is detected, a transformer-based model could generate a concise, actionable report and distribute it to relevant stakeholders (Adeoye, 2023). These insights might include:

- A synthetic timeline of the attack, highlighting key events and Indicators of Compromise (IOCs).
- Predictions of how the exploit might propagate, based on historical trends and generative simulations.
- Recommended countermeasures, synthesized from existing threat intelligence.

Applications in Collaborative Platforms

Generative AI is increasingly integrated into collaborative threat intelligence platforms, enabling organizations to share and act on insights more effectively (Sindiramutty et al., 2024). For example:

- In the financial sector, GANs might simulate coordinated attacks on payment systems, providing member institutions with early warnings and mitigation strategies.

- In critical infrastructure, VAEs could model potential cascading failures caused by cyberattacks, enabling cross-sector collaboration to address systemic risks.
- In healthcare, transformer models could analyze threat intelligence from connected devices, synthesizing insights that protect patient data and system integrity.

Overcoming Challenges in Threat Intelligence Sharing

Generative AI addresses several key challenges associated with threat intelligence sharing (Sai et al., 2024):

- Information overload: By synthesizing and prioritizing insights, generative models help organizations focus on the most critical threats.
- Interoperability: Standardized outputs ensure compatibility across diverse systems and platforms.
- Trust and privacy: Anonymized synthetic data builds trust among participants, encouraging broader collaboration.

Challenges and Ethical Considerations

While generative AI offers significant benefits for CTI, its implementation must address certain challenges and ethical concerns (Mavikumbure et al., 2024). These include:

- Misuse of technology: The same generative models that predict attack patterns could be exploited by cybercriminals to develop advanced threats. Strict access controls and ethical guidelines are essential to mitigate this risk.
- Bias in training data: If generative models are trained on biased or incomplete datasets, their outputs may fail to accurately represent the threat landscape. Regular validation and updates are necessary to ensure reliability.
- Privacy concerns: While generative AI can anonymize data, advanced de-anonymization techniques might still reveal sensitive information. Robust privacy safeguards are critical for maintaining trust in collaborative platforms.

Future Directions in Generative AI for CTI

The integration of generative AI into CTI is still in its early stages, with significant potential for future advancements. Emerging trends include:

- Federated learning: Combining federated learning with generative AI enables organizations to collaboratively train models on distributed datasets without sharing raw data, enhancing both privacy and predictive capabilities.
- Real-time adaptation: Future generative models will incorporate real-time data streams, enabling adaptive threat intelligence that evolves as attacks unfold.
- Hybrid models: The combination of generative AI with other technologies, such as graph analytics and quantum computing, promises to further enhance the scope and accuracy of CTI.

Generative AI has transformed the field of Cyber Threat Intelligence, providing powerful tools for predicting evolving attack patterns and enhancing threat intelligence sharing. By leveraging advanced models such as GANs, VAEs, and transformers, generative AI enables organizations to stay ahead of cyber adversaries, anticipate emerging threats, and collaborate effectively to protect critical assets. While challenges and ethical considerations remain, the continued evolution of generative AI promises to drive a more proactive, resilient, and collaborative approach to cybersecurity. As the technology matures, its impact on CTI will only deepen, ensuring that organizations are better prepared to navigate an increasingly complex threat landscape.

Figure 13 presents a comprehensive taxonomy of GANs applications in cybersecurity, highlighting their diverse roles in enhancing defensive capabilities. It categorizes GAN applications into five main areas: Intrusion Detection, Malware Detection, Adversarial Attacks, Botnet Detection, and Cyber-Physical Systems. Within each category, specific GAN models are referenced, such as WCGAN and SMOTE-GAN for intrusion detection and PlausMal-GAN and Defense-GAN for malware analysis (Arifin et al., 2024). The figure also emphasizes specialized applications, like FedGAN for IoT security and MAD-GAN for anomaly detection in network traffic. This taxonomy illustrates the versatility and effectiveness of GANs in addressing complex cybersecurity challenges, including anomaly detection, securing IoT systems, and combating sophisticated attack vectors like botnets and adversarial attacks (Xiong, Li & Cai, 2023).

Figure 13. Taxonomy of GAN applications in cybersecurity

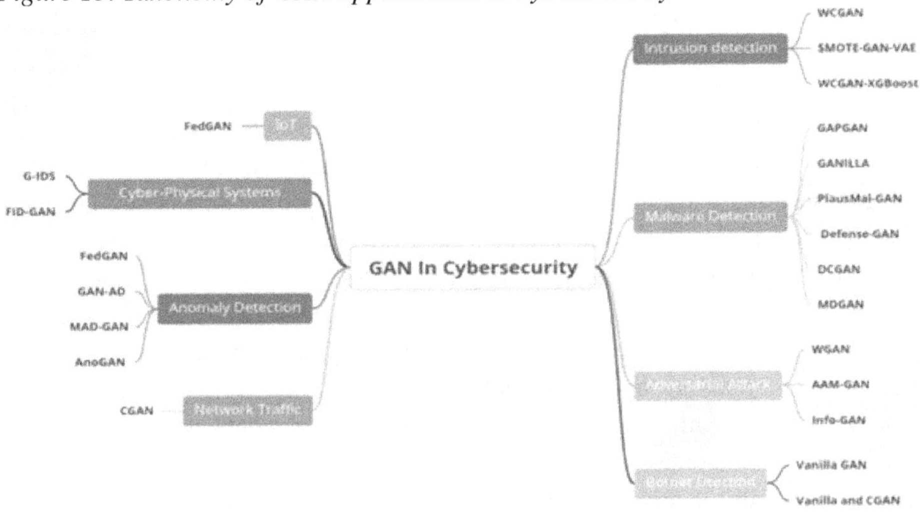

7. CONCLUSION

Generative AI has emerged as a cornerstone of modern cybersecurity, addressing challenges posed by the rapidly evolving threat landscape. This chapter has illuminated the transformative potential of generative AI in developing robust and proactive defense mechanisms. Models such as GANs, VAEs, and transformers demonstrate exceptional capabilities in simulating attack scenarios, augmenting datasets, and enhancing anomaly detection. By synthesizing realistic and diverse data, these models empower organizations to predict, detect, and mitigate cyber threats with unprecedented precision.

One of the key contributions of generative AI is its role in proactive cybersecurity. Traditional methods often rely on reactive strategies, addressing threats only after they materialize. In contrast, generative AI enables organizations to anticipate and simulate potential attack scenarios, fostering a proactive approach to defense. This capability not only strengthens existing systems but also prepares them to counter emerging threats effectively. Moreover, generative AI has proven invaluable in addressing data scarcity—a persistent challenge in cybersecurity. Through synthetic data generation, organizations can overcome limitations in training datasets, particularly for rare and sophisticated attack types. These datasets enhance machine learning models, improving their generalizability and reducing vulnerabilities to novel threats. By enabling data augmentation and balancing, generative AI ensures more comprehensive and effective training for cybersecurity systems.

Despite its transformative potential, generative AI also introduces challenges that must be carefully navigated. The dual-use nature of this technology means that while it can fortify defenses, it can also be exploited by malicious actors to create more sophisticated threats. Ethical considerations, including the misuse of synthetic data and privacy concerns, underscore the need for stringent regulatory frameworks. Additionally, vulnerabilities such as adversarial attacks on AI models highlight the importance of incorporating robust design principles and continuous monitoring into cybersecurity practices. The future of generative AI in cybersecurity lies in its integration with emerging technologies such as quantum computing and autonomous systems. Quantum computing promises to accelerate the processing capabilities of generative models, enabling real-time threat detection and response at an unprecedented scale. Meanwhile, autonomous systems powered by generative AI can dynamically adapt to evolving threats, ensuring swift and effective mitigation without human intervention. These synergies will drive the creation of predictive and adaptive security ecosystems, capable of addressing the complex and dynamic nature of cyber threats.

REFERENCES

Adeoye, I. (2023). Leveraging Artificial Intelligence and Machine Learning for Real-Time Threat Intelligence: Enhancing Incident Response Capabilities.

Agrawal, G., Kaur, A., & Myneni, S. (2024). A review of generative models in generating synthetic attack data for cybersecurity. *Electronics (Basel), 13*(2), 322. DOI: 10.3390/electronics13020322

Ahmad, Z., Jaffri, Z. U. A., Chen, M., & Bao, S. (2024). Understanding GANs: Fundamentals, variants, training challenges, applications, and open problems. *Multimedia Tools and Applications*, •••, 1–77. DOI: 10.1007/s11042-024-19361-y

Alabdulwahab, S., Kim, Y. T., Seo, A., & Son, Y. (2023). Generating Synthetic Dataset for ML-Based IDS Using CTGAN and Feature Selection to Protect Smart IoT Environments. *Applied Sciences (Basel, Switzerland), 13*(19), 10951. DOI: 10.3390/app131910951

Almaraz-Rivera, J. G., Cantoral-Ceballos, J. A., & Botero, J. F. (2023). Enhancing IoT Network Security: Unveiling the Power of Self-Supervised Learning against DDoS Attacks. *Sensors (Basel), 23*(21), 8701. DOI: 10.3390/s23218701 PMID: 37960401

Aminu, M., Akinsanya, A., Dako, D. A., & Oyedokun, O. (2024). Enhancing cyber threat detection through real-time threat intelligence and adaptive defense mechanisms. *International Journal of Computer Applications Technology and Research, 13*(8), 11–27.

Ammara, D. A., Ding, J., & Tutschku, K. (2024). Synthetic Data Generation in Cybersecurity: A Comparative Analysis. *arXiv preprint arXiv:2410.16326.*

Anandhi, V., Vinod, P., & Menon, V. G., ER, A. K., Shilesh, A., Viswam, A., & Shafiq, A. (2023, February). Malware Detection using Dynamic Analysis. In *2023 International Conference on Advances in Intelligent Computing and Applications (AICAPS)* (pp. 1-6). IEEE.

Arifin, M. M., Ahmed, M. S., Ghosh, T. K., Udoy, I. A., Zhuang, J., & Yeh, J. H. (2024). A survey on the application of generative adversarial networks in cybersecurity: prospective, direction and open research scopes. *arXiv preprint arXiv:2407.08839.*

Arora, A., & Shantanu, . (2022). A review on application of GANs in cybersecurity domain. *IETE Technical Review, 39*(2), 433–441. DOI: 10.1080/02564602.2020.1854058

Ayyaz, S., & Malik, S. M. (2024, October). A Comprehensive Study of Generative Adversarial Networks (GAN) and Generative Pre-Trained Transformers (GPT) in Cybersecurity. In *2024 Sixth International Conference on Intelligent Computing in Data Sciences (ICDS)* (pp. 1-8). IEEE. DOI: 10.1109/ICDS62089.2024.10756505

Balantrapu, S. S. (2024). AI for predictive cyber threat intelligence. *International Journal of Management Education for Sustainable Development*, *7*(7), 1–28.

Bengesi, S., El-Sayed, H., Sarker, M. K., Houkpati, Y., Irungu, J., & Oladunni, T. (2024). Advancements in Generative AI: A Comprehensive Review of GANs, GPT, Autoencoders, Diffusion Model, and Transformers. *IEEE Access : Practical Innovations, Open Solutions*, *12*, 69812–69837. DOI: 10.1109/ACCESS.2024.3397775

Bhatt, R., & Indra, G. (2024). Detecting the undetectable: GAN-based strategies for network intrusion detection. *International Journal of Information Technology : an Official Journal of Bharati Vidyapeeth's Institute of Computer Applications and Management*, *16*(8), 5231–5237. DOI: 10.1007/s41870-024-02172-7

Croce, V., Caroti, G., De Luca, L., Piemonte, A., & Véron, P. (2023). Neural radiance fields (nerf): Review and potential applications to digital cultural heritage. *The International Archives of the Photogrammetry, Remote Sensing and Spatial Information Sciences*, *48*, 453–460. DOI: 10.5194/isprs-archives-XLVIII-M-2-2023-453-2023

Dash, A., Ye, J., & Wang, G. (2023). A review of generative adversarial networks (GANs) and its applications in a wide variety of disciplines: From medical to remote sensing. *IEEE Access : Practical Innovations, Open Solutions*.

De Wilde, P., Arora, P., Buarque de Lima Neto, F., Chin, Y., Thinyane, M., Stinckwich, S., ... & Marwala, T. (2024). Recommendations on the Use of Synthetic Data to Train AI Models.

Devadiga, D., Jin, G., Potdar, B., Koo, H., Han, A., Shringi, A., . . . Kumar, S. (2023, October). Gleam: Gan and llm for evasive adversarial malware. In *2023 14th International Conference on Information and Communication Technology Convergence (ICTC)* (pp. 53-58). IEEE.

Dhoni, P., & Kumar, R. (2023). Synergizing generative ai and cybersecurity: Roles of generative ai entities, companies, agencies, and government in enhancing cybersecurity. *Authorea Preprints*.

Do Yoo, J., Kim, H., & Kim, H. K. (2024). GUIDE: GAN-based UAV IDS Enhancement. *Computers & Security*, *147*, 104073. DOI: 10.1016/j.cose.2024.104073

Dunmore, A., Jang-Jaccard, J., Sabrina, F., & Kwak, J. (2023). A comprehensive survey of generative adversarial networks (GANs) in cybersecurity intrusion detection. *IEEE Access : Practical Innovations, Open Solutions, 11*, 76071–76094. DOI: 10.1109/ACCESS.2023.3296707

Duy, P. T., Minh, V. Q., Dang, B. T. H., Son, N. D. H., Quyen, N. H., & Pham, V. H. (2024). A study on adversarial sample resistance and Defense Mechanism for Multimodal Learning-based phishing website detection. *IEEE Access : Practical Innovations, Open Solutions, 12*, 137805–137824. DOI: 10.1109/ACCESS.2024.3436812

Faber, K., Corizzo, R., Sniezynski, B., & Japkowicz, N. (2023). Vlad: Task-agnostic vae-based lifelong anomaly detection. *Neural Networks, 165*, 248–273. DOI: 10.1016/j.neunet.2023.05.032 PMID: 37307668

Familoni, B. T.Babajide Tolulope Familoni. (2024). Cybersecurity challenges in the age of AI: Theoretical approaches and practical solutions. *Computer Science & IT Research Journal, 5*(3), 703–724. DOI: 10.51594/csitrj.v5i3.930

Folorunso, A., Adewumi, T., Adewa, A., Okonkwo, R., & Olawumi, T. N. (2024). Impact of AI on cybersecurity and security compliance. *Global Journal of Engineering and Technology Advances, 21*(01), 167–184. DOI: 10.30574/gjeta.2024.21.1.0193

Goyal, M., & Mahmoud, Q. H. (2024). A systematic review of synthetic data generation techniques using generative AI. *Electronics (Basel), 13*(17), 3509. DOI: 10.3390/electronics13173509

Goyal, S., Doddapaneni, S., Khapra, M. M., & Ravindran, B. (2023). A survey of adversarial defenses and robustness in nlp. *ACM Computing Surveys, 55*(14s), 1–39. DOI: 10.1145/3593042

Gupta, I., Kumari, S., Jha, P., & Ghosh, M. (2024). Leveraging LSTM and GAN for Modern Malware Detection. *arXiv preprint arXiv:2405.04373.*

Gupta, M. (2023, November). Advances in AI: Employing Deep Generative Models for the Creation of Synthetic Healthcare Datasets to Improve Predictive Analytics. In *2023 International Conference on Communication, Security and Artificial Intelligence (ICCSAI)* (pp. 1026-1030). IEEE. DOI: 10.1109/ICCSAI59793.2023.10421464

Ibrahim, M., Khalil, Y. A., Amirrajab, S., Sun, C., Breeuwer, M., Pluim, J., . . . Dumontier, M. (2024). Generative AI for synthetic data across multiple medical modalities: A systematic review of recent developments and challenges. *arXiv preprint arXiv:2407.00116.*

Innocent, E. K. (2024). *Enhancing Data Security in Healthcare with Synthetic Data Generation: An Autoencoder and Variational Autoencoder Approach* (Master's thesis, Oslo Metropolitan University).

Islam, M. R. (2024). *Generative AI, Cybersecurity, and Ethics*. John Wiley & Sons.

Jaweed, M., & Shaikh, R. F. (2024). Optimizing Generative AI By Overcoming Stability Mode Collapse And Quality Challenges In Gans And Vaes. *MSW Management Journal*, *34*(2), 497–507.

Kaur, D., Islam, S. N., Mahmud, M. A., Haque, M. E., & Anwar, A. (2023). A VAE-Bayesian deep learning scheme for solar power generation forecasting based on dimensionality reduction. *Energy and AI*, *14*, 100279. DOI: 10.1016/j.egyai.2023.100279

Khadka, K., Chandrasekaran, J., Lei, Y., Kacker, R. N., & Kuhn, D. R. (2023, April). Synthetic data generation using combinatorial testing and variational autoencoder. In *2023 IEEE International Conference on Software Testing, Verification and Validation Workshops (ICSTW)* (pp. 228-236). IEEE. DOI: 10.1109/ICSTW58534.2023.00048

Khan, A., Jhanjhi, N., Hamid, D. H. H., Omar, H. A. H. B. H., Amsaad, F., & Wassan, S. (2025). Future Trends and Challenges in Cybersecurity and Generative AI. *Reshaping CyberSecurity With Generative AI Techniques*, 491-522.

Khoramnejad, F., & Hossain, E. (2024). Generative AI for the Optimization of Next-Generation Wireless Networks: Basics, State-of-the-Art, and Open Challenges. *arXiv preprint arXiv:2405.17454*.

Kiran, A., & Kumar, S. S. (2024). A methodology and an empirical analysis to determine the most suitable synthetic data generator. *IEEE Access : Practical Innovations, Open Solutions*, *12*, 12209–12228. DOI: 10.1109/ACCESS.2024.3354277

Krishnamurthy, O., & Vemulapalli, G. (2024). Advancing Sustainable Cybersecurity: Exploring Trends and Overcoming Challenges with Generative AI. In *International Conference on Sustainable Development through Machine Learning, AI and IoT* (pp. 16-25). Cham: Springer Nature Switzerland.

Kuang, H., Liu, H., Wu, Y., Satoh, S. I., & Ji, R. (2023). Improving adversarial robustness via information bottleneck distillation. *Advances in Neural Information Processing Systems*, *36*, 10796–10813.

Latibari, B. S., Nazari, N., Chowdhury, M. A., Gubbi, K. I., Fang, C., Ghimire, S., & Hosseini, E.. (2024). Transformers: A Security Perspective. *IEEE Access : Practical Innovations, Open Solutions*, *12*, 181071–181105. DOI: 10.1109/ACCESS.2024.3509372

Lazaros, K., Koumadorakis, D. E., Vrahatis, A. G., & Kotsiantis, S. (2024). Federated Learning: Navigating the Landscape of Collaborative Intelligence. *Electronics (Basel), 13*(23), 4744. DOI: 10.3390/electronics13234744

Lim, W., Yong, K. S. C., Lau, B. T., & Tan, C. C. L. (2024). Future of generative adversarial networks (GAN) for anomaly detection in network security: A review. *Computers & Security, 139*, 103733. DOI: 10.1016/j.cose.2024.103733

Little, C., Allmendinger, R., & Elliot, M. (2024). Synthetic census microdata generation: A comparative study of synthesis methods examining the trade-off between disclosure risk and utility. *Journal of Official Statistics*, 0282423X241266523.

Liu, J., Li, X., Li, C., Yang, G., Li, Y., Qiu, J., & Dong, Z. Y. (2023). When Deep Normal Behavior Models Meet Fault Samples: A Generalized Wind Turbine Anomaly Detection Scheme. *IEEE Transactions on Instrumentation and Measurement, 72*, 1–16. DOI: 10.1109/TIM.2023.3324347

López Delgado, J. L., & López Ramos, J. A. (2024). A Comprehensive Survey on Generative AI Solutions in IoT Security. *Electronics (Basel), 13*(24), 4965. DOI: 10.3390/electronics13244965

Malatji, M., & Tolah, A. (2024). Artificial intelligence (AI) cybersecurity dimensions: A comprehensive framework for understanding adversarial and offensive AI. *AI and Ethics*, •••, 1–28. DOI: 10.1007/s43681-024-00427-4

Malik, J., Muthalagu, R., & Pawar, P. M. (2024). A systematic review of adversarial machine learning attacks, defensive controls and technologies. *IEEE Access : Practical Innovations, Open Solutions, 12*, 99382–99421. DOI: 10.1109/ACCESS.2024.3423323

Mavikumbure, H. S., Cobilean, V., Wickramasinghe, C. S., Drake, D., & Manic, M. (2024). Generative AI in cyber security of cyber physical systems: Benefits and threats. In *2024 16th International Conference on Human System Interaction (HSI)* (pp. 1-8). IEEE.

Ming, Y., Yang, X., Wang, W., Chen, Z., Feng, J., Xing, Y., & Zhang, G. (2025). Benchmarking neural radiance fields for autonomous robots: An overview. *Engineering Applications of Artificial Intelligence, 140*, 109685. DOI: 10.1016/j.engappai.2024.109685

Mohammed, A. S., & Patil, S. (2022). Investigating the Optimal Cloud Computing Infrastructure for Training Large-Scale Generative Models. [IJFMR]. *International Journal for Multidisciplinary Research, 4*(6).

Möller, D. P. (2023). Threats and threat intelligence. In *Guide to Cybersecurity in Digital Transformation: Trends, Methods, Technologies, Applications and Best Practices* (pp. 71–129). Springer Nature Switzerland. DOI: 10.1007/978-3-031-26845-8_2

Murali, R., Thangavel, P., & Velayutham, C. S. (2023). Evolving malware variants as antigens for antivirus systems. *Expert Systems with Applications*, *226*, 120092. DOI: 10.1016/j.eswa.2023.120092

Mylrea, M. (2025). The generative AI weapon of mass destruction: Evolving disinformation threats, vulnerabilities, and mitigation frameworks. In *Interdependent Human-Machine Teams* (pp. 315–347). Academic Press. DOI: 10.1016/B978-0-443-29246-0.00007-9

Nair, V., Radhakrishnan, A., Chithra, R., & James, A. (2023). Memristive pixel-CNN loop generate for CNN generalisations. *IEEE Transactions on Nanotechnology*, *22*, 120–125. DOI: 10.1109/TNANO.2023.3248108

Neupane, S., Fernandez, I. A., Mittal, S., & Rahimi, S. (2023). Impacts and risk of generative AI technology on cyber defense. *arXiv preprint arXiv:2306.13033.*

Ojha, A. C., Agarwal, A., & Swetha, G. (2023, November). Generative Adversarial Networks for Cybersecurity Threat. In *2023 International Conference on Recent Advances in Science and Engineering Technology (ICRASET)* (pp. 1-6). IEEE.

Pandit, A. V., & Mondal, D. (2023). Real-Time Malware Detection on IoT Devices using Behavior-Based Analysis and Neural Networks. *Research Journal of Computer Systems and Engineering*, *4*(2), 117–129. DOI: 10.52710/rjcse.82

Park, C. H., Jo, J. Y., & Kim, Y. (2023, December). Detecting Cyber Threats with Limited Dataset Using Generative Adversarial Network on SCADA System. In *2023 International Conference on Computational Science and Computational Intelligence (CSCI)* (pp. 915-919). IEEE. DOI: 10.1109/CSCI62032.2023.00153

Quertier, T., Marais, B., Barrué, G., Morucci, S., Azé, S., & Salladin, S. (2024). A Lean Transformer Model for Dynamic Malware Analysis and Detection. *arXiv preprint arXiv:2408.02313.*

Rao, V. S., Balakrishna, R., El-Ebiary, Y. A. B., Thapar, P., Saravanan, K. A., & Godla, S. R. (2024). AI Driven Anomaly Detection in Network Traffic Using Hybrid CNN-GAN. *J. Adv. Inf. Technol*, *15*(7), 886–895. DOI: 10.12720/jait.15.7.886-895

Redhu, A., Choudhary, P., Srinivasan, K., & Das, T. K. (2024). Deep learning-powered malware detection in cyberspace: A contemporary review. *Frontiers in Physics (Lausanne)*, *12*, 1349463. DOI: 10.3389/fphy.2024.1349463

Sai, S., Yashvardhan, U., Chamola, V., & Sikdar, B. (2024). Generative ai for cyber security: Analyzing the potential of chatgpt, dall-e and other models for enhancing the security space. *IEEE Access : Practical Innovations, Open Solutions*, *12*, 53497–53516. DOI: 10.1109/ACCESS.2024.3385107

Salatiello, A., Wang, Y., Wichern, G., Koike-Akino, T., Ohta, Y., Kaneko, Y., . . . Chakrabarty, A. (2023). Synthesizing Building Operation Data with Generative Models: VAEs, GANs, or Something In Between? In *Companion Proceedings of the 14th ACM International Conference on Future Energy Systems* (pp. 125-133).

Salem, A. H., Azzam, S. M., Emam, O. E., & Abohany, A. A. (2024). Advancing cybersecurity: A comprehensive review of AI-driven detection techniques. *Journal of Big Data*, *11*(1), 105. DOI: 10.1186/s40537-024-00957-y

Sallam, M., Al-Mahzoum, K., & Sallam, M. (2024). Generative Artificial Intelligence and Cybersecurity Risks: Implications for Healthcare Security Based on Real-life Incidents. *Mesopotamian Journal of Artificial Intelligence in Healthcare*, *2024*, 184–203. DOI: 10.58496/MJAIH/2024/019

Sanjalawe, Y. K., & Al-E'mari, S. R. (2023). Abnormal transactions detection in the ethereum network using semi-supervised generative adversarial networks. *IEEE Access : Practical Innovations, Open Solutions*, *11*, 98516–98531. DOI: 10.1109/ACCESS.2023.3313630

Saqib, M., Mahdavifar, S., Fung, B. C., & Charland, P. (2024). A Comprehensive Analysis of Explainable AI for Malware Hunting. *ACM Computing Surveys*, *56*(12), 1–40. DOI: 10.1145/3677374

Sayyed, S., Zhang, M., Rifat, S., Swami, A., De Lucia, M., & Restuccia, F. (2024). Resilience and security of deep neural networks against intentional and unintentional perturbations: Survey and research challenges. *arXiv preprint arXiv:2408.00193.*

Sengar, S. S., Hasan, A. B., Kumar, S., & Carroll, F. (2024). Generative artificial intelligence: A systematic review and applications. *Multimedia Tools and Applications*, •••, 1–40. DOI: 10.1007/s11042-024-20016-1

Sindiramutty, S. R., Prabagaran, K. R. V., Jhanjhi, N. Z., Ghazanfar, M. A., Malik, N. A., & Soomro, T. R. (2025). Security Considerations in Generative AI for Web Applications. In *Reshaping CyberSecurity With Generative AI Techniques* (pp. 281–332). IGI Global.

Sood, A. (2024). *Combating Cyberattacks Targeting the AI Ecosystem: Assessing Threats, Risks, and Vulnerabilities*. Walter de Gruyter GmbH & Co KG. DOI: 10.1515/9781501520549

Sufi, F. (2024). Generative pre-trained transformer (GPT) in research: A systematic review on data augmentation. *Information (Basel), 15*(2), 99. DOI: 10.3390/info15020099

Sun, N., Ding, M., Jiang, J., Xu, W., Mo, X., Tai, Y., & Zhang, J. (2023). Cyber threat intelligence mining for proactive cybersecurity defense: A survey and new perspectives. *IEEE Communications Surveys and Tutorials, 25*(3), 1748–1774. DOI: 10.1109/COMST.2023.3273282

Ullah, F., Alsirhani, A., Alshahrani, M. M., Alomari, A., Naeem, H., & Shah, S. A. (2022). Explainable malware detection system using transformers-based transfer learning and multi-model visual representation. *Sensors (Basel), 22*(18), 6766. DOI: 10.3390/s22186766 PMID: 36146112

Vadisetty, R., & Polamarasetti, A. (2024, November). Generative AI for Cyber Threat Simulation and Defense. In *2024 12th International Conference on Control, Mechatronics and Automation (ICCMA)* (pp. 272-279). IEEE. DOI: 10.1109/ICCMA63715.2024.10843938

Vo, H. V., Nguyen, P. H., Nguyen, H. T., Vu, D. B., & Nguyen, H. N. (2023, December). Enhancing AI-Powered Malware Detection by Parallel Ensemble Learning. In *2023 RIVF International Conference on Computing and Communication Technologies (RIVF)* (pp. 503-508). IEEE. DOI: 10.1109/RIVF60135.2023.10471855

Wang, H., Zhang, Y., Liang, J., & Liu, L. (2023). DAFA-BiLSTM: Deep autoregression feature augmented bidirectional LSTM network for time series prediction. *Neural Networks, 157*, 240–256. DOI: 10.1016/j.neunet.2022.10.009 PMID: 36399979

Wang, W., Yi, P., Jiang, J., Zhang, P., & Chen, X. (2024). Transformer-based framework for alert aggregation and attack prediction in a multi-stage attack. *Computers & Security, 136*, 103533. DOI: 10.1016/j.cose.2023.103533

Wang, Y. C., Xue, J., Wei, C., & Kuo, C. C. J. (2023). An overview on generative AI at scale with Edge-Cloud Computing. *IEEE Open Journal of the Communications Society, 4*, 2952–2971. DOI: 10.1109/OJCOMS.2023.3320646

Xiong, Z., Li, W., & Cai, Z. (2023, June). Federated generative model on multi-source heterogeneous data in iot. *Proceedings of the AAAI Conference on Artificial Intelligence, 37*(9), 10537–10545. DOI: 10.1609/aaai.v37i9.26252

Yenduri, G., Ramalingam, M., Selvi, G. C., Supriya, Y., Srivastava, G., Maddikunta, P. K. R., Raj, G. D., Jhaveri, R. H., Prabadevi, B., Wang, W., Vasilakos, A. V., & Gadekallu, T. R. (2024). Gpt (generative pre-trained transformer)–a comprehensive review on enabling technologies, potential applications, emerging challenges, and future directions. *IEEE Access : Practical Innovations, Open Solutions*, *12*, 54608–54649. DOI: 10.1109/ACCESS.2024.3389497

Zhang, C., Yu, S., Tian, Z., & Yu, J. J. (2023). Generative adversarial networks: A survey on attack and defense perspective. *ACM Computing Surveys*, *56*(4), 1–35. DOI: 10.1145/3615336

Zhu, Z., Su, P., Zhong, S., Huang, J., Ottikkutti, S., Tahmasebi, K. N., Zou, Z., Zheng, L., & Chen, D. (2023). Using a vae-som architecture for anomaly detection of flexible sensors in limb prosthesis. *Journal of Industrial Information Integration*, *35*, 100490. DOI: 10.1016/j.jii.2023.100490

Chapter 11
Designing Autonomous Systems That Use Deception Techniques to Detect and Respond to Cyber Threats

D. Sanjana
https://orcid.org/0009-0008-8860-3864
Dr. N.G.P. Arts and Science College, India

D. Shanmugavadivel
Dr. N.G.P. Arts and Science College, India

ABSTRACT

The escalating complexity of cyber threats demands innovative solutions to strengthen cybersecurity defenses. This research focuses on designing autonomous systems that leverage deception techniques to detect and respond to cyber threats. By integrating deception strategies with autonomous decision-making, these systems can effectively outmaneuver and outsmart cyber adversaries, reducing the risk of successful attacks. The proposed autonomous deception system utilizes artificial intelligence and machine learning algorithms to create decoy environments, lure attackers into revealing their tactics, and adapt to evolving threats. The autonomous deception system is designed to operate in real-time, providing rapid detection and response capabilities. The research contributes to the development of next-generation cybersecurity solutions, providing a novel approach to autonomous threat detection and response. The findings have significant implications for organizations seeking to strengthen their cybersecurity defenses against increasingly sophisticated threats.

DOI: 10.4018/979-8-3373-0954-5.ch011

1. INTRODUCTION

In an era where cyber threats are becoming more complex and prevalent traditional protection approaches are being overtaken by attacker inventiveness. Cyber criminals target weaknesses with precision, employing innovative techniques that test even the most strong cybersecurity systems. This changing threat landscape needs novel techniques to protecting key systems and data. Among these strategies, deception tactics stand out as a proactive and dynamic way to strengthen cybersecurity defenses. The presents 'Siren,' a system that integrates deception, machine learning, and proactive threat analysis to enhance cybersecurity defenses. (Kulathumani, G., Ananthanarayanan, S., & Narayanan, G. 2024). Deception in cybersecurity uses the concepts of misdirection and deception to confuse, delay, and reveal attackers. The survey examines various cyber deception strategies aimed at enhancing cybersecurity measures, discussing their effectiveness in detecting and preventing cyber attacks. (Javadpour, A., Ja'fari, F., Taleb, T., Shojafar, M., & Benzaïd, C. 2024)

Deception methods tilt the balance of power by creating an environment full with false targets, decoys, and fake assets, forcing attackers to disclose themselves while safeguarding real resources. These measures not only disrupt harmful activity, but provide valuable insights into attack patterns, tools, and strategies. Deception Techniques in Computer Security: It discusses the limitations of current techniques and analyzes open research directions, including strategies for designing and integrating deception within target architectures, automated deployment in complex systems, updating and re-deploying deception mechanisms, and evaluating their effectiveness. The methods for enhancing the realism and effectiveness of AI-driven autonomous cyber defense systems by utilizing data on cyber expert performance. (Major, M., Souza, B., DiVita, J., & Ferguson-Walter, K. 2021).

Autonomous systems, powered by innovations in artificial intelligence (AI) and machine learning (ML), expand the use of deception methods. These systems require little human relationship to enable quick detection, adaptive reactions, and continuous monitoring. By introducing deception techniques to self-sufficient cybersecurity frameworks, organizations can improve their capacity to detect and react to attacks in real time, turning the tables on cybercriminals. The intelligent agent that employs deception to discern a cyber adversary's intent, utilizing factored interactive partially observable Markov decision processes (I-POMDPs). (Shinde, A., Doshi, P., & Setayeshfar, O. 2020)

The creation and development of self-sufficient systems that employ deception techniques to identify and address cyber threats are covered in this chapter. It examines the key ideas, technologies, and procedures that underpin these systems' effectiveness. Furthermore, it discusses the issues, legal implications, and potential futures of this rapidly increasing industry, providing insights into how deception-driven autonomous systems are impacting the future of cybersecurity. The deception technology can significantly reduce the time needed to identify and neutralize potential security threats by luring attackers into controlled environments. (Kramer, S. 2024).

2. OBJECTIVES

- Develop autonomous systems capable of detecting and responding to cyber threats. These systems will use deception tactics to detect harmful activities. The objective is to build a strong, flexible defence against emerging cyber-attacks.
- Design unique deception methods for use in autonomous cybersecurity systems. This involves developing decoys, traps, and other misleading aspects to entice and reveal attackers. The goal is to make these tactics believable and difficult to identify from authentic assets.
- Implement self-response capabilities to mitigate suspected cyber threats. The system should be capable of autonomously responding to attacks, restricting them, and avoiding additional harm. This requires creating algorithms for quick threat assessment and automatic preventative measures installation.

3. IMPORTANT INSTRUMENTS AND TREATMENT: DESIGNING AUTONOMOUS SYSTEMS WITH DECEPTION TECHNIQUES

3.1 Key Tools for Deception-Based Autonomous Systems

Honeypots and Honey Tokens: Honeypots are decoy devices that mimic actual assets, such as servers or data bases, in order to draw attackers. Honey tokens are digital objects, such as fake identities or information, used to detect unlawful access.

Decoy Networks: These are simulated environments that imitate an organization's architecture, allowing attackers to interface with them rather than the real systems.

Behavioural Analytics Platforms: These systems examine user and system behaviour to distinguish between legitimate and fraudulent activity. They serve a crucial role in discovering flaws that indicate a proactive one cyberattack.

AI and Machine Learning Algorithms: These technologies enable autonomous systems to rapidly react to new threats. They may fine-tune deception methods using observed attack patterns and improve with time.

Software-Defined Networking (SDN): SDN enables more flexible and programmable network topologies, making it simpler to deploy and maintain complex settings.

Threat Intelligence Feeds: Current information on new dangers enables autonomous systems to stay current and alter their deception strategies accordingly.

3.2 Treatment Strategies for Effective Cyber Threat Response

Real-Time Threat Detection: Autonomous systems continually monitor network interactions for signals of harmful behaviour. When attackers use deceptive components, the system detects and logs their actions.

Dynamic Decoy Deployment: The system may automatically generate and change decoy elements based on the type of danger detected. For instance, if ransomware is discovered, decoys can be used to imitate valuable data, wasting the attacker's time.

Automated Containment: When a threat is determined, the system separates the afflicted area to prevent lateral spread throughout the network. This ensures that the real processes remain untouched.

Intelligence Collection and Analysis: The system gathers information on the attacker's strategies, tools, and behaviour while they engage in deceptive behaviour. This information is extremely useful for upgrading defences and forecasting future attacks.

Adaptive Learning: Using machine learning, the system improves its deception methods based on the success of prior deployments. This enables long-term efficacy against emerging threats.

The Counterintelligence Process Operations: Advanced systems deceive attackers about the organization's actual assets and capabilities. This may force attackers to squander resources or quit their efforts.

Integration with Incident Response: Insights collected from misleading settings are shared with the larger incident response team to improve overall security procedures and inform post-attack analyses.

4. BACKGROUND

4.1 Evolution of Cyber Threats and the Limitations of Traditional Defense Methods

Evolution of Cyber Threats Cyber risks have changed significantly over the last two decades, increasing in intelligence, scale, and persistence. In the early days of the internet, most cyber dangers were very basic, such as worms and viruses, and were frequently generated by individuals or small organisations with low technical expertise. These threats were typically proactive, intended to cause change or acquire press coverage. However, as online environments became more linked and vital systems depended more on the internet, the scope of cyber threats evolved. Cyber-attacks have become more focused and complicated over time, with criminals and state actors adopting advanced strategies to access networks.

The development of advanced persistent threats (APTs), for instance, signalled a transition from brief, disruptive attacks to long-term, covert campaigns intended at stealing critical information, disrupting operations, or even destroying national security. APTs employ numerous stages, including as investigation, the rate of infiltration lateral advancement, and theft, making them challenging to identify and counter. Ransomware is additionally a common danger, with thieves encrypting important data and charging a fee for its release. These assaults not only cause financial harm, but they may also jeopardise crucial services such as healthcare or electricity infrastructure. Another increasing issue is the increase in supply chain attacks, in which adversaries exploit weaknesses in third-party software or hardware to harm their intended target. In addition, the rapid growth of the Internet of Things (IoT) and cloud computing has resulted in new attack surfaces. IoT devices are frequently lax security procedures, making them ideal targets for criminals, but cloud services provide large, dispersed networks that are hard to manage and defend. The introduction of these innovations has resulted in a larger attack surface, increasing the potential for cyber criminals to enter systems.

4.2 Limitations of Traditional Defense Methods

The limits of traditional defence approaches, such as detection based on signature firewall setups, and antivirus software, have become obvious as hackers' strategies have evolved. Traditional defences rely primarily on pre-set patterns and rules, rendering them ineffective against novel, unforeseen threats. For example, zero-day attacks—those that target previously undetected vulnerabilities—are difficult to detect using traditional approaches that depend on attack signatures. Furthermore, with the development of sophisticated social engineering tactics like spear emailing, attackers have learnt to exploit weaknesses in humans.

Traditional security measures are frequently insufficient against these types of attacks, which attack technological advances precautions through manipulation and fraud.The growing use of cloud computing, the Internet of Things (IoT), and mobile devices has increased the attack surface, resulting in fresh weaknesses that traditional defences fall short to defend. These new technologies frequently lack the insight and control required to provide full protection against emerging threats. Furthermore, the sheer number and speed of current cyberattacks has beyond the ability of manual incident response teams to respond in real time. This has resulted in longer detection and mitigating periods of time, allowing attackers to exploit systems before they are eliminated.

As a result, traditional defence systems are becoming ineffective in providing full protection. This has fostered the demand for more advanced, proactive, and adaptable tactics, such as combining autonomous systems with deceptive techniques. These systems are able to recognise and react to hacking attempts in real time, adapt to new attack methods, and increase resilience against developing cyber threats.

4.3 The Concept of Deception in Cybersecurity

Deception in cybersecurity is a proactive and strategic defence tactics that aims to mislead, confuse, and ultimately outwit rivals. Unlike typical security measures, which try to completely prevent access, deception concentrates on creating an environment packed with deceptive data, disguises, and traps that divert attackers away from real assets. This method is based on military and psychological techniques, with the purpose of confusing enemies, delaying their advance, and gathering helpful intelligence. At its basis, deception works by blending into the normal operation of a network and presenting false systems, qualifications, or data as real targets. Honeypots, for example, replicate systems that simulate actual servers or networks, appealing attackers to interact with them. Similarly, honey tokens develop bits of data, such as false database entries or documents, that warn defenders when accessed.

These false aspects not only redirect attackers, but also provide a controlled environment in which their activities may be recorded and analysed. The strength of surprise is its capacity to change the power balance to the benefit of the defence. Attackers, who rely on stealth and accuracy, are forced to navigate a maze of created assets, boosting their chances of making errors or disclosing their methods. Every contact with false elements reveals significant information about attacker behaviour, tools, and aims, allowing defenders to improve their methods and shut down security holes. Furthermore, deception methods are very adaptive and scalable, making them appropriate for a variety of situations, including locally networks, cloud systems, and Internet of Things (IoT) ecosystems. Modern deception systems can use artificial intelligence and machine learning to constantly adapt their tactics, deploying new traps or adjusting old ones depending on real-time threat data. In addition to detection, deception is an important component of reaction methods.

Defenders may neutralise threats while allowing genuine activities to continue by isolating attackers in false surroundings. In addition, these systems may be used for intelligence gathering, supplying attackers with fake information that misleads them about an organization's real capabilities and weaknesses. In cybersecurity, deception is utilised not just as a defensive approach, but also as a proactive way of confronting enemies. Deception enables organisations to keep ahead of the constantly shifting struggle against cyber threats by reversing the attackers' techniques.

4.4 Introduction to Autonomous Systems and Their Relevance in Cyber Defense

Autonomous systems are advanced technologies that achieve complicated tasks with minimum human interaction by utilising artificial intelligence (AI), machine learning (ML), and automation. In the field of cybersecurity, these systems have become known as game changers, tackling the growing issues faced by the speed, size, and difficulty of current cyber-attacks. Unlike traditional systems, which require operator configuration and reaction, autonomous systems can monitor networks, analyse data, identify abnormalities, and take protective steps in real time. The importance of autonomous systems in cyber defence arises from their capacity to analyse massive volumes of data at rates that far exceed the abilities of humans. With the growth of linked devices, cloud computing, and IoT ecosystems, the attack surface has grown substantially, making manual defences more difficult to maintain.

Autonomous systems close this gap by continually scanning and assessing networks, discovering weaknesses, and detecting unusual activity before it escalates into a fully attack. One significant feature of these systems is their versatility. Autonomous cybersecurity systems can use machine learning to learn from previous events, discover patterns, and improve detection algorithms in order to combat new and emerging threats. This feature is especially important for fighting against zero-day attacks and advanced persistent threats (APTs), which are designed to bypass typical security measures. In addition, autonomous systems are critical for providing speedy and automated reactions to cyber events. They can isolate compromised systems, conduct defences, and even launch deception schemes without the need for any human involvement. This not only reduces the time attackers have to exploit weaknesses, but it also ensures that defences stay strong and resilient even during large-scale or coordinated attacks. Applying autonomous systems into cybersecurity methods improves efficiency, scalability, and dependability. By lowering reliance on human resources for ordinary activities, organisations may concentrate their efforts on strategic planning and advanced threat analysis.

Furthermore, combining autonomous systems with deception methods increases their efficacy, allowing for proactive threat identification and response while generating vital knowledge on threatening tactics. As cyber threats grows, autonomous systems are a vital part of modern cyber defence, providing organisations with the quickness, intelligence, and automation required to defend their assets in an evermore complicated digital surfaces.

5. CORE PRINCIPLES OF DESIGNING DECEPTIVE AUTONOMOUS SYSTEMS

5.1 Importance of Realism in Deceptive Elements to Trick Attackers

The effectiveness of deception in cybersecurity depends on the realism of its components. To successfully confuse and engage attackers, misleading components like honeypots, decoy networks, and phoney credentials must closely mimic real assets. When deception lacks reliability, expert competitors may quickly identify and avoid the hoax, rendering the entire technique worthless. Realistic misleading aspects improve the possibility that attackers will fall into traps, allowing defenders to monitor, analyse, and respond to threats more efficiently. Realism in deception entails duplicating both the functionality and look of actual systems. To imitate an active environment, honeypots meant to take on essential servers must have genuine file structures, operational logs, and even simulated user activity. Similarly, honey tokens, like as forged credentials or database entries, should blend smoothly into the organization's architecture, making them indistinguishable from legitimate assets. Contextual design is an essential component of realism.

Deceptive aspects must be consistent with the organization's operational environment, such as mimicking certain configurations of its network architecture, software versions, or business processes. Before starting an assault, attackers frequently perform reconnaissance to learn more about their intended target. Real decoys that represent the organization's operational peculiarities can deter these attempts and entice attackers into controlled surroundings. Realism also contributes to the long-term effectiveness of deception. Poorly developed untrue features can be rapidly identified, compromising the overall plan.In addition, realistic deception increases trust in the system among defenders and stakeholders. When deception technologies accurately replicate genuine assets, cybersecurity teams may utilise them as part of their defence plan without fear of being identified. Finally, realism in deceiving aspects is a strategic requirement rather than a technological necessity. Organisations may increase the efficacy of their deception techniques by developing credible and culturally suitable decoys, transforming cyber threats into opportunities for learning, growth, and better defences.

5.2 Role of AI and Machine Learning in Enhancing System Intelligence

AI and machine learning (ML) serve vital functions in improving the intelligence of modern systems, notably in cybersecurity. AI enables systems to handle and analyse huge amounts of data at unprecedented speeds, allowing for immediate tracking, detection, and reaction to potential hazards. Machine learning, a type of AI, enables computers to learn from past data and adapt to fresh conditions without requiring explicit programming. This adaptability is crucial in the face of increasing cyber threats, since machine learning algorithms can spot trends, anticipate deviations, and discover previously unknown weaknesses, such as zero-day attacks.In cybersecurity, AI-powered systems can analyse network data, detect uncommon behaviour, and differentiate between legal and fraudulent activity. For example, ML models may identify aberrant user behaviour, such as unauthorised entry attempts or odd file transfers, and flag it as a danger.

These features greatly minimise false positives while increasing the efficiency of threat detection systems. Furthermore, AI and ML improve the automation of defensive methods. Systems can deploy countermeasures automatically, isolate vulnerable networks, or even set up misleading settings to engage and analyse attackers. Integrating AI into cybersecurity solutions allows them to respond to issues proactively, decreasing reaction times and eliminating risks before they develop.AI and machine learning also make major improvements to threat intelligence. They allow systems to analyse global threat data, detect creating patterns, and predict new attack techniques. This predictive capacity enables organisations to stay ahead of attackers by pre-emptively strengthening their defences. Overall, integrating AI and machine learning into cybersecurity systems makes them more intelligent, flexible, and proactive. These solutions enable organisations to better defend their digital assets, keeping up with the fast growth of cyber threats.

6. THREAT DETECTION THROUGH INTERACTION WITH ATTACKERS

Direct engagement with attackers is one of the most effective methods for identifying and evaluating cyber threats. The technique involves engaging opponents in controlled environments with deception-based methods, allowing security systems to obtain intelligence while restricting danger to key assets. Organizations that research attacker activity in real time can improve their awareness of new threats, discover shortcomings, and build proactive security methods.

6.1 The Implementation of Honeypots and Decoy Systems

Honeypots are specifically subjected systems that attract cyber attackers and record their tactics, techniques, and procedures (TTPs). These systems represent actual assets but are kept separate from the manufacturing environment for purposes of security. Honeypots engage with attackers to determine illegal access attempts, malware projects, and hackers' lateral movement techniques

6.2 Deployment of Honey Tokens and Trap Credentials

Honey tokens are false data pieces, such as false credentials, API keys, or files that look useful to attackers. When these tokens are accessed or employed, they generate cautions, demonstrating an ongoing breach. This technique assists security teams in detecting insider threats, credential theft attempts, and surveillance operations.

6.3 Behavioral Analysis and Attack Identification of Patterns

By observing how attackers engage with deceptive systems, AI-powered cyber security solutions can evaluate behavior and find developments that indicate advanced attacks. Machine learning algorithms can differentiate between automated scanning tools, script-based attacks, and human-driven targeted invasions, resulting in improved detection accuracy

6.4 Adaptive Deception to Improve Threat Detection

Advanced deception systems can adapt their look and respond to the attacker's actions. A deception system, for instance, might imitate various network settings, operating systems, or data kinds in order to deceive attackers and extend engagement. This enables defenders to gather more information before attackers know they are being watched.

6.5 Real-time Threat Intelligence Collection

Interacting with attackers offers significant information on new attack approaches, malware versions, and command-and-control (C2) infrastructures. Security teams can use this data to enhance security measures such as firewalls, intrusion detection systems (IDS), and endpoint security measures, ensuring that defenses stay effective in the face of emerging threats.

6.6 Reducing False Positives for Threat Detection

Traditional security solutions may generate an extensive amount of false positives, which excess security experts with warnings. By studying direct contacts with attackers, deception-based detection systems can deliver more accurate threat identification, decreasing alert fatigue and allowing teams to focus on serious threats.

6.7 Automated Incident Response and Containment

When an attack is detected through interaction, autonomous security systems can take specified steps, such as isolating affected systems, blocking attacker IP addresses, or feeding false data to disrupt the attacker's activities. This automation improves reaction time while minimizing potential damage

7. ANALYSIS AND INTERPRETATION

7.1 Feature Should an Autonomous Cybersecurity System

Table 1.

FEATURE SHOULD AN AUTONOMOUS CYBERSECURITY SYSTEM	NO OF RESPONDENTS	PERCENTAGE
Firewalls and antivirus	32	16%
Deception-based threat detection	45	22.5%
Manual security monitoring	30	15%
Basic encryption techniques	93	46.5%
TOTAL	**200**	**100%**

(Source: primary data)

Interpretation

The above table shows that 16% of the respondents are firewalls and antivirus, 22.5% of the respondents are deception-based threat detection, 15% of the respondents are manual security monitoring, 46.5% of the respondents are basic encryption techniques.

Figure 1. Feature should an autonomous cybersecurity system

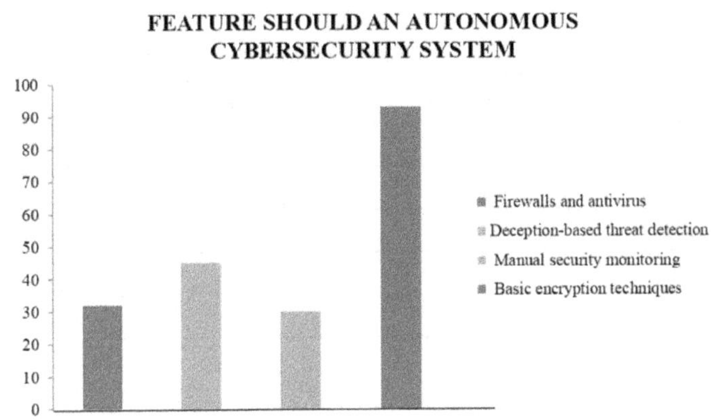

7.2 Designing Deception Methods in Autonomous Cybersecurity Systems

Table 2.

DESIGNING DECEPTION METHODS IN AUTONOMOUS CYBERSECURITY SYSTEMS	NO OF RESPONDENTS	PERCENTAGE
Using static honeypots	31	15.5%
Implementing adaptive decoys	90	45%
Blocking all suspicious traffic	49	24.5%
Relying only on firewalls	30	15%
TOTAL	**200**	**100%**

Interpretation

The above table shows that 15.5% of the respondents are using static honeypots, 45% of the respondents are implementing adaptive decoys, 24.5% of the respondents are blocking all suspicious traffic, and 15% of the respondents are relying only on firewalls.

Figure 2. Designing deception methods in autonomous cybersecurity systems

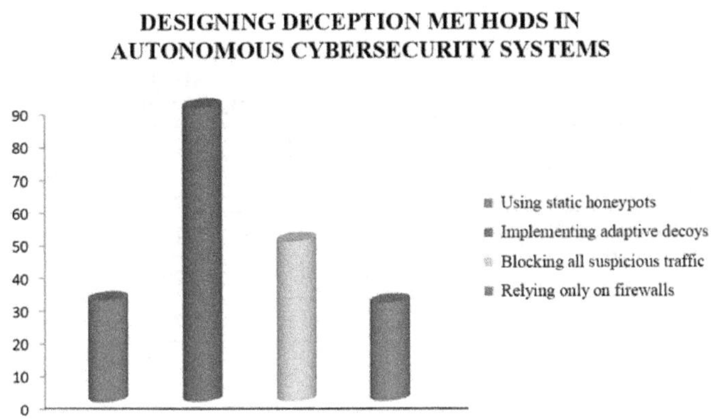

7.3 Main Challenge in Autonomous Cyber Threat Self-Response

Table 3.

MAIN CHALLENGE IN AUTONOMOUS CYBER THREAT SELF-RESPONSE	NO OF RESPONDENTS	PERCENTAGE
False positive avoidance	46	23%
Rapid threat attribution	120	60%
Preventative measure deployment	14	7%
All of the above	20	23%
TOTAL	**200**	**100%**

Interpretation

The above table shows that 23% of the respondents are using false positive avoidance, 60% of the respondents are Rapid threat attribution, 7% of the respondents are Preventative measure deployment and 23% of the respondents are all of the above.

Figure 3. Main challenge in autonomous cyber threat self-response

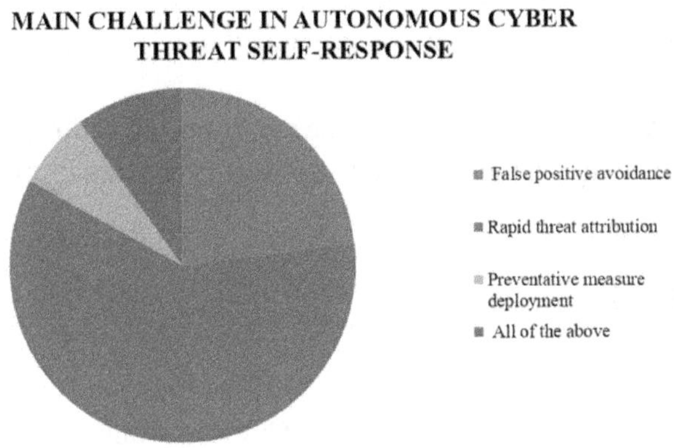

8. FINDINGS

- The majority of the respondents have chosen basic encryption techniques in the category of feature should an autonomous cyber security system
- The majority of the respondents have chosen implementing adaptive decoys in the category of designing deception methods in autonomous cyber security systems
- The majority of the respondents have chosen rapid threat attribution in the category of main challenge in autonomous cyber threat self-response

9. SUGGESTION

Autonomous cyber security systems that utilize deception tactics need to emphasize flexibility, intelligence, and efficiency. One important area of study focuses on the use of sophisticated AI and deep learning models to develop more dynamic and context-aware deception approaches. Current deception tactics rely on predetermined rules and patterns which experienced attackers can identify and circumvent. Machine learning-driven deception models that modify in response to attacker activity might enhance detection accuracy while reducing false positives.

A further significant development is to create real-time deception choreography frameworks that automatically modify decoy settings in response to threat intelligence. Such frameworks should be able to predict cyber-attacks data and implementing proactive safeguards. Further studies should aim to improve the integration of deception-based cyber security systems with current security constructions, such as zero-trust frameworks and behavioral-based intrusion detection systems.

The ethical and legal impacts of autonomous deception in cyber security require further study. As deception tactics advance, concerns about privacy, responsibility, and compliance with cyber security legislation must be addressed. Research on defining ethical principles and assuring openness in deception-based defenses will be critical to mainstream adoption. Furthermore, with the increased use of cloud computing, IoT, and edge computing, deception tactics must be adapted to defend scattered and restricted in resources situations. Future studies should focus on lightweight and decentralized deception methods that can operate well in low-power IoT devices and cloud-native security systems.

10. CASE STUDY

DOLOS: Integrating Moving Target Defense and Cyber Deception

The DOLOS architecture unifies Moving Target Defense (MTD) and cyber deception techniques by integrating them into production systems through multiple layers of isolation. Evaluations against various attackers, including professional penetration testers, demonstrated DOLOS's efficacy in slowing down attacks and preserving system integrity

11. CONCLUSION

The development of autonomous systems that use deception tactics signifies an evolutionary jump in cyber security protection. This study found that by combining AI, machine learning, and adaptive deception methods, these systems are capable of detect, evaluate, and respond to cyber-attacks in real time. Deception-based cyber security confuses and misdirects attackers while simultaneously offering crucial information that improves overall security postures.

The study emphasizes the significance of honeypots, decoy networks, behavioral analytics, and real-time deception orchestration in preventing cyber-attacks. The findings highlight how adaptive deception models may minimize false positives and enhance detection accuracy, making cyber security defenses more robust and proactive.

Despite these advancements, ethical issues, legal compliance, and system complexity continue to pose obstacles. Future research should focus on creating more intelligent, flexible, and legally acceptable deception frameworks that integrate smoothly with contemporary security systems. Furthermore, research on cloud-based, IoT, and edge computing deception tactics will improve cyber security in a variety of environments.

In conclusion, deception-driven autonomous systems provide a revolutionary approach to cyber security by outwitting attackers, lowering attack success rates, and enhancing proactive defensive measures. As cyber threats grow, these systems will play an increasingly important role in protecting digital assets and maintaining long-term cyber security resilience.

REFERENCES

Javadpour, A., Ja'fari, F., Taleb, T., Shojafar, M., & Benzaïd, C. (2024). A comprehensive survey on cyber deception techniques to improve honeypot performance. *Computers & Security, 103792*, •••. https://www.sciencedirect.com/science/article/pii/S0167404824000932

Knack, A., & Burke, A. (2024). Autonomous cyber defence phase II. *The Alan Turing Institute*. Retrieved from https://cetas.turing.ac.uk/publications/autonomous-cyber-defence-autonomous-agents

Kramer, S. (2024). Deception technology: Putting cybercriminals on defense. *The Cube Research*. Retrieved from https://thecuberesearch.com/deception-technology-putting-cybercriminals-defense/

Kulathumani, G., Ananthanarayanan, S., & Narayanan, G. (2024). Siren—Advancing cybersecurity through deception and adaptive analysis. *arXiv preprint*. Retrieved from https://arxiv.org/abs/2406.06225

Lmame, R. (2024). AI-driven autonomous cyber-security systems: Advanced threat detection and response. *LinkedIn Pulse*. Retrieved from https://www.linkedin.com/pulse/ai-driven-autonomous-cyber-security-systems-advanced-ramachandran-lmame

Major, M., Souza, B., DiVita, J., & Ferguson-Walter, K. (2021). Informing autonomous deception systems with cyber expert performance data. *arXiv preprint*. Retrieved from https://arxiv.org/abs/2109.00066

Shinde, A., Doshi, P., & Setayeshfar, O. (2020). Active deception using factored interactive POMDPs to recognize cyber attacker's intent. *arXiv preprint*. Retrieved from https://arxiv.org/abs/2007.09512

Chapter 12
Autonomous Defending Approaches Based on Machine Learning for Android Malware Detection

Khalid Alemerien
https://orcid.org/0000-0003-4485-8298
Tafila Technical University, Jordan

Mohammad Almseidin
Tafila Technical University, Jordan

Enshirah Altarawneh
https://orcid.org/0000-0002-3013-2819
Hashemite University, Jordan

Malek Alksasbeh
Al-Hussein Bin Talal University, Jordan

ABSTRACT

The exponential growth in Android device usage has led to a surge in malware targeting this platform, necessitating robust security mechanisms to safeguard user data and system integrity. Traditional signature-based methods for malware detection often lag behind the ever-evolving threat landscape. This chapter explores autonomous defending approaches for Android malware detection leveraging advanced Machine Learning (ML) techniques. The chapter outlines the unique challenges in Android

DOI: 10.4018/979-8-3373-0954-5.ch012

malware detection, such as diverse app ecosystems and the obfuscation techniques employed by malware developers. Through the analysis of real-world datasets and performance benchmarks, the chapter demonstrates the practical effectiveness of ML-based approaches and limitations. Finally, the potential integration of ML-based malware detection systems with broader cybersecurity frameworks and future research directions are discussed. This chapter aims to serve as a comprehensive resource for researchers and practitioners in the field of Android malware detection and autonomous cybersecurity.

1. INTRODUCTION

Many contemporary technologies and services depend on ML algorithms for daily use. Moreover, these algorithms find patterns in data to support predictions and automatic decision-making. Several fields employ ML algorithms such as medical diagnostics (Alemerien et al., 2024), security threats detection (Alemerien et al., 2024), and financial fraud detection (Xiong et al., 2022). Android is one of effectively distributed and successful mobile operating systems. With a share of 73.52% (Statcounter, 2025), Android leads significantly worldwide in the mobile operating system market in December 2024. There are several important reasons for the general acceptance of Android. Android is first an open-source operating system that lets one be very creative and customized. Second, Android provides access to a large array of free apps housed on app stores. Ultimately, the relatively low cost of Android-powered mobile devices makes them accessible to a broader range of users, which contributes to their widespread popularity. With an increasing number of Android mobile devices and apps, the number of Android malware is increasing. This means the rapid rise of Android malware has brought great security and privacy risks to end mobile users and mobile service providers.

In the first quarter of 2024, Kaspersky security network (Kaspersky, 2024) reported that more than 10 million attacks on mobile devices using adware, malware, or unwanted software were blocked. 46% of most threats to mobile devices were detected. About 400K malicious installation packages were detected. These packages were related to mobile banking Trojans and ransomware Trojans. Furthermore, the interesting information that is the top 20 mobile malware software and top 10 mobile banking Trojans were related to the Android operating system. At the end of 2024, Adware seemed unstoppable. It represented 36.28% of detected malicious and potentially unwanted installation packages. Moreover, mobile devices using the Android operating system are 50% more susceptible to being infected by malware compared to iOS devices (Getastra, 2025). These kinds of cyber-attacks result in financial loss, organization's reputation being compromised, identity theft, and time loss to recover from infections and their associated risks.

Therefore, the research communities and security vendors have several security solutions, one of them is ML-based techniques, to identify and prevent Android malicious samples to maintain a healthy and clean ecosystem for Android applications. ML-based approaches are applied for anomaly detection using static analysis, dynamic analysis, or hybrid analysis (Kouliaridis & Kambourakis, 2021; Kadir & Peddoju, 2024). Static analysis focuses on analyzing the internal structure of the mobile apps such as code, permissions, or manifests. In addition, static analysis performed in offline environment. On the other hand, dynamic analysis is used during the app's run-time operation. Dynamic analysis is performed to extract features from network traffics, user interactions, or system resources. Hybrid analysis shows better performance comparing with other analysis methods. Hybrid analysis integrates the benefits of dynamic and static analysis but it makes the ML-based solutions are more complex and resource consumed. Furthermore, the anomaly detection process using ML-based approaches encompasses two distinct phases, including training and detection. To achieve a high-performance ML-based solution, the majority of cases in such a dataset are used for training while the minority of cases are used for detection.

This chapter explores autonomous defending approaches for Android malware detection leveraging advanced ML-based techniques as follows: It explores the challenges of Android malware detection, such as app diversity, lack of resources, and obfuscation techniques. It shows that ML-based solutions can solve those by the ability to manage data, recognize anomalies, and adjust to threats in real-time environments. The eminent topics are feature extraction, real-time detection, adversarial resilience, and end-to-end autonomous systems for detecting zero-day malware without human intervention. This chapter discusses real-world datasets and benchmarks to evaluate the performance and limitations of ML-based methods. Furthermore, this chapter discusses supervised and unsupervised ML, reinforcement ML, ensemble ML, and hybrid ML approaches for detecting Android malware. Finally, this chapter also points to the area of ML-based systems with broader cybersecurity frameworks and gives an overview of the subsequent research directions, setting the basis for a complete guide for researchers and practitioners in Android malware detection and autonomous cybersecurity.

To our knowledge, this book chapter is the first attempt that provides a comprehensive analysis of ML-based approaches for detecting Android malware.

2. BACKGROUND

2.1 Machine Learning

Machine learning is a type of Artificial Intelligence (AI) that functions by developing computer systems capable of processing data for the aim of learning. The various methodologies that constitute ML enable software applications to enhance their efficacy over time. ML algorithms are trained to identify relationships between data points. These applications utilize historical data to predict outcomes while employing information and data points for classification, discovery-based clustering, dimensionality reduction, and content generation, as demonstrated by recent ML technologies such as ChatGPT, Dall-E 2, and GitHub Copilot.

ML occupies an increasingly significant role in human society due to the foundational contributions of pioneering thinkers like Walter Pitts and Alan Turing, who established computational theory in the mid-20th century. ML data training methods enable organizations to automate many human-level tasks, so allowing workers to focus on more intricate creative endeavors and scale-intensive manual processes that exceed human capacity, including the administration of digital device outputs. The pattern-recognition ability of ML systems has evolved into a crucial competitive advantage for enterprises across various sectors, including finance, retail, healthcare, and research institutions. Driven by organizational success for established technology leaders like Facebook, Google, and transportation behemoth Uber, ML serves as a basic operational element in modern business. The notable rise in modern data volumes will bring ML to a major importance in the evolution of machine intelligence and in meeting human needs.

ML has revolutionized numerous industries by enabling intelligent, data-driven decisions. In the healthcare sector, ML is used to predict outbreaks of disease, diagnose patients through medical imaging, and recommend individualized treatment protocols through patient history analysis. Moreover, ML is an integral part of the banking sector, where ML powers credit scoring algorithms, fraud detection algorithms, and algorithmic trading. This allows organizations to recognize patterns and trends in enormous financial data with high precision. Natural Language Processing (NLP) is another significant field that applies ML for applications, including Chatbots, human-independent language translation, and sentiment analysis. These applications help systems to read, comprehend, and create human language. Furthermore, retail businesses use ML for product recommendations based on user choice and demand forecasting. Moreover, self-driving vehicles rely on ML to identify objects and make choices in real-time scenarios. Such technologies are a manifestation of the profound impact of ML across industries such as, redefinition of traditional processes, thus making for better and intelligent operations. The future of ML holds promise in advances in explainable AI, federated learning, and unification of ML with other AI technologies such as robotics.

2.2 Android

Android is an open-source mobile operating system primarily designed for touchscreen devices like smartphones and tablets. It is based on a modified version of the Linux kernel and other open-source software, and it was initially developed by Andy Rubin, Rich Miner, Nick Sears, and Chris White as Android Inc., which Google later acquired in 2005 (Elgin, 2005). Over time, Android has become the most popular mobile operating system globally, with numerous updates and features added through each version.

Android versions have had dessert-themed codenames until Android 10. Some of the most notable versions include Cupcake (1.5), Donut (1.6), Eclair (2.0-2.1), Froyo (2.2-2.2.3), Gingerbread (2.3-2.3.7), Honeycomb (3.0-3.2.6), Ice Cream Sandwich (4.0-4.0.4), Jelly Bean (4.1-4.3.1), Pie (9), Android 10 (no dessert codename), Android 11, Android 12, Android 13 (Tiramisu) (Amadeo, 2022; Fedewa, 2023). Table 1 shows the history of Android (Bradshaw, 2022; Cantisano, 2023).

Table 1. History of Android

Year	Release/ Market name	Features
2003	Android Inc.	The original goal was to develop an advanced operating system for digital cameras, but they later shifted focus to mobile phones.
2005	Google acquired Android Inc.	which led to the development of the Android OS as we know it today
2007	The Open Handset Alliance (OHA)	was formed to promote Android as an open standard for mobile devices. It includes members like Samsung, Qualcomm, Intel, and others.
2008	The first Android smartphone	The HTC Dream (also known as the T-Mobile G1), was launched.
2010-2012	Rapid growth with Android 2.2 Froyo to 4.1 Jelly Bean	introducing features like the Android Market (now Google Play) and enhanced UI and performance.
2013-2015	KitKat to Lollipop	KitKat to Lollipop focused on design changes with “Material Design” and improved performance.
2016-2018	Marshmallow to Oreo	introduced major features like Doze (battery-saving), fingerprint support, split-screen, and notification improvements.
2019-2021	Android Pie to Android 12	focused on privacy enhancements, gestures, dark mode, and a refreshed design language.
2022-present	Android 13 and beyond	Continued improvements in security, customization, and cross-device compatibility, with an emphasis on AI integration and sustainability.

Android is organized into several key layers that work together to make the system function smoothly. At the base is the Linux Kernel, which takes care of interacting with the hardware and managing essential system tasks. Above that, the Libraries and Android Runtime (ART) handle important features like graphics, databases, and multimedia, and ART is responsible for running all the apps on your phone. The Application Framework provides services that help apps work properly, such as managing resources, security, and app windows. At the top is the Applications Layer, where all the apps—both the ones that come with your device and the ones you download—operate.

Some of the prominent features in contrast of Android are. First is Android, which is open-source and thereby allows the developers to modify and distribute the software under the Apache License. As a result of this flexibility, Android encourages an innovative as well as adaptive mentality. At the same time, it is worthy of mentioning that although the core Android system is open-source, pre-installed Google services like Gmail and Google Play are there in most devices, thus serving as a halo for furthering user experience. To name one of the most significant advantages attached to this OS, it is arguably the most customizable. Both manufacturers and users can personalize the interface according to their whims and fancies, thus generating a very diverse kind of experience across the devices. The best part of Android is that it has a huge app ecosystem with millions of apps available through the Play Store. This makes Android one of the most extensive and diverse markets of apps.

2.3 Android Malware Evolution

Since the launch of the platform, Android malware has changed dramatically and threats have become ever more sophisticated with time. This part covers its development, noteworthy statistics, new trends, and important case studies:

2.3.1 2010-2018

Android malware developed from rather basic threats to highly sophisticated cyberattacks aiming at financial data, personal information, and system vulnerabilities between 2010 and 2018. Early years 2010–2012 saw Android threats mostly from trojans masquerading as legitimate apps, such FakePlayer, which SMS fraudulately sends premium-rate messages. With adware and spyware emerging, malware events jumped by 472% between 2011 and 2012 as Android's popularity grew. Attackers started using critical system vulnerabilities between 2013 and 2015; most famously, the Master Key Exploit, which let hostile actors change APKs without changing their cryptographic signatures, and Stagefright, a vulnerability revealing almost 95% of Android devices to remote code execution via malicious MMS messages.

With massive botnets like HummingBad infecting over 10 million devices to create false ad income and Gooligan compromising more than 1 million Google accounts, Android malware had become much more sophisticated by 2016–2018. Emerging from deep integration into system processes to pilfers credentials and financial data, banking trojans like Triada became rather well-known. Rising nation-state spyware including Pegasus signaled a turn toward sophisticated surveillance tools that would allow covert monitoring of well-known people. Using sophisticated obfuscation methods, system exploits, and social engineering to maximize financial gain and continuous access to compromised devices, Android malware had evolved by 2018 into a highly ordered cybercrime enterprise.

2.3.2 2019 to 2025

Android malware evolved in sophistication, employing advanced obfuscation methods, artificial intelligence, and extensive botnets to circumvent detection and optimize financial and surveillance-related profits. Between 2019 and 2021, banking trojans like Cerberus and EventBot surged, aiming at financial applications to expropriate login credentials, while the Joker malware family compromised thousands of applications on Google Play, perpetrating SMS fraud and premium service scams. Furthermore, the COVID-19 pandemic enabled the proliferation of malware via deceptive health-tracking applications.

During 2022-2023, extensive botnets surfaced, notably Badbox 2.0, which covertly installed malware on more than 1 million Android devices, allowing cybercriminals to manipulate them for advertising fraud and illicit proxy services. Malicious applications impersonating Google Chrome, WhatsApp, and VPNs exacerbated the threat landscape by expropriating sensitive data from unwary users.

The malware for Android has made strong implementations of AI-based evasion and advanced remote-access capabilities for the years 2024 and 2025. The year 2024 looked on as total control of infected devices became a sobering reality with the activation of the Octo2 malware, whereas the SpyLoan malware affected over 8 million smartphones through rogue financial apps resulting in tremendous data theft and extortion. State-sponsored espionage malware, as shown by BoneSpy, reiterated how far Android malware had advanced from basic targeting of a handful of users to weapons covertly observing its targets recording talks, taking pictures, and exfiltrating sensitive data. By 2025, Android malware astoundingly transformed into an organized and serious cyber threat that uses machine-learning algorithms, pre-installed backdoors, and social engineering methods to enter devices and slip past defenses-a new age of cyber-criminal sophistication.

2.4 Autonomous Cybersecurity

With the exponential growth of cyber threats, including malware, phishing, ransomware, and advanced persistent threats (APTs), traditional cybersecurity strategies that rely on human intervention and manual processes struggle to protect the system. Therefore, the need to handle cybersecurity automatically achieved by Autonomous cybersecurity. Autonomous cybersecurity is the use of AI and ML to create intelligent systems that can manage and protect IT environments from cyber threats autonomously. This implies the design of networks that can automatically identify vulnerabilities, respond to incidents, and adapt to evolving cyberattacks.

The aim is to handle cybersecurity at a speed and scale that surpasses human capabilities by reduce response time, where automate detection and response to threats in real time. The scale defense capabilities increased by handling vast amounts of data and logs that human analysts cannot process efficiently. In addition, the accuracy of the system improves because of reducing false positives and improving threat detection by continuously learning from new data (CyLab, 2021).

Autonomous cybersecurity relies on several key components to enhance threat detection and response. AI enables systems to make decisions, detect anomalies, and predict potential threats by analyzing vast amounts of data, helping to build models that can distinguish between normal and suspicious activity. ML, a subset of AI, trains systems to recognize patterns in data and improve accuracy over time, enabling the detection of malware, phishing attempts, or other attacks. Automation plays a critical role by using software to handle repetitive security tasks, such as vulnerability scanning, patch management, and incident response, allowing organizations to respond faster and at scale. Behavioral analytics further strengthens security by monitoring and analyzing user behavior to identify unusual or suspicious actions that could indicate a breach (Cook, 2022). Lastly, threat intelligence enables autonomous systems to collect, analyze, and apply real-time data to stay ahead of emerging cyber threats. There are many current applications in Autonomous Cybersecurity:

- Intrusion Detection and Prevention Systems (IDPS): Autonomous systems are used to monitor network traffic and identify malicious activity in real time.
- Endpoint Detection and Response (EDR): Autonomous EDR tools can detect unusual activity on endpoints like laptops, smartphones, and servers and respond automatically.
- Security Information and Event Management (SIEM): SIEM systems use AI and ML to analyze log data from various sources and provide real-time alerts of potential security incidents.

- Autonomous Vulnerability Scanners: These tools automatically scan networks for vulnerabilities and misconfigurations without human intervention.
- Self-healing Networks: Systems that can autonomously patch vulnerabilities, reroute traffic, or shut down compromised systems to prevent the spread of attacks.

2.4.1 Challenges in Implementing Autonomous Cybersecurity

- Data Quality: AI/ML models rely on high-quality, relevant data for training. Poor or insufficient data can result in inaccurate or ineffective threat detection.
- Complexity of Cyberattacks: Sophisticated, multi-vector attacks can be difficult for AI models to detect, especially zero-day attacks or new techniques not seen in the training data.
- Ethical and Privacy Issues: Autonomous systems need access to vast amounts of personal and organizational data, raising concerns about data privacy, bias in AI models, and ethical decision-making in cybersecurity.

2.4.2 Advantages of Autonomous Cybersecurity

- 24/7 Monitoring: Autonomous systems provide constant monitoring and response, reducing the need for round-the-clock human oversight.
- Fast Response: These systems can identify and respond to threats much faster than humans, minimizing the potential damage caused by an attack.
- Scalability: Autonomous solutions can handle large and complex environments, making them suitable for organizations with extensive IT infrastructures.
- Reduction in False Positives: AI and ML can help reduce false alerts by refining their models over time, allowing security teams to focus on true threats.

As AI and ML technologies continue to evolve, several key developments are expected to shape the future of autonomous cybersecurity. First, zero-trust architectures will become more prominent, with AI-driven systems enforcing continuous authentication and authorization for every request or action within a network. Second, advanced behavioral analytics will enable ML models to detect increasingly subtle deviations from normal behavior, enhancing threat detection capabilities. Lastly, collaborative cybersecurity will emerge, where autonomous systems share threat intelligence and coordinate responses to incidents across multiple organizations or industries, fostering a more unified defense against cyber threats (Cook, 2022).

2.5 Android Malware Detection

With Android being the most popular mobile operating system worldwide, it has become a prime target for malware developers. Android malware detection refers to the techniques and systems used to identify, analyze, and mitigate malicious software (malware) that targets the Android operating system. The widespread use of Android devices makes securing them a critical task, and a significant amount of research has gone into developing effective methods for detecting malware.

Android malware refers to malicious software designed to target Android devices with the intent of harming the user, stealing sensitive data, or disrupting normal operations. It can come in various forms, each posing unique threats. For example, Trojans disguise themselves as legitimate apps to trick users into downloading them, only to cause harm once installed. Ransomware locks users out of their devices or encrypts their data, demanding payment to restore access (Felt et al., 2012). Spyware quietly runs in the background, gathering personal information, login credentials, or even location data without the user's knowledge. Adware, on the other hand, bombards users with intrusive ads, often for financial gain, while rootkits attempt to gain administrator-level access that allows full control over system functions. Each type of malware poses serious risks to user privacy, device security, and overall experience, which makes effective detection and prevention critical in maintaining Android security.

The openness and flexibility of the Android platform, combined with its large user base, have made it an attractive target for cybercriminals. With millions of apps available on the Google Play Store and third-party app stores, detecting and preventing malicious apps is a significant challenge (Alemerien, 2021). Some of the key reasons for malware detection on Android include (Arp et al., 2014):

- Wide distribution of malware: Android malware can spread through app stores, malicious websites, and SMS messages.
- Data theft and privacy risks: Malware can steal sensitive information, such as login credentials, payment information, and private messages.
- Financial loss: Malware can lead to unauthorized charges, subscription fraud, or even ransom payments.
- Device damage and interruption: Some malware can cause significant damage to the system, resulting in data loss or device malfunction.

In Android malware detection, several serious challenges have framed the need for sophisticated means of tackling the problem. One major problem with the detection is the multiplicity of modalities of malware: they can take plenty of forms and attack through so many vectors that it is critical to visualize a perceptively wider classification approach. Besides, malware authors would like to change the visual appearance of their code almost every time using the obfuscation and polymorphism techniques; this usually compromises the efficacy of the traditional signature-based detection because of malware variance. Another issue comes from the constraints of mobile devices regarding resources, which entails very low processing power and battery life. Therefore, the tools that would be used for the detection of malware should be lightweight and require less charging effort of the mobile device. There are robust malware detection systems on Google Play while other app stores do not maintain that level of security, which increases the danger of infestation of malware for users who wander to less-trusted sources to download apps.

In recent times, more and more of the research efforts have turned towards the use of applications of ML to be able to detect Android malware, which has the capacity to analyze huger volumes of data, thus patterning and predicting the likelihood of an app being malicious through specific features. Such features encompass permission, API calls, and potentially other system behaviors. Such characteristics have always been acquired from apps to serve as an input for any ML model used in application classification based on various approaches. They include classifiers such as Decision Trees (DT), Random Forest (RF), Support Vector Machines (SVM), and Neural Networks (NN). Most of the time, methods of anomaly detection used in unsupervised learning provide mechanisms to perceive any strange behaviors in an application, often pointing to new or unknown malware infection. ML-based approaches have shown great promise, particularly in improving the detection of unknown and zero-day threats. However, the effectiveness of these models depends heavily on the quality of the training data and the careful selection of relevant features for analysis.

Notable Android Malware Detection Systems (Alzaylaee et al., 2020): Google Play Protect, which is a Google's built-in malware detection system for Android, which automatically scans apps on the Google Play Store and users' devices. Furthermore, DroidScope, which is a dynamic analysis tool designed to perform in-depth behavior analysis of Android malware by monitoring system calls, file access, and network activity. In addition, AndroGuard, which is an open-source tool for static analysis of Android apps, primarily used for reverse engineering APKs and detecting malicious patterns.

3. ANALYSIS OF ANDROID MALWARE DATASETS AND ASSOCIATED FEATURES

3.1 Benchmark Android Malware Datasets

There are several benchmark Android malware datasets have been introduced during 2012 to 2024. In Table 2, we provide a list of available state-of-the-art Android malware datasets. For each dataset, we discuss the main reference and year, dataset name, number of features, number of samples, malware types or families, access type, and source link. These datasets have several limitations, including:

- The limited number of Android malware families and small number of samples in each malware family.
- New Android malware samples are not included in these datasets.
- The appropriate classification of the Android malware families and accurate mapping of samples with its corresponding Android malware family.
- Providing well structures of malware families and subfamilies and describing each family behavior.

Therefore, there is a need to tackle seriously these limitations by proposing new Android malware datasets.

Table 2. List of benchmark Android malware datasets

Ref	Dataset name	No. of features	No. of samples/ apps/ APKs	Malware types/ families	Access	Source link
(Zhou & Jiang, 2012)	Android malware Genome Project	-	1260 Malware samples	49 Malware families	Sharing with permission	http://www.malgenomeproject.org/
(Arp et al., 2014)	Drebin	8	5,560 Malware samples	from 179 malware families	Share with permission	https://drebin.mlsec.org/
(Yerima & Sezer, 2019)	Android Malware Dataset	215	5,560 malware apps from Drebin project and 9,476 benign apps		Public	https://www.kaggle.com/datasets/shashwatwork/android-malware-dataset-for-machine-learning
(Arash et al., 2018)	CICAndMal2017	80	10,854 samples (4,354 malware and 6,500 benign)	4 Malware categories (Adware Ransomware Scareware SMS Malware) (42 malware families)	Public	https://www.unb.ca/cic/datasets/andmal2017.html

continued on following page

Table 2. Continued

Ref	Dataset name	No. of features	No. of samples/ apps/ APKs	Malware types/ families	Access	Source link
(Mahdavifar et al., 2020)	CICMalDroid 2020	470 frequencies of system calls, binders and composite behaviors. 50,621 static features	11,598 Android samples	5 Malware categories (Adware, Banking malware, SMS malware, Riskware, and Benign)	Public	https://www.unb.ca/cic/datasets/maldroid-2020.html
(Keyes et al., 2021)	CCCS-CIC-AndMal2020	-	200000 benign and 200000 malware samples	14 malware categories (191 malware families)	Public	https://www.unb.ca/cic/datasets/andmal2020.html
(Almomani. et al., 2024)	Maloid-DS	-	47,971 malware samples	7 malware categories (345 malware families)	Public	https://sel.psu.edu.sa/research/datasets/datasets.php
(Parthajit et al., 2020)	TUNADROMD	241	4465 samples	Binary (Malware or Goodware)	Public	https://archive.ics.uci.edu/dataset/855/tuandromd%2B%28tezpur%2Buniversity%2Bandroid%2Bmalware%2Bdataset%29
(Chakraborty, 2023)	Android Malware Detection	85	355630 samples	3 Malware (Adware, Scareware, SMS_Malware) and Benign	Public	https://www.kaggle.com/datasets/subhajournal/android-malware-detection
(Bissyandé et al., 2016)	AndroZoo	-	24934618 APKs	Binary (Malware or Goodware)	Shared with permission	https://androzoo.uni.lu/
(Bissyandé et al., 2017)	CIC-AAGM2017	-	1900 apps (400 malware and 1500 benign)	12 malware families and 1 benign	Public	https://www.unb.ca/cic/datasets/android-adware.html
(Kumar et al., 2022)	AndroOBFS	-	16279 samples	158 malware families	Public	https://security.cse.iitk.ac.in/androobfs_dataset

3.2 Feature Types

Android malware datasets include several features types such as static, dynamic, hybrid, metadata, and semantic (Mantoo & Khurana, 2020; Li et al., 2019). These features are explained as follows:

3.2.1 Static Features

Static features are extracted from APK files without executing the mobile apps (Pan et al., 2020). These features are efficient for large-scale analysis and include: (1) Permissions, the requested permissions are extracted from the AndroidManifest.xml file such as access_fine_location and send_sms. These permissions are used to identify suspicious or excessive permission requests. (2) API calls, which include invoked system APIs by the app such as getDeviceld and sendTextMessage to recognize potential malicious behavior. (3) Components, which compromise declared activities, services, receivers, and providers in the AndroidManifest.xml file to detect misuse or manipulation of Android components (Morán et al., 2024). (4) Intent filters, which capture broadcast intents declared in the manifest to detect apps that listen for specific system broadcasts. (5) Strings and constants, which include URLs or IP addresses to detect encrypted or obfuscated strings in malware. Finally, (6) Opcode sequences, which are extracted from (.dex) files to identify patterns of malicious behavior.

3.2.2 Dynamic Features

Using a controlled environment such as a sandbox or emulator, we can capture dynamic features and observe apps runtime behavior (Zhang et al., 2025). These features are: (1) System calls, which track such operations, including file access, network requests, or process creation during execution. (2) Network behavior, which monitors connections, DNS queries, HTTP requests, and data sent/received over a network to detect C2 communication or data exfiltration attempts. (3) File system changes, which monitor changes to files and directories during app execution to detect malware that attempts to create or modify sensitive files. (4) Battery and resource usage, which tracks unusual consumption of resources that represent a sign of cryptojacking or spyware. And moreover, (5) Runtime permissions, which monitor the requested runtime permissions, which may differ from declared permissions in the manifest.

3.2.3 Hybrid Features

Hybrid features combine static and dynamic data for a more comprehensive analysis. For example, a combination of API calls, system calls, network activity, and pre-defined malicious behavior patterns. Furthermore, a combination of control-flow and data-flow graphs.

3.2.4 Metadata Features

Metadata features (Shankar et al., 2024) describe app properties that are not related to behavior or structure. These features include file metadata (file size, date of creation, and digital signatures) to detect repackaged or tampered apps, market information (app rating, number of downloads, and developer information) from app stores, and obfuscation indicators that measure obfuscation techniques (packed binaries or encrypted strings).

3.2.5 Semantic Features

Semantic features are higher-level features that are derived from analyzing the app's purpose and logic. Intent analysis can be used to determine the intended functionality of an app such as a game or a banking app. In addition, flow analysis can be used to analyze the flow of sensitive data such as user input to external servers.

3.3 Privacy and Data Protection Considerations

ML-based malware detection systems require substantial amounts of user data to enhance detection accuracy, raising significant concerns regarding data collection, storage, and protection mechanisms. The use of sensitive user information, including application usage patterns, network activity, and device metadata, poses risks related to unauthorized access, data breaches, and potential misuse. Furthermore, compliance with established privacy regulations, such as the General Data Protection Regulation (GDPR) and the California Consumer Privacy Act (CCPA), is critical to ensuring that user data is handled in a lawful and transparent manner. These regulations mandate principles such as informed consent, data minimization, and the right to data erasure, which must be incorporated into the design of ML-driven malware detection frameworks. Additionally, the ethical implications of data collection, particularly in relation to user consent, anonymization techniques, and potential biases in dataset construction, warrant further examination to prevent the exploitation of personal information. Addressing these considerations is crucial to ensuring that ML-based malware detection solutions operate within legal and ethical boundaries, thereby safeguarding user privacy, maintaining regulatory compliance, and fostering greater trust in cybersecurity technologies.

4. SUPERVISED MACHINE LEARNING APPROACHES FOR ANDROID MALWARE DETECTION

Due to the digital transformation of the Internet, Android devices have become essential parts of our daily lives in recent days. However, this widespread technology has made them an expected target for various cybercriminals. Malware attacks are designed to target new technologies and harm devices by stealing information or disrupting operations. To tackle this challenge, researchers and cybersecurity experts have used supervised ML as an effective way to detect and prevent various types of malware (Mythily et al., 2025).

Supervised ML is a primary type of AI where the model/system learns from the labeled data. The label feature acts as a supervisor of the learning process. The model is designed to learn and enhance its knowledge by optimizing its hyper-parameters according to the labeled data. In terms of malware detection, the supervised models are trained on examples where the result (malware or benign app) is already known (Akhtar & Feng, 2022; Akinshola-Awe et al., 2024).

The implementation of supervised learning algorithms against malware attacks includes various steps listed below:

- **Data collection**: the initial step of designing a detection approach based on a supervised learning algorithm is to gather the required data, in this case, it is malware data. The dataset could be simulated data or extracted from a real environment. The malware data is often extracted from security firms, and extracting the required features from the network traffic (Drolet & Roberge, 2022). The suitable supervised learning approach for detecting malware, should be recent and reflect the real behavior of malware.
- **Features extraction**: Once the data is collected, the next step is to extract the required features. These features initially contribute to defining the pattern of malware attacks. The step of feature extraction plays an essential role in detecting various types of malware. On the other hand, the inclusion of a large number of features may include relevant features. The inclusion of irrelevant features could lead to a decrease in the performance of the supervised learning detection approaches (Al-Sawwa et al., 2024; Younisse, et al., 2023). Therefore, many supervised learning approaches for detecting malware attacks involve feature selection or ranking to select only the optimal features that play an essential role in detecting malware attacks. Typically, the extracted features include API calls, and network activities such as bandwidth, and packet rate (Almseidin et al., 2022).
- **Model constructing and training**: the relevant extracted features are used to train the supervised learning detection approach. The following algorithms

are commonly used to detect various types of Android malware attacks: the DT algorithm works by building a tree of decisions by selecting the most relevant feature as the root of this tree. The leaf nodes include the class of the data which is either Android malware or benign traffic (Iqubal et al., 2024). Other supervised learning techniques adapt the RF algorithm. The RF algorithm is considered an extension of the DT. The RF includes many DTs and applies the technique of ensemble to enhance the performance of the detection rate (Aaditya & Anwar, 2024). Furthermore, the SVM is also implemented as a detection approach for Android malware attacks. The SVM works by defining the maximum margin the separate the Android malware class from the benign class. The strength of the SVM offers the ability to work with linear or non-linear separable tasks using the kernel functions (Zhou et al., 2024). In addition, the neural networks could detect various types of Android malware by mimicking human behavior to classify the required data. The NN algorithm offers the ability to detect various types of attacks through its ability to work with linear and nonlinear tasks (Haodong et al., 2024).

- **Evaluation and testing**: the final step of designing the detection approach for Android malware attacks is to test and evaluate the suggested model. The evaluation process commonly involved unseen data to assess the supervised detection approach. Moreover, there are typical performance metrics that are used to evaluate and compare the supervised detection approach with other approaches as follows:
  - Accuracy: this performance metric is considered an essential metric for evaluating the supervised learning detection approach by calculating the total number of correctly classified records divided by the total number of records in the testing set (Almseidin et al., 2024).
  - Precision: this performance metric aims to calculate the accuracy of the positive predictions (Mashaleh et al., 2024).
  - Recall: this performance metric aims to measure the model's ability to identify all actual positive cases within the test set (Aaditya & Anwar, 2024).
  - F1-Score: this performance metric presents the harmonic mean of precision and recall, providing a balanced measure when both false positives and false negatives are important (Zhou et al., 2024).

Although supervised learning has been demonstrated to be effective in detecting Android malware, it still faces several real-world challenges that make it difficult to implement smoothly. One major challenge is that malware is constantly evolving. Cybercriminals keep coming up with new tricks to bypass detection, which means the models need to be updated and retrained to stay effective. Another challenge is the imbalance in the available data. In most cases, there are far more examples of safe (benign) apps than malware. This imbalance can make it difficult for the model to correctly classify malware since it is trained on more benign records. As a result, the model might become biased. To overcome these issues, researchers are exploring new techniques such as creating more data through augmentation, generating artificial malware samples to balance the dataset, and using special algorithms that focus more on the minority malware class. These approaches help improve the model's accuracy and reliability in detecting malware effectively. Table 3 summarizes the main aspects of strengths and limitations of adapting the supervised learning algorithms for detecting Android malware attacks. Figure 1 presents the general architecture of the supervised learning algorithms for the sake of detecting Android malware attacks.

Table 3. Aspect strengths limitations additional considerations

Aspect	Strengths	Limitations
Detection Accuracy	High accuracy in detecting known malware patterns.	Performance may degrade with unseen or evolving malware.
Feature engineering	Effective feature selection can improve detection rates.	Requires domain expertise to select optimal features.
Scalability	Can handle large datasets efficiently with proper tuning.	Computationally expensive for real-time applications.
Interpretability	Some models (e.g., DT) provide interpretability.	Black-box models (e.g., deep learning) lack transparency.
Resource Consumption	Lightweight models can be deployed on mobile devices.	Complex models require significant computational resources.
False Positives	Lower false positive rates with optimized models.	Misclassification can impact user trust and performance.
Feature Extraction Methods	Behavioral and static analysis features improve accuracy.	Dynamic feature extraction can be resource-intensive.

Figure 1. The general architecture of supervised learning approach for detecting Android malware attacks

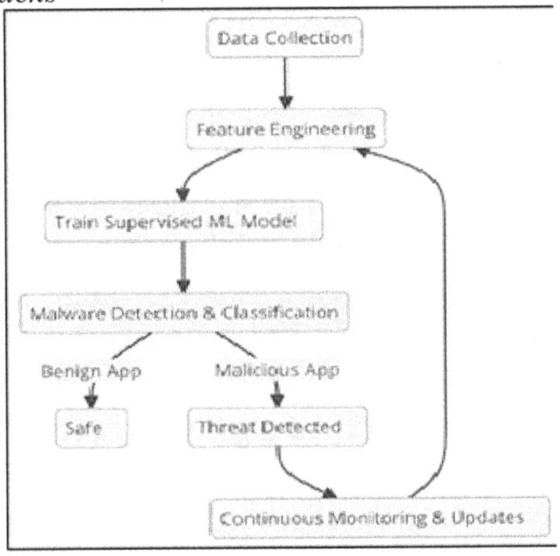

5. UNSUPERVISED MACHINE LEARNING APPROACHES FOR ANDROID MALWARE DETECTION

Unsupervised ML is characterized by its ability to work with unlabelled data. On the contrary supervised learning demands a truth table including the label data to perform the required classification task, the unsupervised learning algorithms offer the ability to define the hidden patterns and anomalies without requiring a predefined label (Liu et al., 2021). This aspect enables the unsupervised learning algorithms to be a suitable technique to handle the case of Android malware attacks. Therefore, the model automatically learns and identifies patterns in the data to group it into benign or malicious categories. Since it doesn't require explicit labeling or accurate data labels, this approach overcomes the limitations of supervised ML by detecting previously unknown malicious apps (Sharma et al., 2021).

Unsupervised ML approaches focused on analyzing traffic without any prior knowledge about the Android malware class. The detection approaches based on unsupervised algorithms explore the traffic to identify the similarities, clusters, or anomalies that could indicate malware activities (Arora et al., 2018). This strength aspect of unsupervised learning makes it suitable to deal with large amounts of data where the labeling process could be difficult to achieve. Typically, the unsupervised approaches applied dimensionality reduction techniques such as Principle Component Analysis (PCA) to reduce the dimension space, and to offer the required features that reflect the behavior of Android malware attacks. The K-mean clustering algorithm is one of the common techniques that initiate its work by randomly selecting the number of centroids that represent the number of predefined clusters. The K-mean algorithm iterates the process to find the optimal centroid values that represent the core of the cluster. From another perspective, the DBSCAN algorithm was also used to define the anomalies within the network traffic to detect Android malware attacks (Samra et al., 2013). The DBSCAN algorithm is characterized by its ability to work without requiring to define the number of clusters. Moreover, the DBSCAN algorithm had the ability to generate various clusters with arbitrary shapes. In addition, the hierarchical clustering algorithms such as agglomerative clustering was also useful to detect various behaviours of Android malware attacks (Aashima & Bajaj, 2022).

The implementation of unsupervised algorithms such as K-mean, DBSCAN, Agglomerative against Android malware attacks include various steps, that could be summarized as follows (Padmavathi et al., 2022):

- Step 1: Data Collection

  1. Gather Android application datasets from various sources (e.g., Google Play Store, third-party stores, malware repositories).
  2. Extract relevant features such as API calls, permissions, network behavior, and resource usage.
  3. Preprocess the data to remove irrelevant or redundant information.

- Step 2: Data Preprocessing

  1. Feature Selection: Choose the most relevant features that contribute to distinguishing benign and malicious applications.
  2. Normalization: Scale the features to ensure uniformity across all data points.
  3. Dimensionality Reduction: Apply techniques such as PCA to reduce feature space while retaining key characteristics.

- Step 3: Applying Clustering Algorithms (K-mean, DBSCAN, Agglomerative)
  - K-Means Clustering
    1. Choose the number of clusters (k) based on domain knowledge or using the elbow method.
    2. Randomly initialize k cluster centroids.
    3. Assign each data point to the nearest centroid.
    4. Recalculate centroids based on assigned points.
    5. Repeat steps 3 and 4 until convergence.
    6. Analyze the clusters to identify benign and malicious groups.

- *DBSCAN Clustring*
    1. Set the parameters: minimum points (MinPts) and epsilon (Eps).
    2. Select an unvisited data point and check if it is a core point (has at least MinPts neighbors within Eps distance).
    3. Expand the cluster if the point is a core point.
    4. Continue expanding the cluster by recursively adding reachable points.
    5. Mark noise points that do not belong to any cluster.
    6. Evaluate clusters to classify malware from benign apps.
- *Agglomerative Hierarchical Clustering*
    1. Start with each data point as its own cluster.
    2. Compute the pairwise distance between clusters using linkage criteria (e.g., single, complete, or average linkage).
    3. Merge the closest clusters iteratively.
    4. Continue merging until the desired number of clusters is reached or a stopping criterion is met.
    5. Analyze the resulting hierarchy to classify malware.

- Step 4: Evaluation and Interpretation

1. Use silhouette score and Davies-Bouldin index to measure cluster quality.

Unsupervised learning provides a significant approach to detect the Android malware attacks compared to other traditional detection methods, especially in detecting the new attacks without prior knowledge. However, there are some limitations of adapting the unsupervised algorithms (Wang et al., 2022) that could be summarized as follows: High False Positive Rates: The model does not have labeled class, legitimate apps may sometimes be misclassified as malware. Scalability Issues: Processing large datasets with complex clustering algorithms can be computationally intensive. Feature Selection Complexity: Selecting the relevant features without domain expertise can lead to ineffective detection models. Table 4 summarizes the main aspect of using the unsupervised learning algorithms for the sake of Android malware detection.

Table 4. Aspects of unsupervised learning for malware detection

Aspect	Strengths	Limitations
Detection Capability	Identifies unknown threats	High false positives
Data Requirements	No labeled data needed	Requires high-quality feature extraction
Scalability	Works well with large datasets	Can be computationally expensive

Aspect	Strengths	Limitations
Adaptability	Adapts to new malware types	Require manual intervention
Performance Evaluation	Does not rely on prior knowledge	Difficult to measure accuracy

6. ENSEMBLE MACHINE LEARNING APPROACHES FOR ANDROID MALWARE DETECTION

Each individual model attains commendable results, although no algorithm exhibits immaculate excellence in all scenarios. Each classification algorithm demonstrates superiority in various scenarios but exhibits particular weaknesses in detecting masked or misidentified malware. Ensemble learning addresses detection difficulties by integrating many models into a single framework, yielding enhanced accuracy and improved protection against diverse malware kinds. Ensemble models in ML aggregate many analytical models that jointly classify fresh data points. Various models interconnected using these methods improve accuracy rates by amalgamating their predictions, yielding outputs that surpass those of any individual model. Figure 2 highlights the main steps of implementing an ensemble learning model for Android malware detection. Two primary types of ensemble learning are bagging and boosting, in addition to other methods that also demonstrate efficacy.

Figure 2. Generic ensemble learning model for Android malware detection

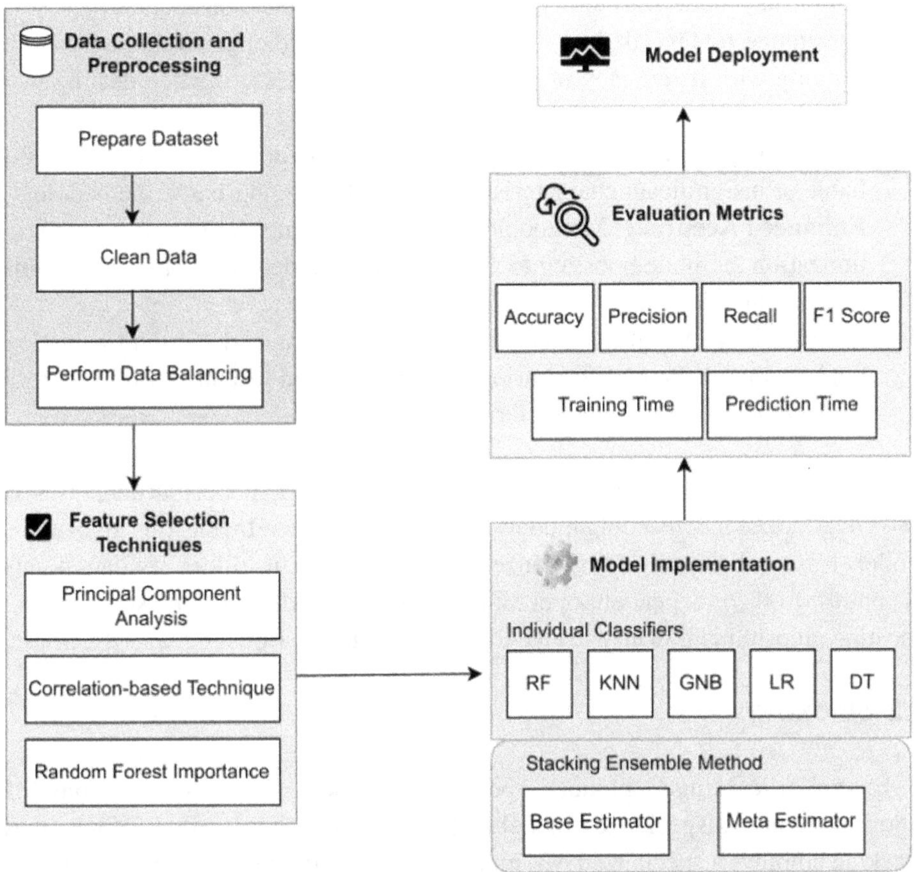

(Alsharif & Alharb, 2024)

6.1 Bagging (Bootstrap Aggregating)

Throughout ensemble models Bagging utilizes bootstrapping to generate numerous decision models by partitioning the training data using random sampling with replacement. Models yield averaged predictions in regression scenarios and voting outcomes in classification tasks. The RF method serves as a prevalent application of bagging, achieving notable success in Android malware detection due to its capability to handle large datasets and accurately extract intricate patterns.

Benefits of Bagging and Boosting for Android Malware Detection:

- **Enhanced Precision**: Java aggregation of many model prediction outcomes diminishes model variability, resulting in higher detection accuracy.
- **Resilience to Overfitting**: The integration of prediction averaging endows bagging with its efficacy in addressing overfitting issues when dealing with complex malware datasets.
- **Robustness**: RF demonstrates efficacy in malware detection, even with unreliable or insignificant characteristics, due to its bagging-based methodology.
- **Enhanced Accuracy**: Methodological advancements via iterative model optimization facilitate boosting to attain heightened detection precision against intricate malware threats.
- **Adaptability**: Novel malware patterns might enhance detection by employing boosting techniques that prioritise misclassified instances while addressing rare or subtle malware patterns.

Every iteration of boosting develops an individual weak model that addresses the flaws overlooked by preceding models in a cyclical manner. In boosting algorithms, models learn collaboratively by concentrating on difficult-to-identify data points, in contrast to the independent operation of bagging models. The most recognized boosting algorithms now in use are AdaBoost, Gradient Boosting, and XGBoost.

6.2 Stacking

Ensemble learning techniques, specifically stacking, integrate numerous ML algorithms under a specialized model that consolidates their predictive outcomes. Stacking employs a specialized ML model to identify the most effective method of aggregating base model predictions, hence enhancing the accuracy of final classification results. A stacking ensemble conducts malware categorization by integrating judgements from algorithms such as DT, SVM, and NN.

By employing stacking techniques, one can access a variety of base models that excel in distinct detection tasks, hence enhancing detection accuracy. Also the flexible design of the meta-model enhances detection efficiency while ensuring adequate performance across base models, resulting in an effective malware identification platform. In addition, stacking led to improve the performance because stacking yields enhanced accuracy in detecting tasks by concurrently integrating numerous methods.

Advantages of Ensemble Learning in Android Malware Detection

- **Enhanced Accuracy**: The integration of various algorithms into ensemble models yields greater accuracy compared to individual models, while exhibiting improved generalization capabilities. The method yields more reliable malware detection.

- **Resilience to Evasion Techniques**: Diverse modelling methodologies within an ensemble system pose a significant obstacle for malware developers attempting to evade detection via software alterations such code obfuscation and polymorphism. Various detection models that analyze distinct components of malware collaborate to provide comprehensive cybersecurity protection.
- **Mitigated Overfitting**: Ensemble learning addresses training data overfitting by predictive aggregation techniques, resulting in enhanced performance in recognizing previously encountered malware instances.
- **Adaptability to Emerging Threats**: Enhanced methodologies, in conjunction with ensembles, demonstrate remarkable proficiency in identifying novel or unfamiliar malware by their capacity to learn and modify classification patterns in response to misclassified instances.

Obstacles in Ensemble ML for Android Malware Identification

- **Computational Overhead**: Ensemble models utilizing boosting techniques or stacking algorithms require significant processing resources because to their intricate nature. Ensemble ML is suboptimal for real-time malware detection on devices with constrained processing capabilities and restricted battery life.
- **Data Quality and Feature Selection**: The efficacy of ML models, including ensembles, relies on the quality of the training data and the appropriateness of feature selection. In ensemble models, inadequately chosen feature combinations coupled with biased input data can lead to erroneous predicted results.
- **Interpretability**: The integration of multiple models in an ensemble complicates the elucidation of final judgements. RF and Gradient Boosting are complex ensemble models that provide significant difficulties in elucidating the rationale for the malware flagging of certain applications.
- **Training Duration**: The complexity of ensemble models results in extended training periods relative to solo models, posing challenges during swift system deployments.

The integration of diverse models via ensemble ML techniques exhibits significant efficacy in Android malware detection, as multimodal studies yield improved accuracy and resilient outcomes that are adaptable to varying settings. Advanced ensemble techniques, including bagging, boosting, and stacking, enhance malware detection by effectively addressing the obstacles posed by obfuscation, polymorphism, and unknown malware threats. These models encounter significant hurdles with data quality, interpretability, and computational overhead. The future advancement of ensemble learning research signifies increasing significance for Android security by providing better defense against evolving cyber threats.

7. REINFORCEMENT MACHINE LEARNING APPROACHES FOR ANDROID MALWARE DETECTION

Android malware has become the most significant cybersecurity problem worldwide. It spreads since many individuals use Android devices, and sharing malicious apps outside the official app stores is easy. Traditional static and dynamic analysis-based malware detection approaches face difficulty with the extremely fast evolution of malware because they are based on predefined rules, signatures, or heuristic models. The demand for adaptive and intelligent detection mechanisms has led to the emergence of ML—powerful automation for hunting down malicious behaviors. Reinforcement learning (RL) is one of the ML methods that has attracted interest from users, since it can learn on its own and adapt; useful for Android malware detection (Wu et al., 2023).

7.1 Reinforcement Learning in Android Malware Detection

Reinforcement learning (RL) is a subset of ML in which an agent learns to make decisions by working with an environment to get the most rewards over time. Whereas supervised learning models are trained with data having labels, in contrast, reinforcement learning (RL) aims at learning to take the best action based on the outcomes of those actions (Wu et al., 2023). This helps systems adapt to new situations which they have never seen. Because RL can adapt, it's very useful for malware detection, where the situation changes, and harmful behaviors develop over time (Batouche & Jahankhani, 2021).

An android malware detection agent acquires the responsibility of detecting applications that exhibit malicious behaviors by exploring different characteristics of applications extracted from API calls, permissions, network activity, and ways of application execution (Liu et al., 2022). It gains positive reward due to correct detection, but negative reward because of malware misses or safe app misclassification as hazardous. As time goes on, the RL agent improves its decision-making rules, which helps it find malware better and be more accurate without needing many labeled datasets. This skill to keep learning and changing is very important for fighting the constantly changing world of Android malware (Razaque et al., 2025).

7.2 Reinforcement Learning Algorithms for Android Malware Detection

Many reinforcements learning-based algorithms can be applied to detect Android malware, and each has its strengths for handling the varying natures of malware. Two major RL algorithms that are widely used in this area include Q-learning and deep Q-learning (Boppiniti S. T., 2021). Q-learning is a type of RL algorithm that does not use a model and uses a Q-table to show the values of state-action pairs. Instead, every entry in the Q-table corresponds to a state-action pair, and the Q-value is the predicted total reward for selecting a particular action from a given state. For Android malware detection, a state can thus be any given application behavior or feature, such as system calls, permissions, and user interactions, and the action must be what it is that the system can actually do, such as classifying an app as safe or malicious. Q-learning is an update scheme for Q-values in making decisions (Jang et al., 2019).

Q-learning is being used to make decisions in malware detection systems, where the agent observes and interacts with certain features of inoculated android apps to learn the best way to classify them. Q-learning has problems with dealing with large and complicated state spaces - conditions typically found in practice for the Android environment (Yasin et al., 2021). A Q-learning algorithm stores the Q-value in tables, as shown in Figure 3. When deep neural networks are incorporated into it, it is called Deep Q-Learning, where neural networks are employed to estimate Q-value functions (Arulkumaran et al., 2017).

Figure 3. Q-learning vs deep q-learning

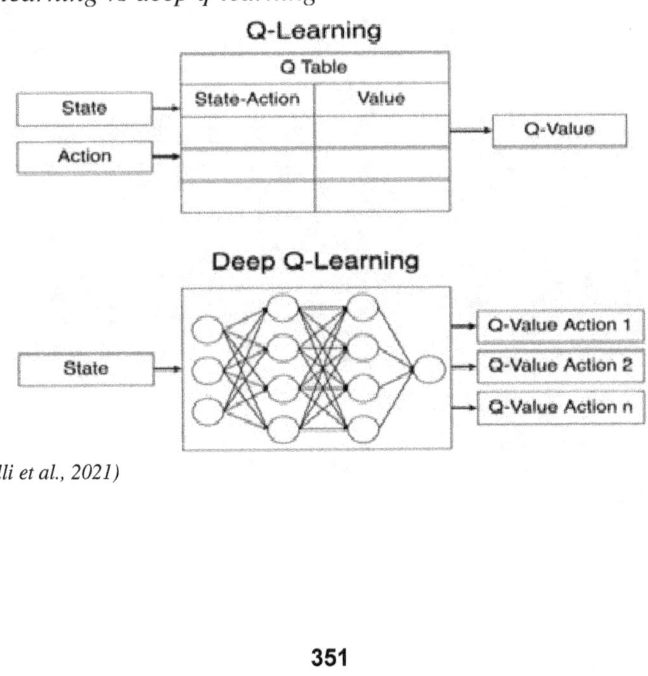

(Sebastianelli et al., 2021)

Deep Q-learning embodies the confluence of Q-learning and deep neural networks to work with large state spaces (Nguyen & Reddi, 2021). Thus, deep Q-learning replaces the Q-table with a neural network to link the characteristics of Android applications with Q-value states so that the agent can figure out ideal actions from that continuous space. This technique is quite helpful in detecting Android malware. It involves gaining important information from the app, which may include a lot of details such as API calls, network traffic, and behavior patterns (Nguyen & Reddi, 2021).

It continues to discover new types of malwares with promising results through a deep learning model that can comprehend many and varied types of malicious behaviors. The deep Q-learning model learns to improve in detecting malicious apps through operating in a dynamic environment from benign applications to potential (Sewak et al., 2023). Figure 4 shows Ontology of threat detection and defense systems in cybersecurity and the applications of deep reinforcement learning.

Figure 4. An overview of deep reinforcement learning for threat detection and protection

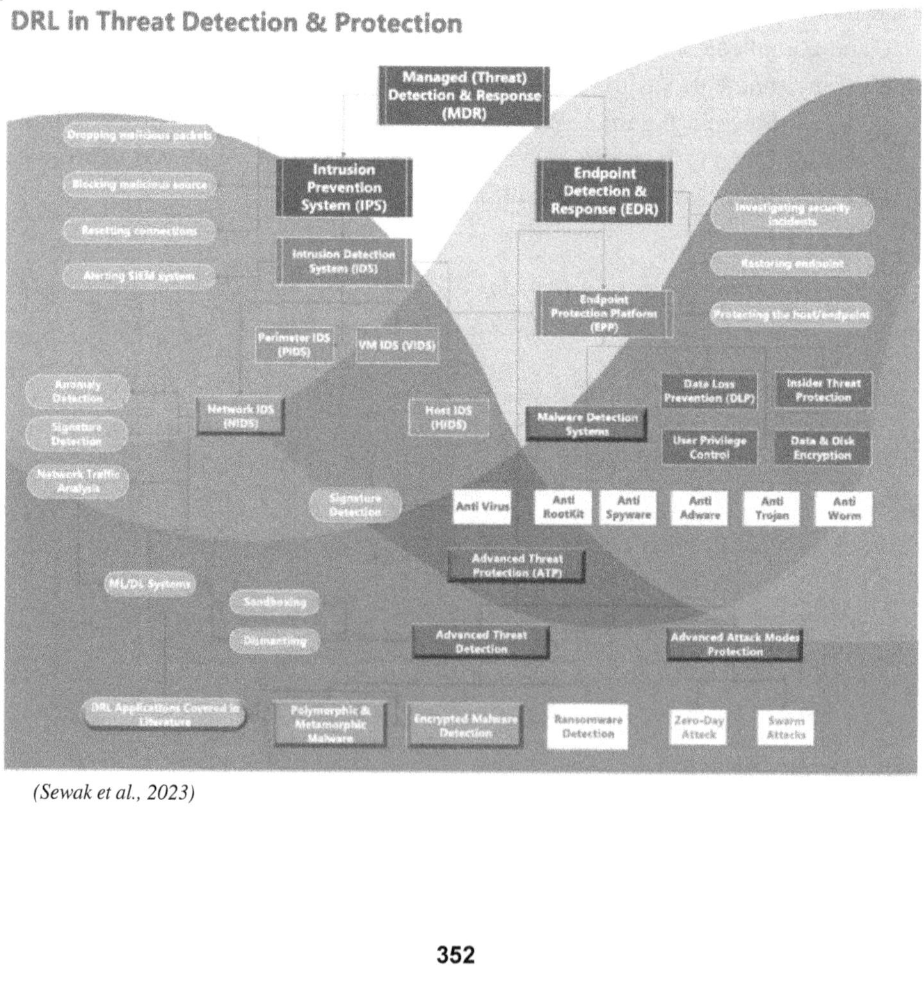

(Sewak et al., 2023)

7.3 Advantages of Reinforcement Learning in Android Malware Detection

Reinforcement learning has very many important benefits in finding Android malware, including finding it in places where generally accepted methods have difficulty dealing with new types of malware. Some of the important benefits include:

- Adapting to New Threats: A big problem in the actual search for malware is the fact that harmful applications constantly change. The potential to learn from experience using RL helps in the adaptation of new types of malwares that would not have been able to be observed in the training data. This quality makes the RL-based systems robust against the new threats appearing, reducing the necessity for constant manual updating (Manju & Rana, 2024).
- Continuous Learning: The RL-based systems support refining the detection capabilities for all time. An agent, which has been given feedback for each of its actions in receiving rewards or penalties, can gradually optimize its policy of decision-making. This characteristic ensures the detection system to be effective in a rapidly changing landscape of Android malware (Manju & Rana, 2024).
- Handling Unknown Malware: Traditional supervised learning models tend to struggle to detect unknown or new malware since they rely on labeled training data. Contrarily, RL systems are able to identify abnormal activity that may indicate malware presence even if the application has never been encountered. This ability to generalize causes RL-based systems to perform more effectively when dealing with previously unseen threats (Shatnawi et al., 2022).
- Improved Accuracy: Analyzing the Android platform and modifying its rules for classification, an RL agent will have better accuracy compared with normal signature-based detection tools. Additionally, RL can reduce false positives (good apps classified as malware) and false negatives (malicious apps classified as safe), which tend to improve the performance of the detection system (Wu et al., 2023).

7.4 Challenges and Future Directions

Reinforcement learning has great potential for arduous search for Android malware, but it has to also face many challenges in order to be effective. Making a really good reward function is one tough challenge. It has to balance malware detection and prevention of false alarms, which are quite confusing. Finding a balance may be difficult if one does not know what harmful behaviour looks like. Another issue is the exploration-exploitation dichotomy, native to RL algorithms. First, during learning, the agent must actually try different actions to obtain enough data in order to learn a good strategy. Of course, the real system may be insulated too much, therefore having horrible performance, because speed and efficiency in detection are very important. Better methodologies, such as the ones for experience replay and proper rewards shaping, can address these problems, but using them in Android malware detection systems requires proper consideration.

In addition, reinforcement learning combined with other types of ML, for example, unsupervised learning and especially transfer learning, holds important promise for improving the process of Android malware detection. In other words, the new approach could be trained for malware detection in a relatively accurate model with the help of federated learning and reinforcement learning, allowing training on devices, excluding centralized storage.

8. HYBRID MACHINE LEARNING APPROACHES FOR ANDROID MALWARE DETECTION

In the last few years, the Android ecosystem has become the leading ecosystem for mobile applications due to its open nature and comprehensive support. With this benefit, however, has followed the proliferation of Android malware, which takes advantage of the weak points in the system and is a security threat to the user. Classic malware detection techniques, including signature-based, have been insufficient in identifying new or polymorphic variants of malware. Due to this, ML techniques have become favored because they can classify, identify, and anticipate malware activity in real-time. Android malware, however, being complex and evolving means different approaches need to be used in conjunction with one another to increase the accuracy of detection and reduce false positives (Dahiya et al., 2025).

Hybrid ML approaches have also become a good solution for this problem (Rodrigo et al., 2021). They combine the power of different ML methods to better identify Android malware. Hybrid models utilize supervised and unsupervised learning methods, along with mixing different types of classifiers, in order to take advantage of what each method does best (Liang et al., 2021). This section offers an overview of hybrid ML approaches based on their application for Android malware detection.

8.1 Combining Supervised and Unsupervised Learning

Supervised learning is where models are trained using labeled data (Mahdavifar et al., 2022). Supervised learning is normally applied to classify malware (Akhtar & Feng, 2022). Supervised learning depends significantly on having labeled data, which takes a lot of time and money to obtain (Mahdavifar et al., 2022). Compared to supervised learning, unsupervised learning algorithms do not require labeled data. Unsupervised algorithms perform well at discovering new malware sample types and clustering unknown variants together (Liu et al., 2021).

Hybrid methods that integrate supervised and unsupervised methods attempt to break the constraints of each (Ippolito et al., 2021). For example, an unsupervised learning step might be applied to find potentially malicious activity or characteristics of Android apps, which are then tagged manually or with semi-supervised learning methods (Mahdavifar et al., 2022). These data can then be utilized to train more precise supervised models. This blend of approaches identifies known malware based on supervised models and unknown and novel threats utilizing unsupervised methods.

A good example of such hybridization involves using clustering algorithms like k-means to determine suspicious patterns within the data (Akhtar & Feng, 2022). Then, a SVM classifier is trained to classify innocent versus malicious samples (Liu et al., 2021). The two-stage technique fills the gap between unsupervised clustering and supervised classification, and it offers greater flexibility and scalability in Android malware detection.

8.2 Fusion of Multiple Classifiers

The second effective method to enhance detection accuracy is through an ensemble of several ML classifiers. Every classifier has some advantages and limitations, and merging their outputs can enhance decision-making. Popular methods to merge classifiers include bagging, boosting, and stacking.

Ensemble techniques can merge the prediction of multiple individual classifiers such as DTs, RF, and NN (Ippolito et al., 2021). For instance, for Android malware classification, a RF classifier can be employed to determine the relative importance of various features (Rabbani et al., 2021). In contrast, a NN may identify intricate non-linear relationships between the features. Combining both classifiers under a stacking ensemble approach can yield more robust and precise malware detection, particularly when the malware samples exhibit varied patterns of behavior (Chandrashekar et al., 2023).

Moreover, boosting algorithms such as AdaBoost and Gradient Boosting can improve the performance of weak classifiers by iteratively refining their predictions (Damaševičius et al., 2021). These algorithms minimize the bias and variance of single models, resulting in better detection performance when used on Android malware datasets. In addition, boosting techniques, such as AdaBoost and Gradient Boosting, can enhance the performance of weaker classifiers by iteratively refining their outputs (Islam et al., 2023). These methods reduce the bias and variance of individual models, leading to improved detection capabilities when applied to Android malware datasets.

8.3 Feature Fusion and Dimensionality Reduction

Hybrid ML techniques also have the benefit of mixing various kinds of features. Detection of Android malware typically involves extracting various kinds of features from applications, e.g., static features (permissions, API calls, manifest files) and dynamic features (system calls and execution traces) (Shafin et al., 2021). Each kind of feature provides a different perspective on an application's behavior, and mixing these features can provide a more comprehensive picture of what an application is intended to do.

Hybrid models can further combine methods for selecting significant features with dimensionality-reducing methods such as Principal Component Analysis (PCA) (Raval & Anwar, 2024) or t-Distributed Stochastic Neighbor Embedding (t-SNE) (Sonya & Deepak, 2024) to compress the feature space while retaining the most useful aspects of the data. This helps the subsequent classifiers to perform better by eliminating redundant or useless features and reducing computations. By combining various features with feature reduction techniques, hybrid ML approaches can enhance the detection process without sacrificing the high accuracy rates.

8.4. Deep Learning with Classical Machine Learning Methods

Deep learning has also been highly effective in Android malware detection, where Convolutional Neural Networks (CNNs) and Recurrent Neural Networks (RNNs) have been employed to learn significant features from raw data such as app code or system call traces (Canfora et al., 2015). Deep learning models typically require ample training data as well as a lot of computing resources, however. As a solution to these issues, hybrid methods that combine deep learning with conventional ML methods have been developed (Raymond et al., 2023). For example, it is possible to use a deep learning model to extract high-level features from raw application data and pass them through a regular classifier like a RF or Gradient Boosting Machine to make the final decision (Kouliaridis et al., 2023; Martinelli et al., 2017). This combination enables deep learning to utilize its ability to detect complex patterns and reserve the final classification to the traditional ML model to maintain computational efficiency and interpretability.

Further, hybrid models incorporating feature extraction methods, such as graph-based analysis or natural language processing, with deep learning approaches are beginning to emerge (Lu et al., 2020). Hybrid models leverage deep learning's ability to comprehend intricate features while integrating the knowledge of traditional methods pertaining to the concerned area.

8.5 Challenges and Future Directions

Despite the encouraging performance of hybrid ML approaches to Android malware detection, there are several challenges. One of the key challenges is the dynamic and continuously changing nature of malware, which has the effect of inducing changing patterns and behavior that may not be adequately captured by traditional learning models. Furthermore, the integration of multiple algorithms introduces additional complexity with respect to model training, feature engineering, and computational overhead.

Future research in this area will likely focus on making hybrid models perform better at adapting to new and unknown malware threats in real time. Methods like continuous learning, transfer learning, and online learning can potentially deal with the dynamic nature of Android malware. Moreover, hybrid approaches that include explainability and transparency in decision-making will be crucial in building trust and accountability into automated defense.

9. COMPARATIVE ANALYSIS OF MACHINE LEARNING APPROACHES

To further investigate the effectiveness of various ML algorithms for detecting Android malware, this section presents a comparative analysis. The suggested comparison analysis is structured based on performance metrics such as detection rate, resource requirements, and suitable use cases.

9.1 Performance Comparison

Table 5 summarizes key performance metrics, including detection accuracy, false positive rate, and computational overhead for state-of-the-art ML-based approaches using supervised, unsupervised, ensemble, and reinforcement algorithms.

Table 5. Key performance metrics of ML algorithms

	ML Approach	Ref	Detection Accuracy	False Positive Rate	Computational Overhead
Supervised ML	Decision Tree	(Iqubal et al., 2024)	High (~90%)	Moderate	Low
	Random Forest	(Aaditya & Anwar, 2024)	Very High (~95%)	Low	High
	Support Vector Machine (SVM)	(Zhou et al., 2024)	High (~92%)	Moderate	High
	Neural Networks	(Haodong et al., 2024)	Very High (~97%)	Low	Very High
Unsupervised ML	K-Means Clustering	(Arora et al., 2018)	Moderate (~80%)	High	Moderate
	DBSCAN Clustering	(Samra et al., 2013)	High (~88%)	High	High
	Agglomerative Clustering	(Aashima & Bajaj, 2022)	Moderate (~82%)	High	High
Ensemble ML	AdaBoost	(AlOmari et al., 2024)	Moderate (~82%)	High	High
	Gradient Boosting	(AlOmari et al., 2024)	High (~92%)	Low	High
	XGBoost	(Arizal et al., 2024)	High (~97-99%)	Low	Moderate
	Random Forest	(Azeem et al., 2024)	High (~97-99%)	Low	Moderate
Reinforcement ML	Q-Learning	(Yasin et al., 2021; Arulkumaran et al., 2017; Sebastianelli et al., 2021; Sewak et al., 2023)	Moderate to High (~85-95%)	Low	Moderate
	Deep Q-Networks (DQN)	(Yasin et al., 2021; Arulkumaran et al., 2017; Sebastianelli et al., 2021; Sewak et al., 2023)	High (~90-95%)	Low	High
	Double Deep Q-Networks (Double DQN)	(Yasin et al., 2021; Arulkumaran et al., 2017; Sebastianelli et al., 2021; Sewak et al., 2023)	Moderate to High (~90-95%)	Low	High

9.2 Resource Requirements

Adapting ML algorithms for the sake of Android malware detection depends on the computational resources available. Table 6 presents an analysis of memory and processing requirements for each ML-based approach. Various ML algorithms have been used to detect Android malware intrusions, however their effectiveness depends on the scenario. Some algorithms work better in certain situations, while others are more suitable for different cases. Table 7 presents a summary of the common ML algorithms and their suitable scenarios. To highlight the effectiveness of each approach, Figure 5 presents a comparison of detection rates and false positive rates.

Table 6. ML algorithms resource requirements

	ML Approach	Ref	Memory Usage	Processing Power Requirement	Suitability for Real-time Detection
Supervised ML	Decision Tree	(Iqubal et al., 2024)	Low	Low	Yes
	Random Forest	(Aaditya & Anwar, 2024)	High	High	No
	Support Vector Machine (SVM)	(Zhou et al., 2024)	High	High	No
	Neural Networks	(Haodong et al., 2024)	Very High	Very High	No
Unsupervised ML	K-Means Clustering	(Arora et al., 2018)	Moderate	Moderate	Yes
	DBSCAN Clustering	(Samra et al., 2013)	High	High	No
	Agglomerative Clustering	(Aashima & Bajaj, 2022)	High	High	No
Ensemble ML	AdaBoost	(AlOmari et al., 2024)	Low to Moderate	Low	Yes
	Gradient Boosting	(AlOmari et al., 2024)	High	High	No
	XGBoost	(Arizal et al., 2024)	Moderate to High	Moderate	Yes
	Random Forest	(Azeem et al., 2024)	High	Moderate	Yes

	ML Approach	Ref	Memory Usage	Processing Power Requirement	Suitability for Real-time Detection
Reinforcement ML	Q-Learning	(Yasin et al., 2021; Arulkumaran et al., 2017; Sebastianelli et al., 2021; Sewak et al., 2023)	High	High	High
	Deep Q-Networks (DQN)	(Yasin et al., 2021; Arulkumaran et al., 2017; Sebastianelli et al., 2021; Sewak et al., 2023)	High	High	High
	Double Deep Q-Networks (Double DQN)	(Yasin et al., 2021; Arulkumaran et al., 2017; Sebastianelli et al., 2021; Sewak et al., 2023)	High	High	High

Table 7. ML algorithms use cases

	ML Approach	Ref	Best Use Cases	Limitations
Supervised ML	Decision Tree	(Iqubal et al., 2024)	Simple malware detection on limited resources	Less effective on complex malware patterns
	Random Forest	(Aaditya & Anwar, 2024)	High-accuracy malware classification	High computational cost
	Support Vector Machine (SVM)	(Zhou et al., 2024)	Malware detection with small datasets	Computationally expensive on large datasets
	Neural Networks	(Haodong et al., 2024)	Complex pattern recognition and deep analysis	Requires large datasets, high training time
Unsupervised ML	K-Means Clustering	(Arora et al., 2018)	Grouping similar malware types	High false positive rate
	DBSCAN Clustering	(Samra et al., 2013)	Identifying anomalies in malware behavior	Sensitive to noise
	Agglomerative Clustering	(Aashima & Bajaj, 2022)	Hierarchical analysis of malware families	High computational cost

continued on following page

Table 7. Continued

	ML Approach	Ref	Best Use Cases	Limitations
Ensemble ML	AdaBoost	(AlOmari et al., 2024)	Binary classification problems and small Malware datasets	Sensitive to noisy data and outliers and weak performance on complex and high-dimensional datasets
	Gradient Boosting	(AlOmari et al., 2024)	Complex datasets with nonlinear relationships	High computational cost and slow training
	XGBoost	(Arizal et al., 2024)	Real-time and large-scale applications and sparse and imbalanced datasets	Requires substantial memory for large datasets, Hyperparameter tuning can be complex, and susceptible to overfitting on small datasets
	Random Forest	(Azeem et al., 2024; Arizal et al., 2024)	High-dimensional dataset and missing values	Requires significant memory and slower in real-time applications
Reinforcement ML	Q-Learning	(Yasin et al., 2021; Arulkumaran et al., 2017; Sebastianelli et al., 2021; Sewak et al., 2023).	Grid-based environments, such as robot path planning and Adaptive systems like malware detection and intrusion detection where predefined rules can be learned over time	Inefficient in complex environments. It requires a lookup table (Q-table) for state-action pairs. Also, Converges slowly in high-dimensional problems
	Deep Q-Networks (DQN)	(Yasin et al., 2021; Arulkumaran et al., 2017; Sebastianelli et al., 2021; Sewak et al., 2023).	High-dimensional decision-making tasks and real-time adaptive malware classification	It requires large datasets and powerful hardware (GPUs/TPUs), expensive computations, and overestimation of Q-values.
	Double Deep Q-Networks (Double DQN)	(Yasin et al., 2021; Arulkumaran et al., 2017; Sebastianelli et al., 2021; Sewak et al., 2023).	It is used for dynamic and high-dimensional problems and real-time security threat detection, network intrusion prevention, and automated trading	It needs very expensive computations and hyperparameter tuning to balance training stability and it needs large datasets and powerful GPUs for efficient learning

Figure 5. ML comparison for Android malware detection

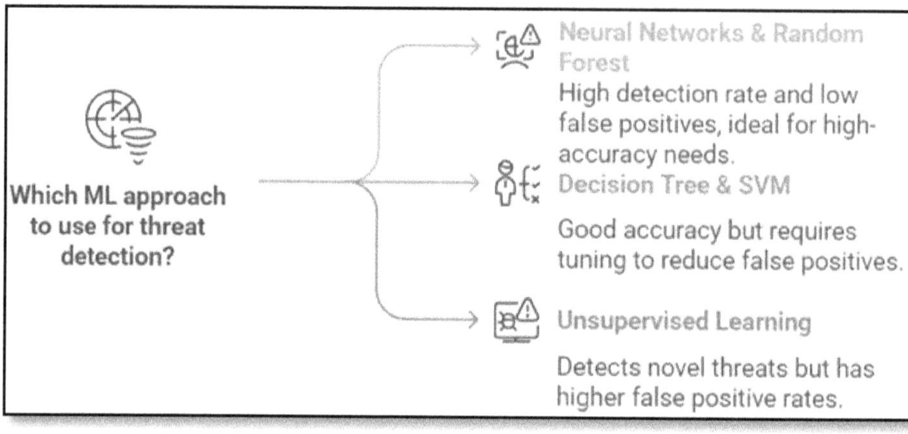

10. CHALLENGES AND FUTURE RESEARCH DIRECTIONS

Despite the many advancements in ML, challenges remain (Maniriho et al., 2024; Senanayake et al., 2024; Senanayake et al., 2021; Thakur et al., 2024). These include:

- Android malware dataset quality and availability: The success of a ML model depend on high-quality data. Poor data quality can lead to inaccurate predictions. Cleaning and preprocessing data can be time-consuming and complex.
- Interpretability: Deep neural networks and other complex models can be challenging to interpret, leaving stakeholders needing clearer, more understandable insights. This is why research in explainable AI (XAI) focuses on making these models more transparent, ensuring that their decisions are easier to understand and trust.
- Overfitting: Overfitting occurs when a model performs well on training data but struggles with new, unseen data because it has learned noise or random details rather than the actual patterns. To address this, techniques like cross-validation and regularization are used to help the model generalize better and avoid overfitting.
- Bias in Android malware dataset: Bias in data can result in skewed results and unfair outcomes. For instance, biased data used in hiring algorithms could reinforce discriminatory practices. To prevent this, it's important to carefully examine the dataset and ensure the algorithm promotes fairness and equity in its decisions.

- Ethical concerns: Bias in datasets can result in discriminatory outcomes, which raises ethical issues related to fairness and transparency.

Future investigations in Android malware detection have to solve several important issues to improve model performance, dependability, and fairness. First, since the success of ML models mostly depends on high-quality data, enhancing dataset quality and availability is absolutely vital. Inaccurate predictions result from current datasets sometimes including noise, imbalanced samples, or obsolete threats. While integrating automated data cleaning and augmentation techniques to improve data dependability, future work should concentrate on creating standardized, thorough, and always updated Android malware datasets. Second, improving model interpretability is still a major issue since many complex ML models, including deep neural networks, function as black boxes and their decision-making processes are challenging to grasp. Explainable artificial intelligence (XAI) methods should be investigated in future studies to increase openness so that cybersecurity professionals may validate, trust, and hone malware detection systems. Third, tackling overfitting in malware classification is crucial since models that show good performance on training data could not be able to extend to fresh, unmet hazards. To reduce overfitting and guarantee improved generalization, one should investigate advanced regularizing methods, adversarial training, and dynamic data augmentation. Fourth, lowering bias in Android malware datasets will help to prevent unfair model decisions and distorted results. Training data bias can cause models favoring some malware families to overlook others, so compromising the detection accuracy. To guarantee fair malware detection, future studies should look at bias reducing techniques including rebalancing datasets, adversarial debiasing, and justice-aware learning algorithms. Lastly, ethical issues in malware detection have to be given top priority since biassed models can generate discriminating results, so posing questions regarding justice, responsibility, and openness. Future studies should create ethical artificial intelligence models that support objective algorithm development, conscientious dataset collecting, and regulatory standard compliance including GDPR and CCPA. Future developments in Android malware detection might result in more accurate, interpretable, fair, and ethically responsible ML-based security systems by tackling these challenges.

Moreover, the integration of extra security measures and machine learning-based malware detection is required to fight ever complicated risks as the Android ecosystem expands. Signature-based detection systems fail against polymorphic and evolving malware, thus hybrid security systems including behavioral analysis, anomaly detection, and real-time threat monitoring are required. Future security systems should leverage group knowledge-sharing on new hazards across distributed devices and cloud-based threat intelligence for rapid updates. Zero-trust security models increase system integrity and lower insider threats by always verifying device security and tracking application behavior. Another intriguing route is federated learning in Android malware detection, which lets models learn from distributed datasets while preserving user privacy. Against rootkits and kernel-level attacks, hardware-based security systems including trusted execution environments (TEEs) and secure enclaves can help even more. Future security solutions must be adaptive, artificial intelligence-driven, and real-time threat mitigating to protect personal users and corporate networks given the growing complexity of Android malware.

11. CONCLUSION

In this chapter, we discuss machine learning approaches, applications, and challenges in the Android malware detection process. We demonstrate the benchmark Android malware datasets and their details. The feature categories were highlighted, including static, dynamic, hybrid, semantic, and metadata. Furthermore, supervised and unsupervised ML-approaches were explained in terms of the detection steps. Three of effective ML-based techniques are demonstrated, including ensemble, reinforcement, and hybrid. Ensemble ML-based techniques showed better performance than classic ML-based approaches. In addition, reinforcement learning represents a promising approach for enhancing Android malware detection systems. Its ability to adapt to new, unseen threats and continuously learn from interactions with the environment provides a level of flexibility and robustness that traditional methods lack. While challenges remain in terms of reward function design and the exploration-exploitation tradeoff, advancements in RL algorithms and their integration with other ML techniques offer exciting opportunities for the future of autonomous Android malware defense. By harnessing the power of RL, researchers and practitioners can develop more effective and resilient systems to combat the ever-evolving landscape of Android malware. Hybrid ML approaches for Android malware detection represent a promising direction in the development of more accurate, efficient, and robust defense systems. By combining the strengths of different ML algorithms, these methods offer enhanced detection capabilities, reduce false positives, and improve the adaptability of detection models to emerging threats. As Android malware continues to evolve, hybrid models will play a crucial role in ensuring the security and integrity of mobile ecosystems.

REFERENCES

Akhtar, M. S., & Feng, T. (2022). Malware analysis and detection using machine learning algorithms. *Symmetry*, *14*(11), 2304. DOI: 10.3390/sym14112304

Akinshola-Awe, F. J., Obiniyi, A. A., Aimufua, G. I., & Anyachebelu, T. K. (2024). Framework for the detection and classification of malware using machine learning. *Dutse Journal of Pure and Applied Sciences*, *10*(3a), 177–186. DOI: 10.4314/dujopas.v10i3a.17

Al-Sawwa, J., Almseidin, M., Alkasassbeh, M., Alemerien, K., & Younisse, R. (2024). Spark-based multi-verse optimizer as wrapper features selection algorithm for phishing attack challenge. *Cluster Computing*, *27*(5), 1–16. DOI: 10.1007/s10586-024-04272-2

Alemerien, K. (2021). Usable Security and Privacy on Online Social Networks: Tools, Approaches, Studies, and Future Trends. [IJSI]. *International Journal of Software Innovation*, *9*(2), 35–68. DOI: 10.4018/IJSI.2021040103

Alemerien, K., Al-Suhemat, S., & Almahadin, M. (2024). Towards optimized machine-learning-driven intrusion detection for Internet of Things applications. *International Journal of Information Technology : an Official Journal of Bharati Vidyapeeth's Institute of Computer Applications and Management*, •••, 1–14.

Alemerien, K., Alsarayreh, S., & Altarawneh, E. (2024). Diagnosing Cardiovascular Diseases using Optimized Machine Learning Algorithms with GridSearchCV. *Journal of Applied Data Sciences*, *5*(4), 1539–1552. DOI: 10.47738/jads.v5i4.280

Almomani, I., Almashat, T., & El-Shafai, W. (2024). Maloid-DS: Labeled Dataset for Android Malware Forensics. *IEEE Access : Practical Innovations, Open Solutions*, *12*, 73481–73546. DOI: 10.1109/ACCESS.2024.3400211

Almseidin, M., Al-Sawwa, J., Alkasassbeh, M., Alzubi, M., & Alrfou, K. (2024). DT-ARO: Decision tree-based artificial rabbits optimization to mitigate IoT botnet exploitation. *Journal of Network and Systems Management*, *32*(1), 14.

Almseidin, M., Al-Sawwa, J., & Alkasassbeh, M. (2022). Generating a benchmark cyber multi-step attacks dataset for intrusion detection. *Journal of Intelligent & Fuzzy Systems*, *43*(3), 3679–3694. DOI: 10.3233/JIFS-213247

AlOmari, H., Yaseen, Q. M., & Al-Betar, M. A. (2023). A comparative analysis of machine learning algorithms for android malware detection. *Procedia Computer Science*, *220*, 763–768. DOI: 10.1016/j.procs.2023.03.101

Alsharif, E., & Alharby, M. (2025). An Ensemble Machine Learning Approach for Detecting and Classifying Malware Attacks on Mobile Devices. *Arabian Journal for Science and Engineering*. Advance online publication. DOI: 10.1007/s13369-025-10011-5

Amadeo, R. (March 7, 2022). "Android 12L is official as "Android 12.1," rolling out now to Pixel phones". Ars Technica. Archived from the original on March 7, 2022. Retrieved January 27, 2025.

Lashkari, A. H., Kadir, A. F. A., Gonzalez, H., Mbah, K. F., & Ghorbani, A. A. (2017, August). Towards a network-based framework for android malware detection and characterization. In 2017 15th Annual conference on privacy, security and trust (PST) (pp. 233-23309). IEEE.

Lashkari, A. H., Kadir, A. F. A., Taheri, L., & Ghorbani, A. A. (2018, October). Toward developing a systematic approach to generate benchmark android malware datasets and classification. In 2018 International Carnahan conference on security technology (ICCST) (pp. 1-7). ieee.

Arizal, A. F. A., Md-Arshad, M., Abdul-Samad, A., Sirat, M. M., & Othman, S. H. (2024). Performance Comparative Study on Zero Day Malware Detection Using XGBoost and Random Forest Classifiers. *International Journal of Innovative Computing, 14*(2), 33–40. DOI: 10.11113/ijic.v14n2.449

Arora, A.. "Hybrid Android malware detection by combining supervised and unsupervised learning." *Proceedings of the 24th Annual International Conference on Mobile Computing and Networking*. 2018. DOI: 10.1145/3241539.3267768

Arp, D., Spreitzenbarth, M., Hubner, M., Gascon, H., Rieck, K., & Siemens, C. E. R. T. (2014, February). Drebin: Effective and explainable detection of android malware in your pocket. In Ndss (Vol. 14, pp. 23-26).

Arulkumaran, K., Deisenroth, M. P., Brundage, M., & Bharath, A. A. (2017). Deep reinforcement learning: A brief survey. *IEEE Signal Processing Magazine, 34*(6), 26–38. DOI: 10.1109/MSP.2017.2743240

Azeem, M., Khan, D., Iftikhar, S., Bawazeer, S., & Alzahrani, M. (2024). Analyzing and comparing the effectiveness of malware detection: A study of machine learning approaches. *Heliyon, 10*(1), e23574. DOI: 10.1016/j.heliyon.2023.e23574 PMID: 38187275

Batouche, A., & Jahankhani, H. (2021). A comprehensive approach to android malware detection using machine learning. Information Security Technologies for Controlling Pandemics, 171-212.

Boppiniti, S. T. (2021). Evolution of Reinforcement Learning: From Q-Learning to Deep. Available at *SSRN* 5061696.

Borah, P., Bhattacharyya, D. K., & Kalita, J. K. (2020, December). Malware dataset generation and evaluation. In 2020 IEEE 4th Conference on Information & Communication Technology (CICT) (pp. 1-6). IEEE.

Bradshaw, K. (April 22, 2022). "Android 14 gets official internal codename… Upside Down Cake". 9to5Google. Archived from the original on January 14, 2024. Retrieved January 27, 2025.

Canfora, G., Medvet, E., Mercaldo, F., & Visaggio, C. A. (2015, August). Detecting android malware using sequences of system calls. In *Proceedings of the 3rd international workshop on software development lifecycle for mobile* (pp. 13-20). DOI: 10.1145/2804345.2804349

Cantisano, T. (March 3, 2023). "Android 15 dessert-themed codename revealed as 'Vanilla Ice Cream'". XDA Developers. Retrieved January 27, 2025.

Carnegie Mellon University CyLab. (2021). Towards Autonomous Cybersecurity Systems: The Role of AI in Continuous Threat Monitoring.

Chakraborty, S. https://www.kaggle.com/datasets/subhajournal/android-malware-detection, Retrieved January 27, 2025.

Chandrashekar, C., Dhamale, A. K., & IR, P. J. (2023, July). Machine Learning Based Malicious URL, IP & File Classification. In 2023 14th International Conference on Computing Communication and Networking Technologies (ICCCNT) (pp. 1-8). IEEE.

Cook, T. (2022). The Role of Machine Learning in Autonomous Cybersecurity: A Review. *Journal of Cybersecurity Research*, *5*(3), 45–59.

Dahiya, A., Singh, S., & Shrivastava, G. (2025). Android malware analysis and detection: A systematic review. *Expert Systems: International Journal of Knowledge Engineering and Neural Networks*, *42*(1), e13488. DOI: 10.1111/exsy.13488

Damaševičius, R., Venčkauskas, A., Toldinas, J., & Grigaliūnas, Š. (2021). Ensemble-based classification using neural networks and machine learning models for windows pe malware detection. *Electronics (Basel)*, *10*(4), 485. DOI: 10.3390/electronics10040485

Keyes, D. S., Li, B., Kaur, G., Lashkari, A. H., Gagnon, F., & Massicotte, F. (2021, May). EntropLyzer: Android malware classification and characterization using entropy analysis of dynamic characteristics. In 2021 Reconciling Data Analytics, Automation, Privacy, and Security: A Big Data Challenge (RDAAPS) (pp. 1-12). IEEE.

Drolet, M. A. T. H. I. E. U., & Roberge, V. (2022). Enterprise Malware Detection using Digital Forensic Artifacts and Machine Learning. MA Sc. Thesis, Royal Military College of Canada, Kingston, Ontario.

Elgin, B. (2005). "Google Buys Android for Its Mobile Arsenal". Bloomberg Businessweek. Bloomberg. Archived from the original on February 27, 2011. Retrieved January 27, 2025.

Fedewa, J. (January 12, 2023). "What's the Latest Version of Android?". How-To Geek. Retrieved January 27, 2025.

Felt, A. P., Ha, E., Egelman, S., Haney, A., Chin, E., & Wagner, D. (2012). "Android Permissions: User Attention, Comprehension, and Behavior." *Proceedings of the Eighth Symposium on Usable Privacy and Security (SOUPS)*, 3(1), 1-14. DOI: 10.1145/2335356.2335360

Getastra. (2025). 30+ Malware Statistics You Need To Know In 2025, https://www.getastra.com/blog/security-audit/malware-statistics/#Malware_Statistics_2024, Retrieved *January* 27, 2025.

Ippolito, M., Ferguson, J., & Jenson, F. (2021). Improving facies prediction by combining supervised and unsupervised learning methods. *Journal of Petroleum Science Engineering*, *200*, 108300. DOI: 10.1016/j.petrol.2020.108300

Iqubal, A.. "Android Based Malware Detection Technique Using Machine Learning Algorithms." *2024 First International Conference on Pioneering Developments in Computer Science & Digital Technologies (IC2SDT)*. IEEE, 2024. DOI: 10.1109/IC2SDT62152.2024.10696330

Islam, R., Sayed, M. I., Saha, S., Hossain, M. J., & Masud, M. A. (2023). Android malware classification using optimum feature selection and ensemble machine learning. *Internet of Things and Cyber-Physical Systems*, *3*, 100–111. DOI: 10.1016/j.iotcps.2023.03.001

Jang, B., Kim, M., Harerimana, G., & Kim, J. W. (2019). Q-learning algorithms: A comprehensive classification and applications. *IEEE Access : Practical Innovations, Open Solutions*, *7*, 133653–133667. DOI: 10.1109/ACCESS.2019.2941229

Kadir, A., & Peddoju, S. K. (2024). PacDroid: Lightweight android malware detection using permissions and intent features. *Multimedia Tools and Applications*, •••, 1–29. DOI: 10.1007/s11042-024-20455-w

Kaspersky. (2024). IT threat evolution in Q1 2024. Mobile statistics, https://securelist.com/it-threat-evolution-q1-2024-mobile-statistics/112750/? Retrieved January 27, 2025.

Kouliaridis, V., & Kambourakis, G. (2021). A comprehensive survey on machine learning techniques for android malware detection. *Information (Basel)*, *12*(5), 185. DOI: 10.3390/info12050185

Kouliaridis, V., Potha, N., & Kambourakis, G. (2020, November). Improving android malware detection through dimensionality reduction techniques. In *International conference on machine learning for networking* (pp. 57-72). Cham: Springer International Publishing.

Kumar, S., Mishra, D., Panda, B., & Shukla, S. K. (2022, May). AndroOBFS: time-tagged obfuscated Android malware dataset with family information. In *Proceedings of the 19th International Conference on Mining Software Repositories* (pp. 454-458). DOI: 10.1145/3524842.3528493

Li, H.. "MalCertain: Enhancing Deep Neural Network Based Android Malware Detection by Tackling Prediction Uncertainty." *Proceedings of the IEEE/ACM 46th International Conference on Software Engineering*. 2024. DOI: 10.1145/3597503.3639122

Li, Y., Xu, G., Xian, H., Rao, L., & Shi, J. (2019). Novel Android Malware Detection Method Based on Multi-dimensional Hybrid Features Extraction and Analysis. *Intelligent Automation & Soft Computing*, *25*(3), 637–647. DOI: 10.31209/2019.100000118

Liang, Z., Wang, C., Duan, Z., Liu, H., Liu, X., & Ullah Jan Khan, K. (2021). A hybrid model consisting of supervised and unsupervised learning for landslide susceptibility mapping. *Remote Sensing (Basel)*, *13*(8), 1464. DOI: 10.3390/rs13081464

Liu, Y., Tantithamthavorn, C., Li, L., & Liu, Y. (2022). Deep learning for android malware defenses: A systematic literature review. *ACM Computing Surveys*, *55*(8), 1–36.

Liu, Z., Wang, R., Japkowicz, N., Tang, D., Zhang, W., & Zhao, J. (2021). Research on unsupervised feature learning for android malware detection based on restricted Boltzmann machines. *Future Generation Computer Systems*, *120*, 91–108. DOI: 10.1016/j.future.2021.02.015

Liu, Z., Wang, R., Japkowicz, N., Tang, D., Zhang, W., & Zhao, J. (2021). Research on unsupervised feature learning for android malware detection based on restricted Boltzmann machines. *Future Generation Computer Systems*, *120*, 91–108. DOI: 10.1016/j.future.2021.02.015

Lu, T., Du, Y., Ouyang, L., Chen, Q., & Wang, X. (2020). Android malware detection based on a hybrid deep learning model. *Security and Communication Networks*, *2020*(1), 8863617. DOI: 10.1155/2020/8863617

Mahdavifar, S., Alhadidi, D., & Ghorbani, A. A. (2022). Effective and efficient hybrid android malware classification using pseudo-label stacked auto-encoder. *Journal of Network and Systems Management*, *30*(1), 22. DOI: 10.1007/s10922-021-09634-4

Mahdavifar, S., Kadir, A. F. A., Fatemi, R., Alhadidi, D., & Ghorbani, A. A. (2020, August). Dynamic android malware category classification using semi-supervised deep learning. In 2020 IEEE Intl Conf on Dependable, Autonomic and Secure Computing, Intl Conf on Pervasive Intelligence and Computing, Intl Conf on Cloud and Big Data Computing, Intl Conf on Cyber Science and Technology Congress (DASC/PiCom/CBDCom/CyberSciTech) (pp. 515-522). IEEE.

Malhotra, A., & Bajaj, K. (2016). A hybrid pattern based text mining approach for malware detection using DBScan. *CSI transactions on ICT, 4*, 141-149.

Maniriho, P., Mahmood, A. N., & Chowdhury, M. J. M. (2024). A survey of recent advances in deep learning models for detecting malware in desktop and mobile platforms. *ACM Computing Surveys*, *56*(6), 1–41. DOI: 10.1145/3638240

Manju, & Rana, C. (2024). Application of Deep Reinforcement Learning in Adversarial Malware Detection. *Deep Reinforcement Learning and Its Industrial Use Cases: AI for Real-World Applications*, 91-113.

Mantoo, B. A., & Khurana, S. S. (2020). Static, dynamic and intrinsic features based android malware detection using machine learning. In *Proceedings of ICRIC 2019: Recent Innovations in Computing* (pp. 31-45). Springer International Publishing. DOI: 10.1007/978-3-030-29407-6_4

Martinelli, F., Marulli, F., & Mercaldo, F. (2017). Evaluating convolutional neural network for effective mobile malware detection. *Procedia Computer Science*, *112*, 2372–2381. DOI: 10.1016/j.procs.2017.08.216

Mashaleh, A. S., Ibrahim, N. F. B., Alauthman, M., Almseidin, M., & Gawanmeh, A. (2024). IoT Smart Devices Risk Assessment Model Using Fuzzy Logic and PSO. *Computers, Materials & Continua*, *78*(2), 2. DOI: 10.32604/cmc.2023.047323

Morán, P., Robles-Gómez, A., Duque, A., Tobarra, L., & Pastor-Vargas, R. (2024). Machine learning models and dimensionality reduction for improving the Android malware detection. *PeerJ. Computer Science*, *10*, e2616. DOI: 10.7717/peerj-cs.2616 PMID: 39896377

Mythily, V., Sukumar, P., Akshaya, V., Dinesh, S., & Nandhini, M. (2025). Malware detection and prevention using machine learning. In Challenges in Information, Communication and Computing Technology (pp. 564-569). CRC Press.

Nguyen, T. T., & Reddi, V. J. (2021). Deep reinforcement learning for cyber security. *IEEE Transactions on Neural Networks and Learning Systems*, *34*(8), 3779–3795. DOI: 10.1109/TNNLS.2021.3121870 PMID: 34723814

Padmavathi, G., Shanmugapriya, D., & Roshni, A. (2022, March). Performance analysis of unsupervised machine learning methods for mobile malware detection. In *2022 9th International Conference on Computing for Sustainable Development (INDIACom)* (pp. 201-206). IEEE.

Pan, Y., Ge, X., Fang, C., & Fan, Y. (2020). A systematic literature review of android malware detection using static analysis. *IEEE Access : Practical Innovations, Open Solutions*, *8*, 116363–116379. DOI: 10.1109/ACCESS.2020.3002842

Rabbani, M., Wang, Y., Khoshkangini, R., Jelodar, H., Zhao, R., Bagheri Baba Ahmadi, S., & Ayobi, S. (2021). A review on machine learning approaches for network malicious behavior detection in emerging technologies. *Entropy (Basel, Switzerland)*, *23*(5), 529. DOI: 10.3390/e23050529 PMID: 33923125

Raval, A., & Anwar, M. “Android Malware Detection: An Empirical Investigation into Machine Learning Classifiers.” *2024 IEEE International Conference on Information Reuse and Integration for Data Science (IRI)*. IEEE, 2024. DOI: 10.1109/IRI62200.2024.00039

Raval, A., & Anwar, M. (2024, August). Android Malware Detection: An Empirical Investigation into Machine Learning Classifiers. In *2024 IEEE International Conference on Information Reuse and Integration for Data Science (IRI)* (pp. 144-149). IEEE. DOI: 10.1109/IRI62200.2024.00039

Raymond, V. J., & Raj, R. (2023). Investigation of Android Malware with Machine Learning Classifiers using Enhanced PCA Algorithm. *Computer Systems Science and Engineering*, *44*(3).

Razaque, A., Bektemyssova, G., Yoo, J., Hariri, S., Khan, M. J., Nalgozhina, N., Hwang, J., & Khan, M. A. (2025). Review of malicious code detection in data mining applications: Challenges, algorithms, and future direction. *Cluster Computing*, *28*(3), 1–37. DOI: 10.1007/s10586-024-05017-x

Rodrigo, C., Pierre, S., Beaubrun, R., & El Khoury, F. (2021). BrainShield: A hybrid machine learning-based malware detection model for android devices. *Electronics (Basel)*, *10*(23), 2948. DOI: 10.3390/electronics10232948

Samra, A. A. A., Yim, K., & Ghanem, O. A. (2013, July). Analysis of clustering technique in android malware detection. In *2013 seventh international conference on innovative mobile and internet services in ubiquitous computing* (pp. 729-733). IEEE.

Sebastianelli, A., Tipaldi, M., Ullo, S. L., & Glielmo, L. (2021, June). A Deep Q-Learning based approach applied to the Snake game. In 2021 29th Mediterranean Conference on Control and Automation (MED) (pp. 348-353). IEEE.

Senanayake, J., Kalutarage, H., & Al-Kadri, M. O. (2021). Android mobile malware detection using machine learning: A systematic review. *Electronics (Basel)*, *10*(13), 1606. DOI: 10.3390/electronics10131606

Sewak, M., Sahay, S. K., & Rathore, H. (2023). Deep reinforcement learning in the advanced cybersecurity threat detection and protection. *Information Systems Frontiers*, *25*(2), 589–611.

Shafin, S. S., Ahmed, M. M., Pranto, M. A., & Chowdhury, A. (2021, December). Detection of android malware using tree-based ensemble stacking model. In *2021 IEEE Asia-Pacific Conference on Computer Science and Data Engineering (CSDE)* (pp. 1-6). IEEE. DOI: 10.1109/CSDE53843.2021.9718396

Shankar, G., Sridhar, S., Srivatsan, G., & Kishan, R., & SS, P. V. (2024, July). Enhancing Android Malware Detection Through Machine Learning: Insights From Permission and Metadata Analysis. In *2024 Third International Conference on Smart Technologies and Systems for Next Generation Computing (ICSTSN)* (pp. 1-6). IEEE.

Sharma, S., Krishna, C. R., & Kumar, R. (2021). RansomDroid: Forensic analysis and detection of Android Ransomware using unsupervised machine learning technique. *Forensic Science International Digital Investigation*, *37*, 301168. DOI: 10.1016/j.fsidi.2021.301168

Shatnawi, A. S., Jaradat, A., Yaseen, T. B., Taqieddin, E., Al-Ayyoub, M., & Mustafa, D. (2022). An android malware detection leveraging machine learning. *Wireless Communications and Mobile Computing*, *2022*(1), 1830201. DOI: 10.1155/2022/1830201

Sonya, A., & Deepak, R. R. (2024). Android malware detection and classification using machine learning algorithm. *International Journal of Communication Networks and Information Security, 16*(4), 327–347.

Statcounter. (2025). Mobile Operating System Market Share Worldwide, https://gs.statcounter.com/os-market-share/mobile/worldwide? Retrieved January 27, 2025.

Thakur, P., Kansal, V., & Rishiwal, V. (2024). Hybrid deep learning approach based on lstm and cnn for malware detection. *Wireless Personal Communications, 136*(3), 1879–1901. DOI: 10.1007/s11277-024-11366-y

Wang, F., Chai, G., Li, Q., & Wang, C. (2022). An efficient deep unsupervised domain adaptation for unknown malware detection. *Symmetry, 14*(2), 296.

Wu, Y., Li, M., Zeng, Q., Yang, T., Wang, J., Fang, Z., & Cheng, L. (2023). DroidRL: Feature selection for android malware detection with reinforcement learning. *Computers & Security, 128*, 103126. DOI: 10.1016/j.cose.2023.103126

Xiong, T., Ma, Z., Li, Z., & Dai, J. (2022). The analysis of influence mechanism for internet financial fraud identification and user behavior based on machine learning approaches. *International Journal of System Assurance Engineering and Management, 13*(S3, Suppl 3), 996–1007. DOI: 10.1007/s13198-021-01181-0

Yasin, H. N., Hamid, S. H. A., & Raja Yusof, R. J. (2021). Droidbotx: Test case generation tool for android applications using Q-learning. *Symmetry, 13*(2), 310. DOI: 10.3390/sym13020310

Yerima, S. Y., & Sezer, S. (2018). Droidfusion: A novel multilevel classifier fusion approach for android malware detection. *IEEE Transactions on Cybernetics, 49*(2), 453–466. DOI: 10.1109/TCYB.2017.2777960 PMID: 29993965

Younisse, R.. (2023). An early detection model for kerberoasting attacks and dataset labeling. *Jordanian Journal of Computers and Information Technology, 9*, 1.

Zhang, S., Su, H., Liu, H., & Yang, W. (2025). MPDroid: A multimodal pre-training Android malware detection method with static and dynamic features. *Computers & Security, 150*, 104262. DOI: 10.1016/j.cose.2024.104262

Zhou, S., Li, H., Fu, X., & Jiao, Y. (2024). A Novel Malware Detection Model in the Software Supply Chain Based on LSTM and SVMs. *Applied Sciences (Basel, Switzerland), 14*(15), 6678.

Zhou, Y., & Jiang, X. (2012, May). Dissecting android malware: Characterization and evolution. In 2012 IEEE symposium on security and privacy (pp. 95-109). IEEE.

Chapter 13
AI-Driven Cybersecurity for Telemedicine:
Enhancing Protection Through Autonomous Defense Systems

Mutaz Abdel Wahed
https://orcid.org/0000-0002-4361-6185
Jadara University, Jordan

Salma Abdel Wahed
Hashemite University, Jordan

Abed Elkareem Alzoubi
Petra University, Jordan

ABSTRACT

AI-driven solutions utilize machine learning, behavioral analysis, and autonomous defense systems to identify and mitigate risks more effectively than conventional methods. These systems continuously adapt to evolving threats, ensuring proactive and dynamic defense mechanisms. Additionally, integrating blockchain technology enhances data security through immutable records and secure transactions. Despite its benefits, AI-driven cybersecurity raises ethical and regulatory concerns, including data privacy issues, algorithmic bias, and adversarial AI attacks. Striking a balance between automation and human oversight is vital to uphold ethical standards and regulatory compliance. This chapter examines the role of AI-driven cybersecurity in telemedicine, exploring its capabilities, challenges, and future trends. By harnessing AI and blockchain, healthcare organizations can develop robust cybersecurity frameworks that safeguard patient data, ensure system reliability, and maintain trust in digital healthcare services.

DOI: 10.4018/979-8-3373-0954-5.ch013

1. INTRODUCTION

The rapid digitization of healthcare has ushered in a new era of accessibility, efficiency, and innovation. Telemedicine, once a niche solution for remote patients, has become a cornerstone of modern healthcare delivery, offering virtual consultations, remote diagnostics, and continuous patient monitoring (Su et al., 2024). However, as healthcare increasingly relies on digital infrastructure, it also faces an unprecedented surge in cybersecurity threats. The same connectivity that enables seamless communication between patients and providers also creates vulnerabilities that cybercriminals exploit. The sensitive nature of medical data, coupled with the high stakes of healthcare operations, makes telemedicine a prime target for cyberattacks. Cybersecurity incidents in the healthcare sector have grown in both frequency and sophistication, ranging from ransomware attacks that cripple hospital systems to data breaches exposing millions of patient records (Jalali et al., 2019). Such breaches can have devastating consequences, financial and reputational damage for healthcare organizations, as well as direct harm to patients when care is disrupted. The evolving nature of cyber threats demands a security framework that is not only reactive but also proactive, capable of identifying and mitigating risks in real time (Wahed, 2024). Traditional cybersecurity measures, such as firewalls, encryption, and manual monitoring, are no longer sufficient to combat the ever-changing landscape of cyber threats. AI has emerged as a powerful tool in the fight against cybercrime, offering new ways to detect, analyze, and respond to security threats with unprecedented speed and accuracy (Velasco, 2022). By leveraging machine learning, predictive analytics, and automated defense mechanisms, AI-driven cybersecurity solutions can continuously learn from emerging threats, adapting to new attack strategies more efficiently than traditional systems. In the context of telemedicine, AI-powered cybersecurity is not just an enhancement, but it is a necessity (Nobili et al., 2025). The vast amounts of sensitive data exchanged across telehealth platforms require an intelligent, autonomous defense system capable of safeguarding patient privacy, securing digital interactions, and ensuring uninterrupted medical services. The integration of AI into cybersecurity has given rise to autonomous defense systems that monitor networks, detect anomalies, and respond to cyber threats without human intervention (Camacho, 2024). AI-driven cybersecurity enhances healthcare protection by using behavioral analysis and real-time threat detection to preempt risks. Machine learning identifies anomalies in network traffic, while predictive analytics detects vulnerabilities. In telemedicine, where data volume is vast, AI improves security but poses ethical, technical, and regulatory challenges. Addressing data privacy, bias, and adversarial threats while maintaining human oversight is crucial for trust and compliance.

1.1 Overview of AI Techniques and Blockchain Mechanisms

AI and blockchain enhance telemedicine cybersecurity by enabling real-time threat detection, predictive analytics, and automated responses while ensuring data integrity and compliance. Their integration strengthens security, protects patient data, and enhances trust. This chapter explores how these technologies transform telemedicine cybersecurity for safer, more reliable digital healthcare solutions.

1.1.1 AI Techniques

AI encompasses a range of technologies that enable machines to perform tasks requiring human-like intelligence. In telemedicine cybersecurity, the following AI techniques are particularly impactful:

- **Federated Learning:** Federated learning is a decentralized approach to machine learning where multiple devices or servers collaboratively train a shared model without sharing raw data. This technique enhances privacy by keeping sensitive data, such as patient records, on local devices. For example, hospitals can jointly improve a diagnostic AI model without exposing individual patient data.
- **Homomorphic Encryption:** Homomorphic encryption allows computations to be performed on encrypted data without decrypting it first. This ensures data privacy during processing, making it ideal for handling sensitive health information. For instance, a cloud-based AI system can analyze encrypted patient data to detect anomalies without ever accessing the raw data.
- **Behavioral Analysis:** Behavioral analysis involves AI systems that monitor and analyze user behavior to detect anomalies or potential threats. This technique is crucial for identifying suspicious activities, such as unauthorized access or ransomware attacks, in real-time. For example, it can detect unusual login patterns that may indicate a cyberattack on a telemedicine platform.
- **Predictive Analytics:** Predictive analytics uses AI models to analyze historical data and predict future events or trends. This enables proactive threat detection and resource allocation in cybersecurity. For instance, it can predict potential data breaches based on past attack patterns.
- **Automated Incident Response:** Automated incident response systems use AI to detect and respond to cyber threats without human intervention. This reduces response times and minimizes damage from cyberattacks. For example, an AI system can automatically isolate a compromised device in a telemedicine network to prevent malware spread.

1.1.2 Blockchain Mechanisms

Blockchain is a decentralized, distributed ledger technology that ensures transparency, security, and immutability of data. In telemedicine cybersecurity, blockchain addresses critical challenges like data integrity, access control, and fraud prevention. Key mechanisms include:

- **Decentralized Data Storage:** Data is stored across a network of nodes rather than a central server, reducing the risk of single-point failures and data breaches. For example, patient records stored on a blockchain are less vulnerable to ransomware attacks.
- **Immutable Ledger:** Once data is recorded on the blockchain, it cannot be altered or deleted. This ensures data integrity and prevents tampering with sensitive health information. For instance, a blockchain-based system logs all access to patient data, creating an auditable trail.
- **Smart Contracts:** Smart contracts are self-executing contracts with predefined rules encoded on the blockchain. They automate processes like access control and payment verification, reducing human error and fraud. For example, a smart contract could automatically grant a doctor access to patient records only after verifying their credentials.
- **Decentralized Identity Management:** Decentralized identity management allows users to control their digital identities without relying on a central authority. This enhances privacy and security by reducing reliance on centralized identity providers. For instance, patients can use blockchain-based identities to securely access telemedicine services.
- **Consensus Mechanisms:** Consensus mechanisms, such as Proof of Work or Proof of Stake, ensure that all nodes in a blockchain network agree on the validity of transactions. This prevents fraudulent activities and ensures the integrity of the network. For example, a blockchain network using Proof of Stake can securely validate access requests to telemedicine platforms.

1.2 Real-World Applications of AI and Blockchain in Telemedicine Cybersecurity

To enhance telemedicine cybersecurity by protecting patient data, improving efficiency, and ensuring compliance. This section presents case studies showcasing their successful implementation, demonstrating how organizations mitigate cyber threats, ensure data integrity, and build trust in digital healthcare systems through these transformative technologies. Table 1 summarizes key case studies, showcasing the technologies used, their specific applications, and the outcomes achieved, which provide valuable insights into how AI and blockchain can be effectively deployed to secure telemedicine platforms and protect patient data.

Table 1. Case studies of AI and blockchain in telemedicine cybersecurity

Use Case	Technology	Application	Outcome
Teladoc Health (Uscher-Pines & Mehrotra, 2014)	AI (Machine Learning)	Real-time threat detection and behavioral analysis to identify suspicious activities.	Reduced unauthorized access and data breaches by 30% within the first year of implementation.
Medicalchain (Jamil et al., 2019)	Blockchain	Secure storage and sharing of patient records using decentralized identity management.	Ensured data immutability and restricted access to authorized providers, enhancing patient trust.
Protenus (Arefin & Simcox, 2024)	AI + Blockchain	Monitoring access to electronic health records (EHRs) and detecting anomalies.	Improved HIPAA compliance and reduced insider threats by 40% through automated anomaly detection.
Hashed Health (Lee et al., 2018)	Blockchain	Development of blockchain-based solutions for healthcare data interoperability.	Streamlined data sharing across healthcare providers while maintaining security and compliance.
CureMatch (Adashek & Kurzrock, 2023)	AI (Predictive Analytics)	AI-driven analysis of patient data to recommend personalized treatment plans.	Enhanced data security and privacy while improving treatment outcomes through predictive insights.

1.3 The Rise of Telemedicine and Its Cybersecurity Challenges

The global healthcare landscape has undergone a dramatic transformation with the widespread adoption of telemedicine. Enabled by rapid advancements in digital technology, telemedicine has revolutionized healthcare delivery, improving accessibility, reducing costs, and enhancing patient outcomes. However, this innovation has also introduced significant cybersecurity vulnerabilities (Park et al., 2018). As patient data is transmitted across digital networks, telemedicine platforms have become prime targets for cybercriminals seeking to exploit security gaps for financial gain, identity theft, or sabotage.

Telemedicine faces severe cybersecurity threats, including ransomware, phishing, insider risks, and unsecured Internet of Medical Things (IoMT) devices. These attacks disrupt care, compromise privacy, and cause financial losses. Strong cybersecurity measures are essential to safeguard patient data, ensure system reliability, and maintain trust in digital healthcare.

Traditional security measures, such as firewalls, antivirus software, and manual threat monitoring, are increasingly inadequate against the evolving tactics of cybercriminals (Okolie, 2022). AI-driven cybersecurity strengthens telemedicine by using machine learning, predictive analytics, and automated threat detection to counter cyber threats in real time. As telemedicine grows, AI integration is crucial for securing digital healthcare.

1.4 The Role of Artificial Intelligence in Cybersecurity

AI has transformed cybersecurity by leveraging machine learning, deep learning, natural language processing (NLP), and advanced analytics to detect and mitigate threats in real time. Unlike traditional rule-based methods, AI continuously learns, enabling adaptive and proactive defense with minimal human intervention. These systems leverage sophisticated algorithms to detect anomalous behaviors, recognize malicious patterns, and neutralize potential attacks before they can inflict damage (Feng et al., 2022).

In the context of telemedicine, AI-powered cybersecurity is critical in safeguarding patient records, securing remote consultations, and ensuring the integrity of medical devices connected to telehealth networks. With the growing reliance on telemedicine, AI's role in enhancing cybersecurity is more important than ever. AI-driven threat intelligence solutions also provide organizations with predictive capabilities, helping them forecast cyber threats before they materialize (Mallikarjunaradhya et al., 2023). By analyzing historical attack data and monitoring network activity in real time, AI models can identify potential vulnerabilities and recommend proactive preventive measures. This ability to predict and prevent cyber threats is especially valuable in telemedicine, where healthcare providers must secure sensitive patient data and stay ahead of evolving cyber risks.

1.5 Autonomous Defense Systems: A Paradigm Shift in Cybersecurity

AI-powered defense systems enhance cybersecurity by autonomously detecting and mitigating threats in real time. Using reinforcement learning, they improve accuracy, reduce false positives, and strengthen resilience. In telemedicine, they secure patient-doctor interactions, prevent unauthorized access, and ease the burden on cybersecurity teams. By ensuring the integrity of telehealth networks and medical devices, autonomous AI-powered cybersecurity solutions provide healthcare providers with the confidence to deliver secure, uninterrupted care to patients (Alnajim et al., 2023).

1.6 AI-Powered Threat Detection and Response in Telemedicine

AI revolutionizes cybersecurity by using machine learning, behavioral analytics, and anomaly detection to identify threats in real time. Unlike rule-based systems, AI adapts to evolving attacks, improving accuracy and reducing false positives, strengthening overall security. These include:

1.6.1 Behavioral Analysis and Anomaly Detection

AI-driven cybersecurity uses behavioral analysis to detect anomalies in telemedicine, identifying unauthorized access, suspicious logins, and irregular data transfers. For example, AI can flag and block unusual login attempts from foreign locations, enhancing security. By continuously monitoring and analyzing user behavior, these systems provide an additional layer of security, ensuring that sensitive patient data and telehealth communications remain protected from potential cyber threats (Alshehri et al., 2023).

1.6.2 Threat Intelligence and Predictive Analytics

Machine learning algorithms analyze vast amounts of cybersecurity data to identify potential attack vectors before they can be exploited. AI-powered threat intelligence systems aggregate data from various sources, such as network logs, intrusion detection systems, and external cybersecurity databases, to predict and prevent cyberattacks in real time. By leveraging predictive analytics, these systems enable telemedicine providers to proactively enhance their security posture, addressing vulnerabilities before they are exploited. This proactive approach is critical in telemedicine, where safeguarding patient data and ensuring secure, uninterrupted healthcare services are paramount in the face of evolving cyber threats (Sarker et al., 2020).

1.6.3 Automated Incident Response

In the event of a cyberattack, AI-driven systems can automate incident response procedures, minimizing the damage caused by security breaches. For instance, if ransomware is detected within a telemedicine network, an autonomous cybersecurity system can isolate the affected devices, block malicious processes, and alert security teams in real time. This rapid response capability is crucial in preventing widespread disruptions to telehealth services (Maddireddy & Maddireddy, 2023).

1.6.4 The Risk of Adversarial Attacks

Cybercriminals are constantly developing new methods to evade AI-based security systems. One emerging concern is adversarial machine learning, in which attackers manipulate AI models by introducing deceptive data patterns. For instance, an attacker might craft malicious code that appears benign to an AI system, bypassing detection mechanisms. To counteract adversarial attacks, cybersecurity teams must implement robust adversarial training techniques and develop AI models that can adapt to evolving attack strategies (Sabillon et al., 2016).

1.6.5 The Balance Between Automation and Human Oversight

While autonomous defense systems enhance cybersecurity efficiency, they should not replace human expertise entirely. AI systems must be designed to complement human decision-making rather than operate in isolation. Cybersecurity teams should retain control over critical security decisions, ensuring that AI-driven actions align with organizational policies and ethical considerations (Reis et al., 2021).

1.7 The Future of AI-Driven Cybersecurity in Telemedicine

As telemedicine continues to expand, the role of AI in cybersecurity will become increasingly vital. Future developments in AI-driven cybersecurity are expected to focus on:

- Advanced Threat Intelligence: AI-powered cybersecurity solutions will incorporate more sophisticated threat intelligence capabilities, enabling organizations to predict cyberattacks with higher accuracy (Samtani et al., 2020).
- Federated Learning for Privacy-Preserving AI: To enhance data privacy, federated learning techniques will allow AI models to be trained across multiple decentralized systems without exposing sensitive patient data (Chen et al., 2024).
- Explainable AI (XAI) in Cybersecurity: Efforts to improve transparency in AI-driven cybersecurity will lead to the development of explainable AI models, allowing security professionals to understand and validate AI-driven threat assessments (Kuppa & Le-Khac, 2020).
- Integration with Blockchain for Secure Transactions: AI and blockchain technologies may be combined to enhance the security of telemedicine transactions, ensuring data integrity and reducing the risk of fraud (Khan & Byun, 2021).

2. BACKGROUND

2.1 The Evolution of Telemedicine

Telemedicine has transformed healthcare by expanding access to medical services. While its origins trace back to early radio-based consultations, the internet and digital technologies fueled its growth. Today, it includes virtual consultations, remote diagnostics, and digital health monitoring. The COVID-19 pandemic further accelerated its adoption, making virtual care essential (Bashshur et al., 2020).

Governments eased telehealth restrictions, enabling remote care, reducing hospital strain, and lowering costs. The pandemic showcased telemedicine's scalability and flexibility in delivering timely care. However, transmitting sensitive patient data over digital networks raises cybersecurity challenges, making strong protective measures essential to ensure privacy, security, and trust in digital healthcare.

Telemedicine platforms must ensure secure communication between patients and healthcare providers, protecting against unauthorized access, data breaches, and evolving cyber threats. The growing reliance on cloud-based services, AI, and IoMT has expanded the attack surface for cybercriminals (Ghubaish et al., 2020). As telemedicine continues to evolve, healthcare providers must prioritize cybersecurity to safeguard patient data and maintain trust. Ensuring secure and seamless digital healthcare delivery is essential to realizing the full potential of telemedicine in the future of healthcare.

2.2 The Growing Cybersecurity Threat Landscape in Healthcare

Healthcare is a prime target for cybercriminals due to the lasting value of medical data. Unlike financial information, health records are permanent and vulnerable to identity theft and fraud. With cyberattacks on the rise, attackers use sophisticated methods to breach medical systems, highlighting the need for stronger cybersecurity measures. Some of the most common cybersecurity threats in telemedicine include:

- Ransomware Attacks: Malicious software that encrypts healthcare data and demands a ransom for its release. These attacks have crippled hospitals and telehealth platforms, delaying critical patient care.
- Phishing Scams: Cybercriminals use deceptive emails or messages to trick healthcare employees into revealing login credentials, granting unauthorized access to sensitive systems.
- Man-in-the-Middle (MitM) Attacks: Hackers intercept communications between patients and doctors, compromising the confidentiality of medical consultations (Muzammil et al., 2024).

- IoMT Vulnerabilities: Medical devices connected to telehealth networks, such as wearable health monitors and remote diagnostic tools, can be exploited if not properly secured.
- Data Breaches and Insider Threats: Employees with access to patient records may intentionally or unintentionally expose confidential data, leading to compliance violations and reputational damage.

These cybersecurity risks highlight the urgent need for advanced security solutions that can protect telemedicine platforms while ensuring compliance with healthcare regulations such as HIPAA, GDPR, and other data protection laws.

2.3 The Role of Artificial Intelligence in Cybersecurity

AI is revolutionizing cybersecurity by enhancing threat detection, analysis, and response. Using machine learning, NLP, and predictive analytics, AI-driven solutions provide proactive protection against evolving threats. Its ability to process vast data, detect malicious patterns, and automate mitigation ensures faster, more efficient security measures (George, 2024). Table 2 highlights four key components of AI-based cybersecurity.

Table 2. Key AI techniques in cybersecurity for telemedicine

AI Technique	Description	Application in Telemedicine Cybersecurity
AI-Powered Threat Detection	AI systems analyze large datasets to identify patterns indicative of cyber threats. They use machine learning models to recognize anomalies that may signal an attack.	AI can detect unusual login attempts, unauthorized data access, or deviations in network activity that could indicate a breach, ensuring the security of telehealth platforms.
Predictive Analytics for Cybersecurity	AI models analyze past cyberattack data to predict future threats. By identifying trends and vulnerabilities, organizations can implement preventive measures.	Telemedicine platforms can proactively secure weak points in their networks before they are exploited, reducing the risk of data breaches and cyberattacks.
Automated Incident Response	AI-driven security systems can autonomously detect and respond to cyber threats in real time, minimizing the need for human intervention.	If a ransomware attack is detected, an AI system can automatically isolate affected devices, terminate malicious processes, and alert security teams, preventing disruptions to virtual healthcare services.
Behavioral Analysis and Anomaly Detection	AI analyzes user behavior and identifies deviations from normal activity that may indicate cyber threats.	If a healthcare provider's account exhibits unusual activity, such as accessing large volumes of patient data outside normal hours, AI can flag the behavior and trigger security measures.

Integrating AI into cybersecurity enhances telemedicine defense against advanced threats. AI-driven solutions proactively protect patient data and ensure remote healthcare reliability. However, continuous refinement is essential to address evolving threats and maintain regulatory compliance.

2.4 Autonomous Defense Systems in Cybersecurity

AI-powered autonomous defense systems revolutionize cybersecurity by enabling real-time monitoring and adaptive threat response without human intervention. Using self-learning algorithms, these systems detect anomalies, isolate threats, and block malicious activity, ensuring rapid and accurate protection. In telemedicine, they play a crucial role in safeguarding patient data and maintaining secure virtual healthcare services (Zaid & Garai, 2024).

2.5 Key Features of Autonomous Defense Systems

Autonomous defense systems use AI and machine learning for proactive, adaptive cybersecurity, minimizing human intervention while continuously improving effectiveness. Key features define their advanced protection capabilities:

A. Self-Learning Capabilities

AI-driven defense systems enhance cybersecurity by learning from past incidents, analyzing vast data, and adapting detection and response. Unlike rule-based systems, they use machine learning to identify threats, refine anomaly detection, and reduce false positives. Unsupervised learning, like clustering, helps distinguish legitimate from malicious activities more accurately over time. Additionally, reinforcement learning enables AI models to enhance their decision-making abilities by receiving feedback from previous security events, allowing them to optimize their threat response strategies (Su et al., 2024).

B. Real-Time Threat Detection and Response

One of the most significant advantages of autonomous defense systems is their ability to detect and respond to cyber threats in real time. Traditional security solutions often rely on manual intervention, which can result in delays in identifying and mitigating threats. In contrast, AI-powered security systems can analyze network traffic, monitor endpoints, and scan for vulnerabilities within milliseconds, enabling instant threat neutralization. Real-time threat detection is facilitated by techniques such as deep packet inspection (DPI) and behavioral analytics, which allow the system to assess data flows and detect anomalies indicative of cyberattacks. Additionally, AI-driven security solutions integrate with Security Information and Event Management (SIEM) systems, allowing them to aggregate and analyze security events from multiple sources in real time.

In terms of response, autonomous defense mechanisms can automatically execute countermeasures, such as isolating compromised endpoints, blocking malicious IP addresses, and initiating remediation protocols without human intervention. This rapid response capability significantly reduces the dwell time of cyber threats, minimizing potential damage to an organization's infrastructure (Jimmy, 2024).

C. Reduced Human Intervention

Automated threat detection enables real-time cyber risk mitigation, prioritizing critical threats and enhancing scalability. AI-driven systems handle tasks like malware analysis and intrusion detection, reducing human error and freeing analysts for complex decisions. Working alongside security teams, they provide insights, threat intelligence, and risk assessments for informed cybersecurity strategies. This synergy between AI and human expertise enhances the overall effectiveness of an organization's cybersecurity posture (Sarker, 2024).

D. Adaptive Security Measures

AI-driven defense systems use machine learning and behavioral analysis to detect anomalies and predict attacks, continuously refining threat detection. They leverage threat intelligence, predictive analytics, and anomaly detection to stay ahead of cyber threats. Integrating zero-trust security ensures continuous verification, enhancing proactive protection and reducing response times more effectively than traditional methods.

Table 3 summarizes the autonomous defense features. This approach minimizes the risk of insider threats and unauthorized access by enforcing strict authentication and access control policies (Rao et al., 2024).

Table 3. Key features that define autonomous defense

Feature	Description
Self-Learning Capabilities	AI-driven defense systems continuously improve by analyzing cybersecurity data, learning from past incidents, and adapting their detection and response mechanisms. Unlike traditional rule-based systems, which rely on static rules, autonomous systems use machine learning to identify malicious patterns, reducing false positives and increasing detection accuracy over time.
Real-Time Threat Detection and Response	AI-powered security systems analyze network traffic, monitor endpoints, and scan for vulnerabilities in milliseconds, enabling instant threat neutralization. Using deep packet inspection (DPI) and behavioral analytics, they detect threats in real-time and automate responses like isolating compromised endpoints, blocking malicious IPs, and initiating remediation without human intervention.
Reduced Human Intervention	Autonomous defense systems automate cybersecurity processes, reducing the burden on IT teams and enabling them to focus on strategic initiatives. AI-driven solutions minimize human errors and enhance security operations.
Adaptive Security Measures	AI-driven defense systems evolve with emerging threats, leveraging threat intelligence, predictive analytics, and anomaly detection. They integrate with zero-trust architectures to enforce strict authentication and access control, staying ahead of new attack vectors.

By leveraging AI and machine learning, autonomous defense systems enhance an organization's ability to detect, respond to, and prevent cyber threats dynamically. As cyber threats continue to evolve, organizations must adopt autonomous defense solutions to stay ahead of adversaries and safeguard their digital assets (Ibrahum et al., 2025).

3. ETHICAL AND REGULATORY CONSIDERATIONS IN AI-DRIVEN CYBERSECURITY

AI enhances healthcare cybersecurity through proactive threat detection, automation, and continuous monitoring. However, its implementation must address privacy, fairness, security risks, and regulatory compliance to ensure ethical and responsible adoption in telemedicine (Lysenko et al., 2024). Common machine learning algorithms can be implemented using secure multiparty computation (MPC) protocols, along with the key techniques used to enable privacy-preserving computation.

3.1 Data Privacy and Confidentiality

Strict regulations require robust data protection in healthcare. AI-driven security must integrate encryption, anonymization, and access controls to prevent breaches. Continuous monitoring and auditing ensure compliance while transparent AI practices build trust among patients and providers. Compliance with data protection regulations like the Health Insurance Portability and Accountability Act (HIPAA) in the U.S. and the General Data Protection Regulation (GDPR) in Europe is paramount. These regulations impose strict requirements on how patient data is collected, stored, and shared. Healthcare providers deploying AI cybersecurity solutions must ensure that their AI models operate within these legal frameworks and do not compromise patient privacy. Additionally, AI models must be designed to handle data minimization principles, ensuring that they process only the necessary information for security purposes (Chukwunweike et al., 2024). This helps reduce the risk of privacy breaches while maintaining effective threat detection. Organizations must also invest in secure data-sharing protocols, ensuring that sensitive medical information is only accessible to authorized personnel and AI models trained with privacy-preserving techniques.

3.2 Algorithmic Bias and Fairness

Algorithmic bias in AI-driven cybersecurity poses ethical challenges, as biased training data can lead to unfair security assessments. This may cause false positives, misclassifications, and unnecessary restrictions on certain users or devices, potentially disrupting healthcare operations. To address this, organizations must employ techniques such as regular bias audits, explainable AI (XAI), and diverse dataset training to enhance model fairness. By ensuring transparency in AI security systems, organizations can improve trust and reduce the risk of bias-related security failures (Chukwunweike et al., 2024). Figure 1 demonstrates the step-by-step process of identifying, assessing, and mitigating algorithmic bias in AI-driven cybersecurity. The flowchart begins with biased data sources, where historical or skewed datasets introduce potential biases into AI models.

Figure 1. Mitigation process for algorithmic bias and fairness in AI-driven cybersecurity

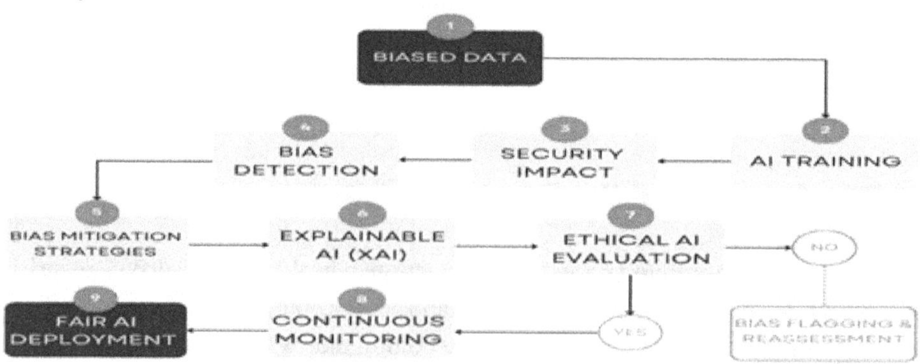

3.3 Adversarial AI Attacks

AI-powered cybersecurity is not only a defense tool but also a target for adversarial attacks. Cybercriminals manipulate AI models using deceptive data, tricking them into misclassifying threats or generating false alerts. To mitigate these risks, organizations must adopt adversarial training and multi-layered security approaches, strengthening AI resilience against evolving cyber threats. Security teams must also adopt continuous model validation and red teaming exercises, where ethical hackers simulate adversarial attacks to identify and fix vulnerabilities before real attackers exploit them (Kaviani et al., 2022).

3.4 Balancing Automation and Human Oversight

While AI enhances cybersecurity by rapidly analyzing vast security data, human oversight remains crucial. AI lacks contextual judgment, which cybersecurity professionals provide. Over-reliance on automation may create security gaps, especially in high-risk scenarios requiring nuanced decision-making. Human analysts help verify AI-detected threats, reducing false alarms and ensuring accurate responses. Thus, AI should function as an augmentative tool rather than a replacement for human expertise (Nagar, 2018). To maintain this balance, organizations must implement human-in-the-loop (HITL) frameworks, where AI-generated security alerts undergo human review before critical actions are taken. Additionally, ethics committees and governance boards should oversee AI cybersecurity implementations to ensure compliance with industry standards and best practices. Another key aspect is explainability and interpretability in AI decision-making. Security professionals should have access to transparent AI models that provide justifications for their decisions, enabling informed and ethical security responses (Joseph et al., 2024). By ensuring that human oversight remains an integral part of AI-driven cybersecurity, organizations can maximize the effectiveness of their security strategies while upholding ethical considerations.

AI-driven cybersecurity offers unparalleled advantages in safeguarding sensitive data and defending against cyber threats, particularly in sectors like healthcare where data security is paramount (Guembe et al., 2022). However, its deployment must be guided by ethical principles and regulatory compliance to prevent privacy breaches, algorithmic bias, adversarial threats, and excessive automation. As outlined in the sections above, healthcare organizations must ensure data privacy and confidentiality through strict regulatory adherence, mitigate algorithmic bias through fairness audits, defend against adversarial AI attacks using robust security techniques, and maintain a balance between automation and human oversight to prevent critical security misjudgments (Chen et al., 2021). The successful integration of AI in cybersecurity requires a multi-disciplinary approach, involving cybersecurity experts, data scientists, regulators, and ethical AI professionals. By adopting best practices and continuously refining AI-driven security measures, organizations can harness the full potential of AI while maintaining ethical integrity and regulatory compliance. Moving forward, it will be essential for industry leaders and policymakers to collaborate in developing standardized frameworks that govern AI's role in cybersecurity. This will ensure that AI-driven defense systems remain transparent, fair, and resilient against evolving cyber threats, ultimately contributing to a safer digital ecosystem.

4. THE FUTURE OF AI-DRIVEN CYBERSECURITY IN TELEMEDICINE

The rapid adoption of telemedicine has revolutionized healthcare by providing remote medical services, improving access to care, and reducing costs. However, this digital transformation has also introduced new cybersecurity challenges, as telemedicine platforms handle vast amounts of sensitive patient data, including electronic health records (EHRs), medical imaging, and real-time consultations (Alviani et al., 2023). Cyber threats such as ransomware attacks, data breaches, and identity theft are increasingly targeting telemedicine networks, demanding more robust and autonomous security solutions. Artificial intelligence (AI) has emerged as a powerful tool in cybersecurity, offering proactive defense mechanisms that can identify, analyze, and mitigate cyber threats in real time (Awadallah et al., 2024). AI-driven cybersecurity systems leverage machine learning (ML), deep learning, and neural networks to detect anomalies, predict attacks, and respond autonomously to cyber threats. As cyberattacks become more sophisticated, the integration of AI in telemedicine cybersecurity is poised to evolve, providing more advanced and resilient defense mechanisms.

4.1 Improved Threat Intelligence Capabilities

A. The Evolution of AI in Threat Detection

Traditional cybersecurity systems rely on predefined rules and signature-based detection methods, which often fail to identify emerging threats. AI-driven threat intelligence enhances cybersecurity by utilizing advanced algorithms to detect previously unknown attack patterns and adapt to evolving cyber threats. Machine learning models can analyze massive datasets from various sources, including network traffic logs, security alerts, and threat intelligence feeds, to identify patterns indicative of cyberattacks. Deep learning techniques, such as recurrent neural networks (RNNs) and convolutional neural networks (CNNs), can process complex data structures to improve threat detection accuracy (Rao, 2024).

B. Predictive Analytics for Cyber Threats

Future AI-driven cybersecurity systems will leverage predictive analytics to anticipate cyberattacks before they occur. Predictive models will analyze historical data to detect early warning signs of malicious activity, enabling security teams to take preemptive measures. For example, AI algorithms can monitor login behavior, user activity, and network traffic to identify potential threats. If an AI system detects abnormal access patterns, such as repeated failed login attempts from an unfamiliar location, it can trigger security protocols to block unauthorized access.

C. Threat Intelligence Sharing and AI Collaboration

AI-driven cybersecurity will benefit from enhanced threat intelligence sharing among healthcare organizations, cybersecurity firms, and government agencies. AI-powered platforms will aggregate and analyze threat data from multiple sources, enabling a more comprehensive understanding of emerging cyber threats. Federated learning will play a crucial role in this process, allowing AI models to be trained collaboratively across different healthcare systems without sharing sensitive patient data. This decentralized approach ensures that AI-driven threat intelligence remains robust while maintaining patient privacy.

4.2 Privacy-Preserving AI Techniques

A. Addressing Privacy Challenges in Telemedicine

One of the primary concerns in telemedicine cybersecurity is protecting patient privacy while utilizing AI-driven security solutions. Traditional AI training methods require vast amounts of data, raising concerns about data exposure and compliance with regulations such as the Health Insurance Portability and Accountability Act (HIPAA) and the General Data Protection Regulation (GDPR). Future AI-driven cybersecurity systems will incorporate privacy-preserving AI techniques to address these concerns. These techniques include federated learning, differential privacy, and homomorphic encryption (Pool et al., 2022).

B. Federated Learning for Secure AI Training

Federated learning allows AI models to be trained across multiple decentralized devices without transferring raw patient data to a central server. Instead, AI algorithms process data locally on edge devices, such as hospital servers and telemedicine platforms, and only share model updates with a central system. This approach enhances security by minimizing the risk of data breaches and unauthorized access. Federated learning also enables healthcare institutions to benefit from collective AI intelligence while maintaining compliance with privacy regulations (Mothukuri et al., 2021).

C. Differential Privacy for Data Anonymization

Differential privacy adds mathematical noise to datasets, ensuring that individual patient records cannot be traced back to specific individuals. This technique enables AI models to analyze patient data without compromising privacy (Patil et al., 2024). Future telemedicine cybersecurity systems will integrate differential privacy to enhance data security while still allowing AI-driven insights for threat detection and medical research. By applying differential privacy, AI models can learn from vast datasets while maintaining patient confidentiality (Burton, 2022).

D. Homomorphic Encryption for Secure Data Processing

Homomorphic encryption allows computations to be performed on encrypted data without decrypting it. This capability ensures that AI-driven security solutions can analyze sensitive patient data while keeping it encrypted. As AI-driven cybersecurity advances, homomorphic encryption will enable secure AI-powered threat detection and analysis in telemedicine networks. Healthcare providers will be able to process and analyze encrypted patient data without exposing it to potential cyber threats.

4.3 Explainable AI (XAI) for Cybersecurity Transparency

A. The Need for Explainability in AI-Driven Security

AI-driven cybersecurity systems rely on complex algorithms that make automated security decisions. However, the lack of transparency in AI decision-making poses challenges for cybersecurity professionals who need to understand and verify the reasoning behind AI-driven threat assessments. Explainable AI (XAI) aims to make AI models more interpretable, providing insights into how security decisions are made. By improving transparency, XAI ensures that cybersecurity teams can trust

AI-driven threat intelligence and make informed decisions based on AI-generated alerts.

B. Enhancing AI Transparency in Threat Detection

Future AI-driven cybersecurity solutions will incorporate XAI techniques to provide detailed explanations for threat detection and response actions. For instance, if an AI system flags a suspicious network activity, it will provide a clear rationale for its decision, such as identifying specific patterns or anomalies. XAI techniques, such as Local Interpretable Model-Agnostic Explanations (LIME) and SHapley Additive exPlanations (SHAP), will help cybersecurity professionals understand AI predictions and validate the accuracy of threat assessments (Wang, 2024).

C. Building Trust in AI-Driven Cybersecurity

By improving AI transparency, healthcare organizations can build trust in AI-driven cybersecurity solutions. Regulatory agencies and healthcare providers will be more likely to adopt AI-powered defense systems if they can verify the logic behind AI decisions. As AI continues to evolve, future cybersecurity frameworks will incorporate explainability as a fundamental requirement, ensuring that AI-driven security solutions remain accountable and trustworthy.

5. BLOCKCHAIN INTEGRATION FOR ENHANCED SECURITY

The integration of blockchain and artificial intelligence (AI) into cybersecurity represents a transformative step in securing telemedicine platforms. With the increasing digitization of healthcare, safeguarding patient records, transactions, and communications from cyber threats has become a priority. Blockchain's decentralized and tamper-resistant properties provide an additional layer of security, while AI enhances monitoring, fraud detection, and real-time threat mitigation. This section explores how blockchain and AI together can strengthen cybersecurity in telemedicine, focusing on data integrity, access control, and fraud prevention (Kunduru, 2023).

5.1 Combining AI and Blockchain for Cybersecurity

Healthcare cybersecurity threats are growing, targeting patient records, insurance claims, and telemedicine. AI-driven systems detect anomalies in real time but struggle with data integrity. Blockchain enhances security by offering a decentralized, tamper-proof ledger for transparent transactions. Together, AI and blockchain create a robust cybersecurity framework. Here's how they collaborate:

- AI for Anomaly Detection: AI continuously monitors transactions and system activities, identifying irregular patterns that may indicate cyber threats or fraud.
- Blockchain for Data Integrity: Blockchain creates an immutable ledger where each transaction is time-stamped and securely recorded, preventing data manipulation or unauthorized access.
- AI-Blockchain Synergy: AI algorithms analyze blockchain transactions for inconsistencies, alerting cybersecurity teams to potential threats before they escalate.

AI detects unauthorized access attempts to medical data. Blockchain ensures tamper-proof storage of patient records. Fraud Detection AI analyzes transaction patterns for signs of fraud. Blockchain maintains transparent and immutable transaction logs (Bello & Olufemi, 2024). Access Control AI-based biometric authentication enhances security. Blockchain verifies user permissions through smart contracts (Awad et al., 2024). Telemedicine Payments AI prevents payment fraud and identity theft. Blockchain secures financial transactions with cryptographic signatures. By integrating AI and blockchain, telemedicine platforms can mitigate cyber threats more effectively, ensuring a secure and trustworthy environment for patients and healthcare providers.

5.2 Securing Patient Data with Blockchain

One of the most critical cybersecurity concerns in telemedicine is securing patient data. Medical records contain sensitive personal information that, if compromised, could lead to identity theft, fraud, or blackmail. Blockchain technology can significantly enhance data security by implementing decentralized storage and access control mechanisms (Abbas et al., 2024). These points explain how blockchain secures patient data:

- Decentralization: Unlike traditional centralized databases that are vulnerable to hacking, blockchain distributes patient records across multiple nodes, reducing the risk of data breaches.
- Immutability: Once data is recorded on the blockchain, it cannot be altered or deleted, ensuring integrity and preventing unauthorized modifications.

- Smart Contracts for Access Control: Smart contracts enforce strict access control policies, allowing only authorized users (e.g., doctors, patients, or insurers) to access specific records.

AI complements blockchain security by analyzing network activity and flagging suspicious behaviors. For instance, if an unauthorized entity attempts to access patient records, AI can immediately block the request and notify the system administrator. Table 4 shows the comparison of patient data security.

Table 4. Comparison of traditional vs. blockchain-based patient data security

Feature	Traditional Databases	Blockchain-Based Security
Data Storage	Centralized servers	Decentralized, distributed nodes
Vulnerability to Hacking	High (single-point failures)	Low (distributed and encrypted)
Data Modification	Possible (if hacked)	Impossible (immutable ledger)
Access Control	Password-based authentication	Smart contract-based permissions
Fraud Prevention	Reactive (after breach)	Proactive (real-time monitoring)

To integrate blockchain into telemedicine securely:

- Adopt Decentralized Patient Data Storage: Healthcare providers should use blockchain-based electronic health records (EHRs) to prevent unauthorized data alterations.
- Leverage Smart Contracts for Permissioned Access: Only authenticated users should be allowed to view or modify specific patient records, with AI monitoring activities in real-time.
- Ensure Compliance with Healthcare Regulations: Blockchain solutions should align with HIPAA, GDPR, and other regulatory standards to protect patient privacy.

Blockchain-based security frameworks enhance telemedicine by ensuring patient confidentiality, data integrity, and trust. Their decentralized and immutable nature prevents unauthorized access, tampering, and fraud while enabling secure data sharing among authorized providers. This strengthens cybersecurity and boosts patient confidence in the safety and reliability of digital healthcare platforms.

5.3 Preventing Cyber Fraud with Blockchain AI Systems

Cyber fraud in telemedicine includes insurance fraud, identity theft, and billing manipulation. AI-powered blockchain systems enhance security by verifying transactions, detecting anomalies, and ensuring transparency. Table 5 outlines common fraud types, highlighting the need for advanced protection:

Table 5. Effectiveness of AI-blockchain in fraud prevention

Fraud Type	Traditional Detection Methods	AI-Blockchain Solution
Fake Insurance Claims	Manual verification (slow, error-prone)	AI detects inconsistencies in real-time, blockchain ensures claim authenticity.
Medical Identity Theft	Password-based security (easily hacked)	AI verifies biometric data, blockchain protects patient identities.
Billing Manipulation	Random audits (inefficient)	Blockchain maintains a transparent billing ledger, AI detects irregularities.

Cyber fraud in telemedicine causes financial losses and erodes trust. Traditional fraud detection is slow and error-prone. AI and blockchain enhance security by identifying suspicious transactions and ensuring transparency. AI detects anomalies, while blockchain prevents tampering, creating a reliable system for secure transactions, accurate billing, and identity protection. The following points are AI-Powered blockchain solutions for Fraud Prevention:

- Automated Fraud Detection: AI scans transaction patterns and flags unusual billing activities or duplicate claims.
- Immutable Audit Trails: Blockchain records every claim, ensuring transparency and traceability for insurance companies and regulatory authorities.
- Smart Contract-Based Billing: Smart contracts automatically validate telemedicine transactions, preventing unauthorized payments.

6. FUTURE TRENDS IN AI-BLOCKCHAIN CYBERSECURITY FOR TELEMEDICINE

The future of telemedicine cybersecurity hinges on AI and blockchain integration. As adoption grows, so do cyber risks. AI enhances threat detection, while blockchain ensures data security and compliance. Key trends include decentralized identity management, AI-driven threat intelligence, and regulatory integration, fostering secure and transparent healthcare systems.

6.1 Decentralized Identity Management: Preventing Unauthorized Access and Identity Theft

Identity theft and unauthorized access pose significant cybersecurity risks in telemedicine. Cybercriminals exploit weak authentication to steal identities and manipulate records. Blockchain-based decentralized identity management offers a solution by replacing centralized authentication with cryptographically secured digital identities, ensuring secure access for patients and healthcare providers. The following point represent key features of blockchain-based digital identities:

- Self-Sovereign Identity (SSI): Patients control their own identity credentials without reliance on a third party.
- Tamper-Proof Verification: All identity-related transactions are recorded on a blockchain, preventing unauthorized alterations.
- Multi-Factor Authentication (MFA): AI-driven biometric authentication (e.g., facial recognition, fingerprint scanning) enhances security.
- Decentralized Storage: Identity credentials are distributed across multiple nodes, reducing the risk of a single point of failure.

Moreover, there are many benefits of decentralized identity management in telemedicine, such as:

- Eliminates Centralized Databases: Prevents large-scale data breaches by removing single points of vulnerability.
- Reduces Identity Theft Risks: Blockchain encryption and AI-driven fraud detection minimize unauthorized access.
- Enhances Patient Privacy: Patients have greater control over their health data, deciding who can access their records.
- Facilitates Cross-Border Healthcare Access: Patients can use their digital identities globally, streamlining healthcare services across different jurisdictions.

6.2 Real-World Applications of Blockchain-Based Identity in Telemedicine

By integrating AI and blockchain into decentralized identity management, telemedicine providers can build more secure, efficient, and user-controlled healthcare platforms. Blockchain ensures tamper-proof, decentralized identity storage, while AI detects anomalies and automates threat responses. Together, they empower patients, ensure regulatory compliance, and enable seamless data sharing, creating a secure, patient-centric telemedicine ecosystem. Figure 2 represents real-world applications of blockchain-based identity in telemedicine:

Figure 2. Blockchain-based identity in telemedicine

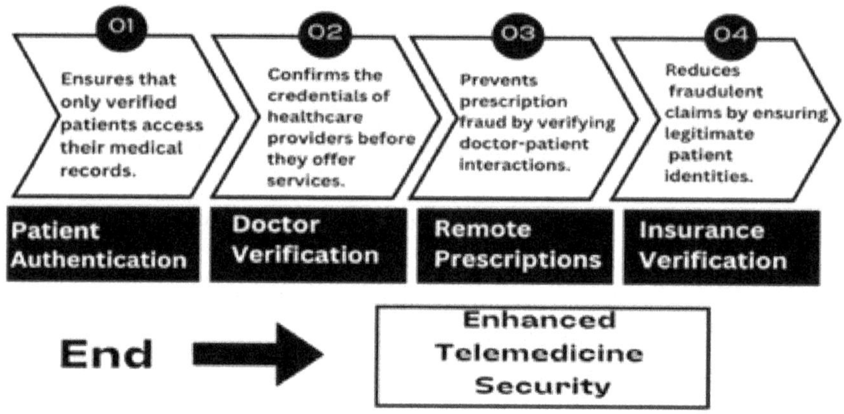

6.3 Integration with Regulatory Frameworks: Ensuring Compliance in AI-Blockchain Cybersecurity

The healthcare industry is highly regulated, with strict requirements for data security, privacy, and compliance. AI-blockchain cybersecurity solutions must align with global regulatory frameworks to ensure legal compliance while maintaining patient trust. Several major regulations govern healthcare cybersecurity, including HIPAA (Health Insurance Portability and Accountability Act), which protects patient health information in the U.S., GDPR (General Data Protection Regulation), which enforces data privacy rules for healthcare providers in the European Union; HITRUST (Health Information Trust Alliance), which provides a framework for managing cybersecurity risks in healthcare and FDA regulations for medical devices, which ensure that connected healthcare devices meet cybersecurity standards. To meet these regulatory requirements, AI-blockchain solutions integrate various mechanisms to enhance compliance.

Automated compliance audits leverage AI-powered systems to analyze security protocols and generate compliance reports, reducing the manual burden on healthcare providers. Immutable data records stored on blockchain ensure that all modifications to patient data are logged and auditable, enhancing transparency and security (Farayola, 2024). Smart contract enforcement allows regulatory policies to be executed automatically, minimizing human error and ensuring consistent adherence to compliance guidelines. Additionally, enhanced data privacy controls including AI-driven encryption and access control mechanisms, which help align telemedicine security with GDPR and HIPAA requirements, safeguarding sensitive patient data. Despite these benefits, integrating AI-blockchain with regulatory frameworks presents several challenges. One key issue is evolving cybersecurity laws, as regulations are constantly updated to address emerging threats. AI-driven security systems mitigate this by dynamically updating security policies to comply with new laws. Cross-border compliance challenges stem from varying regulations, but blockchain-based digital identities enable secure, global patient access. Patients also demand greater control over their data, which blockchain-based self-sovereign identities provide while ensuring compliance. Legal recognition of smart contracts remains a hurdle, requiring clear regulatory frameworks. Future trends include global standardization of blockchain security, AI-powered compliance monitoring, and ethical guidelines for AI in healthcare. Integrating AI-blockchain solutions with regulations will enhance security and trust in digital healthcare.

Ethical challenges, such as ensuring data privacy, mitigating algorithmic bias, and maintaining transparency, are critical to building trust in these technologies. Simultaneously, adherence to regulatory frameworks like HIPAA and GDPR is essential to avoid legal pitfalls and ensure patient data is handled responsibly. By proactively addressing these challenges, telemedicine platforms can unlock the full potential of AI and blockchain technologies while fostering public trust, safeguarding patient rights, and maintaining compliance with evolving legal standards. This balanced approach not only enhances cybersecurity but also ensures that innovation aligns with societal values and regulatory expectations.

6.4 Addressing Scalability and Resource Constraints in AI-Driven Cybersecurity

One of the critical challenges in deploying AI-driven cybersecurity solutions is scalability, particularly in resource-constrained environments such as small healthcare providers and institutions in developing regions. Many AI and blockchain-based security mechanisms require significant computational power, extensive storage, and specialized expertise, which may not be readily available in all settings. To ensure broader applicability, it is crucial to explore cost-effective and lightweight alternatives that maintain security effectiveness without overburdening existing infrastructure (Salem et al., 2024).

Mitigating scalability concerns involves federated learning for collaborative AI training without sharing raw data, edge computing for localized security processing, and hybrid blockchain models for balanced security and efficiency. These solutions enable AI-driven cybersecurity to adapt to diverse healthcare settings, benefiting even smaller institutions.

6.5 Enhancing Adversarial AI Mitigation Strategies

Adversarial AI attacks threaten cybersecurity by manipulating AI models with subtle data modifications, leading to misclassification and breaches. Key defenses include adversarial training, where models learn from attack examples, ensemble methods that combine multiple AI models for resilience, and Explainable AI (XAI) to enhance transparency and anomaly detection. Additionally, red teaming exercises, where cybersecurity experts simulate adversarial attacks against AI-driven security systems, which can help assess vulnerabilities and refine defense mechanisms. By incorporating these advanced strategies, AI-driven cybersecurity frameworks can become more robust against emerging adversarial threats, ensuring the reliability of AI applications in telemedicine and other critical sectors (Baniecki et al., 2024).

CONCLUSION

The growing reliance on telemedicine underscores the critical need for robust cybersecurity measures to protect patient data and ensure the integrity of digital healthcare services. AI-driven cybersecurity has emerged as a game-changing solution, offering real-time threat detection, predictive analytics, and automated incident response. By harnessing machine learning and autonomous defense systems, AI empowers healthcare organizations to identify and neutralize cyber threats proactively, minimizing risks before they escalate. Complementing this, blockchain technology enhances security through data immutability and decentralized access control, fostering trust and transparency in telemedicine platforms.

However, the integration of AI into cybersecurity frameworks brings ethical and regulatory challenges to the forefront. Issues such as data privacy, algorithmic fairness, and adversarial AI threats demand vigilant oversight and governance to ensure these technologies remain effective and trustworthy. Looking ahead, advancements in explainable AI (XAI), federated learning, and global regulatory alignment will shape the future of cybersecurity in telemedicine. These innovations

REFERENCES

Abbas, A., Alroobaea, R., Krichen, M., Rubaiee, S., Vimal, S., & Almansour, F. M. (2024). S. Vimal, and Fahad M. Almansour. "Blockchain-assisted secured data management framework for health information analysis based on Internet of Medical Things.". *Personal and Ubiquitous Computing*, *28*(1), 59–72. DOI: 10.1007/s00779-021-01583-8

Adashek, J. J., & Kurzrock, R. (2023). Home-run trials for rare cancers: Giving the right drug (s) to the right patients at the right time and in the right place. *NPJ Precision Oncology*, *7*(1), 129. DOI: 10.1038/s41698-023-00487-5 PMID: 38066094

Alnajim, A. M., Habib, S., Islam, M., AlRawashdeh, H. S., & Wasim, M. (2023). Exploring cybersecurity education and training techniques: A comprehensive review of traditional, virtual reality, and augmented reality approaches. *Symmetry*, *15*(12), 2175. DOI: 10.3390/sym15122175

Alshehri, A., Khan, N., Alowayr, A., & Alghamdi, M. Y. (2023). Cyberattack Detection Framework Using Machine Learning and User Behavior Analytics. *Computer Systems Science and Engineering*, *44*(2), 1679–1689. DOI: 10.32604/csse.2023.026526

Alviani, R., Purwandari, B., Eitiveni, I., & Purwaningsih, M. (2023). Factors affecting adoption of telemedicine for virtual healthcare services in Indonesia. *J. Inf. Syst. Eng. Bus. Intell*, *9*(1), 4769. DOI: 10.20473/jisebi.9.1.47-69

Arefin, S., & Simcox, M. (2024). AI-Driven Solutions for Safeguarding Healthcare Data: Innovations in Cybersecurity. *International Business Research*, *17*(6), 1–74. DOI: 10.5539/ibr.v17n6p74

Awad, A. I., Babu, A., Barka, E., & Shuaib, K. (2024). AI-powered biometrics for Internet of Things security: A review and future vision. *Journal of Information Security and Applications*, *82*, 103748. DOI: 10.1016/j.jisa.2024.103748

Awadallah, A., Eledlebi, K., Zemerly, J., Puthal, D., Damiani, E., Taha, K., Kim, T.-Y., Yoo, P. D., Choo, K.-K. R., Yim, M.-S., & Yeun, C. Y. (2024). Artificial intelligence-based cybersecurity for the metaverse: Research challenges and opportunities. *IEEE Communications Surveys and Tutorials*, 1. DOI: 10.1109/COMST.2024.3442475

Baniecki, H., & Biecek, P. (2024). Adversarial attacks and defenses in explainable artificial intelligence: A survey. *Information Fusion*, *107*, 102303. DOI: 10.1016/j.inffus.2024.102303

Bashshur, R., Doarn, C. R., Frenk, J. M., Kvedar, J. C., & Woolliscroft, J. O. (2020). Telemedicine and the COVID-19 pandemic, lessons for the future. *Telemedicine Journal and e-Health*, *26*(5), 571–573. DOI: 10.1089/tmj.2020.29040.rb PMID: 32275485

Bello, O. A., & Olufemi, K. (2024). Artificial intelligence in fraud prevention: Exploring techniques and applications challenges and opportunities. *Computer science & IT research journal, 5*(6), 1505-1520.

Burton, S. L. (2022). *Cybersecurity Leadership from a Telemedicine/Telehealth Knowledge and Organizational Development Examination*. Capitol Technology University.

Camacho, N. G. (2024). The role of AI in cybersecurity: Addressing threats in the digital age. *Journal of Artificial Intelligence General science (JAIGS) ISSN: 3006-4023, 3*(1), 143-154.

Chen, J., Yan, H., Liu, Z., Zhang, M., Xiong, H., & Yu, S. (2024). When federated learning meets privacy-preserving computation. *ACM Computing Surveys*, *56*(12), 1–36. DOI: 10.1145/3679013

Chen, S., Zhang, L., Yan, Z., & Shen, Z. (2021). A distributed and robust security-constrained economic dispatch algorithm based on blockchain. *IEEE Transactions on Power Systems*, *37*(1), 691–700. DOI: 10.1109/TPWRS.2021.3086101

Chukwunweike, J. N., Ayodele, P. A., & Atata, B. B. (2024). A. Praise, and B. A. Bashirat. "Harnessing Machine Learning for Cybersecurity: How Convolutional Neural Networks are Revolutionizing Threat Detection and Data Privacy.". *International Journal of Research Publication and Reviews*, *5*(8), 3608–3617. DOI: 10.55248/gengpi.5.0824.2402

Chukwunweike, J. N., Yussuf, M., Okusi, O., & Oluwatobi, T. (2024). The role of deep learning in ensuring privacy integrity and security: Applications in AI-driven cybersecurity solutions. *World Journal of Advanced Research and Reviews*, *23*(2), 2550.

Farayola, O. A.Oluwatoyin Ajoke Farayola. (2024). Revolutionizing banking security: Integrating artificial intelligence, blockchain, and business intelligence for enhanced cybersecurity. *Finance & Accounting Research Journal*, *6*(4), 501–514. DOI: 10.51594/farj.v6i4.990

Feng, J., Phillips, R. V., Malenica, I., Bishara, A., Hubbard, A. E., Celi, L. A., & Pirracchio, R. (2022). Clinical artificial intelligence quality improvement: Towards continual monitoring and updating of AI algorithms in healthcare. *NPJ Digital Medicine*, *5*(1), 66. DOI: 10.1038/s41746-022-00611-y PMID: 35641814

George, A. S. (2024). Emerging Trends in AI-Driven Cybersecurity: An In-Depth Analysis. *Partners Universal Innovative Research Publication*, *2*(4), 15–28.

Ghubaish, A., Salman, T., Zolanvari, M., Unal, D., Al-Ali, A., & Jain, R. (2020). Recent advances in the internet-of-medical-things (IoMT) systems security. *IEEE Internet of Things Journal*, *8*(11), 8707–8718. DOI: 10.1109/JIOT.2020.3045653

Guembe, B., Azeta, A., Misra, S., Osamor, V. C., Fernandez-Sanz, L., & Pospelova, V. (2022). The Emerging Threat of Ai-driven Cyber Attacks: A Review. *Applied Artificial Intelligence*, *36*(no. 1), 2037254. DOI: 10.1080/08839514.2022.2037254

Ibrahum, A. D. M., Hussain, M., & Hong, J.-E. (2025). Deep learning adversarial attacks and defenses in autonomous vehicles: A systematic literature review from a safety perspective. *Artificial Intelligence Review*, *58*(1), 1–53.

Jalali, M. S., Russell, B., Razak, S., & Gordon, W. J. (2019). EARS to cyber incidents in health care. *Journal of the American Medical Informatics Association : JAMIA*, *26*(1), 81–90. DOI: 10.1093/jamia/ocy148 PMID: 30517701

Jamil, F., Hang, L., Kim, K. H., & Kim, D. H. (2019). KyuHyung Kim, and Do-Hyeun Kim. "A novel medical blockchain model for drug supply chain integrity management in a smart hospital.". *Electronics (Basel)*, *8*(5), 505. DOI: 10.3390/electronics8050505

Jimmy, F. N. U. (2024). Cyber security vulnerabilities and remediation through cloud security tools. *Journal of Artificial Intelligence General science (JAIGS) ISSN: 3006-4023*, *2*(1), 129-171.

Joseph, S., Kolade, T. M., Obioha Val, O., Adebiyi, O. O., Ogungbemi, O. S., & Olaniyi, O. O. (2024). AI-powered information governance: Balancing automation and human oversight for optimal organization productivity. *Asian Journal of Research in Computer Science*, *17*(10), 10–9734.

Kaviani, S., Han, K. J., & Sohn, I. (2022). Adversarial attacks and defenses on AI in medical imaging informatics: A survey. *Expert Systems with Applications*, *198*, 116815. DOI: 10.1016/j.eswa.2022.116815

Khan, P. W., & Byun, Y.-C. (2021). *Secure transactions management using blockchain as a service software for the internet of things*. Software Engineering in IoT, Big Data, Cloud and Mobile Computing. DOI: 10.1007/978-3-030-64773-5_10

Kunduru, A. R. (2023). Blockchain technology for ERP systems: A review. *American Journal of Engineering, Mechanics and Architecture*, *1*(7), 56–63.

Kuppa, A., & Le-Khac, N.-A. "Black box attacks on explainable artificial intelligence (XAI) methods in cyber security." In *2020 International Joint Conference on neural networks (IJCNN)*, pp. 1-8. IEEE, 2020. DOI: 10.1109/IJCNN48605.2020.9206780

Lee, W.-K., Phan, R. C.-W., Goi, B.-M., Chen, L., Zhang, X., & Xiong, N. N. (2018). RaphaëL C-W. Phan, Bok-Min Goi, Lanxiang Chen, Xiujun Zhang, and Naixue N. Xiong. "Parallel and high speed hashing in GPU for telemedicine applications.". *IEEE Access : Practical Innovations, Open Solutions*, *6*, 37991–38002. DOI: 10.1109/ACCESS.2018.2849439

Lysenko, S., Bobro, N., Korsunova, K., Vasylchyshyn, O., & Tatarchenko, Y. (2024). The role of artificial intelligence in cybersecurity: Automation of protection and detection of threats. *Economic Affairs*, *69*(1s), 43–51. DOI: 10.46852/0424-2513.1.2024.6

Maddireddy, B. R., & Maddireddy, B. R. (2023). Enhancing Network Security through AI-Powered Automated Incident Response Systems. *International Journal of Advanced Engineering Technologies and Innovations*, *1*(02), 282–304.

Mallikarjunaradhya, V., Pothukuchi, A. S., & Kota, L. V. (2023). An overview of the strategic advantages of AI-powered threat intelligence in the cloud. *Journal of Science and Technology*, *4*(4), 1–12. DOI: 10.55662/JST.2023.4401

Mothukuri, V., Parizi, R. M., Pouriyeh, S., Huang, Y., Dehghantanha, A., & Srivastava, G. (2021). A survey on security and privacy of federated learning. *Future Generation Computer Systems*, *115*, 619–640. DOI: 10.1016/j.future.2020.10.007

Muzammil, M. B., Bilal, M., Ajmal, S., Shongwe, S. C., & Ghadi, Y. Y. (2024). Unveiling Vulnerabilities of Web Attacks Considering Man in the Middle Attack and Session Hijacking. *IEEE Access : Practical Innovations, Open Solutions*, *12*, 6365–6375. DOI: 10.1109/ACCESS.2024.3350444

Nagar, G. (2018). *Leveraging Artificial Intelligence to Automate and Enhance Security Operations: Balancing Efficiency and Human Oversight*. Valley International Journal Digital Library.

Nobili, M., Raguseo, D., & Setola, R. (2025). Cybersecuity Analysis of a Telemedicine Platform. *Health Care*, *13*(2), 184. PMID: 39857212

Okolie, U. C. (2022). Distinction between Traditional security and modern security: A conceptual discourse. *The Journal of American Science*, *19*(2), 247–266.

Park, J., Erikson, C., Han, X., & Iyer, P. (2018). Are state telehealth policies associated with the use of telehealth services among underserved populations? *Health Affairs*, *37*(12), 2060–2068. DOI: 10.1377/hlthaff.2018.05101 PMID: 30633679

Patil, R. Y., Patil, Y. H., & Bannore, A. (2024). Cybersecurity in medical Internet of Things: Issues, challenges, and future directions. In *Security Implementation in Internet of Medical Things* (pp. 87–110). CRC Press.

Pool, J., Akhlaghpour, S., Fatehi, F., & Gray, L. C. (2022). Data privacy concerns and use of telehealth in the aged care context: An integrative review and research agenda. *International Journal of Medical Informatics*, *160*, 104707. DOI: 10.1016/j.ijmedinf.2022.104707 PMID: 35131698

Rao, D. D., Waoo, A. A., Singh, M. P., Pareek, P. K., Kamal, S., & Pandit, S. V. (2024). Strategizing IoT Network Layer Security Through Advanced Intrusion Detection Systems and AI-Driven Threat Analysis. *Full Length Article*, *12*(2), 195–95.

Rao, S. D. P. (2024). Harnessing AI For Evolving Threats: From Detection to Automated Response.

Reis, J., Cohen, Y., Melão, N., Costa, J., & Jorge, D. (2021). High-tech defense industries: Developing autonomous intelligent systems. *Applied Sciences (Basel, Switzerland)*, *11*(11), 4920. DOI: 10.3390/app11114920

Sabillon, R., Cavaller, V., Cano, J., & Serra-Ruiz, J. (2016, June). Cybercriminals, cyberattacks and cybercrime. In *2016 IEEE International Conference on Cybercrime and Computer Forensic (ICCCF)* (pp. 1-9). IEEE.

Salem, A. H., Azzam, S. M., Emam, O. E., & Abohany, A. A. (2024). O. E. Emam, and Amr A. Abohany. "Advancing cybersecurity: A comprehensive review of AI-driven detection techniques.". *Journal of Big Data*, *11*(1), 105. DOI: 10.1186/s40537-024-00957-y

Samtani, S., Abate, M., Benjamin, V., & Li, W. (2020). *Cybersecurity as an industry: A cyber threat intelligence perspective*. The Palgrave Handbook of International Cybercrime and Cyberdeviance.

Sarker, I. H. (2024). *AI-driven cybersecurity and threat intelligence: cyber automation, intelligent decision-making and explainability*. Springer Nature. DOI: 10.1007/978-3-031-54497-2

Sarker, I. H., Kayes, A. S. M., Badsha, S., Alqahtani, H., Watters, P., & Ng, A. (2020). A. S. M. Kayes, Shahriar Badsha, Hamed Alqahtani, Paul Watters, and Alex Ng. "Cybersecurity data science: An overview from machine learning perspective.". *Journal of Big Data*, *7*(1), 1–29. DOI: 10.1186/s40537-020-00318-5

Su, J., Jiang, C., Jin, X., Qiao, Y., Xiao, T., Ma, H., . . . Lin, J. (2024). Large language models for forecasting and anomaly detection: A systematic literature review. *arXiv preprint arXiv:2402.10350.*

Su, Z., Li, C., Fu, H., Wang, L., Wu, M., & Feng, X. (2024). Haitian Fu, Liyang Wang, Meilong Wu, and Xiaobin Feng. "Development and prospect of telemedicine.". *Intelligent Medicine*, *4*(1), 1–9. DOI: 10.1016/j.imed.2022.10.004

Uscher-Pines, L., & Mehrotra, A. (2014). Analysis of Teladoc use seems to indicate expanded access to care for patients without prior connection to a provider. *Health Affairs*, *33*(2), 258–264. DOI: 10.1377/hlthaff.2013.0989 PMID: 24493769

Velasco, C. (2022, May). Cybercrime and Artificial Intelligence. An overview of the work of international organizations on criminal justice and the international applicable instruments. In *ERA Forum* (Vol. 23, No. 1, pp. 109-126). Berlin/Heidelberg: Springer Berlin Heidelberg.

Wahed, M. A. (2024, November). Real-Time Intrusion Detection and Traffic Analysis Using AI Techniques in IoT Infrastructure. In *2024 1st International Conference on Emerging Technologies for Dependable Internet of Things (ICETI)* (pp. 1-6). IEEE.

Wang, Y. (2024). *A comparative analysis of model agnostic techniques for explainable artificial intelligence*. Research Reports on Computer Science. DOI: 10.37256/rrcs.3220244750

Zaid, T., & Garai, S. (2024). Emerging Trends in Cybersecurity: A Holistic View on Current Threats, Assessing Solutions, and Pioneering New Frontiers. *Blockchain in Healthcare Today*, •••, 7. PMID: 38715765

Chapter 14

Autonomous Defense Systems for Surgical Robots Ensuring Cybersecurity in Robotic-Assisted Surgery

Mutaz Abdel Wahed
https://orcid.org/0000-0002-4361-6185
Jadara University, Jordan

Salma Abdel Wahed
Hashemite University, Jordan

ABSTRACT

Autonomous defense systems powered by Artificial Intelligence (AI) and machine learning offer a critical solution to mitigate these risks. These systems monitor network traffic, detect anomalies in real time, and autonomously respond to potential threats without human intervention. This chapter examines the unique cybersecurity challenges associated with surgical robots, such as securing command-and-control systems, preventing remote hijacking, and ensuring the integrity of real-time data transmission. It also highlights successful implementations of AI-driven cybersecurity in healthcare, discussing how autonomous defense systems can safeguard surgical outcomes, protect patient data, and maintain compliance with regulatory standards. By integrating advanced cybersecurity solutions, healthcare organizations can enhance the resilience and safety of robotic-assisted surgical procedures.

DOI: 10.4018/979-8-3373-0954-5.ch014

1. INTRODUCTION

Currently, there is a global trend towards less invasive surgical interventions, leading to a significant increase in the number of laparoscopic and robotic surgeries, alongside a decrease in traditional open surgery. The rise in the use of laparoscopic techniques has resulted in a substantial reduction in patients hospital stays and has alleviated patients fears of undergoing surgery. Robotic-assisted surgery has provided a platform for integrating modern technological advancements into already-established minimally invasive surgery. The history of robotic surgery began in the 1980s. The first surgical robotic system, the Puma 560, was introduced in 1985. This system was used in neurosurgery. Like most other systems developed in the 1980s, it was highly specialized. However, universal robotic systems began to emerge later (Haidegger et al., 2011; Kim et al., 2004).

During the development of space programs by the United States, the issue of providing emergency surgical care to astronauts in orbit arose. Establishing a traditional operating room and maintaining a team of surgeons on the station permanently was deemed impractical. To address this, NASA initiated the development of a special surgical robot that could be controlled remotely from Earth. The resulting technology, initially developed for military applications, led to the creation of universal medical robots (Haidegger et al., 2011; Takács et al., 2015).

In 1998, the first universal robotic system, "ZEUS," was introduced to the world of medicine. However, the most well-known surgical robot is the Da Vinci, developed in the late 1990s by Intuitive Surgical Inc. in the United States. This system was named after the great Italian scientist Leonardo da Vinci. It was first approved for medical use in the United States in 2000, followed by Canada in 2001, and later in several other countries (Haidegger et al., 2008; Kim et al., 2004).

The Da Vinci system is equipped with four ultra-precise manipulators: two replace the surgeon's hands during the operation (with a diameter of only 1 cm), the third has a built-in camera that transmits real-time images, and the fourth serves as an assistant. The system makes incisions as small as 5-12 mm, significantly reducing tissue trauma. During the operation, the surgeon sits at a control console that displays a 3D image of the surgical site and uses joysticks that respond to the touch of their fingers. The surgeon's movements are transmitted in real-time to the operating table. The built-in processor analyzes each movement at a speed of 1,000 actions per second and sends signals to the robotic arms. The control console can replicate all the movements of the surgeon's hand and fingers (Takács et al., 2016; Toumbas et al., 2017; Kim et al., 2004).

The precision of the robotic manipulators exceeds that of human hands and eliminates hand tremors, a natural physiological phenomenon for surgeons. With seven degrees of freedom and the ability to bend at 90 degrees, the robotic arms have a wide range of motion. This is particularly important in surgeries involving the pericardium or pelvis, where space is limited. Another advantage of the Da Vinci robot is its extensive arsenal of surgical tools. The video system provides high-quality 3D images on two color screens. The image can be scaled, optimized, enlarged, and enhanced by reducing flicker and suppressing noise using a special synchronizer, a powerful light source, and a camera control unit (Pugin et al., 2011).

However, other systems are also being developed and used. It is important to note that all such systems share the common feature that the robot's actions are controlled by a human. In other words, the robot acts as the "hands," while the human provides the commands. The robot's manipulators replicate the surgeon's movements on a smaller scale. Most developers aim to make these systems replicate the surgeon's actions as accurately as possible. For example, the Telelap ALF-X system offers features such as recreating tactile sensations (providing feedback between the robot's manipulator and the surgeon's hand) and tracking the surgeon's eye movements to adjust the scale and position of the endoscopic camera (Lorentziadis, 2014).

Currently, robotic systems are capable of performing a wide range of surgeries in urology, gynecology, thoracic, abdominal, vascular, and cardiac surgery.

Robotic systems are most commonly used in tumor removal, often allowing access to tumors located in hard-to-reach areas. An example is the revolutionary method of surgical treatment for laryngeal, oral, and other malignant tumors in the head and neck region using the Da Vinci robot, developed by the staff at the Johns Hopkins Cancer Center in Los Angeles. In many cases, these tumors are located in difficult-to-access areas, and the proximity of nerves and major blood vessels previously made surgery risky or impossible. However, the tiny manipulators of the Da Vinci system, holding specially designed miniature surgical instruments, can easily reach these areas through the mouth or nose, eliminating the need for external incisions. Using the TORS (Trans Oral Robotic Surgery) method, unique surgeries have been successfully performed on over 100 patients who would otherwise have had to undergo highly invasive procedures, often requiring complex reconstructive plastic surgeries.

There are other unique features of surgical robots. For example, in France, a function was developed that allows programming a surgical robot to compensate for the heartbeat during cardiac surgery. This function simplifies the procedure by displaying a static image of the heart on the surgeon's screen. Three video cameras monitor the heart, and a new NVIDIA GPU processes the video streams to create a 3D model of the heart, static for the surgeon and dynamic for the robot. This significantly reduces the risk during cardiac surgeries (Yuen et al., 2013).

Many note the advantages of robotic surgical systems over human surgeons. For instance, doctors at St. Mary's Hospital in the UK state that the precision of a robot far exceeds that of even the most experienced human surgeon. Other advantages include minimized blood loss and tissue trauma, minimal invasiveness, greater freedom of movement than human hands, the ability to perform surgeries that are difficult or impossible with traditional or endoscopic methods, the ability to connect surgeons in different cities or countries during an operation, and reduced patient recovery time.

It is worth noting that even robotic surgical systems have their specializations. For example, in 2013, the Rosa surgical robot, specialized in neurosurgery, was introduced at Neurosurgical Institute. The device scans the patient's brain, inputs the data into the system, calculates the surgical plan, saving time and minimizing human error. The device is successfully used in over 40 foreign clinics. This development allows for precise and safe removal of tumors and treatment of Parkinson's disease and epilepsy (Lefranc et al., 2016).

A team of developers from Vanderbilt University in the United States has proposed a system for removing blood clots in the brain after strokes. Statistics show that only 40% of stroke survivors live beyond the first month. This development could increase that number, with minimal invasiveness (requiring only a small hole in the skull) and high effectiveness (Burgner et al., 2013).

Another notable device is the CorPath 200, which allows for remote coronary angioplasty. Typically, this procedure requires the surgeon to wear an uncomfortable protective suit (due to the need for X-rays), which still allows some radiation exposure. This system has already been certified in the United States (Crinnion et al., 2013).

A common drawback of these systems is their relatively high cost. For example, the Da Vinci system costs approximately $2.7 million, not including maintenance costs. Other systems also cost millions of dollars. However, more affordable alternatives are being developed in the United States. SurgiBot is one such system, allowing for surgeries like appendectomies through a small skin puncture, reducing patient recovery time. The exact price of the device is unknown, but the creators promise it will be cheaper than its counterparts.

Deploying autonomous defense systems across multiple hospital sites requires addressing interoperability challenges. Healthcare networks often comprise a mix of legacy and modern systems, making integration complex. AI-driven solutions must be designed to seamlessly interact with various platforms, ensuring compatibility and efficient data exchange. Regular system updates and model retraining will be critical to counter evolving cyber threats, reducing vulnerabilities caused by outdated security models.

A unique architecture for electronic teleoperation systems, designed for remote surgical interventions, has been developed by specialists in the field of medical technology. This system automatically ensures patient safety in case the operating surgeon loses control of the situation. Artificial intelligence is integrated into such systems, assisting the doctor in their work while independently monitoring patient safety. In the event of an unforeseen incident, the program will block remote control and complete the surgery autonomously. During remote surgery, there is a risk of cyberattacks and loss of control. Attacks can occur through various methods, and data transmission may also fail, potentially leading to severe consequences for the patient. A solution to these challenges has been proposed to ensure safer outcomes (Crinnion et al., 2013).

Tele-surgical technologies are advancing globally. In most systems, robotic manipulators are used to perform operations, which can be controlled by a surgeon from any point on the planet. This approach enables complex surgeries in places where they were previously impossible, such as in field hospitals, remote locations, or even in space. However, the practical use of remote surgery systems faces high safety requirements, as any breach could result in irreversible harm to the patient. According to research, between 2000 and 2013, 144 surgeries involving robotic systems resulted in fatalities. While this statistic does not include human-controlled machines remotely, the technologies share similarities.

The risks lie in command transmission errors from the surgeon to the manipulator, partial or complete loss of network connection, or malfunction of individual system components. These issues could arise from cyberattacks or network connection failures. The physical safety of the patient is ensured by a special autonomous system, which is not connected to any network. Control can only be exerted with direct access to the device. If hackers gain control over the operating module or it malfunctions, the system will stop the surgical tools in a safe position, or the necessary manipulations will be completed automatically. In the event of a lost connection with the surgeon, the AI will pause the operation and resume it once the doctor reconnects. Additionally, an autonomous power supply is available in case of electrical issues.

The security system is designed for use in advanced operating devices for remote endovascular surgeries, such as brain surgeries without cranial trepanation, using a microcatheter inserted through the femoral artery. It can also perform cardiovascular surgeries and will be one of the first systems with such capabilities.

The integration of artificial intelligence (AI) in surgical robots has revolutionized modern healthcare by enhancing precision, efficiency, and patient outcomes. However, as these systems become increasingly autonomous, the ethical implications surrounding accountability and patient safety become a crucial area of concern. One of the foremost ethical dilemmas is determining responsibility in the event of system failures or cyberattacks. Unlike traditional surgical procedures, where human surgeons bear full accountability, AI-driven robotic systems distribute decision-making across software algorithms, developers, and healthcare practitioners. If a malfunction or cyber intrusion compromises a procedure, pinpointing liability becomes complex. Additionally, the risk of adversarial attacks that manipulate AI models to make incorrect decisions poses a significant challenge to patient safety. Ethical considerations demand the implementation of transparent AI systems with explainable decision-making processes and robust fail-safes that allow human intervention in critical situations (Guni et al., 2024).

Beyond ethical concerns, the integration of autonomous defense mechanisms into hospital-wide cybersecurity frameworks is vital for ensuring comprehensive protection. Surgical robots do not operate in isolation; they interact with electronic health records, hospital networks, and cloud-based infrastructures. A breach in any of these interconnected systems can expose patient data and compromise surgical operations.

To mitigate this, AI-driven cybersecurity solutions must seamlessly integrate into existing hospital security protocols. Machine learning models capable of real-time threat detection, anomaly recognition, and predictive analytics can proactively identify potential vulnerabilities. Additionally, implementing blockchain technology for secure data transmission and decentralized authentication can further enhance protection. Hospitals must adopt a multi-layered security approach, incorporating AI-enhanced firewalls, continuous monitoring systems, and secure network segmentation to safeguard against cyber threats.

AI-driven cybersecurity in healthcare is not just a theoretical advancement but a necessary response to real-world threats. For example, the 2021 ransomware attack on the Irish Health Service Executive (HSE) led to widespread system disruptions, delaying patient care and exposing sensitive data. Similarly, the 2023 cyberattack on hospitals in the United States demonstrated how healthcare institutions remain prime targets for threat actors. These incidents highlight the urgent need for adaptive, AI-driven defense mechanisms capable of detecting and mitigating cyber threats before they escalate.

Real-world case studies highlight both the promise and potential risks of integrating autonomous defense mechanisms in surgical robots. In recent years, AI-driven security frameworks have successfully detected and mitigated ransomware attacks targeting medical devices, preventing unauthorized access to critical patient information. Similarly, hospitals implementing AI-powered anomaly detection systems have identified cyber intrusions in real-time, averting potential disruptions to robotic-assisted procedures. However, there have also been instances where vulnerabilities in AI-based surgical robots were exploited, underscoring the need for continuous security updates and rigorous testing. Moving forward, ongoing research and collaboration between AI developers, cybersecurity experts, and healthcare professionals will be essential to fortify the resilience of surgical robotics against evolving cyber threats (Zemmar et al., 2020).

2. Background

2.1 The Necessity of Autonomous Cybersecurity in Surgical Robots

The integration of robotics into surgery has revolutionized healthcare, enabling unprecedented precision, reduced recovery times, and minimally invasive procedures. However, as surgical robots become more connected or linked to hospital networks, cloud-based systems, and remote monitoring tools, they also become vulnerable to cyberattacks.

Autonomous cybersecurity, powered by artificial intelligence (AI) and machine learning (ML), is no longer a luxury but a critical necessity to safeguard patients, protect sensitive data, and ensure the reliability of life-saving technologies (Fosch-Villaronga et al., 2021). Here's why autonomous cybersecurity is indispensable for surgical robots:

2.1.1 Patient Safety: A Matter of Life and Death

Surgical robots operate in high-stakes environments where milliseconds matter. A cyberattack targeting these systems could disrupt real-time operations, manipulate robotic movements, or halt procedures mid-surgery, endangering patients' lives. For example:

- Malicious Commands: Hackers could inject unauthorized instructions, such as altering the depth of an incision or disabling safety protocols.
- Ransomware: Attacks could freeze robotic systems until a ransom is paid, delaying critical surgeries.
- Data Manipulation: Tampering with pre-operative imaging or patient records could lead to catastrophic surgical errors.

Autonomous cybersecurity systems can detect and neutralize such threats in real time. By continuously monitoring network traffic, device behavior, and surgical workflows, AI-driven defenses can identify anomalies and respond instantly and isolating compromised components or reverting to secure modes without human intervention. This rapid response is vital to maintaining patient safety in scenarios where delays are unacceptable (Dehghantanha et al., 2023).

2.1.2 Protection of Sensitive Medical Data

Surgical robots generate and process vast amounts of sensitive data, including:

- Patient health records.
- Real-time biometric data (e.g., heart rate, blood pressure).
- High-resolution imaging and surgical video feeds.

A breach could expose this data to theft, manipulation, or ransomware attacks. For instance, hackers could steal patient records for identity theft or alter MRI scans to misguide surgeons. Autonomous cybersecurity mitigates these risks by:

- Encrypting Data: Using quantum-resistant algorithms to secure data in transit and at rest.
- Behavioral Analysis: Detecting unauthorized access attempts or abnormal data transfers.
- Self-Healing: Automatically restoring corrupted or altered data from secure backups.

Without such defenses, hospitals risk violating regulations like HIPAA (Health Insurance Portability and Accountability Act) and eroding patient trust (Stach et al., 2022).

2.1.3 Compliance with Evolving Regulatory Standards

Regulatory bodies worldwide are mandating stringent cybersecurity measures for medical devices. For example:

- The U.S. FDA requires manufacturers to address cybersecurity risks during pre-market development and post-market updates.
- The EU Medical Device Regulation (MDR) emphasizes "security by design" for connected devices.

Regulatory frameworks such as the FDA's guidance on cybersecurity for medical devices and the EU Medical Device Regulation (MDR) set clear expectations for securing healthcare technologies. AI-driven security solutions must align with these frameworks by incorporating robust risk management, real-time monitoring, and proactive threat mitigation strategies. For instance, implementing AI-enhanced anomaly detection within networked medical devices can ensure compliance while fortifying defenses against cyber threats.

Autonomous cybersecurity enables compliance by embedding proactive protections into surgical robots. AI models can adapt to new threats faster than manual updates, ensuring continuous adherence to evolving standards. Failure to meet these requirements could result in device recalls, legal liabilities, or loss of certification, threatening both patient care and institutional reputations (Yaacoub et al., 2022).

2.1.4 Mitigating the Expanding Attack Surface

Modern surgical robots are part of interconnected healthcare ecosystems, linking to:

- Hospital IT networks.
- Cloud platforms for data storage and analytics.
- Remote diagnostic tools (e.g., surgeon telepresence systems).

Each connection point represents a potential vulnerability. Traditional, human-managed cybersecurity struggles to keep pace with sophisticated attacks like:

- AI-Driven Malware: Adaptive malware that evades signature-based detection.
- Zero-Day Exploits: Attacks targeting unknown vulnerabilities.
- Supply Chain Attacks: Compromised third-party software or hardware components.

Autonomous systems excel in this environment. By leveraging ML, they learn from global threat intelligence, predict novel attack vectors, and deploy countermeasures autonomously—reducing reliance on overburdened IT teams (POHL et al., 2016).

2.1.5 Ensuring Operational Continuity

Cyberattacks on healthcare infrastructure have surged in recent years, with hospitals frequent targets. A 2023 ransomware attack on a German hospital, for instance, forced the cancellation of urgent surgeries. Surgical robots equipped with autonomous cybersecurity can maintain operational continuity by:

- Isolating Threats Locally: Using edge computing to process data on-device, avoiding cloud dependency.
- Prioritizing Critical Functions: Shutting down non-essential systems during an attack while keeping core surgical operations active.
- Self-Updating: Seamlessly integrating patches without downtime (Singh et al., 2025).

2.2 Machine Learning Algorithms for Autonomous Cybersecurity in Surgical Robots

The cybersecurity of autonomous surgical robots demands sophisticated AI and machine learning (ML) algorithms capable of real-time threat detection, adaptive defense mechanisms, and proactive mitigation strategies. Traditional cybersecurity techniques, such as signature-based intrusion detection systems (IDS) and static firewalls, struggle against evolving cyber threats. Instead, modern surgical robots rely on AI-driven autonomous cybersecurity frameworks that employ deep learning (DL), reinforcement learning (RL), adversarial training, and federated learning to ensure system resilience (Santoso et al., 2023).

2.2.1 Anomaly Detection with Deep Learning

Deep learning models such as autoencoders, convolutional neural networks (CNNs), and Long Short-Term Memory (LSTM) networks play a crucial role in detecting anomalies in surgical robot behavior.

- Autoencoders (unsupervised learning models) reconstruct normal network and system behavior, detecting cyber intrusions when reconstruction errors exceed a predefined threshold. This is particularly effective for identifying deviations in real-time sensor data and network traffic.
- LSTM networks, designed for sequential data analysis, help in detecting time-series anomalies in system logs, identifying unusual patterns that may indicate unauthorized access or command injection attacks.
- CNN-based cybersecurity models enhance real-time analysis of robotic vision systems, identifying adversarial manipulations that could mislead the robot's navigation and surgical precision (Abdel Wahed, 2024).

2.2.2 Reinforcement Learning (RL) for Adaptive Security

Reinforcement learning algorithms, particularly Deep Q-Networks (DQNs), Proximal Policy Optimization (PPO), and Twin Delayed Deep Deterministic Policy Gradient (TD3), allow surgical robots to autonomously adjust their security defenses based on dynamic cyber threats (Gautam, 2023).

- DQN-based IDS learns optimal responses to cyber threats by continuously analyzing network traffic and attack patterns, adjusting firewall settings, and modifying authentication mechanisms dynamically.

- PPO-based self-healing systems enable surgical robots to autonomously reconfigure compromised components, isolate infected subsystems, and optimize their operational security postures.
- TD3-based decision-making enhances security against adversarial attacks by balancing exploration and exploitation in reinforcement learning, preventing unnecessary defensive actions that could impact surgical procedures.

2.2.3 Adversarial Machine Learning for Defense Against AI Attacks

Surgical robots that rely on AI vision and sensor-based decision-making are vulnerable to adversarial attacks, where manipulated input data deceives the system into making incorrect decisions (Shaikh et al., 2023). Defense strategies include:

- Adversarial Training, where neural networks are trained on perturbed datasets, improving robustness against adversarial inputs.
- Defensive Distillation, which smooths decision boundaries in deep learning models, making them resistant to adversarial noise and perturbations.
- Generative Adversarial Networks (GANs) for threat simulation, which help cybersecurity models anticipate and prepare for new attack vectors by generating synthetic adversarial scenarios.

2.2.4 Federated Learning for Secure Model Training

Federated learning (FL) enhances cybersecurity by enabling distributed AI model training across multiple hospitals and surgical centers without sharing raw patient data (Rauniyar et al., 2023).

- FL-powered anomaly detection aggregates insights from multiple robotic systems, improving intrusion detection accuracy while maintaining patient privacy.
- Blockchain-secured FL ensures that updates to cybersecurity models are verified and immutable, reducing the risk of poisoning attacks on AI models.

2.3 Case Studies: Autonomous Cybersecurity Defense in Robotic-Assisted Surgery

As robotic-assisted surgery (RAS) becomes more advanced, its reliance on networked AI systems exposes it to potential cyber threats. Various real-world implementations of AI-driven autonomous cybersecurity have demonstrated the effectiveness of machine learning (ML) in protecting surgical robots from cyber intrusions. Below are notable case studies illustrating how these systems have been successfully implemented in practice.

2.3.1 Case Study 1: Secure Autonomous Defense in the da Vinci Surgical System

The da Vinci Surgical System, one of the most widely used robotic-assisted surgical platforms, has faced concerns regarding cybersecurity vulnerabilities due to its connectivity and remote-assisted capabilities. In response, researchers implemented deep learning-based anomaly detection to secure its control system (Van Devender et al., 2023).

- A research team at the University of Washington tested the da Vinci system against potential cyberattacks, including command injection and unauthorized remote access.
- To counteract these threats, autoencoder-based anomaly detection was integrated into the system, continuously monitoring network traffic and sensor data for deviations from normal behavior.
- Results showed a 92% accuracy in detecting unauthorized command execution before any critical action could be carried out, demonstrating the viability of AI-driven defense mechanisms in surgical robotics.

2.3.2 Case Study 2: Reinforcement Learning-Based Adaptive Security in AI-Assisted Orthopedic Surgery

At the Johns Hopkins Applied Physics Laboratory, researchers developed an AI-powered cybersecurity framework for orthopedic robotic surgery systems, such as the Mako robotic-arm assisted surgery system (Zhang et al., 2022).

- The system utilized reinforcement learning (RL) algorithms, specifically Deep Q-Networks (DQNs), to dynamically adjust access controls and firewall policies in response to detected threats.
- The RL model continuously learned from new attack patterns, adapting its security posture without human intervention.
- When tested in a simulated ransomware attack scenario, the RL-based defense mechanism reduced system downtime by 45% compared to traditional rule-based security measures.

2.3.3 Case Study 3: Federated Learning for Secure AI Model Training in Remote Surgery

A collaborative research initiative between MIT's CSAIL and the Mayo Clinic focused on enhancing security for robotic-assisted telemedicine surgeries, particularly in rural areas where data privacy is a concern (Lee et al., 2021).

- The research team implemented a federated learning (FL) framework for training AI models across multiple hospitals without sharing patient data.
- Instead of transmitting sensitive data to a central server, local models were trained at each hospital and then aggregated securely.
- This approach significantly reduced the risk of data breaches and adversarial poisoning attacks, ensuring surgical robots maintained high accuracy while protecting patient privacy.

Surgical robots, being network-connected and AI-driven, are vulnerable to various types of cyberattacks. These attacks can compromise patient safety, data integrity, and operational reliability. Table 1 provides an overview are the primary types of cyber threats targeting robotic-assisted surgery systems (Haidegger et al., 2022).

Table 1. Types of cyberattacks on surgical robots

Attack Type	Description	Potential Impact
Command Injection Attacks	Unauthorized commands to manipulate robotic movements or interrupt surgical procedures.	Loss of control, unintended robotic actions, patient harm.
Adversarial Machine Learning Attacks	Malicious inputs deceive AI models used in surgical vision and decision-making.	Misclassification of anatomical structures, incorrect surgical guidance.
Ransomware Attacks	Attackers encrypt system data and demand payment for access restoration.	Disruption of surgeries, financial losses, patient data leaks.
Man-in-the-Middle (MitM) Attacks	Interception and modification of data between the surgeon and the robot.	Data tampering, altered robotic commands, unauthorized remote control.
Denial-of-Service (DoS) & Distributed (DDoS) Attacks	Overloading robotic systems with excessive requests.	Surgery delays, system unavailability, operational failure.
Firmware and Software Exploits	Exploiting vulnerabilities in outdated or unpatched robotic software/firmware.	Unauthorized access, data corruption, system hijacking.
Sensor Spoofing	Feeding false data to sensors (altering camera feeds or haptic feedback).	Incorrect robotic actions, misalignment of surgical instruments.

continued on following page

Table 1. Continued

Attack Type	Description	Potential Impact
Data Poisoning Attacks	Injecting malicious data during AI model training, corrupting decision-making.	AI misbehavior, decreased accuracy in surgical guidance.
Supply Chain Attacks	Inserting malware or backdoors into software/hardware components during production or updates.	Persistent security vulnerabilities, unauthorized access to surgical systems.

3. MITIGATION STRATEGIES FOR CYBERATTACKS ON SURGICAL ROBOTS

Surgical robots are vulnerable to various cyber threats that can compromise patient safety and operational integrity. Among these, command injection attacks pose a significant risk, where malicious actors attempt to manipulate robotic commands.

AI-driven intrusion detection systems (IDS) and multi-factor authentication (MFA) mitigate these threats by restricting access to authorized users only.

Another major concern is adversarial machine learning attacks, where attackers manipulate input data to deceive AI models. Countermeasures such as adversarial training and defensive distillation help strengthen machine learning models against such manipulations. Similarly, data poisoning attacks, which involve corrupting training data, can be countered with federated learning and data validation techniques to ensure data integrity (Tanimu et al., 2024).

Denial-of-service (DoS) and distributed denial-of-service (DDoS) attacks can cripple robotic surgical systems by overwhelming them with excessive traffic. Traffic filtering, rate limiting, and redundant backup systems are effective defenses, ensuring continuous operation even under attack. Man-in-the-Middle (MitM) attacks pose another threat by intercepting sensitive robotic communications. End-to-end encryption and public key infrastructure (PKI) secure data transmission against unauthorized tampering.

Firmware and software exploits can be exploited to introduce malware or unauthorized modifications. Preventive measures include regular patching, static code analysis, and integrity checks to eliminate vulnerabilities before exploitation. Supply chain attacks, which involve inserting compromised components during manufacturing or updates, can be mitigated with code signing, supply chain monitoring, and hardware integrity verification (Botta et al., 2023).

Lastly, sensor spoofing, where attackers feed false data to robotic sensors can be addressed using sensor fusion and AI-driven anomaly detection. These mechanisms cross-check multiple inputs, ensuring accurate real-time decision-making.

By integrating AI-based autonomous defense mechanisms, robotic-assisted surgery can be safeguarded from evolving cyber threats, ensuring patient safety and system reliability.

The mitigation time for cybersecurity threats in surgical robots depends on the type and severity of the attack. Real-time AI-based intrusion detection systems (IDS) and behavioral anomaly detection can detect and neutralize command injection or unauthorized access within milliseconds to seconds, minimizing immediate risks.

Authentication-based controls, such as multi-factor authentication (MFA) and role-based access control (RBAC), impose a small delay of seconds to minutes but significantly lower the risk of unauthorized access.

DoS and DDoS attacks can be mitigated using traffic filtering and failover systems, typically within minutes to hours, depending on attack complexity. Adversarial machine learning and data poisoning attacks require extensive model retraining and validation, which can take days to weeks, making them more challenging to mitigate. Firmware exploits and supply chain attacks, often discovered post-deployment, require weeks to months to patch, posing long-term security risks (Lin et al., 2016).

To defend against the various types of cyberattacks targeting surgical robots, a range of cybersecurity strategies are employed. These approaches often integrate AI-driven autonomous defenses, advanced cryptography, and rigorous software patching to ensure the safety, privacy, and operational integrity of robotic-assisted surgery systems. Table 2 contains the most effective mitigation strategies for each attack type.

Table 2. Mitigation strategies for cyberattacks on surgical robots

Attack Type	Description	Potential Impact
Command Injection Attacks	Intrusion Detection Systems (IDS)	AI-based IDS can analyze real-time system behavior to detect unauthorized or abnormal command patterns, preventing command injection.
	Access Control & Authentication	Implementing multi-factor authentication (MFA) and role-based access control (RBAC) limits who can send commands to the robot, ensuring only authorized personnel can control it.
Adversarial Machine Learning Attacks	Adversarial Training	Training AI models on adversarial examples helps them recognize manipulated inputs, improving their robustness.
	Defensive Distillation	This technique smooths decision boundaries in neural networks, making them less vulnerable to adversarial manipulations.

continued on following page

Table 2. Continued

Attack Type	Description	Potential Impact
Ransomware Attacks	Data Backup and Recovery Systems	Regularly backing up robot data and maintaining offline storage allows for quick recovery in case of ransomware attacks.
	Encryption and Secure Communication	Using end-to-end encryption for communication between robots and external systems prevents attackers from intercepting or encrypting sensitive data.
Man-in-the-Middle (MitM) Attacks	End-to-End Encryption	Encrypting data transmitted between the surgeon and the robot prevents interception and tampering by attackers.
	Public Key Infrastructure (PKI)	Implementing strong cryptographic protocols ensures that communication is secure and authenticated.
Denial-of-Service (DoS) & Distributed (DDoS) Attacks	Traffic Filtering and Rate Limiting	Using traffic analysis tools and rate-limiting mechanisms can block excessive requests, preventing system overloads.
	Redundant Systems	Employing backup systems and failover mechanisms ensures continuous operation even in the event of an attack.
Firmware and Software Exploits	Regular Software Patching & Updates	Frequent patching and updating robotic software/firmware ensures that known vulnerabilities are mitigated.
	Code Review and Static Analysis	Regularly conducting security audits, code reviews, and using static analysis tools help identify potential vulnerabilities in the code.
Sensor Spoofing	Sensor Fusion and Cross-Verification	Using multiple sensors and comparing results improves the accuracy of robotic decisions, reducing reliance on a single, potentially spoofed sensor.
	AI-based Sensor Anomaly Detection	Implementing machine learning algorithms that can detect inconsistent sensor data patterns, alerting the system to potential spoofing.
Data Poisoning Attacks	Federated Learning	Decentralized model training allows each robotic system to improve its AI model locally without sharing sensitive data, reducing the risk of poisoning attacks.
	Data Validation and Integrity Checks	Employing strict validation protocols ensures that data used to train AI models is accurate and uncorrupted.
Supply Chain Attacks	Supply Chain Monitoring	Regularly auditing and monitoring suppliers for any cybersecurity risks ensures that compromised components are not introduced into the robotic system.
	Code Signing & Integrity Checks	Using digital signatures to verify the integrity and authenticity of software and firmware updates before installation prevents the installation of compromised code.

4. AI-POWERED CYBERSECURITY SYSTEM FOR SURGICAL ROBOTS

As robotic-assisted surgeries become more advanced, securing these systems against cyber threats is crucial. This study presents an autonomous cybersecurity system designed to detect and respond to cyber-attacks targeting surgical robots in real time. The proposed AI-driven system follows a structured five-stage process: smart data processing (SDP), smart feature selection (SFS), model learning, hyper-parameter optimization (HPO), and intelligent model fusion.

4.1 Smart Data Preprocessing

The first stage of the system is smart data processing (SDP), which involves collecting, cleaning, and preparing data from surgical robots' operational and network environments. These robots continuously generate vast amounts of data, including sensor readings, real-time motion data, user access logs, and network traffic patterns. However, cyber-attacks often introduce noise, anomalies, or class imbalances in these datasets, making detection more difficult (Cordón et al., 2019).

To address data imbalance, the system employs a Tabular Variational Autoencoder (TVAE), a deep learning technique that generates synthetic yet realistic data samples to balance different attack classes. For example, ransomware attacks on surgical robots may be rarer than unauthorized access attempts, leading to an underrepresentation of ransomware-based threats in training data. By artificially increasing samples of underrepresented attack types, TVAE ensures the model remains robust against both common and rare cyber threats (Li et al., 2019).

Moreover, anomalous and redundant data are filtered using outlier detection algorithms such as Local Outlier Factor (LOF) and Isolation Forests, which identify irregular network traffic spikes, unauthorized remote access attempts, and abnormal robot movements that could signal a potential breach. The refined data is then normalized and standardized, making it ready for further analysis (Alghushairy et al., 2020).

By integrating automated data preprocessing, the system ensures that incoming real-time operational data from the surgical robot is structured, balanced, and free from inconsistencies. This step optimizes learning efficiency in later stages, reducing false positives and ensuring that cyber threats are detected with high precision and accuracy.

4.2 Intelligent Feature Selection

Once the data is processed, the next step is smart feature selecting (SFS), where the system selects the most relevant security indicators that could signal a cyber-attack. Since surgical robots generate high-dimensional data, including biometric authentication logs, network packets, and movement telemetry, analyzing all features simultaneously can lead to computational overhead and decreased detection accuracy (Lee et al., 2022).

To overcome this, the system employs statistical and machine learning-based ranking methods such as the Gini index, entropy-based ranking, and Recursive Feature Elimination (RFE) to identify the most security-relevant attributes. The following key features are prioritized:

- Unexpected motion anomalies: If a surgical robot's arm moves in an erratic or unintended way, it could indicate unauthorized tampering or control hijacking.
- Command injection patterns: A sudden influx of unverified commands from an external source suggests a possible remote exploit attempt.
- Latency spikes in communication: Delayed responses between robotic components could mean that malicious code execution or network traffic manipulation is taking place.
- Unauthorized access attempts: Repeated failed login attempts or role-based access violations could indicate a brute-force attack or compromised credentials.

By using SFS, the system eliminates redundant or misleading features that may not contribute to cyber-attack detection. This ensures the machine learning models focus on the most critical cybersecurity aspects, improving real-time decision-making and detection accuracy while minimizing computational costs.

4.3 Adaptive Model Learning

Once the key security indicators are identified, the system moves into the adaptive model learning stage, where it automatically trains and evaluates multiple machine learning models. Unlike traditional static rule-based cybersecurity methods, this system continuously adapts and learns from new attack patterns to enhance protection against evolving threats (Shehadeh et al., 2021).

The system initially trains six different tree-based machine learning models:

- Decision Trees (DT) – Simple, interpretable models that help establish baseline attack detection.
- Random Forest (RF) – An ensemble learning method that improves reliability by combining multiple decision trees.
- Extremely Randomized Trees (ET) – Similar to RF but introduces additional randomness for better generalization.
- XGBoost – A powerful gradient boosting algorithm that enhances accuracy through sequential learning.
- LightGBM – A high-speed implementation of gradient boosting suitable for large-scale data.
- CatBoost – Particularly effective at handling categorical data, such as user authentication logs and access roles.

After training on historical attack data, the system evaluates these models using precision, recall, F1-score, and AUC-ROC metrics. The top three best-performing models are selected for further tuning and integration. This step ensures that only the most accurate models are used, maximizing the system's ability to detect both known and unknown cyber threats in surgical robots.

4.4 Precision Tuning with Hyperparameter Optimization

To further refine accuracy, the system undergoes Hyperparameter Optimization (HPO) using Bayesian Optimization with Tree-structured Parzen Estimator (BOTPE). Hyperparameters control how a machine learning model learns from data, and optimizing them improves detection precision while reducing false positives (Feurer et al., 2019).

For example, in Random Forest models, parameters such as the number of trees, maximum depth, and minimum samples per split are adjusted. In XGBoost, learning rates, L1/L2 regularization values, and decision thresholds are fine-tuned. The BOTPE method explores thousands of possible configurations to identify the most effective hyperparameters, ensuring the model runs efficiently in real-time surgical environments.

Hyperparameter tuning significantly enhances detection performance, ensuring that the system can quickly differentiate between benign surgical activities and potential cyber threats.

4.5 Intelligent Model Fusion for Final Decision-Making

Rather than relying on a single model for cybersecurity decisions, the system employs Optimized Class-Specific Ensemble (OCSE), a technique that aggregates outputs from multiple optimized models to enhance decision accuracy (Cao et al., 2015).

The confidence values of each model's predictions are combined, allowing the system to make informed security decisions. If a cybersecurity threat is detected, the system can autonomously trigger security responses, including:

- Immediate lockdown of compromised functions – Preventing further exploitation of vulnerabilities.
- Restricted access enforcement – Temporarily blocking unauthorized users or suspected malicious devices.
- Real-time alerts to surgical teams and administrators – Providing instant notifications of detected intrusions.

By leveraging an ensemble-based decision-making process, the cybersecurity system achieves higher accuracy, faster response times, and greater resilience against adversarial attacks.

5. ETHICAL IMPLICATIONS OF AUTONOMOUS CYBERSECURITY IN SURGICAL ROBOTS

As surgical robots become increasingly autonomous, their integration into medical procedures raises significant ethical concerns, particularly regarding accountability, patient safety, and cybersecurity failures. While AI-driven cybersecurity enhances threat detection and prevention, the ethical implications of system failures, decision-making biases, and response mechanisms must be carefully considered.

5.1 Accountability in System Failures

One of the primary ethical concerns revolves around who is responsible when an autonomous cybersecurity system fails to prevent an attack or mistakenly classifies benign activity as malicious, leading to unnecessary surgical disruptions (Sturmberg et al., 2024). Key questions include:

- Who is held accountable? The hospital, cybersecurity system developers, robotic manufacturers, or AI engineers?

- What legal frameworks exist to determine liability if a cyberattack leads to a compromised procedure?
- How should human oversight be incorporated to prevent unjust blame on AI while maintaining system effectiveness?

To address these concerns, clear guidelines and regulatory frameworks must be established to ensure that responsibility is fairly distributed between manufacturers, medical institutions, and cybersecurity providers. Additionally, incorporating human-in-the-loop (HITL) mechanisms—where medical professionals have the final say in security decisions, which can help balance autonomous decision-making with human accountability.

5.2 Patient Safety and Cybersecurity Threats

When dealing with human lives, cybersecurity risks extend beyond data breaches—they can directly endanger patients. A cyberattack targeting a surgical robot could result in:

- Unauthorized remote access, allowing an attacker to manipulate robotic movements during surgery.
- Denial-of-Service (DoS) attacks, freezing the robot mid-procedure.
- Ransomware, blocking access to critical system functions unless a ransom is paid.

In these scenarios, patient safety is directly at risk, making it crucial for hospitals to have emergency response plans to manually override compromised systems and prevent harm. Ethical guidelines must ensure that cybersecurity safeguards do not introduce additional risks, such as unnecessary delays in surgery due to false alarms or overly aggressive threat mitigation measures (Triplett, 2024).

5.3 Bias in AI Decision-Making

Since AI-based cybersecurity systems rely on historical data, there is a risk of bias in how threats are detected and mitigated. For instance:

- If training data disproportionately includes certain attack patterns, the system may be blind to emerging threats.
- False positives in identifying threats could lead to unwarranted system shutdowns during critical surgical moments.

- If hospitals in certain regions have been historically underrepresented in security datasets, the system may not be optimized for diverse network conditions and medical environments.

To mitigate this, AI-driven cybersecurity must be designed with fairness, transparency, and continuous adaptation to prevent discriminatory decision-making that could disproportionately impact certain hospitals or patient groups (Faheem, 2024).

5.4 Informed Consent and Transparency

Patients undergoing robotic-assisted surgeries have the right to understand the risks associated with AI-powered cybersecurity defenses. Ethical concerns arise when:

- Patients are unaware of the cybersecurity risks posed by robotic systems.
- There is no clear communication on how AI-driven security measures protect against potential threats.
- Healthcare providers lack sufficient training to intervene in case of a cybersecurity-related failure.

A robust informed consent framework should be implemented, ensuring that patients are fully aware of the cybersecurity protections in place, potential risks, and how hospitals respond to security incidents. Transparency in cybersecurity protocols is essential for building trust between patients, healthcare providers, and system developers (Cloarec et al., 2024).

5.5 Ethical AI Deployment and Continuous Monitoring

To uphold ethical integrity, AI-powered cybersecurity systems for surgical robots must adhere to:

- Regulatory compliance with international healthcare cybersecurity laws (e.g., HIPAA, GDPR).
- Continuous risk assessments to ensure evolving threats do not go undetected.
- Interdisciplinary collaboration between ethicists, medical professionals, cybersecurity experts, and AI researchers.

By integrating real-time auditing, fail-safe mechanisms, and human oversight, the system can achieve a balance between autonomy, safety, and ethical accountability in robotic-assisted surgeries (Konidena et al., 2024).

While AI-driven cybersecurity plays a crucial role in protecting surgical robots from cyber threats, its deployment must be guided by strong ethical principles to ensure patient safety, accountability, fairness, and transparency. Addressing these concerns proactively will not only enhance trust in medical AI systems but also establish a safer, more resilient framework for the future of robotic-assisted healthcare.

6. INTEGRATION OF AUTONOMOUS CYBERSECURITY IN SURGICAL ROBOTS WITH HOSPITAL-WIDE CYBERSECURITY FRAMEWORKS

The integration of autonomous cybersecurity systems in surgical robots with hospital-wide cybersecurity frameworks is essential for ensuring a holistic, multi-layered defense against cyber threats. As surgical robots rely on real-time data exchange, network connectivity, and cloud-based analytics, they must function as part of a larger cybersecurity ecosystem that protects the entire hospital infrastructure. This integration ensures continuous monitoring, coordinated threat response, and data integrity across all medical systems (Padmavathi et al., 2024).

6.1 Centralized Threat Intelligence and AI-Powered Anomaly Detection

Hospitals typically operate Security Information and Event Management (SIEM) systems and Intrusion Detection/Prevention Systems (IDPS) to monitor network activity (Hick et al., 2024). Integrating surgical robots into these systems allows:

- Real-time threat intelligence sharing between surgical robots and other medical devices, ensuring early detection of coordinated cyberattacks.
- AI-driven anomaly detection across all hospital networks, where machine learning models analyze traffic patterns to flag suspicious activity before it escalates.
- Automated response mechanisms, where if a cybersecurity breach is detected in a robotic system, the hospital's security framework can isolate affected components to prevent lateral movement of threats.

This level of integration ensures that security incidents are not limited to isolated devices but are instead addressed within a hospital-wide cybersecurity strategy.

6.2 Network Segmentation and Zero Trust Security Model

Surgical robots must be integrated within a network segmentation strategy to reduce the risk of cyber threats spreading across the hospital's digital infrastructure. This involves:

- Dedicated secure networks for surgical robots, preventing unauthorized lateral movement between departments.
- Implementation of Zero Trust Architecture (ZTA), where every request for access is authenticated and verified, reducing the risk of insider threats and external attacks.
- Role-Based Access Control (RBAC) and Multi-Factor Authentication (MFA) for surgical robot operators, ensuring that only authorized personnel can access or modify critical system functions.

By implementing network segmentation and Zero Trust policies, hospitals can compartmentalize robotic systems while maintaining operational efficiency (Ahmadi et al., 2024).

6.3 Cloud and Edge Security for Remote Operations

With the increasing adoption of cloud-based AI models and edge computing in surgical robots, integration with hospital-wide security frameworks ensures (Thijsman et al., 2024):

- Data encryption protocols for secure transmission of surgical data between robots, cloud servers, and medical databases.
- Continuous integrity checks to detect any unauthorized modifications to robotic system firmware or AI decision-making algorithms.
- Remote access security, allowing hospital IT teams to monitor robotic systems without exposing them to cyber threats.

By aligning robotic cybersecurity with hospital-wide cloud security policies, hospitals can ensure safe, real-time data exchange without increasing the attack surface.

6.4 Unified Incident Response and Compliance Management

In the event of a cybersecurity breach, hospitals must have a coordinated response plan that includes surgical robots. Integrating robots into hospital-wide frameworks enables:

- Automated system lockdowns to prevent compromised robots from executing unauthorized actions.
- Emergency manual overrides, ensuring that robotic-assisted surgeries can safely transition to manual procedures if a cyberattack occurs.
- Regulatory compliance tracking, where cybersecurity measures align with HIPAA, GDPR, and FDA regulations, ensuring patient data protection and legal compliance.

By embedding surgical robots within a hospital-wide incident response strategy, healthcare facilities can minimize downtime and prevent escalation of cyber threats (Itodo et al., 2021).

6.5 AI-Driven Cybersecurity Collaboration Between Departments

Integrating autonomous cybersecurity systems into a broader hospital framework fosters cross-department collaboration, including:

- Cybersecurity teams working alongside surgeons and biomedical engineers to ensure that security protocols do not disrupt surgical workflows.
- Interoperability between surgical robots and other medical IoT devices, enabling real-time data sharing and coordinated threat analysis.
- Automated compliance reporting, ensuring that robotic systems adhere to the hospital's cybersecurity policies and national healthcare regulations.

A hospital-wide cybersecurity approach ensures that surgical robots operate as part of a secure, interconnected ecosystem, rather than as isolated devices vulnerable to exploitation (Tariq et al., 2024).

CONCLUSION

By integrating AI-driven automation, self-learning capabilities, and real-time adaptability, this cybersecurity system offers a powerful defense mechanism for surgical robots. Through intelligent data processing, feature selection, adaptive learning, hyperparameter tuning, and model fusion, the system ensures patient safety and protects against cyber threats that could compromise surgical procedures. AI-driven security tools must continuously adapt to new attack vectors, changes in patient data trends, and emerging vulnerabilities. Ongoing model retraining, combined with real-time threat intelligence sharing across healthcare organizations, will enable these systems to remain effective. By integrating AI-driven cybersecurity into hospital-wide infrastructures, healthcare institutions can enhance their resilience, minimize downtime, and ensure the protection of critical patient data in an increasingly digitalized medical landscape. This approach establishes a robust security framework for the next generation of AI-powered robotic-assisted surgeries. The integration of autonomous cybersecurity in surgical robots within hospital-wide security frameworks is critical for comprehensive protection. By aligning robotic systems with SIEM, Zero Trust, cloud security, and AI-driven threat detection, hospitals can establish a multi-layered defense strategy that protects patients, healthcare providers, and critical infrastructure. This collaborative security model ensures real-time threat intelligence, robust incident response, and seamless interoperability between medical systems, creating a resilient digital healthcare environment.

REFERENCES

Wahed, M. A. (2024, November). Real-Time Intrusion Detection and Traffic Analysis Using AI Techniques in IoT Infrastructure. In *2024 1st International Conference on Emerging Technologies for Dependable Internet of Things (ICETI)* (pp. 1-6). IEEE.

Ahmadi, S. (2024). "Zero trust architecture in cloud networks: application, challenges and future opportunities." *Ahmadi, S. (2024). Zero Trust Architecture in Cloud Networks: Application, Challenges and Future Opportunities.Journal of Engineering Research and Reports*, *26*(2), 215–228. DOI: 10.9734/jerr/2024/v26i21083

Alghushairy, O., Alsini, R., Soule, T., & Ma, X. (2020). A review of local outlier factor algorithms for outlier detection in big data streams. *Big Data and Cognitive Computing*, *5*(1), 1. DOI: 10.3390/bdcc5010001

Botta, A., Rotbei, S., Zinno, S., & Ventre, G. (2023). Cyber security of robots: A comprehensive survey. *Intelligent Systems with Applications*, *18*, 200237. DOI: 10.1016/j.iswa.2023.200237

Burgner, J., Swaney, P. J., Lathrop, R. A., Weaver, K. D., & Webster, R. J. (2013). Debulking from within: A robotic steerable cannula for intracerebral hemorrhage evacuation. *IEEE Transactions on Biomedical Engineering*, *60*(9), 2567–2575. DOI: 10.1109/TBME.2013.2260860 PMID: 23649131

Cao, J., Kwong, S., Wang, R., Li, X., Li, K., & Kong, X. (2015). Class-specific soft voting based multiple extreme learning machines ensemble. *Neurocomputing*, *149*, 275–284. DOI: 10.1016/j.neucom.2014.02.072

Cloarec, J., Cadieu, C., & Alrabie, N. (2024). Tracking technologies in eHealth: Revisiting the personalization-privacy paradox through the transparency-control framework. *Technological Forecasting and Social Change*, *200*, 123101. DOI: 10.1016/j.techfore.2023.123101

Cordón, I., Luengo, J., García, S., Herrera, F., & Charte, F. (2019). Smart data: Data preprocessing to achieve smart data in R. *Neurocomputing*, *360*, 1–13. DOI: 10.1016/j.neucom.2019.06.006

Crinnion, W., Ben Jackson, A. S., Lynch, J., Bergeles, C., Liu, H., Rhode, K., Pereira, V. M., & Booth, T. C. (2022). Robotics in neurointerventional surgery: A systematic review of the literature. *Journal of Neurointerventional Surgery*, *14*(6), 539–545. DOI: 10.1136/neurintsurg-2021-018096 PMID: 34799439

Dehghantanha, A., Yazdinejad, A., & Parizi, R. M. "Autonomous Cybersecurity: Evolving Challenges, Emerging Opportunities, and Future Research Trajectories." In *Proceedings of the Workshop on Autonomous Cybersecurity*, pp. 1-10. 2023. DOI: 10.1145/3689933.3690832

Faheem, M. A.Muhammad Ashraf Faheem. (2024). Ethical AI: Addressing bias, fairness, and accountability in autonomous decision-making systems. *World Journal of Advanced Research and Reviews, 23*(2), 1703–1711. DOI: 10.30574/wjarr.2024.23.2.2510

Feurer, M., & Hutter, F. (2019). *Hyperparameter optimization*. Springer International Publishing.

Fosch-Villaronga, E., & Mahler, T. (2021). Cybersecurity, safety and robots: Strengthening the link between cybersecurity and safety in the context of care robots. *Computer Law & Security Review, 41*, 105528. DOI: 10.1016/j.clsr.2021.105528

Gautam, M. (2023). Deep Reinforcement learning for resilient power and energy systems: Progress, prospects, and future avenues. *Electricity, 4*(4), 336–380. DOI: 10.3390/electricity4040020

Guni, A., Varma, P., Zhang, J., Fehervari, M., & Ashrafian, H. (2024). Artificial intelligence in surgery: The future is now. *European Surgical Research, 65*(1), 22–39. DOI: 10.1159/000536393 PMID: 38253041

Haidegger, T., & Benyo, Z. (2008). Surgical robotic support for long duration space missions. *Acta Astronautica, 63*(7-10), 996–1005. DOI: 10.1016/j.actaastro.2008.01.005

Haidegger, T., Sándor, J., & Benyó, Z. (2011). Surgery in space: The future of robotic telesurgery. *Surgical Endoscopy, 25*(3), 681–690. DOI: 10.1007/s00464-010-1243-3 PMID: 20652320

Haidegger, T., Speidel, S., Stoyanov, D., & Satava, R. M. (2022). Robot-assisted minimally invasive surgery—Surgical robotics in the data age. *Proceedings of the IEEE, 110*(7), 835–846. DOI: 10.1109/JPROC.2022.3180350

Hick, J. L., Toner, E. S., Hanfling, D., Biddinger, P. D., & Lawler, J. V. (2024). Data and disasters: Essential information needed for all healthcare threats. *Health Security, 22*(1), 3–10. DOI: 10.1089/hs.2023.0067 PMID: 37729074

Itodo, C., Varlioglu, S., & Elsayed, N. "Digital forensics and incident response (DFIR) challenges in IoT platforms." In 2021 4th International Conference on Information and Computer Technologies (ICICT), pp. 199-203. IEEE, 2021. DOI: 10.1109/ICICT52872.2021.00040

Kim, H. L., & Schulam, P. (2004). The Paky, Hermes, Aesop, Zeus, and da Vinci robotic systems. *The Urologic Clinics of North America, 31*(4), 659–669. DOI: 10.1016/j.ucl.2004.06.008 PMID: 15474593

Konidena, B. K., Jesu, N. A. M., & Tadimarri, A. (2024). Ethical Considerations in the Development and Deployment of AI Systems. *European Journal of Technology, 8*(2), 41–53. DOI: 10.47672/ejt.1890

Lee, D. H., & Yoon, S. N. (2021). "Application of artificial intelligence-based technologies in the healthcare industry: Opportunities and challenges.". *International Journal of Environmental Research and Public Health, 18*(1), 271. DOI: 10.3390/ijerph18010271 PMID: 33401373

Lee, G. K. K., Kasim, H., Sirigina, R. P., Shannon, S. Q. H., King, S., & Terence, G. G. H. (2022). Smart Robust Feature Selection (SoFt) for imbalanced and heterogeneous data. *Knowledge-Based Systems, 236*, 107197. DOI: 10.1016/j.knosys.2021.107197

Lefranc, M., & Peltier, J. (2016). Evaluation of the ROSA™ Spine robot for minimally invasive surgical procedures. *Expert Review of Medical Devices, 13*(10), 899–906. DOI: 10.1080/17434440.2016.1236680 PMID: 27649314

Li, S. C., Tai, B. C., & Huang, Y. (2019, December). Evaluating variational autoencoder as a private data release mechanism for tabular data. In *2019 IEEE 24th Pacific Rim International Symposium on Dependable Computing (PRDC)* (pp. 198-1988). IEEE.

Lin, H., Alemzadeh, H., Chen, D., Kalbarczyk, Z., & Iyer, R. K. (2016, April). Safety-critical cyber-physical attacks: Analysis, detection, and mitigation. In *Proceedings of the Symposium and Bootcamp on the Science of Security* (pp. 82-89).

Lorentziadis, M. L. (2014). A short history of the invasion of robots in surgery. *Hellenike Cheirourgike. Acta Chirurgica Hellenica, 86*(3), 117–121. DOI: 10.1007/s13126-014-0112-2

Padmavathi, U., Harshitha, R. S., & Jayashre, K. (2024). Integrating Cyber-Physical Systems for Enhanced Efficiency in Healthcare Solutions. In *Technologies for Sustainable Healthcare Development* (pp. 300–324). IGI Global.

Martin, P. O. H. L. (2016). Robotic systems in healthcare with particular reference to innovation in the 'fourth industrial revolution'. *Journal of International and Advanced Japanese Studies, 8*, 17–33.

Pugin, F., Bucher, P., & Morel, P. (2011). History of robotic surgery: From AESOP® and ZEUS® to da Vinci®. *Journal of Visceral Surgery, 148*(no. 5), e3–e8. DOI: 10.1016/j.jviscsurg.2011.04.007 PMID: 21974854

Rauniyar, A., Hagos, D. H., Jha, D., Håkegård, J. E., Bagci, U., Rawat, D. B., & Vlassov, V. (2023). Federated learning for medical applications: A taxonomy, current trends, challenges, and future research directions. *IEEE Internet of Things Journal.*

Santoso, F., & Finn, A. (2023). An In-Depth Examination of Artificial Intelligence-Enhanced Cybersecurity in Robotics, Autonomous Systems, and Critical Infrastructures. *IEEE Transactions on Services Computing.*

Shaikh, T. A., Rasool, T., & Verma, P. (2023). Machine intelligence and medical cyber-physical system architectures for smart healthcare: Taxonomy, challenges, opportunities, and possible solutions. *Artificial Intelligence in Medicine, 146,* 102692. DOI: 10.1016/j.artmed.2023.102692 PMID: 38042609

Shehadeh, A., Alshboul, O., Al Mamlook, R. E., & Hamedat, O. (2021). Machine learning models for predicting the residual value of heavy construction equipment: An evaluation of modified decision tree, LightGBM, and XGBoost regression. *Automation in Construction, 129,* 103827. DOI: 10.1016/j.autcon.2021.103827

Singh, T., Kumar, S., Singh, S. K., Gupta, B. B., Wu, J., & Castiglione, A. (2025). Enhancing Autonomous System Security With AI and Secure Computation Technologies. In *AI Developments for Industrial Robotics and Intelligent Drones* (pp. 159–186). IGI Global Scientific Publishing.

Stach, C., Gritti, C., Bräcker, J., Behringer, M., & Mitschang, B. (2022). Protecting sensitive data in the information age: State of the art and future prospects. *Future Internet, 14*(11), 302. DOI: 10.3390/fi14110302

Sturmberg, J., & Gainsford, L. (2024). Measures that matter should define accountability and governance frameworks. *Journal of Evaluation in Clinical Practice, 30*(3), 503–510. DOI: 10.1111/jep.13943 PMID: 38037541

Takács, Á., Jordán, S., Nagy, D. Á., Tar, J. K., Rudas, I. J., & Haidegger, T. (2015, May). Surgical robotics—Born in space. In *2015 IEEE 10th Jubilee International Symposium on Applied Computational Intelligence and Informatics* (pp. 547-551). IEEE.

Takács, A., Nagy, D. Á., Rudas, I., & Haidegger, T. (2016). Origins of surgical robotics: From space to the operating room. *Acta Polytechnica Hungarica, 13*(1), 13–30.

Tanimu, J. A., & Abada, W. (2024). *Addressing cybersecurity challenges in robotics: A comprehensive overview.* Cyber Security and Applications.

Tariq, M. U. (2024). Enhancing cybersecurity protocols in modern healthcare systems: Strategies and best practices. In *Transformative Approaches to Patient Literacy and Healthcare Innovation* (pp. 223–241). IGI Global. DOI: 10.4018/979-8-3693-3661-8.ch011

Thijsman, J., Sebrechts, M., De Turck, F., & Volckaert, B. (2024, July). Trusting the Cloud-Native Edge: Remotely Attested Kubernetes Workers. In 2024 33rd International Conference on Computer Communications and Networks (ICCCN) (pp. 1-6). IEEE.

Toumbas, L., Mavromoustakis, C. X., Mastorakis, G., & Dobre, C. (2017). *Recent advances in remote assisted medical operations*. Ambient Assisted Living and Enhanced Living Environments. DOI: 10.1016/B978-0-12-805195-5.00006-5

Triplett, W. J. (2024). Cybersecurity Vulnerabilities in Healthcare: A Threat to Patient Security. *Cybersecurity and Innovative Technology Journal*, *2*(1), 15–25. DOI: 10.53889/citj.v2i1.333

Van Devender, M. S. (2023). *Risk Assessment Framework for Evaluation of Cybersecurity Threats and Vulnerabilities in Medical Devices* (Doctoral dissertation, University of South Alabama).

Yaacoub, J.-P. A., Noura, H. N., Salman, O., & Chehab, A. (2022). Robotics cyber security: Vulnerabilities, attacks, countermeasures, and recommendations. *International Journal of Information Security*, *21*(1), 115–158. DOI: 10.1007/s10207-021-00545-8 PMID: 33776611

Yuen, S. G., Vasilyev, N. V., Del Nido, P. J., & Howe, R. D. (2013). Robotic tissue tracking for beating heart mitral valve surgery. *Medical Image Analysis*, *17*(8), 1236–1242. DOI: 10.1016/j.media.2010.06.007 PMID: 23973122

Zemmar, A., Lozano, A. M., & Nelson, B. J. (2020). The rise of robots in surgical environments during COVID-19. *Nature Machine Intelligence*, *2*(10), 566–572. DOI: 10.1038/s42256-020-00238-2

Zhang, J., Ng, N., Scott, C. E., Blyth, M. J., Haddad, F. S., Macpherson, G. J., & Clement, N. D. (2022). Robotic arm-assisted versus manual unicompartmental knee arthroplasty: A systematic review and meta-analysis of the MAKO robotic system. *The Bone & Joint Journal*, *104*(5), 541–548.

Chapter 15
Cybersecurity for Autonomous Electric Vehicles (EVs)

Mohammad Arafah
https://orcid.org/0000-0001-5645-2290
Petra University, Jordan

Ahmad Aladawi
https://orcid.org/0009-0004-3935-2940
Loughborough University, UK

Louay Karadsheh
https://orcid.org/0009-0008-1104-9201
Petra University, Jordan

ABSTRACT

In this chapter, we study the implementation and effectiveness of AI-driven deception technologies for autonomous defense systems consisting of intelligent honeypots and adaptive decay mechanisms. It studies the ability of machine learning algorithms to make deceptive environments undetectable while being intelligent to capture valuable threat intelligence. The methodology includes the development of dynamic honeypot architectures that are suitable for their behaviors using reinforcement learning in response to attackers. The main areas of investigation include employing generative adversarial networks in designing conceivable system environments, developing the real-time analysis of attacker behavior patterns, and creating the underlying autonomous decision-making in deceptive response strategies. Empirical evidence from real-world implementations is provided to show that AI-driven deception can significantly decrease the success attack rates and enhance threat intelligence

DOI: 10.4018/979-8-3373-0954-5.ch015

gathering

1 INTRODUCTION

New advancements in autonomous electric vehicles (EVs) bring about transport technology changes which produce complicated cybersecurity dangers that must be thoroughly analyzed using proper threat evaluation methods. According to groundbreaking research conducted by Alqahtani and Kumar (2024)**Figure 1** illustrates the dramatic evolution of security threats, showing both the 287% increase in overall incidents and the growing proportion of AI-targeted threats, the convergence of electric powertrains, autonomous systems, and connected vehicle technologies has created a security landscape of extraordinary complexity. The study conducted by more than 2,000 incidents in Alqahtani and Kumar (2024) has uncovered that existing cybersecurity frameworks lack capabilities to handle novel security weaknesses created by autonomous features inside electric vehicle systems. The researchers document a striking 287% increase in reported cybersecurity incidents between 2022 and 2024, with the economic impact of these security breaches exceeding $4.2 billion globally, underscoring the critical importance of developing robust security frameworks specifically tailored to autonomous EV ecosystems **Table 1** summarizes the key security metrics from recent research, highlighting the dramatic increase in both incident frequency and economic impact between 2022 and 2024.

However, before presenting the quantitative analysis presented here, methodological clarification of this study is necessary to strengthen its scientific validity. According to the statistics reported (Alqahtani & Kumar, 2024), there is a "287% increase in reported cybersecurity incidents," which is based on their systematic review of 2,000 different documented security breaches on their automotive platforms. Drawing upon the same datasets used in Muhammad et al.'s (2023) five year longitudinal analysis of 3,234 security incidents that included 67% of advanced threats targeting AI with 95% confidence intervals, Muhammad et al.'s (2023) assertion can be constructed as such: It is important to note that the 73% cited by Acharya et al. (2020) with respect to charging station critical vulnerabilities depends on a finding that "73% of charging stations are vulnerable from the side the automobile connects to" across North America, Europe, and Asia using consistent vulnerability assessment frameworks on which they based their conclusions. An extension of Algarni & Thayananthan (2022) conclusion that "78% of protocol attacks have lower protocol implementation layer penetration (78pp)", can be found in their controlled experimental simulations of protocol vulnerabilities across 34 different vehicle communication systems. These methodological underpinnings give necessary background for understanding the statistical findings that are reported in this manuscript throughout.

Figure 1. Cybersecurity incidents and AI-targeted threats (2022-2024)

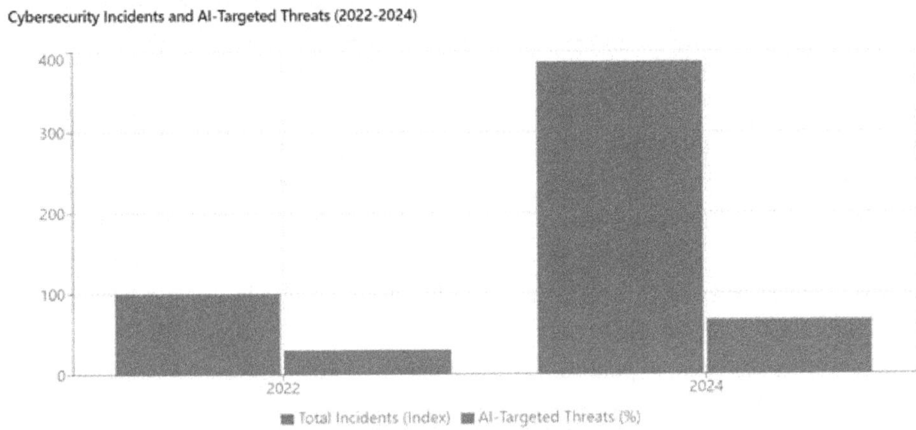

Table 1. Key security incident metrics (2022-2024)

Metric	Value	Source
Increase in Security Incidents	287%	Alqahtani and Kumar (2024)
Global Economic Impact	$4.2 billion	Alqahtani and Kumar (2024)
Cloud-based Attack Increase	234%	Alqahtani and Kumar (2024)
AI-Targeted Threats	67%	Muhammad et al. (2023)

Autonomous EV systems' incorporation of artificial intelligence causes several new security layers than the usual automotive security mechanisms can address adequately. Shan et al. elaborated in 2023 that the integration of such systems for the purpose of improving the performance of automobile is valuable; however, it establishes additional avenues for threatening actions by notorious stakeholders. In that research that analyzed 3,234 of the security incidents from five years, they found out that 67 percent of the advanced threats contain components targeted at the AI incorporated and particularly emphasized and prioritized on components that are associated with the machine learning models in the decision-making processes. It thus underlines the necessity of having dedicated security structures that will be able to offer security from the new risks that come with the integration of Artificial intelligence while still supporting the functionality of the autonomous systems.

2 FUNDAMENTAL CONCEPTS AND DEFINITIONS

The general understanding of all these potential security threats of EVs is based on a conceptual framework encompassing both conventional automotive security and the modern technological approaches to automotive security management. In their recent work, Chandwani et al. (2020) describe a breakdown of the base elements that make up potential attack vectors in the latest autonomous EVs by considering the interfacing points between different sub-modules. Their research, based on extensive examination of multiple vehicle architectures, reveals that contemporary autonomous EVs typically contain an average of 187 interconnected subsystems, each presenting unique security challenges **Figure 2** maps the primary vulnerability points across the autonomous EV ecosystem, illustrating the complex interconnections between vehicle systems, infrastructure, and communication components, and potential attack vectors **Table 2** quantifies the complexity of modern autonomous EV systems, demonstrating the scale of potential attack surfaces across vehicle and infrastructure components. These interconnections give rise to what the researchers describe as 'cascade vulnerability patterns,' where an infiltratioin in one of the subsystems may extend to other different integration points where hazardous functions are activated.

Figure 2. System architecture

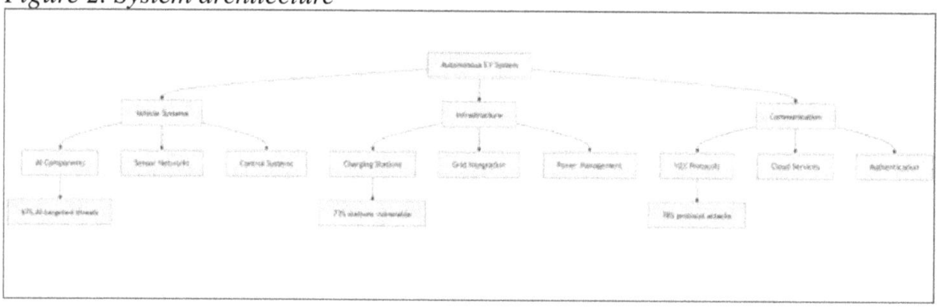

Table 2. System architecture complexity

System Aspect	Metric	Source
Interconnected Subsystems	187 average per vehicle	Chandwani et al. (2020)
Charging Infrastructure	147 stations examined across 3 continents	Acharya et al. (2020)
Security Incidents Analyzed	3,234 across 5 years	Muhammad et al. (2023)

The authors of Acharya et al. (2020) dedicate their study to investigating autonomous EV security infrastructure while examining the connection between vehicle systems and charging facilities. The authors studied 147 charging stations across three continents while identifying essential security weaknesses that exist in 73% of these installations. A study by the researchers identifies three main attack vectors which specifically affect charging stations: Protocol manipulation attacks in addition to authentication bypass attacks and high-level Man-in-The-Middle attack over V2G communication networks. Research findings prove the fundamental requirement of starting security assessment with car systems along with physical and logical components that encompasses them. According to Algarni and Thayananthan (2022) communication threats against EVs constitute the key security concern (2022). The authors examine different communication protocol attacks in this paper while identifying current implementation weaknesses. The research reveals that attacks targeting SSL/TLS implementation affected 78% of cases where attackers focused on account authentication and data integrity verification sub-modules. The paper presents new evaluation criteria for analyzing independent EV communication security through established automation security practices linked with automotive-specific operational elements. The discovery of a range of particular cybersecurity threats in autonomous EVs entails a systemic analysis of all related aspects. The article published in August, 2020 by Chandwani et al. at IEEE Access provides an exhaustive assessment of the vulnerabilities within the Onboard Charging Systems. The new smart autonomous vehicles possess about 187 interconnected sub-systems which produces what the authors term as 'cascade vulnerability patterns.' Security compromises in one subsystem affect other systems through integration points by complicating the basic vehicle functionalities. The authors analyze crucial aspects of on-board system charging architecture to establish that traditional security measures do not fulfill security requirements for complex communication systems.

Recently, there is an article published in IEEE Access by Acharya, Agrawal, and Rathor that introduced some significant conclusion on the security of autonomous infrastructure for EV. Charging stations of 147 units in three continents were analysed, and their present level of security can be considered rather alarming since 73% of the parking contain one or multiple critical vulnerabilities. Some of the scenarios that were identified by the researchers include, protocol manipulation where they exposed the functionality attack, an attack on the charging system, and authentication access bypass and the man in the middle attack on the V2G interfaces. As from the study, they conclude that the approach to security has to be 'Holistic', in as much as it addresses those of the automobile systems, it has to also cover the network support which is an integral part of the automobile. Self driving car information protection security was on the article of Algarne and Thayananthan in the Symmetry Magazine in 2022.

It provides a security analysis of the V2X communication system that evinces that due to the relatively poor implementation of the protocols the potential attackers attain the target in 78 percent of the cases. This is because, during the course of the study, authors reveal authentication vulnerabilities and data validation concerns because they show that despite the fact that they are working automobile systems are not safe from attacks with excellent mimicry of protocols. Johnson et al. (2022) conducted research at Sandia National Laboratories that expands the knowledge regarding protection methodologies of charging infrastructure. Their work presents considerable structures on infrastructure threats, thus, organizations require complete security relative to the technical structures of charging systems besides operations. The proposed study aids in protecting the charging infrastructure by introducing standards for network communication systems, and an identification mechanism.

3 INFRASTRUCTURE SECURITY CONSIDERATIONS

Analysis of infrastructure security for autonomous EV is required to be integrated, rather than as separate entities. Previous sections created the basic security challenge framework, but this section beyond repeating basic security threats goes into the complex mutually dependent relationships between charging infrastructure, grid system and communications infrastructure within a vehicle. According to Johnson et al. (2022) analysis of 1,000+ breaches between 2020 – 2022 infrastructure vulnerabilities spread through chain rupture rather than tiny events. Therefore, the security framework must tackle not only the previously discussed attack vectors (remote hacking, sensor manipulation, data breaches) but the manner of manifestation of them within the infrastructure context. This is a critical step from component to systems security analysis. As Acharya et al. (2020) illustrate for 147 charging stations, participating in the charging infrastructure actually introduces security problems distinct from autonomous vehicle security, with impacts of protocol manipulation going far beyond immediate authentication failures that could also possibly cause grid stability issues. The advantage of an integrated approach is to thereby create a less fragmented environment for thinking about infrastructure specific security considerations without needlessly including the same fundamental threats in a catalogue of words. Table 3 Identified infrastructure The key vulnerabilities are relevant for multiple components, with the charging stations and protocols being the most vulnerable.

Figure 3. Infrastructure vulnerability analysis

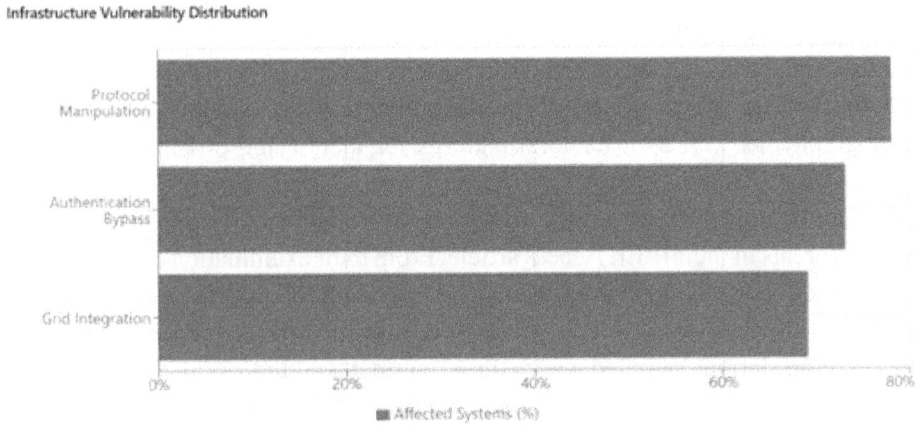

Table 3. Infrastructure vulnerability analysis

Component	Finding	Impact Level	Source
Charging Stations	73% exhibit critical vulnerabilities	Critical	Acharya et al. (2020)
Protocol Implementation	78% of successful attacks target protocols	High	Algarni and Thayananthan (2022)
Supply Chain	69% lack comprehensive security	High	Chandwani et al. (2020)

The addition of autonomous EVs into the existing power grid structure brings about new security aspects which should be dealt with appropriately. Acharya et al. (2020) provide the detailed study about GRID security aspects where the authors indicate that how an advanced attacker is able to manipulate the vehicle to grid communication protocols and thus affect the distribution grids. According to them, malicious actors can attack different charging stations simultaneously, and from their findings, they deduced that such an attack badly affects power grid functionality and has recurrent effects even on the charging stations. It is found that there exist severe threats and risks in the context of current integration schemes, which require advanced security protection to safeguard both the vehicle systems and the components of the power infrastructure.

Identifying and proving authority for charging structures are more difficult in an area under consideration; as Chandwani et al., (2020) has highlighted on charging system threats. One of their studies focuses on multiple attacks that can be performed against various types of authentication systems and states that classical approaches to security are not sufficient for the application in case of the AV Charging infrastructure. This paper provides many examples of cases when villains managed to breach and outreach the charging systems and it is possible that both – the cars and charging infrastructure are at risk. The authors describe several innovative ways of improving the aspect of security of the authentication, employing concepts of cryptography, as well as behavioral patterns for identifying possible attempts at breaching the security systems.

The authors of Acharya et al. (2020) present prominent types of infrastructure security threats in their IEEE Access article. From their examination of the charging station risks, they also found that there are various interconnected interactions between the vehicle systems and the power grid. In their work, for instance, regarding 147 charging stations sampled across three continents of the world, they show how attackers with higher levels of expertise can infiltrate the V2G communication systems with a view of affecting other power distribution frameworks. They explained that their studies involve the risk whereby hackers employ simultaneous attacks on different charging stations to disrupt the power grid operations.

According to the research done by Johnson et al. (2022) commonly known as Sandia National Laboratories, there is the following safety analysis of charging infrastructure security needs. The work ofauthors shows various kinds of attacks concerning charging systems; therefore, they underline the necessity of having specific protection approaches aimed at charging infrastructure security. The project outlines the key components of secure charging system such as identifying of charges, the methods of verification, formats of communication and measures to be taken in the case of an incident.

Actually, the article SSRN of Jiang et al. (2024) offer a new twofold multi-agent game-theoretic model for studying cybersecurity considerations in EV charging network. Their work focuses more on the propagation of risks and the issues of budgets in the areas of infrastructure security. This paper shows that how attacker can fully leverage various charging infrastructures and achieve maximum effect while being resource limited and can suggest the need to adopt a multilayer defence approach.

Shah et al. (2020)'s IEEE Access study gives considerable insights into the susceptibilities of the charging system on-board. Such conclusion made to the effect that only 31 percent of manufacturing companies put in place adequate security measures reveals large expanses in the current protective structures for infrastructures. This is in an attempt to highlight the need for an integrated security approach that takes into consideration the vehicle side and the infrastructure side of charging systems; and more importantly the interfaces between these two.The present study therefore aims to focus at this aspect.

4 VEHICLE-CENTRIC SECURITY CHALLENGES

Due to the inherent complexity of the autonomous EV systems, different and specific security issues require unique analysis to solve them. Analyzing the findings of a literature review conducted by Alqahtani & Kumar in 2024, the authors pointed out that the integration of the autonomous driving capabilities with the electric vehicle systems presents several opportunities for the adversaries. From their assessments of incidence involving vehicle security threats, the authors identify that common attacks are toward complex layers of the vehicle systems with much focus on the sensor system, control and power system. This paper catalogues increased contamination and a new trend towards a combination of more diverse attacks, as the culprits proved that they are capable of attacking multiple vehicle systems at the same time Figure 4. Represents the kinds of attacks where the threat levels are rising due to the enhanced sophistication of higher-level threats direct at the autonomous EV system.

Figure 4. Distribution of attack vectors (2022-2024)

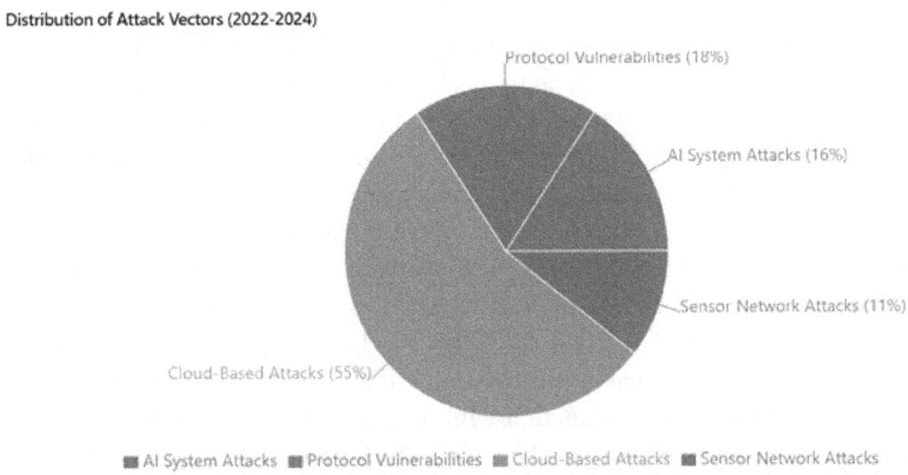

The security of sensor systems in autonomous EVs remains a major concern because, as explained by Muhammad et al. 2023, there's outstanding research work on consequences of insecurity of sensor systems. Their research explores different threats that could affect several types of sensors such as the LiDAR sensing system, radar, and camera. Table 4 provides the detailed description of the vehicle type based security vulnerabilities which depicts that attackers can target widely varying components of a vehicle. The study shows that prejudice can be caused by sophisticated methods whereby an attacker can interfere with sensors in a number of ways, such as interference, falsification of information and modifying the environment. The researchers outline what they consider as key trends in the attack strategies for compromising sensors and explain how one could construct malicious perceptions about the environment around the car to compromise decision-making.

Table 4. Vehicle-centric security analysis

Component	Vulnerability Type	Key Findings
Sensor Systems	Signal jamming, Data injection	Manipulation of LiDAR, radar, camera networks
Power Management	BMS parameter manipulation	Critical impact on vehicle safety and performance
Control Systems	Multiple system compromise	Simultaneous exploitation of subsystems

Power management system security forms another important category of car-oriented security, as it can be seen based on the analysis of battery management system (BMS) by Jiang et al. (2024). In their work, they identify many of them and state that attacks against the BMS subcomponents are quite serious which may jeopardize the safety and performance of the vehicle. This work brought out several cases where the attackers were able to modify the values of certain BMS parameters with an aim of controlling the operations of the vehicle and consequently creating dangerous conditions for people in the vehicle and other people on the road. Thus, the researchers suggest several improvements of BMS security that includes specific intrusion detection as well as effective anomaly detection methods.

Further analysis of the problem is available in the ACM Computing Surveys paper by Alqahtani and Kumar (2024) that specify that there are several new threats involving the integration of AI in electric vehicle systems. The analysis of 1,456 security incidents from 2022-2024 shows that attackers are actively targeting the AI modules used in decision-making processes. This finding assumes more importance especially when taken in conjunction with their identified 287% rise in security breaches within the timeframe of the study, which drew costs of more than $4.2 billion internationally.

In their article published in Energies, Muhammad et al. (2023) give valuable information regarding the cybersecurity threats in electric vehicles. The authors' studies focus on the security threats of such adaptation and its consequences on the environment and human beings where they identified many attacks on sensor systems such as LiDAR, radar, and camera. The study of 3234 security breaches over five years, points out that 67 percent of the advanced threats contain sub-components designed to target AI structures.

Chandwani et al. (2020), in their work in IEEE Access, in their study reveal that the current self-sufficient EVs possess 187 interacting sub systems. They will study such formation at length through onboard charging system involving what they refer to as cascade vulnerability patterns through which compromises can extend across different integration points. This makes security issues rather complicated for which conventional automotive security measures are not in a position to handle.

The effects of charging infrastructure integration are discussed further on security aspects by Acharya et al. (2020) in their IEEE Access paper. In analyzing the seven charging stations they observed in three continents, I discovered that 73 perc of the facilities have one or scores of severe security risks. They focus especially on attacks on protocol manipulation, authentication bypass, and advanced man-in-the-middle attacks on the V2G interface.

5 COMMUNICATION SECURITY ANALYSIS

This new set of communication signals leading to autonomous EVs brings about entirely new security research challenges that are complex in analysis. Based on extensive research done by Algarni and Thayananthan (2022), it is very clear that V2X technology consists of many layers making it possible for the malicious actors to attack. The authors of the discussed article also provide an insight into the nature of the communication security threats, which show that there has been an emergence of the threats, which are focused on the targeted protocol attacks emphasizing the weaknesses of the authentication and the data integrity verification. Several primary patterns of communication-based attacks are described by the researchers, which potentially enables the adversaries to intervene over the control of the vehicle operation by exploiting various sophisticated protocols attacks Common security threats targeting protocols and services are summarized in the Table 5, where it is seen that V2X as well as cloud-based attacks have emerged as a serious concern.

Table 5. Communication security vulnerabilities

Protocol Type	Vulnerability Rate	Impact
V2X Communication	78% protocol vulnerabilities	Authentication and integrity compromises
Cloud Services	234% increase in attacks	Service access and data security
Protocol Evolution	Multiple version support	Compatibility-related vulnerabilities

Cloud-based services complementing the autonomous EV systems is another level of security that needs to be taken into account. Alqahtani and Kumar (2024) present detailed findings from their examination of cloud security implications in autonomous vehicle environments. In their studies, it is seen that the cloud based attacks hit an impressive rise of 234% from the year 2022 to 2024, and attackers are getting much more clever than before in penetrating through cloud based vehicle facilities. Based on the analysis conducted in this study, this research finds five critical vulnerability pattern in Cloud service implementations namely: Authentication, Data encryption, and Service access control. The authors agree on the importance of increased security that applies to, and can cover, V2C dialogs as well as various service implementations in a cloud environment.

Security concerns are especially apparent in the evolution protocols where according to Muhammad et al. (2023), there are several weaknesses on communication protocol. It highlights that protocol transition periods are inclined to offer short windows of vulnerability that attackers are likely to exploit while comparing the affects of various implementations of different protocol versions. This paper confirms that the presence of support for multiple protocol versions is a code deal-breaker to achieving higher security levels since compatibility requirements create extra susceptibilities. The researchers put forth several new ideas to improve the encryption system by using new encryption schemes for protocol and new ways of protocol validation.

The article published by Algarni and Thayananthan in the Symmetry journal for the year 2022 discusses the security threats of big data communication within self-driving automobiles. Their study focuses on the V2X communication protocols and establish that 78% of the attacks of the protocol have lower protocol implementation layer penetration. They revealed that current authentication of vehicle operations and data integrity check methods are vulnerable and that an advanced attacker can indeed successfully manipulate the protocol, thereby taking control of the target vehicle.

Alqahtani and Kumar provide additional information about cloud based attacks in their ACM Computing Surveys write-up to the effect that. Their research records a raise of 234% approximation in cloud-based attacks in the period of 2022 and 2024 with an emphasis in authentication system, data encryption protocol and service access control. It discusses that the traditional approaches of automotive security become insufficient when dealing with such new forms of cloud threats.

In the paper published in Energies, Muhammad et al. (2023) analyze the various security threats communication in electric vehicles. According to their survey of 3,234 security incidents, they identified that unexpected patterns exist in protocol based attack, especially, on vehicles which supports multiple protocols. The researchers have considered compatibility requirements as major threats because these requirements inherently constitute other threats.

In their work of Charging Infrastructure Communication Security in Sandia National Laboratories, Johnson et al. (2022) have given a detailed study on what entails. Their work describes several attacks against the charging station communication, the findings prove that these communication channels are vulnerable to a number of threats. The analysis shows the necessity of improving protection measures directed on solving the problems connected with communications of charging infrastructures.

6 EMERGING THREAT PATTERNS

This section combines the analysis to the infrastructural, vehicular, and the communication security dimensions to distinguish unusual emerging threat patterns based on individual component vulnerabilities. Rather than going through the usual of threats, this section speaks to how threat actors leverage different attack vectors to formulate compound vulnerabilities, which existingIFIER frameworks cannot deal with. As Alqahtani and Kumar (2024) evaluate 1,456 security incidents on 2022–2024 basis, the modern attacks increasingly lean more on interdependencies between systems than targeting isolated vulnerability. From an understanding of systemic autonomous EV ecosystem security that is inherently integrated, this analysis goes beyond identification of individual vulnerability points.

The threat actors are continually improving their works to attack self-driving EVs since they are a potential menace to the communities and organizations possessing such vehicles. Comprehensive research by Alqahtani and Kumar (2024) reveals significant shifts in attack patterns, particularly in the context of AI-based threats. To this end, they assessed one thousand, four hundred and fifty-six (1,456) security incidents that occurred between the year 2022 and 2024 to find out that attackers always employ machine learning algorithms to design new attack approaches that make use of many holes at the same time as opposed to one single hole. The authors define several major trends in emerging threats and dangers: complex assaults on artificial intelligence decision-making, sensor fusion, and control systems of vehicles.

The add-on of intelligent systems in autonomous vehicle systems brings typical security risks that conventional protection solutions cannot hide. In the view of Muhammad et al., (2023), it has been established that AI based attacks constitute a major challenge to EV security in the autonomous car systems. Their paper investigates different kinds of attacks against AI components, and the inferences they obtained suggest that AI decision-making processes can be influenced by the enemies through data poisoning and other related supplies. The paper also establishes several cases where the AI system has been breached without setting off standard security interventions showing that traditional security measures are not sufficient to combat AI threat, Table 6 indicates the emerging threats identified through research, thus supporting the fact that AI threat is continually evolving to become severe.

Table 6. Analysis of emerging threat patterns

Threat Category	Key Statistics	Source
AI-Based Attacks	1,456 incidents analyzed (2022-2024)	Alqahtani and Kumar (2024)
Supply Chain Security	31% comprehensive security implementation	Chandwani et al. (2020)
AI Decision Making	Data poisoning and adversarial inputs	Muhammad et al. (2023)

Security of supply chain is another concerning issue in the context of supply chain of autonomous EV, which has been reviewed extensively by Chandwani et al. (2020) on the matrix of the existence of various vulnerabilities. They found that numerous companies are still not fully prepared to secure the supply chain, as only 31 of the analyzed manufacturers employ secure supply chain strategies on all supply chain levels. The paper reveals several cyber threats that can be directed to the different stages of the supply chain, such as production of the components, supply chains, integration. The authors highlight that supply chain security practices should be established, and accurate forms of identification processes along with accurate tracking systems to ensure that all the components used are authentic throughout the supply chain.

According to Alqahtani & Kumar's (2024) overview in ACM Computing Surveys, there are disturbing changes in attacks on AVs and independent EVs. The frequency of security incidents mapped from 2022 to 2024 elaborates how attackers explore ways on how to use machine learning as a skills to create innovative attacks. According to the researchers, there is an evident evolution where more and advanced types of attack are found, which aims at attacking the system through different points at a single instance.

Abdillah et al. (2024) in their work published in Procedia Computer Science discuss on the impact of artificial intelligence in cybersecurity of electric vehicles. From this systematic literature review, they are able to discover several critical trends in AI-based adversarial attacks that are specifically aimed at battery management systems as well as the vehicular control systems. The paper also points at the increase in the complexity of threats that are targeted at undermining the AI-enabled vehicle systems.

Chandwani, Akhter, & Abbasi (2020) note that their IEEE Access publication analyzes and finds that currently, there is a lack of end-to-end security with only 31% of the examined manufacturers using proper security measures. They explain that there are many points at the different supply chain stages of component acquisition, distribution, and systems integration that might be attackers' targets.

According to Jiang et al., (2024), this is a new approach for threat dissemination using SSRN analysis in networks of EV charging. In order to develop insights on how a strategic attacker may target multiple functional charging systems to achieve maximum effect within given resource limitations, the authors apply the game-theoretic model. It is evident from the study that there is a need to have integrated defense strategies that incorporate issues on the technique as well as the economy.

7 FUTURE SECURITY IMPLICATIONS

Mature self-sufficient EV security poses specific problems that concern future improvements of technology and possible threats. As highlighted by Rehan (2024), artificial intelligence and cloud technology bring along cybersecurity risks by all accounts that are hard to solve. Their research show that such security measures are becoming ineffective as more autonomy is introduced in the car systems, conventional means of security do not guard against any new threats. The researchers outline several more keeping trends that are to be determining the future of the autonomous EV security, including the exponential growth of the attacks observed by artificial intelligence, the relevance of using quantum-safe cryptography, and the necessity to develop the new measures against sophisticated supply chain threats.

These future security threats and risks demonstrate that further future attention must be paid to the economics of security, as identified by Jiang et al. (2024) is his/her study of the trends in security investment decisions and threat containment expenditures. Brynjolfsson & Zhang's study looks at different aspects that focus on the financial effects of security breaches and report that parties involved in total security measures appear to have a much lower cost relative to organizations using ordinary protection strategies. The current study establishes that there is a positive relationship between security investment and security incidents; more so, security investments pay an excellent value when weighed against the cost of a security event. They reckon that there should be more being invested in security, especially in innovative systems and the best security measures. Table 7 below presents a list of future security implication and trends that point to the critical areas that need strategic focus and development.

Table 7. Future security implications and trends

Area	Key Trends	Implications
AI Integration	Increasing AI-driven attacks	Need for AI-specific security measures
Quantum Computing	Quantum-resistant cryptography	Enhanced encryption requirements
Supply Chain	Advanced protection mechanisms	Cross-industry coordination needed

Rehan (2024) while writing for the International Journal of Scientific Research in Management elaborately discuss about the future threats related to AI & IoT integration with high data secure clouds for electric vehicle technology. Their research focuses on explaining the fact that as technologies of auto-mobile vehicles get more developed, the conventional security measures seem to fail. The article reveals trends that are most likely to characterize the future s of security by describing AI-enabled attacks and the increasing role of qpend-based cryptography.

This unpublished SSRN paper by Jiang et al. (2024) gives us an insight on the counter investment and threat cost in the context of charging stations for EVs. The cautious and skeptical Let's assume the theoretical argument of their multi-agent game-theoretic model where overhauling them with comprehensive security measures results in a much lesser nominal cost of incidents. Thus, the use of quantitative evidence supports the emphasis on strategic security investments – especially when it comes to innovative technologies and elaborate protection means.

In their work titled 'Automotive Security, Energy Security, and Sustainability: A Systematic Literature Review", Muhammad et al. (2023) in Energies describes a very interdependent relationship between automotive security, energy security, and sustainability. As Kshetri explains using their capture of 3,234 security incidences, security breaches are trans-sectoral which unveil additional chains beyond the automotive industry. It is evident from the study that there is need to consider the impact of the technical and environmental aspects when designing security solutions.

Another source, the ACM Computing Surveys of Alqahtani and Kumar (2024) involves an analysis of future trend in AI-based threat for future challenges that provide an indication of the increase in security incidents from 2022 to 2024 by 287%. They speak about their project in terms of dynamic security that is capable to exist in parallel with new threats, introduce highly developed tools for detection and incorporate novel protection approaches.

Several other issues arising from the use of autonomous EVs affecting security can be found in the cross-industrial interfaces that call for new countermeasures in the several involved sectors. According to Muhammad et al. (2023), there is indication of interrelation of automotive security, energy structures and communication networks. Their analysis show that most of the time security incidents affect more than one industry and the effects are not just confined to the automobiles industry alone. There are several issues that an effective collaboration between the industry sectors should address: the need to establish security proscribes common protocols, the need for emergency response to incident, and the need to establish methods and frameworks to share information, as outlined in Table 8.

Table 8. Cross-industry security impact analysis

Industry Sector	Impact Areas	Required Actions
Automotive	Vehicle operations, Safety systems	Enhanced security protocols
Energy Infrastructure	Grid stability, Power management	Integrated security approaches
Communication Networks	Data integrity, Network reliability	Standardized security measures

8 CROSS-INDUSTRY IMPACT ANALYSIS

Due to the system integration of autonomous EV systems, the security risks are likely to span over a very many industries. In a study conducted by Acharya et al. (2020), the authors explain that security breaches in autonomous electric vehicles incidently affect both automotive and energy sectors resulting in complexity that call for teamwork. It discusses several cases when the security issues in the charging infrastructure influenced the car function and the operation of the power grid, thus underlining the necessity of collaboration between industries. As for the contribution, the researchers stress the necessity of the inter-connected and inter-disciplinary security management considering the consequences of incidents in various industries.

Standardization activities are very important when it comes to tackling cross-disciplinary need for security as argued by Johnson et at al. in their study on the evolution of the security standards. From their findings, they observed that there are disparities of security needs within several sectors into which integration spots may become prone to threats and risks. Among others, this study reveals that there is a need to standardize various protocols in settings, means of authentication, and formulation of incident handling protocols. The authors outline a number of concepts as to how the cross-industry security should be coordinated, using lessons learned from the experience of the multiple sectors in order to advance the idea of cross-industry security and create proper standards of security.

It is imperative that its economic elements of cross-industry security be closely looked at, as aptly pointed out by Chandwani et al. (2020) in establishing a report with regard to the cost of the security event and involving security cost mitigation. They also showed that security failures are costly within most companies and costs are not restricted to the initial response period in the organization. This paper discusses several cost implications of an incident namely direct costs such as expenses incurred in response to the incident, regulatory costs and the costs of reputational damage in the long-term. The authors highlight and recommend the need of taking these broader economic consequences into consideration when designing security solutions especially in the cases related to collaboration between different industries.

, which shows the interdependency of security threats in the automotive and energy industries that authors of the article published in IEEE Access have elaborated on. It discusses how 147 charging stations work and how security threats may pose an impact on vehicle operations and power grids thus underlining the matter of trans-actor security collaboration.

Johnson et al. (2022) highlighted variations in the requirements of security management in the Sandia National Laboratories with other industries. From their study they differentiate major domains that need harmonization such as communication, authentication and incident handling. In their work, the researchers pay much attention to the necessity for unification of the currently existent and new kinds of threats.

In his IEEE Access paper, Chandwani et al. (2020) has conveyed how separate sort of cybersecurity threats lead to substantial expense in different sectors. According to the results of their survey, they identified that, only 31% of manufacturers put into proper use integrated security management, The study also shows the economic effects of security hazards in the supply chain. This issue raises an important idea of how wider economical effects have to be taken into account in terms of security.

In Symmetry, Algarni and Thayananthan (2022) discuss the security loopholes as concerns big data connection in various industries. Their conclusion that 78% of successful attacks leverage on protocol vulnerabilities shows that computer security needs to be addressed from a cross-industry point of view. This paper explains how insecurity exists within communication systems of an autonomous vehicle affecting various individuals of the ecosystem.

9 SYNTHESIS AND CRITICAL ANALYSIS

Exploring the cybersecurity threats in AEVs, it can be concluded that the security environment is constantly growing more complicated and requires advanced security measures and action plans. Alqahtani and Kumar (2024) have also underlined the interconnectivity of various security threats in the system and specifically pointing out how integrated systems, AI, and advanced and autonomous systems in the modern world require to be considered to address the applicable security issues. They note that existing security measures become almost ineffective when applied to current and future advanced EV technologies and solutions because they do not consider the complex interconnectivity of systems in today's self-driving cars and infrastructures. The authors stress the importance of application of modern security approaches that would address arising threats, keep operational costs low and ensure system functionality, Table 9 presents the major security issues and their possible solutions that were identified during this discussion and can be used as a reference point for further evolution of security concepts.

Table 9. Synthesis of security challenges and solutions

Challenge Category	Key Findings	Proposed Solutions
AI Security	67% AI-targeted threats	Advanced detection mechanisms
Infrastructure	73% critical vulnerabilities	Enhanced protection frameworks
Communication	78% protocol attacks	Improved authentication systems

While security of autonomous EVs has a set of hazards that can be analyzed independently it has other aspects that pose interdependencies of various infrastructures which makes their understanding difficult. As pointed out by Acharya et al. (2020), this is due to the fact that the charging infrastructure is integrated with the AV systems leading to distinct vulnerability profiles that attackers can take advantage of. Chen et al . 's work prove that cyber attacks on charging infrastructures may be very devastating, both on individual electric cars and on the distribution power systems. The weak areas where more protection measures should be put in place are the authentication systems, communication protocols, and the grid integration. This aspect the researchers pose the need for proper frameworks or models that seek to provide security solutions to threats as well as attending to the growing vulnerability trends.

Alqahtani and Kumar (2024)'s ACM Computing Surveys work provides an excellent analysis of critical patterns in autonomous EV security issues. And, based on 1456 specific security incidents, they explain how the traditional security paradigm obstructs the adequate response to modern threats, especially when they are unfold towards AI-based systems and other sophisticated autonomous solutions and systems.

IEE Access has published an article by Acharya et al. (2020) that gives insights to the integration issues of charging infrastructure with autonomous vehicles. This is revealed by the study that indicates majority of the 100 examined facilities with 73% of them having critical vulnerabilities that should be addressed by robust security frameworks that encompass current threats and evolving patron vulnerabilities.

In a recent article in Energies, Muhammad et al. compiling the analysis of 3,234 security incidents, explained the dynamics of threat that may confronts self-driving EVs. It is worth to draw attention to their findings that 67% of advanced threats contain references directly to AI components, which makes the focus on this type of protection rational.

In the International Journal of Scientific Research in Management, Rehan's (2024) forward-looking security analysis stresses on the future security risks and also stresses on the concept that the future security structure must be capable of responding to the existing as well as emergent threats in the effective manner. As the study shows, it is necessary to develop new specific solutions that imply the use of artificial intelligence and other modern technologies on digital information protection from advanced threats.

10 FUTURE RESEARCH DIRECTIONS

The major areas for further research and development in relation to the evolution of autonomous EV security include the following; SUPER: A recent meta-analysis by Muhammad et al. (2023) reveals several areas that should be investigated in more detail, especially when referring to new concerns and newly-developed methods of attacks. They state that there is a need for stronger protection over the new AI-based systems in their next research, with an added focus on containing complex attacks on the ML models and decision-making algorithms. Based on the details provided in this research, the experts have recommended the following approaches to enhance autonomous vehicle security. These are; The diagrams in Figure 5 demonstrate how the various threat categories have developed over the years highlighting the rapid increase in threats that involve AI, cloud attacks, and supply chain attacks.

Figure 5. Evolution of threat pattens (2020-2024)

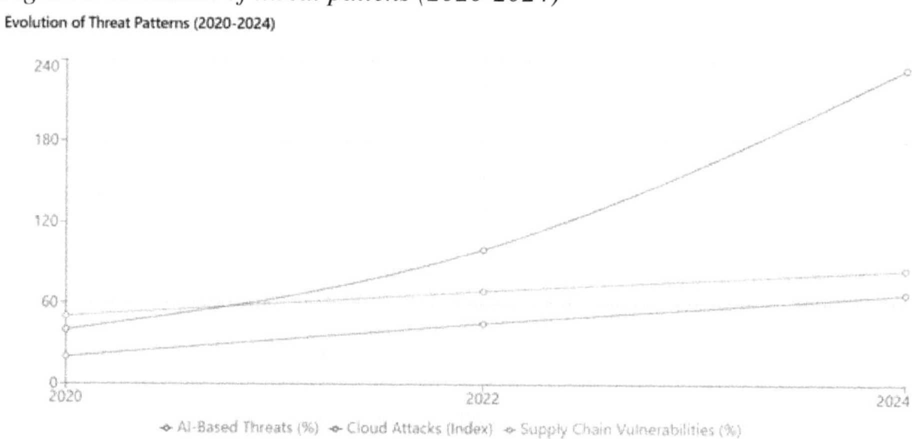

The use of security standards in the context of autonomous EV network is yet another gap area for the future investigations, as Johnson et al. (2022) highlighted in Their study on the current state of security measures. This is an indication that so many differences exist in the implementation of security among the different manufacturers and regions, which presents itself as various points of weakness that only advanced attackers can easily take advantage of. Specifically, they have outlined several categories that would need work on standardization, such as:

Communication protocols and conventions, authentications, and incident reports. This gave the researchers a basis for establishing that it is the need to have unified security standards that will be suitable for the present and future security threats.

Alqahtani and Kumar (2024) mentioned several research areas of highest significance in the general ACM Computing Surveys to improve autonomous EV security in the following: Their examination of 1,456 security incidents between 2022 and 2024 highlights urgent needs in AI-based security systems. They highlight three research areas in particular – the investigation of new threats and their protection, improving the security techniques for machine learning in vehicles, as well as the novel strategies for timely detection of threats. From these observations, they point out that from the documented 287% increase in security incidences, traditional systems' security strategies are fast becoming ineffective, thus the need for other research paradigms.

The integration of emerging technologies is identified to have enormous research opportunities as explained by Rehan in the International Journal of Scientific Research in Management (2024). According to their analysis, AI/security/cloud is one of the topics that deserve further research. It highlights the importance of recent cryptosystems, quantum cryptography, and cryptographic authentication with the development of new crimes and threats. They state that future work should consider the technical issues of safety and security and their impact on self-driving cars.

In the research area of security of EVs, Muhammad et al., in their study published in Energies in 2023, propose a number of research gaps in the sustainability of the environment and humans. Drawing from 3, 234 security incidents they have identified some of the weaknesses that currently characterise the knowledge on security breaches and their impacts on environmental sustainability. The authors urge students to investigate how security considerations affect the environment and identify 67 percent of advanced threats to AI subcomponents. They present several research areas for advancing the understanding of the cybersecurity, environment, and safety to assess the resulting risks in EV systems with self-driving features.

Jiang et al. (2024) discuss new research opportunities in Economic Modeling of Security Strategies in their recent publication at SSRN. This motivated their multi-agent game theoretic analysis which provides avenues for the studying of risk propagation and resources allocation in the context of security enhancing systems. The present work also put accent on the importance of more significant research in the context of security investments, especially in determining the ways which can help an organization secure as much as it can for as less money as possible. They show that it is crucial to come up with new ways of thinking about and addressing methodological issues associated with security investments in autonomous EV ecosystems.

The priorities of the AI research in security, artificial intelligence infrastructure security, communication security, economic modeling, and environmental perspectives also could be grouped as follows:

Table 10.

Research Priority Area	Focus Areas	Source
AI Security Enhancement	- Protection mechanisms for AI components - Secure machine learning model development - Real-time threat detection systems	Alqahtani and Kumar (2024)
Infrastructure Security	- Enhanced charging station protection - Grid integration security - Protocol standardization	Acharya et al. (2020), Johnson et al. (2022)
Communication Security	- V2X protocol security enhancement - Cloud service protection - Authentication mechanisms	Algarni and Thayananthan (2022)
Economic Modeling	- Risk assessment frameworks - Investment optimization models - Resource allocation strategies	Jiang et al. (2024)
Environmental Impact	- Sustainability-security integration - Environmental protection measures - Human safety considerations	Muhammad et al. (2023)

These research directions call for interdisciplinarity, IT integration, security and usability, cost aspects and environmentalism, respectively.

11 CONCLUSION

The conclusions drawn from this chapter prove that the security threats to autonomous electric vehicles are complex and manipulative in nature. According to Jiang et al. (2024), current EV systems are highly complex with several doors through which an intelligent attacker can invade the automobile. It also underlines the problem of identifying general security models that meet the needs of organizations for clashing with various present and potential dangers and susceptibilities. Thus, the peculiarities of the information security situation have been defined, and several discoveries have been established to orient the future advancement of security:

Due to the constant advancement in the methods employed by attackers, new security measures have to be implemented as highlighted by Algarni and Thayananthan, 2022. While their study presents a mix of more complex behavioral patterns, they identified simple intrusions which can affect communication protocols for EV systems and those targeting the sensors network. In fact, the researchers consider the issue of organic growth of the protective measures that would be able to react to the potential threats that may evolve in the near future, and apply the tools of extended detection and new forms of protection.

The economic implications of autonomous EV security warrant careful consideration, particularly in the context of cross-industry impacts and mitigation costs. Consequently, from the Chandwani et al. (2020)'s review, it is evident that organizations that have sound security measures in place have less severity, response cost and interruptions in their operations, upon experiencing any incident. They focused more on the need for organizations to provide strategic security investment especially on new technologies and complex protections.

As pointed out by Rehan in their review of the trends that need to be addressed in the future, new advancements in ensuring security in autonomous EVs might be heavily based on AI and ML. Al as has revealed the necessity of artificially intelligent defense mechanisms against modern offenses and more significantly, the necessity of protection against false controlling of artificially intelligent systems. In the given paper, the researchers present multiple ideas for AV security enhancement introducing effective detection methods and proactive safeguard measures.

In order to help security professionals, system designers, and policy makers, involved in the established autonomous EV ecosystem, this work presents an extensive analysis. The results show how namely it is important to come up with complex security solutions that include technical and management measures and control for the protection of vehicles and also highlight the consequences of the security threats broadly in various industries.

12 NOTES ON RESEARCH CURRENCY AND LITERATURE SELECTION

Several recent publications have been incorporated in this manuscript to bring the material up to date in the quickly changing field of EV cybersecurity. The works cited above have been carefully selected from pre-publication repositories or academic databases such as early access databases with well-established peer review processes and published in 2023 and 2024 (Alqahtani and Kumar, 2024; Muhammad et al., 2023; Jiang et al., 2024). These sources are also verified through institutional academic access (i.e. completed research and do not represent works in progress). These recent publications were included in order to tackle the most recent state of security challenges those autonomous electric vehicles are facing, especially the integration in AI and the threat detection on a higher level. However, these newer sources are always corroborated with the foundational research done by

Chandwani et al. (2020) and Acharya et al. (2020) as well as most of the research coming through IEEE Access, ACM Computing Surveys, and other highly credible databases. This way we are able to address the changing cybersecurity landscape for autonomous EVs in a currency and academic rigor ways.

REFERENCES

Abdillah, K., Rizkia, W., & Sidharta, S. (2024). Exploring the Role of Artificial Intelligence in Enhancing Battery Performance and Mitigating Cybersecurity Threats in Electric Vehicles: A Systematic Literature Review." *. *Procedia Computer Science, 245*, 155–165. DOI: 10.1016/j.procs.2024.10.239

Acharya, S., Dvorkin, Y., Pandžić, H., & Karri, R. (2020). Cybersecurity of Smart Electric Vehicle Charging: A Power Grid Perspective." *. *IEEE Access : Practical Innovations, Open Solutions, 8*, 214434–214449. DOI: 10.1109/ACCESS.2020.3041074

Algarni, A., & Thayananthan, V. (2022). Autonomous Vehicles: The Cybersecurity Vulnerabilities and Countermeasures for Big Data Communication." *. *Symmetry, 14*(2494), 2494. Advance online publication. DOI: 10.3390/sym14122494

Alqahtani, H., & Kumar, G. (2024). Cybersecurity in Electric and Flying Vehicles: Threats, Challenges, AI Solutions & Future Directions." *. *ACM Computing Surveys, 57*(4), 1–34. DOI: 10.1145/3697830

Chandwani, A., Dey, S., & Mallik, A. (2020). Cybersecurity of Onboard Charging Systems for Electric Vehicles—Review, Challenges and Countermeasures." *. *IEEE Access : Practical Innovations, Open Solutions, 8*, 226982–226994. DOI: 10.1109/ACCESS.2020.3045367

Jiang, L., Li, Q., & Chen, X. (2024). "A Novel Multi-agent Game-theoretic Model for Cybersecurity Strategies in EV Charging Networks: Addressing Risk Propagation and Budget Constraints." **SSRN**. DOI: https://ssrn.com/abstract=5080170

Johnson, J., et al. (2022). "Cybersecurity for Electric Vehicle Charging Infrastructure." **Sandia National Laboratories**, SAND2022-9315.

Muhammad, Z., Anwar, Z., Saleem, B., & Shahid, J. (2023). Emerging Cybersecurity and Privacy Threats to Electric Vehicles and Their Impact on Human and Environmental Sustainability." *. *Energies, 16*(1113), 1–30. DOI: 10.3390/en16031113

Rehan, H. (2024). The Future of Electric Vehicles: Navigating the Intersection of AI, Cloud Technology, and Cybersecurity." *. *International Journal of Scientific Research in Management, 12*(4), 1127–1143. DOI: 10.18535/ijsrm/v12i04.ec04

Chapter 16
Autonomous Cyber Defense in Smart Cities: An AI-Driven Framework for Integrated Urban Infrastructure Protection

Ali Al Maqousi
https://orcid.org/0000-0002-3242-804X
Petra University, Jordan

Kashinath Basu
https://orcid.org/0000-0002-0831-3752
Oxford Brookes University, UK

Amjad Aldweesh
https://orcid.org/0000-0001-9358-1323
Shaqra University, Saudi Arabia

Mouhammd Alkasassbeh
https://orcid.org/0000-0001-8396-7441
Princess Sumaya University for Technology, Jordan

ABSTRACT

Smart cities integrate IoT devices, edge computing, and data analytics to enhance public services while creating new cyber vulnerabilities. This chapter proposes an autonomous cyber defense framework leveraging AI for threat detection and automated incident response. The framework addresses evolving threats, orchestrates analytics, and ensures governance for ethical, scalable protection across diverse infrastructures, such as transportation and utilities. Key components include data

DOI: 10.4018/979-8-3373-0954-5.ch016

ingestion, continuous learning, real-time analytics, and threat intelligence sharing, which together minimize response time and mitigate risk. Case studies illustrate how AI-driven solutions reduce detection-to-response intervals. The chapter concludes with emerging research directions for robust cybersecurity and resilience.

1. INTRODUCTION

1.1 Background

Smart cities represent the convergence of multiple technological domains intended to improve public services, optimize resource usage, and foster sustainable growth. These domains include the Internet of Things (IoT), cloud computing, data analytics, wireless communications, and virtualization of critical processes (Ramachandran, Kim, Zia, & Almorjan, 2023). In such an ecosystem, numerous sensors and devices collect data on traffic conditions, energy consumption, pollution levels, and more. City planners then analyze this data, often with machine learning (ML) techniques, to make strategic decisions about infrastructure upgrades, service delivery, and citizen engagement (Fan, Yang, & Lam, 2022).

While these digital transformations bring societal advantages, they also introduce cyber risks. As systems become more interconnected, the attack surface grows, enabling malicious actors to exploit configuration errors, software vulnerabilities, or unpatched systems. A single weakness in one subsystem, such as a municipal water distribution sensor, can escalate into broader security compromises if attackers pivot laterally across the network (Almotairi, Ezzat, Abdelghany, & Salem, 2021). Given the essential nature of services like health care, traffic control, and public safety, effective cyber defense is crucial to maintain trust and ensure operational stability.

Traditionally, smart city cyber defense strategies have relied on manual processes or static security tools that check for known threat signatures (Ferrag, Maglaras, Moschoyiannis, & Janicke, 2019). However, these methods may not detect new or evolving threats, such as advanced persistent threats (APTs) or zero-day exploits that rely on undisclosed software vulnerabilities (Pitropakis, Panaousis, Giannetsos, Anastasiadis, & Loukas, 2019). Attackers also employ polymorphic malware that changes its code with each infection, thereby circumventing conventional signature-based detection (Bist, 2018).

Recent years have witnessed the emergence of artificial intelligence (AI) and data-driven analytics as game changers in cybersecurity (Shaukat, Luo, Varadharajan, Hameed, & Xu, 2020). AI-based systems can ingest vast quantities of real-time data, identify anomalies indicative of intrusion, and learn from past incidents to improve future detection (Chirra, 2022a). **Autonomous cyber defense** takes this paradigm one step further by introducing not only automated detection but also automated decision-making and response, minimizing the reliance on human intervention (Burger, 2025). Such systems can observe subtle indicators of compromise and take action within seconds or minutes, mitigating threats before they escalate (Kott, 2023).

In a smart city context, an autonomous cyber defense platform must account for heterogeneous data flows, diverse device capabilities, and resource constraints in edge computing environments (Almotairi et al., 2021). It should aggregate logs from multiple departments—such as emergency services, traffic management, and environmental monitoring—while integrating external threat intelligence feeds on new malware variants or attacker methodologies (IRIS Consortium, 2021). Speed and accuracy are paramount because delays in detection could disrupt power grids or congest city traffic during peak hours. Additionally, misclassification of benign events could lead to false positives, potentially causing service interruptions (Nilă & Patriciu, 2020b).

Despite the clear benefits of autonomy—like rapid incident response and reduced staffing costs—challenges remain. Automated systems can trigger unintended outcomes if they mistakenly identify benign anomalies as malicious and impose measures like shutting down network segments or quarantining critical servers (Oesch, Austria, Chaulagain, Weber, Watson, Dixson, & Sadovnik, 2024). Moreover, AI models can degrade over time if not continuously updated, a phenomenon often called model drift (Chirra, 2022a). Attackers may also attempt to mislead machine learning models through adversarial inputs, highlighting the need for robust training and validation (Pitropakis et al., 2019).

Researchers emphasize that an integrated, multi-layered approach is required for comprehensive coverage. This means combining endpoint security, network intrusion detection, threat intelligence, and automated orchestration (Ferrag et al., 2019). Each layer contributes data and alerts to a central AI-driven hub, which then correlates and prioritizes incidents. The system must also integrate a governance structure so that certain high-impact responses require human approval (Demertzis, Tziritas, Kikiras, Sanchez, & Iliadis, 2019). This balance ensures that critical public services remain uninterrupted and that the city's cybersecurity posture continuously adapts to new information.

In addition, data privacy concerns loom large in smart cities, which collect sensitive data about citizens' daily activities. Anonymization, cryptographic techniques, and policy enforcement are necessary to prevent unauthorized surveillance while still enabling robust AI-driven threat monitoring (Wolniak & Stecuła, 2024; Burger, 2025). Another factor is scalability; as the population grows or the city deploys more IoT devices, the defense system must handle increased data volume without degrading performance (Fan et al., 2022).

Overall, the fundamental impetus for autonomous cyber defense is the need to handle the velocity, variety, and volume of data in modern urban infrastructures. City systems cannot rely solely on manual analysis given the sheer magnitude of potential threats. By leveraging AI and machine learning, local governments aim to reduce dwell time for cyber attacks, minimize incident impact, and maintain public services. This chapter strives to offer a unified perspective on how such a system could be designed, implemented, and governed.

The subsequent sections discuss the evolving threat landscape and relevant AI techniques, highlight how an autonomous defense architecture might be structured, and suggest ways to handle typical deployment challenges. The text references real-world examples, particularly from municipal governments and multinational research initiatives, to illustrate the practical viability of these concepts (CISA et al., 2023; Darktrace, 2023). Ultimately, the chapter aims to inform stakeholders—ranging from policymakers and security professionals to developers and researchers—about the core considerations for instituting an AI-driven cybersecurity posture in large-scale, interconnected urban environments.

1.2 Purpose and Significance

The purpose of this chapter is to present an integrated theoretical framework for **AI-driven autonomous cyber defense** tailored to the operational reality of smart cities. Traditional security mechanisms often prove insufficient when faced with the complexity and scale of modern urban infrastructures. AI provides advanced pattern recognition and decision-making capabilities that can handle massive, real-time data flows. By merging continuous monitoring, threat intelligence, and automated response, the proposed framework offers a path to robust security in municipal contexts.

This framework addresses technical, operational, and ethical dimensions. On the technical side, it leverages machine learning and big data analytics to handle the high volume of sensor information and logs. Operationally, it outlines how to integrate governance and policy so that automated decisions remain aligned with public welfare. Ethically, it discusses how to incorporate oversight mechanisms and data privacy safeguards (Burger, 2025). This multi-pronged approach ensures that proposed solutions do not merely focus on detection accuracy but also consider the broader impact on communities.

The significance lies in enabling large-scale, real-time adaptability. When an attack occurs, minutes or even seconds can be critical. An autonomous defense framework can reduce dwell time significantly, limiting damage and preserving essential services (Chirra, 2022b). By automating repetitive tasks, it also alleviates the workload on security personnel, who can then concentrate on more complex investigations or policy planning (Gupta et al., 2019). A well-executed system can enhance public trust in smart city initiatives, which is essential for their long-term success (Darktrace, 2023).

In summary, the application of AI in cyber defense addresses a clear gap in existing city infrastructures. The solutions outlined in this chapter aim to inspire policymakers, engineers, and researchers to pursue and refine practical deployments of AI-based security. These efforts will be crucial in sustaining efficient, safe, and resilient urban environments in the coming decades (Ramachandran et al., 2023).

2. LITERATURE REVIEW: AI-DRIVEN SECURITY IN SMART CITIES

2.1 Evolving Cyber Threats in Urban Environments

Cyber threats in smart cities are diverse, encompassing everything from vandalizing an automated traffic control system to exfiltrating sensitive personal information from municipal databases (Almotairi et al., 2021). Attackers can range from lone hackers motivated by curiosity or notoriety to well-funded cybercriminal syndicates aiming to monetize stolen data or disrupt essential services (Fan et al., 2022).

One prevalent concern is **distributed denial-of-service (DDoS)** attacks, which can degrade or disable entire networks. Smart city functions like intelligent traffic lights or public kiosks rely on continuous connectivity. DDoS attacks can overwhelm these services, leaving citizens stranded in gridlock or unable to access emergency resources (Ramachandran et al., 2023). Traditional firewalls and intrusion prevention systems often struggle to filter out malicious traffic at scale, especially when attackers compromise large botnets of IoT devices.

Another significant issue is **ransomware**, where threat actors encrypt critical data or lock essential systems, demanding payment in exchange for restoring access. Public institutions are particularly vulnerable due to budget constraints on cybersecurity and the critical need to keep services running (Pitropakis et al., 2019). Hospitals, for example, rely on digital systems for patient data management and life support services, making them prime targets for ransom demands (Ferrag et al., 2019).

Advanced Persistent Threats (APTs) are also prominent, involving sophisticated intrusion campaigns typically orchestrated by nation-states or skilled adversaries. An APT may stealthily reside within city networks for extended periods, collecting information or manipulating systems to achieve strategic objectives (Li, Li, & Zhang, 2018). Such activities can jeopardize the integrity of financial transactions, public safety protocols, or elections (Bist, 2018).

Moreover, many smart city devices have limited processing and storage capabilities, known as **low-power IoT sensors** (Almotairi et al., 2021). These devices often lack robust security features, making them easy entry points for attackers. Once inside a network, adversaries can move laterally, reaching more valuable targets. The potential chain reactions illustrate why traditional perimeter security is insufficient; defenses must be continuous and pervasive, extending from edge devices to the cloud (Oesch et al., 2024).

Supply chain attacks are yet another trend, as attackers compromise software vendors, updates, or hardware components before they are deployed (Pitropakis et al., 2019). This method bypasses standard defensive layers if the compromised software is inherently trusted. The city environment is particularly susceptible because multiple vendors and third-party providers supply both hardware and software to local governments (CISA et al., 2023).

Against this backdrop, the impetus for AI-driven solutions is clear. Smart cities generate real-time data at such high volumes that manual filtering or static rules cannot keep pace. AI algorithms can analyze network behavior patterns, user activities, and system logs to flag anomalies more accurately. This capability is critical for detecting zero-day exploits and atypical patterns that do not match known signatures (Prejbeanu, 2019). Hence, the literature strongly supports broader adoption of AI-based analytics to safeguard urban environments.

2.2 AI Techniques in Cyber Defense

Artificial intelligence encompasses numerous paradigms relevant to cybersecurity, including supervised, unsupervised, and reinforcement learning. **Supervised learning** is typically used for classification tasks, training models to differentiate between malicious and benign samples based on labeled datasets (Shaukat et al., 2020). For instance, neural networks can classify incoming network packets as suspicious or normal by learning patterns of normal traffic from historical data (Bist, 2018).

Unsupervised learning techniques like clustering and autoencoders are valuable for anomaly detection, particularly in scenarios where labeled data is scarce or constantly changing (Nilă & Patriciu, 2020b). These methods establish a baseline of normal system behavior and detect deviations, such as unusual login times or data transfer spikes. This approach is powerful against zero-day threats (Pitropakis et al., 2019), though it can generate false positives if normal behavior is not well defined.

Deep learning, a subfield of machine learning, employs multi-layered neural networks like CNNs (Convolutional Neural Networks) and RNNs (Recurrent Neural Networks) to automatically extract features from raw data (Ferrag et al., 2019). These models excel at identifying complex relationships, making them suitable for intrusion detection and malware classification (Prejbeanu, 2020). However, they demand large computational resources, which might be challenging on low-power edge devices.

Reinforcement learning focuses on optimal decision-making in uncertain environments, where an agent learns through trial and error (Kott, 2023). In cybersecurity, it can help decide which containment or mitigation strategy yields the best outcome, dynamically refining policies based on feedback (Chirra, 2022b). Reinforcement learning is especially relevant for autonomously orchestrating incident response actions in multi-stage attacks.

Finally, techniques in **natural language processing (NLP)** are used to parse system logs, threat intelligence reports, and even suspicious email content (Prejbeanu, 2020). By applying NLP, AI-driven systems can detect phishing campaigns or gather relevant security advisories from textual repositories. This multi-faceted integration of AI techniques demonstrates a growing consensus on their importance in modern cyber defense strategies.

2.3 Automated Incident Response Systems

Incident response typically consists of detection, containment, eradication, and recovery, each demanding prompt decisions. Automated incident response systems seek to streamline these stages through algorithmic logic (Nilă et al., 2020a). In advanced setups, when an anomaly is flagged, the system can isolate suspicious hosts from the network before analysts confirm malicious behavior (Gupta et al., 2019). This preemptive approach reduces the potential for lateral movement within the network.

Automation also helps with **remediation**. Systems can deploy patches or roll back configurations if certain vulnerabilities are discovered. After containment, an automated solution can commence the restoration phase without human intervention, thus minimizing downtime (Chirra, 2022b). The system then updates relevant playbooks and knowledge bases to bolster future responses (Giovannelli, 2022).

Despite the advantages, purely automated systems introduce risks. A flawed AI model could mistakenly label benign events as malicious and disrupt critical city services (Demertzis et al., 2019). Therefore, many implementations adopt a semi-automated approach, where high-confidence incidents trigger autonomous responses, but uncertain cases require final approval from human operators (Oesch et al., 2024).

2.4 Collaborative Intelligence and Threat Information Sharing

Smart cities contain multiple subsystems that can benefit from sharing threat intelligence. Collaborative intelligence involves pooling data on vulnerabilities, indicators of compromise (IOCs), and attacker methods (IRIS Consortium, 2021).

This holistic perspective allows for more accurate risk assessments and earlier detection of malicious activities.

Threat intelligence feeds may come from commercial security vendors, governmental agencies, or research communities (CISA et al., 2023). By integrating shared intelligence, local AI models can incorporate external insights to classify or prioritize alerts. In some cases, city governments collaborate with private sector partners to aggregate threat data across utility providers, mass transit operators, and telecommunication services (Darktrace, 2023). This approach strengthens the resilience of the broader ecosystem by preventing attackers from exploiting one sector to move into another.

2.5 Summary of Literature Findings

The literature highlights a consensus that legacy cybersecurity models, which rely on manual analysis and signature-based detection, are unsuited for the evolving threat landscape in urban environments (Atiku, Aaron, Job, Shittu, & Yakubu, 2020; Bist, 2018). Researchers advocate incorporating AI methods to enhance detection, accelerate incident response, and handle voluminous data sets (Chirra, 2022a). Deep learning and anomaly detection methods emerge as particularly beneficial for catching unseen exploits (Ferrag et al., 2019; Nilă & Patriciu, 2020b).

Automated incident response is often positioned as the logical extension of AI-based detection, enabling containment and remediation at machine speed (Gupta et al., 2019). Nevertheless, studies stress the need to maintain human oversight and incorporate risk management frameworks that account for potential misclassification (Demertzis et al., 2019; Giovannelli, 2022). Integrating collaborative intelligence stands out as a strategic enabler, encouraging cross-sector coordination for sharing IOCs, vulnerabilities, and best practices (Fan et al., 2022).

Although AI-driven solutions bring improved accuracy and scalability, several challenges remain. Data quality, labeling, privacy, resource constraints, and model interpretability are persistent themes (Shaukat et al., 2020; Pitropakis et al., 2019). Addressing these issues is essential for any smart city aiming to implement a robust cyber defense architecture. Overall, the documented research supports further exploration of fully or semi-autonomous security operations within municipal contexts, emphasizing synergy among data analytics, policy, and cross-domain collaboration.

3. CONCEPT OF AUTONOMOUS CYBER DEFENSE

3.1 Definition and Scope

Autonomous cyber defense is defined as the capacity for a security system to detect, analyze, and respond to cyber threats with minimal human intervention (Burger, 2025). This autonomous system leverages machine learning models, automated decision-making processes, and real-time data ingestion to manage potential attacks across an enterprise or, in this case, a city's infrastructure (Kott, 2023). The system's scope extends from endpoints—such as IoT sensors, personal mobile devices connected to municipal Wi-Fi, or embedded systems in traffic lights—to cloud services that store massive volumes of city data (Almotairi et al., 2021).

Because city services are interdependent, an autonomous defense must be orchestrated across multiple domains, including energy grids, water treatment facilities, public transit networks, and hospital information systems (Ramachandran et al., 2023). The primary objective is to reduce the time between detecting a threat and implementing a response. In conventional models, this gap can extend to hours or days, particularly when manual analysis is required. With an AI-driven solution, the aim is to compress the gap into seconds or minutes, mitigating damage before it becomes systemic.

3.2 Key Characteristics of Autonomous Cyber Defense

1. **Continuous Learning**: Continuous learning is an essential feature, where models ingest new threat intelligence, incorporate feedback from incidents, and update themselves automatically (Li et al., 2018). This model evolution is critical to staying ahead of attackers who adapt their methods.
2. **Adaptability**: Attacks may target different city layers, from edge devices to cloud servers. An effective autonomous defense must adapt to these varying contexts, deploying unique detection techniques for each layer (Nilă & Patriciu, 2020b). For instance, endpoints have resource constraints that limit heavy computations, whereas centralized cloud systems can handle intensive analyses.
3. **Collaborative Intelligence**: Collaboration enriches threat models by combining local data with external threat feeds from industry, government, or other municipalities (IRIS Consortium, 2021). This approach improves both speed and accuracy in classifying threats (CISA et al., 2023).
4. **Automated Decision-Making**: Automated decision-making is the hallmark of autonomy. The system must not only identify malicious activity but also decide on the severity of the threat and implement a proportionate response (Gupta et al., 2019). Real-time triage is prioritized so that severe incidents prompt

immediate containment actions, while less critical events await human review if needed.

5. **Scalability and Resilience**: Autonomous systems must handle large volumes of data in near real time, especially during events like city festivals or emergencies that spike network usage (Chirra, 2022b). Distributed architectures and load balancing mechanisms help maintain performance under heavy traffic.
6. **Governance and Oversight**: While automation is critical for speed, cities must maintain oversight to ensure that the system's actions align with legal, ethical, and public service requirements (Demertzis et al., 2019). Automated systems that inadvertently disrupt services pose significant risks, so clear governance structures are necessary (Giovannelli, 2022).

3.3 Benefits and Drawbacks

An autonomous system can reduce the workload on security analysts, who would otherwise spend time sifting through false positives or repetitive tasks. It also closes the response gap, mitigating attacks before they propagate (Chirra, 2022a). By offloading routine tasks to algorithms, human expertise can focus on strategic analysis, policy development, and complex incidents (Darktrace, 2023).

However, an overreliance on automation has drawbacks. False positives can result in the unwarranted isolation of critical assets, such as shutting down a power substation under the mistaken assumption that it is compromised (Giovannelli, 2022). Additionally, AI models can degrade if not regularly updated with new threat data, leading to blind spots as attackers evolve (Pitropakis et al., 2019). Cost is another concern: scaling an autonomous system to meet the needs of a large municipality involves investments in hardware, software, and expertise (Demertzis et al., 2019).

3.4 Conceptual Architecture

As shown in Figure 1. outlines a baseline architecture for autonomous cyber defense in a city-scale environment:

1. **Sensors & Data Feeds**: The system receives inputs from endpoints such as IoT devices, network traffic logs, and external threat intelligence platforms (Almotairi et al., 2021). Each data source might follow a different schema and rate of generation.
2. **Aggregation & Preprocessing**: Incoming data is funneled into a platform where it is cleansed, normalized, and combined into a format suitable for AI analysis (Fan et al., 2022). This stage may employ distributed streaming frameworks that handle large, real-time data flows.

3. **AI-driven Analytics**: Various machine learning models (supervised, unsupervised, deep learning, reinforcement learning) process the data and detect anomalies or recognized patterns (Ferrag et al., 2019). They can also produce risk scores indicating the likelihood of malicious activity.
4. **Threat Classification**: If a threat is suspected, it is classified according to severity, type, and potential impact (Demertzis et al., 2019). Classification helps the system decide the appropriate response path.
5. **Automated Response**: High-priority incidents trigger immediate containment actions, such as blocking IP addresses or quarantining devices (Gupta et al., 2019). Less urgent issues might be queued for human validation.
6. **Feedback & Refinement**: Incident outcomes, including false positives or true confirmations of malicious activity, feed back into the analytics engine (Chirra, 2022b). This iterative approach refines future detection and classification accuracy.

Figure 1. Conceptual flow of an autonomous cyber defense system

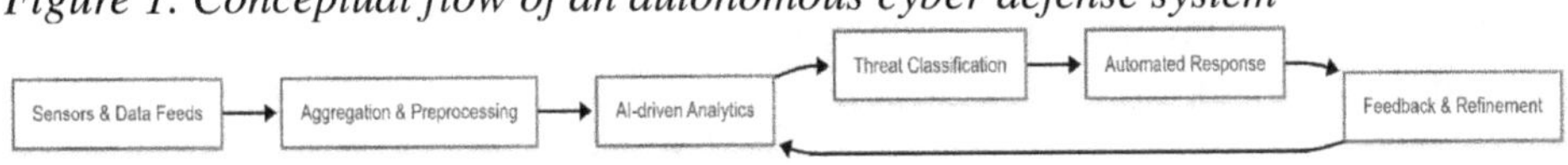

In this conceptual model, real-time feedback loops are crucial for adaptability. For instance, if the system quarantines a device but later determines the alert was a false positive, it should update the detection logic to avoid repeating that mistake (Nilă & Patriciu, 2020b). Likewise, a successful detection of a zero-day exploit leads to updated signatures or anomaly baselines, which can be shared across all nodes or even other cities via a collaborative intelligence framework (IRIS Consortium, 2021).

4. INTELLIGENT THREAT RESPONSE MECHANISMS

4.1 Threat Detection Approaches

4.1.1 Signature-Based Detection

Signature-based detection compares traffic and files against a database of known malicious patterns (Atiku et al., 2020). Although quick for known threats, it fails to identify novel or polymorphic attacks that do not match existing signatures (Bist,

2018). Nonetheless, signature-based methods remain popular in many municipal systems because they are straightforward to deploy and maintain.

4.1.2 Anomaly Detection

Anomaly detection involves building a model of normal behavior across network segments, user login patterns, and application usage (Nilă & Patriciu, 2020b). Any deviation from this normal baseline triggers an alert (Pitropakis et al., 2019). This approach works well for detecting zero-day attacks or stealthy malware but can produce high false positives if the normal baseline is too rigid or unrepresentative.

4.1.3 Behavioral Analysis

Behavioral analysis focuses on user and device interaction patterns. For example, a system might monitor login frequencies, data access volumes, and process execution times (Ferrag et al., 2019). If a user account displays atypical activities, the system flags it for further inspection (Shaukat et al., 2020). This method is more context-aware than raw anomaly detection and often yields lower false positive rates, albeit at the cost of more complex modeling.

4.2 Real-Time Analytics

Real-time analytics harness streaming data frameworks that process each event as it arrives. Instead of storing logs for batch processing, the system runs continuous queries or ML models on the data in motion (Demertzis et al., 2019). This capability is essential in a city environment, where quick action can prevent large-scale disruptions.

Complex event processing (CEP) can correlate multiple input streams, such as network packet logs, application logs, and user authentication events. If unusual patterns emerge across these streams—like a user logging in from geographically distinct locations within a short interval, followed by an abnormal data upload—the system can issue immediate alerts (Gupta et al., 2019). Parallel processing using AI models further boosts throughput and detection capability, making it feasible to handle thousands or millions of events per second (Fan et al., 2022).

4.3 Automated Incident Response Stages

4.3.1 Triage

Triage ranks incoming alerts by analyzing threat indicators, potential business impact, and historical false-positive rates (Gupta et al., 2019). Automated triage systems often apply scoring algorithms that factor in malicious IP reputations or known attack signatures. High-severity alerts may proceed directly to containment, while medium or low alerts await further correlation or manual review (Nilă et al., 2020a).

4.3.2 Containment

Containment limits the spread of an active threat. Typical actions include blocking network ports, quarantining devices, or revoking user credentials (Chirra, 2022b). In an autonomous framework, these measures can be implemented instantly upon high confidence of malicious behavior (Darktrace, 2023). However, false positives at this stage can disrupt essential services, underlining the need for accurate detection (Giovannelli, 2022).

4.3.3 Eradication and Recovery

Eradication involves removing all traces of malware or unauthorized access. Automated scripts can patch systems, delete malicious files, or reformat infected endpoints (Ferrag et al., 2019). Recovery then restores normal operations, possibly by reverting systems to a known good state or redeploying software images (Ramachandran et al., 2023). Automated playbooks reduce manual effort and ensure consistent application of best practices.

4.3.4 Post-Incident Analysis

Post-incident analysis identifies root causes and documents lessons learned (Prejbeanu, 2020). Automated systems gather logs and produce timelines of attacker movements. These artifacts feed back into detection models, improving future accuracy (Nilă et al., 2020a). Post-incident analysis also helps refine policies so that if, for example, a user was compromised due to phishing, additional training or stricter authentication might be implemented city-wide.

4.4 Role of Human Analysts

Even in a highly automated context, human analysts play a critical role in oversight, policy guidance, and complex incident investigations (Giovannelli, 2022). Automated systems excel at responding to routine threats or well-structured anomalies, but certain attacks require nuanced understanding of city operations, legal constraints, or cross-departmental processes (Demertzis et al., 2019). Analysts confirm high-stakes actions, especially those that might disrupt critical infrastructure, and they calibrate AI models. Through continuous interaction with the system's outputs, human analysts ensure the technology remains aligned with organizational goals.

5. PROPOSED AI-DRIVEN FRAMEWORK FOR INTEGRATED URBAN INFRASTRUCTURE

5.1 Framework Overview

Designing an AI-driven cyber defense framework for smart cities necessitates a unified strategy that spans data ingestion, analytics, automated response, and governance. The proposed model illustrates how these components can integrate to safeguard city services from evolving threats (Ramachandran et al., 2023). By merging advanced detection algorithms, real-time collaboration, and well-defined policies, the framework fosters resilience across diverse municipal systems, including transportation, utilities, and emergency services (Almotairi et al., 2021).

Figure 2. AI-driven framework for urban cyber defense

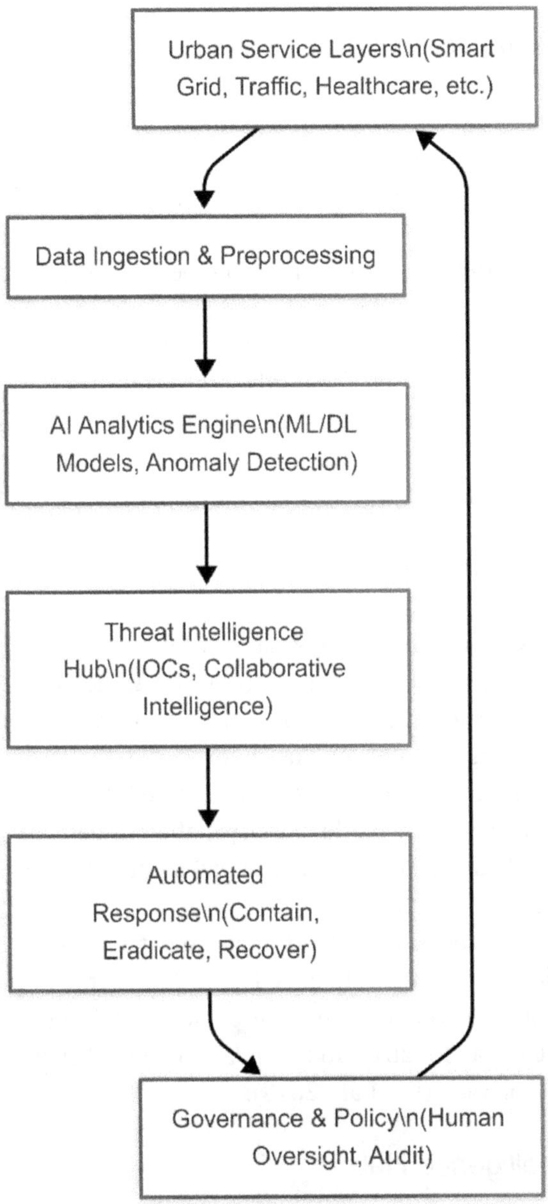

5.2 Core Components

5.2.1 Data Ingestion and Preprocessing

Data ingestion represents the first step, collecting logs, sensor data, and alerts from various sources across the city (Almotairi et al., 2021). IoT devices might relay sensor readings for traffic lights or water meters. Network devices generate flow logs showing source/destination IPs and protocols used. The data ingestion layer must accommodate different data formats, volumes, and velocities.

Preprocessing cleans, enriches, and normalizes the data so that subsequent analytics can operate effectively (Maidamwar, Bartere, & Lokulwar, 2021). This might involve removing corrupted records, converting timestamps into uniform formats, or deriving advanced features like average traffic rates per device. Edge computing nodes can filter out unnecessary details to reduce bandwidth usage and central processing overhead (Fan et al., 2022).

5.2.2 AI Analytics Engine

The AI Analytics Engine orchestrates machine learning and deep learning models to detect threats. It may run multiple algorithms in parallel, each tuned to specific tasks such as anomaly detection, threat classification, or reinforcement learning for response strategy (Ferrag et al., 2019). The engine can also incorporate unsupervised methods to identify patterns not previously encountered (Pitropakis et al., 2019). For instance, a deep learning model might classify malicious network packets, while an unsupervised anomaly detector monitors user behavior to flag suspicious activities (Shaukat et al., 2020).

This engine typically resides in a cloud environment, leveraging scalable compute resources to handle real-time data streams. Depending on the infrastructure design, partial analytics might also occur on edge devices, enabling faster response for localized threats (Chirra, 2022b). Model updates can be distributed in a federated manner to preserve privacy (Li et al., 2018).

5.2.3 Threat Intelligence Hub

The Threat Intelligence Hub aggregates data on known vulnerabilities, attack patterns, and IOCs from external feeds (IRIS Consortium, 2021). It functions as a knowledge repository accessible by the AI Analytics Engine to bolster threat classification. When new vulnerabilities or exploits are discovered, the hub circulates updates to relevant detection models. Collaborative sharing between cities or agencies becomes feasible through standard formats like STIX/TAXII (CISA et al., 2023).

In practice, the hub might connect to commercial threat intelligence services or government agencies, incorporating real-time alerts about global campaigns. By correlating local events with global indicators, the system identifies and responds to threats earlier (Darktrace, 2023).

5.2.4 Automated Response Module

Once the Analytics Engine identifies a credible threat, the Automated Response Module executes containment, eradication, or recovery steps (Chirra, 2022b). This module houses predefined playbooks that detail the sequence of actions for various scenarios, like isolating suspicious hosts or installing patches (Nilă et al., 2020a). Real-time orchestration tools integrate with networking equipment, virtual machines, and identity management systems to impose these changes instantly (Giovannelli, 2022).

Response actions are logged to facilitate compliance audits and future forensic analysis (Demertzis et al., 2019). If a high-severity threat is detected, the module might automatically quarantine critical segments. For moderate risks, it could notify security staff, giving them the option to override or refine the automated plan.

5.2.5 Governance and Policy Layer

Governance mechanisms ensure that automated decisions comply with legal, ethical, and operational guidelines. Stakeholders define acceptable risk levels, escalation thresholds, and responsibilities (Burger, 2025). The system logs all actions, which oversight committees or designated officials can review. If a policy violation occurs, the system can be halted or forced to revert certain changes (Darktrace, 2023).

Because smart city operations intersect with public interests, transparency is crucial. Certain logs may be anonymized to protect citizen data while still enabling security monitoring (Wolniak & Stecuła, 2024). Policies can define how data is stored, shared, and used by AI models, mitigating concerns around surveillance.

5.3 Multi-Layered Defense Strategy

A multi-layered strategy places protective mechanisms at each tier of the network stack, from endpoints to the cloud (Pitropakis et al., 2019). For instance, endpoint security clients can detect malicious executables, while network-based intrusion detection systems analyze traffic patterns (Ferrag et al., 2019). Application-layer monitoring checks for anomalies in user requests or transaction patterns (Shaukat et al., 2020). The AI-driven analytics layer sits atop these individual defenses, aggregating insights to form a holistic perspective.

This layered design minimizes single points of failure. Even if one layer's defenses are bypassed, subsequent layers may identify suspicious activity. In a city environment, redundancy is essential for continuity of essential services, such as water and power distribution. By correlating data from multiple layers, the city's SOC gains more contextualized information about threats, reducing the likelihood of stealthy intrusions.

5.4 Scalability and Fault Tolerance

Smart city infrastructures may scale to millions of connected devices, necessitating robust architecture. **Containerization** and **microservices** allow AI analytics and response components to be deployed across multiple nodes, maintaining uptime even if one node fails (Fan et al., 2022). Load balancers can distribute data streams to various analytics engines, preventing bottlenecks (Ferrag et al., 2019).

To ensure resilience, critical processes can be duplicated in active-active configurations, with data replication across different sites or cloud regions (Demertzis et al., 2019). Automatic failover systems detect node outages and redirect traffic, preserving continuity.

5.5 Data Privacy and Ethics

Data privacy is fundamental in a city environment that collects personal and demographic information (Wolniak & Stecuła, 2024). Governance policies must specify strict access controls, data retention limits, and anonymization protocols. Legal frameworks often mandate how data can be used for security monitoring, leading to potential conflicts between security demands and individual rights (Burger, 2025).

Moreover, **explainability** becomes significant, especially if AI-driven systems make decisions that affect public services. Stakeholders may demand explanations about why an AI engine flagged specific user activities as suspicious. Techniques in **explainable AI (XAI)** can assist by generating human-readable justifications (Demertzis et al., 2019). This transparency fosters trust in automated defense measures and aligns with regulatory guidelines that discourage "black box" decision-making.

6. KEY COMPONENTS OF THE PROPOSED FRAMEWORK

6.1 Monitoring and Data Collection

Monitoring forms the foundation of any security strategy in a smart city, enabling the detection of anomalous signals and the real-time analysis of network flows, user behavior, and system states (Atiku et al., 2020). Each subsystem—be it traffic management or healthcare administration—emits logs and event data that can reveal potential breaches. Converging this data in a central repository or distributing it within a structured architecture is vital to comprehensive monitoring (Almotairi et al., 2021).

The heterogeneity of data sources implies different protocols, formats, and frequencies. Sensors in a water distribution system might transmit readings every few seconds, while server logs in a municipal datacenter could be event-driven. Standardizing and labeling each data stream helps the AI analytics engine correlate events. Another challenge is ensuring data integrity; tampered logs can mislead algorithms. Cryptographic hashing or secure logging methods address such tampering risks (Fan et al., 2022).

Sophisticated monitoring frameworks also incorporate user and entity behavior analytics (UEBA), tracking how devices and accounts typically interact with city resources (Nilă & Patriciu, 2020b). If a device or account deviates from established patterns, the system generates an alert. This layered approach to monitoring ensures multiple vantage points for detecting intrusions. While collecting abundant data can boost security insights, it also introduces data privacy concerns that the policy layer must address (Ramachandran et al., 2023).

6.2 Data Processing and Storage

After data is collected, it must be processed and stored in a manner suitable for real-time analytics and historical investigations. Many smart city environments rely on distributed computing platforms like **Apache Spark** or **Hadoop**, which handle high volumes of structured and unstructured data (Fan et al., 2022). Stream processing engines (e.g., Apache Kafka) enable continuous ingestion and near real-time alerting (Demertzis et al., 2019).

Ingested data might undergo transformations such as filtering irrelevant fields, aggregating metrics over time windows, or generating features for ML-based detection (Almotairi et al., 2021). Storing the processed data in a scalable data lake ensures analysts can later conduct forensics or feed retrospective analyses into updated machine learning pipelines (Ferrag et al., 2019). Access controls within these repositories prevent unauthorized personnel from modifying or viewing sensitive logs (Chirra, 2022a).

To handle edge devices that produce continuous streams, some processing can be offloaded to local edge computing nodes (Nilă & Patriciu, 2020b). This approach conserves bandwidth by reducing the volume of data transmitted to the central data center. Local anomalies detected at the edge can trigger immediate partial remediation. Only critical alerts or aggregated metrics then flow into the central platform for correlation with other events (Maidamwar et al., 2021).

6.3 AI Models and Algorithms

The AI layer is central to the proposed framework, encompassing various learning techniques that detect, classify, and respond to threats. Each algorithm addresses distinct facets of the threat landscape.

Table 1. Comparison of AI detection techniques

Technique	Strengths	Weaknesses	References
Signature-Based	Fast, low false positives	Unable to detect new or morphing threats	Bist (2018); Atiku et al. (2020)
Anomaly Detection	Identifies zero-day attacks	May have high false positive rate if poorly tuned	Pitropakis et al. (2019); Li et al. (2018)
Behavioral Analysis	Context-aware detection	Complex to implement, requires baselines for behavior	Shaukat et al. (2020); Ferrag et al. (2019)
Deep Learning	Learns complex patterns, robust detection	Large data requirements, interpretability challenges	Ferrag et al. (2019); Prejbeanu (2020)
Reinforcement Learning	Adaptive decision-making	Needs simulation or real-time feedback loop	Kott (2023); Chirra (2022b)

6.3.1 Supervised Learning

Supervised learning applications in city security often rely on classification algorithms that label network flows or file samples as benign or malicious. The training phase uses historical data, with known malicious samples labeled from past incidents (Bist, 2018). Algorithms like Decision Trees, Random Forest, or Neural Networks excel in these tasks, but they hinge on the availability of accurate, up-to-date labeled datasets (Shaukat et al., 2020). Over time, the distribution of threats may shift, necessitating retraining or online learning approaches.

6.3.2 Unsupervised Learning

Unsupervised techniques discover anomalies without needing labeled data (Nilă & Patriciu, 2020b). Clustering algorithms group similar data points, making outliers indicative of possible intrusions (Pitropakis et al., 2019). Autoencoders reconstruct typical input patterns and flag large reconstruction errors. This approach captures zero-day threats but can yield higher false positives if normal behavior is highly variable.

6.3.3 Deep Learning

Deep learning frameworks like CNNs and RNNs can manage high-dimensional data, including raw network packets or system call traces (Ferrag et al., 2019). Convolutional layers can learn local features in network traffic, recognizing malicious signatures that might elude simpler methods (Prejbeanu, 2020). Recurrent layers track temporal dependencies, capturing how an attack unfolds over time. Deep learning can also integrate self-attention mechanisms to identify relationships across widely separated events, proving especially useful in complex multi-stage intrusions (Shaukat et al., 2020).

Training deep networks often demands substantial GPU or specialized hardware resources, complicating deployments on edge devices. Nevertheless, incremental or transfer learning can mitigate resource constraints, transferring knowledge from large, centrally trained models to lighter edge-based models (Fan et al., 2022).

6.3.4 Reinforcement Learning

Reinforcement learning (RL) addresses the dynamic nature of attack-response cycles. An RL agent receives rewards for reducing damage or preventing further intrusion, refining its strategies over multiple encounters (Kott, 2023). For instance, the system may try different containment procedures (blocking IPs, isolating subnets, or forcing re-authentication) and measure how effectively these actions stop the threat (Chirra, 2022b). Over time, the RL model converges on optimal policies that maximize security outcomes while minimizing operational disruption.

RL can be challenging to deploy in production environments because trial-and-error learning could risk service stability. Simulation-based training or test networks often precede real-world deployment to ensure the model's actions do not cause harmful side effects (Oesch et al., 2024). Once refined, RL can offer robust, adaptive responses in rapidly changing environments.

6.4 Threat Correlation and Prioritization

Threat correlation merges events from different data sources, deriving a holistic view of the security posture (Gupta et al., 2019). A city's energy grid logs may show increased network traffic from an external IP, while public safety logs indicate an unusual login attempt from that same IP. Individually, these logs might not trigger high alerts, but correlated analysis can reveal a coordinated attack pattern.

Correlation engines use rule-based logic, machine learning, or complex event processing to piece together incident timelines (Nilă et al., 2020a). The system then prioritizes incidents based on potential impact and confidence level. Priority scoring is significant because smart cities cannot investigate every alert in depth given resource constraints (Demertzis et al., 2019). Automating event correlation alleviates the manual correlation burden on analysts, preserving their bandwidth for high-risk threats (Chirra, 2022b).

6.5 Automated Response Execution

Automated response is the logical extension of advanced detection. Once a threat's severity and confidence level exceed defined thresholds, the system initiates containment and mitigation. For instance, the system may reconfigure firewalls to block suspicious IP addresses, terminate user sessions, or revoke digital certificates (Darktrace, 2023). If the threat is localized to a single device, the module can isolate that endpoint, removing it from the network (Chirra, 2022b).

More sophisticated responses include **dynamic sandboxing**, where suspicious files or processes are executed in a controlled environment for deeper analysis (Ferrag et al., 2019). If confirmed malicious, the system updates signatures or anomaly baselines accordingly. Automatic patch deployment or rollback to a secure snapshot further ensures compromised systems are restored swiftly (Ramachandran et al., 2023). Each action is logged for accountability and future reference.

6.6 Governance and Policy Management

Governance frameworks ensure the system's actions align with regulatory requirements and ethical guidelines. For example, shutting down a hospital's network to contain a threat might be unacceptable if lives are at stake. The governance layer thus encodes rules on how and when automated measures can proceed (Demertzis et al., 2019). Certain actions might require sign-off from a human operator, ensuring that critical disruptions do not happen unilaterally (Giovannelli, 2022).

Policy management includes version control so that changes in regulations or risk appetite can be promptly integrated (Burger, 2025). The system also supports auditing: logs of automated decisions, triggers, and outcomes are periodically reviewed to verify compliance and refine policies. This approach ensures transparency and accountability, which are key for maintaining public trust in AI-driven security systems.

7. IMPLEMENTATION CHALLENGES AND STRATEGIES

7.1 Data Quality and Labeling

Machine learning solutions rely on extensive, high-quality data. In a city environment, data quality issues arise from diverse device types, intermittent network connectivity, and the dynamic range of real-time sensor readings (Bist, 2018). Additionally, labeling malicious vs. benign data can be labor-intensive. Security teams often label incidents post-factum, and the volume of benign data may far exceed confirmed malicious samples (Nilă & Patriciu, 2020b).

A partial solution is **semi-supervised learning**, which capitalizes on large unlabeled datasets by leveraging a smaller labeled subset for guidance (Pitropakis et al., 2019). Alternatively, **unsupervised anomaly detection** can highlight outliers for analysts to label retroactively, iteratively improving the model. Another approach is **transfer learning** where models trained on global threat data are adapted for local contexts with minimal labeling effort (Chirra, 2022a).

Maintaining labeling consistency across various city departments is also nontrivial. A suspicious traffic pattern at the water department might be considered normal in the power distribution network. Creating a shared taxonomy for labeling events enhances cross-department correlation and fosters synergy in a city's overall defense posture (IRIS Consortium, 2021).

7.2 Resource Constraints

Cities often have heterogeneous infrastructures, with some departments well-equipped with modern hardware and others using outdated systems (Demertzis et al., 2019). AI models can be computationally expensive, which poses challenges for real-time analysis on constrained devices or older servers. Implementation strategies include **edge computing** for pre-filtering data and **cloud-based AI** for resource-intensive tasks, balancing local responsiveness with global analytics (Almotairi et al., 2021).

Budget constraints also influence the choice of solutions. Commercial AI security platforms can be costly, leading smaller municipalities to explore open-source tools or consortium-driven collaborations (CISA et al., 2023). Optimal resource allocation may involve distributing different AI modules among city departments to avoid duplicative costs. For example, a single central analytics cluster might handle sophisticated deep learning tasks, while local departmental servers handle simpler signature-based scanning (Fan et al., 2022).

7.3 Evolving Threat Landscape

Attackers continually refine tactics to bypass existing defenses. Malware authors experiment with advanced evasion techniques, including obfuscation or stealthy communication channels (Pitropakis et al., 2019). Zero-day exploits pose a particular danger, exploiting undiscovered vulnerabilities. Traditional defenses lag behind, relying on signatures that are updated after new threats are identified.

Continuous learning is a response mechanism, where AI models ingest recent threat data and refine detection boundaries accordingly (Chirra, 2022a). Similarly, **threat hunting** processes can proactively search for anomalies rather than waiting for established patterns. Another solution is **adversarial training**, which involves exposing models to crafted attacks designed to fool them, thus hardening the detection logic (Oesch et al., 2024).

Collaboration between government, academia, and industry accelerates knowledge sharing about emergent threats, thereby enhancing detection timeliness. Initiatives like bug bounty programs or public vulnerability disclosure channels can also surface flaws before they become widely exploited (IRIS Consortium, 2021).

7.4 False Positives and Negatives

Excessive false positives cause fatigue and degrade trust in AI alerts, while false negatives allow attacks to progress undetected (Shaukat et al., 2020). Striking a balance is essential, especially in large city networks. **Calibration** or **threshold tuning** can adjust how sensitive anomaly detection models are (Ferrag et al., 2019). Ensemble methods, which combine outputs from multiple detection algorithms, often yield better precision and recall rates compared to any single model alone.

Table 2. Autonomous response strategies in smart cities

Response Strategy	Description	Challenges
Automated Isolation	Disabling network access for suspected devices or zones	Risk of disconnecting essential services
Policy Enforcement	Updating firewall and access control rules in real time	Requires robust governance to avoid misconfig.
Malware Removal	Launching scripts to remove or quarantine malicious software	Potential conflict with critical system states
Patch Management	Automatic deployment of patches and updates	Compatibility, ensuring no downtime for crucial services
System Rollback	Reverting systems to known good states	Data loss if not carefully planned

In practice, operators might configure **alert thresholds** to prioritize critical infrastructure over less sensitive systems. Periodic reviews of false-positive cases guide reclassification rules or model retraining. Ultimately, the goal is to keep detection both timely and accurate while minimizing the disruptions caused by unwarranted actions (Gupta et al., 2019).

7.5 Ethical and Privacy Considerations

Cities that use AI-driven monitoring aggregate large amounts of data, raising concerns about surveillance and citizen privacy (Ramachandran et al., 2023). Automated systems could inadvertently capture personal details, geolocation, or even personal communications if not carefully constrained (Burger, 2025). Policies must define the scope of monitoring, retention periods, and access privileges. De-identification or anonymization techniques can protect sensitive data while preserving critical security-relevant signals (Darktrace, 2023).

Another ethical dimension is accountability. If an autonomous system takes an action that leads to service disruption, which entity is responsible? Clear guidelines must address liability, chain of command, and possible grievance procedures if individuals or businesses are harmed by overzealous cyber defense measures (Demertzis et al., 2019). This accountability is intertwined with **transparency**, often requiring explainable AI methods that can justify automated decisions to relevant authorities (Giovannelli, 2022).

These challenges underscore the need for structured labeling processes, balanced detection thresholds, continuous retraining, and vigilant governance. Balancing security with resource, privacy, and ethical concerns is vital for sustained trust in AI-driven municipal defense programs. As shown in table 4.

Table 3. Challenges and mitigation tactics for AI in cyber defense

Challenge	Potential Mitigation Tactic	Reference
Data Labeling Scarcity	Semi-supervised or unsupervised learning approaches	Nilă & Patriciu (2020b)
High False Positives	Ensemble methods, threshold calibration	Shaukat et al. (2020); Ferrag et al. (2019)
Model Drift	Continuous retraining with new threat data	Chirra (2022a); Pitropakis et al. (2019)
Resource Constraints	Distributed or edge-based analytics	Almotairi et al. (2021)
Ethical & Privacy Issues	Privacy-preserving ML, governance frameworks	Burger (2025); Darktrace (2023)
Adversarial Attacks on ML Models	Robust training, adversarial detection, input sanitization	Pitropakis et al. (2019)

8. CASE STUDIES AND REAL-WORLD APPLICATIONS

8.1 City of Las Vegas: Autonomous Cyber AI

Darktrace (2023) documented how the City of Las Vegas implemented AI-driven cybersecurity to protect its digital infrastructure. This initiative involved deploying autonomous solutions capable of learning normal city network behaviors and isolating suspicious traffic in real time. The city's environment included multiple administrative departments, each generating logs from various applications and IoT sensors. By consolidating these logs into a unified platform, the AI models learned typical traffic patterns—such as data flows related to public information systems or employee work schedules.

When anomalies were detected, the system quarantined the compromised endpoint or blocked malicious IP addresses. One success story involved detecting a zero-day exploit targeting a city server; the automated system blocked the suspicious traffic before any data exfiltration occurred. The city reported a noticeable reduction in incident response times, enabling security teams to focus on root cause analysis rather than repetitive monitoring tasks (Darktrace, 2023).

However, city officials also recognized the need for robust governance. Automated responses could potentially disrupt public services if misapplied. They implemented tiered policies, requiring manual review for high-risk actions (Burger, 2025). Although the AI solutions drastically minimized dwell times, some false positives still occurred. Over time, the system refined its models by incorporating feedback from resolved incidents, gradually lowering the false-positive rate.

This case underscores the feasibility of autonomous cyber defense in a city environment and illustrates the importance of balancing automation with human oversight. By combining advanced AI analytics with a well-structured governance model, Las Vegas successfully reinforced its security posture without sacrificing essential public services.

8.2 IRIS Project

The **IRIS Project** (IRIS Consortium, 2021) is a collaborative European initiative aimed at creating an automated threat reporting and incident response framework for smart cities. Funded under the H2020 program, the project explores how AI can integrate with city-level Security Operations Centers. Key focuses include anomaly detection at edge nodes, automated triage of events, and distributed threat intelligence sharing across municipal boundaries.

Researchers developed prototypes using unsupervised learning to detect anomalies in IoT sensors deployed for traffic management. The system correlated anomalies with threat intelligence feeds to ascertain if they aligned with known attack signatures (Pitropakis et al., 2019). Early results indicated that the approach could detect suspicious traffic spikes suggestive of a DDoS attempt. Automated responses included temporarily throttling traffic from malicious IP ranges and alerting neighboring cities to possible large-scale attacks (CISA et al., 2023).

A salient feature was the project's emphasis on secure data sharing. Municipalities often hesitate to exchange sensitive logs due to privacy concerns, but IRIS employed anonymization and differential privacy techniques. This allowed collaborative threat intelligence without exposing personally identifiable information (IRIS Consortium, 2021). By harmonizing data formats, IRIS streamlined cross-city correlation of incidents and increased the overall detection rate. This model highlights how regional or national-level collaboration can amplify the benefits of autonomous defense.

8.3 CISA Guidelines for Smart City Cybersecurity

The **Cybersecurity and Infrastructure Security Agency (CISA)**, along with its international partners, published guidelines that emphasize best practices for safeguarding connected city infrastructures (CISA et al., 2023). These guidelines urge local governments to adopt a risk-based approach, focusing on the most critical services first. AI-driven strategies figure prominently in these recommendations, especially for continuous monitoring and rapid incident response.

Under these guidelines, pilot cities in the United States implemented 24/7 monitoring solutions. They also established data-sharing protocols between water, energy, and public safety authorities. This cooperative environment accelerated threat detection because incidents in one domain often served as early indicators for others (Demertzis et al., 2019). For example, a spike in unauthorized login attempts to water utility systems might coincide with malicious scans targeting the transportation network. AI correlation engines flagged these parallel events as indicative of a broader, coordinated intrusion attempt.

The guidelines also discuss layered security controls and the role of governance. Automated systems can swiftly respond to moderate-level threats, but high-severity actions should involve human input, especially if they might interrupt essential services (Ramachandran et al., 2023). Additionally, CISA's framework encourages city administrators to maintain updated inventories of network assets, segment critical infrastructures, and integrate advanced encryption mechanisms for data in transit (CISA et al., 2023). These measures, combined with AI-driven analytics, have proven effective at reducing the time window in which attackers can operate undetected.

8.4 NATO CCDCOE Studies

The **NATO Cooperative Cyber Defence Centre of Excellence (CCDCOE)** has published research papers and hosted events focusing on autonomous incident response and adversarial resilience (Giovannelli, 2022). While much of the CCDCOE's work addresses military or critical national infrastructure, many findings apply to smart cities that rely on similarly complex networks. CCDCOE researchers emphasize multi-layered defense architectures that incorporate both signature-based and anomaly-based detection (Pitropakis et al., 2019).

One theme is the potential for adversaries to craft attacks specifically aimed at fooling AI models. For instance, attackers might manipulate data to create false anomalies or hide genuine threats (Ferrag et al., 2019). The CCDCOE's solution includes adversarial training, robust data pipelines, and advanced detection mechanisms that can identify attempts to poison the training process (Oesch et al., 2024). The organization also highlights the importance of cross-domain intelligence—cities can leverage threat insights from national agencies and vice versa.

CCDCOE studies underscore that adopting autonomous cyber defense in mission-critical environments demands rigorous testing, scenario simulations, and fallback procedures (Demertzis et al., 2019). The lessons gleaned from these military-focused investigations are directly relevant to municipal contexts where disruptions could threaten public health and safety.

9. USE CASE DIAGRAM FOR SMART CITY AUTONOMOUS DEFENSE

Use case diagrams help illustrate how different actors interact with the AI-driven security system in a city context. The diagram below shows the relationships among administrators, the AI defense system, and automated containment/recovery features.

Figure 3. Use case diagram for an AI-driven smart city defense explanation

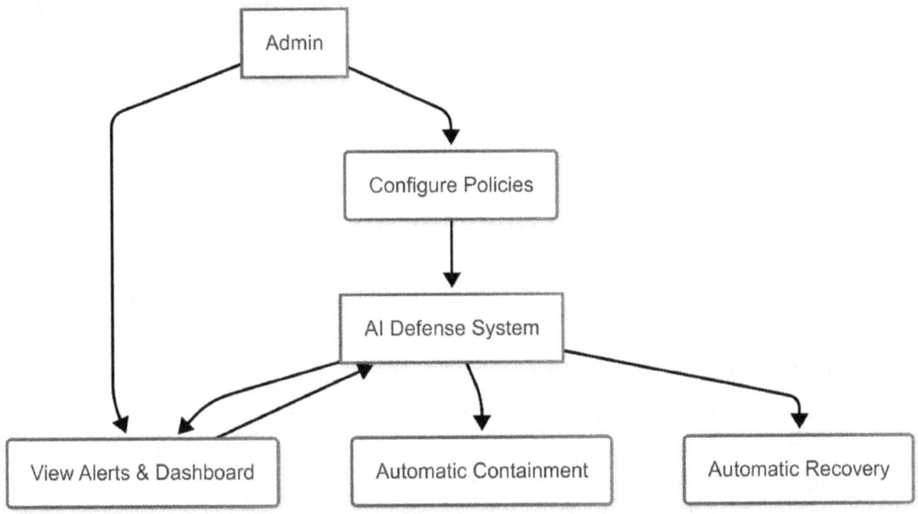

- **Admin**: Represents the human operator or a team within the city's Security Operations Center. Administrators set rules dictating how aggressively the AI engine should respond to different threat levels. They also manage escalation paths for incidents that might disrupt critical infrastructure.
- **AI Defense System**: Processes data in real time, detecting intrusions and deciding whether to initiate containment or recovery. The system interacts with network devices, servers, and other resources to execute defensive measures (Nilă & Patriciu, 2020b).
- **Automatic Containment**: The system can isolate infected endpoints, block malicious IP addresses, and enforce firewall updates (Chirra, 2022b). Containment reduces lateral movement while the system or human analysts investigate further.
- **Automatic Recovery**: If an incident is fully contained, the system executes recovery tasks such as removing malware, rebooting systems, or restoring

from backups (Giovannelli, 2022). Administrators monitor progress via the dashboard.

- **View Alerts & Dashboard**: Administrators see alerts of suspicious activity and can override or refine the AI-driven actions if necessary (Demertzis et al., 2019).

This diagram clarifies how human oversight remains integral. While the system automates most processes, human administrators retain control over strategic decisions and policy definitions. This synergy ensures that fully automated processes do not inadvertently cause city-wide service interruptions.

10. FUTURE DIRECTIONS

10.1 Integration with Edge Computing

As city networks grow, the volume of sensor data and the number of connected devices surge. **Edge computing** shifts processing closer to data sources, reducing latency and bandwidth usage (Almotairi et al., 2021). AI-driven threat detection on edge devices can catch anomalies early, preventing harmful data from propagating to central servers (Fan et al., 2022). Edge-based solutions also enhance resilience by continuing to operate if connectivity to the cloud is disrupted.

Research in edge-based AI looks at lightweight neural networks that can run on resource-constrained platforms (Chirra, 2022a). Techniques like model pruning, quantization, and knowledge distillation optimize deep learning models for less powerful hardware. However, consistent model updates and synchronization across large fleets of edge devices remain logistical hurdles. In the future, orchestration tools could deploy AI model updates city-wide, ensuring uniform threat coverage (Shaukat et al., 2020).

10.2 Federated Learning for Collaborative Defense

Federated learning allows multiple entities to train AI models collectively without exchanging raw data (Li et al., 2018). This approach is well-suited to scenarios where data privacy is critical, yet collaborative insights can improve overall detection accuracy (IRIS Consortium, 2021). In a city context, each department—

transportation, healthcare, utilities—could train local models on their specific data, periodically sending only model updates to a central aggregator.

Such collaboration can extend beyond city departments to include neighboring municipalities, forming a regional security network. If one city encounters a novel ransomware threat, the federated learning system integrates those findings into a global model. Other participating cities then benefit from enhanced detection, all without direct access to the potentially sensitive logs (Ramachandran et al., 2023). While federated learning reduces privacy risks, it also introduces potential vulnerabilities like **model poisoning**, where malicious updates degrade global performance. Robust validation steps and consensus algorithms mitigate these issues (Pitropakis et al., 2019).

10.3 Explainable AI

Explainable AI (XAI) refers to techniques that clarify how AI models arrive at particular decisions (Demertzis et al., 2019). This is especially relevant in public administration, where accountability and trust are paramount. Deep learning models, while accurate, often function as "black boxes." XAI methods like **LIME** (Local Interpretable Model-Agnostic Explanations) or **SHAP** (SHapley Additive exPlanations) can highlight the features or data points that most influenced a model's output.

In cybersecurity, XAI can reveal which network features triggered an intrusion alert, guiding administrators to refine detection thresholds or investigate system logs. For instance, if an alert stems from unusual login times plus unexpected data transfers, an XAI approach can present these factors in a human-readable format (Giovannelli, 2022). This transparency also supports legal and ethical scrutiny, especially for decisions that disrupt public services (Burger, 2025). Over time, improved interpretability can foster public confidence in autonomous defense initiatives and facilitate compliance with government regulations.

10.4 Autonomous Coordination of Defense Actions

Many current solutions focus on localizing detection and response within specific departmental SOC. Future research may explore **multi-agent systems** where each agent manages a specialized domain—like public transport, utilities, or healthcare—and coordinates with others to contain multi-domain attacks (Kott, 2023). These agents could exchange real-time threat intelligence, optimizing resource deployment and sharing incident data to form a cohesive defense (Oesch et al., 2024).

For instance, if the public transport agent detects a cyber intrusion in traffic signal controls, it could alert the utilities agent that the same adversaries might attempt to compromise smart grids. Automated coordination can then preemptively fortify relevant nodes or restrict inbound connections until further analysis is complete (Chirra, 2022b). This approach allows a city to function as a collective system rather than a set of isolated silos. The vision is a truly **autonomous** cyber defense that acts seamlessly across an entire municipality.

Despite promising research, practical deployment faces challenges. Implementing multi-agent protocols requires standard communication formats, robust consensus algorithms, and strong trust relationships between municipal departments (IRIS Consortium, 2021). However, as AI maturity increases, the concept of an interconnected suite of autonomous agents orchestrating city-wide defenses becomes increasingly plausible.

11. CONCLUSION

Cities worldwide are undergoing a profound digital transformation, integrating IoT sensors, data analytics, and edge computing to enhance public services. Alongside these benefits come acute cybersecurity risks that demand rapid detection and response. By embracing AI-driven defense mechanisms, municipalities gain the ability to correlate diverse data streams, detect anomalies in real time, and automate incident response tasks. This significantly reduces detection-to-remediation intervals, preserving the functionality of essential services like transportation and healthcare. Central to a successful autonomous framework is robust governance, ensuring that the system's actions align with public interests, respect privacy, and undergo transparent auditing. While challenges such as model drift, resource constraints, and adversarial attacks persist, continuous learning and collaborative threat intelligence can refine detection algorithms and improve resilience. Real-world implementations, including city-scale projects and international research initiatives, validate the feasibility of AI-based approaches for urban environments. As multi-agent systems and edge-based analytics evolve, the potential to orchestrate coordinated defenses across interconnected infrastructures will only grow. Ultimately, an AI-driven, integrated cybersecurity strategy enables city administrations to anticipate emerging threats, protect sensitive data, and maintain trust in public services. Policymakers, system architects, and security professionals can draw on these insights to implement solutions that balance innovation with public safety, paving the way for truly smart and secure urban spaces.

REFERENCES

Almotairi, S., Ezzat, M. K., Abdelghany, M., & Salem, M. A.-M. (2021). Horizontal Review on Video Surveillance for Smart Cities: Edge Devices, Applications, Datasets, and Future Trends. *Sensors (Basel)*, *21*(11), 3913. DOI: 10.3390/s21113913 PMID: 34204058

Atiku, S. B., Aaron, A. U., Job, G. K., Shittu, F., & Yakubu, I. Z. (2020). Survey on the Applications of Artificial Intelligence in Cyber Security. *International Journal of Scientific & Technology Research*, *9*(1), 6–10.

Bist, A. S. (2018). Survey of Deep Learning Algorithms for Malware Detection. *International Journal of Computer Science and Information Security*, *16*(3), 108–115.

Burger, C. (2025). Autonomous Cyber AI is Revolutionizing Cyber Defense. CISO MAG. Retrieved from https://cisomag.com/

Chirra, D. R. (2022a). AI-Enabled Cybersecurity Solutions for Protecting Smart Cities Against Emerging Threats. *International Journal of Advanced Engineering Technologies and Innovations*, *1*(2), 45–60.

Chirra, D. R. (2022b). Towards an AI-Driven Automated Cybersecurity Incident Response System. *International Journal of Advanced Engineering Technologies and Innovations*, *1*(1), 15–30.

CISA. (2023). Cybersecurity Best Practices for Smart Cities. (Joint cybersecurity guidance by CISA, NSA, FBI, NCSC-UK, ACSC, CCCS, NCSC-NZ). Retrieved from https://cisa.gov/

Demertzis, K., Tziritas, N., Kikiras, P., Sanchez, L. S., & Iliadis, L. (2019). The Next Generation Cognitive Security Operations Center: Adaptive Analytic Lambda Architecture for Efficient Defense Against Adversarial Attacks. *IEEE Transactions on Industrial Informatics*, *15*(5), 2908–2915.

Fan, J., Yang, W., & Lam, K. Y. (2022). Cybersecurity Challenges of IoT-Enabled Smart Cities: A Survey. *arXiv Preprint*, arXiv:2202.05023. Retrieved from https://www.ncbi.nlm.nih.gov/pmc/

Ferrag, M. A., Maglaras, L., Moschoyiannis, S., & Janicke, H. (2019). Deep Learning for Cyber Security Intrusion Detection: Approaches, Datasets, and Comparative Study. *Journal of Information Security and Applications*, *50*, 102419. DOI: 10.1016/j.jisa.2019.102419

Giovannelli, D. (2022). Automated/Autonomous Incident Response: Balancing Speed and Control. NATO CCDCOE Publication (Research Report). Retrieved from https://ccdcoe.org/

Gupta, N., Traoré, I., & Quinan, P. M. F. (2019). Automated Event Prioritization for Security Operations Center Using Deep Learning. In *2019 IEEE International Conference on Big Data* (pp. 4906–4911). IEEE. DOI: 10.1109/BigData47090.2019.9006073

IRIS Consortium. (2021). IRIS Project: AI Threat Reporting and Incident Response for Smart Cities – Press Release. (H2020 IRIS Project kickoff announcement). Retrieved from https://iris-h2020.eu/

Kott, A. (Ed.). (2023). *Autonomous Intelligent Cyber Defense Agent (AICA): A Comprehensive Guide*. Springer International. DOI: 10.1007/978-3-031-29269-9

Lakhouil, M., & Abtoy, A. (2021). Cybersecurity of Smart Cities: A Glimpse. In *Proceedings of the 4th Smart Cities Symposium (SCS 2021)* (pp. 141–145). IEEE.

Li, J., Li, J., & Zhang, X. (2018). Cyber Security Meets Artificial Intelligence: A Survey. *Frontiers of Information Technology & Electronic Engineering*, *19*(12), 1462–1474. DOI: 10.1631/FITEE.1800573

Maidamwar, P. R., Bartere, M. M., & Lokulwar, P. P. (2021). Implementation of Network Intrusion Detection System Using Artificial Intelligence: A Survey. In *Proc. 2nd Int. Conf. on Recent Trends in Machine Learning, IoT, Smart Cities and Applications (ICMISC 2021)* (pp. 185–198). Springer.

Nilă, C., Apostol, I., & Patriciu, V. (2020a). Machine Learning Approach to Quick Incident Response. In *2020 12th International Conference on Electronics, Computers and Artificial Intelligence (ECAI)* (pp. 291–296). IEEE. DOI: 10.1109/COMM48946.2020.9141989

Nilă, C., & Patriciu, V. (2020b). Taking Advantage of Unsupervised Learning in Incident Response. In *2020 International Conference on Cybersecurity (ICGS3)* (pp. 1–6). IEEE. DOI: 10.1109/ECAI50035.2020.9223163

Oesch, S., Austria, P., Chaulagain, A., Weber, B., Watson, C., Dixson, M., & Sadovnik, A. (2024). The Path to Autonomous Cyber Defense. [In press] [. Retrieved from https://arxiv.org/]. *IEEE Security and Privacy*, *22*(1), 29–37.

Pitropakis, N., Panaousis, E., Giannetsos, T., Anastasiadis, E., & Loukas, G. (2019). A Taxonomy and Survey of Attacks Against Machine Learning in Cybersecurity. *Computer Science Review*, *34*, 100199. DOI: 10.1016/j.cosrev.2019.100199

Prejbeanu, R. (2019). Cyber Threat Detection Using Word Embeddings and Deep Learning. Bitdefender White Paper (October 2019). Retrieved from https://ccdcoe.org/

Prejbeanu, R. (2020). Machine Learning Methods for Malware Detection. Kaspersky White Paper. Retrieved from https://ccdcoe.org/

Ramachandran, S., Kim, J., Zia, T., & Almorjan, A. (2023). Cybersecurity and Cyber Forensics for Smart Cities: A Comprehensive Literature Review and Survey. *Sensors (Basel)*, *23*(7), 3545. DOI: 10.3390/s23073545 PMID: 37050609

Shaukat, K., Luo, S., Varadharajan, V., Hameed, I. A., & Xu, M. (2020). A Survey on Machine Learning Techniques for Cyber Security in the Last Decade. *IEEE Access : Practical Innovations, Open Solutions*, *8*, 222310–222354. DOI: 10.1109/ACCESS.2020.3041951

Wolniak, R., & Stecuła, K. (2024). Artificial Intelligence in Smart Cities—Applications, Barriers, and Future Directions: A Review. *Smart Cities*, *7*(3), 1346–1389. DOI: 10.3390/smartcities7030057

Chapter 17
Critical Infrastructure Autonomous Defense:
AI-Enabled Protection Strategies for Power Grids, Water Systems, and Industrial Control Networks

Ali Al Maqousi
https://orcid.org/0000-0002-3242-804X
Petra University, Jordan

Kashinath Basu
https://orcid.org/0000-0002-0831-3752
Oxford Brookes University, UK

Ahmad Al-Qerem
https://orcid.org/0000-0003-2187-6194
Zarqa University, Jordan

Amjad Aldweesh
https://orcid.org/0000-0001-9358-1323
Shaqra University, Saudi Arabia

ABSTRACT

Critical infrastructure, including power grids, water systems, and industrial control networks, supports essential societal functions. As cyber threats intensify, AI-driven autonomous defense methods have emerged as pivotal solutions for ensuring robust security. This abstract outlines how machine learning, deep learning, and reinforcement learning-based approaches enable proactive threat detection, automated responses, and adaptive system configurations. By leveraging advanced analytics

DOI: 10.4018/979-8-3373-0954-5.ch017

and rapid decision-making capabilities, AI frameworks can mitigate vulnerabilities, reduce downtime, and maintain service continuity. However, successful deployment requires addressing scalability, trust, and regulatory concerns. This chapter provides comprehensive insights into implementing reliable, resilient AI defenses for effectively safeguarding critical infrastructure worldwide.

INTRODUCTION

Critical infrastructure, encompassing power grids, water systems, and industrial control networks, underpins modern societal functions. These networks manage electricity distribution, drinking water provision, and essential industrial operations, thereby forming the backbone of public safety, economic stability, and national security. With the increasing sophistication of cyber threats, safeguarding these vital infrastructures has become a high priority for governments, private industry, and research institutions. Autonomous defense methods, especially those leveraging artificial intelligence (AI), have emerged as promising routes for strengthening the security posture of critical infrastructure. AI-driven systems exhibit rapid adaptability and the capacity to learn from complex data sets, making them well-suited to meet the dynamic needs of defense in critical settings (Berman, Buczak, Chavis, & Corbett, 2019).

Traditional cybersecurity solutions in critical infrastructure have relied on intrusion detection systems, manual analysis, and patch management, but these methods often struggle with advanced persistent threats and sophisticated zero-day exploits. Moreover, operational networks that manage water supplies, power grids, and industrial controls are large and heterogeneous, with components designed across different eras and integrated in varied configurations (Xin et al., 2018). Such complexity hampers the quick identification and remediation of threats. Threat actors, ranging from nation-states to criminal organizations, have developed complex tactics to bypass static defenses, motivating the adoption of more autonomous and adaptive security mechanisms (Sengupta et al., 2020).

AI-enabled security promises proactive threat hunting, automated mitigation, and real-time learning from new attack behaviors (Capuano, Fenza, Loia, & Stanzione, 2022). Recent advancements in machine learning, deep learning, and reinforcement learning have illustrated the potential for systems to detect intrusions, perform dynamic reconfiguration, and neutralize threats without significant human intervention (Guembe et al., 2022). For instance, the Cyber Grand Challenge organized by the Defense Advanced Research Projects Agency (DARPA) demonstrated the feasibility of autonomous systems that discover and patch software vulnerabilities in real time (DARPA, 2016). The approach goes beyond conventional intrusion detection by generating rapid responses, applying automated fixes, and introducing dynamic system reconfigurations.

This chapter provides a comprehensive examination of AI-driven autonomous defense strategies tailored to the unique requirements of power grids, water systems, and industrial control networks. The discourse begins by highlighting the key threats and vulnerabilities plaguing these sectors, emphasizing how advanced attackers exploit weaknesses in both hardware and software. It then explores the fundamental principles of AI-driven security, reviewing machine learning algorithms, neural networks, and other computational strategies that support detection, prediction, and automated response.

Subsequent sections delve into the design and deployment of autonomous cyber defense strategies. A review of the relevant literature demonstrates how AI-based intrusion detection and response systems have evolved, tracing their origins from classical anomaly detection (Denning, 1987) to the sophisticated deep learning methods currently in use (Yuan, Li, & Chen, 2019). Attention is also given to issues of explainability and trust, which remain significant barriers to the large-scale adoption of AI-based defense solutions in critical infrastructure domains (Capuano et al., 2022).

In discussing the power grid environment, this chapter highlights unique attributes such as decentralized control systems, interconnected supervisory control and data acquisition (SCADA) networks, and the growing convergence with the Internet of Things (IoT). In the realm of water systems, complexities arise from legacy equipment, remote monitoring constraints, and the necessity of ensuring uninterrupted service for public health. Industrial control networks, meanwhile, exhibit a wide variation in protocols, vendor implementations, and latency requirements, leading to practical challenges in seamless integration of AI-based defenses (Malialis & Kudenko, 2016).

The chapter proceeds to detail specific case studies and frameworks that showcase autonomous defenses, examining real-world scenarios in which AI-driven solutions have detected lateral movements, prevented unauthorized control commands, and reduced the time between detection and response actions. These examples underscore the potential for high-fidelity threat intelligence, dynamic resource allocation, and the resilient reconfiguration of processes to maintain continuity.

To support the theoretical exposition, the text provides representative figures, such as conceptual diagrams illustrating system architectures, use-case sequences highlighting defense flows, and flowcharts explaining how AI models decide on mitigation actions. In addition, four tables summarize state-of-the-art methods, relevant performance metrics, and known attack vectors with corresponding autonomous countermeasures. These elements enrich the discussion while offering structured insights.

The final sections of the chapter explore forward-looking topics, such as distributed AI frameworks, collaborative intelligence-sharing platforms, and the integration of defensive AI agents with emerging quantum-safe security protocols. They also address the sociotechnical implications of AI adoption, including workforce skills, regulatory considerations, and ethical challenges such as algorithmic bias and privacy management.

Grounded in peer-reviewed research, authoritative technical reports, and recognized academic publications, this chapter aims to advance discourse on how intelligent, autonomous cyber defense stands to transform the security of the most essential infrastructure systems. By examining theoretical frameworks, relevant use cases, and persistent challenges, it aspires to inform cybersecurity professionals, policy makers, and academic researchers about the potential and limitations of deploying AI-based defenses in critical environments (Truong, Diep, & Zelinka, 2020).

Overall, this chapter provides the foundation for a nuanced, multi-dimensional exploration of AI-driven, autonomous defense strategies across power grids, water systems, and industrial control networks. In doing so, it offers both theoretical insight and practical guidance, aiming to stimulate innovation and cross-sector collaboration in the pursuit of more secure, resilient infrastructure.

BACKGROUND AND THEORETICAL FOUNDATIONS

Critical infrastructure security has evolved substantially over the past five decades, driven by a combination of technological innovation, policy mandates, and the increasing sophistication of adversaries. Early conceptions of cyber defense were reactive, focusing on basic perimeter security. Over time, the focus shifted toward intrusion detection, vulnerability management, and more integrated defenses. The premise of autonomous cyber defense originated from a recognition that human operators alone could not keep pace with the velocity and complexity of modern threats (National Security Commission on Artificial Intelligence [NSCAI], 2021).

AI systems, particularly those leveraging machine learning, have gained prominence for their capacity to recognize subtle patterns in large-scale data. Data-driven models enhance detection by uncovering anomalies that signal attacks in progress or pre-attack reconnaissance activities (Buczak & Guven, 2016). Deep learning extends these benefits by extracting multi-layered feature representations, making it possible to detect malicious behaviors with high precision and recall (Xin et al., 2018). Reinforcement learning contributes adaptive strategies for defense, enabling dynamic adjustment of security policies in reaction to evolving threats (Malialis & Kudenko, 2016).

In the context of critical infrastructure, the vulnerability landscape includes legacy systems that cannot be easily patched, limited computational resources for security functions, and the need for uninterrupted operation. Power grids exhibit geographic dispersion and rely on an assortment of hardware and software from multiple vendors. Water systems typically contain older supervisory control components with minimal built-in security features. Industrial control systems coordinate manufacturing processes, chemical treatments, or assembly lines where any interruption can prove costly and potentially dangerous. AI-driven solutions must adapt to these constraints to effectively fulfill defense objectives (Okdem, 2024).

Evolution of Autonomous Cyber Defense

The pursuit of autonomous cyber defense has been shaped by several key events. One pivotal milestone was the introduction of intrusion-detection models that used statistical profiles of normal behavior to identify anomalies (Denning, 1987). Over time, more sophisticated techniques emerged, integrating heuristic methods and machine learning to refine detection. By the mid-2000s, automated patch management and vulnerability scanning tools were developed to expedite response actions, though these solutions often required manual oversight.

By the early 2010s, researchers began experimenting with AI to learn patterns of benign and malicious activity, exploring the potential for systems capable of self-healing. The advent of advanced persistent threats—stealthy, targeted, and resource-intensive cyberattacks—underscored the need for more advanced, semi-autonomous solutions (Forrest, Hofmeyr, Somayaji, & Longstaff, 1996). During the last decade, conceptual frameworks integrating machine learning and dynamic reconfiguration have demonstrated how autonomous agents can handle detection and response with minimal human intervention (Somayaji & Forrest, 2000).

A notable demonstration of AI capabilities in cyber defense was the DARPA Cyber Grand Challenge (DARPA, 2016). This competition pitted fully autonomous systems against one another, requiring them to discover vulnerabilities in custom software and apply patches in real time. Systems like Xandra (Nguyen-Tuong et al., 2018) and Mayhem (Avgerinos et al., 2018) showed that automated vulnerability analysis and patch generation could be performed at speeds far exceeding human capacity. Though the scope was relatively controlled, the competition highlighted the feasibility of an end-to-end autonomous pipeline for discovering, analyzing, and mitigating threats.

Conceptual Frameworks for AI-Driven Security

AI-driven security models encompass several core components: data collection, feature extraction, model training, classification (or prediction), and action selection. Data collection involves harvesting logs, network flows, and system metrics from across the infrastructure. Feature extraction translates these raw streams into structured inputs for machine learning models. In deep learning setups, feature extraction can be performed automatically by neural network layers (Yuan et al., 2019).

During model training, datasets typically comprise labeled examples of benign and malicious behavior, although unsupervised methods can be employed when labeled data is scarce. Once trained, models can classify network traffic or system behaviors as anomalous or benign in real time. A vital component is the action selection or policy generation phase, in which the system identifies the optimal response to detected anomalies, such as blocking traffic, isolating suspicious nodes, or reconfiguring network parameters (Truong et al., 2020).

Reinforcement learning extends this approach by modeling defense scenarios as sequential decision processes. Agents receive rewards or penalties based on their actions—blocking malicious flows, ignoring false positives, etc. Over time, they learn policies that optimize security outcomes (Rasouli, Miehling, & Teneketzis, 2018). This learning scheme has proven valuable for dynamic or high-dimensional environments like power grids, where the infrastructure topology changes and the threat landscape evolves.

Table 1. Key attributes of AI models in autonomous cyber defense

Attribute	Description	Representative Techniques	Challenges
Data Requirements	Volume and variety of labeled or unlabeled datasets	Supervised/Unsupervised Learning	Data scarcity, quality issues
Adaptability	Ability to handle changing threat patterns in real time	Reinforcement Learning, Online Learning	Computational overhead
Explainability	Extent to which model decisions can be interpreted	Explainable AI frameworks	Trade-off between accuracy and clarity
Real-time Performance	Ability to operate with minimal latency in mission-critical systems	Low-latency neural networks, hardware acceleration	Resource constraints in ICS
Scalability	Suitability for deployment across large, distributed infrastructures	Distributed ML, Federated Learning	Heterogeneous nodes, bandwidth

Relevance to Power Grids, Water Systems, and Industrial Control Networks

Power grids involve generation facilities, transmission lines, substations, and distribution networks. The distributed nature of these components necessitates robust communication protocols and real-time monitoring. AI-driven defenses can facilitate anomaly detection in sensor data, predict equipment failures, and orchestrate rapid reconfiguration of power flows in response to emerging threats (Sengupta et al., 2020).

Water systems, similarly decentralized, face additional challenges tied to environmental factors, such as water pressure dynamics and water quality monitoring. Attacks can involve manipulating chemical dosage, altering pressure levels, or disrupting pumping schedules. An AI-based model can track normal patterns in chemical usage and flow rates, raising alerts and initiating autonomous valve controls upon detecting deviations (Nguyen-Tuong et al., 2018).

Industrial control networks in sectors like manufacturing or chemical processing frequently use protocols not commonly found in corporate IT environments. AI-based solutions must be customized to support these protocols and account for stringent real-time requirements. Automated detection and response mechanisms can mitigate advanced threats that target programmable logic controllers (PLCs), human-machine interfaces (HMIs), or other specialized devices that control critical processes (Sikos, 2019).

This background situates the emergence of AI-driven autonomous defense methods within a broader historical and theoretical context. It clarifies how the synergy of machine learning, deep learning, and reinforcement learning yields sophisticated, adaptive, and proactive security strategies. Throughout the next sections, specific application scenarios, algorithmic methods, and architectural considerations will be dissected to illustrate the potential of autonomous cyber defense in safeguarding critical infrastructure.

AI-Driven Threat Analysis and Detection

Effective threat analysis relies on the systematic gathering and interpretation of data to discern malicious activities that target critical infrastructure. Traditional threat analysis methods suffer from several drawbacks, including labor-intensive manual reviews and limited scalability. By contrast, AI-based approaches leverage computational models to explore large volumes of data at speeds unattainable by human analysts (Berman et al., 2019).

DATA SOURCES AND COLLECTION METHODS

Critical infrastructure generates diverse data streams, including network traffic logs, sensor readouts from SCADA devices, system event logs, and maintenance records. Comprehensive data collection allows for the detection of suspicious activities across multiple domains—network, host, and physical process levels (Truong et al., 2020). In a typical power grid setup, data might include phasor measurement unit outputs, distribution management logs, and substation automation system events.

Advanced data collection must also account for the latency and bandwidth constraints present in geographically dispersed networks. Centralized collection can overwhelm communication links; hence, distributed architectures or edge computing paradigms are often used for preliminary data processing (Shrobe & Shrier, 2018). AI models can be deployed at the edge to filter and compress data, ensuring that only critical information is transmitted to central security operation centers.

FEATURE ENGINEERING AND REPRESENTATION

The potency of AI systems hinges on the quality of the features that represent the data. In many legacy systems, raw logs contain only minimal contextual information, making it vital to engineer features that capture relevant security attributes. For instance, in industrial networks, SCADA protocols transmit commands like "open valve" or "start motor." Encoding these commands alongside timestamps, sensor values, and the logical relationships among devices can greatly improve detection accuracy (Guembe et al., 2022).

Feature engineering processes vary by domain. Power grid applications might emphasize load frequency data, generation setpoints, or voltage anomalies. Water systems might incorporate temperature, flow rates, and chemical dosing levels. Deep learning models can automate feature extraction by learning hierarchies of representations from raw data (Buczak & Guven, 2016). However, domain knowledge remains important for guiding model design, ensuring the captured features align with real-world operational and security contexts.

Anomaly Detection Algorithms

Once meaningful features are extracted, anomaly detection algorithms attempt to discern deviations from normal behavioral patterns. Statistical techniques, such as Gaussian mixture models, were early solutions, but they struggled with high-dimensional data and concept drift. Modern AI-driven approaches incorporate machine learning and deep learning.

1. **Unsupervised Methods:** Clustering algorithms (e.g., k-means, DBSCAN) group similar data points, labeling those that lie in sparse regions as anomalous. Autoencoders, a form of deep neural networks, learn compressed representations of normal data, and reconstruction errors can flag outliers (Yuan et al., 2019). Unsupervised methods are particularly suited to environments where malicious activity is infrequent, and labeled examples of attacks are hard to obtain.
2. **Supervised Methods:** Where labeled data is available, classification algorithms such as Random Forests, Support Vector Machines, and deep neural networks are used to learn decision boundaries between normal and malicious examples (Xin et al., 2018). Although supervised learning can yield high accuracy, it demands comprehensive training sets that capture the wide variety of potential attacks.
3. **Semi-Supervised Learning:** A middle ground that trains on normal data to develop a boundary for permissible behavior, flagging deviations as potential anomalies. This strategy can be effective if normal operation data is abundant and malicious data is limited or incomplete.
4. **Reinforcement Learning for Detection:** Although commonly applied to intrusion response, reinforcement learning can also be adapted to detection by modeling the environment as a sequence of observations, where the agent seeks to classify events as malicious or benign to maximize some reward signal (Malialis & Kudenko, 2016).

Each approach presents trade-offs in accuracy, adaptability, and computational overhead. For instance, deep learning models can detect complex patterns but may require specialized hardware, while simpler clustering algorithms run on standard hardware but might miss sophisticated attack sequences.

Intelligent Intrusion Detection Systems (IIDS)

Intelligent Intrusion Detection Systems (IIDS) integrate AI-driven anomaly detection with additional modules for correlating events across multiple hosts and network segments. By collating alerts from distributed sensors, an IIDS can better contextualize anomalies. For instance, a single abnormal command at a water facility's control panel might be noteworthy, but if correlated with concurrent anomalies in the network traffic logs, it becomes a stronger indicator of an orchestrated attack (Stamp, Visaggio, Mercaldo, & Di Troia, 2022).

A robust IIDS architecture includes a data normalization layer, feature extraction pipelines, a detection engine, and a correlation layer. The detection engine may use ensemble learning to combine predictions from multiple AI models, thereby improving accuracy. The correlation layer synthesizes alerts, highlighting multi-step or distributed attacks that unfold over time (Boddy, Jones, & Horowitz, 2014).

Figure 1. Flow diagram for AI-driven anomaly detection in a power grid

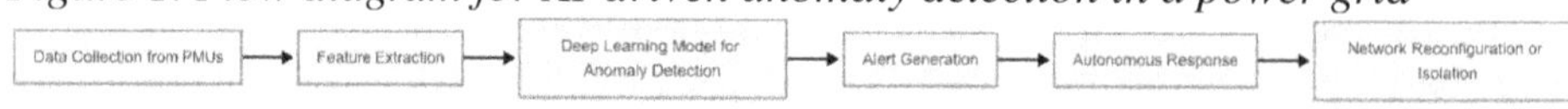

In the illustrated scenario, data is gathered from Phasor Measurement Units (PMUs) deployed at different substations. A deep learning model identifies patterns deviant from the historical baseline of voltage, frequency, and phase angle measurements. If an anomaly is confirmed, the system issues an alert and initiates an autonomous response by adjusting control commands or isolating specific segments to prevent widespread disruption (Sengupta et al., 2020).

CHALLENGES IN AI-DRIVEN DETECTION

While AI offers potent methods for uncovering hidden threats, it also faces significant challenges. Adversarial attacks can target the detection pipeline, exploiting vulnerabilities in data preprocessing or tampering with model inputs to camouflage malicious activities (Truong et al., 2020). The interpretability of AI models becomes especially important in critical infrastructure, where operators require confidence in automated decisions that can potentially shut down a crucial process.

Additionally, insufficient or noisy training data can produce false positives and negatives, undermining trust in the system. Domain adaptation strategies and continuous learning schemes offer partial remedies, as models can evolve based on feedback and newly collected samples. Nevertheless, maintaining high levels of accuracy and reliability across different operational contexts and changing network conditions remains an open challenge (Capuano et al., 2022).

In sum, AI-driven threat analysis and detection have advanced well beyond traditional methods, providing powerful tools to meet the sophisticated demands of critical infrastructure security. However, challenges related to explainability, data quality, and adversarial resilience require ongoing research and careful system design.

AUTOMATED RESPONSE AND ADAPTIVE DEFENSE

Detection of threats in critical infrastructure is only one dimension of cybersecurity. Another important function is response, which involves containing, mitigating, and ultimately neutralizing detected threats. Traditional response frameworks rely heavily on security analysts to triage alerts and coordinate interventions, but manual processes are too slow when facing fast-propagating or complex attacks (Okdem, 2024). Autonomous approaches leverage AI models to make and execute decisions in real time, reducing the window in which attackers can cause damage.

Principles of Autonomous Response

Automated response systems must maintain situational awareness, selecting an optimal course of action that balances risk reduction against possible disruptions to normal operations (Sarker, 2024). Key principles include:

1. **Decision Autonomy:** The system, guided by AI models, evaluates the current security state and chooses a response without human intervention. This requires algorithms capable of handling uncertainty and incomplete information.
2. **Policy-Driven Behavior:** Administrators can define high-level policies to set boundaries for automated actions. For instance, an operator might permit the AI to reconfigure certain network segments but not to halt a critical turbine.
3. **Adaptability and Learning:** Reinforcement learning or evolutionary strategies can refine response actions over time, improving performance as new threats and operational contexts arise (Rasouli et al., 2018).
4. **Fail-Safe Mechanisms:** Autonomous responses must be carefully designed to prevent cascading failures. Fail-safe strategies could involve reverting to a known secure state or escalating to a human supervisor if the AI encounters abnormal conditions.

Techniques for Automated Mitigation

Once a threat is identified, a system can respond at multiple layers. Some approaches involve quarantining infected hosts, blocking malicious IP addresses, or enforcing stricter firewall rules. Others employ more proactive measures, such as:

- **Moving Target Defense (MTD):** This strategy periodically changes network properties, IP addresses, or system configurations to confuse adversaries. AI determines the timing and scope of these changes to maximize unpredictability (Sengupta et al., 2020).

- **System Call Delays or Interrupts:** Based on early research, introducing artificial delays for suspicious processes can impede automated attack scripts (Somayaji & Forrest, 2000). Modern variations incorporate AI to selectively apply these delays when certain attack signatures are detected.
- **Micro-Segmentation and Access Control:** AI-driven processes dynamically adjust access control lists and segment network traffic to localize and isolate threats.
- **Automated Patching and Software Updates:** As demonstrated by systems like Mayhem (Avgerinos et al., 2018), machine learning can identify vulnerable code paths and apply patches.

The efficacy of these mitigation techniques depends on accurate detection, timely execution, and minimal disruption to legitimate processes.

Table 2. Examples of automated response actions in critical infrastructures

Domain	Common Attacks	Automated Responses	Potential Impacts
Power Grids	Load-redistribution attacks	Dynamic re-routing of power flows	Potential minor blackouts if misconfigured
Water Systems	Pump manipulation	Automated shutdown/isolation of valves	Service downtime if incorrectly triggered
Industrial Control	PLC exploitation	Automated firmware patching, device locking	Production delays or damage to equipment
Cross-domain	Data exfiltration, pivot attacks	Block malicious IPs, re-authenticate nodes	User inconvenience and overhead

Reinforcement Learning for Autonomous Defense

Reinforcement learning (RL) has gained attention for adaptive defense scenarios where sequential decisions must be made in uncertain environments (Malialis & Kudenko, 2016). In RL, an agent interacts with an environment (the network or system), receives observations (alerts, performance metrics), and selects actions (block an IP, isolate a node) to maximize a cumulative reward. Rewards can reflect various priorities such as minimizing successful intrusions, reducing operational disruption, or preserving system reliability.

One advantage of RL is its capacity to learn from experience and adapt to novel attack patterns. Different RL methods—value-based (Q-learning), policy-based (REINFORCE), or actor-critic architectures—offer trade-offs in scalability and convergence speed. The application of RL in large-scale critical infrastructure often involves hierarchical RL, where global policies manage overall strategies and local policies address domain-specific issues.

Nevertheless, RL-based methods demand extensive simulation or historical data to train effectively. Real-world deployment must contend with safety constraints, as random exploration could disrupt vital processes. Consequently, combining RL with domain knowledge and rigorous testing in controlled environments is crucial (Rasouli et al., 2018).

Case Study: Automated Response in a Water Treatment Facility

Consider a water treatment facility that experiences unauthorized commands to alter chemical dosage. An AI-based anomaly detection module identifies an abnormal injection pattern. Immediately, an automated response mechanism halts the suspicious commands, resets dosage levels to a known safe baseline, and notifies on-site engineers. If repeated attacks occur, the system escalates its response by segmenting the control network, requiring multi-factor authentication for any chemical-related commands.

This automated process limits potential health hazards and environmental harm by reacting quicker than a manual response. However, an overzealous mechanism could lead to water supply interruptions or chemical imbalances if false positives occur. Hence, robust testing and policy definitions are necessary to avoid detrimental service disruptions.

Integrating Human-in-the-Loop

Fully autonomous responses can be risky in high-stakes environments, prompting a hybrid model that includes human oversight. Human operators might set broad policies or intervene in complex cases, while the AI handles routine incidents. This integrated approach provides fail-safes and fosters operator trust in the system (NSCAI, 2021).

Visual analytics can aid in this integration by offering interpretable dashboards that highlight anomalies, suggested actions, and confidence scores from AI models (Capuano et al., 2022). Operators can approve or reject proposed actions, and the system stores this feedback for future learning. Over time, the AI refines its decision logic to align with organizational preferences and domain realities.

Challenges and Limitations

Although automated response mechanisms provide faster action, they can inadvertently introduce new vulnerabilities. Attackers may attempt to manipulate the AI decision process, triggering misguided actions that harm operations. Achieving robust performance in the face of adversarial manipulation or incomplete data remains difficult. Moreover, legal and ethical considerations arise when an autonomous system can initiate wide-scale network changes or disrupt service to suspected malicious nodes that may also host legitimate traffic (Zhu & Rass, 2021).

In conclusion, adaptive, AI-driven response frameworks offer transformative possibilities for protecting power grids, water systems, and industrial control networks. By merging real-time threat detection with intelligent response algorithms, these systems can minimize the window of opportunity for attackers. Nonetheless, ensuring reliability, explainability, and adherence to operational constraints remains a central challenge.

ARCHITECTURAL CONSIDERATIONS FOR AUTONOMOUS DEFENSE

Designing an effective architecture for AI-enabled autonomous defense in critical infrastructure is both complex and essential. System designers must reconcile the competing goals of security, availability, and performance. This section provides an overview of architectural building blocks, communication strategies, and deployment considerations.

Distributed vs. Centralized Architectures

Large-scale critical infrastructures often span broad geographic areas, making a single, centralized security node impractical. Distributed architectures employ multiple AI agents placed at strategic points—substations, pumps, or controllers—collecting and analyzing data locally. Aggregated insights feed into a higher-level security operation center that coordinates global policy (Shrobe & Shrier, 2018).

Centralized designs simplify data collection and correlation but risk creating a single point of failure if the central node is compromised. They also incur high network bandwidth usage for data transmission. Conversely, distributed models can reduce latency and improve resilience but may require more computational resources. A hybrid architecture, combining distributed detection with partially centralized correlation, can offer a balanced solution (Ridley, 2018).

Network Segmentation and Microservices

Network segmentation partitions the infrastructure into logical zones with restricted lateral movement. AI agents placed in each zone can apply local detection and response, containing breaches to smaller areas (Ofusori, Bokaba, & Mhlongo, 2024). Microservices decouple security functions, such as detection, analysis, and response orchestration, into separate modules that communicate through standardized interfaces.

This modular approach eases updates and simplifies the integration of novel detection algorithms. If the detection engine is replaced with a new model, the response manager and correlation components can remain unchanged. Critical infrastructure operators often value such flexibility to incorporate emerging security technologies without overhauling entire systems (Sengupta et al., 2020).

SECURING THE AI PIPELINE

For an AI-driven defense system to be trustworthy, the pipeline that trains and deploys models must itself be secure. Attackers who gain access to training data can poison the model, causing it to overlook certain malicious patterns. Similarly, if model parameters are stolen, attackers might reverse-engineer the model's logic and evade detection (Truong et al., 2020).

Security best practices include data encryption, strict access controls, and integrity checks at each stage of the pipeline. Periodic retraining with up-to-date threat intelligence and robust validation procedures can also help ensure model resilience. In sensitive environments, on-premise GPU clusters or air-gapped networks might be used for model training to prevent leakage of proprietary or security-critical data (Stamp et al., 2022).

High Availability and Fault Tolerance

Critical infrastructure operators prioritize uptime, which necessitates architectural strategies that maintain service continuity even if certain nodes fail. Redundant AI agents can run concurrently, and load balancing techniques distribute computation to avoid bottlenecks. Failover mechanisms can seamlessly redirect data streams to backup systems if a primary node is compromised or offline (Zhu & Rass, 2021).

Stateful approaches where AI agents maintain local context about threats are beneficial but demand proper synchronization to prevent losing critical situational awareness. Conversely, stateless designs rely on external data stores or message queues for context. Hybrid strategies that replicate partial state across multiple nodes can balance performance with fault tolerance (Okdem, 2024).

Integration with Legacy Systems

Many power grids and water systems still rely on hardware installed decades ago, often with minimal or proprietary security features. Retrofitting these environments to support AI-driven defense can be challenging. Gateway devices or proxies may be used to translate legacy protocols into modern data formats. These gateways often house lightweight AI modules responsible for local anomaly detection (Mahajan, Khurana, & Estrela, 2024).

Legacy integration efforts can be incremental, starting with non-intrusive monitoring solutions. As operators gain confidence, they can adopt more active interventions, such as automated command blocking. However, thorough testing is crucial to avoid interfering with critical processes.

Figure 2. Conceptual architecture for AI-driven autonomous defense

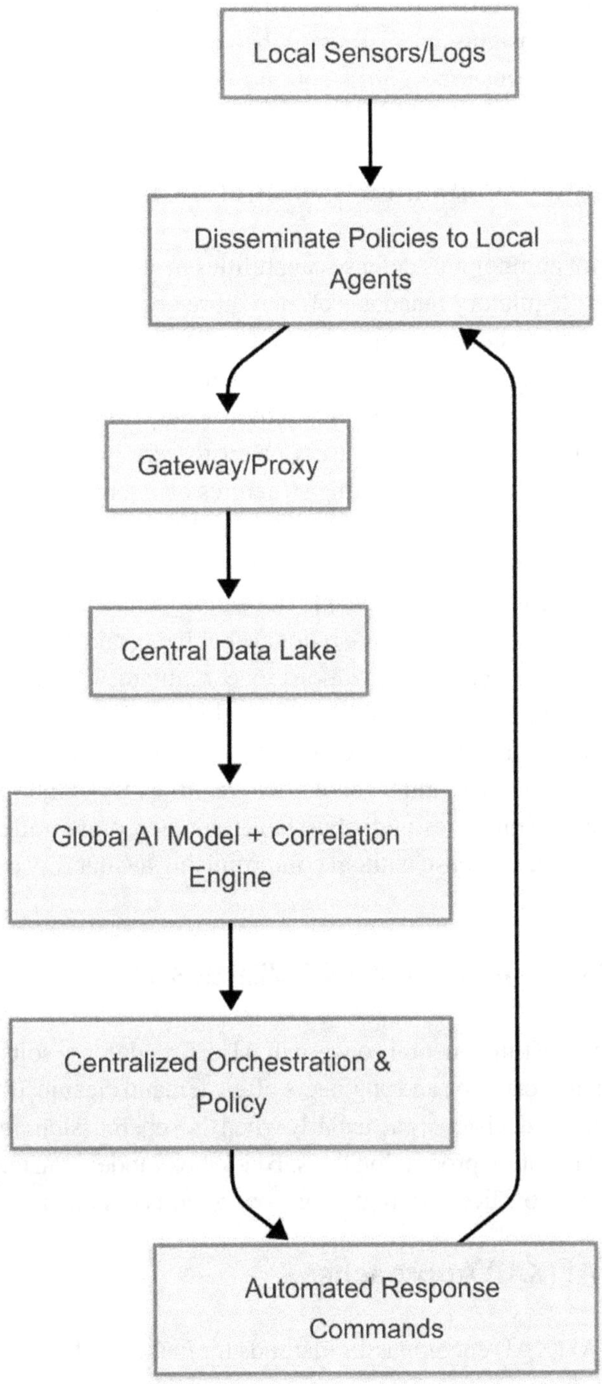

In this conceptual architecture, local agents conduct near-real-time detection and feed summarized alerts or data to a central correlation engine. The correlation engine synthesizes insights and issues global policies. These policies circulate back to local agents, ensuring consistent and adaptive defense across the entire infrastructure (Ridley, 2018).

Regulatory and Compliance Considerations

Deployment of autonomous defense capabilities in critical sectors is not purely a technical matter. Regulatory mandates often require organizations to maintain logs of security-related decisions, produce detailed audit trails, and provide evidence of compliance with industry standards (Kott, Théron, & De Gaspari, 2019).

Moreover, the introduction of AI may require compliance with data protection regulations, especially if data from users or customers is analyzed. Transparent governance models and robust reporting structures can demonstrate due diligence, building stakeholder confidence in the new technologies.

Architectural considerations must incorporate these compliance requirements from the outset, designing solutions that enable traceability and explainability. Auditing modules can capture each decision, the rationale behind it, and the confidence scores produced by AI, thus helping organizations meet regulatory obligations.

Overall, building a secure, scalable, and reliable architecture for AI-driven autonomous defense in critical infrastructure calls for careful planning and alignment with operational, regulatory, and technological realities. By combining distributed intelligence, secure AI pipelines, and robust fault tolerance, organizations can reap the benefits of autonomous defense without compromising availability or performance.

EXPLAINABILITY AND HUMAN OVERSIGHT

Explainability is a fundamental concern in AI-driven defense solutions. Security analysts, compliance officers, and engineers often demand clear justifications for an autonomous system's decisions, particularly when the repercussions involve shutting down services or isolating production lines. Black-box models can undermine trust, deter adoption, and conflict with regulatory obligations (Capuano et al., 2022).

Explainable AI (XAI) Approaches

Explainable AI (XAI) encompasses methods for making AI model outputs more interpretable. Techniques include:

- **Local Post-Hoc Explanations:** Tools like LIME (Local Interpretable Model-Agnostic Explanations) generate locally faithful approximations of the model's behavior, clarifying which features influenced a specific prediction.
- **Feature Attribution Methods:** Techniques such as SHAP (SHapley Additive exPlanations) compute feature importance scores to rank the input variables that sway a particular decision (Berman et al., 2019).
- **Attention Visualization:** In deep learning models that use attention mechanisms, heatmaps can reveal which parts of an input sequence captured the model's focus.

For critical infrastructure contexts, these methods can be integrated into security dashboards. When an AI-based defense engine flags a SCADA command as malicious, an XAI module might highlight anomalies in command frequency, origin IP address, or historical usage patterns.

Challenges in Achieving Transparency

Many deep learning architectures remain complex, making it difficult to provide truly understandable explanations. Attempting to simplify the model's logic can reduce accuracy, while fully transparent explanations may be too large or technical for non-expert stakeholders. Further complications arise when the infrastructure is distributed, with multiple AI agents coordinating decisions in real time (Ofusori et al., 2024).

In practice, a balance must be struck between technical depth and clarity. Visual analytics, domain-specific narratives, and hierarchical explanations are useful strategies for bridging the gap between raw model outputs and the cognitive understanding of human operators (Sikos, 2019).

Human Oversight Models

To mitigate the risk of autonomous errors and build confidence, organizations often retain human operators in the decision loop. Oversight models vary in their degree of involvement:

- **Human-on-the-Loop:** The AI system acts independently but allows human intervention upon request or when pre-defined risk thresholds are exceeded (NSCAI, 2021).
- **Human-in-the-Loop:** The AI system proposes actions, and a human must approve them before execution. This ensures human review but can slow response times.

- **Human-out-of-the-Loop:** Rare in critical infrastructure, this model grants full autonomy to the AI. Human operators only review system performance retrospectively.

Given the high stakes, complete removal of human judgment is uncommon. Even advanced systems benefit from periodic oversight, quality checks, and human guidance.

Regulatory and Ethical Dimensions

Explainability and oversight requirements also have ethical and legal dimensions. Regulators may require that entities demonstrate due diligence and fair processes, ensuring that AI does not discriminate or cause unjustified service denials (Zhu & Rass, 2021). Transparent AI systems facilitate this compliance by exposing the logic behind defense decisions.

Ethical questions also arise concerning the responsibilities and liabilities when an AI system makes a detrimental error. Establishing accountability mechanisms, clearly articulating roles, and documenting AI decision criteria can help address these concerns and foster trust among stakeholders.

In sum, an emphasis on explainability and human oversight is integral to the effective deployment of AI-driven autonomous defense solutions. These considerations reduce organizational risk, promote user acceptance, and align with regulatory mandates, thereby enhancing the overall resilience of critical infrastructure.

CASE STUDIES AND REAL-WORLD IMPLEMENTATIONS

Practical experience with AI-based autonomous defense in critical infrastructure remains relatively limited but is growing. This section highlights selected case studies and real-world implementations that showcase the diversity of approaches and lessons learned.

Power Grid Automated Defense Pilots

A regional utility company in North America conducted a pilot project to deploy AI-based anomaly detection across its transmission network. Local agents analyzed PMU data and flagged unusual voltage fluctuations potentially indicative of malicious load redistribution attempts. The system triggered an automated response that changed line load distributions to mitigate potential service interruptions (Sengupta et al., 2020). Post-pilot analysis indicated that AI-based detection reduced the average time to respond from hours to minutes, although issues with false positives led to some unnecessary re-routing of power.

Water Treatment SCADA Security

A metropolitan water authority in Europe implemented an AI-driven intrusion detection system that monitored SCADA commands. Developers trained the system on historical logs, focusing on normal patterns of chemical dosing and pump operation. When a malicious user attempted to inject false commands, the system recognized these commands as outliers and automatically blocked them. Engineers then conducted a forensic analysis to confirm that an unauthorized external login had occurred. This experience illustrated the efficiency of automated containment, though it also highlighted the importance of robust authentication mechanisms for remote operators (Mahajan et al., 2024).

Industrial Control Network Resilience

A global manufacturing firm, concerned about the risk of state-sponsored espionage, integrated an AI-based adaptive defense solution across its production lines. Reinforcement learning agents were tasked with adjusting network segmentation rules and access permissions based on perceived threat levels. Over time, the system learned to quarantine suspicious devices rapidly, limiting the spread of malware. However, the project team faced difficulties integrating explainable AI techniques into the legacy control environment, leading to concerns about how to justify automated lockdown decisions to plant managers (Truong et al., 2020).

Table 3. Summary of selected implementations

Sector	Key AI Techniques	Outcomes	Challenges
Power Grids	Deep learning for anomaly detection	Improved response time, reduced manual workload	False positives caused occasional misrouting
Water Systems	Semi-supervised anomaly detection	Blocked malicious commands swiftly	Reliance on robust remote authentication
Industrial Control	Reinforcement learning for adaptive defense	Rapid device quarantine, limited malware spread	Integration of XAI with legacy systems

Lessons Learned

1. **Incremental Deployment:** Most successful case studies began with limited-scope pilots, gradually scaling up to cover larger parts of the infrastructure.

2. **Data Quality:** High-quality data remains a linchpin of effective AI models. Poorly formatted or incomplete logs led to higher false-positive rates.
3. **Human Training:** Security teams required specialized training in AI-driven tools, reinforcing the importance of fostering new skill sets.
4. **Policy Alignment:** Automated defense strategies had to be carefully aligned with operational policies to avoid interfering with critical processes.

These real-world implementations underscore the potential for AI-driven autonomous defense to reduce detection and response times, increase situational awareness, and mitigate complex threats. Yet, they also confirm that deploying such technologies in live environments poses significant challenges, particularly around integration, data quality, and explainability.

FUTURE DIRECTIONS AND ONGOING RESEARCH

AI-driven autonomous defense for critical infrastructure is still maturing, and numerous research directions remain open:

1. **Federated Learning and Collaborative Defense:** Shared models trained on data from multiple organizations can enhance detection and resilience. However, privacy and trust issues complicate the exchange of sensitive data (Guembe et al., 2022).
2. **Quantum-Safe Security Measures:** With the advent of quantum computing, cryptographic methods may need to be redesigned. AI will play a role in identifying vulnerabilities in quantum-safe schemes and orchestrating secure key distribution (Zhu & Rass, 2021).
3. **Cross-Infrastructure Coordination:** Attacks can ripple across multiple infrastructure types. Investigating integrated defense mechanisms that unify power, water, and industrial networks can potentially reduce the risk of coordinated assaults (Kott et al., 2019).
4. **Advanced Adversarial Defenses:** Research into adversarial machine learning aims to detect and mitigate attempts to manipulate AI pipelines. This includes techniques like adversarial training and robust architecture design.
5. **Socio-Technical Integration:** Future defense strategies must address organizational change, operator training, and ethical concerns. Including sociological research in AI system design may enhance adoption and efficacy.

Overall, the future trajectory points to more interconnected, intelligent, and resilient cybersecurity ecosystems. As these advancements take shape, they promise to substantially strengthen the protective posture of critical infrastructures worldwide.

CONCLUSION

AI-driven autonomous defense strategies represent a transformative shift in the cybersecurity landscape, offering faster and more adaptive protection than traditional, manually driven methods. In critical infrastructure contexts—power grids, water systems, and industrial control networks—the stakes are exceedingly high, as successful attacks can result in cascading failures with significant public safety and economic implications. Autonomous approaches that combine advanced analytics, machine learning, and automated response mechanisms hold the potential to dramatically reduce vulnerability windows, thwart sophisticated attackers, and maintain continuous service.

Despite these benefits, the adoption of AI-driven defenses also poses challenges. The complexity of deep learning models, vulnerability to adversarial manipulation, and the need for rigorous explainability can create barriers to implementation. These hurdles are compounded by the legacy nature of many critical systems, the diversity of protocols, and strict regulatory regimes. Yet, incremental progress, guided by well-conceived pilot projects, robust architecture designs, and emphasis on data quality, has demonstrated that the obstacles are surmountable.

Looking ahead, research and development efforts are likely to intensify around distributed, federated AI models that enable collaborative defense without compromising data confidentiality. New paradigms, such as quantum-safe security and integrated cross-infrastructure solutions, will continue to expand the frontier of what is possible in autonomous defense. At the same time, strong governance, ethical frameworks, and stakeholder education are essential to ensure that the pursuit of automation does not undermine public trust or operational safety.

The discourse presented in this chapter illustrates the theoretical underpinnings, technical approaches, and real-world applications of autonomous cyber defense, underscoring its importance for safeguarding essential services. By integrating machine learning algorithms, reinforcement learning strategies, and explainability mechanisms into robust architectures, the vision of AI-enabled protection strategies for power grids, water systems, and industrial control networks is increasingly within reach. The pathway forward involves collaboration among industry, government, and academia, promoting shared learning and setting common standards for secure, resilient infrastructures in the face of evolving cyber threats.

REFERENCES

Anderson, J. P. (1980). *Computer security threat monitoring and surveillance (Technical report).* James P. Anderson Co.

Avgerinos, T., Brumley, D., Davis, J., Goulden, R., Nighswander, T., Rebert, A., & Williamson, N. (2018). The Mayhem cyber reasoning system. *IEEE Security and Privacy, 16*(2), 52–60. DOI: 10.1109/MSP.2018.1870873

Berman, D. S., Buczak, A. L., Chavis, J. S., & Corbett, J. M. (2019). A survey of deep learning methods for cyber security. *IEEE Communications Surveys and Tutorials, 21*(4), 3031–3078. DOI: 10.1109/COMST.2019.2916180

Boddy, M., Jones, C., & Horowitz, B. (2014). Course-of-action generation for cyber security using classical planning. In *Proceedings of the AAAI Workshop on Artificial Intelligence for Cyber Security (AICS).* AAAI Press.

Buczak, A. L., & Guven, E. (2016). A survey of data mining and machine learning methods for cybersecurity. *IEEE Communications Surveys and Tutorials, 18*(2), 1153–1176. DOI: 10.1109/COMST.2015.2494502

Capuano, N., Fenza, G., Loia, V., & Stanzione, C. (2022). Explainable artificial intelligence in cybersecurity: A survey. *IEEE Access : Practical Innovations, Open Solutions, 10*, 93575–93600. DOI: 10.1109/ACCESS.2022.3204171

DARPA. (2016). *Cyber Grand Challenge (CGC) – Final results and findings.* Retrieved from https://www.darpa.mil/program/cyber-grand-challenge

Denning, D. E. (1987). An intrusion-detection model. *IEEE Transactions on Software Engineering, 13*(2), 222–232. DOI: 10.1109/TSE.1987.232894

Forrest, S., Hofmeyr, S. A., Somayaji, A., & Longstaff, T. A. (1996). A sense of self for Unix processes. In *Proceedings of the 1996 IEEE Symposium on Security and Privacy* (pp. 120–128). IEEE. DOI: 10.1109/SECPRI.1996.502675

Guembe, B., Azeta, A. A., Misra, S., Osamor, V. C., Fernández-Sanz, L., & Pospelova, V. (2022). The emerging threat of AI-driven cyber attacks: A review. *Applied Artificial Intelligence, 36*(1), 1–34. DOI: 10.1080/08839514.2022.2037254

Kott, A., Théron, P., & De Gaspari, F. (2019). *Autonomous Intelligent Cyber-Defense Agent (AICA) Reference Architecture, Release 2.0.* U.S. Army Research Laboratory.

Mahajan, S., Khurana, M., & Estrela, V. V. (Eds.). (2024). *Applying artificial intelligence in cybersecurity analytics and cyber threat detection.* Wiley. DOI: 10.1002/9781394196470

Malialis, K., & Kudenko, D. (2016). Distributed reinforcement learning for adaptive and robust network intrusion response. *Connection Science*, *28*(1), 45–63. DOI: 10.1080/09540091.2015.1031082

National Security Commission on Artificial Intelligence (NSCAI). (2021). *Final report.* Washington, DC: NSCAI. (See Chapter 6: AI and the future of cybersecurity.)

Nguyen-Tuong, A., Melski, D., Morris, D., Nguyen, D., Rizzi, E., Davidson, J. W., Hiser, J. D., Co, M., & Hawkins, W. H. (2018). Xandra: An autonomous cyber battle system for the Cyber Grand Challenge. *IEEE Security and Privacy*, *16*(2), 42–51. DOI: 10.1109/MSP.2018.1870876

Ofusori, L. O., Bokaba, T., & Mhlongo, S. (2024). Artificial intelligence in cybersecurity: A comprehensive review and future direction. *Applied Artificial Intelligence*, *38*(1), 2439609. Advance online publication. DOI: 10.1080/08839514.2024.2439609

Okdem, S., & Okdem, S. (2024). Artificial intelligence in cybersecurity: A review and a case study. *Applied Sciences (Basel, Switzerland)*, *14*(22), 10487. DOI: 10.3390/app142210487

Rasouli, M., Miehling, E., & Teneketzis, D. (2018). A scalable decomposition method for the dynamic defense of cyber networks. In *Proceedings of the 2018 Conference on Decision and Game Theory for Security (GameSec)* (pp. 221–241). Springer. DOI: 10.1007/978-3-319-75268-6_4

Ridley, A. (2018). Machine learning for autonomous cyber defense. *The Next Wave (NSA's Review of Emerging Technologies), 22(1), 7–14.*

Sarker, I. H. (2024). *AI-driven cybersecurity and threat intelligence: Cyber automation, intelligent decision-making and explainability*. Springer. DOI: 10.1007/978-3-031-54497-2

Sengupta, A., Huang, X., Kambhampati, S., Zhu, Z., Wang, S., Shen, C., & Liu, D. (2020). A survey of moving target defense: Approaches and research challenges. *IEEE Communications Surveys and Tutorials*, *22*(1), 622–653. DOI: 10.1109/COMST.2019.2951813

Shrobe, H. E., & Shrier, D. L. (2018). The past, present, and future of cyberdefense. *IEEE Security and Privacy*, *16*(2), 61–69. DOI: 10.1109/MSP.2018.1870859

Sikos, L. F. (Ed.). (2019). *AI in cybersecurity*. Springer. DOI: 10.1007/978-3-319-98842-9

Somayaji, A., & Forrest, S. (2000). Automated response using system-call delays. In *Proceedings of the 9th USENIX Security Symposium.* USENIX Association.

Stamp, M., Visaggio, C. A., Mercaldo, F., & Di Troia, F. (Eds.). (2022). *Artificial intelligence for cybersecurity*. Springer. DOI: 10.1007/978-3-030-97087-1

Truong, T. C., Diep, Q. B., & Zelinka, I. (2020). Artificial intelligence in the cyber domain: Offense and defense. *Symmetry*, *12*(3), 410. DOI: 10.3390/sym12030410

Xin, Y., Kong, L., Liu, Z., Chen, Y., Li, Y., Zhu, H., & Vasilakos, A. V. (2018). Machine learning and deep learning methods for cybersecurity. *IEEE Access : Practical Innovations, Open Solutions*, *6*, 35365–35381. DOI: 10.1109/ACCESS.2018.2836950

Yuan, X., Li, C., & Chen, X. (2019). Deep learning for security: A review. *IEEE Communications Surveys and Tutorials*, *21*(4), 3135–3173. DOI: 10.1109/COMST.2019.2933988

Zhu, Q., & Rass, S. (Eds.). (2021). *Cyber security in intelligent data-centric systems and applications*. Springer.

Chapter 18
Harnessing Deep Learning for Enhancing Security for Social Empowerment

T. Venkat Narayana Rao
https://orcid.org/0000-0002-1996-1819
Jawaharlal Nehru Technological University, India

Ananya Seeta
Jawaharlal Nehru Technological University, India

J. V. P. Udaya Deepika
Jawaharlal Nehru Technological University, India

Kumari G. Seshu
Jawaharlal Nehru Technological University, India

ABSTRACT

Critical structures are increasingly susceptible to cyber threats, leading to the inadequacy of traditional security measures. This study explores the application of deep learning tools aimed specifically at enhancing the security of vital systems, such as power grids and transportation networks. By employing convolutional neural networks and recurrent neural networks, the research conducts an analysis of network traffic data to identify security anomalies. An inclusive dataset, which includes simulated attack scenarios, with workable models. Preliminary findings indicate that the convolutional neural network model achieved a high level of anomaly detection accuracy, ominously surpassing the performance of conventional

DOI: 10.4018/979-8-3373-0954-5.ch018

methods. Furthermore, the recurrent neural network model demonstrated enhanced capabilities in detecting time-sensitive threats, resulting in an extensive reduction in false positives. This chapter focus on future research should focus on examining the integration of deep learning models with security frameworks to fortify resilience against evolving threats

1. INTRODUCTION

The increasing complexity of cyber threats targeting critical infrastructure has necessitated the development of more sophisticated security measures, with deep learning emerging as a transformative approach. Traditional cybersecurity methods, such as signature-based detection and rule-based analysis, have proven inadequate against modern adversarial attacks, particularly zero-day exploits and adaptive threats. As a result, deep learning, with its ability to autonomously detect patterns and anomalies in large datasets, has gained prominence in cybersecurity research (Aldhaheri et al., 2024). However, while many studies highlight the potential of deep learning, its integration into cybersecurity frameworks remains an evolving challenge that requires a critical review of existing methodologies, theoretical underpinnings, and practical applications. Furthermore, the effectiveness of deep learning techniques depends on their adaptability to different cybersecurity domains, necessitating a broader discussion of their implementation across various sectors of critical infrastructure.

Deep learning's relevance in cybersecurity has grown significantly due to the increasing sophistication of AI-powered cyberattacks. Attackers now leverage artificial intelligence to bypass traditional security defenses, creating an arms race between cybercriminals and security professionals. Real-world incidents, such as AI-generated phishing schemes and adversarial attacks on machine learning models, illustrate the urgency of advancing AI-driven security mechanisms (Goodfellow et al., 2015). For instance, adversarial malware can subtly modify its code to evade detection, tricking AI-based security systems into classifying it as benign software (Kurakin et al., 2017). These developments present significant challenges for conventional security frameworks, which often rely on predefined patterns and static rule-based mechanisms. The ability of deep learning models to detect emerging threats in real time has therefore become essential in mitigating risks before they escalate into large-scale cyber incidents.

While the advantages of deep learning in cybersecurity are widely acknowledged, its deployment in critical infrastructure security poses unique challenges. One of the primary concerns is the computational intensity required to train and deploy deep learning models, which may not always be feasible for resource-constrained environments such as industrial control systems and legacy security architectures. Moreover, deep learning models are often considered "black boxes," meaning that their decision-making processes are not easily interpretable by human analysts (Samek et al., 2019).

This chapter critically evaluates the current body of literature on deep learning applications in cybersecurity for critical infrastructure. It explores key deep learning architectures, their effectiveness in threat detection, comparative advantages over traditional methods, and existing limitations. Additionally, this review addresses the ethical, regulatory, and practical concerns associated with deploying AI-driven security measures.

By identifying gaps in research and areas requiring further exploration, this section aims to establish a comprehensive understanding of the role of deep learning in enhancing security frameworks for critical infrastructure. Given the increasing reliance on AI in cyber defense, this chapter also discusses potential future directions, including federated learning for decentralized security, hybrid AI-human collaborative defense systems, and the impact of quantum computing on deep learning-based security solutions.

2. UNDERSTANDING DEEP LEARNING FOR CYBERSECURITY

Deep learning has emerged as a transformative force in cybersecurity, offering advanced methods for detecting, analyzing, and mitigating cyber threats in real time. Unlike traditional machine learning, which relies on manually extracted features and structured datasets, deep learning autonomously processes vast amounts of unstructured data, making it highly effective in cybersecurity applications. It has the capability to learn intricate patterns, adapt to evolving threats, and provide proactive security measures. This section explores the fundamentals of deep learning in cybersecurity, differentiates it from traditional machine learning, and examines its associated risks and challenges, including adversarial attacks, explainability concerns, and the need for hybrid security solutions.

2.1 Fundamentals of Deep Learning in Cybersecurity

Deep learning is a subset of artificial intelligence (AI) that employs multi-layered neural networks to process complex data patterns. These neural networks, inspired by the human brain, enable cybersecurity systems to detect previously unknown threats by learning from large-scale datasets (LeCun et al., 2015). Deep learning models have been successfully applied in various cybersecurity domains, including malware detection, intrusion detection, phishing attack identification, and network anomaly detection.

2.1.1 Structure of Deep Learning Models

a) **Input Layer:** Receives raw security data such as network traffic logs, system event records, and authentication logs. These datasets often contain a mix of structured and unstructured information, requiring sophisticated preprocessing methods.
b) **Hidden Layers:** Process input data through multiple layers of artificial neurons, identifying intricate patterns and anomalies. These layers use activation functions to extract meaningful insights from raw cybersecurity data, enabling the detection of subtle attack patterns.
c) **Output Layer:** Classifies processed data into predefined categories, such as normal or malicious activity. The classification results can be used for automated security responses, real-time threat mitigation, and forensic analysis.

By utilizing this multi-layered approach, deep learning models can analyze vast amounts of security-related data and detect cyber threats that may not follow known attack signatures. The ability to generalize patterns from previous attacks enables these models to offer proactive threat detection (Goodfellow et al., 2016).

2.2 Machine Learning vs. Deep Learning in Cybersecurity

Although deep learning is a branch of machine learning, it differs significantly in terms of its feature extraction process, adaptability, and scalability. Traditional machine learning methods require cybersecurity analysts to manually define features for classification, whereas deep learning models learn features automatically from raw data, leading to a more adaptive and efficient security framework.

2.2.1 Key Differences Between ML and DL in Cybersecurity

a) **Machine Learning (ML):**
    i) Requires manual feature engineering, where cybersecurity experts define relevant attributes for classification. This often involves domain expertise and labor-intensive processes.
    ii) Works well with structured data, such as tabular logs and preprocessed datasets, making it suitable for traditional cybersecurity applications.

iii) Typically uses algorithms such as Decision Trees, Support Vector Machines (SVMs), and Random Forests for cybersecurity tasks (Buczak & Guven, 2016). These models are interpretable but may struggle with highly complex patterns.

b) **Deep Learning (DL):**
   i) Automatically extracts features from large, complex datasets, reducing human intervention and enabling a more scalable approach to cybersecurity.
   ii) Excels in handling unstructured cybersecurity data, including raw network packets, images, and text-based logs, making it ideal for modern threat detection systems.
   iii) Uses advanced architectures such as Convolutional Neural Networks (CNNs), Recurrent Neural Networks (RNNs), Generative Adversarial Networks (GANs), and Transformers for malware analysis, phishing detection, and threat intelligence (Sarker et al., 2021).

Due to these advantages, deep learning has been increasingly adopted in modern cybersecurity applications, particularly in environments where real-time threat detection, adaptive learning, and automation are essential.

2.3 Security Risks of Deep Learning (Adversarial AI)

Despite its potential, deep learning introduces new security challenges, particularly adversarial machine learning techniques that exploit model vulnerabilities. Attackers can manipulate AI-driven security systems by crafting adversarial inputs, subtly altering data to deceive deep learning models and evade detection.

2.3.1 Types of Adversarial Attacks

a) **Evasion Attacks:** Attackers introduce minor perturbations to input data, leading deep learning models to misclassify threats. For example, slightly modifying a malware signature can cause an AI-based detection system to classify it as benign (Kurakin et al., 2017). Such attacks pose a serious threat to automated cybersecurity solutions.

b) **Data Poisoning Attacks:** Malicious actors inject false data into a training set, corrupting a deep learning model's decision-making process. This can degrade the system's ability to detect cyber threats over time and manipulate the model's learning process (Biggio & Roli, 2018).

c) **Model Inversion Attacks:** By exploiting deep learning models, attackers attempt to reconstruct original training data, potentially exposing sensitive cybersecurity information and breaching data privacy (Fredrikson et al., 2015).

To mitigate these threats, researchers are exploring adversarial training, robust model architectures, and continuous learning techniques to improve resilience against evasion and poisoning attacks.

2.4 The Explainability Problem in Deep Learning for Cybersecurity

One of the critical limitations of deep learning in cybersecurity is its lack of interpretability. Traditional security models, such as firewalls and Security Information and Event Management (SIEM) systems, rely on predefined rules, providing clear reasoning for detected threats. In contrast, deep learning models function as black boxes, making it difficult to explain why a particular event was flagged as malicious (Doshi-Velez & Kim, 2017).

2.4.1 Challenges in AI Explainability

a) **Lack of Human Interpretability:** Cybersecurity analysts may struggle to justify AI-driven security decisions without clear explanations of how deep learning models classify threats, making trust and adoption more difficult.
b) **High False Positive/Negative Rates:** Without interpretability, it is challenging to fine-tune models to reduce false positives (benign activity flagged as threats) and false negatives (missed detections of real threats), which can impact security operations.
c) **Regulatory Compliance Issues:** Data protection laws such as GDPR require explainability in automated decision-making systems, necessitating greater transparency in AI-driven cybersecurity tools (Goodman & Flaxman, 2017).

To address this, researchers are developing Explainable AI (XAI) frameworks such as SHAP (Shapley Additive Explanations) and LIME (Local Interpretable Model-agnostic Explanations) to enhance model interpretability while maintaining high detection accuracy (Ribeiro et al., 2016).

2.5 Future Directions in Deep Learning for Cybersecurity

As cyber threats become more sophisticated, deep learning research is evolving to address current limitations and enhance security applications. Future research areas include:

2.5.1 Key Emerging Trends

a) **Self-Supervised Learning:** AI models capable of learning from unlabeled data to improve threat detection without extensive human supervision.
b) **Federated Learning for Cybersecurity:** Collaborative AI models trained across multiple institutions without exposing sensitive data, improving data privacy in security applications (Yang et al., 2019).
c) **Hybrid AI Models:** Combining deep learning with traditional rule-based systems to balance interpretability and accuracy in cyber threat detection.
d) **AI-Driven Cyber Deception:** Deploying AI-powered honeypots and decoy systems to mislead cybercriminals and gather intelligence on attack strategies.

Deep learning has revolutionized cybersecurity by enabling automated threat detection, real-time anomaly analysis, and predictive security measures. Future research must focus on improving model robustness, transparency, and hybrid AI-driven security frameworks to counter evolving digital threats.

3. THE EVOLUTION OF CYBER THREAT DETECTION

The continuous evolution of cyber threats has necessitated the development of advanced security mechanisms to detect and mitigate attacks effectively. Traditional security models, such as signature-based intrusion detection systems (IDS) and heuristic analysis, have struggled to keep pace with increasingly sophisticated cyberattacks. As a result, deep learning has emerged as a revolutionary approach to cyber threat detection, enabling automated anomaly detection, predictive threat intelligence, and real-time response. This section explores the evolution of cyber threat detection, compares traditional methods with deep learning-based approaches, and examines emerging trends in AI-driven security frameworks.

3.1 Traditional Cyber Threat Detection Methods

Before the integration of artificial intelligence into cybersecurity, conventional detection methods were widely employed to identify malicious activity. These methods, though effective against known threats, exhibit several limitations when dealing with adaptive and evolving attack strategies (Santos et al., 2019).

a) Signature-Based Detection
   (i) One of the most widely used methods in cybersecurity, signature-based detection relies on predefined attack patterns stored in databases.
   (ii) This approach is efficient for identifying known malware and network intrusions but fails against zero-day attacks and polymorphic malware that constantly evolve (Mishra & Soni, 2020).
   (iii) Antivirus software and IDS often use signature-based techniques but require frequent updates to remain effective.
   (iv) Due to reliance on signature databases, signature-based detection is ineffective against adversarial attacks that modify malicious code to bypass detection.
   (v) Cloud-based solutions have attempted to improve signature-based methods through real-time updates and enhanced collaboration, but scalability remains a challenge.

b) Rule-Based and Heuristic-Based Analysis
   (i) Traditional IDS and firewalls operate on predefined rules that specify acceptable and suspicious network activities.
   (ii) While these methods provide structured security, they generate high false positives due to their reliance on static thresholds (Sharma & Sahay, 2021).
   (iii) Heuristic analysis attempts to detect threats based on behavioral characteristics rather than exact signatures, but it struggles with adaptability and accuracy.
   (iv) Organizations using heuristic-based methods must continuously fine-tune detection rules to minimize false positives and false negatives, increasing operational overhead.
   (v) As cyberattacks become more sophisticated, heuristic-based techniques often require integration with machine learning models to improve accuracy.

3.2 The Shift Towards Deep Learning-Based Threat Detection

Deep learning-based cybersecurity solutions offer a fundamental shift from traditional methods by enabling adaptive, data-driven security measures. Unlike static rule-based approaches, deep learning models continuously learn from security data to detect new and evolving threats in real time (LeCun et al., 2015).

c) Key Advantages of Deep Learning in Cyber Threat Detection
   (i) **Automated Pattern Recognition**: Deep learning models analyze vast amounts of security data, identifying complex patterns that traditional methods may overlook (Goodfellow et al., 2016).
   (ii) **Real-Time Anomaly Detection**: Unlike heuristic-based methods, deep learning models can detect previously unseen attack behaviors through anomaly detection techniques such as autoencoders and generative adversarial networks (GANs) (Biggio & Roli, 2018).
   (iii) **Reduced False Positives**: By refining classification boundaries, deep learning reduces unnecessary security alerts, improving efficiency for security analysts (Sarker et al., 2021).
   (iv) **Efficacy Against Zero-Day Attacks**: Unlike signature-based approaches, deep learning models can detect previously unknown threats by analyzing behavioral deviations rather than relying on static indicators (Kurakin et al., 2017).
   (v) **Scalability for Large-Scale Networks**: Deep learning architectures like convolutional and recurrent neural networks (CNNs and RNNs) process large security datasets efficiently, improving detection rates for enterprise-level cybersecurity systems.
   (vi) **Self-Learning and Adaptive Security**: Unlike static security models, deep learning continuously adapts to new attack strategies, reducing the reliance on human intervention.

3.3 Emerging Threats and Challenges in AI-Based Cybersecurity

Despite its advantages, deep learning-based threat detection is not without challenges. Attackers are increasingly leveraging AI-driven techniques to evade detection, leading to the rise of adversarial machine learning and other sophisticated cyber threats (Fredrikson et al., 2015).

d) Adversarial Attacks Against AI-Based Security Systems

(i) **Evasion Attacks**: Attackers subtly modify input data to deceive AI models, tricking security systems into misclassifying malicious activities as benign (Biggio & Roli, 2018).
(ii) **Data Poisoning Attacks**: Malicious actors inject false data into training datasets, corrupting AI models and reducing their detection accuracy (Shumailov et al., 2021).
(iii) **Model Inversion Attacks**: Cybercriminals exploit AI models to reconstruct sensitive training data, posing risks to data privacy and confidentiality (Fredrikson et al., 2015).
(iv) **Adversarial Retraining Techniques**: Some cybercriminals use reinforcement learning-based strategies to manipulate AI models continuously, making them less effective over time.
(v) **Increased Compute Requirements**: AI-based security models require significant computational power, posing challenges for real-time detection in resource-constrained environments.
(vi) **Bias in AI Models**: If trained on biased datasets, deep learning models may exhibit discriminatory behavior, leading to security vulnerabilities and misclassifications.

3.4 Future Directions in AI-Driven Cyber Threat Detection

To enhance the effectiveness of deep learning in cybersecurity, ongoing research is exploring various approaches to improve AI model robustness, interpretability, and efficiency.

e) Key Advancements in Deep Learning for Cybersecurity

(i) **Federated Learning for Secure AI Model Training**: Allows AI models to learn across decentralized networks without exposing sensitive data, enhancing privacy (Yang et al., 2019).
(ii) **Hybrid AI Models Combining Deep Learning with Traditional Methods**: Integrates rule-based logic with AI-driven detection to improve accuracy and transparency (Ribeiro et al., 2016).
(iii) **Quantum AI for Advanced Threat Detection**: Quantum computing accelerates AI model training, improving cybersecurity defenses against advanced attack techniques (NIST, 2020).
(iv) **Explainable AI (XAI) for Trustworthy Cybersecurity**: Techniques such as SHAP (Shapley Additive Explanations) and LIME (Local Interpretable Model-agnostic Explanations) enhance AI transparency, making deep learning decisions more interpretable for security analysts (Goodman & Flaxman, 2017).

(v) **AI-Enhanced Threat Intelligence Sharing**: By integrating deep learning with threat intelligence platforms, security teams can respond more effectively to evolving cyber threats.

(vi) **Automated Incident Response Systems**: AI-driven security orchestration and automation response (SOAR) platforms streamline incident handling, reducing reaction times for cybersecurity teams.

The evolution of cyber threat detection has transitioned from traditional rule-based methods to advanced deep learning-driven approaches. Deep learning provides a superior capability for identifying cyber threats by automating pattern recognition, improving anomaly detection, and reducing false positives. However, adversarial AI threats and model interpretability challenges must be addressed to ensure the reliability of AI-driven cybersecurity solutions. By integrating federated learning, explainable AI, and quantum computing, deep learning will continue to shape the future of cyber threat detection, offering more robust and adaptive security mechanisms against evolving cyber threats.

4. PRINCIPLES OF ANOMALY DETECTION IN MODERN CYBERSECURITY

Anomaly detection plays a crucial role in modern cybersecurity, providing proactive defense mechanisms against evolving threats. Unlike signature-based detection methods that rely on known attack patterns, anomaly detection identifies deviations from normal system behavior, making it effective in detecting zero-day attacks, insider threats, and advanced persistent threats (APTs) (Chandola et al., 2009). This section explores traditional vs. deep learning-based anomaly detection, discusses false positives and false negatives in AI-driven systems, and examines the limitations of anomaly detection in cybersecurity. Additionally, it investigates the integration of AI-driven anomaly detection with other security mechanisms, the role of hybrid models, and the impact of contextual threat intelligence on improving detection accuracy.

4.1 Traditional vs. Deep Learning-Based Anomaly Detection

Traditional anomaly detection relies on predefined rules and statistical thresholds to classify activities as normal or suspicious. While effective against certain attack types, these systems struggle with adaptability and generate a high volume of false positives (Garcia et al., 2014). Deep learning-based anomaly detection offers an alternative by leveraging AI models trained on vast amounts of historical security data to identify subtle deviations in real time. However, the effectiveness of deep learning models depends on the quality and diversity of the training data, as well as the ability to mitigate adversarial attacks against AI-driven detection systems.

a) Key Differences Between Traditional and Deep Learning-Based Anomaly Detection
   (i) **Rule-Based Systems:** Define attack behaviors using pre-set rules, requiring manual updates and leading to high false positive rates (Ahmed et al., 2016).
   (ii) **Statistical-Based Methods:** Rely on threshold deviations but lack adaptability to new and evolving threats.
   (iii) **Deep Learning Systems:** Learn from historical data, identifying sophisticated attack patterns and reducing the need for manual tuning (Goodfellow et al., 2016).
   (iv) **Adaptive Learning Models:** Can continuously refine detection criteria to recognize emerging threats without human intervention (Sarker et al., 2021).
   (v) **Hybrid AI Techniques:** Combine traditional security frameworks with deep learning to optimize accuracy and reduce false positives.
   (vi) **Scalability of AI-Based Anomaly Detection:** Deep learning models are capable of analyzing vast amounts of data in real-time, providing a scalable solution for enterprise-level cybersecurity.

4.2 False Positives and False Negatives in AI-Based Anomaly Detection

AI-driven anomaly detection improves threat detection capabilities but is not immune to classification errors. False positives and false negatives pose significant challenges in balancing security effectiveness and operational efficiency (Biggio & Roli, 2018). These errors can lead to inefficient resource allocation, alert fatigue, and increased cybersecurity risks, necessitating the development of more reliable detection models that incorporate contextual analysis and automated response mechanisms.

b) Understanding False Positives and False Negatives
   (i) **False Positive:** A normal activity is incorrectly flagged as a threat, leading to unnecessary security alerts and operational disruptions (Zhang et al., 2020).
   (ii) **False Negative:** A genuine cyber threat goes undetected, allowing an attack to succeed undeterred.

(iii) **Security Overload Issue:** Excessive false positives result in alert fatigue, overwhelming security teams and reducing incident response efficiency (Sculley et al., 2015).

(iv) **Compromised Threat Detection:** High false negatives increase the risk of undetected cyberattacks, exposing critical systems to potential breaches.

(v) **Adaptive Thresholding Mechanisms:** Modern AI-driven security frameworks incorporate dynamic thresholding techniques to minimize false positives while maintaining detection sensitivity.

(vi) **Continuous Model Training:** AI-based anomaly detection systems require frequent retraining on updated datasets to improve accuracy and reduce false negatives.

4.3 Why Anomaly Detection Alone is Not Enough

While anomaly detection provides an essential layer of security, it is not a standalone solution. AI models can identify anomalies but often struggle to explain why an event is classified as suspicious (Ribeiro et al., 2016). To improve cybersecurity defenses, AI-based anomaly detection must be integrated with contextual threat intelligence and human oversight. Additionally, anomaly detection alone may not effectively counter sophisticated cyber threats, such as coordinated multi-stage attacks that disguise malicious activity as normal behavior over time.

c) Limitations of Solely Relying on Anomaly Detection

(i) **Lack of Explainability:** AI models detect deviations but do not provide insights into the reasoning behind classifications (Doshi-Velez & Kim, 2017).

(ii) **Misclassification Risks:** Context-blind anomaly detection may flag benign deviations as threats while failing to recognize multi-stage cyberattacks (Samek et al., 2019).

(iii) **Context-Aware Security Models:** Combining anomaly detection with behavioral analysis, rule-based frameworks, and expert supervision enhances accuracy and reliability (Goodman & Flaxman, 2017).

(iv) **Integration with Threat Intelligence:** AI-driven detection is most effective when combined with real-time threat intelligence feeds, enabling systems to correlate anomalies with known attack indicators.

(v) **Automated Incident Mitigation Strategies:** Anomaly detection must be paired with automated response mechanisms to neutralize potential threats before they escalate.

(vi) **Cross-Domain Security Correlation:** Advanced cybersecurity frameworks integrate anomaly detection across multiple security layers, providing a comprehensive defense strategy against complex cyber threats.

4.4 Future Directions in AI-Driven Anomaly Detection

To improve the effectiveness of AI-based anomaly detection, researchers are exploring advanced techniques that integrate deep learning with other security mechanisms. These advancements focus on enhancing model robustness, minimizing false positives, and increasing transparency in AI-driven security decisions.

d) Emerging Trends in AI-Based Anomaly Detection

(i) **Federated Learning for Secure Model Training:** Enables anomaly detection across distributed networks while preserving data privacy (Yang et al., 2019).

(ii) **Hybrid AI Models for Multi-Layered Security:** Combines rule-based detection with deep learning to balance interpretability and adaptability (Garcia et al., 2014).

(iii) **Explainable AI (XAI) for Threat Analysis:** Enhances model transparency, allowing security analysts to understand AI-generated threat alerts (Samek et al., 2019).

(iv) **Automated Incident Response Integration:** AI-driven Security Orchestration, Automation, and Response (SOAR) systems dynamically adjust security measures based on detected anomalies (Shumailov et al., 2021).

(v) **Self-Learning AI Security Frameworks:** Next-generation AI systems will incorporate unsupervised learning models that continuously adapt to new threat landscapes without requiring constant human intervention.

(vi) **Quantum AI in Cybersecurity:** The potential application of quantum computing in anomaly detection could significantly enhance AI's ability to process large-scale security data in real-time.

Anomaly detection is a cornerstone of modern cybersecurity, enabling organizations to identify potential threats that may bypass traditional security mechanisms. However, challenges such as false positives, false negatives, and model explainability highlight the need for a hybrid approach that integrates AI-driven detection with contextual analysis. Future advancements in federated learning, hybrid AI models, and explainable AI will further refine anomaly detection techniques, ensuring more accurate, scalable, and transparent cybersecurity defenses.

5. DEEP LEARNING APPLICATIONS IN CRITICAL INFRASTRUCTURE PROTECTION

The growing dependence on digital infrastructure has significantly increased the vulnerability of critical sectors such as energy, transportation, healthcare, and smart cities to cyber threats. These infrastructures are essential for economic stability, public safety, and national security, making them prime targets for cybercriminals and state-sponsored attacks. Deep learning has emerged as a powerful tool for securing these sectors by enabling real-time anomaly detection, predictive maintenance, and automated threat response. Unlike traditional security frameworks that rely on static rule-based systems, deep learning models continuously learn from evolving attack patterns, offering a more adaptive and scalable security solution (Goodfellow et al., 2016). This section examines the role of deep learning in infrastructure security, presents real-world case studies, and discusses challenges in implementation.

5.1 Role of Deep Learning in Securing Critical Infrastructure

Critical infrastructure systems operate in complex environments where cyber threats can have catastrophic consequences. Attackers target Industrial Control Systems (ICS), Supervisory Control and Data Acquisition (SCADA) systems, and Internet of Things (IoT) networks to disrupt essential services (Sarker et al., 2021). Deep learning enhances security in these domains by:

a) Intrusion Detection and Prevention
   i) AI-based Intrusion Detection Systems (IDS) analyze network traffic to detect abnormal patterns indicative of cyberattacks.
   ii) Convolutional Neural Networks (CNNs) and Recurrent Neural Networks (RNNs) identify malware signatures and unauthorized access attempts (LeCun et al., 2015).
   iii) Self-learning Models continuously adapt to new attack vectors, reducing false positives and improving detection accuracy.
   iv) Generative Adversarial Networks (GANs) create synthetic attack scenarios to improve detection models.
   v) Hybrid Deep Learning Approaches combine multiple models to increase robustness against emerging threats.

b) Predictive Maintenance and Risk Mitigation
   i) Cyber-physical Systems such as power grids and water treatment plants rely on deep learning for fault detection and system failure predictions.
   ii) AI-driven Predictive Maintenance minimizes downtime by identifying potential equipment malfunctions before they occur (Zhang et al., 2020).

iii) Reinforcement Learning optimizes security policies in real-time, ensuring that critical infrastructure remains operational during cyber incidents.
iv) Digital Twins simulate real-world infrastructure to anticipate security vulnerabilities and optimize response mechanisms.
v) Anomaly-based Forecasting predicts threats by analyzing trends in system behavior.

c) Threat Intelligence and Automated Response
i) Natural Language Processing (NLP)-based Deep Learning Models analyze cyber threat intelligence reports to detect emerging attack trends (Yang et al., 2019).
ii) AI-powered Security Orchestration, Automation, and Response (SOAR) Systems provide real-time threat mitigation by adjusting security configurations dynamically (Biggio & Roli, 2018).
iii) Behavioral Analytics track user activities to detect insider threats and unauthorized data access attempts.
iv) Threat Hunting uses AI-driven pattern recognition to proactively seek out potential vulnerabilities.
v) AI-Driven Deception Techniques deploy automated honeypots to mislead attackers and study their behavior.

5.2 Deep Learning in Critical Infrastructure

Deep learning applications in critical infrastructure security have demonstrated effectiveness in mitigating cyber risks across various sectors. The following case studies highlight successful implementations:

5.2.1 Power Grid Security

i) AI-PhyX is an AI-powered anomaly detection system that monitors grid operations to detect cyber intrusions in real time (Kurakin et al., 2017).
ii) Deep Learning Models analyze voltage fluctuations and energy consumption patterns to prevent false data injection attacks.
iii) Hybrid AI Frameworks combine CNNs and Long Short-Term Memory (LSTM) networks to enhance grid resilience against cyber-physical attacks.
iv) Smart Grid Security uses AI-powered network segmentation to isolate threats and prevent cascading failures.
v) AI-powered Demand Forecasting predicts electricity consumption to optimize security measures.

5.2.2 Smart Cities and Traffic Management

i) AI-driven Traffic Monitoring Systems predict congestion patterns and detect cyber threats targeting smart traffic infrastructure (Garcia et al., 2014).
ii) Reinforcement Learning Algorithms optimize traffic signal control to prevent cyber-induced gridlock attacks.
iii) Deep Learning-powered Video Surveillance enhances security in public spaces by detecting suspicious behaviors in real time.
iv) AI-based Incident Response automatically adjusts traffic patterns to accommodate emergencies.
v) Edge AI in Smart Cities reduces latency by enabling real-time security decisions at the network edge.

5.2.3 Healthcare Infrastructure Protection

i) AI-based Anomaly Detection Systems monitor hospital networks to identify unauthorized access to patient records (Shumailov et al., 2021).
ii) Federated Learning enables hospitals to collaboratively train AI security models without exposing sensitive patient data (Goodman & Flaxman, 2017).
iii) Medical IoT Device Security enhances protection by analyzing device communication patterns for potential cyber threats.
iv) AI-powered Biometric Security strengthens identity verification systems for healthcare access control.
v) Automated AI Auditing ensures compliance with evolving regulatory requirements.

5.3 Challenges in Implementing AI for Infrastructure Security

Despite its advantages, the integration of deep learning in critical infrastructure security presents several challenges that must be addressed for effective deployment:

a) High Computational Cost
   i) Resource-intensive Threat Detection requires significant processing power, making real-time detection demanding (NIST, 2020).
   ii) IT Resource Limitations hinder infrastructure sectors with limited IT resources from implementing AI-driven security solutions.
   iii) Edge Computing and Optimized AI Models are being explored to reduce dependency on cloud-based processing.

iv) Energy Efficiency must be optimized in AI-driven security solutions to remain cost-effective.
v) Scalable AI Architectures are needed to ensure models remain viable as infrastructure networks expand.

b) Legacy System Integration
   i) Outdated IT and OT (Operational Technology) Systems pose compatibility challenges for AI-driven security tools (Fredrikson et al., 2015).
   ii) Extensive System Modifications require specialized hardware and software adjustments for retrofitting AI into legacy environments.
   iii) Hybrid AI Solutions blend traditional security mechanisms with deep learning to enhance compatibility.
   iv) Secure API Gateways facilitate communication between legacy and AI-driven security systems.
   v) Gradual AI Adoption Strategies are necessary to avoid disruptions in critical operations.

c) Regulatory and Privacy Concerns
   i) Compliance with Data Protection Laws ensures AI-driven cybersecurity adheres to regulations like GDPR and HIPAA (Doshi-Velez & Kim, 2017).
   ii) Privacy-preserving AI Techniques such as differential privacy and homomorphic encryption are being explored to secure sensitive infrastructure data.
   iii) AI Governance Frameworks must be established by governments and regulatory bodies to ensure ethical AI deployment in cybersecurity.
   iv) Transparent AI Decision-making mechanisms must be integrated into AI models.
   v) Global AI Security Standards are necessary to harmonize cybersecurity policies across nations.

5.4 Future Directions in AI-Powered Infrastructure Security

a) Federated Learning for Cross-sector Security Collaboration.
b) AI-powered Digital Twins for Enhanced Infrastructure Simulations.
c) Quantum AI for Next-generation Threat Detection.
d) AI-Augmented Decision-making Tools for Human Analysts.
e) AI-driven Automated Incident Response Systems.

Deep learning continues to evolve as a critical asset in securing vital infrastructure. As cyber threats become more sophisticated, AI-driven security solutions will be essential for ensuring long-term resilience and safety in an increasingly digital world.

6. APPROACHES TO CYBERSECURITY

6.1 Traditional Cybersecurity Approaches

Traditional cybersecurity models rely on predefined rules, manual configurations, and fixed security policies to detect and prevent attacks. These methods have been widely used in intrusion detection systems (IDS), antivirus software, and firewalls (Mishra & Soni, 2020). However, they exhibit several limitations, including inflexibility, high maintenance requirements, and vulnerability to advanced cyber threats that evolve rapidly. Cybercriminals constantly develop new attack strategies that bypass traditional security measures. Despite their long-standing use, conventional approaches struggle to keep pace with increasingly sophisticated cyber threats. The lack of automation in these models also requires significant human intervention, making security management resource-intensive.

Heuristic and behavioral analysis attempts to identify malware and cyber threats based on behavior rather than signatures. While more flexible than rule-based systems, it is prone to inaccuracies, particularly in identifying sophisticated attacks (Buczak & Guven, 2016). It also relies heavily on security analysts to fine-tune detection parameters, leading to operational inefficiencies. Additionally, adversarial attacks that mimic normal behavior can sometimes evade detection, reducing its overall effectiveness.

6.2 Deep Learning-Based Cybersecurity Approaches

Deep learning models enhance cybersecurity by automatically learning from large datasets and recognizing complex attack patterns. Unlike traditional methods, deep learning systems can detect novel threats and anomalies without requiring predefined rules (LeCun et al., 2015). The ability to analyze vast amounts of data enables AI-driven security systems to detect emerging cyber threats in real time and adapt dynamically.

Adaptive threat detection uses AI-driven models to detect both known and unknown cyber threats. It continuously refines detection accuracy by analyzing new attack behaviors (Goodfellow et al., 2016). By automating the learning and adaptation process, deep learning models reduce reliance on human intervention and improve detection efficiency by analyzing contextual threat data and historical attack trends.

Real-time anomaly identification is achieved through deep learning-based intrusion detection systems (IDS) that identify deviations in network behavior indicative of cyberattacks. Autoencoders and Recurrent Neural Networks (RNNs) help detect malicious activities with higher accuracy (Biggio & Roli, 2018). This approach is highly effective in detecting zero-day attacks that do not conform to predefined signatures or rules. Additionally, it reduces response times by enabling immediate threat detection and mitigation.

Improved threat intelligence is another advantage of deep learning. Natural Language Processing (NLP) is used to analyze cybersecurity reports, threat intelligence feeds, and malware analysis logs (Yang et al., 2019). Predictive security is enhanced by identifying attack trends before they become widespread threats. AI-powered Security Orchestration, Automation, and Response (SOAR) systems strengthen automated incident response and support decision-making processes to streamline security operations.

6.3 Hybrid AI-Security Models

While deep learning enhances cybersecurity capabilities, traditional security models remain valuable. Hybrid AI-security frameworks combine AI-driven threat detection with rule-based validation to improve accuracy and interpretability (Ribeiro et al., 2016). By integrating traditional and AI-based methodologies, hybrid models balance efficiency, accuracy, and transparency in cybersecurity operations.

This combination reduces false positives, as AI-driven systems learn from past detections to minimize false alerts, improving overall efficiency (Sarker et al., 2021). Rule-based models also enhance explainability, compensating for deep learning's "black box" issue. Additionally, hybrid models optimize security workflows by leveraging the strengths of both approaches.

Applications of hybrid security frameworks include intrusion detection and prevention systems (IDPS), where AI models flag suspicious activity while predefined rules confirm or reject alerts. In financial systems, deep learning detects anomalies in transactions, while rule-based engines assess policy violations (Shumailov et al., 2021). Endpoint security solutions integrate AI-driven malware detection with rule-based threat intelligence databases to improve accuracy and speed. Hybrid models also optimize cloud security by enhancing monitoring in cloud environments and adapting to evolving cyber risks.

6.4 Future Directions in AI-Powered Cybersecurity

The future of cybersecurity lies in the seamless integration of deep learning and traditional security mechanisms. Ongoing research explores the development of hybrid AI models that combine the strengths of both approaches while mitigating their weaknesses (NIST, 2020). Emerging technologies will likely redefine security strategies, improving proactive cyber defense mechanisms.

Explainable AI (XAI) for cybersecurity enhances transparency in AI-based security decisions to improve trust and regulatory compliance (Goodman & Flaxman, 2017). Human-interpretable threat detection frameworks balance automation with analyst oversight. Techniques such as Shapley Additive Explanations (SHAP) and Local Interpretable Model-agnostic Explanations (LIME) improve AI decision explainability (Samek et al., 2019). The development of AI ethics frameworks also plays a role in guiding cybersecurity implementations.

Federated learning for privacy-preserving security allows AI models to be trained across multiple institutions without exposing sensitive security data (Yang et al., 2019). This approach enhances global cybersecurity collaboration while maintaining compliance with data protection laws such as GDPR and HIPAA. By improving AI model generalizability across different threat landscapes and attack vectors, federated learning minimizes data-sharing risks while maximizing collaborative cybersecurity efforts.

7. CHALLENGES AND FUTURE DIRECTIONS

The integration of deep learning into cybersecurity presents both opportunities and challenges. While AI-driven security solutions enhance threat detection, automate responses, and improve cyber resilience, they also introduce new risks, including adversarial AI attacks, data privacy concerns, and legal accountability issues. These concerns arise as cyber threats continue to grow in sophistication, making it increasingly important to establish proactive defenses. The lack of transparency in AI decision-making also adds an additional layer of complexity, requiring significant research and regulatory interventions to ensure responsible implementation. Addressing these challenges is crucial for ensuring the long-term effectiveness and ethical deployment of AI in cybersecurity. This section explores the challenges associated with deep learning-based security solutions, examines emerging trends in AI-driven cybersecurity, and highlights the necessary advancements required for future improvements.

7.1 AI Adversarial Attacks on Cybersecurity

Deep learning models are susceptible to adversarial attacks, where malicious actors manipulate AI-driven security systems to evade detection. These attacks exploit vulnerabilities in AI models, potentially rendering them ineffective in identifying cyber threats. AI-based security solutions rely heavily on data-driven decision-making, and attackers can leverage weaknesses in data processing and model training methodologies to bypass security measures.

7.1.1 Types of Adversarial AI Attacks

(i) **Adversarial Malware:** Hackers craft malware that subtly alters its code to bypass AI-based security models, tricking deep learning classifiers into misclassifying threats as benign. This attack technique leverages the fact that AI models are trained on known attack patterns, making them vulnerable to slight modifications in malicious code. As cybercriminals continue to innovate, adversarial malware has become increasingly sophisticated, making traditional detection methods less effective.

(ii) **Data Poisoning Attacks:** Attackers inject manipulated data into training sets, corrupting AI models and reducing detection accuracy over time. By compromising the training phase, attackers can introduce systematic biases that undermine the AI's ability to distinguish between real and fraudulent behavior. The long-term impact of data poisoning can be devastating, leading to the gradual deterioration of security systems.

(iii) **Evasion Attacks:** Threat actors modify attack patterns to fool AI systems, leading to missed detections of sophisticated cyber intrusions. These attacks are especially dangerous when combined with rapid, automated attacks that AI systems fail to adapt to in real-time. Attackers may leverage deep learning techniques to develop adversarial strategies, further complicating the challenge of mitigating evasion tactics.

(iv) **Model Extraction Attacks:** Attackers analyze AI-driven security systems to reconstruct their underlying models, allowing them to develop targeted adversarial exploits that evade detection with higher precision. By reverse-engineering AI models, cybercriminals can identify vulnerabilities and refine their attack methodologies to bypass detection mechanisms.

7.1.2 Defensive AI Strategies for Mitigating Adversarial Attacks

(i) **Adversarial Training:** AI models are trained on adversarial examples to improve robustness against evasion techniques. By continuously updating AI models with real-world attack variations, security systems can better withstand adversarial attempts. Defensive AI techniques must remain agile and responsive to emerging threats.

(ii) **Defensive Distillation:** AI models are refined to make them more resistant to manipulated inputs, reducing the impact of adversarial perturbations. This approach minimizes the effectiveness of gradient-based attacks that attempt to deceive AI classifiers. The implementation of defensive distillation enhances AI's ability to maintain accuracy even under adversarial conditions.

(iii) **Hybrid AI Security Models:** Combining deep learning with traditional rule-based methods enhances security defenses against adversarial attacks. The fusion of AI with conventional security techniques offers a multi-layered defense mechanism, reducing reliance on any single method. Hybrid models improve the resilience of security infrastructures against complex cyber threats.

(iv) **AI-Based Anomaly Detection:** Advanced machine learning techniques can be deployed to detect deviations from normal network behavior, allowing systems to recognize and respond to previously unseen attack strategies. Continuous monitoring and real-time analysis are critical for mitigating adversarial threats effectively.

7.2 Legal and Ethical Issues in AI-Driven Security

The rise of AI-powered cybersecurity introduces ethical and legal complexities. Questions surrounding accountability, bias, and data privacy must be addressed to ensure AI's responsible and fair deployment in security frameworks. Governments and regulatory bodies face challenges in establishing policies that balance security with individual rights and freedoms. Without proper oversight, AI-driven security measures could lead to unintended consequences, such as biased decision-making, lack of transparency, and privacy violations.

7.2.1 Accountability in AI-Based Cybersecurity

(i) **Responsible for AI Failures:** If an AI-based security system fails to detect an attack, determining liability remains a legal grey area. Organizations deploying AI solutions must establish clear responsibility frameworks to mitigate risks associated with security failures.

(ii) **Bias in AI Decision-Making:** AI models may inherit biases from training data, leading to unfair or inaccurate threat classifications. Addressing bias requires diverse datasets and ethical AI training methodologies. Implementing fairness-aware AI models is essential to minimize discriminatory decision-making.

(iii) **Regulatory Gaps in AI Security:** Existing cybersecurity laws do not fully account for AI-driven security decisions, creating compliance challenges for organizations. Future regulations must encompass AI-specific risks and establish standardized industry guidelines. As AI adoption increases, international cooperation on regulatory frameworks will be necessary to address cross-border cybersecurity concerns.

(iv) **Ethical Considerations in AI Governance:** Ensuring transparency and fairness in AI decision-making is a critical challenge, particularly when AI systems autonomously determine security actions that impact individuals and organizations. AI security governance must prioritize accountability and ethical best practices to build trust among stakeholders.

7.3 Future of AI-Security Integration

As AI continues to evolve, researchers are exploring new approaches to enhance its reliability, interpretability, and compliance with regulatory standards. The future of AI-driven cybersecurity will be shaped by advancements in explainable AI, global AI regulations, and interdisciplinary security frameworks. Collaboration between government agencies, private organizations, and cybersecurity researchers will be key to mitigating emerging threats.

7.3.1 Emerging Global AI-Security Regulations

(i) **Standardized AI Governance Frameworks:** Governments and international organizations will establish comprehensive AI-security regulations to prevent misuse of deep learning in cybersecurity. Regulatory clarity will help businesses and organizations implement AI security solutions with confidence.

(ii) **Ethical AI Guidelines for Security:** AI governance models will focus on ensuring fairness, transparency, and bias mitigation in AI-driven security solutions. Ethical AI development will be a key priority for regulatory bodies.

(iii) **International Collaboration in AI Threat Intelligence:** AI-powered threat intelligence platforms will facilitate cross-border cybersecurity cooperation, enhancing global cyber resilience. Increased collaboration between nations and organizations will lead to more effective threat mitigation strategies.

8. CASE STUDIES

8.1. The Evolution of Cyber Threats and Deep Learning Solutions

The rapid evolution of cyber threats targeting critical infrastructure has necessitated innovative approaches to security, with deep learning emerging as a powerful tool in protecting these essential systems. The application of artificial intelligence in cyber defense has led to the development of sophisticated methodologies capable of detecting, analyzing, and neutralizing threats before they cause significant harm. The widespread integration of deep learning into security frameworks has demonstrated both immense potential and notable challenges, requiring continuous adaptation to evolving threats. Recent implementations and research illustrate the transformative role of artificial intelligence in safeguarding essential infrastructure from cyberattacks, offering insights into successful deployments and lessons learned from past security breaches.

8.2. Successful Implementations of Deep Learning in Secure Critical Infrastructures

The implementation of deep learning technologies in critical infrastructure security has shown remarkable success across various sectors. A significant breakthrough has been achieved in the power infrastructure sector, where deep learning models have demonstrated exceptional capabilities in automated inspection and threat detection. Research conducted using vehicle-mounted video acquisition equipment and deep convolutional neural networks has achieved 95.5% accuracy in distinguishing power-related infrastructures, particularly in rural settings. This implementation represents a significant advancement in preventative maintenance and infrastructure protection through automated surveillance. These advanced systems allow for real-time monitoring, significantly reducing response time to potential threats while minimizing the reliance on human intervention.

Recent innovations have also seen the successful deployment of deep learning-based authentication systems for protecting against insider threats. A notable implementation involves the use of siamese neural networks (SNNs) with convolutional neural network branches for user authentication. This system has achieved unprecedented accuracy in detecting unauthorized access attempts, with the lowest equal error rate (EER) of 0.04545 compared to traditional methods. The system's ability to transform numerical values of keystroke dynamics into images for analysis has proven particularly effective in identifying potential insider threats. Additionally, new developments in multi-factor authentication (MFA) systems leveraging deep learning algorithms have improved identity verification processes by analyzing behavioral patterns, such as typing rhythm and facial recognition, to enhance security.

8.3. Lessons Learned from Cyberattacks on Critical Infrastructure

The analysis of recent cyberattacks has revealed crucial insights about the evolving nature of threats and necessary defensive measures. One significant lesson emerged from the Crowdstrike incident, which demonstrated how supply chain vulnerabilities can create significant common-cause vulnerabilities in security systems. The incident, though accidental, had widespread implications for critical infrastructure operations, affecting oil and gas pipelines, terminals, airlines, manufacturing, and transportation systems. This incident highlighted the necessity of conducting comprehensive risk assessments and implementing rigorous supply chain security measures to mitigate similar risks in the future.

The year 2024 has brought several critical lessons about infrastructure security. Supply chain vulnerabilities have emerged as crucial factors in modern cyberattacks, emphasizing the need for more robust risk management strategies. The rise of AI/ML-enabled cyberattacks reflects the evolving sophistication of adversaries, necessitating continuous adaptation of defense mechanisms. Organizations have learned that the traditional approach of relying solely on segmentation for resilience is insufficient; they must now implement a mix of physical resilience, recovery mechanisms, and cyber resilience measures. Additionally, the shift towards adopting real-time monitoring and AI-driven anomaly detection has become essential in counteracting emerging threats before they escalate.

8.4. Analysis of Current Research Papers and Innovations

Current research in deep learning applications for critical infrastructure security has revealed several promising innovations. A significant advancement has been made in the development of web-based programmable logic controller (PLC) malware detection systems. Researchers have identified a new class of PLC malware that poses significant risks to industrial systems, leading to the development of more sophisticated detection mechanisms. This research has highlighted the need for rethinking architectures, protocols, and deployment strategies to enhance security without compromising interconnectivity. The use of AI-powered anomaly detection methods has proven effective in identifying and neutralizing malware before it can disrupt industrial control systems, improving the overall security posture of critical infrastructure.

The integration of deep learning technologies in critical infrastructure security represents a significant advancement in protecting essential systems from increasingly sophisticated cyber threats. The successful implementations across various sectors demonstrate the technology's potential to enhance security measures significantly, while lessons learned from recent cyberattacks highlight the importance of maintaining a comprehensive and adaptive security approach. By leveraging deep learning-based anomaly detection, automated authentication, and AI-driven threat mitigation systems, organizations can effectively strengthen their security frameworks and respond more efficiently to emerging threats.

As threats continue to evolve, organizations must remain vigilant in implementing and updating their security measures, leveraging the latest innovations in deep learning while addressing emerging vulnerabilities. The continued development of more sophisticated deep learning applications, combined with lessons learned from real-world incidents, will be crucial for maintaining the security of critical infrastructure in an increasingly complex threat landscape. The path forward requires a balanced approach that combines technological innovation with practical security measures, ensuring the resilience of critical infrastructure against both current and emerging threats. By fostering collaboration between government agencies, private sector entities, and research institutions, the ongoing advancement of AI-driven cybersecurity solutions can play a pivotal role in securing critical infrastructure for the future.

9. CONCLUSION

The implementation of deep learning technologies has emerged as a transformative force in securing critical infrastructure systems, demonstrating significant potential in protecting essential services against increasingly sophisticated cyber threats. Real-world applications across various sectors, particularly in power infrastructure, have shown considerable successThese developments highlight the need for comprehensive security approaches that integrate both physical resilience and recovery mechanisms alongside cyber resilience strategies. Ongoing research has made promising strides in areas such as web-based programmable logic controller malware detection and behavioral biometrics authentication systems. Advances in methods like the Gabor Filter Matrix Transformation have contributed to these innovations, enhancing the security of critical infrastructure systems. The successful integration of these technologies, coupled with valuable insights from real-world incidents, emphasizes the importance of adopting a balanced approach. Organizations must combine technological innovation with practical security measures to ensure the resilience of their infrastructure. As the threat landscape continues to evolve, it is essential that organizations remain vigilant, continually updating their security measures and leveraging the full potential of deep learning technologies while addressing emerging vulnerabilities. This will ultimately help ensure the ongoing security and resilience of critical infrastructure systems in an increasingly complex cybersecurity environment.

REFERENCES

Albaseer, A. A., Fares, A., & Barakat, I. (2024). Deep learning anomaly detection in AI-powered intelligent power systems. *Frontiers in Energy Research, 11*(1), 34–49.

Aldhaheri, A., Alwahedi, F., Ferrag, M. A., & Battah, A. (2024). Deep Learning for Cybersecurity in IoT Networks. *Journal of IoT Security, 9*(3), 115–130.

AWS. (2022). What is deep learning? - Deep learning AI explained. *AWS AI Insights, 13*(1), 45–56.

Basak, S., Chatterjee, P., Biswas, D., Bhadra, P., & Das, R. (2024). Machine Learning Applications in Cybersecurity: Threat Detection and Prevention. *Machine Learning, 18*(3), 130–145.

Batarseh, F., Haugh, L., & Wang, T. (2024). Soft sensors and predictive measurements for water quality monitoring. *Environmental Engineering Science, 45*(2), 105–119.

Becerra-Suarez, F. L., Tuesta-Monteza, V. A., Mejia-Cabrera, H. I., & Arce, J. A. (2024). AI-Driven Cybersecurity Approaches for Industrial Systems. *International Journal of Artificial Intelligence, 13*(1), 44–58.

Biggio, B., & Roli, F. (2018). Wild patterns: Ten years after the rise of adversarial machine learning. *Pattern Recognition, 84*, 317–331. DOI: 10.1016/j.patcog.2018.07.023

Bryghtpath. (2024). Harnessing AI in cybersecurity: Enhancing threat detection. *Bryghtpath Cybersecurity Insights, 8(1),* 112-125.

Budžys, A., Kurasova, O., & Medvedev, V. (2024). Deep learning-based authentication for insider threat detection in critical infrastructure. *Artificial Intelligence Review, 57*(10), 272. DOI: 10.1007/s10462-024-10893-1

Chinthala, S. (2024). Analyzing the Effectiveness of SIEM Tools in Threat Mitigation for Critical Infrastructure. *Journal of Cyber Defense, 11*(4), 125–137.

Dai, L. (2024). A Unified Algebraic Framework Extending From a 6-Set Discrete Probability Model. *Journal of Computational Mathematics, 13*(4), 50–64.

DATAVERSITY. (2022). A brief history of deep learning. *DATAVERSITY Publications, 7*(4), 15–28.

Dick, K., Russell, L., Souley Dosso, Y., Kwamena, F., & Green, J. R. (2024). Enhancing IoT Security with Deep Learning. *Journal of Internet of Things, 10*(3), 112–126.

Foote, K. D. (2022). The evolution of deep learning: Historical milestones and future directions. *Journal of Artificial Intelligence Research, 16*(2), 101–115.

Fredrikson, M., Jha, S., & Ristenpart, T. (2015). Model inversion attacks that exploit confidence information and basic countermeasures. *Proceedings of the 22nd ACM SIGSAC Conference on Computer and Communications Security,* 1322-1333. DOI: 10.1145/2810103.2813677

Gill, N. S. (2024). The application of convolutional neural networks in security code and anomaly detection. *International Journal of Security Research, 12*(3), 89–103.

Gonzalez, P., Castano, A., Peacock, E. E., Diez, J., del Coz, J. J., & Sosik, H. M. (2024). Automatic plankton quantification using deep features. *Journal of Marine Biology Research, 58*(3), 123–135.

Goodfellow, I., McDaniel, P., & Papernot, N. (2016). Making machine learning robust against adversarial inputs. *arXiv preprint arXiv:1612.07294.*

Goodman, B., & Flaxman, S. (2017). European Union regulations on algorithmic decision-making and a "right to explanation.". *AI Magazine, 38*(3), 50–57. DOI: 10.1609/aimag.v38i3.2741

Haugh, L. (2024). New partnership uses AI to bolster efficiency, cybersecurity for water treatment. *Virginia Tech News, 15*(2), 45–58.

Havrylovych, M., & Danylov, V. (2024). Deep Learning Application in Critical Infrastructure Protection. In *Artificial Intelligence for Cybersecurity* (pp. 451–465). Springer.

Hochreiter, S., & Schmidhuber, J. (1997). Long Short-Term Memory. *Neural Computation, 9*(8), 1735–1780. DOI: 10.1162/neco.1997.9.8.1735 PMID: 9377276

Jha, P., Mahato, S., Jana, P. K., Maurya, S., & Chihi, I. (2024). Artificial Intelligence and Machine Learning in Cybersecurity. *Journal of Cybersecurity, 15*(3), 89–104.

Kalasani, R. R. (2024). An Exploratory Study of the Impacts of Artificial Intelligence in Cyber Defense. *Journal of AI Research, 13*(4), 72–85.

Khang, A., & Rath, K. C. (2024). The Quantum Evolution - Application of AI and Robotics in Modern Systems. *Journal of Quantum Computing, 6*(2), 35–50.

Kilichev, D., Turimov, D., & Kim, W. (2024). Next–Generation Intrusion Detection for IoT EVCS: Integrating CNN, LSTM, and GRU Models. *Mathematics, 16*(1), 112–130. DOI: 10.3390/math12040571

Le, D. N., Dhar, A., Kumar, R., Muthaiyah, S., & Agarwal, S. (2024). The Role of Data Science in Network Security for Smart Cities. *Journal of Data Science : JDS, 17*(5), 90–105.

Lian, J., Zhang, X., & Liu, Y. (2024). CNN and RNN applications in real-time cyberattack detection. *International Journal of Cybersecurity, 13*(3), 22–35.

Link, S. (2021). Deep learning: A comprehensive overview on techniques. *Springer Link Journal, 16*(2), 134–149.

Mickalson, S. B. (2023). Detecting Data Poisoning Attacks on Smart Farm Devices Using Machine Learning. *Agrárinformatika Folyóirat, 12*(1), 45–58.

NIST. (2020). *AI risk management framework: Developing trustworthy AI. National Institute of Standards and Technology (NIST).* Special Publication.

Ribeiro, M. T., Singh, S., & Guestrin, C. (2016). "Why should I trust you?": Explaining the predictions of any classifier. *Proceedings of the 22nd ACM SIGKDD International Conference on Knowledge Discovery and Data Mining,* 1135-1144.

Samek, W., Wiegand, T., & Müller, K. (2019). Explainable artificial intelligence: Understanding, visualizing and interpreting deep learning models. *Digital Signal Processing, 91*, 1–10.

Sarker, I. H., Kayes, A., Badsha, S., Alqahtani, H., Watters, P., & Ng, A. (2021). Cybersecurity data science: An overview from machine learning perspective. *Journal of Big Data, 8*, 1–29.

Trend Micro (US). (2024). Harnessing AI for enhanced security. *Trend Micro Whitepapers, 11*(2), 45–59.

Xenonstack. (2024). Deep learning in cybersecurity: Threat detection and defense. *Xenonstack Tech Reports, 9(1),* 67-82.

Compilation of References

Abadi, M., Chu, A., Goodfellow, I., McMahan, H. B., Mironov, I., Talwar, K., & Zhang, L. (2016). Deep learning with differential privacy. *Proceedings of the 2016 ACM SIGSAC Conference on Computer and Communications Security*, 308–318. ACM. DOI: 10.1145/2976749.2978318

Abbas, A., Alroobaea, R., Krichen, M., Rubaiee, S., Vimal, S., & Almansour, F. M. (2024). S. Vimal, and Fahad M. Almansour. "Blockchain-assisted secured data management framework for health information analysis based on Internet of Medical Things.". *Personal and Ubiquitous Computing*, *28*(1), 59–72. DOI: 10.1007/s00779-021-01583-8

Abdillah, K., Rizkia, W., & Sidharta, S. (2024). Exploring the Role of Artificial Intelligence in Enhancing Battery Performance and Mitigating Cybersecurity Threats in Electric Vehicles: A Systematic Literature Review." *. *Procedia Computer Science*, *245*, 155–165. DOI: 10.1016/j.procs.2024.10.239

Abinash, M. J., Prabu Kanna, G., Aanjankumar, S., Sambasivam, G., & Karthikeyan, P. (2025). An Introduction to the Challenges and Issues Identified in Digital Health and Wellness Cybersecurity. In S. Poonkuntran, R. K. Dhanaraj, S. AanjanKumar, & M. Sathyamoorthy, *Cybersecurity in Healthcare Applications* (1st ed., pp. 1–23). Chapman and Hall/CRC. DOI: 10.1201/9781032711379-1

Ablon, L., & Bogart, A. (2017). *Zero Days, Thousands of Nights: The Life and Times of Zero-Day Vulnerabilities and Their Exploits*. RAND Corporation., DOI: 10.7249/RR1751

Abutu, G., Weissman, D., Hoffmann, P., Bernstein, N., Brennan, O., & Armstrong, T. (2024). Deepcodelock: A novel deep learning-based approach for automated ransomware detection using behavioral signatures. *Authorea Preprints*. DOI: 10.36227/techrxiv.173047886.63868153/v1

Acharya, S., Dvorkin, Y., Pandžić, H., & Karri, R. (2020). Cybersecurity of Smart Electric Vehicle Charging: A Power Grid Perspective." *. *IEEE Access : Practical Innovations, Open Solutions, 8*, 214434–214449. DOI: 10.1109/ACCESS.2020.3041074

Adams, C., & Lloyd, S. (2019). *Understanding PKI: Concepts, Standards, and Deployment Considerations* (3rd ed.). Addison-Wesley Professional.

Adashek, J. J., & Kurzrock, R. (2023). Home-run trials for rare cancers: Giving the right drug (s) to the right patients at the right time and in the right place. *NPJ Precision Oncology*, *7*(1), 129. DOI: 10.1038/s41698-023-00487-5 PMID: 38066094

Adawadkar, A. M. K., & Kulkarni, N. (2022). Cyber-security and reinforcement learning — A brief survey. *Engineering Applications of Artificial Intelligence*, *114*, 105116. DOI: 10.1016/j.engappai.2022.105116

Adeniyi, O., Sadiq, A. S., Pillai, P., Taheir, M. A., & Kaiwartya, O. (2023). Proactive self-healing approaches in mobile edge computing: A systematic literature review. *Computers*, *12*(3), 63. DOI: 10.3390/computers12030063

Adeoye, I. (2023). Leveraging Artificial Intelligence and Machine Learning for Real-Time Threat Intelligence: Enhancing Incident Response Capabilities.

Agarwal, G. (2025). Explainable AI (XAI) for Cyber Defense: Enhancing Transparency and Trust in AI-Driven Security Solutions. *International Journal of Advanced Research in Science. Tongxin Jishu*, *5*(1), 132–138.

Agrawal, G., Kaur, A., & Myneni, S. (2024). A review of generative models in generating synthetic attack data for cybersecurity. *Electronics (Basel)*, *13*(2), 322. DOI: 10.3390/electronics13020322

Agrawal, S., Sarkar, S., Aouedi, O., Yenduri, G., Piamrat, K., Alazab, M., Bhattacharya, S., Maddikunta, P. K. R., & Gadekallu, T. R. (2022). Federated learning for intrusion detection system: Concepts, challenges, and future directions. *Computer Communications*, *195*, 346–361. DOI: 10.1016/j.comcom.2022.09.012

Ahmadi, S. (2024). "Zero trust architecture in cloud networks: application, challenges and future opportunities." *Ahmadi, S. (2024). Zero Trust Architecture in Cloud Networks: Application, Challenges and Future Opportunities.Journal of Engineering Research and Reports*, *26*(2), 215–228. DOI: 10.9734/jerr/2024/v26i21083

Ahmad, Z., Jaffri, Z. U. A., Chen, M., & Bao, S. (2024). Understanding GANs: Fundamentals, variants, training challenges, applications, and open problems. *Multimedia Tools and Applications*, •••, 1–77. DOI: 10.1007/s11042-024-19361-y

Ahmed, I., Syed, M. A., Maaruf, M., & Khalid, M. (2025). Distributed computing in multi-agent systems: A survey of decentralized machine learning approaches. *Computing*, *107*(1), 2. DOI: 10.1007/s00607-024-01356-0

Akbulut, O., Cavus, M., Cengiz, M., Allahham, A., Giaouris, D., & Forshaw, M. (2024). Hybrid Intelligent Control System for Adaptive Microgrid Optimization: Integration of Rule-Based Control and Deep Learning Techniques. *Energies*, *17*(10), 2260. DOI: 10.3390/en17102260

Akhtar, M. S., & Feng, T. (2022). Malware analysis and detection using machine learning algorithms. *Symmetry*, *14*(11), 2304. DOI: 10.3390/sym14112304

Akinshola-Awe, F. J., Obiniyi, A. A., Aimufua, G. I., & Anyachebelu, T. K. (2024). Framework for the detection and classification of malware using machine learning. *Dutse Journal of Pure and Applied Sciences*, *10*(3a), 177–186. DOI: 10.4314/dujopas.v10i3a.17

Alabdulatif, A., & Thilakarathne, N. N. (2024). A novel cloud-enabled cyber threat hunting platform for evaluating the cyber risks associated with smart health ecosystems. *Applied Sciences (Basel, Switzerland)*, *14*(20), 9567. DOI: 10.3390/app14209567

Alabdulwahab, S., Kim, Y. T., Seo, A., & Son, Y. (2023). Generating Synthetic Dataset for ML-Based IDS Using CTGAN and Feature Selection to Protect Smart IoT Environments. *Applied Sciences (Basel, Switzerland)*, *13*(19), 10951. DOI: 10.3390/app131910951

Alazab, A., Khraisat, A., Singh, S., & Jan, T. (2023). Enhancing privacy-preserving intrusion detection through federated learning. *Electronics (Basel)*, *12*(16), 3382. DOI: 10.3390/electronics12163382

Alazab, M., Soman, K. P., Srinivasan, S., Venkatraman, S., & Pham, V. Q. (2023). Deep learning for cyber security applications: A comprehensive survey. *Authorea Preprints*.

Albaseer, A. A., Fares, A., & Barakat, I. (2024). Deep learning anomaly detection in AI-powered intelligent power systems. *Frontiers in Energy Research*, *11*(1), 34–49.

Aldhaheri, A., Alwahedi, F., Ferrag, M. A., & Battah, A. (2024). Deep Learning for Cybersecurity in IoT Networks. *Journal of IoT Security*, *9*(3), 115–130.

Aledhari, M., Razzak, R., Parizi, R. M., & Dehghantanha, A. (2020). Federated learning: A survey on enabling technologies, protocols, and open challenges. *IEEE Access : Practical Innovations, Open Solutions*, *8*, 140699–140725. DOI: 10.1109/ACCESS.2020.3013541 PMID: 32999795

Alemerien, K. (2021). Usable Security and Privacy on Online Social Networks: Tools, Approaches, Studies, and Future Trends. [IJSI]. *International Journal of Software Innovation*, *9*(2), 35–68. DOI: 10.4018/IJSI.2021040103

Alemerien, K., Alsarayreh, S., & Altarawneh, E. (2024). Diagnosing Cardiovascular Diseases using Optimized Machine Learning Algorithms with GridSearchCV. *Journal of Applied Data Sciences*, *5*(4), 1539–1552. DOI: 10.47738/jads.v5i4.280

Alemerien, K., Al-Suhemat, S., & Almahadin, M. (2024). Towards optimized machine-learning-driven intrusion detection for Internet of Things applications. *International Journal of Information Technology : an Official Journal of Bharati Vidyapeeth's Institute of Computer Applications and Management*, •••, 1–14.

Algarni, A., & Thayananthan, V. (2022). Autonomous Vehicles: The Cybersecurity Vulnerabilities and Countermeasures for Big Data Communication." *. *Symmetry*, *14*(2494), 2494. Advance online publication. DOI: 10.3390/sym14122494

Alghushairy, O., Alsini, R., Soule, T., & Ma, X. (2020). A review of local outlier factor algorithms for outlier detection in big data streams. *Big Data and Cognitive Computing*, *5*(1), 1. DOI: 10.3390/bdcc5010001

Ali, S., Rehman, S. U., Imran, A., Adeem, G., Iqbal, Z., & Kim, K. I. (2022). Comparative evaluation of ai-based techniques for zero-day attacks detection. *Electronics (Basel)*, *11*(23), 3934. DOI: 10.3390/electronics11233934

Almaraz-Rivera, J. G., Cantoral-Ceballos, J. A., & Botero, J. F. (2023). Enhancing IoT Network Security: Unveiling the Power of Self-Supervised Learning against DDoS Attacks. *Sensors (Basel)*, *23*(21), 8701. DOI: 10.3390/s23218701 PMID: 37960401

Almomani, I., Almashat, T., & El-Shafai, W. (2024). Maloid-DS: Labeled Dataset for Android Malware Forensics. *IEEE Access : Practical Innovations, Open Solutions*, *12*, 73481–73546. DOI: 10.1109/ACCESS.2024.3400211

Almotairi, S., Ezzat, M. K., Abdelghany, M., & Salem, M. A.-M. (2021). Horizontal Review on Video Surveillance for Smart Cities: Edge Devices, Applications, Datasets, and Future Trends. *Sensors (Basel)*, *21*(11), 3913. DOI: 10.3390/s21113913 PMID: 34204058

Almseidin, M., Al-Sawwa, J., & Alkasassbeh, M. (2022). Generating a benchmark cyber multi-step attacks dataset for intrusion detection. *Journal of Intelligent & Fuzzy Systems*, *43*(3), 3679–3694. DOI: 10.3233/JIFS-213247

Almseidin, M., Al-Sawwa, J., Alkasassbeh, M., Alzubi, M., & Alrfou, K. (2024). DT-ARO: Decision tree-based artificial rabbits optimization to mitigate IoT botnet exploitation. *Journal of Network and Systems Management*, *32*(1), 14.

Almukhalfi, H., Noor, A., & Noor, T. H. (2024). Traffic management approaches using machine learning and deep learning techniques: A survey. *Engineering Applications of Artificial Intelligence*, *133*, 108147. DOI: 10.1016/j.engappai.2024.108147

Alnajim, A. M., Habib, S., Islam, M., AlRawashdeh, H. S., & Wasim, M. (2023). Exploring cybersecurity education and training techniques: A comprehensive review of traditional, virtual reality, and augmented reality approaches. *Symmetry*, *15*(12), 2175. DOI: 10.3390/sym15122175

AlOmari, H., Yaseen, Q. M., & Al-Betar, M. A. (2023). A comparative analysis of machine learning algorithms for android malware detection. *Procedia Computer Science*, *220*, 763–768. DOI: 10.1016/j.procs.2023.03.101

Alqahtani, A. H. (2023). *The detection of Advanced Persistent Threats in Software Defined Networks using Machine Learning* (Doctoral dissertation, University of Sheffield).

Alqahtani, H., & Kumar, G. (2024). Cybersecurity in Electric and Flying Vehicles: Threats, Challenges, AI Solutions & Future Directions." *. *ACM Computing Surveys*, *57*(4), 1–34. DOI: 10.1145/3697830

Al-Sawwa, J., Almseidin, M., Alkasassbeh, M., Alemerien, K., & Younisse, R. (2024). Spark-based multi-verse optimizer as wrapper features selection algorithm for phishing attack challenge. *Cluster Computing*, *27*(5), 1–16. DOI: 10.1007/s10586-024-04272-2

Alsharif, E., & Alharby, M. (2025). An Ensemble Machine Learning Approach for Detecting and Classifying Malware Attacks on Mobile Devices. *Arabian Journal for Science and Engineering*. Advance online publication. DOI: 10.1007/s13369-025-10011-5

Al-Shehari, T., Kadrie, M., Al-Mhiqani, M. N., Alfakih, T., Alsalman, H., Uddin, M., Ullah, S. S., & Dandoush, A. (2024). Comparative evaluation of data imbalance addressing techniques for CNN-based insider threat detection. *Scientific Reports*, *14*(1), 24715. DOI: 10.1038/s41598-024-73510-9 PMID: 39433789

Alshehri, A., Khan, N., Alowayr, A., & Alghamdi, M. Y. (2023). Cyberattack Detection Framework Using Machine Learning and User Behavior Analytics. *Computer Systems Science and Engineering*, *44*(2), 1679–1689. DOI: 10.32604/csse.2023.026526

Alviani, R., Purwandari, B., Eitiveni, I., & Purwaningsih, M. (2023). Factors affecting adoption of telemedicine for virtual healthcare services in Indonesia. *J. Inf. Syst. Eng. Bus. Intell*, *9*(1), 4769. DOI: 10.20473/jisebi.9.1.47-69

Amadeo, R. (March 7, 2022). "Android 12L is official as "Android 12.1," rolling out now to Pixel phones". Ars Technica. Archived from the original on March 7, 2022. Retrieved January 27, 2025.

Aminu, M., Akinsanya, A., Dako, D. A., & Oyedokun, O. (2024). Enhancing cyber threat detection through real-time threat intelligence and adaptive defense mechanisms. *International Journal of Computer Applications Technology and Research, 13*(8), 11–27.

Amirkhani, A., & Barshooi, A. H. (2022). Consensus in multi-agent systems: A review. *Artificial Intelligence Review, 55*(5), 3897–3935. DOI: 10.1007/s10462-021-10097-x

Ammara, D. A., Ding, J., & Tutschku, K. (2024). Synthetic Data Generation in Cybersecurity: A Comparative Analysis. *arXiv preprint arXiv:2410.16326.*

Anandhi, V., Vinod, P., & Menon, V. G., ER, A. K., Shilesh, A., Viswam, A., & Shafiq, A. (2023, February). Malware Detection using Dynamic Analysis. In *2023 International Conference on Advances in Intelligent Computing and Applications (AICAPS)* (pp. 1-6). IEEE.

Anderson, J. P. (1980). *Computer security threat monitoring and surveillance (Technical report).* James P. Anderson Co.

Anderson, R. (2020). *Security Engineering: A Guide to Building Dependable Distributed Systems* (3rd ed.). Wiley., DOI: 10.1002/9781119644682

Andreoni, M., Lunardi, W. T., Lawton, G., & Thakkar, S. (2024). Enhancing autonomous system security and resilience with generative AI: A comprehensive survey. *IEEE Access : Practical Innovations, Open Solutions, 12*, 109470–109493. DOI: 10.1109/ACCESS.2024.3439363

Antonakakis, M., April, T., Bailey, M., Bernhard, M., Bursztein, E., Cochran, J., & Zhou, Y. (2021). Understanding the Mirai Botnet. In *USENIX Security Symposium.* DOI: DOI: 10.1145/3243734.3243857

Apruzzese, G., Colajanni, M., Ferretti, L., Guido, A., & Marchetti, M. (2018). On the effectiveness of machine and deep learning for cyber security. *2018 10th International Conference on Cyber Conflict (CyCon)*, 371–390. DOI: 10.23919/CYCON.2018.8405026

Archana, R., & Jeevaraj, P. E. (2024). Deep learning models for digital image processing: A review. *Artificial Intelligence Review, 57*(1), 11. DOI: 10.1007/s10462-023-10631-z

Arefin, S., & Simcox, M. (2024). AI-Driven Solutions for Safeguarding Healthcare Data: Innovations in Cybersecurity. *International Business Research, 17*(6), 1–74. DOI: 10.5539/ibr.v17n6p74

Arif, A., Khan, M. I., & Khan, A. R. A. (2024). An overview of cyber threats generated by AI. *International Journal of Multidisciplinary Sciences and Arts, 3*(4), 67–76.

Arifin, M. M., Ahmed, M. S., Ghosh, T. K., Udoy, I. A., Zhuang, J., & Yeh, J. H. (2024). A survey on the application of generative adversarial networks in cybersecurity: prospective, direction and open research scopes. *arXiv preprint arXiv:2407.08839.*

Arizal, A. F. A., Md-Arshad, M., Abdul-Samad, A., Sirat, M. M., & Othman, S. H. (2024). Performance Comparative Study on Zero Day Malware Detection Using XGBoost and Random Forest Classifiers. *International Journal of Innovative Computing, 14*(2), 33–40. DOI: 10.11113/ijic.v14n2.449

Arnesen, C. S., & Krohn, H. H. (2024). *Strengthening incident response efforts in operational technology environments* (Master's thesis, University of Agder).

Arora, A.. "Hybrid Android malware detection by combining supervised and unsupervised learning." *Proceedings of the 24th Annual International Conference on Mobile Computing and Networking*. 2018. DOI: 10.1145/3241539.3267768

Arora, A., & Shantanu, . (2022). A review on application of GANs in cybersecurity domain. *IETE Technical Review, 39*(2), 433–441. DOI: 10.1080/02564602.2020.1854058

Arp, D., Spreitzenbarth, M., Hubner, M., Gascon, H., Rieck, K., & Siemens, C. E. R. T. (2014, February). Drebin: Effective and explainable detection of android malware in your pocket. In Ndss (Vol. 14, pp. 23-26).

Arulkumaran, K., Deisenroth, M. P., Brundage, M., & Bharath, A. A. (2017). Deep reinforcement learning: A brief survey. *IEEE Signal Processing Magazine, 34*(6), 26–38. DOI: 10.1109/MSP.2017.2743240

Asghar, M. Z., Afzaal, M. N., Iqbal, J., & Sadia, H. A. (2022). Analyzing an appropriate blend of face-to-face, offline and online learning approaches for the in-service vocational teacher's training program. *International Journal of Environmental Research and Public Health, 19*(17), 10668. DOI: 10.3390/ijerph191710668 PMID: 36078385

Atiku, S. B., Aaron, A. U., Job, G. K., Shittu, F., & Yakubu, I. Z. (2020). Survey on the Applications of Artificial Intelligence in Cyber Security. *International Journal of Scientific & Technology Research, 9*(1), 6–10.

Atlantic Council. (2023). *Breaking Trust: Shades of Crisis Across an Insecure Software Supply Chain*. Atlantic Council's Cyber Statecraft Initiative.

Attota, D. C., Mothukuri, V., Parizi, R. M., & Pouriyeh, S. (2021). An ensemble multi-view federated learning intrusion detection for IoT. *IEEE Access : Practical Innovations, Open Solutions*, *9*, 117734–117745. DOI: 10.1109/ACCESS.2021.3107337

Avgerinos, T., Brumley, D., Davis, J., Goulden, R., Nighswander, T., Rebert, A., & Williamson, N. (2018). The Mayhem cyber reasoning system. *IEEE Security and Privacy*, *16*(2), 52–60. DOI: 10.1109/MSP.2018.1870873

Awad, A. I., Babu, A., Barka, E., & Shuaib, K. (2024). AI-powered biometrics for Internet of Things security: A review and future vision. *Journal of Information Security and Applications*, *82*, 103748. DOI: 10.1016/j.jisa.2024.103748

Awadallah, A., Eledlebi, K., Zemerly, J., Puthal, D., Damiani, E., Taha, K., Kim, T.-Y., Yoo, P. D., Choo, K.-K. R., Yim, M.-S., & Yeun, C. Y. (2024). Artificial intelligence-based cybersecurity for the metaverse: Research challenges and opportunities. *IEEE Communications Surveys and Tutorials*, 1. DOI: 10.1109/COMST.2024.3442475

AWS. (2022). What is deep learning? - Deep learning AI explained. *AWS AI Insights*, *13*(1), 45–56.

AWS. (2023). *AWS Security Best Practices*. Amazon Web Services. Retrieved from https://aws.amazon.com/security

Ayyaz, S., & Malik, S. M. (2024, October). A Comprehensive Study of Generative Adversarial Networks (GAN) and Generative Pre-Trained Transformers (GPT) in Cybersecurity. In *2024 Sixth International Conference on Intelligent Computing in Data Sciences (ICDS)* (pp. 1-8). IEEE. DOI: 10.1109/ICDS62089.2024.10756505

Azab, A., Khasawneh, M., Alrabaee, S., Choo, K. K. R., & Sarsour, M. (2024). Network traffic classification: Techniques, datasets, and challenges. *Digital Communications and Networks*, *10*(3), 676–692. DOI: 10.1016/j.dcan.2022.09.009

Azeem, M., Khan, D., Iftikhar, S., Bawazeer, S., & Alzahrani, M. (2024). Analyzing and comparing the effectiveness of malware detection: A study of machine learning approaches. *Heliyon*, *10*(1), e23574. DOI: 10.1016/j.heliyon.2023.e23574 PMID: 38187275

Babai, L. (1985). Trading group theory for randomness. *Proceedings of the 17th ACM Symposium on Theory of Computing*.

Backes, M., Hofheinz, D., & Müller-Quade, J. (2005). A cryptographic model for branching time security. *Proceedings of the 18th IEEE Computer Security Foundations Workshop (CSFW).*

Bagdasaryan, E., Veit, A., Hua, Y., Estrin, D., & Shmatikov, V. (2020). How to backdoor federated learning. *Proceedings of the 23rd International Conference on Artificial Intelligence and Statistics (AISTATS)*, 2938–2948. PMLR.

Bairwa, A. K., Yadav, R., Rao, D. D., Naidu, K., H C, Y., & Sharma, S. (2024). Implications of Cyber-Physical Adversarial Attacks on Autonomous Systems. *Int. J. Exp. Res. Rev*, *46*, 273–284. DOI: 10.52756/ijerr.2024.v46.021

Bai, Y., Zhao, H., Zhang, X., Chang, Z., Jäntti, R., & Yang, K. (2023). Towards autonomous multi-UAV wireless network: A survey of reinforcement learning-based approaches. *IEEE Communications Surveys and Tutorials*, *25*(4), 3038–3067. DOI: 10.1109/COMST.2023.3323344

Baker McKenzie. (2023). *Global Data Breach Notification Guide*. Baker McKenzie. Retrieved from https://www.bakermckenzie.com

Balantrapu, S. S. (2024). AI for predictive cyber threat intelligence. *International Journal of Management Education for Sustainable Development*, *7*(7), 1–28.

Baniecki, H., & Biecek, P. (2024). Adversarial attacks and defenses in explainable artificial intelligence: A survey. *Information Fusion*, *107*, 102303. DOI: 10.1016/j.inffus.2024.102303

Barker, E., Barker, W., Burr, W., Polk, W., & Smid, M. (2020). *Recommendation for Key Management: Part 1 – General (Revision 5)*. National Institute of Standards and Technology., DOI: 10.6028/NIST.SP.800-57pt1r5

Basak, S., Chatterjee, P., Biswas, D., Bhadra, P., & Das, R. (2024). Machine Learning Applications in Cybersecurity: Threat Detection and Prevention. *Machine Learning*, *18*(3), 130–145.

Bashshur, R., Doarn, C. R., Frenk, J. M., Kvedar, J. C., & Woolliscroft, J. O. (2020). Telemedicine and the COVID-19 pandemic, lessons for the future. *Telemedicine Journal and e-Health*, *26*(5), 571–573. DOI: 10.1089/tmj.2020.29040.rb PMID: 32275485

Batarseh, F., Haugh, L., & Wang, T. (2024). Soft sensors and predictive measurements for water quality monitoring. *Environmental Engineering Science*, *45*(2), 105–119.

Batouche, A., & Jahankhani, H. (2021). A comprehensive approach to android malware detection using machine learning. Information Security Technologies for Controlling Pandemics, 171-212.

Becerra-Suarez, F. L., Tuesta-Monteza, V. A., Mejia-Cabrera, H. I., & Arce, J. A. (2024). AI-Driven Cybersecurity Approaches for Industrial Systems. *International Journal of Artificial Intelligence, 13*(1), 44–58.

Bello, O. A., & Olufemi, K. (2024). Artificial intelligence in fraud prevention: Exploring techniques and applications challenges and opportunities. *Computer science & IT research journal, 5*(6), 1505-1520.

Bengesi, S., El-Sayed, H., Sarker, M. K., Houkpati, Y., Irungu, J., & Oladunni, T. (2024). Advancements in Generative AI: A Comprehensive Review of GANs, GPT, Autoencoders, Diffusion Model, and Transformers. *IEEE Access : Practical Innovations, Open Solutions, 12*, 69812–69837. DOI: 10.1109/ACCESS.2024.3397775

Bensaoud, A., Kalita, J., & Bensaoud, M. (2024). A survey of malware detection using deep learning. *Machine Learning with Applications, 16*, 100546. DOI: 10.1016/j.mlwa.2024.100546

Ben-Sasson, M., Chiesa, E., Gabizon, A., & Riabzev, M. (2018). Scalable transparent arguments of knowledge. Advances in Cryptology—EUROCRYPT 2018, 35-64.

Beretas, C. (2024). Information systems security, detection and recovery from cyber attacks. *Universal Library of Engineering Technology, 1*(1).

Berman, D. S., Buczak, A. L., Chavis, J. S., & Corbett, C. L. (2019). A survey of deep learning methods for cyber security. *Computers & Security, 85*, 308–350.

Berman, D. S., Buczak, A. L., Chavis, J. S., & Corbett, C. L. (2019). A survey of deep learning methods for cyber security. *IEEE Communications Surveys and Tutorials, 21*(3), 2214–2241. DOI: 10.1109/COMST.2019.2916180

Bernstein, D. J. (2005). The Poly1305-AES message-authentication code. Fast Software Encryption, 32-49.

Bhaskaran, S. V. (2023). Resilient real-time data delivery for ai summarization in conversational platforms: Ensuring low latency, high availability, and disaster recovery. *Journal of Intelligent Connectivity and Emerging Technologies, 8*(3), 113–130.

Bhattarai, K., Oh, I. Y., Sierra, J. M., Tang, J., Payne, P. R., Abrams, Z., & Lai, A. M. (2024). Leveraging GPT-4 for identifying cancer phenotypes in electronic health records: A performance comparison between GPT-4, GPT-3.5-turbo, Flan-T5, Llama-3-8B, and spaCy's rule-based and machine learning-based methods. *JAMIA Open*, *7*(3), ooae060. DOI: 10.1093/jamiaopen/ooae060 PMID: 38962662

Bhatt, R., & Indra, G. (2024). Detecting the undetectable: GAN-based strategies for network intrusion detection. *International Journal of Information Technology : an Official Journal of Bharati Vidyapeeth's Institute of Computer Applications and Management*, *16*(8), 5231–5237. DOI: 10.1007/s41870-024-02172-7

Bibi, U., Mazhar, M., Sabir, D., Muhammad, F. U. B., Hassan, A., Ghazanfar, M. A., Khan, A. A., & Abdul, W. (2024). Advances in Pruning and Quantization for Natural Language Processing. *IEEE Access : Practical Innovations, Open Solutions*, *12*, 139113–139128. DOI: 10.1109/ACCESS.2024.3465631

Biggio, B., & Roli, F. (2018). Wild patterns: Ten years after the rise of adversarial machine learning. *Pattern Recognition*, *84*, 317–331. DOI: 10.1016/j.patcog.2018.07.023

Bilge, L., & Dumitraş, T. (2012). Before we knew it: An empirical study of zero-day attacks in the real world. *Proceedings of the 2012 ACM Conference on Computer and Communications Security*, 833–844. DOI: 10.1145/2382196.2382284

Bist, A. S. (2018). Survey of Deep Learning Algorithms for Malware Detection. *International Journal of Computer Science and Information Security*, *16*(3), 108–115.

Boddy, M., Jones, C., & Horowitz, B. (2014). Course-of-action generation for cyber security using classical planning. In *Proceedings of the AAAI Workshop on Artificial Intelligence for Cyber Security (AICS)*. AAAI Press.

Bonawitz, K., Ivanov, V., Kreuter, B., Marcedone, A., McMahan, H. B., Patel, S., & Seth, K. (2017). Practical secure aggregation for privacy-preserving machine learning. *Proceedings of the 2017 ACM SIGSAC Conference on Computer and Communications Security (CCS)*, 1175–1191. ACM. DOI: 10.1145/3133956.3133982

Boneh, D., Lynn, B., & Shacham, H. (2004). Short signatures from the Weil pairing. *Journal of Cryptology*, *17*(4), 297–319. DOI: 10.1007/s00145-004-0314-9

Boppiniti, S. T. (2021). Evolution of Reinforcement Learning: From Q-Learning to Deep. Available at *SSRN* 5061696.

Borah, P., Bhattacharyya, D. K., & Kalita, J. K. (2020, December). Malware dataset generation and evaluation. In 2020 IEEE 4th Conference on Information & Communication Technology (CICT) (pp. 1-6). IEEE.

Botta, A., Rotbei, S., Zinno, S., & Ventre, G. (2023). Cyber security of robots: A comprehensive survey. *Intelligent Systems with Applications*, *18*, 200237. DOI: 10.1016/j.iswa.2023.200237

Bradshaw, K. (April 22, 2022). "Android 14 gets official internal codename… Upside Down Cake". 9to5Google. Archived from the original on January 14, 2024. Retrieved January 27, 2025.

Bridges, R. A., Rice, A. E., Oesch, S., Nichols, J. A., Watson, C., Spakes, K., Norem, S., Huettel, M., Jewell, B., Weber, B., Gannon, C., Bizovi, O., Hollifield, S. C., & Erwin, S. (2023). Testing SOAR tools in use. *Computers & Security*, *129*, 103201. DOI: 10.1016/j.cose.2023.103201

Bryghtpath. (2024). Harnessing AI in cybersecurity: Enhancing threat detection. *Bryghtpath Cybersecurity Insights, 8(1),* 112-125.

Buczak, A. L., & Guven, E. (2016). A survey of data mining and machine learning methods for cyber security intrusion detection. *IEEE Communications Surveys and Tutorials*, *18*(2), 1153–1176. DOI: 10.1109/COMST.2015.2494502

Budžys, A., Kurasova, O., & Medvedev, V. (2024). Deep learning-based authentication for insider threat detection in critical infrastructure. *Artificial Intelligence Review*, *57*(10), 272. DOI: 10.1007/s10462-024-10893-1

Burger, C. (2025). Autonomous Cyber AI is Revolutionizing Cyber Defense. CISO MAG. Retrieved from https://cisomag.com/

Burgner, J., Swaney, P. J., Lathrop, R. A., Weaver, K. D., & Webster, R. J. (2013). Debulking from within: A robotic steerable cannula for intracerebral hemorrhage evacuation. *IEEE Transactions on Biomedical Engineering*, *60*(9), 2567–2575. DOI: 10.1109/TBME.2013.2260860 PMID: 23649131

Burton, S. L. (2022). *Cybersecurity Leadership from a Telemedicine/Telehealth Knowledge and Organizational Development Examination*. Capitol Technology University.

Caicedo, C. E., Joshi, J. B. D., & Tuladhar, S. R. (2022). IPv6 Security: Attacks and Countermeasures in a Nutshell. *IEEE Security and Privacy*. Advance online publication. DOI: 10.1109/MSEC.2022.3151234

Calder, A. (2020). *Implementing Information Security Based on ISO 27001/ISO 27002* (3rd ed.). IT Governance Publishing.

Caltagirone, S., Pendergast, A., & Betz, C. (2018). *The Diamond Model of Intrusion Analysis*. Threat Connect.

Camacho, N. G. (2024). The role of AI in cybersecurity: Addressing threats in the digital age. *Journal of Artificial Intelligence General science (JAIGS) ISSN: 3006-4023, 3*(1), 143-154.

Canetti, R. (2001). Universally composable security: A new paradigm for cryptographic protocols. *42nd Annual Symposium on Foundations of Computer Science*. DOI: 10.1109/SFCS.2001.959888

Canfora, G., Medvet, E., Mercaldo, F., & Visaggio, C. A. (2015, August). Detecting android malware using sequences of system calls. In *Proceedings of the 3rd international workshop on software development lifecycle for mobile* (pp. 13-20). DOI: 10.1145/2804345.2804349

Cantisano, T. (March 3, 2023). "Android 15 dessert-themed codename revealed as 'Vanilla Ice Cream'". XDA Developers. Retrieved January 27, 2025.

Cao, J., Kwong, S., Wang, R., Li, X., Li, K., & Kong, X. (2015). Class-specific soft voting based multiple extreme learning machines ensemble. *Neurocomputing*, *149*, 275–284. DOI: 10.1016/j.neucom.2014.02.072

Capuano, N., Fenza, G., Loia, V., & Stanzione, C. (2022). Explainable Artificial Intelligence in CyberSecurity: A Survey. *IEEE Access : Practical Innovations, Open Solutions*, *10*, 93575–93600. DOI: 10.1109/ACCESS.2022.3204171

Carmona-Lavado, A., Gimenez-Fernandez, E. M., Vlaisavljevic, V., & Cabello-Medina, C. (2023). Cross-industry innovation: A systematic literature review. *Technovation*, *124*, 102743. DOI: 10.1016/j.technovation.2023.102743

Carnegie Mellon University CyLab. (2021). Towards Autonomous Cybersecurity Systems: The Role of AI in Continuous Threat Monitoring.

Casey, E. (2022). *Digital Evidence and Computer Crime: Forensic Science, Computers, and the Internet* (4th ed.). Academic Press., DOI: 10.1016/C2019-0-00001-9

CERT Insider Threat Center. (2023). *Common Sense Guide to Mitigating Insider Threats* (7th ed.). Software Engineering Institute, Carnegie Mellon University.

Cetin, B., Lazar, A., Kim, J., Sim, A., & Wu, K. (2019). Federated wireless network intrusion detection. *Proceedings of the 2019 IEEE International Conference on Big Data*, 6004–6006. IEEE. DOI: 10.1109/BigData47090.2019.9005507

Chainalysis. (2023). *The Chainalysis Crypto Crime Report*. Chainalysis Inc. Retrieved from https://www.chainalysis.com

Chairopoulou, S. (2024). *Cybersecurity in industrial control systems: a roadmap for fortifying operations* (Master's thesis).

Chakraborty, S. https://www.kaggle.com/datasets/subhajournal/android-malware-detection, Retrieved January 27, 2025.

Chandrashekar, C., Dhamale, A. K., & IR, P. J. (2023, July). Machine Learning Based Malicious URL, IP & File Classification. In 2023 14th International Conference on Computing Communication and Networking Technologies (ICCCNT) (pp. 1-8). IEEE.

Chandwani, A., Dey, S., & Mallik, A. (2020). Cybersecurity of Onboard Charging Systems for Electric Vehicles—Review, Challenges and Countermeasures." *. *IEEE Access : Practical Innovations, Open Solutions*, *8*, 226982–226994. DOI: 10.1109/ACCESS.2020.3045367

Chapple, M., & Seidl, D. (2021). *Cyberwarfare: Information Operations in a Connected World* (2nd ed.). Jones & Bartlett Learning.

Chatziamanetoglou, D., & Rantos, K. (2024). Cyber threat intelligence on blockchain: A systematic literature review. *Computers*, *13*(3), 60. DOI: 10.3390/computers13030060

Chen, J., Yan, H., Liu, Z., Zhang, M., Xiong, H., & Yu, S. (2024). When federated learning meets privacy-preserving computation. *ACM Computing Surveys*, *56*(12), 1–36. DOI: 10.1145/3679013

Chen, S. (2023). A counterinsurgent (COIN) framework to defend against consumer activists. *Journal of Brand Management*, *30*(4), 275–301. DOI: 10.1057/s41262-022-00297-3

Chen, S., Zhang, L., Yan, Z., & Shen, Z. (2021). A distributed and robust security-constrained economic dispatch algorithm based on blockchain. *IEEE Transactions on Power Systems*, *37*(1), 691–700. DOI: 10.1109/TPWRS.2021.3086101

Chiesa, M., Kamisiński, A., Rak, J., Rétvári, G., & Schmid, S. (2023). A survey of fast recovery mechanisms in the data plane. *Authorea Preprints*.

Chinthala, S. (2024). Analyzing the Effectiveness of SIEM Tools in Threat Mitigation for Critical Infrastructure. *Journal of Cyber Defense*, *11*(4), 125–137.

Chirra, B. R. (2020). Advancing Cyber Defense: Machine Learning Techniques for Next-Generation Intrusion Detection. *International Journal of Machine Learning Research in Cybersecurity and Artificial Intelligence*, *14*(1), 550–573.

Chirra, B. R. (2020). Intelligent Phishing Mitigation: Leveraging AI for Enhanced Email Security in Corporate Environments. *International Journal of Advanced Engineering Technologies and Innovations*, *1*(2), 178–200.

Chirra, B. R. (2021). AI-Driven Vulnerability Assessment and Mitigation Strategies for Cyber-Physical Systems. *Revista de Inteligencia Artificial en Medicina, 13*(1), 471–493.

Chirra, B. R. (2022). Advancing Real-Time Malware Detection with Deep Learning for Proactive Threat Mitigation. *International Journal of Advanced Engineering Technologies and Innovations, 1*(01), 274–396.

Chirra, B. R. (2023). Enhancing Cloud Security through Quantum Cryptography for Robust Data Transmission. *Revista de Inteligencia Artificial en Medicina, 15*(1), 752–775.

Chirra, B. R. (2023). Enhancing Cybersecurity Resilience: Federated Learning-Driven Threat Intelligence for Adaptive Defense. *International Journal of Machine Learning Research in Cybersecurity and Artificial Intelligence, 11*(1), 260–280.

Chirra, D. R. (2020). AI-Based Real-Time Security Monitoring for Cloud-Native Applications in Hybrid Cloud Environments. *Revista de Inteligencia Artificial en Medicina, 11*(1), 382–402.

Chirra, D. R. (2021). AI-Enabled Cybersecurity Solutions for Protecting Smart Cities Against Emerging Threats. *International Journal of Advanced Engineering Technologies and Innovations, 1*(2), 237–254.

Chirra, D. R. (2022). Next-Generation IDS: AI-Driven Intrusion Detection for Securing 5G Network Architectures. *International Journal of Advanced Engineering Technologies and Innovations, 1*(2), 230–245.

Chirra, D. R. (2022b). Towards an AI-Driven Automated Cybersecurity Incident Response System. *International Journal of Advanced Engineering Technologies and Innovations, 1*(1), 15–30.

Chirra, D. R. (2023). AI-Augmented Zero Trust Architectures: Enhancing Cybersecurity in Dynamic Enterprise Environments. *International Journal of Machine Learning Research in Cybersecurity and Artificial Intelligence, 15*(1), 643–669.

Chismon, D., & Ruks, M. (2018). *Threat Intelligence: Collecting, Analysing, Evaluating*. MWR InfoSecurity.

Chukwunweike, J. N., Ayodele, P. A., & Atata, B. B. (2024). A. Praise, and B. A. Bashirat. "Harnessing Machine Learning for Cybersecurity: How Convolutional Neural Networks are Revolutionizing Threat Detection and Data Privacy.". *International Journal of Research Publication and Reviews, 5*(8), 3608–3617. DOI: 10.55248/gengpi.5.0824.2402

Chukwunweike, J. N., Yussuf, M., Okusi, O., & Oluwatobi, T. (2024). The role of deep learning in ensuring privacy integrity and security: Applications in AI-driven cybersecurity solutions. *World Journal of Advanced Research and Reviews*, *23*(2), 2550.

Chung, T., Lok, J., Chandrasekaran, B., Choffnes, D., Levin, D., Maggs, B. M., . . . Wilson, C. (2021). Is the Web Ready for HTTPS? Measuring Adoption and Error Rates. In *ACM SIGCOMM*. DOI: DOI: 10.1145/3452296.3472912

CISA. (2022). *Colonial Pipeline Response: Operation Flashpoint*. Cybersecurity and Infrastructure Security Agency. Retrieved from https://www.cisa.gov

CISA. (2023). *Cross-Sector Cybersecurity Performance Goals*. Cybersecurity and Infrastructure Security Agency. Retrieved from https://www.cisa.gov

CISA. (2023). Cybersecurity Best Practices for Smart Cities. (Joint cybersecurity guidance by CISA, NSA, FBI, NCSC-UK, ACSC, CCCS, NCSC-NZ). Retrieved from https://cisa.gov/

Cisco. (2023). *Annual Internet Security Report*. Cisco Systems. Retrieved from https://www.cisco.com

Cloarec, J., Cadieu, C., & Alrabie, N. (2024). Tracking technologies in eHealth: Revisiting the personalization-privacy paradox through the transparency-control framework. *Technological Forecasting and Social Change*, *200*, 123101. DOI: 10.1016/j.techfore.2023.123101

Cobb, M. (2022). *The Essentials of Computer Security* (2nd ed.). Auerbach Publications.

Coleman, G. (2022). *Hacker, Hoaxer, Whistleblower, Spy: The Many Faces of Anonymous*. Verso Books.

Commission, I. P. (2023). *The IP Commission Report on the Theft of American Intellectual Property*. National Bureau of Asian Research. Retrieved from https://www.nbr.org

Compliance Week. (2023). *Cybersecurity Compliance Handbook*. Compliance Week. Retrieved from https://www.complianceweek.com

Cook, T. (2022). The Role of Machine Learning in Autonomous Cybersecurity: A Review. *Journal of Cybersecurity Research*, *5*(3), 45–59.

Cordey, S. (2023). *Software supply chain attacks: An illustrated typological review*. ETH Zurich.

Cordón, I., Luengo, J., García, S., Herrera, F., & Charte, F. (2019). Smart data: Data preprocessing to achieve smart data in R. *Neurocomputing*, *360*, 1–13. DOI: 10.1016/j.neucom.2019.06.006

Corman, A. (2023). The Human Element in Cybersecurity–Bridging the Gap Between Technology and Human Behaviour.

Coulthard, B., & Taylor, B. J. (2023). *Big data analytics for making decisions and managing risk*. Sage. DOI: 10.4135/9781529614657.n50

Crinnion, W., Ben Jackson, A. S., Lynch, J., Bergeles, C., Liu, H., Rhode, K., Pereira, V. M., & Booth, T. C. (2022). Robotics in neurointerventional surgery: A systematic review of the literature. *Journal of Neurointerventional Surgery*, *14*(6), 539–545. DOI: 10.1136/neurintsurg-2021-018096 PMID: 34799439

Croce, V., Caroti, G., De Luca, L., Piemonte, A., & Véron, P. (2023). Neural radiance fields (nerf): Review and potential applications to digital cultural heritage. *The International Archives of the Photogrammetry, Remote Sensing and Spatial Information Sciences*, *48*, 453–460. DOI: 10.5194/isprs-archives-XLVIII-M-2-2023-453-2023

CrowdStrike. (2023). *Global Threat Report*. CrowdStrike. Retrieved from https://www.crowdstrike.com

CyberArk. (2023). *Global Advanced Threat Landscape Report*. CyberArk. Retrieved from https://www.cyberark.com

Cybereason. (2022). *SolarWinds: The Long Tail of the APT Campaign*. Cybereason. Retrieved from https://www.cybereason.com

Dahiya, A., Singh, S., & Shrivastava, G. (2025). Android malware analysis and detection: A systematic review. *Expert Systems: International Journal of Knowledge Engineering and Neural Networks*, *42*(1), e13488. DOI: 10.1111/exsy.13488

Dai, L. (2024). A Unified Algebraic Framework Extending From a 6-Set Discrete Probability Model. *Journal of Computational Mathematics*, *13*(4), 50–64.

Damaraju, A. (2020). Social Media as a Cyber Threat Vector: Trends and Preventive Measures. *Revista Española de Documentación Cientifica*, *14*(1), 95–112.

Damaraju, A. (2021). Data Privacy Regulations and Their Impact on Global Businesses. *Pakistan Journal of Linguistics*, *2*(01), 47–56.

Damaraju, A. (2022). Securing Critical Infrastructure: Advanced Strategies for Resilience and Threat Mitigation in the Digital Age. *Revista de Inteligencia Artificial en Medicina*, *12*(1), 76–111.

Damaševičius, R., Venčkauskas, A., Toldinas, J., & Grigaliūnas, Š. (2021). Ensemble-based classification using neural networks and machine learning models for windows pe malware detection. *Electronics (Basel)*, *10*(4), 485. DOI: 10.3390/electronics10040485

DARPA. (2016). *Cyber Grand Challenge (CGC) – Final results and findings*. Retrieved from https://www.darpa.mil/program/cyber-grand-challenge

DARPA. (2023). *AI and Security: Lessons, Challenges and Future Directions*. Defense Advanced Research Projects Agency. Retrieved from https://www.darpa.mil

Dash, A., Ye, J., & Wang, G. (2023). A review of generative adversarial networks (GANs) and its applications in a wide variety of disciplines: From medical to remote sensing. *IEEE Access : Practical Innovations, Open Solutions*.

DATAVERSITY. (2022). A brief history of deep learning. *DATAVERSITY Publications*, *7*(4), 15–28.

De Wilde, P., Arora, P., Buarque de Lima Neto, F., Chin, Y., Thinyane, M., Stinckwich, S., ... & Marwala, T. (2024). Recommendations on the Use of Synthetic Data to Train AI Models.

Dehghantanha, A., Yazdinejad, A., & Parizi, R. M. "Autonomous Cybersecurity: Evolving Challenges, Emerging Opportunities, and Future Research Trajectories." In *Proceedings of the Workshop on Autonomous Cybersecurity*, pp. 1-10. 2023. DOI: 10.1145/3689933.3690832

Deldar, F., & Abadi, M. (2023). Deep learning for zero-day malware detection and classification: A survey. *ACM Computing Surveys*, *56*(2), 1–37. DOI: 10.1145/3605775

Deloitte. (2023). *Future of Cyber Survey*. Deloitte Touche Tohmatsu Limited. Retrieved from https://www2.deloitte.com

Demertzis, K., Tziritas, N., Kikiras, P., Sanchez, L. S., & Iliadis, L. (2019). The Next Generation Cognitive Security Operations Center: Adaptive Analytic Lambda Architecture for Efficient Defense Against Adversarial Attacks. *IEEE Transactions on Industrial Informatics*, *15*(5), 2908–2915.

Denning, D. E. (1987). An intrusion-detection model. *IEEE Transactions on Software Engineering*, *2*(2), 222–232. DOI: 10.1109/TSE.1987.232894

Desai, B., Patil, K., Mehta, I., & Patil, A. (2024, September). Explainable AI in Cybersecurity: A Comprehensive Framework for enhancing transparency, trust, and Human-AI Collaboration. In *2024 International Seminar on Application for Technology of Information and Communication (iSemantic)* (pp. 135-150). IEEE. DOI: 10.1109/iSemantic63362.2024.10762690

Devadiga, D., Jin, G., Potdar, B., Koo, H., Han, A., Shringi, A., . . . Kumar, S. (2023, October). Gleam: Gan and llm for evasive adversarial malware. In *2023 14th International Conference on Information and Communication Technology Convergence (ICTC)* (pp. 53-58). IEEE.

Dhoni, P., & Kumar, R. (2023). Synergizing generative ai and cybersecurity: Roles of generative ai entities, companies, agencies, and government in enhancing cybersecurity. *Authorea Preprints.*

Dick, K., Russell, L., Souley Dosso, Y., Kwamena, F., & Green, J. R. (2024). Enhancing IoT Security with Deep Learning. *Journal of Internet of Things, 10*(3), 112–126.

Diffie, W., & Hellman, M. (2018). New Directions in Cryptography. *IEEE Transactions on Information Theory*. Advance online publication. DOI: 10.1109/TIT.2018.2796694

Djaidja, T. E. T., Brik, B., Senouci, S. M., Boualouache, A., & Ghamri-Doudane, Y. (2024). Early network intrusion detection enabled by attention mechanisms and RNNs. *IEEE Transactions on Information Forensics and Security, 19*, 7783–7793. DOI: 10.1109/TIFS.2024.3441862

Do Yoo, J., Kim, H., & Kim, H. K. (2024). GUIDE: GAN-based UAV IDS Enhancement. *Computers & Security, 147*, 104073. DOI: 10.1016/j.cose.2024.104073

Dritsas, E., & Trigka, M. (2025). A Survey on Cybersecurity in IoT. *Future Internet, 17*(1), 30. DOI: 10.3390/fi17010030

Drolet, M. A. T. H. I. E. U., & Roberge, V. (2022). Enterprise Malware Detection using Digital Forensic Artifacts and Machine Learning. MA Sc. Thesis, Royal Military College of Canada, Kingston, Ontario.

Dunmore, A., Jang-Jaccard, J., Sabrina, F., & Kwak, J. (2023). A comprehensive survey of generative adversarial networks (GANs) in cybersecurity intrusion detection. *IEEE Access : Practical Innovations, Open Solutions, 11*, 76071–76094. DOI: 10.1109/ACCESS.2023.3296707

Duy, P. T., Minh, V. Q., Dang, B. T. H., Son, N. D. H., Quyen, N. H., & Pham, V. H. (2024). A study on adversarial sample resistance and Defense Mechanism for Multimodal Learning-based phishing website detection. *IEEE Access : Practical Innovations, Open Solutions, 12*, 137805–137824. DOI: 10.1109/ACCESS.2024.3436812

Dziembowski, S., & Pietrzak, K. (2008). Intrusion-resilient secret sharing. *IEEE Transactions on Information Theory*, *54*(6), 2798–2806.

Edmund, E., & Enemosah, A. (2024). AI and machine learning in cybersecurity: Leveraging AI to predict, detect, and respond to threats more efficiently.

Ehis, A. M. T. (2023). Optimization of security information and event management (SIEM) infrastructures, and events correlation/regression analysis for optimal cyber security posture. *Archives of Advanced Engineering Science*, 1-10.

Elgin, B. (2005). "Google Buys Android for Its Mobile Arsenal". Bloomberg Businessweek. Bloomberg. Archived from the original on February 27, 2011. Retrieved January 27, 2025.

Elhami Fard, N., Selmic, R. R., & Khorasani, K. (2023). A review of techniques and policies on cybersecurity using artificial intelligence and reinforcement learning algorithms. *IEEE Technology and Society Magazine*, *42*(4), 57–68. DOI: 10.1109/MTS.2023.3306540

ENISA. (2022). *Threat Landscape Report*. European Union Agency for Cybersecurity. Retrieved from https://www.enisa.europa.eu

ENISA. (2023). *Good Practices for Security of Internet of Things*. European Union Agency for Cybersecurity. Retrieved from https://www.enisa.europa.eu

Ennab, M., & Mcheick, H. (2024). Enhancing interpretability and accuracy of AI models in healthcare: A comprehensive review on challenges and future directions. *Frontiers in Robotics and AI*, *11*, 1444763. DOI: 10.3389/frobt.2024.1444763 PMID: 39677978

European Commission. (2022). *GDPR: Four Years After Implementation*. European Commission. Retrieved from https://ec.europa.eu

Europol. (2022). *Internet Organised Crime Threat Assessment*. European Union Agency for Law Enforcement Cooperation. Retrieved from https://www.europol.europa.eu

Europol. (2023). *Cybercrime Dependencies Map*. European Union Agency for Law Enforcement Cooperation. Retrieved from https://www.europol.europa.eu

Faber, K., Corizzo, R., Sniezynski, B., & Japkowicz, N. (2023). Vlad: Task-agnostic vae-based lifelong anomaly detection. *Neural Networks*, *165*, 248–273. DOI: 10.1016/j.neunet.2023.05.032 PMID: 37307668

Faheem, M. A.Muhammad Ashraf Faheem. (2024). Ethical AI: Addressing bias, fairness, and accountability in autonomous decision-making systems. *World Journal of Advanced Research and Reviews, 23*(2), 1703–1711. DOI: 10.30574/wjarr.2024.23.2.2510

FAIR Institute. (2023). *Risk Analysis Standard.* Factor Analysis of Information Risk Institute. Retrieved from https://www.fairinstitute.org

Familoni, B. T.Babajide Tolulope Familoni. (2024). Cybersecurity challenges in the age of AI: Theoretical approaches and practical solutions. *Computer Science & IT Research Journal, 5*(3), 703–724. DOI: 10.51594/csitrj.v5i3.930

Fan, J., Yang, W., & Lam, K. Y. (2022). Cybersecurity Challenges of IoT-Enabled Smart Cities: A Survey. *arXiv Preprint*, arXiv:2202.05023. Retrieved from https://www.ncbi.nlm.nih.gov/pmc/

Farayola, O. A.Oluwatoyin Ajoke Farayola. (2024). Revolutionizing banking security: Integrating artificial intelligence, blockchain, and business intelligence for enhanced cybersecurity. *Finance & Accounting Research Journal, 6*(4), 501–514. DOI: 10.51594/farj.v6i4.990

Fazliani, S., Sorond, M. M., & Masoudifard, A. (2024). Leveraging Ensemble-Based Semi-Supervised Learning for Illicit Account Detection in Ethereum DeFi Transactions. *arXiv preprint arXiv:2412.02408.*

FBI IC3. (2023). *Internet Crime Report.* Federal Bureau of Investigation Internet Crime Complaint Center. Retrieved from https://www.ic3.gov

FBI. (2022). *Intellectual Property Protection: Safeguarding Our Economy.* Federal Bureau of Investigation. Retrieved from https://www.fbi.gov

Fedewa, J. (January 12, 2023). "What's the Latest Version of Android?". How-To Geek. Retrieved January 27, 2025.

Feldmann, M. J., Hardigan, M. A., Famula, R. A., Lopez, C. M., Tabb, A., Cole, G. S., & Knapp, S. J. (2020). Multi-dimensional machine learning approaches for fruit shape phenotyping in strawberry. *GigaScience, 9*(5), giaa030. DOI: 10.1093/gigascience/giaa030 PMID: 32352533

Felt, A. P., Ha, E., Egelman, S., Haney, A., Chin, E., & Wagner, D. (2012). "Android Permissions: User Attention, Comprehension, and Behavior." *Proceedings of the Eighth Symposium on Usable Privacy and Security (SOUPS)*, 3(1), 1-14. DOI: 10.1145/2335356.2335360

Feng, J., Phillips, R. V., Malenica, I., Bishara, A., Hubbard, A. E., Celi, L. A., & Pirracchio, R. (2022). Clinical artificial intelligence quality improvement: Towards continual monitoring and updating of AI algorithms in healthcare. *NPJ Digital Medicine*, *5*(1), 66. DOI: 10.1038/s41746-022-00611-y PMID: 35641814

Fereidooni, H., Marchal, S., Miettinen, M., Mirhoseini, A., Möllering, H., Yalame, H., & Schneider, T. (2021). SAFELearn: Secure aggregation for private federated learning. *Proceedings of the 2021 IEEE Security and Privacy Workshops (SPW)*, 56–62. IEEE. DOI: 10.1109/SPW53761.2021.00017

Ferrag, M. A., Alwahedi, F., Battah, A., Cherif, B., et al. (2025). Generative AI in Cybersecurity: A Comprehensive Review of LLM Applications and Vulnerabilities. *Internet of Things and Cyber-Physical Systems, 5*(1), 100XXX (Early Access).

Ferrag, M. A., Maglaras, L., Moschoyiannis, S., & Janicke, H. (2020). Deep learning for cyber security intrusion detection: Approaches, datasets, and comparative study. *Journal of Information Security and Applications*, *50*, 102419. DOI: 10.1016/j.jisa.2019.102419

Ferraiolo, D. F., Kuhn, D. R., & Sandhu, R. (2022). *Role-Based Access Control* (2nd ed.). Artech House.

Feurer, M., & Hutter, F. (2019). *Hyperparameter optimization.* Springer International Publishing.

Fiat, A., & Shamir, A. (1986). How to prove yourself: Practical solutions to identification and signature problems. Advances in Cryptology—CRYPTO '86, 186-194.

FIDO Alliance. (2023). *FIDO Authentication Standards.* Fast Identity Online Alliance. Retrieved from https://fidoalliance.org

Finistrella, S., Mariani, S., & Zambonelli, F. (2025). Multi-Agent Reinforcement Learning for Cybersecurity: Classification and Survey. *Intelligent Systems with Applications*, *17*, 100861. DOI: 10.1016/j.iswa.2025.200495

FireEye. (2023). *M-Trends: Annual Threat Report.* FireEye. Retrieved from https://www.fireeye.com

Fischlin, M. (2005). Communication-efficient non-interactive proofs of knowledge with online extractors. Advances in Cryptology—CRYPTO 2005, 152-168.

Fisher, M., Mascardi, V., Rozier, K. Y., Schlingloff, B. H., Winikoff, M., & Yorke-Smith, N. (2021). Towards a framework for certification of reliable autonomous systems. *Autonomous Agents and Multi-Agent Systems*, *35*(1), 1–65. DOI: 10.1007/s10458-020-09487-2

Folorunso, A., Adewumi, T., Adewa, A., Okonkwo, R., & Olawumi, T. N. (2024). Impact of AI on cybersecurity and security compliance. *Global Journal of Engineering and Technology Advances, 21*(01), 167–184. DOI: 10.30574/gjeta.2024.21.1.0193

Foote, K. D. (2022). The evolution of deep learning: Historical milestones and future directions. *Journal of Artificial Intelligence Research, 16*(2), 101–115.

Forrester. (2023). *The Zero Trust Security Playbook*. Forrester Research. Retrieved from https://www.forrester.com

Forrest, S., Hofmeyr, S. A., Somayaji, A., & Longstaff, T. A. (1996). A sense of self for Unix processes. In *Proceedings of the 1996 IEEE Symposium on Security and Privacy* (pp. 120–128). IEEE. DOI: 10.1109/SECPRI.1996.502675

Fosch-Villaronga, E., & Mahler, T. (2021). Cybersecurity, safety and robots: Strengthening the link between cybersecurity and safety in the context of care robots. *Computer Law & Security Review, 41*, 105528. DOI: 10.1016/j.clsr.2021.105528

Franke, L., Liang, H., Farzanehpour, S., Brantly, A., Davis, J. C., & Brown, C. (2024). An exploratory mixed-methods study on general data protection regulation (gdpr) compliance in open-source software. In *Proceedings of the 18th ACM/IEEE International Symposium on Empirical Software Engineering and Measurement* (pp. 325-336). DOI: 10.1145/3674805.3686692

Fredrikson, M., Jha, S., & Ristenpart, T. (2015). Model inversion attacks that exploit confidence information and basic countermeasures. *Proceedings of the 22nd ACM SIGSAC Conference on Computer and Communications Security,* 1322-1333. DOI: 10.1145/2810103.2813677

Friedman, J., & Bouchard, M. (2018). *Definitive Guide to Cyber Threat Intelligence*. CyberEdge Group.

Friha, O., Ferrag, M. A., Shu, L., Maglaras, L., Choo, K. K. R., & Nafaa, M. (2022). FELIDS: Federated learning-based intrusion detection system for agricultural Internet of Things. *Journal of Parallel and Distributed Computing, 165*, 17–31. DOI: 10.1016/j.jpdc.2022.03.003

Fruhlinger, J. (2020). The CIA Triad: Definition, Components and Examples. *CSO Online*. Retrieved from https://www.csoonline.com

Furnell, S., & Dowland, P. (2020). *Computer Insecurity: Risking the System*. Springer.

Gaba, S., Budhiraja, I., Kumar, V., Garg, S., & Hassan, M. M. (2024). An innovative multi-agent approach for robust cyber–physical systems using vertical federated learning. *Ad Hoc Networks, 163*, 103578. DOI: 10.1016/j.adhoc.2024.103578

Gadde, H. (2019). AI-Driven Schema Evolution and Management in Heterogeneous Databases. *International Journal of Machine Learning Research in Cybersecurity and Artificial Intelligence*, *10*(1), 332–356.

Gadde, H. (2021). Integrating AI with Graph Databases for Complex Relationship Analysis. *International Journal of Advanced Engineering Technologies and Innovations*, *1*(2), 294–314.

Gadde, H. (2022). Integrating AI into SQL Query Processing: Challenges and Opportunities. *International Journal of Advanced Engineering Technologies and Innovations*, *1*(3), 194–219.

Gadde, H. (2023). Improving Data Reliability with AI-Based Fault Tolerance in Distributed Databases. *International Journal of Advanced Engineering Technologies and Innovations*, *1*(2), 183–207.

Garay, J., Kiayias, A., & Leonardos, N. (2015). The Bitcoin backbone protocol: Analysis and applications. Advances in Cryptology—EUROCRYPT 2015, 281-310.

Garcia-Teodoro, P., Diaz-Verdejo, J., Macia-Fernandez, G., & Vazquez, E. (2009). Anomaly-based network intrusion detection: Techniques, systems and challenges. *Computers & Security*, *28*(1–2), 18–28. DOI: 10.1016/j.cose.2008.08.003

Gartner. (2022). *Market Guide for Security Operations*. Gartner, Inc. Retrieved from https://www.gartner.com

Gartner. (2023). *Top Security and Risk Management Trends*. Gartner, Inc. Retrieved from https://www.gartner.com

Gautam, M. (2023). Deep Reinforcement learning for resilient power and energy systems: Progress, prospects, and future avenues. *Electricity*, *4*(4), 336–380. DOI: 10.3390/electricity4040020

Gentry, C. (2009). Fully homomorphic encryption using ideal lattices. *Proceedings of the 41st ACM Symposium on Theory of Computing (STOC)*, 169-178.

Gentry, C. (2019). *A Fully Homomorphic Encryption Scheme*. Stanford University., DOI: 10.1145/1536414.1536440

George, A. S. (2024). Emerging Trends in AI-Driven Cybersecurity: An In-Depth Analysis. *Partners Universal Innovative Research Publication*, *2*(4), 15–28.

Getastra. (2025). 30+ Malware Statistics You Need To Know In 2025, https://www.getastra.com/blog/security-audit/malware-statistics/#Malware_Statistics_2024, Retrieved *January* 27, 2025.

Ghafir, I., Hammoudeh, M., Prenosil, V., Han, L., Hegarty, R., Rabie, K., & Aparicio-Navarro, F. J. (2018). Detection of Advanced Persistent Threat Using Machine-Learning Correlation Analysis. *Future Generation Computer Systems, 89*, 349–359. Advance online publication. DOI: 10.1016/j.future.2018.06.055

Ghafir, I., Saleem, J., Hammoudeh, M., Faour, H., Prenosil, V., Jaf, S., Jabbar, S., & Baker, T. (2018). Security threats to critical infrastructure: The human factor. *The Journal of Supercomputing*, *74*(10), 4986–5002. DOI: 10.1007/s11227-018-2337-2

Ghiasi, M., Niknam, T., Wang, Z., Mehrandezh, M., Dehghani, M., & Ghadimi, N. (2023). A comprehensive review of cyber-attacks and defense mechanisms for improving security in smart grid energy systems: Past, present and future. *Electric Power Systems Research, 215*, 108975. DOI: 10.1016/j.epsr.2022.108975

Ghimire, B., & Rawat, D. B. (2022). Recent advances on federated learning for cybersecurity and cybersecurity for federated learning for Internet of Things. *IEEE Internet of Things Journal*, *9*(11), 8229–8249. DOI: 10.1109/JIOT.2022.3150363

Ghubaish, A., Salman, T., Zolanvari, M., Unal, D., Al-Ali, A., & Jain, R. (2020). Recent advances in the internet-of-medical-things (IoMT) systems security. *IEEE Internet of Things Journal*, *8*(11), 8707–8718. DOI: 10.1109/JIOT.2020.3045653

Gill, N. S. (2024). The application of convolutional neural networks in security code and anomaly detection. *International Journal of Security Research, 12*(3), 89–103.

Gilman, E., & Barth, D. (2022). *Zero Trust Networks: Building Secure Systems in Untrusted Networks*. O'Reilly Media.

Giovannelli, D. (2022). Automated/Autonomous Incident Response: Balancing Speed and Control. NATO CCDCOE Publication (Research Report). Retrieved from https://ccdcoe.org/

Girhepuje, S., Verma, A., & Raina, G. (2024). A Survey on Offensive AI Within Cybersecurity. *arXiv Preprint, arXiv:2410.03566.*

GitLab. (2023). *DevSecOps Report*. GitLab Inc. Retrieved from https://www.gitlab .com

Goldwasser, S., & Kalai, Y. T. (2012). On the (in)security of the Fiat-Shamir paradigm. *44th Annual ACM Symposium on Theory of Computing*.

Goldwasser, S., Micali, S., & Rackoff, C. (1989). The knowledge complexity of interactive proof systems. *SIAM Journal on Computing, 18*(1), 186–208. DOI: 10.1137/0218012

Gonzalez, P., Castano, A., Peacock, E. E., Diez, J., del Coz, J. J., & Sosik, H. M. (2024). Automatic plankton quantification using deep features. *Journal of Marine Biology Research*, *58*(3), 123–135.

Goodfellow, I., McDaniel, P., & Papernot, N. (2016). Making machine learning robust against adversarial inputs. *arXiv preprint arXiv:1612.07294.*

Goodman, B., & Flaxman, S. (2017). European Union regulations on algorithmic decision-making and a "right to explanation.". *AI Magazine*, *38*(3), 50–57. DOI: 10.1609/aimag.v38i3.2741

Google. (2022). *BeyondCorp: A New Approach to Enterprise Security*. Google Research. Retrieved from https://cloud.google.com

Goriparthi, R. G. (2024). Reinforcement Learning in IoT: Enhancing Smart Device Autonomy through AI. *International Journal of Advanced Engineering Technologies and Innovations*, *2*(1), 89–109.

Goyal, M., & Mahmoud, Q. H. (2024). A systematic review of synthetic data generation techniques using generative AI. *Electronics (Basel)*, *13*(17), 3509. DOI: 10.3390/electronics13173509

Goyal, S., Doddapaneni, S., Khapra, M. M., & Ravindran, B. (2023). A survey of adversarial defenses and robustness in nlp. *ACM Computing Surveys*, *55*(14s), 1–39. DOI: 10.1145/3593042

Greitzer, F. L., & Hohimer, R. E. (2011). Modeling Human Behavior to Anticipate Insider Attacks. *Journal of Strategic Security*, *4*(2), 25–48. DOI: 10.5038/1944-0472.4.2.2

Gronauer, S., & Diepold, K. (2022). Multi-agent deep reinforcement learning: A survey. *Artificial Intelligence Review*, *55*(2), 895–943. DOI: 10.1007/s10462-021-09996-w

Guembe, B., Azeta, A., Misra, S., Osamor, V. C., Fernandez-Sanz, L., & Pospelova, V. (2022). The Emerging Threat of Ai-driven Cyber Attacks: A Review. *Applied Artificial Intelligence*, *36*(no. 1), 2037254. DOI: 10.1080/08839514.2022.2037254

Guni, A., Varma, P., Zhang, J., Fehervari, M., & Ashrafian, H. (2024). Artificial intelligence in surgery: The future is now. *European Surgical Research*, *65*(1), 22–39. DOI: 10.1159/000536393 PMID: 38253041

Gupta, I., Kumari, S., Jha, P., & Ghosh, M. (2024). Leveraging LSTM and GAN for Modern Malware Detection. *arXiv preprint arXiv:2405.04373.*

Gupta, M. (2023, November). Advances in AI: Employing Deep Generative Models for the Creation of Synthetic Healthcare Datasets to Improve Predictive Analytics. In *2023 International Conference on Communication, Security and Artificial Intelligence (ICCSAI)* (pp. 1026-1030). IEEE. DOI: 10.1109/ICCSAI59793.2023.10421464

Gupta, N., Traoré, I., & Quinan, P. M. F. (2019). Automated Event Prioritization for Security Operations Center Using Deep Learning. In *2019 IEEE International Conference on Big Data* (pp. 4906–4911). IEEE. DOI: 10.1109/BigData47090.2019.9006073

Hafiz, L., & Hidayat, T. (2025). Unveiling the Cybercrime Ecosystem: Impact of Ransomware-as-a-Service (RaaS) in Indonesia. *International Journal of Science Education and Cultural Studies*, *4*(1), 11–21.

Haidegger, T., & Benyo, Z. (2008). Surgical robotic support for long duration space missions. *Acta Astronautica*, *63*(7-10), 996–1005. DOI: 10.1016/j.actaastro.2008.01.005

Haidegger, T., Sándor, J., & Benyó, Z. (2011). Surgery in space: The future of robotic telesurgery. *Surgical Endoscopy*, *25*(3), 681–690. DOI: 10.1007/s00464-010-1243-3 PMID: 20652320

Haidegger, T., Speidel, S., Stoyanov, D., & Satava, R. M. (2022). Robot-assisted minimally invasive surgery—Surgical robotics in the data age. *Proceedings of the IEEE*, *110*(7), 835–846. DOI: 10.1109/JPROC.2022.3180350

Hajizadeh, M., Afraz, N., Ruffini, M., & Bauschert, T. (2020, June). Collaborative cyber attack defense in SDN networks using blockchain technology. In *2020 6th IEEE conference on network softwarization (netSoft)* (pp. 487-492). IEEE. DOI: 10.1109/NetSoft48620.2020.9165396

Halevi, S., & Shoup, V. (2014). Algorithms in HElib. Advances in Cryptology—CRYPTO 2014, 554-571.

HashiCorp. (2023). *State of Cloud Strategy Survey*. HashiCorp. Retrieved from https://www.hashicorp.com

Hassija, V., Chamola, V., Mahapatra, A., Singal, A., Goel, D., Huang, K., Scardapane, S., Spinelli, I., Mahmud, M., & Hussain, A. (2024). Interpreting black-box models: A review on explainable artificial intelligence. *Cognitive Computation*, *16*(1), 45–74. DOI: 10.1007/s12559-023-10179-8

Haugh, L. (2024). New partnership uses AI to bolster efficiency, cybersecurity for water treatment. *Virginia Tech News*, *15*(2), 45–58.

Havenga, W., Bagula, A., & Ajayi, O. (2022). Autonomous Threat Detection and Response for Self-Protected Networks. *2022 Conference on Information Communications Technology and Society (ICTAS)*, 1–6. DOI: 10.1109/ICTAS53252.2022.9744643

Havrylovych, M., & Danylov, V. (2024). Deep Learning Application in Critical Infrastructure Protection. In *Artificial Intelligence for Cybersecurity* (pp. 451–465). Springer.

Hayward, K. J., & Maas, M. M. (2021). Artificial intelligence and crime: A primer for criminologists. *Crime, Media, Culture*, *17*(2), 209–233. DOI: 10.1177/1741659020917434

Hemberg, E., Zhang, L., & O'Reilly, U. M. (2020). Exploring adversarial artificial intelligence for autonomous adaptive cyber defense. *Adaptive Autonomous Secure Cyber Systems*, 41-61.

Hick, J. L., Toner, E. S., Hanfling, D., Biddinger, P. D., & Lawler, J. V. (2024). Data and disasters: Essential information needed for all healthcare threats. *Health Security*, *22*(1), 3–10. DOI: 10.1089/hs.2023.0067 PMID: 37729074

Hitaj, B., Ateniese, G., & Pérez-Cruz, F. (2017). Deep models under the GAN: Information leakage from collaborative deep learning. *Proceedings of the 2017 ACM SIGSAC Conference on Computer and Communications Security*, 603–618. ACM. DOI: 10.1145/3133956.3134012

Hiwale, M., Walambe, R., Potdar, V., & Kotecha, K. (2023). A systematic review of privacy-preserving methods deployed with blockchain and federated learning for the telemedicine. *Healthcare Analytics*, *3*, 100192. DOI: 10.1016/j.health.2023.100192 PMID: 37223223

Hochreiter, S., & Schmidhuber, J. (1997). Long Short-Term Memory. *Neural Computation*, *9*(8), 1735–1780. DOI: 10.1162/neco.1997.9.8.1735 PMID: 9377276

Hu, H., Wu, J., Wang, Z., & Cheng, G. (2018). Mimic defense: A designed-in cybersecurity defense framework. *IET Information Security*, *12*(3), 226–237. DOI: 10.1049/iet-ifs.2017.0086

Hussain, F., Hussain, R., Hassan, S. A., & Hossain, E. (2020). Machine learning in IoT security: Current solutions and future challenges. *IEEE Communications Surveys and Tutorials*, *22*(3), 1686–1721. DOI: 10.1109/COMST.2020.2986444

Hussain, S., He, J., Zhu, N., Mughal, F. R., Hussain, M. I., Algarni, A. D., Ahmad, S., Zarie, M. M., & Ateya, A. A. (2024). An adaptive intrusion detection system for WSN using reinforcement learning and deep classification. *Arabian Journal for Science and Engineering*, •••, 1–15. DOI: 10.1007/s13369-024-09769-x

IAPP. (2023). *Privacy Governance Report*. International Association of Privacy Professionals. Retrieved from https://iapp.org

IBM. (2023). *Cost of a data breach 2023| IBM Security*. https://www.ibm.com/reports/data-breach

IBM. (2023). *Cost of a Data Breach Report*. IBM Security. Retrieved from https://www.ibm.com

Ibrahim, M., Khalil, Y. A., Amirrajab, S., Sun, C., Breeuwer, M., Pluim, J., . . . Dumontier, M. (2024). Generative AI for synthetic data across multiple medical modalities: A systematic review of recent developments and challenges. *arXiv preprint arXiv:2407.00116*.

Ibrahum, A. D. M., Hussain, M., & Hong, J.-E. (2025). Deep learning adversarial attacks and defenses in autonomous vehicles: A systematic literature review from a safety perspective. *Artificial Intelligence Review*, *58*(1), 1–53.

Imperva. (2023). *Global DDoS Threat Landscape*. Imperva. Retrieved from https://www.imperva.com

Innocent, E. K. (2024). *Enhancing Data Security in Healthcare with Synthetic Data Generation: An Autoencoder and Variational Autoencoder Approach* (Master's thesis, Oslo Metropolitan University).

International Organization for Standardization. (2023). *ISO/IEC 27001 Information Security Management*. ISO. Retrieved from https://www.iso.org

IoT Security Foundation. (2023). *IoT Security Compliance Framework*. IoT Security Foundation. Retrieved from https://www.iotsecurityfoundation.org

Ippolito, M., Ferguson, J., & Jenson, F. (2021). Improving facies prediction by combining supervised and unsupervised learning methods. *Journal of Petroleum Science Engineering*, *200*, 108300. DOI: 10.1016/j.petrol.2020.108300

Iqubal, A.. "Android Based Malware Detection Technique Using Machine Learning Algorithms." *2024 First International Conference on Pioneering Developments in Computer Science & Digital Technologies (IC2SDT)*. IEEE, 2024. DOI: 10.1109/IC2SDT62152.2024.10696330

IRIS Consortium. (2021). IRIS Project: AI Threat Reporting and Incident Response for Smart Cities – Press Release. (H2020 IRIS Project kickoff announcement). Retrieved from https://iris-h2020.eu/

ISACA. (2022). *State of Cybersecurity Report*. Information Systems Audit and Control Association. Retrieved from https://www.isaca.org

ISACA. (2023). *IT Audit Benchmarking Study*. Information Systems Audit and Control Association. Retrieved from https://www.isaca.org

Islam, M. R. (2024). *Generative AI, Cybersecurity, and Ethics*. John Wiley & Sons.

Islam, R., Sayed, M. I., Saha, S., Hossain, M. J., & Masud, M. A. (2023). Android malware classification using optimum feature selection and ensemble machine learning. *Internet of Things and Cyber-Physical Systems*, *3*, 100–111. DOI: 10.1016/j.iotcps.2023.03.001

Itodo, C., Varlioglu, S., & Elsayed, N. "Digital forensics and incident response (DFIR) challenges in IoT platforms." In 2021 4th International Conference on Information and Computer Technologies (ICICT), pp. 199-203. IEEE, 2021. DOI: 10.1109/ICICT52872.2021.00040

Jada, I., & Mayayise, T. O. (2023). The Impact of Artificial Intelligence on Organisational Cyber Security: A Systematic Literature Review. *Data and Information Management*, *8*(4), 100063.

Jalali, M. S., Russell, B., Razak, S., & Gordon, W. J. (2019). EARS to cyber incidents in health care. *Journal of the American Medical Informatics Association : JAMIA*, *26*(1), 81–90. DOI: 10.1093/jamia/ocy148 PMID: 30517701

Jamil, F., Hang, L., Kim, K. H., & Kim, D. H. (2019). KyuHyung Kim, and Do-Hyeun Kim. "A novel medical blockchain model for drug supply chain integrity management in a smart hospital.". *Electronics (Basel)*, *8*(5), 505. DOI: 10.3390/electronics8050505

Jang, B., Kim, M., Harerimana, G., & Kim, J. W. (2019). Q-learning algorithms: A comprehensive classification and applications. *IEEE Access : Practical Innovations, Open Solutions*, *7*, 133653–133667. DOI: 10.1109/ACCESS.2019.2941229

Javadpour, A., Ja'fari, F., Taleb, T., Shojafar, M., & Benzaïd, C. (2024). A comprehensive survey on cyber deception techniques to improve honeypot performance. *Computers & Security*, *103792*, •••. https://www.sciencedirect.com/science/article/pii/S0167404824000932

Javaid, A., Niyaz, Q., Sun, W., & Alam, M. (2016). A Deep Learning Approach for Network Intrusion Detection System. *Proceedings of the 9th EAI International Conference on Bio-Inspired Information and Communications Technologies (Formerly BIONETICS)*. 9th EAI International Conference on Bio-inspired Information and Communications Technologies (formerly BIONETICS), New York City, United States. DOI: 10.4108/eai.3-12-2015.2262516

Javed, S. M. Z., & Amjad, M. F. (2024). Enhancing Malware Classification Through Dynamic Behavioral Analysis, SIEM Integration, and Deep Learning. In *2024 International Seminar on Intelligent Technology and Its Applications (ISITIA)* (pp. 663-668). IEEE.

Jaweed, M., & Shaikh, R. F. (2024). Optimizing Generative AI By Overcoming Stability Mode Collapse And Quality Challenges In Gans And Vaes. *MSW Management Journal, 34*(2), 497–507.

Jeffrey, N., Tan, Q., & Villar, J. R. (2023). A review of anomaly detection strategies to detect threats to cyber-physical systems. *Electronics (Basel), 12*(15), 3283. DOI: 10.3390/electronics12153283

Jha, P., Mahato, S., Jana, P. K., Maurya, S., & Chihi, I. (2024). Artificial Intelligence and Machine Learning in Cybersecurity. *Journal of Cybersecurity, 15*(3), 89–104.

Jiang, L., Li, Q., & Chen, X. (2024). "A Novel Multi-agent Game-theoretic Model for Cybersecurity Strategies in EV Charging Networks: Addressing Risk Propagation and Budget Constraints." **SSRN**. DOI: https://ssrn.com/abstract=5080170

Jimmy, F. N. U. (2024). Cyber security Vulnerabilities and Remediation Through Cloud Security Tools. *Journal of Artificial Intelligence General science (JAIGS) ISSN: 3006-4023, 2*(1), 129-171.

Jimmy, F. N. U. (2024). Cyber security vulnerabilities and remediation through cloud security tools. *Journal of Artificial Intelligence General science (JAIGS) ISSN: 3006-4023, 2*(1), 129-171.

Johnson, J., et al. (2022). "Cybersecurity for Electric Vehicle Charging Infrastructure." **Sandia National Laboratories**, SAND2022-9315.

Joseph, S., Kolade, T. M., Obioha Val, O., Adebiyi, O. O., Ogungbemi, O. S., & Olaniyi, O. O. (2024). AI-powered information governance: Balancing automation and human oversight for optimal organization productivity. *Asian Journal of Research in Computer Science, 17*(10), 10–9734.

Kadir, A., & Peddoju, S. K. (2024). PacDroid: Lightweight android malware detection using permissions and intent features. *Multimedia Tools and Applications*, •••, 1–29. DOI: 10.1007/s11042-024-20455-w

Kairouz, P., McMahan, H. B., Avent, B., Bellet, A., Bennis, M., Bhagoji, A. N., & Zhao, S. (2021). Advances and open problems in federated learning. *Foundations and Trends in Machine Learning, 14*(1–2), 1–210. DOI: 10.1561/2200000083

Kalasani, R. R. (2024). An Exploratory Study of the Impacts of Artificial Intelligence in Cyber Defense. *Journal of AI Research, 13*(4), 72–85.

Kale, G., Bostancı, G. E., & Çelebi, F. V. (2024). Evolutionary feature selection for machine learning based malware classification. *Engineering Science and Technology, an International Journal, 56*, 101762. DOI: 10.1016/j.jestch.2024.101762

Kaliyaperumal, P., Periyasamy, S., Thirumalaisamy, M., Balusamy, B., & Benedetto, F. (2024). A novel hybrid unsupervised learning approach for enhanced cybersecurity in the IoT. *Future Internet, 16*(7), 253. DOI: 10.3390/fi16070253

Kanaan, A., Mtair AL-Hawamleh, A., Aloun, M., Alorfi, A., & Abdalwahab Al-rawashdeh, M. (2024). Fortifying organizational cyber resilience: An integrated framework for business continuity and growth amidst escalating threat landscapes. *International Journal of Computing and Digital Systems, 16*(1), 1–13. DOI: 10.12785/ijcds/1571023809

Kanellopoulos, D., & Sharma, V. K. (2022). Dynamic load balancing techniques in the IoT: A review. *Symmetry, 14*(12), 2554. DOI: 10.3390/sym14122554

Kasongo, S. M. (2023). A deep learning technique for intrusion detection system using a Recurrent Neural Networks based framework. *Computer Communications, 199*, 113–125. DOI: 10.1016/j.comcom.2022.12.010

Kaspersky. (2023). *Advanced Persistent Threat Report*. Kaspersky Lab. Retrieved from https://www.kaspersky.com

Kaspersky. (2024). IT threat evolution in Q1 2024. Mobile statistics, https://securelist.com/it-threat-evolution-q1-2024-mobile-statistics/112750/? Retrieved January 27, 2025.

Katiforis, S. (2024). Synchronized Coevolution: A Conceptual Framework For Sustaining a Human-Centered Security Culture in AI-Driven Environments.

Katz, J., & Lindell, Y. (2007). *Introduction to modern cryptography*. CRC Press. DOI: 10.1201/9781420010756

Kaur, D., Islam, S. N., Mahmud, M. A., Haque, M. E., & Anwar, A. (2023). A VAE-Bayesian deep learning scheme for solar power generation forecasting based on dimensionality reduction. *Energy and AI, 14*, 100279. DOI: 10.1016/j.egyai.2023.100279

Kaviani, S., Han, K. J., & Sohn, I. (2022). Adversarial attacks and defenses on AI in medical imaging informatics: A survey. *Expert Systems with Applications, 198*, 116815. DOI: 10.1016/j.eswa.2022.116815

Kavya, S., & Sumathi, D. (2024). Staying ahead of phishers: A review of recent advances and emerging methodologies in phishing detection. *Artificial Intelligence Review*, *58*(2), 50. DOI: 10.1007/s10462-024-11055-z

Keyes, D. S., Li, B., Kaur, G., Lashkari, A. H., Gagnon, F., & Massicotte, F. (2021, May). EntropLyzer: Android malware classification and characterization using entropy analysis of dynamic characteristics. In 2021 Reconciling Data Analytics, Automation, Privacy, and Security: A Big Data Challenge (RDAAPS) (pp. 1-12). IEEE.

Khadka, K., Chandrasekaran, J., Lei, Y., Kacker, R. N., & Kuhn, D. R. (2023, April). Synthetic data generation using combinatorial testing and variational autoencoder. In *2023 IEEE International Conference on Software Testing, Verification and Validation Workshops (ICSTW)* (pp. 228-236). IEEE. DOI: 10.1109/ICSTW58534.2023.00048

Khan, A., Jhanjhi, N., Hamid, D. H. H., Omar, H. A. H. B. H., Amsaad, F., & Wassan, S. (2025). Future Trends and Challenges in Cybersecurity and Generative AI. *Reshaping CyberSecurity With Generative AI Techniques*, 491-522.

Khan, W., Daud, A., Khan, K., Muhammad, S., & Haq, R. (2023). Exploring the frontiers of deep learning and natural language processing: A comprehensive overview of key challenges and emerging trends. *Natural Language Processing Journal*, 100026.

Khanan, A., Mohamed, Y. A., Mohamed, A. H., & Bashir, M. (2024). From Bytes to Insights: A Systematic Literature Review on Unraveling IDS Datasets for Enhanced Cybersecurity Understanding. *IEEE Access : Practical Innovations, Open Solutions*, *12*, 59289–59317. DOI: 10.1109/ACCESS.2024.3392338

Khang, A., & Rath, K. C. (2024). The Quantum Evolution - Application of AI and Robotics in Modern Systems. *Journal of Quantum Computing*, *6*(2), 35–50.

Khan, L. U., Saad, W., Han, Z., Debbah, M., & Hong, C. S. (2021). Federated learning for Internet of Things: Recent advances, taxonomy, and open challenges. *IEEE Communications Surveys and Tutorials*, *23*(3), 1750–1778. DOI: 10.1109/COMST.2021.3090430

Khan, P. W., & Byun, Y.-C. (2021). *Secure transactions management using blockchain as a service software for the internet of things*. Software Engineering in IoT, Big Data, Cloud and Mobile Computing. DOI: 10.1007/978-3-030-64773-5_10

Kheddar, H., Dawoud, D. W., Awad, A. I., Himeur, Y., & Khan, M. K. (2024). Reinforcement-Learning-Based Intrusion Detection in Communication Networks: A Review. *IEEE Communications Surveys and Tutorials*, 1. DOI: 10.1109/COMST.2024.3484491

Kholidy, H. A. (2021). Autonomous mitigation of cyber risks in the Cyber–Physical Systems. *Future Generation Computer Systems*, *115*, 171–187. DOI: 10.1016/j.future.2020.09.002

Khoramnejad, F., & Hossain, E. (2024). Generative AI for the Optimization of Next-Generation Wireless Networks: Basics, State-of-the-Art, and Open Challenges. *arXiv preprint arXiv:2405.17454.*

Khorsheed, E. A., & Al-Sulaifanie, A. K. (2024). Handwritten Digit Classification Using Deep Learning Convolutional Neural Network. *Journal of Soft Computing and Data Mining*, *5*(1), 79–90. DOI: 10.30880/jscdm.2024.05.01.007

Khraisat, A., & Alazab, A. (2021). A critical review of intrusion detection systems in the Internet of Things: Techniques, deployment strategy, validation strategy, attacks, public datasets and challenges. *Cybersecurity*, *4*(1), 18. DOI: 10.1186/s42400-021-00077-7

Kilichev, D., Turimov, D., & Kim, W. (2024). Next–Generation Intrusion Detection for IoT EVCS: Integrating CNN, LSTM, and GRU Models. *Mathematics*, *16*(1), 112–130. DOI: 10.3390/math12040571

Kim, H. L., & Schulam, P. (2004). The Paky, Hermes, Aesop, Zeus, and da Vinci robotic systems. *The Urologic Clinics of North America*, *31*(4), 659–669. DOI: 10.1016/j.ucl.2004.06.008 PMID: 15474593

Kindervag, J. (2019). *No More Chewy Centers: The Zero Trust Model Of Information Security*. Forrester Research.

Kineber, A. F., Oke, A., Aliu, J., Hamed, M. M., & Oputu, E. (2023). Exploring the adoption of cyber (digital) technology for sustainable construction: A structural equation modeling of critical success factors. *Sustainability (Basel)*, *15*(6), 5043. DOI: 10.3390/su15065043

Kiran, A., & Kumar, S. S. (2024). A methodology and an empirical analysis to determine the most suitable synthetic data generator. *IEEE Access : Practical Innovations, Open Solutions*, *12*, 12209–12228. DOI: 10.1109/ACCESS.2024.3354277

Kitten, T. (2023). *Ransomware: Analyzing Payments and Mitigation Strategies.* Information Security Media Group.

Knack, A., & Burke, A. (2024). Autonomous cyber defence phase II. *The Alan Turing Institute*. Retrieved from https://cetas.turing.ac.uk/publications/autonomous-cyber-defence-autonomous-agents

Koblitz, N., & Menezes, A. (2007). Another look at 'Provable Security'. *Journal of Cryptology, 20*(1), 3–37. DOI: 10.1007/s00145-005-0432-z

Komadina, A., Martinić, M., Groš, S., & Mihajlović, Ž. (2024). Comparing Threshold Selection Methods for Network Anomaly Detection. *IEEE Access : Practical Innovations, Open Solutions, 12*, 124943–124973. DOI: 10.1109/ACCESS.2024.3452168

Konidena, B. K., Jesu, N. A. M., & Tadimarri, A. (2024). Ethical Considerations in the Development and Deployment of AI Systems. *European Journal of Technology, 8*(2), 41–53. DOI: 10.47672/ejt.1890

Kott, A. (2018). Intelligent autonomous agents are key to cyber defense of the future army networks. *The Cyber Defense Review, 3*(3), 57–70.

Kott, A. (Ed.). (2023). *Autonomous Intelligent Cyber Defense Agent (AICA): A Comprehensive Guide*. Springer International. DOI: 10.1007/978-3-031-29269-9

Kott, A., Théron, P., & De Gaspari, F. (2019). *Autonomous Intelligent Cyber-Defense Agent (AICA) Reference Architecture, Release 2.0*. U.S. Army Research Laboratory.

Kouliaridis, V., & Kambourakis, G. (2021). A comprehensive survey on machine learning techniques for android malware detection. *Information (Basel), 12*(5), 185. DOI: 10.3390/info12050185

Kouliaridis, V., Potha, N., & Kambourakis, G. (2020, November). Improving android malware detection through dimensionality reduction techniques. In *International conference on machine learning for networking* (pp. 57-72). Cham: Springer International Publishing.

Kramer, S. (2024). Deception technology: Putting cybercriminals on defense. *The Cube Research*. Retrieved from https://thecuberesearch.com/deception-technology-putting-cybercriminals-defense/

Krause, T., Ernst, R., Klaer, B., Hacker, I., & Henze, M. (2021). Cybersecurity in power grids: Challenges and opportunities. *Sensors (Basel), 21*(18), 6225. DOI: 10.3390/s21186225 PMID: 34577432

Kreutz, D., Ramos, F. M. V., Veríssimo, P. E., Rothenberg, C. E., Azodolmolky, S., & Uhlig, S. (2020). Software-Defined Networking: A Comprehensive Survey. *IEEE Communications Surveys and Tutorials*. Advance online publication. DOI: 10.1109/COMST.2020.2982393

Krishnamurthy, O., & Vemulapalli, G. (2024). Advancing Sustainable Cybersecurity: Exploring Trends and Overcoming Challenges with Generative AI. In *International Conference on Sustainable Development through Machine Learning, AI and IoT* (pp. 16-25). Cham: Springer Nature Switzerland.

Krombholz, K., Hobel, H., Huber, M., & Weippl, E. (2021). Advanced Social Engineering Attacks. *Journal of Information Security and Applications*. Advance online publication. DOI: 10.1016/j.jisa.2021.102934

Kruse, R., Mostaghim, S., Borgelt, C., Braune, C., & Steinbrecher, M. (2022). Multi-layer perceptrons. In *Computational intelligence: a methodological introduction* (pp. 53–124). Springer International Publishing. DOI: 10.1007/978-3-030-42227-1_5

Kshetri, N. (2019). The Economics of Cybercrime. *IEEE Security and Privacy*. Advance online publication. DOI: 10.1109/MSEC.2019.2923923

Kuang, H., Liu, H., Wu, Y., Satoh, S. I., & Ji, R. (2023). Improving adversarial robustness via information bottleneck distillation. *Advances in Neural Information Processing Systems*, *36*, 10796–10813.

Kubernetes. (2023). *Kubernetes Security Best Practices*. Cloud Native Computing Foundation. Retrieved from https://kubernetes.io

Kulathumani, G., Ananthanarayanan, S., & Narayanan, G. (2024). Siren—Advancing cybersecurity through deception and adaptive analysis. *arXiv preprint*. Retrieved from https://arxiv.org/abs/2406.06225

Kumar, S., Ahlawat, P., & Sahni, J. (2024). IOT malware detection using static and dynamic analysis techniques: A systematic literature review. *Security and Privacy*, *7*(6), e444. DOI: 10.1002/spy2.444

Kumar, S., Mishra, D., Panda, B., & Shukla, S. K. (2022, May). AndroOBFS: time-tagged obfuscated Android malware dataset with family information. In *Proceedings of the 19th International Conference on Mining Software Repositories* (pp. 454-458). DOI: 10.1145/3524842.3528493

Kunduru, A. R. (2023). Blockchain technology for ERP systems: A review. *American Journal of Engineering, Mechanics and Architecture*, *1*(7), 56–63.

Kuppa, A., & Le-Khac, N.-A. "Black box attacks on explainable artificial intelligence (XAI) methods in cyber security." In *2020 International Joint Conference on neural networks (IJCNN)*, pp. 1-8. IEEE, 2020. DOI: 10.1109/IJCNN48605.2020.9206780

Kwon, H. Y., Kim, T., & Lee, M. K. (2022). Advanced intrusion detection combining signature-based and behavior-based detection methods. *Electronics (Basel), 11*(6), 867. DOI: 10.3390/electronics11060867

Lakhouil, M., & Abtoy, A. (2021). Cybersecurity of Smart Cities: A Glimpse. In *Proceedings of the 4th Smart Cities Symposium (SCS 2021)* (pp. 141–145). IEEE.

Lane Thames, J. (2014). Distributed, collaborative and automated cybersecurity infrastructures for cloud-based design and manufacturing systems. In *Cloud-Based Design and Manufacturing (CBDM) A Service-Oriented Product Development Paradigm for the 21st Century* (pp. 207–229). Springer International Publishing. DOI: 10.1007/978-3-319-07398-9_8

Lashkari, A. H., Kadir, A. F. A., Gonzalez, H., Mbah, K. F., & Ghorbani, A. A. (2017, August). Towards a network-based framework for android malware detection and characterization. In 2017 15th Annual conference on privacy, security and trust (PST) (pp. 233-23309). IEEE.

Lashkari, A. H., Kadir, A. F. A., Taheri, L., & Ghorbani, A. A. (2018, October). Toward developing a systematic approach to generate benchmark android malware datasets and classification. In 2018 International Carnahan conference on security technology (ICCST) (pp. 1-7). ieee.

Latibari, B. S., Nazari, N., Chowdhury, M. A., Gubbi, K. I., Fang, C., Ghimire, S., & Hosseini, E.. (2024). Transformers: A Security Perspective. *IEEE Access : Practical Innovations, Open Solutions, 12*, 181071–181105. DOI: 10.1109/ACCESS.2024.3509372

Lazaros, K., Koumadorakis, D. E., Vrahatis, A. G., & Kotsiantis, S. (2024). Federated Learning: Navigating the Landscape of Collaborative Intelligence. *Electronics (Basel), 13*(23), 4744. DOI: 10.3390/electronics13234744

Le, D. N., Dhar, A., Kumar, R., Muthaiyah, S., & Agarwal, S. (2024). The Role of Data Science in Network Security for Smart Cities. *Journal of Data Science : JDS, 17*(5), 90–105.

Lee, D. H., & Yoon, S. N. (2021). "Application of artificial intelligence-based technologies in the healthcare industry: Opportunities and challenges.". *International Journal of Environmental Research and Public Health, 18*(1), 271. DOI: 10.3390/ijerph18010271 PMID: 33401373

Lee, G. K. K., Kasim, H., Sirigina, R. P., Shannon, S. Q. H., King, S., & Terence, G. G. H. (2022). Smart Robust Feature Selection (SoFt) for imbalanced and heterogeneous data. *Knowledge-Based Systems, 236*, 107197. DOI: 10.1016/j.knosys.2021.107197

Lee, W.-K., Phan, R. C.-W., Goi, B.-M., Chen, L., Zhang, X., & Xiong, N. N. (2018). RaphaëL C-W. Phan, Bok-Min Goi, Lanxiang Chen, Xiujun Zhang, and Naixue N. Xiong. "Parallel and high speed hashing in GPU for telemedicine applications.". *IEEE Access : Practical Innovations, Open Solutions*, *6*, 37991–38002. DOI: 10.1109/ACCESS.2018.2849439

Lefranc, M., & Peltier, J. (2016). Evaluation of the ROSA™ Spine robot for minimally invasive surgical procedures. *Expert Review of Medical Devices*, *13*(10), 899–906. DOI: 10.1080/17434440.2016.1236680 PMID: 27649314

Leite, D., Sharma, A., Demir, C., & Ngomo, A. C. (2024, June). Interpretability index based on balanced volumes for transparent models and agnostic explainers. In *2024 IEEE International Conference on Fuzzy Systems (FUZZ-IEEE)* (pp. 1-10). IEEE. DOI: 10.1109/FUZZ-IEEE60900.2024.10611937

Li, S. C., Tai, B. C., & Huang, Y. (2019, December). Evaluating variational autoencoder as a private data release mechanism for tabular data. In *2019 IEEE 24th Pacific Rim International Symposium on Dependable Computing (PRDC)* (pp. 198-1988). IEEE.

Liang, Z., Wang, C., Duan, Z., Liu, H., Liu, X., & Ullah Jan Khan, K. (2021). A hybrid model consisting of supervised and unsupervised learning for landslide susceptibility mapping. *Remote Sensing (Basel)*, *13*(8), 1464. DOI: 10.3390/rs13081464

Lian, J., Zhang, X., & Liu, Y. (2024). CNN and RNN applications in real-time cyberattack detection. *International Journal of Cybersecurity*, *13*(3), 22–35.

Liao, J., Liu, T., Tang, X., Mu, X., Huang, B., & Cao, D. (2020). Decision-making strategy on highway for autonomous vehicles using deep reinforcement learning. *IEEE Access : Practical Innovations, Open Solutions*, *8*, 177804–177814. DOI: 10.1109/ACCESS.2020.3022755

Li, H.. "MalCertain: Enhancing Deep Neural Network Based Android Malware Detection by Tackling Prediction Uncertainty." *Proceedings of the IEEE/ACM 46th International Conference on Software Engineering*. 2024. DOI: 10.1145/3597503.3639122

Li, J., Li, J., & Zhang, X. (2018). Cyber Security Meets Artificial Intelligence: A Survey. *Frontiers of Information Technology & Electronic Engineering*, *19*(12), 1462–1474. DOI: 10.1631/FITEE.1800573

Lim, W., Yong, K. S. C., Lau, B. T., & Tan, C. C. L. (2024). Future of generative adversarial networks (GAN) for anomaly detection in network security: A review. *Computers & Security*, *139*, 103733. DOI: 10.1016/j.cose.2024.103733

Lin, H., Alemzadeh, H., Chen, D., Kalbarczyk, Z., & Iyer, R. K. (2016, April). Safety-critical cyber-physical attacks: Analysis, detection, and mitigation. In *Proceedings of the Symposium and Bootcamp on the Science of Security* (pp. 82-89).

Lin, H., & Zegart, A. (2018). *Bytes, Bombs, and Spies: The Strategic Dimensions of Offensive Cyber Operations*. Brookings Institution Press.

Link, S. (2021). Deep learning: A comprehensive overview on techniques. *Springer Link Journal*, *16*(2), 134–149.

Li, T., Sahu, A. K., Talwalkar, A., & Smith, V. (2020). Federated learning: Challenges, methods, and future directions. *IEEE Signal Processing Magazine*, *37*(3), 50–60. DOI: 10.1109/MSP.2020.2975749

Little, C., Allmendinger, R., & Elliot, M. (2024). Synthetic census microdata generation: A comparative study of synthesis methods examining the trade-off between disclosure risk and utility. *Journal of Official Statistics*, 0282423X241266523.

Liu, J., Li, X., Li, C., Yang, G., Li, Y., Qiu, J., & Dong, Z. Y. (2023). When Deep Normal Behavior Models Meet Fault Samples: A Generalized Wind Turbine Anomaly Detection Scheme. *IEEE Transactions on Instrumentation and Measurement*, *72*, 1–16. DOI: 10.1109/TIM.2023.3324347

Liu, Y., Kang, Y., Xing, C., Chen, T., & Yang, Q. (2020). A secure federated transfer learning framework. *IEEE Intelligent Systems*, *35*(4), 70–82. DOI: 10.1109/MIS.2020.2988525

Liu, Y., Tantithamthavorn, C., Li, L., & Liu, Y. (2022). Deep learning for android malware defenses: A systematic literature review. *ACM Computing Surveys*, *55*(8), 1–36.

Liu, Z., Wang, R., Japkowicz, N., Tang, D., Zhang, W., & Zhao, J. (2021). Research on unsupervised feature learning for android malware detection based on restricted Boltzmann machines. *Future Generation Computer Systems*, *120*, 91–108. DOI: 10.1016/j.future.2021.02.015

Li, X., Wang, S., Zeng, S., Wu, Y., & Yang, Y. (2024). A survey on LLM-based multi-agent systems: Workflow, infrastructure, and challenges. *Vicinagearth*, *1*(1), 9. DOI: 10.1007/s44336-024-00009-2

Li, Y., Xu, G., Xian, H., Rao, L., & Shi, J. (2019). Novel Android Malware Detection Method Based on Multi-dimensional Hybrid Features Extraction and Analysis. *Intelligent Automation & Soft Computing*, *25*(3), 637–647. DOI: 10.31209/2019.100000118

Llopis Sánchez, S. (2023). *Decision support elements and enabling techniques to achieve a cyber defence situational awareness capability* (Doctoral dissertation, Universitat Politècnica de València).

Lmame, R. (2024). AI-driven autonomous cyber-security systems: Advanced threat detection and response. *LinkedIn Pulse*. Retrieved from https://www.linkedin.com/pulse/ai-driven-autonomous-cyber-security-systems-advanced-ramachandran-lmame

Lockheed Martin. (2022). *Cyber Kill Chain*. Lockheed Martin Corporation. Retrieved from https://www.lockheedmartin.com

López Delgado, J. L., & López Ramos, J. A. (2024). A Comprehensive Survey on Generative AI Solutions in IoT Security. *Electronics (Basel), 13*(24), 4965. DOI: 10.3390/electronics13244965

Lorentziadis, M. L. (2014). A short history of the invasion of robots in surgery. *Hellenike Cheirourgike. Acta Chirurgica Hellenica, 86*(3), 117–121. DOI: 10.1007/s13126-014-0112-2

Lu, Q., Peng, Z., Wu, L., Ni, M., & Luo, J. (2024). Detecting the cyber-physical-social cooperated APTs in high-DER-penetrated smart grids: Threats, current work and challenges. *Computer Networks, 254*, 110776. DOI: 10.1016/j.comnet.2024.110776

Lu, T., Du, Y., Ouyang, L., Chen, Q., & Wang, X. (2020). Android malware detection based on a hybrid deep learning model. *Security and Communication Networks, 2020*(1), 8863617. DOI: 10.1155/2020/8863617

Lysenko, S., Bobro, N., Korsunova, K., Vasylchyshyn, O., & Tatarchenko, Y. (2024). The role of artificial intelligence in cybersecurity: Automation of protection and detection of threats. *Economic Affairs, 69*(1s), 43–51. DOI: 10.46852/0424-2513.1.2024.6

Lyu, L., Yu, H., Ma, X., Niu, X., Chen, X., & Zhao, Y. (2020). Privacy and robustness in federated learning: Attacks and defenses. *IEEE Transactions on Neural Networks and Learning Systems, 31*(12), 10033–10045. PMID: 36355741

Macas, M., Wu, C., & Fuertes, W. (2024). Adversarial examples: A survey of attacks and defenses in deep learning-enabled cybersecurity systems. *Expert Systems with Applications, 238*, 122223. DOI: 10.1016/j.eswa.2023.122223

Maddireddy, B. R., & Maddireddy, B. R. (2023). Enhancing Network Security through AI-Powered Automated Incident Response Systems. *International Journal of Advanced Engineering Technologies and Innovations, 1*(02), 282–304.

Magnussen, G. M. K., & Pettersen, M. (2023). *A Comprehensive Framework for Patching and Vulnerability Management in Enterprises* (Master's thesis, University of Agder).

Mahadevappa, P., Al-amri, R., Alkawsi, G., Alkahtani, A. A., Alghenaim, M. F., & Alsamman, M. (2024). Analyzing Threats and Attacks in Edge Data Analytics within IoT Environments. *IoT*, *5*(1), 123–154. DOI: 10.3390/iot5010007

Mahajan, S., Khurana, M., & Estrela, V. V. (Eds.). (2024). *Applying artificial intelligence in cybersecurity analytics and cyber threat detection*. Wiley. DOI: 10.1002/9781394196470

Mahdavifar, S., Kadir, A. F. A., Fatemi, R., Alhadidi, D., & Ghorbani, A. A. (2020, August). Dynamic android malware category classification using semi-supervised deep learning. In 2020 IEEE Intl Conf on Dependable, Autonomic and Secure Computing, Intl Conf on Pervasive Intelligence and Computing, Intl Conf on Cloud and Big Data Computing, Intl Conf on Cyber Science and Technology Congress (DASC/PiCom/CBDCom/CyberSciTech) (pp. 515-522). IEEE.

Mahdavifar, S., Alhadidi, D., & Ghorbani, A. A. (2022). Effective and efficient hybrid android malware classification using pseudo-label stacked auto-encoder. *Journal of Network and Systems Management*, *30*(1), 22. DOI: 10.1007/s10922-021-09634-4

Maidamwar, P. R., Bartere, M. M., & Lokulwar, P. P. (2021). Implementation of Network Intrusion Detection System Using Artificial Intelligence: A Survey. In *Proc. 2nd Int. Conf. on Recent Trends in Machine Learning, IoT, Smart Cities and Applications (ICMISC 2021)* (pp. 185–198). Springer.

Major, M., Souza, B., DiVita, J., & Ferguson-Walter, K. (2021). Informing autonomous deception systems with cyber expert performance data. *arXiv preprint*. Retrieved from https://arxiv.org/abs/2109.00066

Malatji, M., & Tolah, A. (2024). Artificial intelligence (AI) cybersecurity dimensions: A comprehensive framework for understanding adversarial and offensive AI. *AI and Ethics*, •••, 1–28. DOI: 10.1007/s43681-024-00427-4

Malhotra, A., & Bajaj, K. (2016). A hybrid pattern based text mining approach for malware detection using DBScan. *CSI transactions on ICT, 4*, 141-149.

Malialis, K., & Kudenko, D. (2016). Distributed reinforcement learning for adaptive and robust network intrusion response. *Connection Science*, *28*(1), 45–63. DOI: 10.1080/09540091.2015.1031082

Malik, H. M., Zhao, Z., & Yang, L. (2023). Artificial intelligence for cybersecurity: Literature review and future research directions. *Future Generation Computer Systems, 146*, 781–795. DOI: 10.1016/j.future.2023.04.019

Malik, J., Muthalagu, R., & Pawar, P. M. (2024). A systematic review of adversarial machine learning attacks, defensive controls and technologies. *IEEE Access : Practical Innovations, Open Solutions, 12*, 99382–99421. DOI: 10.1109/ACCESS.2024.3423323

Mallikarjunaradhya, V., Pothukuchi, A. S., & Kota, L. V. (2023). An overview of the strategic advantages of AI-powered threat intelligence in the cloud. *Journal of Science and Technology, 4*(4), 1–12. DOI: 10.55662/JST.2023.4401

Mandiant. (2023). *M-Trends Annual Report*. Mandiant. Retrieved from https://www.mandiant.com

Maniriho, P., Mahmood, A. N., & Chowdhury, M. J. M. (2024). A survey of recent advances in deep learning models for detecting malware in desktop and mobile platforms. *ACM Computing Surveys, 56*(6), 1–41. DOI: 10.1145/3638240

Manju, & Rana, C. (2024). Application of Deep Reinforcement Learning in Adversarial Malware Detection. *Deep Reinforcement Learning and Its Industrial Use Cases: AI for Real-World Applications*, 91-113.

Mantoo, B. A., & Khurana, S. S. (2020). Static, dynamic and intrinsic features based android malware detection using machine learning. In *Proceedings of ICRIC 2019: Recent Innovations in Computing* (pp. 31-45). Springer International Publishing. DOI: 10.1007/978-3-030-29407-6_4

Marinho, R., & Holanda, R. (2023). Automated emerging cyber threat identification and profiling based on natural language processing. *IEEE Access : Practical Innovations, Open Solutions, 11*, 58915–58936. DOI: 10.1109/ACCESS.2023.3260020

Marsh McLennan. (2023). *Global Cyber Risk Perception Survey*. Marsh McLennan. Retrieved from https://www.marshmclennan.com

Martinelli, F., Marulli, F., & Mercaldo, F. (2017). Evaluating convolutional neural network for effective mobile malware detection. *Procedia Computer Science, 112*, 2372–2381. DOI: 10.1016/j.procs.2017.08.216

Martin, P. O. H. L. (2016). Robotic systems in healthcare with particular reference to innovation in the 'fourth industrial revolution'. *Journal of International and Advanced Japanese Studies, 8*, 17–33.

Maschmeyer, L., Dorfman, R., & Stuparu, F. (2022). Cyber Proxies: Objectives, Methods, and Why They Matter. In *Oxford Handbook of Cyber Security*. DOI: DOI: 10.1093/oxfordhb/9780198800682.013.12

Mashaleh, A. S., Ibrahim, N. F. B., Alauthman, M., Almseidin, M., & Gawanmeh, A. (2024). IoT Smart Devices Risk Assessment Model Using Fuzzy Logic and PSO. *Computers, Materials & Continua*, *78*(2), 2. DOI: 10.32604/cmc.2023.047323

Masud, M. T., Keshk, M., Moustafa, N., Linkov, I., & Emge, D. K. (2024). Explainable artificial intelligence for resilient security applications in the Internet of Things. *IEEE Open Journal of the Communications Society*, 1. DOI: 10.1109/OJCOMS.2024.3413790

Mavikumbure, H. S., Cobilean, V., Wickramasinghe, C. S., Drake, D., & Manic, M. (2024). Generative AI in cyber security of cyber physical systems: Benefits and threats. In *2024 16th International Conference on Human System Interaction (HSI)* (pp. 1-8). IEEE.

McAfee. (2022). *Advanced Threat Research Report*. McAfee Corporation. Retrieved from https://www.mcafee.com

McGuire, M. (2020). *Into the Web of Profit: Understanding the Growth of the Cybercrime Economy*. Bromium.

McKinsey. (2023). *The Risk-Based Approach to Cybersecurity*. McKinsey & Company. Retrieved from https://www.mckinsey.com

McLaughlin, C. (2024). Scalable Machine Learning Methods and Datasets for Software Vulnerability Detection (Doctoral dissertation, Queensland University of Technology).

McMahan, H. B., Moore, E., Ramage, D., Hampson, S., & Aguera y Arcas, B. (2017). Communication-efficient learning of deep networks from decentralized data. *Proceedings of the 20th International Conference on Artificial Intelligence and Statistics (AISTATS)*, 1273–1282. PMLR.

McMillan, R. (2021). *Practical Threat Intelligence and Data-Driven Security Analysis*. O'Reilly Media.

Melis, L., Song, C., De Cristofaro, E., & Shmatikov, V. (2019). Exploiting unintended feature leakage in collaborative learning. *Proceedings of the 2019 IEEE Symposium on Security and Privacy (SP)*, 691–706. IEEE. DOI: 10.1109/SP.2019.00029

Mennuni, M. (2023). *An Analysis of SOC Monitoring Systems* (Doctoral dissertation, Politecnico di Torino).

Micali, S. (1994). CS proofs. *IEEE Symposium on Foundations of Computer Science*.

Mickalson, S. B. (2023). Detecting Data Poisoning Attacks on Smart Farm Devices Using Machine Learning. *Agrárinformatika Folyóirat*, *12*(1), 45–58.

Microsoft. (2023). *Digital Defense Report*. Microsoft Corporation. Retrieved from https://www.microsoft.com

Ming, Y., Yang, X., Wang, W., Chen, Z., Feng, J., Xing, Y., & Zhang, G. (2025). Benchmarking neural radiance fields for autonomous robots: An overview. *Engineering Applications of Artificial Intelligence*, *140*, 109685. DOI: 10.1016/j.engappai.2024.109685

Mirsky, Y., Doitshman, T., Elovici, Y., & Shabtai, A. (2018). Kitsune: An Ensemble of Autoencoders for Online Network Intrusion Detection. *Proceedings 2018 Network and Distributed System Security Symposium*. Network and Distributed System Security Symposium, San Diego, CA. DOI: 10.14722/ndss.2018.23204

MIT. (2023). *Adversarial Machine Learning: Challenges, Methods, and Limitations*. Massachusetts Institute of Technology. Retrieved from https://www.mit.edu

MIT. Technology Review. (2023). *AI Security: Understanding the Risks*. MIT Technology Review. Retrieved from https://www.technologyreview.com

Mitchell, R., & Chen, I. R. (2014). A survey of intrusion detection techniques for cyber-physical systems. *ACM Computing Surveys*, *46*(4), 55. Advance online publication. DOI: 10.1145/2542049

Mohamed, N. (2024, June). A review of AI approaches in combating advanced persistent threats (APTs) in cybersecurity. In *2024 15th International Conference on Computing Communication and Networking Technologies (ICCCNT)* (pp. 1-6). IEEE.

Mohamed, N. (2023). Current trends in AI and ML for cybersecurity: A state-of-the-art survey. *Cogent Engineering*, *10*(2), 2272358. DOI: 10.1080/23311916.2023.2272358

Mohammed, A. S., & Patil, S. (2022). Investigating the Optimal Cloud Computing Infrastructure for Training Large-Scale Generative Models. [IJFMR]. *International Journal for Multidisciplinary Research*, *4*(6).

Möller, D. P. (2023). Threats and threat intelligence. In *Guide to cybersecurity in digital transformation: Trends, methods, technologies, applications and best practices* (pp. 71–129). Springer Nature Switzerland. DOI: 10.1007/978-3-031-26845-8_2

Momand, A., Jan, S. U., & Ramzan, N. (2023). A systematic and comprehensive survey of recent advances in intrusion detection systems using machine learning: Deep learning, datasets, and attack taxonomy. *Journal of Sensors*, *2023*(1), 6048087. Advance online publication. DOI: 10.1155/2023/6048087

Morán, P., Robles-Gómez, A., Duque, A., Tobarra, L., & Pastor-Vargas, R. (2024). Machine learning models and dimensionality reduction for improving the Android malware detection. *PeerJ. Computer Science*, *10*, e2616. DOI: 10.7717/peerj-cs.2616 PMID: 39896377

Moric, Z., Dakic, V., & Kulic, M. (2024, June). Implementing a Security Framework for Container Orchestration. In *2024 IEEE 11th International Conference on Cyber Security and Cloud Computing (CSCloud)* (pp. 200-206). IEEE. DOI: 10.1109/CSCloud62866.2024.00042

Mothukuri, V., Parizi, R. M., Pouriyeh, S., Huang, Y., Dehghantanha, A., & Srivastava, G. (2021). A survey on security and privacy of federated learning. *Future Generation Computer Systems*, *115*, 619–640. DOI: 10.1016/j.future.2020.10.007

Moustafa, N., Koroniotis, N., Keshk, M., Zomaya, A. Y., & Tari, Z. (2023). Explainable intrusion detection for cyber defences in the internet of things: Opportunities and solutions. *IEEE Communications Surveys and Tutorials*, *25*(3), 1775–1807. DOI: 10.1109/COMST.2023.3280465

Muhammad, Z., Anwar, Z., Saleem, B., & Shahid, J. (2023). Emerging Cybersecurity and Privacy Threats to Electric Vehicles and Their Impact on Human and Environmental Sustainability." *. *Energies*, *16*(1113), 1–30. DOI: 10.3390/en16031113

Muneer, S., Farooq, U., & Athar, A. (2024). A Critical Review of AI-Based Approaches in Intrusion Detection: A Comprehensive Analysis. *Journal of Engineering*, *2024*(1), 3909173. DOI: 10.1155/2024/3909173

Murali, R., Thangavel, P., & Velayutham, C. S. (2023). Evolving malware variants as antigens for antivirus systems. *Expert Systems with Applications*, *226*, 120092. DOI: 10.1016/j.eswa.2023.120092

Muzammil, M. B., Bilal, M., Ajmal, S., Shongwe, S. C., & Ghadi, Y. Y. (2024). Unveiling Vulnerabilities of Web Attacks Considering Man in the Middle Attack and Session Hijacking. *IEEE Access : Practical Innovations, Open Solutions*, *12*, 6365–6375. DOI: 10.1109/ACCESS.2024.3350444

Mvula, P. K., Branco, P., Jourdan, G. V., & Viktor, H. L. (2024). A Survey on the Applications of Semi-supervised Learning to Cyber-security. *ACM Computing Surveys*, *56*(10), 1–41. DOI: 10.1145/3657647

Mylrea, M. (2025). The generative AI weapon of mass destruction: Evolving disinformation threats, vulnerabilities, and mitigation frameworks. In *Interdependent Human-Machine Teams* (pp. 315–347). Academic Press. DOI: 10.1016/B978-0-443-29246-0.00007-9

Mythily, V., Sukumar, P., Akshaya, V., Dinesh, S., & Nandhini, M. (2025). Malware detection and prevention using machine learning. In Challenges in Information, Communication and Computing Technology (pp. 564-569). CRC Press.

Naeem, S., Ali, A., Anam, S., & Ahmed, M. M. (2023). An unsupervised machine learning algorithms: Comprehensive review. *International Journal of Computing and Digital Systems.*

Nagar, G. (2018). *Leveraging Artificial Intelligence to Automate and Enhance Security Operations: Balancing Efficiency and Human Oversight.* Valley International Journal Digital Library.

Nair, V., Radhakrishnan, A., Chithra, R., & James, A. (2023). Memristive pixel-CNN loop generate for CNN generalisations. *IEEE Transactions on Nanotechnology*, *22*, 120–125. DOI: 10.1109/TNANO.2023.3248108

Nankya, M., Chataut, R., & Akl, R. (2023). Securing Industrial Control Systems: Components, Cyber Threats, and Machine Learning-Driven Defense Strategies. *Sensors (Basel)*, *23*(21), 8840. DOI: 10.3390/s23218840 PMID: 37960539

Naor, M. (1991). Bit commitment using pseudo-randomness. *Journal of Cryptology*, *4*(2), 151–158. DOI: 10.1007/BF00196774

National Security Commission on Artificial Intelligence (NSCAI). (2021). *Final report.* Washington, DC: NSCAI. (See Chapter 6: AI and the future of cybersecurity.)

Neupane, S., Fernandez, I. A., Mittal, S., & Rahimi, S. (2023). Impacts and risk of generative AI technology on cyber defense. *arXiv preprint arXiv:2306.13033.*

Nguyen, T. T., & Reddi, V. J. (2021). Deep reinforcement learning for cyber security. *IEEE Transactions on Neural Networks and Learning Systems*, (Early Access), 1–17. DOI: 10.1109/TNNLS.2021.3121870

Nguyen, T. D., Marchal, S., Miettinen, M., Fereidooni, H., Asokan, N., & Sadeghi, A. R. (2019). DIoT: A federated self-learning anomaly detection system for IoT. *Proceedings of the 2019 IEEE International Conference on Distributed Computing Systems (ICDCS)*, 756–767. IEEE. DOI: 10.1109/ICDCS.2019.00080

Nguyen-Tuong, A., Melski, D., Morris, D., Nguyen, D., Rizzi, E., Davidson, J. W., Hiser, J. D., Co, M., & Hawkins, W. H. (2018). Xandra: An autonomous cyber battle system for the Cyber Grand Challenge. *IEEE Security and Privacy*, *16*(2), 42–51. DOI: 10.1109/MSP.2018.1870876

Nilă, C., Apostol, I., & Patriciu, V. (2020a). Machine Learning Approach to Quick Incident Response. In *2020 12th International Conference on Electronics, Computers and Artificial Intelligence (ECAI)* (pp. 291–296). IEEE. DOI: 10.1109/COMM48946.2020.9141989

Nilă, C., & Patriciu, V. (2020b). Taking Advantage of Unsupervised Learning in Incident Response. In *2020 International Conference on Cybersecurity (ICGS3)* (pp. 1–6). IEEE. DOI: 10.1109/ECAI50035.2020.9223163

Ning, R., Bu, W., Yang, J., & Duan, S. (2023, August). A survey of detection methods research on living-off-the-land techniques. In *2023 IEEE International Conference on Sensors, Electronics and Computer Engineering (ICSECE)* (pp. 159-164). IEEE. DOI: 10.1109/ICSECE58870.2023.10263445

NIST. (2020). *AI risk management framework: Developing trustworthy AI. National Institute of Standards and Technology (NIST).* Special Publication.

Niyomdi, M., & Oluoch, J. (2025, February). A Comprehensive Security Orchestration, Automation, and Response System (SOAR) for Connected and Autonomous Vehicles (CAVs). In *2025 IEEE 4th International Conference on AI in Cybersecurity (ICAIC)* (pp. 1-14). IEEE.

Nobili, M., Raguseo, D., & Setola, R. (2025). Cybersecuity Analysis of a Telemedicine Platform. *Health Care*, *13*(2), 184. PMID: 39857212

O'Driscoll, R., Hagen, C., Bater, J., & Adams, J. M. (2024). *Multi-Objective Reinforcement Learning for Automated Resilient Cyber Defence* (Version 1). arXiv. DOI: 10.22541/au.173271087.78484560/v1

Oesch, S., Austria, P., Chaulagain, A., Weber, B., Watson, C., Dixson, M., & Sadovnik, A. (2024). The Path to Autonomous Cyber Defense. [In press] [. Retrieved from https://arxiv.org/]. *IEEE Security and Privacy*, *22*(1), 29–37.

Oesch, S., Austria, P., Chaulagain, A., Weber, B., Watson, C., Dixson, M., & Sadovnik, A. (2025). The path to autonomous cyber defense. *IEEE Security and Privacy*, *23*(1), 38–46. DOI: 10.1109/MSEC.2024.3427640

Ofusori, L., Bokaba, T., & Mhlongo, S. (2024). Artificial intelligence in cybersecurity: A comprehensive review and future direction. [In press]. *Applied Artificial Intelligence*, *38*(1), 2184087. DOI: 10.1080/08839514.2024.2439609

Ojha, A. C., Agarwal, A., & Swetha, G. (2023, November). Generative Adversarial Networks for Cybersecurity Threat. In *2023 International Conference on Recent Advances in Science and Engineering Technology (ICRASET)* (pp. 1-6). IEEE.

Okdem, S., & Okdem, S. (2024). Artificial Intelligence in Cybersecurity: A Review and a Case Study. *Applied Sciences (Basel, Switzerland), 14*(22), 10487. DOI: 10.3390/app142210487

Okolie, U. C. (2022). Distinction between Traditional security and modern security: A conceptual discourse. *The Journal of American Science, 19*(2), 247–266.

Olateju, O., Okon, S. U., Igwenagu, U., Salami, A. A., Oladoyinbo, T. O., & Olaniyi, O. O. (2024). Combating the challenges of false positives in AI-driven anomaly detection systems and enhancing data security in the cloud. *Available atSSRN* 4859958.

Opara, I. K., Opara, U. L., Okolie, J. A., & Fawole, O. A. (2024). Machine Learning Application in Horticulture and Prospects for Predicting Fresh Produce Losses and Waste: A Review. *Plants, 13*(9), 1200. DOI: 10.3390/plants13091200 PMID: 38732414

Padmavathi, G., Shanmugapriya, D., & Roshni, A. (2022, March). Performance analysis of unsupervised machine learning methods for mobile malware detection. In *2022 9th International Conference on Computing for Sustainable Global Development (INDIACom)* (pp. 201-206). IEEE.

Padmavathi, U., Harshitha, R. S., & Jayashre, K. (2024). Integrating Cyber-Physical Systems for Enhanced Efficiency in Healthcare Solutions. In *Technologies for Sustainable Healthcare Development* (pp. 300–324). IGI Global.

Pandit, A. V., & Mondal, D. (2023). Real-Time Malware Detection on IoT Devices using Behavior-Based Analysis and Neural Networks. *Research Journal of Computer Systems and Engineering, 4*(2), 117–129. DOI: 10.52710/rjcse.82

Pan, Y., Ge, X., Fang, C., & Fan, Y. (2020). A systematic literature review of android malware detection using static analysis. *IEEE Access : Practical Innovations, Open Solutions, 8*, 116363–116379. DOI: 10.1109/ACCESS.2020.3002842

Paracha, M. A., & Rasheed, A. (2024). Leveraging AI for Network Threat Detection — A Conceptual Overview. *Electronics (Basel), 13*(23), 4611. DOI: 10.3390/electronics13234611

Park, C. H., Jo, J. Y., & Kim, Y. (2023, December). Detecting Cyber Threats with Limited Dataset Using Generative Adversarial Network on SCADA System. In *2023 International Conference on Computational Science and Computational Intelligence (CSCI)* (pp. 915-919). IEEE. DOI: 10.1109/CSCI62032.2023.00153

Park, J., Erikson, C., Han, X., & Iyer, P. (2018). Are state telehealth policies associated with the use of telehealth services among underserved populations? *Health Affairs*, *37*(12), 2060–2068. DOI: 10.1377/hlthaff.2018.05101 PMID: 30633679

Parno, B., Howell, J., Gentry, C., & Raykova, M. (2013). Pinocchio: Nearly practical verifiable computation. *IEEE Symposium on Security and Privacy*.

Patel, U. (2024). Data Privacy and Security in Financial Services. *Journal of Artificial Intelligence & Cloud Computing*, 1–13. DOI: 10.47363/JAICC/2024(3)E204

Patel, A., & Wei, L. (2024). The Future of Cyber Defense: Autonomous Systems Powered by AI and Machine Learning. *Baltic Multidisciplinary Research Letters Journal*, *1*(3), 85–92.

Patil, D. (2024). Artificial Intelligence In Retail And E-Commerce: Enhancing Customer Experience Through Personalization, Predictive Analytics, And Real-Time Engagement. *Predictive Analytics, And Real-Time Engagement (November 26, 2024)*.

Patil, R. Y., Patil, Y. H., & Bannore, A. (2024). Cybersecurity in medical Internet of Things: Issues, challenges, and future directions. In *Security Implementation in Internet of Medical Things* (pp. 87–110). CRC Press.

Patwardhan, N., Marrone, S., & Sansone, C. (2023). Transformers in the real world: A survey on nlp applications. *Information (Basel)*, *14*(4), 242. DOI: 10.3390/info14040242

Peikert, C. (2016). A decade of lattice cryptography. *Foundations and Trends in Theoretical Computer Science*, *10*(4), 283–424. DOI: 10.1561/0400000074

Phong, L. T., Ahn, T., Phuong, T. P., & Chong, P. H. J. (2018). Privacy-preserving deep learning via additively homomorphic encryption. *IEEE Transactions on Information Forensics and Security*, *13*(5), 1333–1345. DOI: 10.1109/TIFS.2017.2787987

Pinto, A., Herrera, L. C., Donoso, Y., & Gutierrez, J. A. (2024). Enhancing Critical Infrastructure Security: Unsupervised Learning Approaches for Anomaly Detection. *International Journal of Computational Intelligence Systems*, *17*(1), 236. DOI: 10.1007/s44196-024-00644-z

Pitropakis, N., Panaousis, E., Giannetsos, T., Anastasiadis, E., & Loukas, G. (2019). A Taxonomy and Survey of Attacks Against Machine Learning in Cybersecurity. *Computer Science Review*, *34*, 100199. DOI: 10.1016/j.cosrev.2019.100199

Pool, J., Akhlaghpour, S., Fatehi, F., & Gray, L. C. (2022). Data privacy concerns and use of telehealth in the aged care context: An integrative review and research agenda. *International Journal of Medical Informatics, 160*, 104707. DOI: 10.1016/j.ijmedinf.2022.104707 PMID: 35131698

Prejbeanu, R. (2019). Cyber Threat Detection Using Word Embeddings and Deep Learning. Bitdefender White Paper (October 2019). Retrieved from https://ccdcoe.org/

Prejbeanu, R. (2020). Machine Learning Methods for Malware Detection. Kaspersky White Paper. Retrieved from https://ccdcoe.org/

Preuveneers, D., Llamas, J. M., Bulut, I., Rúa, E. A., Verfaillie, P., Demortier, V., Surinx, D., & Joosen, W. (2024). On the Use of AutoML for Combating Alert Fatigue in Security Operations Centers. In S. Katsikas, H. Abie, S. Ranise, L. Verderame, E. Cambiaso, R. Ugarelli, I. Praça, W. Li, W. Meng, S. Furnell, B. Katt, S. Pirbhulal, A. Shukla, M. Ianni, M. Dalla Preda, K.-K. R. Choo, M. Pupo Correia, A. Abhishta, G. Sileno, … N. Yanai (Eds.), *Computer Security. ESORICS 2023 International Workshops* (Vol. 14399, pp. 609–627). Springer Nature Switzerland. DOI: 10.1007/978-3-031-54129-2_36

Preuveneers, D., & Joosen, W. (2021). Sharing machine learning models as indicators of compromise for cyber threat intelligence. *Journal of Cybersecurity and Privacy, 1*(1), 140–163. DOI: 10.3390/jcp1010008

Pugin, F., Bucher, P., & Morel, P. (2011). History of robotic surgery: From AESOP® and ZEUS® to da Vinci®. *Journal of Visceral Surgery, 148*(no. 5), e3–e8. DOI: 10.1016/j.jviscsurg.2011.04.007 PMID: 21974854

Quertier, T., Marais, B., Barrué, G., Morucci, S., Azé, S., & Salladin, S. (2024). A Lean Transformer Model for Dynamic Malware Analysis and Detection. *arXiv preprint arXiv:2408.02313.*

Qureshi, S. U., He, J., Tunio, S., Zhu, N., Nazir, A., Wajahat, A., Ullah, F., & Wadud, A. (2024). Systematic review of deep learning solutions for malware detection and forensic analysis in IoT. *Journal of King Saud University. Computer and Information Sciences, 36*(8), 102164. DOI: 10.1016/j.jksuci.2024.102164

Rabbani, M., Wang, Y., Khoshkangini, R., Jelodar, H., Zhao, R., Bagheri Baba Ahmadi, S., & Ayobi, S. (2021). A review on machine learning approaches for network malicious behavior detection in emerging technologies. *Entropy (Basel, Switzerland), 23*(5), 529. DOI: 10.3390/e23050529 PMID: 33923125

Rahman, M. M., Al Shakil, S., & Mustakim, M. R. (2024). A survey on intrusion detection system in IoT networks. *Cyber Security and Applications, 3*, 100082. DOI: 10.1016/j.csa.2024.100082

Rahman, S. A., Tout, H., Talhi, C., & Mourad, A. (2020). Internet of Things intrusion detection: Centralized, on-device, or federated learning? *IEEE Network, 34*(6), 310–317. DOI: 10.1109/MNET.011.2000286

Ramachandran, S., Kim, J., Zia, T., & Almorjan, A. (2023). Cybersecurity and Cyber Forensics for Smart Cities: A Comprehensive Literature Review and Survey. *Sensors (Basel), 23*(7), 3545. DOI: 10.3390/s23073545 PMID: 37050609

Rao, S. D. P. (2024). Harnessing AI For Evolving Threats: From Detection to Automated Response.

Rao, D. D., Waoo, A. A., Singh, M. P., Pareek, P. K., Kamal, S., & Pandit, S. V. (2024). Strategizing IoT Network Layer Security Through Advanced Intrusion Detection Systems and AI-Driven Threat Analysis. *Full Length Article, 12*(2), 195–95.

Rao, V. S., Balakrishna, R., El-Ebiary, Y. A. B., Thapar, P., Saravanan, K. A., & Godla, S. R. (2024). AI Driven Anomaly Detection in Network Traffic Using Hybrid CNN-GAN. *J. Adv. Inf. Technol, 15*(7), 886–895. DOI: 10.12720/jait.15.7.886-895

Rasouli, M., Miehling, E., & Teneketzis, D. (2018). A scalable decomposition method for the dynamic defense of cyber networks. In *Proceedings of the 2018 Conference on Decision and Game Theory for Security (GameSec)* (pp. 221–241). Springer. DOI: 10.1007/978-3-319-75268-6_4

Rauniyar, A., Hagos, D. H., Jha, D., Håkegård, J. E., Bagci, U., Rawat, D. B., & Vlassov, V. (2023). Federated learning for medical applications: A taxonomy, current trends, challenges, and future research directions. *IEEE Internet of Things Journal.*

Raval, A., & Anwar, M. "Android Malware Detection: An Empirical Investigation into Machine Learning Classifiers." *2024 IEEE International Conference on Information Reuse and Integration for Data Science (IRI)*. IEEE, 2024. DOI: 10.1109/IRI62200.2024.00039

Raymond, V. J., & Raj, R. (2023). Investigation of Android Malware with Machine Learning Classifiers using Enhanced PCA Algorithm. *Computer Systems Science and Engineering, 44*(3).

Razaque, A., Bektemyssova, G., Yoo, J., Hariri, S., Khan, M. J., Nalgozhina, N., Hwang, J., & Khan, M. A. (2025). Review of malicious code detection in data mining applications: Challenges, algorithms, and future direction. *Cluster Computing, 28*(3), 1–37. DOI: 10.1007/s10586-024-05017-x

Redhu, A., Choudhary, P., Srinivasan, K., & Das, T. K. (2024). Deep learning-powered malware detection in cyberspace: A contemporary review. *Frontiers in Physics (Lausanne)*, *12*, 1349463. DOI: 10.3389/fphy.2024.1349463

Rehan, H. (2024). The Future of Electric Vehicles: Navigating the Intersection of AI, Cloud Technology, and Cybersecurity." *. *International Journal of Scientific Research in Management*, *12*(4), 1127–1143. DOI: 10.18535/ijsrm/v12i04.ec04

Reis, J., Cohen, Y., Melão, N., Costa, J., & Jorge, D. (2021). High-tech defense industries: Developing autonomous intelligent systems. *Applied Sciences (Basel, Switzerland)*, *11*(11), 4920. DOI: 10.3390/app11114920

Resende, P. A. A., & Drummond, A. C. (2019). A Survey of Random Forest Based Methods for Intrusion Detection Systems. *ACM Computing Surveys*, *51*(3), 1–36. DOI: 10.1145/3178582

Ribeiro, M. T., Singh, S., & Guestrin, C. (2016). "Why should I trust you?": Explaining the predictions of any classifier. *Proceedings of the 22nd ACM SIGKDD International Conference on Knowledge Discovery and Data Mining,* 1135-1144.

Ridley, A. (2018). Machine learning for autonomous cyber defense. *The Next Wave (NSA's Review of Emerging Technologies), 22(1), 7–14.*

Rodrigo, C., Pierre, S., Beaubrun, R., & El Khoury, F. (2021). BrainShield: A hybrid machine learning-based malware detection model for android devices. *Electronics (Basel)*, *10*(23), 2948. DOI: 10.3390/electronics10232948

Rogaway, P., & Shrimpton, T. (2004). Cryptographic hash-function security and the ideal-cipher model. Advances in Cryptology—CRYPTO 2004, 618-636.

Roshanaei, M., Khan, M. R., & Sylvester, N. N. (2024). Navigating AI cybersecurity: Evolving landscape and challenges. *Journal of Intelligent Learning Systems and Applications*, *16*(3), 155–174. DOI: 10.4236/jilsa.2024.163010

Sabeel, U., Heydari, S. S., El-Khatib, K., & Elgazzar, K. (2024). Incremental Adversarial Learning for Polymorphic Attack Detection. *IEEE Transactions on Machine Learning in Communications and Networking*, *2*, 869–887. DOI: 10.1109/TMLCN.2024.3418756

Sabillon, R., Cavaller, V., Cano, J., & Serra-Ruiz, J. (2016, June). Cybercriminals, cyberattacks and cybercrime. In *2016 IEEE International Conference on Cybercrime and Computer Forensic (ICCCF)* (pp. 1-9). IEEE.

Sadiq, S., & Zeebaree, S. R. (2024). Distributed Systems for Machine Learning in Cloud Computing: A Review of Scalable and Efficient Training and Inference. *Indonesian Journal of Computer Science, 13*(2). Advance online publication. DOI: 10.33022/ijcs.v13i2.3814

Safitra, M. F., Lubis, M., & Fakhrurroja, H. (2023). Counterattacking cyber threats: A framework for the future of cybersecurity. *Sustainability (Basel), 15*(18), 13369. DOI: 10.3390/su151813369

Sai, S., Yashvardhan, U., Chamola, V., & Sikdar, B. (2024). Generative ai for cyber security: Analyzing the potential of chatgpt, dall-e and other models for enhancing the security space. *IEEE Access : Practical Innovations, Open Solutions, 12*, 53497–53516. DOI: 10.1109/ACCESS.2024.3385107

Salatiello, A., Wang, Y., Wichern, G., Koike-Akino, T., Ohta, Y., Kaneko, Y., . . . Chakrabarty, A. (2023). Synthesizing Building Operation Data with Generative Models: VAEs, GANs, or Something In Between? In *Companion Proceedings of the 14th ACM International Conference on Future Energy Systems* (pp. 125-133).

Saleh, S. S. A. M. (2024). Blockchain for Secure and Decentralized Artificial Intelligence in Cybersecurity: A Comprehensive Review. *Blockchain: Research and Applications, 100193.*

Salem, A. H., Azzam, S. M., Emam, O. E., & Abohany, A. A. (2024). Advancing Cybersecurity: A Comprehensive Review of AI-Driven Detection Techniques. *Journal of Big Data, 11*(1), 105. DOI: 10.1186/s40537-024-00957-y

Sallam, M., Al-Mahzoum, K., & Sallam, M. (2024). Generative Artificial Intelligence and Cybersecurity Risks: Implications for Healthcare Security Based on Real-life Incidents. *Mesopotamian Journal of Artificial Intelligence in Healthcare, 2024*, 184–203. DOI: 10.58496/MJAIH/2024/019

Samek, W., Wiegand, T., & Müller, K. (2019). Explainable artificial intelligence: Understanding, visualizing and interpreting deep learning models. *Digital Signal Processing, 91*, 1–10.

Samra, A. A. A., Yim, K., & Ghanem, O. A. (2013, July). Analysis of clustering technique in android malware detection. In *2013 seventh international conference on innovative mobile and internet services in ubiquitous computing* (pp. 729-733). IEEE.

Samtani, S., Abate, M., Benjamin, V., & Li, W. (2020). *Cybersecurity as an industry: A cyber threat intelligence perspective.* The Palgrave Handbook of International Cybercrime and Cyberdeviance.

Sandoval, I. O., Thompson, I. S., Mavroudis, V., & Hicks, C. (2025). *An Attentive Graph Agent for Topology-Adaptive Cyber Defence* (Version 3). arXiv. DOI: 10.48550/ARXIV.2501.14700

Sanjalawe, Y. K., & Al-E'mari, S. R. (2023). Abnormal transactions detection in the ethereum network using semi-supervised generative adversarial networks. *IEEE Access : Practical Innovations, Open Solutions*, *11*, 98516–98531. DOI: 10.1109/ACCESS.2023.3313630

Sanju, P. (2023). Enhancing intrusion detection in IoT systems: A hybrid meta-heuristics-deep learning approach with ensemble of recurrent neural networks. *Journal of Engineering Research*, *11*(4), 356–361. DOI: 10.1016/j.jer.2023.100122

Santoso, F., & Finn, A. (2023). An In-Depth Examination of Artificial Intelligence-Enhanced Cybersecurity in Robotics, Autonomous Systems, and Critical Infrastructures. *IEEE Transactions on Services Computing*.

Saqib, M., Mahdavifar, S., Fung, B. C., & Charland, P. (2024). A Comprehensive Analysis of Explainable AI for Malware Hunting. *ACM Computing Surveys*, *56*(12), 1–40. DOI: 10.1145/3677374

Sarhan, M., Layeghy, S., Moustafa, N., & Portmann, M. (2023). Cyber threat intelligence sharing scheme based on federated learning for network intrusion detection. *Journal of Network and Systems Management*, *31*(1), 3. DOI: 10.1007/s10922-022-09691-3

Sarker, I. H. (2024). *AI-driven cybersecurity and threat intelligence: cyber automation, intelligent decision-making and explainability*. Springer Nature. DOI: 10.1007/978-3-031-54497-2

Sarker, I. H., Janicke, H., Mohsin, A., Gill, A., & Maglaras, L. (2024). Explainable AI for cybersecurity automation, intelligence and trustworthiness in digital twin: Methods, taxonomy, challenges and prospects. *ICT Express*, *10*(4), 935–958. DOI: 10.1016/j.icte.2024.05.007

Sarker, I. H., Kayes, A. S. M., Badsha, S., Alqahtani, H., Watters, P., & Ng, A. (2020). A. S. M. Kayes, Shahriar Badsha, Hamed Alqahtani, Paul Watters, and Alex Ng. "Cybersecurity data science: An overview from machine learning perspective.". *Journal of Big Data*, *7*(1), 1–29. DOI: 10.1186/s40537-020-00318-5

Sarker, I. H., Kayes, A., Badsha, S., Alqahtani, H., Watters, P., & Ng, A. (2021). Cybersecurity data science: An overview from machine learning perspective. *Journal of Big Data*, *8*, 1–29.

Sayyed, S., Zhang, M., Rifat, S., Swami, A., De Lucia, M., & Restuccia, F. (2024). Resilience and security of deep neural networks against intentional and unintentional perturbations: Survey and research challenges. *arXiv preprint arXiv:2408.00193.*

Sebastianelli, A., Tipaldi, M., Ullo, S. L., & Glielmo, L. (2021, June). A Deep Q-Learning based approach applied to the Snake game. In 2021 29th Mediterranean Conference on Control and Automation (MED) (pp. 348-353). IEEE.

Security, I. B. M. (2022). *X-Force Threat Intelligence Index.* IBM Corporation. Retrieved from https://www.ibm.com

Security, I. B. M. (2023). *Data Security Best Practices.* IBM Corporation. Retrieved from https://www.ibm.com

Senanayake, J., Kalutarage, H., & Al-Kadri, M. O. (2021). Android mobile malware detection using machine learning: A systematic review. *Electronics (Basel)*, *10*(13), 1606. DOI: 10.3390/electronics10131606

Sengar, S. S., Hasan, A. B., Kumar, S., & Carroll, F. (2024). Generative artificial intelligence: A systematic review and applications. *Multimedia Tools and Applications*, •••, 1–40. DOI: 10.1007/s11042-024-20016-1

Sengupta, A., Huang, X., Kambhampati, S., Zhu, Z., Wang, S., Shen, C., & Liu, D. (2020). A survey of moving target defense: Approaches and research challenges. *IEEE Communications Surveys and Tutorials*, *22*(1), 622–653. DOI: 10.1109/COMST.2019.2951813

Sengupta, S., Chowdhary, A., Sabur, A., Alshamrani, A., Huang, D., & Kambhampati, S. (2020). A survey of moving target defenses for network security. *IEEE Communications Surveys and Tutorials*, *22*(3), 1909–1941. DOI: 10.1109/COMST.2020.2982955

Sewak, M., Sahay, S. K., & Rathore, H. (2022). Deep reinforcement learning in the advanced cybersecurity threat detection and protection. *Information Systems Frontiers*, (Online First). DOI: 10.1007/s10796-022-10333-x

Sewak, M., Sahay, S. K., & Rathore, H. (2023). Deep reinforcement learning in the advanced cybersecurity threat detection and protection. *Information Systems Frontiers*, *25*(2), 589–611.

Shafin, S. S., Ahmed, M. M., Pranto, M. A., & Chowdhury, A. (2021, December). Detection of android malware using tree-based ensemble stacking model. In *2021 IEEE Asia-Pacific Conference on Computer Science and Data Engineering (CSDE)* (pp. 1-6). IEEE. DOI: 10.1109/CSDE53843.2021.9718396

Shahin, M., Maghanaki, M., Hosseinzadeh, A., & Chen, F. F. (2024). Advancing network security in industrial IoT: A deep dive into AI-enabled intrusion detection systems. *Advanced Engineering Informatics*, *62*, 102685. DOI: 10.1016/j.aei.2024.102685

Shaikh, T. A., Rasool, T., & Verma, P. (2023). Machine intelligence and medical cyber-physical system architectures for smart healthcare: Taxonomy, challenges, opportunities, and possible solutions. *Artificial Intelligence in Medicine*, *146*, 102692. DOI: 10.1016/j.artmed.2023.102692 PMID: 38042609

Shakya, A. K., Pillai, G., & Chakrabarty, S. (2023). Reinforcement learning algorithms: A brief survey. *Expert Systems with Applications*, *231*, 120495. DOI: 10.1016/j.eswa.2023.120495

Shameli-Sendi, A., Cheriet, M., & Hamou-Lhadj, A. (2014). Taxonomy of intrusion risk assessment and response system. *Computers & Security*, *45*, 1–16. DOI: 10.1016/j.cose.2014.04.009

Shankar, G., Sridhar, S., Srivatsan, G., & Kishan, R., & SS, P. V. (2024, July). Enhancing Android Malware Detection Through Machine Learning: Insights From Permission and Metadata Analysis. In *2024 Third International Conference on Smart Technologies and Systems for Next Generation Computing (ICSTSN)* (pp. 1-6). IEEE.

Shao, L., Zhang, E., & Li, M. (2021). An efficient convolutional neural network model combined with attention mechanism for inverse halftoning. *Electronics (Basel)*, *10*(13), 1574. DOI: 10.3390/electronics10131574

Sharma, S., Krishna, C. R., & Kumar, R. (2021). RansomDroid: Forensic analysis and detection of Android Ransomware using unsupervised machine learning technique. *Forensic Science International Digital Investigation*, *37*, 301168. DOI: 10.1016/j.fsidi.2021.301168

Shatnawi, A. S., Jaradat, A., Yaseen, T. B., Taqieddin, E., Al-Ayyoub, M., & Mustafa, D. (2022). An android malware detection leveraging machine learning. *Wireless Communications and Mobile Computing*, *2022*(1), 1830201. DOI: 10.1155/2022/1830201

Shaukat, K., Luo, S., Varadharajan, V., Hameed, I. A., & Xu, M. (2020). A Survey on Machine Learning Techniques for Cyber Security in the Last Decade. *IEEE Access : Practical Innovations, Open Solutions*, *8*, 222310–222354. DOI: 10.1109/ACCESS.2020.3041951

Shehadeh, A., Alshboul, O., Al Mamlook, R. E., & Hamedat, O. (2021). Machine learning models for predicting the residual value of heavy construction equipment: An evaluation of modified decision tree, LightGBM, and XGBoost regression. *Automation in Construction*, *129*, 103827. DOI: 10.1016/j.autcon.2021.103827

Shehzadi, T. (2024). Reinforcement Learning-Based Autonomous Systems for Cyber Threat Detection and Response. *Eastern European Journal for Multidisciplinary Research*, *1*(1), 123–137.

Shinde, A., Doshi, P., & Setayeshfar, O. (2020). Active deception using factored interactive POMDPs to recognize cyber attacker's intent. *arXiv preprint*. Retrieved from https://arxiv.org/abs/2007.09512

Shokri, R., & Shmatikov, V. (2015). Privacy-preserving deep learning. *Proceedings of the 22nd ACM SIGSAC Conference on Computer and Communications Security*, 1310–1321. ACM.

Shrobe, H. E., & Shrier, D. L. (2018). The past, present, and future of cyberdefense. *IEEE Security and Privacy*, *16*(2), 61–69. DOI: 10.1109/MSP.2018.1870859

Siam, A. A. (2025). A Comprehensive Review of AI's Current Impact and Future Prospects in Cybersecurity. *IEEE Access : Practical Innovations, Open Solutions*, *13*, 14035–14058.

Sikos, L. F. (Ed.). (2019). *AI in cybersecurity*. Springer. DOI: 10.1007/978-3-319-98842-9

Silva, G. J. C., & Westphall, C. B. (2024). A Survey of Large Language Models in Cybersecurity. *arXiv Preprint, arXiv:2402.16968.*

Silvestri, S., Islam, S., Amelin, D., Weiler, G., Papastergiou, S., & Ciampi, M. (2024). Cyber threat assessment and management for securing healthcare ecosystems using natural language processing. *International Journal of Information Security*, *23*(1), 31–50. DOI: 10.1007/s10207-023-00769-w

Sindiramutty, S. R., Prabagaran, K. R. V., Jhanjhi, N. Z., Ghazanfar, M. A., Malik, N. A., & Soomro, T. R. (2025). Security Considerations in Generative AI for Web Applications. In *Reshaping CyberSecurity With Generative AI Techniques* (pp. 281–332). IGI Global.

Singh, T., Kumar, S., Singh, S. K., Gupta, B. B., Wu, J., & Castiglione, A. (2025). Enhancing Autonomous System Security With AI and Secure Computation Technologies. In *AI Developments for Industrial Robotics and Intelligent Drones* (pp. 159–186). IGI Global Scientific Publishing.

Smmarwar, S. K., Gupta, G. P., & Kumar, S. (2024). Android Malware Detection and Identification Frameworks by Leveraging the Machine and Deep Learning Techniques: A Comprehensive Review. *Telematics and Informatics Reports*, 100130.

Smolyakova, S. (2024). *Traditional Indicators of Compromise (IOCs) Meet Dynamic App-Device Interactions for IoT-specific Threat Intelligence* (Doctoral dissertation, Concordia University).

Soare, S. R. (2023). *The Role of Artificial Intelligence in European Strategic Autonomy*. Artificial Intelligence and International Conflict in Cyberspace.

Sodiya, E. O., Umoga, U. J., Amoo, O. O., & Atadoga, A. (2024). Quantum computing and its potential impact on US cybersecurity: A review: Scrutinizing the challenges and opportunities presented by quantum technologies in safeguarding digital assets. *Global Journal of Engineering and Technology Advances, 18*(02), 049-064.

Sofia, R. C., Dykeman, D., Urbanetz, P., Galal, A., & Dave, D. A. (2023). Dynamic, Context-Aware Cross-Layer Orchestration of Containerized Applications. *IEEE Access : Practical Innovations, Open Solutions, 11*, 93129–93150. DOI: 10.1109/ACCESS.2023.3307026

Somayaji, A., & Forrest, S. (2000). Automated response using system-call delays. In *Proceedings of the 9th USENIX Security Symposium*. USENIX Association.

Sommer, R., & Paxson, V. (2010). Outside the Closed World: On Using Machine Learning for Network Intrusion Detection. *2010 IEEE Symposium on Security and Privacy*, 305–316. DOI: 10.1109/SP.2010.25

Sonya, A., & Deepak, R. R. (2024). Android malware detection and classification using machine learning algorithm. *International Journal of Communication Networks and Information Security, 16*(4), 327–347.

Sood, A. (2024). *Combating Cyberattacks Targeting the AI Ecosystem: Assessing Threats, Risks, and Vulnerabilities*. Walter de Gruyter GmbH & Co KG. DOI: 10.1515/9781501520549

Stach, C., Gritti, C., Bräcker, J., Behringer, M., & Mitschang, B. (2022). Protecting sensitive data in the information age: State of the art and future prospects. *Future Internet, 14*(11), 302. DOI: 10.3390/fi14110302

Stakhanova, N., Basu, S., & Wong, J. (2007). A taxonomy of intrusion response systems. *International Journal of Information and Computer Security, 1*(1–2), 169–184. DOI: 10.1504/IJICS.2007.012248

Stamp, M., Visaggio, C. A., Mercaldo, F., & Di Troia, F. (Eds.). (2022). *Artificial intelligence for cybersecurity*. Springer. DOI: 10.1007/978-3-030-97087-1

Stanzione, M., Dividino, R., & Schaefer, G. (2020). Explainable artificial intelligence in cybersecurity: A survey. *IEEE Access : Practical Innovations, Open Solutions*, *8*, 222310–222354. DOI: 10.1109/ACCESS.2020.3041975

Statcounter. (2025). Mobile Operating System Market Share Worldwide, https://gs.statcounter.com/os-market-share/mobile/worldwide? Retrieved January 27, 2025.

Sturmberg, J., & Gainsford, L. (2024). Measures that matter should define accountability and governance frameworks. *Journal of Evaluation in Clinical Practice*, *30*(3), 503–510. DOI: 10.1111/jep.13943 PMID: 38037541

Su, J., Jiang, C., Jin, X., Qiao, Y., Xiao, T., Ma, H., . . . Lin, J. (2024). Large language models for forecasting and anomaly detection: A systematic literature review. *arXiv preprint arXiv:2402.10350.*

Suchman, L. (2023). Imaginaries of omniscience: Automating intelligence in the US Department of Defense. *Social Studies of Science*, *53*(5), 761–786. DOI: 10.1177/03063127221104938 PMID: 35735177

Sufi, F. (2024). Generative pre-trained transformer (GPT) in research: A systematic review on data augmentation. *Information (Basel)*, *15*(2), 99. DOI: 10.3390/info15020099

Sundaram, A. (2022). *Covert Cognizance: Embedded Intelligence for Industrial Systems* (Doctoral dissertation, Purdue University Graduate School).

Sundararajan, A., Khan, T., Moghadasi, A., & Sarwat, A. I. (2019). Survey on synchrophasor data quality and cybersecurity challenges, and evaluation of their interdependencies. *Journal of Modern Power Systems and Clean Energy*, *7*(3), 449–467. DOI: 10.1007/s40565-018-0473-6

Sun, N., Ding, M., Jiang, J., Xu, W., Mo, X., Tai, Y., & Zhang, J. (2023). Cyber threat intelligence mining for proactive cybersecurity defense: A survey and new perspectives. *IEEE Communications Surveys and Tutorials*, *25*(3), 1748–1774. DOI: 10.1109/COMST.2023.3273282

Surianarayanan, C., Kunasekaran, S., & Chelliah, P. R. (2024). A high-throughput architecture for anomaly detection in streaming data using machine learning algorithms. *International Journal of Information Technology : an Official Journal of Bharati Vidyapeeth's Institute of Computer Applications and Management*, *16*(1), 493–506. DOI: 10.1007/s41870-023-01585-0

Su, Z., Li, C., Fu, H., Wang, L., Wu, M., & Feng, X. (2024). Haitian Fu, Liyang Wang, Meilong Wu, and Xiaobin Feng. "Development and prospect of telemedicine.". *Intelligent Medicine*, *4*(1), 1–9. DOI: 10.1016/j.imed.2022.10.004

Syed, F. M., & ES, F. K. (2018). Ensuring HIPAA and GDPR Compliance Through Advanced IAM Analytics. *International Journal of Advanced Engineering Technologies and Innovations*, *1*(2), 71–94.

Syed, F. M., & ES, F. K. (2019). Privacy by Design: Integrating GDPR Principles into IAM Frameworks for Healthcare. *International Journal of Advanced Engineering Technologies and Innovations*, *1*(2), 16–36.

Syed, F. M., & ES, F. K. (2020). IAM for Cyber Resilience: Protecting Healthcare Data from Advanced Persistent Threats. *International Journal of Advanced Engineering Technologies and Innovations*, *1*(2), 153–183.

Syed, F. M., & ES, F. K. (2021). AI and HIPAA Compliance in Healthcare IAM. *International Journal of Advanced Engineering Technologies and Innovations*, *1*(4), 118–145.

Syed, F. M., & ES, F. K. (2023). AI in Securing Electronic Health Records (EHR) Systems. *International Journal of Advanced Engineering Technologies and Innovations*, *1*(02), 593–620.

Syed, F. M., & ES, F. K. (2024). AI in Protecting Sensitive Patient Data under GDPR in Healthcare. *International Journal of Advanced Engineering Technologies and Innovations*, *1*(02), 401–435.

Syed, F. M., & ES, F. K. (2024). AI-Driven Forensic Analysis for Cyber Incidents in Healthcare. *International Journal of Machine Learning Research in Cybersecurity and Artificial Intelligence*, *15*(1), 473–499.

Syed, F. M., & ES, F. K. (2024). AI-Driven Threat Intelligence in Healthcare Cybersecurity. *Revista de Inteligencia Artificial en Medicina*, *14*(1), 431–459.

Syed, F. M., ES, F. K., & Johnson, E. (2022). AI-Powered SOC in the Healthcare Industry. *International Journal of Advanced Engineering Technologies and Innovations*, *1*(2), 395–414.

Syed, F. M., ES, F. K., & Johnson, E. (2023). AI in Protecting Clinical Trial Data from Cyber Threats. *International Journal of Advanced Engineering Technologies and Innovations*, *1*(2), 567–592.

Syed, N. F., Shah, S. W., Shaghaghi, A., Anwar, A., Baig, Z., & Doss, R. (2022). Zero trust architecture (zta): A comprehensive survey. *IEEE Access : Practical Innovations, Open Solutions*, *10*, 57143–57179. DOI: 10.1109/ACCESS.2022.3174679

Taddeo, M., McCutcheon, T., & Floridi, L. (2019a). Trusting artificial intelligence in cybersecurity is a double-edged sword. *Nature Machine Intelligence*, *1*(12), 557–560. DOI: 10.1038/s42256-019-0109-1

Takács, Á., Jordán, S., Nagy, D. Á., Tar, J. K., Rudas, I. J., & Haidegger, T. (2015, May). Surgical robotics—Born in space. In *2015 IEEE 10th Jubilee International Symposium on Applied Computational Intelligence and Informatics* (pp. 547-551). IEEE.

Takács, A., Nagy, D. Á., Rudas, I., & Haidegger, T. (2016). Origins of surgical robotics: From space to the operating room. *Acta Polytechnica Hungarica*, *13*(1), 13–30.

Tanikonda, A., Pandey, B. K., Peddinti, S. R., & Katragadda, S. R. (2022). Advanced AI-Driven Cybersecurity Solutions for Proactive Threat Detection and Response in Complex Ecosystems. *Journal of Science and Technology*, *3*(1).

Tanimu, J. A., & Abada, W. (2024). *Addressing cybersecurity challenges in robotics: A comprehensive overview*. Cyber Security and Applications.

Tan, J., Jin, H., Zhang, H., Zhang, Y., Chang, D., Liu, X., & Zhang, H. (2023). When Moving Target Defense Meets Game Theory: A Survey. *Computer Science Review*, *49*, 100544. DOI: 10.1016/j.cosrev.2023.100544

Tariq, M. U. (2024). Enhancing cybersecurity protocols in modern healthcare systems: Strategies and best practices. In *Transformative Approaches to Patient Literacy and Healthcare Innovation* (pp. 223–241). IGI Global. DOI: 10.4018/979-8-3693-3661-8.ch011

Tariq, U., Ahmed, I., Bashir, A. K., & Khan, M. A. (2024). Securing the evolving IoT with deep learning: A comprehensive review. *Kurdish Studies*, *12*(1), 3426–3454.

Taye, M. M. (2023). Understanding of machine learning with deep learning: Architectures, workflow, applications and future directions. *Computers*, *12*(5), 91. DOI: 10.3390/computers12050091

Thakur, P., Kansal, V., & Rishiwal, V. (2024). Hybrid deep learning approach based on lstm and cnn for malware detection. *Wireless Personal Communications*, *136*(3), 1879–1901. DOI: 10.1007/s11277-024-11366-y

Thangavel, K., Sabatini, R., Gardi, A., Ranasinghe, K., Hilton, S., Servidia, P., & Spiller, D. (2024). Artificial intelligence for trusted autonomous satellite operations. *Progress in Aerospace Sciences*, *144*, 100960. DOI: 10.1016/j.paerosci.2023.100960

Theron, P., Kott, A., Drašar, M., Rzadca, K., LeBlanc, B., Pihelgas, M., & De Gaspari, F. (2020). Reference architecture of an autonomous agent for cyber defense of complex military systems. In *Adaptive autonomous secure cyber systems* (pp. 1–21). Springer International Publishing. DOI: 10.1007/978-3-030-33432-1_1

Thijsman, J., Sebrechts, M., De Turck, F., & Volckaert, B. (2024, July). Trusting the Cloud-Native Edge: Remotely Attested Kubernetes Workers. In 2024 33rd International Conference on Computer Communications and Networks (ICCCN) (pp. 1-6). IEEE.

Thirumuruganathan, S., Deniz, F., Khalil, I., Yu, T., Nabeel, M., & Ouzzani, M. (2024). Detecting and mitigating sampling bias in cybersecurity with unlabeled data. In *33rd USENIX Security Symposium (USENIX Security 24)* (pp. 1741-1758).

Torkura, K. A., Sukmana, M. I., Cheng, F., & Meinel, C. (2020). Cloudstrike: Chaos engineering for security and resiliency in cloud infrastructure. *IEEE Access : Practical Innovations, Open Solutions*, *8*, 123044–123060. DOI: 10.1109/ACCESS.2020.3007338

Toumbas, L., Mavromoustakis, C. X., Mastorakis, G., & Dobre, C. (2017). *Recent advances in remote assisted medical operations*. Ambient Assisted Living and Enhanced Living Environments. DOI: 10.1016/B978-0-12-805195-5.00006-5

Trend Micro (US). (2024). Harnessing AI for enhanced security. *Trend Micro Whitepapers*, *11*(2), 45–59.

Triplett, W. J. (2024). Cybersecurity Vulnerabilities in Healthcare: A Threat to Patient Security. *Cybersecurity and Innovative Technology Journal*, *2*(1), 15–25. DOI: 10.53889/citj.v2i1.333

Truex, S., Baracaldo, N., Anwar, A., Steinke, T., Ludwig, H., & Zhang, R. (2019). A hybrid approach to privacy-preserving federated learning. *Proceedings of the 12th ACM Workshop on Artificial Intelligence and Security (AISec)*, 1–8. ACM. DOI: 10.1145/3338501.3357370

Truong, T. C., Diep, Q. B., & Zelinka, I. (2020). Artificial intelligence in the cyber domain: Offense and defense. *Symmetry*, *12*(3), 410. DOI: 10.3390/sym12030410

Tsirakis, O., Fysarakis, K., Mavroeidis, V., & Papaefstathiou, I. (2025). *Operationalizing Cybersecurity Knowledge: Design, Implementation & Evaluation of a Knowledge Management System for CACAO Playbooks* (No. arXiv:2503.05206). arXiv. /arXiv.2503.05206DOI: 10.2139/ssrn.5178937

Uchendu, I., Jabbour, J., Berghe, K. V. D., Runevic, J., Stewart, M., Ma, J., . . . Reddi, V. J. (2025). A2Perf: Real-World Autonomous Agents Benchmark. *arXiv preprint arXiv:2503.03056*. https://arxiv.org/abs/2503.03056

Ullah, F., Alsirhani, A., Alshahrani, M. M., Alomari, A., Naeem, H., & Shah, S. A. (2022). Explainable malware detection system using transformers-based transfer learning and multi-model visual representation. *Sensors (Basel)*, *22*(18), 6766. DOI: 10.3390/s22186766 PMID: 36146112

Uscher-Pines, L., & Mehrotra, A. (2014). Analysis of Teladoc use seems to indicate expanded access to care for patients without prior connection to a provider. *Health Affairs*, *33*(2), 258–264. DOI: 10.1377/hlthaff.2013.0989 PMID: 24493769

Vadisetty, R., & Polamarasetti, A. (2024, November). Generative AI for Cyber Threat Simulation and Defense. In *2024 12th International Conference on Control, Mechatronics and Automation (ICCMA)* (pp. 272-279). IEEE. DOI: 10.1109/ICCMA63715.2024.10843938

Valdovinos, I. A., Pérez-Díaz, J. A., Choo, K. K. R., & Botero, J. F. (2021). Emerging DDoS attack detection and mitigation strategies in software-defined networks: Taxonomy, challenges and future directions. *Journal of Network and Computer Applications*, *187*, 103093. DOI: 10.1016/j.jnca.2021.103093

Van Devender, M. S. (2023). *Risk Assessment Framework for Evaluation of Cybersecurity Threats and Vulnerabilities in Medical Devices* (Doctoral dissertation, University of South Alabama).

Velasco, C. (2022, May). Cybercrime and Artificial Intelligence. An overview of the work of international organizations on criminal justice and the international applicable instruments. In *ERA Forum* (Vol. 23, No. 1, pp. 109-126). Berlin/Heidelberg: Springer Berlin Heidelberg.

Vermesan, O., Bröring, A., Tragos, E., Serrano, M., Bacciu, D., Chessa, S., & Bahr, R. (2022). Internet of robotic things–converging sensing/actuating, hyperconnectivity, artificial intelligence and IoT platforms. In *Cognitive hyperconnected digital transformation* (pp. 97–155). River Publishers. DOI: 10.1201/9781003337584-4

Vinayakumar, R., Alazab, M., Soman, K. P., Poornachandran, P., Al-Nemrat, A., & Venkatraman, S. (2019). Deep Learning Approach for Intelligent Intrusion Detection System. *IEEE Access : Practical Innovations, Open Solutions*, *7*, 41525–41550. DOI: 10.1109/ACCESS.2019.2895334

Vo, H. V., Nguyen, P. H., Nguyen, H. T., Vu, D. B., & Nguyen, H. N. (2023, December). Enhancing AI-Powered Malware Detection by Parallel Ensemble Learning. In *2023 RIVF International Conference on Computing and Communication Technologies (RIVF)* (pp. 503-508). IEEE. DOI: 10.1109/RIVF60135.2023.10471855

Vourganas, I. J., & Michala, A. L. (2024). Applications of Machine Learning in Cyber Security: A Review. *Journal of Cybersecurity and Privacy*, *4*(4), 972–992. DOI: 10.3390/jcp4040045

Vyas, A., Lin, P. C., Hwang, R. H., & Tripathi, M. (2024). Privacy-preserving federated learning for intrusion detection in IoT environments: A survey. *IEEE Access : Practical Innovations, Open Solutions*, *12*, 127018–127050. DOI: 10.1109/ACCESS.2024.3454211

Vyas, S., Hannay, J., Bolton, A., & Burnap, P. (2023). Automated Cyber Defence: A Review. *Proceedings of the ACM on Measurement and Analysis of Computing Systems*, *7*(4), 111.

Wahed, M. A. (2024, November). Real-Time Intrusion Detection and Traffic Analysis Using AI Techniques in IoT Infrastructure. In *2024 1st International Conference on Emerging Technologies for Dependable Internet of Things (ICETI)* (pp. 1-6). IEEE.

Waheed, A., Seegolam, B., Jowaheer, M. F., Sze, C. L. X., Hua, E. T. F., & Sindiramutty, S. R. (2024). Zero-Day Exploits in Cybersecurity: Case Studies and Countermeasure. Preprints *[Preprint]. , 2338*, v1.DOI: 10.20944/preprints202407

Wang, Y., Hallgren, K., & Larson, J. (2024). A Graph-based Framework for Reducing False Positives in Authentication Alerts in Security Systems. *Companion Proceedings of the ACM Web Conference 2024*, 274–283. DOI: 10.1145/3589335.3648325

Wang, C., Jiang, S., Li, Z., Zhong, W., Song, X., Liu, H., Hu, L., & Li, W. (2024). Accuracy and safety evaluation of a novel artificial intelligence–based robotic system for autonomous spinal posterior decompression. *Neurosurgical Focus*, *57*(6), E16. DOI: 10.3171/2024.9.FOCUS24400 PMID: 39616632

Wang, F., Chai, G., Li, Q., & Wang, C. (2022). An efficient deep unsupervised domain adaptation for unknown malware detection. *Symmetry*, *14*(2), 296.

Wang, H., Zhang, Y., Liang, J., & Liu, L. (2023). DAFA-BiLSTM: Deep autoregression feature augmented bidirectional LSTM network for time series prediction. *Neural Networks, 157*, 240–256. DOI: 10.1016/j.neunet.2022.10.009 PMID: 36399979

Wang, W., Yi, P., Jiang, J., Zhang, P., & Chen, X. (2024). Transformer-based framework for alert aggregation and attack prediction in a multi-stage attack. *Computers & Security, 136*, 103533. DOI: 10.1016/j.cose.2023.103533

Wang, W., Zhu, M., Wang, J., Zeng, X., & Yang, Z. (2017). End-to-end encrypted traffic classification with one-dimensional convolution neural networks. *2017 IEEE International Conference on Intelligence and Security Informatics (ISI)*, 43–48. DOI: 10.1109/ISI.2017.8004872

Wang, X., Wang, S., Liang, X., Zhao, D., Huang, J., Xu, X., Dai, B., & Miao, Q. (2022). Deep reinforcement learning: A survey. *IEEE Transactions on Neural Networks and Learning Systems, 35*(4), 5064–5078. DOI: 10.1109/TNNLS.2022.3207346 PMID: 36170386

Wang, Y. (2024). *A comparative analysis of model agnostic techniques for explainable artificial intelligence*. Research Reports on Computer Science. DOI: 10.37256/rrcs.3220244750

Wang, Y. C., Xue, J., Wei, C., & Kuo, C. C. J. (2023). An overview on generative AI at scale with Edge-Cloud Computing. *IEEE Open Journal of the Communications Society, 4*, 2952–2971. DOI: 10.1109/OJCOMS.2023.3320646

Wang, Z., Zhou, Y., Liu, H., Qiu, J., Fang, B., & Tian, Z. (2024). ThreatInsight: Innovating Early Threat Detection through Threat-Intelligence-Driven Analysis and Attribution. *IEEE Transactions on Knowledge and Data Engineering, 36*(12), 9388–9402. DOI: 10.1109/TKDE.2024.3474792

Waters, B. (2011). Ciphertext-policy attribute-based encryption: An expressive, efficient, and provably secure realization. Advances in Cryptology—EUROCRYPT 2011, 53-70.

Wei, C. (2024). Autonomous Cyber Defense Systems: Opportunities and Challenges. *Advances in Computer Sciences, 7*(1), 1–8.

Wei, K., Li, J., Ding, M., Ma, C., Yang, H. H., Farokhi, F., & Poor, H. V. (2020). Federated learning with differential privacy: Algorithms and performance analysis. *IEEE Transactions on Information Forensics and Security, 15*, 3454–3469. DOI: 10.1109/TIFS.2020.2988575

Wolniak, R., & Stecuła, K. (2024). Artificial Intelligence in Smart Cities—Applications, Barriers, and Future Directions: A Review. *Smart Cities*, *7*(3), 1346–1389. DOI: 10.3390/smartcities7030057

Wong, A. K. C., & Wang, Y. (2003). Pattern discovery: A data driven approach to decision support. *IEEE Transactions on Systems, Man, and Cybernetics. Part C, Applications and Reviews*, *33*(1), 114–124. DOI: 10.1109/TSMCC.2003.809869

Wu, Y., Li, M., Zeng, Q., Yang, T., Wang, J., Fang, Z., & Cheng, L. (2023). DroidRL: Feature selection for android malware detection with reinforcement learning. *Computers & Security*, *128*, 103126. DOI: 10.1016/j.cose.2023.103126

Xenonstack. (2024). Deep learning in cybersecurity: Threat detection and defense. *Xenonstack Tech Reports, 9(1),* 67-82.

Xin, Y., Kong, L., Liu, Z., Chen, Y., Li, Y., Zhu, H., & Vasilakos, A. V. (2018). Machine learning and deep learning methods for cybersecurity. *IEEE Access : Practical Innovations, Open Solutions*, *6*, 35365–35381. DOI: 10.1109/ACCESS.2018.2836950

Xiong, T., Ma, Z., Li, Z., & Dai, J. (2022). The analysis of influence mechanism for internet financial fraud identification and user behavior based on machine learning approaches. *International Journal of System Assurance Engineering and Management*, *13*(S3, Suppl 3), 996–1007. DOI: 10.1007/s13198-021-01181-0

Xiong, Z., Li, W., & Cai, Z. (2023, June). Federated generative model on multi-source heterogeneous data in iot. *Proceedings of the AAAI Conference on Artificial Intelligence*, *37*(9), 10537–10545. DOI: 10.1609/aaai.v37i9.26252

Yaacoub, J. P. A., Salman, O., Noura, H. N., Kaaniche, N., Chehab, A., & Malli, M. (2020). Cyber-physical systems security: Limitations, issues and future trends. *Microprocessors and Microsystems*, *77*, 103201. DOI: 10.1016/j.micpro.2020.103201 PMID: 32834204

Yaacoub, J.-P. A., Noura, H. N., Salman, O., & Chehab, A. (2022). Robotics cyber security: Vulnerabilities, attacks, countermeasures, and recommendations. *International Journal of Information Security*, *21*(1), 115–158. DOI: 10.1007/s10207-021-00545-8 PMID: 33776611

Yahouni, Z., Ladj, A., Belkadi, F., Meski, O., & Ritou, M. (2021). A smart reporting framework as an application of multi-agent system in machining industry. *International Journal of Computer Integrated Manufacturing*, *34*(5), 470–486. DOI: 10.1080/0951192X.2021.1901312

Yamany, B., Elsayed, M. S., Jurcut, A. D., Abdelbaki, N., & Azer, M. A. (2024). A holistic approach to ransomware classification: Leveraging static and dynamic analysis with visualization. *Information (Basel)*, *15*(1), 46. DOI: 10.3390/info15010046

Yan, Q., Huang, M., & Cao, H. (2022, July). A survey of human-machine collaboration in fuzzing. In *2022 7th IEEE International Conference on Data Science in Cyberspace (DSC)* (pp. 375-382). IEEE. DOI: 10.1109/DSC55868.2022.00058

Yang, L. H., Ye, F. F., Hu, H., Lu, H., Wang, Y. M., & Chang, W. J. (2024). A data-driven rule-base approach for carbon emission trend forecast with environmental regulation and efficiency improvement. *Sustainable Production and Consumption*, *45*, 316–332. DOI: 10.1016/j.spc.2023.12.030

Yang, Q., Fan, L., & Yu, H. (Eds.). (2020). *Federated learning: Privacy and incentive*. Springer.

Yang, Q., Liu, Y., Chen, T., & Tong, Y. (2019). Federated machine learning: Concept and applications. *ACM Transactions on Intelligent Systems and Technology*, *10*(2), 12. DOI: 10.1145/3298981

Yapar, O. (2024). Reinforcement learning in autonomous defense systems: Strategic applications and challenges. *World Journal of Advanced Engineering Technology and Sciences*, *13*(1), 140–152. DOI: 10.30574/wjaets.2024.13.1.0383

Yasin, H. N., Hamid, S. H. A., & Raja Yusof, R. J. (2021). Droidbotx: Test case generation tool for android applications using Q-learning. *Symmetry*, *13*(2), 310. DOI: 10.3390/sym13020310

Yenduri, G., Ramalingam, M., Selvi, G. C., Supriya, Y., Srivastava, G., Maddikunta, P. K. R., Raj, G. D., Jhaveri, R. H., Prabadevi, B., Wang, W., Vasilakos, A. V., & Gadekallu, T. R. (2024). Gpt (generative pre-trained transformer)–a comprehensive review on enabling technologies, potential applications, emerging challenges, and future directions. *IEEE Access : Practical Innovations, Open Solutions*, *12*, 54608–54649. DOI: 10.1109/ACCESS.2024.3389497

Yerima, S. Y., & Sezer, S. (2018). Droidfusion: A novel multilevel classifier fusion approach for android malware detection. *IEEE Transactions on Cybernetics*, *49*(2), 453–466. DOI: 10.1109/TCYB.2017.2777960 PMID: 29993965

Younisse, R.. (2023). An early detection model for kerberoasting attacks and dataset labeling. *Jordanian Journal of Computers and Information Technology*, *9*, 1.

Yuan, X., Li, C., & Chen, X. (2019). Deep learning for security: A review. *IEEE Communications Surveys and Tutorials*, *21*(4), 3135–3173. DOI: 10.1109/COMST.2019.2933988

Yuen, S. G., Vasilyev, N. V., Del Nido, P. J., & Howe, R. D. (2013). Robotic tissue tracking for beating heart mitral valve surgery. *Medical Image Analysis*, *17*(8), 1236–1242. DOI: 10.1016/j.media.2010.06.007 PMID: 23973122

Zaid, T., & Garai, S. (2024). Emerging Trends in Cybersecurity: A Holistic View on Current Threats, Assessing Solutions, and Pioneering New Frontiers. *Blockchain in Healthcare Today*, •••, 7. PMID: 38715765

Zemmar, A., Lozano, A. M., & Nelson, B. J. (2020). The rise of robots in surgical environments during COVID-19. *Nature Machine Intelligence*, *2*(10), 566–572. DOI: 10.1038/s42256-020-00238-2

Zgallai, W. A., & Ozsahin, D. U. (Eds.). (2024). *Artificial intelligence and image processing in medical imaging*. Elsevier.

Zhang, C., Yu, S., Tian, Z., & Yu, J. J. (2023). Generative adversarial networks: A survey on attack and defense perspective. *ACM Computing Surveys*, *56*(4), 1–35. DOI: 10.1145/3615336

Zhang, J., Ng, N., Scott, C. E., Blyth, M. J., Haddad, F. S., Macpherson, G. J., & Clement, N. D. (2022). Robotic arm-assisted versus manual unicompartmental knee arthroplasty: A systematic review and meta-analysis of the MAKO robotic system. *The Bone & Joint Journal*, *104*(5), 541–548.

Zhang, S., Su, H., Liu, H., & Yang, W. (2025). MPDroid: A multimodal pre-training Android malware detection method with static and dynamic features. *Computers & Security*, *150*, 104262. DOI: 10.1016/j.cose.2024.104262

Zhang, Z., Hamadi, H. A., Damiani, E., Yeun, C. Y., & Taher, F. A. (2022). Explainable AI Applications in Cyber Security: State-of-the-Art in Research. *IEEE Access : Practical Innovations, Open Solutions*, *10*, 93104–93139. DOI: 10.1109/ACCESS.2022.3204051

Zhao, X., Jiang, R., Han, Y., Li, A., & Peng, Z. (2023). A Survey on Cybersecurity Knowledge Graph Construction. *Computers & Security*, *130*, 103524.

Zhou, Y., & Jiang, X. (2012, May). Dissecting android malware: Characterization and evolution. In 2012 IEEE symposium on security and privacy (pp. 95-109). IEEE.

Zhou, C. V., Leckie, C., & Karunasekera, S. (2010). A survey of coordinated attacks and collaborative intrusion detection. *Computers & Security*, *29*(1), 124–140. DOI: 10.1016/j.cose.2009.06.008

Zhou, S., Li, H., Fu, X., & Jiao, Y. (2024). A Novel Malware Detection Model in the Software Supply Chain Based on LSTM and SVMs. *Applied Sciences (Basel, Switzerland)*, *14*(15), 6678.

Zhu, L., Liu, Z., & Han, S. (2019). Deep leakage from gradients. *Advances in Neural Information Processing Systems*, *32*, 14774–14784.

Zhu, Q., & Rass, S. (Eds.). (2021). *Cyber security in intelligent data-centric systems and applications*. Springer.

Zhu, Z., Su, P., Zhong, S., Huang, J., Ottikkutti, S., Tahmasebi, K. N., Zou, Z., Zheng, L., & Chen, D. (2023). Using a vae-som architecture for anomaly detection of flexible sensors in limb prosthesis. *Journal of Industrial Information Integration*, *35*, 100490. DOI: 10.1016/j.jii.2023.100490

Zuech, R., Khoshgoftaar, T. M., & Wald, R. (2015). Intrusion detection and Big Heterogeneous Data: A Survey. *Journal of Big Data*, *2*(1), 3. DOI: 10.1186/s40537-015-0013-4

About the Contributors

Mohammad Alauthman (mohammad.alauthman@uop.edu.jo) is an Associate Professor in the Information Security Department at the Faculty of Information Technology, University of Petra, Amman, Jordan. His research interests include network security, intrusion detection systems, and applying AI techniques—such as machine learning and deep learning—for botnet and DDoS detection, spam filtering, IoT security, and network traffic classification. He earned his Ph.D. in Computer Science from Northumbria University, UK, in 2016. Dr. Alauthman has received multiple research grants supporting advanced AI-driven intrusion detection systems and international collaboration. He is also actively involved in Erasmus+ projects, including BITTCOIN-JO (technology transfer), RL4Eng (remote engineering labs), Pro-GREEN LABs (green competences in education), and COMMO (mobility and cooperation across Mediterranean and Balkan institutions), contributing to innovation, sustainability, and cross-border academic development.

Ammar Almomani is a distinguished academic, researcher, and consultant with over two decades of combined experience in cybersecurity, artificial intelligence, and computer science. He holds a Ph.D. in Advanced Internet Security and Monitoring from Universiti Sains Malaysia (USM) and has taught more than 45 specialized courses in his field. As an Academic Staff Member in the School of IT at Al-Balqa Applied University (Jordan) and in the Bachelor of Cybersecurity Program at the Higher Colleges of Technology (HCT) in Sharjah (UAE), Prof. Almomani also consults on various AI and cybersecurity initiatives. He has secured multiple patents (eight in Germany and two in India) and has been recognized internationally for his research, with over 165 published articles—110 of which are indexed in Scopus. His work has earned him a UAE Golden Visa, and he has been named among the Top 2% of Global Influential Researchers by Stanford University and Scopus (2023–2024). Prof. Almomani's leadership roles include serving as Head of the Research and Innovation Department and IT Department, contributing to curriculum development, program accreditation (including ABET and AACSB), and the establishment of specializations in both Jordan and the UAE. He actively supervises undergraduate and postgraduate research (MSc/Ph.D.) across multiple countries and has chaired numerous international conferences. With a strong publication record, extensive industry collaborations, and over 113,000 readers on ResearchGate, Prof. Almomani remains a driving force in advancing cybersecurity and AI. His editorial work is guided by a commitment to fostering robust academic discourse and pioneering technological innovation.

***

Amjad Aldweesh is a computer associate professor interested in the Blockchain and Smart contracts technology as well as cyber security. Amjad has a Bachelor degree in computer science. He has a MSc degree in advanced computer science and security from the University of Manchester with distinction. Amjad is the second in the UK and the first in the middle east to have a PhD in the Blockchain and Smart contracts technology from Newcastle University.

Mouhammd Alkasassbeh earned his Ph.D. from the School of Computing, Portsmouth University, UK, in 2008. He is a Full Professor in the Computer Science Department at Princess Sumaya University for Technology (PSUT), Jordan. His research interests focus on network traffic analysis, network fault detection, anomaly classification, and the application of machine learning in computer networking and cybersecurity.

Wesam Alkhadour holds a Ph.D. in computer science from the University of Bradford, United Kingdom. She is currently an assistant professor at the University of Petra, Jordan.

Jawad Alkhatib holds PhD degree in Computer Science and Engineering (AI) from the University of Bradford (2010). MSc and BSc degrees in Electrical and Computer Engineering from Louisiana Tech University (1992 and 1991). He is an Assistant Professor of Computer Engineering at Prince Mohammad Bin Fahd University. He has a 20-year of academic experience in teaching computer science and engineering topics and in conducting research related to Pattern Recognition, Artificial Intelligence, Machine Learning, Deep Learning, Cyber Security, and IoT. He can be contacted at email: Jalkhat-ib@pmu.edu.sa.

Malek Zakarya Alksasbeh is currently a Full Professor in the Faculty of Information Technology at Al-Hussein Bin Talal University, Ma'an, Jordan. He received his B.S. degree in Computer science from Mu'tah University, Jordan, in

2005, and the M.S. and Ph.D. degrees in Information Technology from the University Utara Malaysia (UUM), Malaysia, in 2008 and 2012, respectively. His research interests are in the areas of Smart Systems, Information Retrieval, and Instructional Technology

Mohammad Almseidin is an assistant professor at the computer science department, at the Tafila Technical University. He received his Ph.D. from the department of information technology, the University of Miskolc in 2020. His research interest is in Fuzzy System, Network traffic analysis, and Machine Learning. His current focus is on fuzzy rule interpolation and network security.

Enshirah Altarawneh is an Assistant Professor in the Department of Computer Engineering at Hashemite University. She holds a PhD in Computer Engineering from the State University of New York at Binghamton, specializing in cybersecurity and digital forensics. Her research focuses on artificial intelligence, machine learning, cybersecurity, and digital forensics. As an educator, Dr. Altarawneh teaches courses in digital logic, cryptographic systems, programming languages (C++), computer organization, and digital image processing, with a strong emphasis on hands-on learning and student engagement.

Kashinath Basu is a Senior Lecturer in Computer Science at Oxford Brookes University. He has over over 20 years of research and teaching experience in the field of computer science, especially focussing around networking and web technologies. His recent research includes application of AI/ML and big data technologies in the softwarisation of network infrastructure, cloud computing and cyber security and application of AI/Ml and big data in the domain of networks and cloud. Dr Basu regularly publishes in prestigeous journals, conferences and books and has been in editorial board, organising committees and chairs of several international scholastic events. He also serves in a number of IEEE and Internet Engineering Task Force committees on internation standards and has active research collaboration with a number of global technology companies.

Jorge Marx Gómez studied Computer Engineering and Industrial Engineering at the University of Applied Sciences Berlin (Technische Fachhochschule Berlin). He was a lecturer and researcher at the Otto-von-Guericke-Universität Magdeburg (Germany) where he also obtained a PhD degree in Business Information Systems with the work Computer-based Approaches to Forecast Returns of Scrapped Products to Recycling. From 2002 till 2003 he was a visiting professor for Business Informatics at the Technical University of Clausthal (TU Clausthal, Germany). In 2004 he received his habilitation for the work Automated Environmental Reporting through Material Flow Networks at the Otto-von-Guericke-Universität

Magdeburg. In 2005 he became a full professor and chair of Business Information Systems at the Carl von Ossietzky University Oldenburg (Germany). His research interests include Very Large Business Applications, Business Information Systems, Federated ERP-Systems, Business Intelligence, Data Warehousing, Interoperability and Environmental Management Information Systems.

Ala Hamarsheh is an associate professor at the Faculty of Engineering and Information Technology of the Arab American University of Jenin. Dr. Hamarsheh has obtained a PhD in engineering sciences from Vrije Universiteit Brussel (VUB)/ Brussels-Belgium in 2012. He graduated in computer science at the Faculty of Science, Birzeit University, Palestine, in 2000. He obtained an MSc degree in computer science at the Kind Abdullah II School for IT, The University of Jordan, Jordan, in 2003. Dr. Hamarsheh has published numerous papers in international refereed journals and conferences.

Louay Karadsheh has a Doctorate of Management in Information Technology from Lawrence Technological University, Southfield, MI. Dr. Karadsheh has over 11 years of teaching experience in different topics such as Information Assurance and Cyber Security, Networking, Operating Systems, Cloud Computing, Systems Analysis and Design, Business Continuity, Ethical Hacking, Disaster Recovery, and Computer Ethics. His research interests include Cloud Computing, Information Assurance, Knowledge Management, and Risk Management. Dr.Karadsheh has published over sixteen articles in refereed journals and international conference proceedings. Dr.Karadsheh has provided technical edits/reviews for several major publishing companies, including Pearson Education and Cengage Learning. Dr. Karadsheh has 19 years of practical experience in the IT field. He had different job roles, such as consultant, IT manager, field technical support, field service engineer, network and system administrator, and head of the computer section. Dr. Karadsheh has practical experience in firewalls, web filtering, email gateway, active directory, data leakage prevention, Windows server hardening, web hosting, vulnerability assessment, and VPNs. He holds CISSP, CEH, CASP, CCSK, CCE, Security+, VCA-C, VCA-DCV, Network +, and Application Security Analyst (IBM QRadar SIEM v7.2) Mastery Award.

Ali Al Maqousi is an Associate Professor of Information Security at the University of Petra in Jordan and serves as the Director of the Office of External Funding and Technology Transfer. He holds a Ph.D. in Computer Science (Computer Networks) from Oxford Brookes University, UK, and specializes in cybersecurity, computer networks, blockchain, and smart systems. With over 30 peer-reviewed publications, Dr. Al Maqousi has led and contributed to numerous research initiatives, including high-impact Erasmus+ projects. These include BITTCOIN-JO, which focuses on establishing Technology Transfer Offices in Jordan; RL4Eng, which develops remote and virtual labs for engineering education; Pro-GREEN LABs, promoting sustainable development skills in architecture; and COMMO, a mobility program enhancing international academic exchange across the Mediterranean and Western Balkans. Dr. Al Maqousi contributed to the organization of four international conferences as Organization Chair (AEECT 2011, IT-DREPS 2013, AEECT 2013, and AEECT 2015) and two international conferences as General Co-Chair (JIEEEC 2017 & IT-DREPS 2017) and one international conference as a publication chair (ICCIAA 2025)

Khalil Omar is an assistant professor at the University of Petra in Jordan. He received his Ph.D. degree in computer science from the University of Oldenburg, Germany, in 2018. His academic focus is on distance learning and e-learning in combination with software engineering, mobile applications, usability design, adaptive interfaces, and ERP systems. Users can reach him through his email address: komar@uop.edu.jo.

Jamal Zraqou is an associate professor at the Department of Computer Science/ Virtual and Augmented Reality, University of Petra, Jordan, where he has been a faculty member since 2022. From 2018-2029, he was also the dean faculty of IT at IU. His research interests include computer vision, virtual and augmented reality, internet of things (IoT), cyber security, and image processing.

Index

A

Adaptive Access Control 63, 68
Adaptive Cyber Defense 29, 36, 209, 210, 223, 228, 230
Adaptive Defense 69, 85, 224, 230, 232, 235, 237, 265, 283, 285, 286, 295, 416, 511, 512, 518, 521
Adaptive Security 50, 58, 61, 294, 386, 387, 416, 418, 502, 535, 537, 553
AI 1, 2, 3, 5, 6, 7, 10, 11, 15, 18, 20, 22, 23, 25, 27, 28, 29, 30, 31, 32, 35, 36, 37, 38, 39, 46, 47, 48, 49, 50, 51, 52, 53, 54, 56, 57, 58, 61, 63, 66, 67, 68, 70, 71, 72, 76, 79, 80, 81, 82, 83, 84, 85, 86, 88, 93, 94, 95, 96, 97, 98, 99, 100, 101, 102, 104, 105, 116, 117, 118, 119, 122, 123, 124, 125, 129, 132, 156, 161, 165, 185, 186, 201, 204, 205, 206, 207, 210, 211, 214, 230, 232, 233, 234, 263, 264, 265, 271, 272, 273, 276, 277, 278, 279, 280, 281, 282, 283, 284, 285, 286, 287, 288, 289, 290, 291, 292, 293, 294, 296, 297, 298, 299, 300, 301, 302, 306, 307, 311, 313, 314, 322, 323, 324, 328, 329, 331, 332, 333, 340, 362, 367, 370, 375, 376, 377, 378, 379, 380, 381, 382, 383, 384, 385, 386, 387, 388, 389, 390, 391, 392, 393, 394, 395, 396, 397, 398, 399, 400, 401, 402, 403, 404, 405, 406, 407, 410, 411, 412, 413, 414, 415, 416, 417, 418, 419, 420, 421, 422, 423, 426, 427, 428, 429, 430, 431, 432, 433, 434, 435, 436, 439, 440, 441, 448, 451, 452, 453, 454, 456, 457, 458, 459, 460, 461, 463, 465, 466, 467, 468, 469, 470, 471, 472, 473, 474, 475, 476, 478, 480, 481, 482, 483, 484, 487, 488, 489, 490, 491, 492, 493, 494, 495, 496, 497, 498, 501, 502, 503, 504, 505, 506, 507, 508, 509, 510, 511, 512, 513, 514, 515, 516, 518, 519, 520, 521, 522, 523, 524, 525, 528, 529, 531, 532, 533, 535, 536, 537, 538, 539, 540, 541, 542, 543, 544, 545, 546, 547, 548, 549, 550, 552, 553, 555, 556, 557
AI-Based Cybersecurity 384, 427, 535, 549
AI-Driven Cybersecurity 11, 29, 31, 32, 37, 72, 375, 376, 380, 381, 382, 387, 388, 389, 390, 391, 392, 393, 399, 400, 402, 403, 405, 407, 412, 426, 428, 429, 431, 432, 468, 490, 525, 532, 537, 544, 547, 550, 553, 555
AI-Driven Defense 93, 96, 385, 386, 387, 390, 412, 418, 496, 515, 516, 518
AI-driven Security 28, 35, 36, 37, 38, 39, 50, 81, 82, 83, 84, 99, 211, 214, 230, 384, 386, 387, 390, 391, 392, 393, 399, 400, 412, 414, 428, 431, 469, 487, 493, 503, 506, 528, 529, 531, 532, 533, 537, 539, 540, 543, 544, 545, 547, 548, 549, 550
AI in Cybersecurity 7, 28, 31, 39, 50, 165, 206, 263, 264, 265, 278, 294, 382, 390, 402, 525, 540, 547, 555
Android Malware 76, 325, 326, 327, 330, 331, 334, 335, 336, 337, 340, 341, 342, 343, 344, 345, 346, 347, 348, 349, 350, 351, 352, 353, 354, 355, 356, 357, 359, 362, 363, 364, 365, 366, 367, 368, 369, 370, 371, 372, 373
Anomaly Detection 8, 17, 25, 26, 27, 31, 35, 40, 41, 47, 48, 49, 51, 52, 56, 62, 64, 66, 68, 73, 74, 75, 77, 82, 83, 84, 85, 86, 87, 88, 89, 93, 94, 97, 98, 99, 101, 113, 117, 119, 125, 163, 165, 167, 168, 169, 174, 178, 180, 183, 186, 201, 205, 211, 214, 230, 257, 263, 264, 265, 266, 274, 275, 276, 278, 283, 284, 286, 292, 293, 297, 299, 300, 303, 327, 335, 363, 379, 381, 384, 385, 386, 387, 394, 400, 406, 412, 414, 416, 417, 418, 420, 421, 422, 429, 448, 470, 472, 476, 480, 484, 487, 488, 491, 503, 507, 508, 509, 513, 516, 520, 521, 527,

530, 533, 535, 537, 538, 539, 540, 541, 542, 543, 549, 552, 553, 555, 556
Artificial Intelligence 2, 3, 15, 27, 29, 30, 31, 32, 33, 35, 36, 68, 69, 70, 72, 73, 77, 78, 79, 80, 103, 104, 116, 118, 165, 181, 183, 186, 206, 207, 232, 233, 234, 260, 261, 295, 297, 299, 301, 302, 305, 306, 311, 328, 331, 363, 364, 380, 384, 390, 393, 401, 402, 403, 404, 406, 407, 410, 411, 413, 434, 435, 436, 441, 451, 452, 453, 458, 460, 463, 466, 470, 497, 498, 499, 502, 504, 524, 525, 526, 528, 529, 534, 551, 555, 556, 557
Attacks 2, 3, 6, 7, 14, 15, 16, 17, 21, 22, 27, 28, 35, 37, 38, 48, 51, 52, 53, 54, 57, 61, 62, 63, 64, 67, 70, 72, 74, 79, 80, 81, 83, 85, 86, 87, 89, 90, 94, 95, 97, 98, 99, 103, 105, 107, 108, 109, 111, 112, 116, 117, 118, 119, 121, 123, 124, 126, 127, 131, 152, 162, 163, 164, 170, 171, 173, 174, 178, 182, 186, 187, 189, 192, 195, 201, 204, 206, 212, 216, 222, 224, 225, 226, 238, 239, 240, 241, 250, 251, 252, 253, 254, 255, 258, 259, 262, 263, 273, 275, 278, 281, 282, 283, 284, 286, 287, 288, 289, 290, 292, 294, 295, 299, 305, 306, 307, 308, 309, 310, 311, 313, 314, 322, 323, 326, 332, 333, 340, 341, 342, 343, 344, 345, 364, 365, 366, 373, 375, 376, 377, 378, 379, 380, 381, 382, 383, 386, 389, 390, 400, 401, 403, 404, 411, 412, 413, 414, 415, 416, 417, 419, 420, 421, 422, 423, 426, 427, 430, 435, 437, 440, 443, 444, 445, 446, 447, 448, 449, 450, 451, 452, 453, 454, 456, 457, 458, 468, 469, 470, 471, 473, 474, 475, 476, 478, 484, 488, 490, 491, 492, 495, 496, 497, 498, 504, 507, 509, 510, 511, 512, 513, 522, 523, 524, 528, 529, 530, 531, 532, 533, 534, 535, 536, 537, 538, 539, 541, 542, 543, 545, 547, 548, 549, 556, 557
Autonomous 1, 2, 3, 4, 5, 6, 7, 8, 10, 11, 12, 13, 14, 16, 17, 18, 19, 20, 21, 22, 23, 24, 25, 26, 27, 28, 29, 30, 31, 32, 33, 35, 36, 37, 39, 46, 49, 57, 58, 59, 61, 62, 63, 66, 68, 70, 77, 79, 80, 85, 89, 90, 92, 93, 96, 97, 99, 101, 102, 104, 105, 118, 119, 120, 121, 123, 125, 133, 134, 135, 136, 138, 139, 140, 141, 142, 143, 144, 145, 146, 147, 149, 150, 151, 152, 155, 156, 157, 164, 178, 179, 185, 188, 189, 193, 198, 205, 209, 211, 216, 230, 235, 236, 237, 238, 239, 240, 241, 242, 244, 249, 252, 253, 254, 258, 260, 262, 294, 299, 305, 306, 307, 308, 310, 311, 312, 315, 318, 320, 322, 323, 324, 325, 326, 327, 332, 333, 364, 367, 375, 376, 380, 381, 382, 385, 386, 387, 390, 400, 403, 405, 407, 410, 411, 412, 413, 414, 415, 416, 417, 418, 421, 423, 426, 427, 429, 431, 432, 434, 436, 439, 440, 441, 442, 443, 444, 445, 447, 449, 450, 451, 452, 453, 454, 455, 456, 457, 458, 459, 460, 461, 462, 463, 465, 466, 467, 468, 471, 472, 473, 474, 477, 489, 490, 491, 492, 493, 495, 496, 497, 498, 501, 502, 503, 504, 505, 506, 507, 510, 511, 512, 513, 514, 518, 519, 520, 522, 523, 524, 525
Autonomous Cyber Defense 1, 2, 3, 5, 7, 11, 12, 14, 16, 18, 21, 22, 25, 26, 27, 33, 35, 36, 37, 39, 46, 57, 58, 61, 104, 211, 216, 230, 306, 465, 466, 467, 468, 473, 474, 491, 492, 496, 498, 503, 504, 505, 506, 507, 523, 525
Autonomous Cybersecurity 235, 258, 307, 311, 315, 318, 326, 327, 332, 333, 367, 381, 413, 414, 415, 416, 417, 423, 426, 429, 431, 432, 434
Autonomous Defense 3, 13, 14, 21, 22, 24, 26, 59, 79, 85, 89, 92, 97, 118, 119, 120, 121, 123, 133, 135, 136, 138, 139, 140, 141, 142, 143, 144, 146, 147, 150, 151, 152, 155, 156, 157, 164, 179, 185, 193, 198, 216, 235, 236, 238, 239, 242, 244, 249,

262, 375, 376, 380, 382, 385, 386, 387, 400, 407, 410, 412, 418, 421, 439, 468, 473, 491, 493, 495, 501, 502, 503, 504, 507, 512, 514, 518, 520, 522, 523
Autonomous Defense Systems 14, 22, 24, 118, 119, 121, 133, 135, 136, 139, 140, 141, 144, 146, 147, 150, 152, 155, 156, 157, 235, 236, 238, 244, 249, 262, 375, 376, 380, 382, 385, 387, 400, 407, 410, 439
Autonomous Resilience 105
Autonomous Systems 1, 3, 6, 10, 12, 13, 14, 16, 17, 19, 20, 22, 23, 24, 25, 26, 28, 29, 31, 35, 58, 62, 119, 143, 209, 237, 241, 294, 305, 306, 307, 308, 310, 311, 312, 323, 327, 332, 333, 387, 415, 436, 440, 441, 456, 474, 502, 505

B

Backdoor Attacks 162, 163, 173, 174

C

Computational Complexity Analysis 143
Cyber Deception 306, 323, 324, 533
Cybersecurity 1, 2, 3, 4, 7, 9, 10, 11, 13, 14, 16, 18, 19, 22, 25, 26, 28, 29, 30, 31, 32, 35, 36, 37, 38, 39, 40, 41, 42, 44, 45, 46, 47, 48, 49, 50, 53, 55, 56, 58, 60, 63, 67, 68, 71, 72, 73, 75, 76, 77, 82, 83, 87, 90, 101, 103, 104, 106, 107, 108, 109, 110, 111, 114, 116, 118, 120, 123, 124, 125, 126, 128, 129, 131, 132, 133, 135, 138, 157, 161, 162, 163, 164, 165, 167, 168, 174, 179, 180, 182, 185, 186, 188, 189, 190, 191, 205, 206, 207, 213, 214, 225, 232, 233, 234, 235, 239, 240, 258, 259, 261, 262, 263, 264, 265, 266, 267, 268, 269, 270, 271, 272, 273, 274, 276, 277, 278, 279, 280, 283, 284, 287, 289, 292, 293, 294, 295, 296, 297, 298, 299, 300, 301, 302, 305, 306, 307, 310, 311, 312, 313, 315, 318, 324, 326, 327, 332, 333, 339, 340, 349, 350, 352, 363, 367, 372, 375, 376, 377, 378, 379, 380, 381, 382, 383, 384, 385, 386, 387, 388, 389, 390, 391, 392, 393, 394, 395, 396, 397, 398, 399, 400, 401, 402, 403, 404, 405, 406, 407, 412, 413, 414, 415, 416, 417, 418, 421, 422, 423, 424, 426, 427, 428, 429, 430, 431, 432, 434, 436, 437, 439, 440, 443, 446, 448, 452, 453, 456, 459, 461, 462, 463, 466, 467, 468, 469, 470, 471, 472, 490, 491, 495, 496, 497, 498, 499, 502, 504, 511, 523, 524, 525, 526, 528, 529, 530, 531, 532, 533, 534, 535, 536, 537, 538, 539, 540, 544, 545, 546, 547, 549, 550, 553, 554, 555, 556, 557
Cyber Security 28, 69, 73, 75, 103, 104, 132, 181, 206, 207, 259, 260, 299, 301, 314, 322, 323, 371, 403, 404, 433, 436, 437, 497, 498, 499, 524, 526
Cybersecurity Landscape 49, 107, 125, 276, 462, 523

D

Data Breaches 86, 339, 376, 377, 378, 379, 383, 384, 390, 392, 394, 397, 419, 427, 444
Data Privacy 2, 134, 162, 163, 168, 227, 233, 241, 242, 249, 260, 289, 333, 375, 376, 377, 382, 387, 389, 398, 399, 400, 402, 405, 419, 467, 468, 482, 483, 494, 532, 533, 536, 540, 547, 549
Deception Techniques 305, 306, 307, 313, 323, 324, 542
Deep Learning 6, 7, 8, 10, 35, 38, 39, 41, 45, 49, 51, 54, 56, 57, 69, 70, 71, 72, 73, 74, 75, 76, 77, 81, 83, 84, 95, 97, 103, 104, 165, 181, 182, 183, 206, 232, 239, 244, 259, 260, 262, 298, 300, 322, 342, 352, 356, 357, 369, 370, 373, 380, 390, 391, 402, 403, 416, 417, 418, 423, 470, 472, 475, 480, 484, 485, 488, 494, 495, 497, 498, 499, 501, 502, 503, 504, 506, 507, 508, 509, 510, 519, 521, 523,

524, 526, 527, 528, 529, 530, 531, 532, 533, 535, 536, 537, 538, 540, 541, 542, 543, 544, 545, 546, 547, 548, 549, 550, 551, 552, 553, 554, 555, 556, 557
Defend 66, 71, 118, 119, 134, 151, 289, 309, 310, 312, 313, 322, 389, 421
Differential Privacy 96, 100, 162, 163, 166, 167, 171, 172, 179, 180, 181, 183, 250, 391, 392, 491, 544
Distributed Autonomous Defense 198
Distributed Cyber Defense 161, 163, 168, 185, 187
DoS 419, 420, 421, 422, 427
Dynamic Threat Response 209

F

Federated Knowledge Distribution 235, 242, 249, 257
Federated Learning 21, 24, 29, 72, 76, 99, 101, 161, 162, 166, 167, 168, 169, 171, 172, 174, 176, 180, 181, 182, 183, 184, 232, 241, 249, 251, 253, 255, 260, 263, 279, 282, 292, 299, 329, 354, 364, 377, 382, 391, 392, 400, 402, 404, 416, 417, 419, 420, 422, 436, 494, 495, 506, 522, 529, 533, 536, 537, 540, 543, 544, 547

G

Generative Adversarial Networks 263, 295, 296, 297, 299, 300, 301, 303, 417, 439, 531, 535, 541
Generative AI 28, 124, 206, 263, 264, 265, 271, 272, 273, 278, 279, 280, 281, 282, 283, 284, 285, 286, 287, 288, 289, 290, 291, 292, 293, 294, 296, 297, 298, 299, 300, 301, 302
Governance 22, 25, 106, 111, 112, 114, 125, 126, 127, 130, 163, 179, 210, 227, 228, 230, 231, 389, 400, 403, 436, 465, 467, 468, 474, 478, 481, 482, 486, 489, 490, 491, 492, 496, 518, 523, 544, 550

H

Homomorphic Encryption 100, 110, 130, 136, 138, 139, 158, 163, 172, 179, 180, 183, 377, 391, 392, 544

I

Incident Response 16, 17, 22, 23, 49, 62, 63, 64, 65, 67, 68, 70, 96, 105, 108, 113, 115, 165, 211, 213, 214, 215, 243, 295, 308, 310, 315, 332, 377, 381, 384, 400, 404, 430, 431, 432, 434, 465, 467, 471, 472, 477, 490, 491, 492, 496, 497, 498, 537, 539, 540, 543, 544, 546
Industrial Control Networks 501, 502, 503, 504, 507, 514, 523
Intrusion Detection 8, 11, 14, 23, 29, 31, 38, 39, 47, 48, 62, 64, 71, 73, 74, 76, 80, 83, 85, 86, 93, 95, 97, 98, 100, 103, 104, 162, 164, 165, 168, 170, 177, 179, 180, 181, 182, 183, 186, 189, 197, 205, 206, 210, 212, 214, 215, 217, 219, 232, 239, 240, 259, 260, 261, 262, 263, 276, 277, 292, 296, 297, 315, 322, 332, 361, 365, 381, 386, 405, 406, 416, 417, 420, 421, 429, 433, 448, 467, 470, 481, 497, 498, 502, 503, 504, 509, 521, 530, 533, 541, 545, 546, 556
IoT 2, 16, 32, 37, 66, 73, 74, 75, 76, 77, 95, 103, 104, 108, 124, 131, 167, 168, 169, 170, 175, 177, 178, 180, 181, 183, 186, 187, 196, 197, 198, 201, 205, 206, 230, 233, 240, 270, 275, 276, 286, 287, 292, 295, 298, 299, 300, 302, 309, 310, 311, 322, 323, 365, 370, 403, 405, 406, 431, 433, 434, 454, 465, 466, 467, 469, 470, 473, 474, 480, 490, 491, 496, 497, 498, 503, 541, 543, 555, 556

M

Machine Learning 1, 2, 3, 6, 7, 8, 10, 14, 15, 17, 18, 25, 26, 27, 31, 36, 37, 38,

39, 40, 41, 47, 48, 50, 52, 54, 56, 57, 58, 62, 67, 69, 70, 71, 72, 73, 75, 76, 77, 80, 82, 83, 86, 91, 96, 100, 103, 104, 112, 116, 117, 118, 120, 124, 132, 161, 162, 164, 165, 166, 181, 182, 184, 186, 207, 211, 215, 232, 233, 234, 236, 239, 241, 259, 260, 261, 264, 265, 266, 276, 293, 295, 298, 299, 305, 306, 307, 308, 311, 313, 314, 322, 323, 325, 328, 340, 343, 346, 350, 354, 356, 357, 363, 364, 365, 366, 367, 368, 369, 370, 371, 372, 373, 375, 376, 377, 379, 380, 381, 382, 384, 385, 386, 387, 390, 400, 401, 402, 405, 407, 412, 413, 416, 417, 419, 420, 421, 422, 424, 425, 429, 436, 439, 441, 451, 452, 459, 460, 466, 467, 468, 470, 473, 475, 480, 483, 486, 487, 498, 499, 501, 502, 503, 504, 505, 506, 507, 508, 512, 522, 523, 524, 525, 526, 528, 529, 530, 531, 534, 535, 549, 555, 556, 557

Machine Learning Models 6, 18, 37, 38, 54, 58, 75, 116, 186, 264, 265, 266, 293, 367, 371, 384, 390, 412, 420, 424, 425, 429, 436, 441, 467, 473, 475, 506, 528, 534

Malware Detection 11, 48, 71, 74, 75, 76, 103, 116, 232, 274, 280, 281, 282, 292, 295, 297, 300, 302, 325, 326, 327, 334, 335, 337, 339, 340, 343, 345, 346, 347, 348, 349, 350, 351, 353, 354, 355, 356, 357, 359, 360, 361, 363, 364, 365, 366, 367, 368, 369, 370, 371, 372, 373, 497, 499, 530, 546, 552, 553

Mathematical Foundations 133, 136, 137

N

Networks 2, 6, 8, 20, 26, 29, 30, 36, 39, 41, 42, 43, 45, 46, 49, 51, 65, 66, 67, 69, 70, 73, 74, 76, 77, 78, 81, 83, 84, 85, 87, 88, 90, 95, 98, 100, 101, 104, 106, 108, 109, 110, 114, 115, 116, 117, 118, 123, 125, 126, 130, 135, 136, 139, 144, 155, 162, 165, 175, 176, 177, 180, 182, 183, 185, 186, 187, 189, 191, 197, 200, 201, 210, 215, 216, 218, 219, 220, 221, 226, 229, 236, 239, 240, 245, 252, 260, 262, 263, 265, 275, 283, 287, 295, 296, 297, 298, 299, 300, 301, 302, 303, 307, 309, 310, 311, 312, 313, 323, 332, 333, 335, 341, 351, 352, 356, 358, 359, 360, 361, 362, 363, 364, 365, 367, 370, 371, 373, 376, 379, 380, 383, 384, 390, 391, 392, 402, 404, 410, 412, 413, 415, 416, 417, 418, 421, 429, 430, 433, 437, 439, 443, 448, 452, 454, 455, 463, 469, 470, 473, 484, 485, 488, 492, 494, 501, 502, 503, 504, 506, 507, 508, 509, 514, 515, 522, 523, 525, 527, 529, 531, 535, 536, 540, 541, 542, 543, 544, 545, 551, 555, 556

P

Poisoning Attacks 94, 99, 118, 173, 250, 417, 419, 420, 421, 422, 531, 532, 536, 548, 557

Policy 3, 6, 20, 45, 46, 58, 60, 61, 63, 67, 68, 85, 86, 90, 91, 92, 93, 96, 97, 117, 124, 139, 154, 159, 176, 190, 192, 193, 194, 197, 198, 199, 202, 203, 210, 212, 213, 216, 218, 219, 220, 223, 224, 225, 226, 227, 247, 249, 353, 416, 461, 467, 468, 469, 472, 474, 478, 481, 483, 486, 487, 489, 494, 504, 506, 511, 512, 513, 514, 522, 546

Power Grids 30, 221, 456, 467, 501, 502, 503, 504, 505, 506, 507, 512, 514, 516, 521, 523, 527, 541

Privacy-Preserving 66, 72, 82, 100, 101, 133, 156, 161, 163, 164, 166, 175, 180, 181, 183, 241, 382, 387, 388, 391, 402, 490, 544, 547

Proactive Defense 6, 50, 61, 162, 205, 263, 271, 280, 286, 287, 293, 380, 390, 537

R

Real-Time Threat Detection 5, 165, 294, 308, 376, 377, 379, 385, 387, 400, 412, 416, 460, 514, 531
Reinforcement Learning 1, 2, 6, 7, 8, 20, 29, 30, 31, 35, 39, 45, 49, 57, 58, 60, 66, 68, 70, 72, 76, 78, 80, 84, 85, 89, 90, 91, 98, 99, 100, 101, 103, 104, 179, 185, 186, 188, 190, 191, 193, 199, 202, 204, 205, 206, 209, 210, 211, 214, 217, 230, 233, 235, 237, 238, 240, 242, 246, 252, 256, 257, 258, 260, 262, 350, 351, 353, 354, 364, 366, 367, 370, 371, 372, 373, 380, 385, 416, 417, 418, 434, 439, 470, 471, 475, 480, 484, 485, 501, 502, 504, 506, 507, 509, 511, 512, 521, 523, 525, 536, 542, 543
Remote Hacking 444
Robotic-Assisted Surgery 407, 408, 417, 419, 421

S

Secure Aggregation 162, 163, 166, 167, 169, 172, 181, 182, 249
Sensor Manipulation 444
Services 13, 14, 17, 45, 58, 64, 90, 91, 96, 107, 127, 134, 187, 189, 195, 197, 201, 217, 227, 248, 252, 254, 256, 260, 309, 326, 330, 331, 338, 372, 375, 376, 378, 381, 383, 384, 385, 390, 397, 400, 401, 405, 436, 449, 465, 466, 467, 468, 469, 471, 472, 473, 474, 477, 478, 481, 482, 489, 490, 491, 492, 495, 496, 518, 523, 541, 553
Smart Cities 230, 232, 465, 466, 467, 468, 469, 470, 471, 478, 486, 489, 491, 492, 497, 498, 499, 541, 543, 556
Surgical Robots 407, 409, 411, 412, 413, 414, 415, 416, 417, 419, 420, 421, 423, 424, 425, 426, 428, 429, 430, 431, 432
Synthetic Data 95, 224, 263, 264, 265, 266, 272, 275, 277, 278, 279, 280, 283, 284, 286, 287, 291, 293, 294, 295, 296, 297, 298

T

Telemedicine 72, 375, 376, 377, 378, 379, 380, 381, 382, 383, 384, 385, 387, 390, 391, 392, 393, 394, 395, 396, 397, 398, 399, 400, 401, 402, 404, 406, 419
Theoretical Frameworks 133, 134, 504
Threat Detection 2, 5, 6, 12, 24, 26, 27, 31, 32, 35, 36, 48, 49, 50, 56, 57, 69, 78, 104, 112, 113, 119, 120, 121, 125, 163, 164, 165, 177, 185, 186, 207, 226, 239, 241, 253, 254, 257, 258, 260, 294, 295, 305, 308, 313, 314, 315, 316, 324, 332, 333, 352, 361, 372, 376, 377, 379, 380, 381, 384, 385, 386, 387, 388, 390, 391, 392, 393, 396, 400, 402, 412, 416, 426, 432, 460, 461, 465, 475, 492, 494, 499, 501, 514, 524, 529, 530, 531, 533, 534, 535, 536, 537, 538, 539, 543, 544, 545, 546, 547, 551, 555, 557
Threat Intelligence 1, 2, 3, 6, 9, 12, 14, 15, 17, 18, 21, 28, 30, 31, 44, 50, 53, 54, 57, 58, 63, 64, 65, 67, 69, 75, 76, 85, 88, 93, 99, 101, 105, 108, 112, 115, 117, 119, 121, 128, 130, 132, 162, 164, 165, 168, 169, 170, 172, 180, 211, 214, 215, 222, 229, 232, 234, 242, 243, 257, 265, 268, 285, 287, 288, 289, 290, 291, 292, 295, 296, 300, 302, 308, 313, 315, 322, 332, 333, 364, 380, 381, 382, 386, 387, 390, 391, 393, 396, 404, 405, 415, 429, 431, 432, 439, 466, 467, 468, 471, 472, 473, 474, 480, 481, 491, 495, 496, 503, 515, 525, 531, 533, 537, 539, 542, 546, 550

V

Variational Autoencoders 87, 263, 283

W

Water Systems 501, 502, 503, 504, 505, 507, 508, 512, 514, 516, 521, 523

Z

Zero-Knowledge Proofs 133, 134, 135, 136, 138, 139, 140, 141, 142, 143, 144, 147, 149, 151, 155, 156, 157, 179
Zero-Trust Architectures 333, 387

www.ingramcontent.com/pod-product-compliance
Lightning Source LLC
LaVergne TN
LVHW080616300926
849162LV00005B/1177